Icon and Devotion

Icon and Devotion

Sacred Spaces in Imperial Russia

OLEG TARASOV

Translated and edited by
Robin Milner-Gulland

REAKTION BOOKS

For Pauline

Published by Reaktion Books Ltd
33 Great Sutton Street
London ECIV ODX, UK

www.reaktionbooks.co.uk

First published in English in 2002
Transferred to digital printing 2014

English translation by Robin Milner-Gulland

Designed and typeset by Libanus Press, Marlborough

Printed and bound in Great Britain by CPI Group (UK) Ltd, Croydon CRO 4YY

Tarasov, Oleg
Icon and devotion : sacred spaces in Imperial Russia
1. Icons - Russia (Federation) - History
I. Title
246.5'3'0947

ISBN 978 1 86189 118 1

Contents

Editor's Foreword

It rarely happens, but when it does it is enriching and astonishing: that a subject you thought you knew something about is illuminated from a quite new angle, casting light on different features, bringing out new significances and connections that you feel you *should* have recognized all along, but never did. This was what I felt when I first encountered *Icon and Devotion*. There are plenty of serviceable accounts of Russian icon painting, several excellent museum collections that anyone interested in the topic will know, plenty of attractive illustrated albums; but the picture they conspire to give can seem repetitive and limited, concentrating overwhelmingly on a rather small number of fine, demonstrably early works (pre 1500), treated mostly from the viewpoints of style and iconography.

Oleg Tarasov's approach declares its difference from the start. Certainly he has at his fingertips the tools and methodology of conventional art history, as also a great knowledge of theology and iconography, all of which are put to good effect. But his aim emerges as nothing less than to rewrite the cultural history of Russia since the 16th century. This he achieves through close study of the belief systems, the religion, in which every pre-modern or early-modern Russian's world outlook was rooted, and above all of the icons that were its constant 'objective correlative', its visible aspect and in certain respects even its motive force. At the same time he grapples with the ever-intractable problem of artistic change – how and why old codes are supplanted by new ones, or are themselves revived in new circumstances.

Out of this emerges a sort of intimate social history of Russia, primarily 'from below', revealing the innermost concerns of the supposedly inarticulate masses. Yet the cultural history that is being explored is by no means exclusively Russian: particularly in its second half, Tarasov's study continually evokes Western European (and Oriental Orthodox) experience, demonstrating how apparently specific Russian cultural phenomena were often part of far more extensive movements. At the end of the book the narrative is carried forward to the 1917 Revolution and beyond, showing how 'iconicity' affected the luminaries of Russian modernism as well as mass-circulation prints and posters.

For anyone familiar with previous icon literature, the range and nature of the large amount of illustrative material that Tarasov provides and analyzes must be astonishing. The showpiece medieval icons are completely absent (even the quasi-obligatory Rublyov 'Old Testament Trinity'!); instead, the popular icon-art of the three centuries preceding the Revolution – deeply unfashionable in the 20th century, generally dismissed by art history as styleless and repetitive – is displayed in all its variegation and (often) strangeness, and set in a context of 'high' art, of popular prints, book illustrations, vernacular Western painting, etc. None of this material is familiar, much is published for the first time: the reader may well feel as if invited onto a huge untrodden territory. Since negotiating this territory is best done with a fairly clear idea of what the word 'icon' implies, what follows is a brief account that may help the Western reader to get his or her bearings in the topic: naturally, many of the points touched on are greatly amplified in the course of Tarasov's study. Thereafter I attempt to sketch its historical and cultural context.

Icons

An 'icon' means an image (it is a Greek word, taken over into Russian and other Slavonic languages as *ikona*). Early in the Christian period it came to imply the image of a sacred person or event used as a focus for prayer. Legend has it that Christ miraculously produced the first such icon, the self-image 'Not Made By Hands', on a cloth sent to heal King Abgar of Edessa; St Luke was supposedly the first icon painter. Icons were thought of as accurate, realistic representations of holy personages and events from biblical times and subsequently; medieval people, visited by saints in their dreams, would recognize them from their iconic images.

Icons almost occasioned a civil war in the East Roman (Byzantine) Empire, when in the early 8th century the state and Church authorities – following the Second Commandment, against 'graven images' and 'likenesses' (Exodus 20:4) – banned them, so instigating the long period of iconoclasm. This was resisted by the poor and unprivileged, by monks, by women, by provincials, and ultimately (in 843) the iconoclast elite capitulated: icons were restored in what was commemorated as the Feast of Orthodoxy. Since then icons have been (in theory, at least) not superstitiously worshipped, but *venerated* as a two-way channel of communication with the supernatural world. For the Orthodox believer, 'seeing was believing': every saint has to have an iconic image. Icons – accessible to all classes of a largely illiterate society – were an enormous force for social cohesion in the Orthodox lands, which stretched from Venice to Eastern Siberia (even Alaska), and from the Nile to beyond the Arctic Circle.

The term *icon* can have a broad sense, including devotional objects of many kinds, wall-paintings, mosaics, whole buildings, monasteries, cities (above all Constantinople and Jerusalem), certain written texts and musical compositions, even holy persons. More commonly and more narrowly, though, it applies to paintings for veneration of sacred subjects on portable wooden panels. This is not surprising: millions upon millions of them were produced, above all in Russia (for centuries the one free Orthodox country, whose people perceived it as sanctified and protected by the heavenly grace that flowed through its countless churches and icons). The 'icon-screen' (iconostasis), with its 'royal doors' leading through to the sanctuary, became the focal point of Russian church architecture. Icons often depicted other icons and the miracles they wrought; icons of icons of icons are not uncommon.

Panel icons consist of one or more boards (usually of lime or cypress wood) secured at the back by wooden struts, sometimes with the facial side slightly hollowed; with time the panel would usually become 'bowed' i.e., convex, though this was not intended. Painting would be done in egg tempera on a carefully prepared fine plaster base; then an olive oil-based varnish (which would usually darken in a few decades) would be applied.

Old icons would seldom be discarded, but either scraped down for reuse or, more often, overpainted, perhaps many times.

From the painter's point of view he was 'revealing' an already extant image rather than exercising his own creativity. He was performing a traditional task in an established way, and images were not subject to alteration at whim. Nevertheless, stylistic changes did happen over the course of time, and many variant local manners and types of icon evolved. All, though, are ultimately rooted in Byzantine artistic practice, itself a development of the classical art of late antiquity. However stiff, stylized or anti-naturalistic icons may sometimes look to us, their clear, harmonious colours, rhythmic poses, their ordering of gesture, folds of drapery and so on speak of a classic heritage. The strangest aspect of their pictorial language is the so-called 'reverse perspective' often apparent in the settings of iconic figures: unlike in post-Renaissance 'true' perspective, there seems to be a vanishing-point projected forward from the picture surface, drawing the spectator into a transcendental realm.

Icons may be 'gateways into another world', but they are also emphatically physical objects: their materials – wood, sometimes elaborate metal casings, even jewels, pigments – are 'obvious' and unconcealed. Domestic icons were objects of household utility, indeed almost members of a household (thanked when things went well, occasionally blamed when they went badly): guests would greet them and be seated near them. Villagers and townsfolk would have icons in church that they held in special affection and reverence; a few might be 'wonder-working', a channel for miracles. They were an essential, rather than optional or decorative, part of Orthodox culture: they were indeed works of art, yet more importantly belonged to a realm of experience different from – superior to – the merely 'artistic'.

This chimed with the quest of many figures in 'modernist' art-movements from the turn of the 19th/20th centuries onwards, beginning with the Symbolists, who strove like icon painters for artistic transcendence. Bored by the superficiality of the 19th-century realism, sickened by the slickness of 19th-century techniques, they found in icons an art whose qualities went beyond style, individualism, representationalism or mere decoration. Simultaneously, modern restoration methods began to reveal medieval icons in their full nobility and power. Matisse (in 1911) was one of the first whose enthusiasm for icons spread their repute and influence far beyond the Orthodox lands; it has continued rippling outwards ever since, embracing more and more diverse forms of art.

Historical Context

The story that Tarasov tells begins in the mid-17th century, though naturally with many references to earlier events and figures (e.g., to the Fathers of the Church and defenders of icons; to the Ottoman Turkish conquest of Byzantium and the Balkans; particularly to early 16th-century dissension in the Russian Church and to the major Church council of 1551).

As a work of detailed scholarship, *Icon and Devotion* assumes the sort of historical, religious and cultural background knowledge that an educated Russian would find natural, but many Western readers, unfamiliar with over 1,000 years of Russian history, would not. Clearly this is not the place for any attempt at a comprehensive cultural–historical survey: but it may not come amiss to tell or remind the non-Russian reader of some of the historical landmarks that lead up to Tarasov's close study and provide it with its frame.

Early Russia (Rus) seems to have formed as a recognizable entity in the 9th century. Slav agriculturalists, organized into clans, had gradually colonized the Eastern European plain (forested to the north, grassland to the south), mingling with a scattering of earlier inhabitants, hunter-gatherers and stockbreeders. A more organized polity arose when Viking adventurers started crossing the Baltic from *c.* 800, set up bases and began to exploit the Eastern European river-system for long-distance trade – first with Central Asia via the Volga, soon afterwards with Constantinople (Byzantium) via the Dnieper. High-value products (e.g., furs and amber from the north, Arab silver, Byzantine luxury fabrics) were the objects of this trade, which continued to lure Vikings southwards; some went into military service in the Byzantine Empire. There does not appear to have been large scale colonization by Scandinavians (they seem to have been quickly assimilated), but significantly Vikings provided the first ruling dynasty of Rus (which did not die out till 1598), and set up strongpoints, some of which became capitals of principalities within a loose federation – notably Novgorod in the north and Kiev, 'mother of Russian cities', in the south.

The contact with Constantinople, the 'Great City' of early medieval Europe, proved fateful for the cultural history of Rus and indeed for instigating the whole set of processes dealt with in this book. From the Byzantine viewpoint, trade with Rus was lucrative and to be encouraged, but the pagan northerners also represented a considerable threat (they 'entered history' with a raid on Constantinople itself in 860) – a threat that would be minimized if Rus could be drawn into the Byzantine civilizational orbit. From the 860s, systematic attempts were made to secure the conversion of Rus (or anyhow the elite) to Christianity on the Byzantine model. Ultimate success came in 988/9 when Vladimir I, Prince of Kiev (later canonized), had himself and his population baptized – a process in which (according to the long and fascinating account in the Russian 'Primary Chronicle') an icon of the Last Judgment played a significant role.

Both sides gained much from the Conversion. Byzantium gained an ally (at least in theory), and greatly extended its influence at a time when there was already rivalry between Rome and Constantinople: the Great Schism between Orthodoxy and Catholicism was formalized in 1054. As for Rus, it was immediately plugged into the 'family' of civilized nations (*oikoumene*), acquiring in the process not only a religion but a new art (centred on the icon) and architecture, a music, a written literature with its tailor-made literary language (known nowadays as 'Church Slavonic'), a modified legal system and new political principles, particularly with respect to international relations and to the concept of rulership. Though features of Russia's pre-literate and pre-Christian culture did survive, especially in a peasant milieu, fusing or coexisting with the newer forms, the overall cultural dislocation was immense – giving Russians the sense that the Conversion was the crucial event of their early history, and that their late calling to the fellowship of Christian nations implied a special providential favour and responsibility.

The senior figure of the Russian Church was the Metropolitan of Kiev and All Rus, at first a Byzantine Greek appointee (with rare exceptions). In 1300 the Metropolitan moved his residence to Vladimir (Kiev having been devastated by the Tatars), and in 1326 to Moscow, whose growing prestige was much enhanced by this. In 1448 Moscow – shocked by the Council of Florence that had attempted to patch up the Great Schism – started to choose its metropolitans independently of Constantinople (which itself fell to the Turks in 1453). The Metropolitan of Moscow was raised to the title of Patriarch – highest of Orthodox church dignitaries – in 1589; but after 1700 Peter I let the Patriarchate lapse (it was restored in 1918). Peter's reforms reduced the Church – previously proud of its autonomy – to a branch of state, controlled by a Synod that was effectively a Government ministry.

The Byzantine connection profoundly, if only gradually, modified the notion of what Rus itself was or should be. Early Rus seems to have been run as a sort of family concern by the Ryurikid dynasty (Richard Pipes compares it with later outfits such as the Hudson's Bay Company): the senior prince ruled (until the mid-12th century) in Kiev, while his juniors were installed in other main cities, swapping their residences around when one died, though their temptation to put down roots in one place grew stronger with time. Some cities managed to set up contractual relations with their rulers: in Novgorod the citizenry (from 1136 on) hired and fired its princes – who were little more than military commanders – at will (the leading Novgorod citizen was its Archbishop). Hence arose the later perception – not wholly misguided – of the 'freedom-loving' and 'democratic' Novgorodians. In the 13th century most Russian cities were devastated in Tatar (i.e., Mongol) assaults: Novgorod was spared, and even prospered as the easterly terminus of the Hanseatic Baltic trade-route (its western end was London). The Tatars controlled most of the rest of Rus through native rulers, a situation that encouraged the fragmentation of large principalities into ever smaller units. Much of Western Rus (what later became Belarus and Ukraine), however, passed into the control of Lithuania and thereafter became part of the Catholic-dominated Polish–Lithuanian commonwealth, while itself remaining Orthodox and even gaining its own Metropolitan: a situation with many repercussions on the processes described in the second part of Tarasov's study. With the slow healing of the trauma of the Tatar invasion, Rus both began to reinvent itself and also re-establish and reassess its Byzantine cultural heritage.

This 'reinvention', to some extent a 'repositioning', of Rus, took several interconnected forms in the political, social, cultural and religious fields.

Most visibly, it involved a reversal of the process of fragmentation mentioned above, whereby Rus (with debilitating consequences) subdivided itself into ever-smaller political units. From the early 14th century to the late 15th the Moscow principality's policy of 'gathering in' the Russian lands – whether by purchase, inheritance, cajolery, marriage, conquest – brought it from the position of an obscure backwater of the Vladimir-Suzdal territory to the centre of power of resurgent Rus. Its Grand Princes, once little more than tax-gatherers for the Tatars, were able to portray themselves as liberators after defeating a Tatar army at Kulikovo (1380).

From the mid-15th century several crucial events took place in a short span of time: Constantinople fell to the Turks (1453), Moscow annexed Novgorod (appropriating the landholdings of its aristocrats and enlisting them into Muscovite state service), and the Tatar 'Golden Horde', itself fragmented, proved unable to enforce its power to exact tribute from Muscovy. The long reign of the Grand Prince Ivan III (1462–1505) witnessed a heightening of Byzantine-inspired ceremonial, the rebuilding of the Moscow Kremlin as an awe-inspiring citadel for a new capital, diplomatic and practical contacts with Western Europe, and a determined publicistic effort to portray Muscovy not just as legitimate inheritor of the remembered glories of the Russian pre-Tatar past, but – being the one free Orthodox country – as successor to Constantinople itself (the notorious formula of Moscow as the 'Third Rome', a variant of this, had its main impact later, in the 17th century). The polarization of the ancient Russian lands between their Western sector (controlled by Lithuania, subsequently the Polish Commonwealth, and undergoing 'feudal' social developments) on the one hand, and on the other Muscovy (fast becoming a 'service state', though serfdom proper was still a long way in the future), became more starkly apparent.

The related religious and cultural processes of the 14th and 15th centuries were just as momentous. Orthodoxy as a whole, faced with a crushing double threat from Islam in the East and expansionist Roman Catholicism in the West, reinvigorated itself in the 14th century most strikingly through the mystic theology of Hesychasm (literally 'quietism'), whose doctrine, derived from certain of the Church Fathers, held that the individual might, through arduous spiritual exercises, attain to unmediated apprehension of the Divine Energy. After fierce debate this was accepted as Orthodox doctrine, and has remained a persistent and powerful element within Orthodox experience. Its affirmation owed much to the rise of the significance of the 'monastic republic' of Mt Athos, the 'Holy Mountain' far from centres of population, as meeting-place and spiritual focus for the whole Orthodox world. Hesychasm affected Orthodox iconic art, literature, spirituality and indeed public life (though precisely *how* remains controversial).

In Russia religious renewal took an astonishing form from the mid-14th/mid-15th centuries: an explosive growth of monasticism and individual eremitism, resulting in the establishment of ever more remote hermitages and monasteries – a couple of hundred at least – in the northern forest zone, spearheading colonization of a vast tract of country (of which Moscow eventually took advantage). Its instigator was St Sergius of Radonezh, later considered the country's patron saint, whose great Trinity Monastery – for a few decades around 1400, the 'golden age' of Russian classic icon-painting – was the real cultural centre of Rus, within which Moscow was not yet overwhelmingly dominant. In time Sergius' followers, and their own further followers, the 'Trans-Volga elders' whose guiding spirit was St Nil Sorsky, would come into conflict with a state whose urge for centralization was disturbed by their individualism and nonconformity. This period – *c.* 1350 to 1500 – was the greatest age of Russian sainthood: many of the figures commemorated in icons analyzed in this book, fantastical as their stories may seem, were historical figures associated with the movement instigated by Sergius. But in the 16th century, the 'age of regulated piety', embodied in the figure of St Joseph of Volokolamsk, with its Byzantine-style compact of 'harmony' between Church and state, was already under way. Thereafter, the chief type of Russian saint would be the 'holy fool' (neither simpleton nor lunatic, but a wise person who put on the mask of 'foolishness' to shock the powerful out their complacency): a truly popular phenomenon that has lived on ever since in various guises.

Ivan III's grandson, Ivan IV ('The Terrible', really 'Awesome'), in his even longer reign, set the 'Realm of Special Charisma' (as Tarasov calls 'idealized' Muscovy) in place. He was crowned Tsar (Emperor) with Byzantine-derived ritual in 1547: now the monarch was God's anointed, not just a 'super-proprietor' of the Russian land. The last two decades of his reign were characterized by military reverses, national impoverishment through war and famine, the Tsar's wanton violence if not paranoia; but none of this blots out (for the Russian popular imagination) the bright image of his early years as a 'Renaissance prince' in Orthodox garb, when he led successful 'crusades' against the Tatars of Kazan and Astrakhan, his Cossack forces crossed the Urals, his merchants established trading links from England to Siberia, his cities were given institution of local government, his churchmen–scholars made great compendia of Russian historical and religious knowledge, and he himself set up the great 'Council of a Hundred Chapters' (*Stoglav*, 1551) to settle problems of Church life definitively. This was the period to which, a hundred years and more later, the 'Old Believer' schismatics would look back with a nostalgia that never abated.

We approach the point at which Tarasov's detailed study begins, and can cover the intervening territory swiftly. With the death of Ivan IV's one surviving son, Fyodor I (1598), the first dynasty of Russian rulers ended (though unfounded rumours of the survival of another child, Dmitriy, gave rise to pretenders of whom one briefly reached the throne). In the subsequent fifteen years of the 'Time of Troubles', central authority was disastrously weakened, famine was rife, armed bands roamed the countryside and there were major interventions by Sweden (in the North) and Poland (which occupied Moscow and came close to acquiring the throne). Eventually (1613) an alliance between a popular provincial militia and the great monasteries of central Russia stabilized the situation sufficiently for an 'Assembly of the Land' to be held. This huge gathering – many hundreds of representative of all classes – gave general legitimation to the election of the young Mikhail Romanov (from the family of Ivan IV's popular first wife) as Tsar, founder of the final Russian dynasty. By a bold stroke his father (who had become a monk, and was then a Polish captive) was elected Patriarch.

The relief was general; divine grace seemed to have spared Rus (it is at this time that the expression 'Holy Russia', implying a sanctity independent of any given ruler in power, becomes common). But, as when any former regime is restored, times had moved on, and old Muscovy, inward-looking and exclusivist, could not long be viable in a crisis-ridden 17th century. The intelligent Tsar Aleksey Mikhaylovich (reigned 1645–76), at heart (it would seem) 'medieval' in his tastes and attitudes – the 'last Byzantine' – nevertheless turned out to be an innovator of sorts. His reign had an early, unforeseen success when rebellious Orthodox Cossacks brought much of what is now Ukraine under Muscovite control: intellectually, Ukrainians instigated, and for at least half a century dominated, the process of 'Westernization' that long preceded Peter the Great's more glamorous reforms. At first Aleksey was much influenced by the older, imperious Patriarch Nikon (1605–81), who had his own reform agenda, based on Greek and Venetian practices, unacceptable to traditionalist Muscovites. Nikon and Aleksey fell out in 1658, probably over control of the Ukrainian church, but it was too late to avert the 'Great Schism' (formalized in a Council of 1666–7) between the Old and New Ritualists. The consequences form much of the matter of Tarasov's book. Peter the Great (who learned much from his father Aleksey) was by no means hostile to religion, but judged its institutions (like everything else) by a yardstick of 'utility'. Some of his successors (notably his daughter Elisabeth, reigned 1741–61) were favourably inclined towards Orthodoxy; Catherine the Great's wise consort Potyomkin aimed to heal the Schism. But religion (not necessarily Orthodox) had to wait till the time of Alexander I (1801–25) to enjoy a considerable revival. Under Alexander III (1881–94) and particularly Nicholas II (1894–1917) there was a state-directed effort to revive Russian Orthodoxy, including iconic art: too late, as events all too evidently proved. Though all these vicissitudes, as Tarasov demonstrates, the icon enjoyed amazing productivity, and offers us a way into the thoughts and feelings of the multitude.

Oleg Tarasov's *Ikona i blagochestie: ocherki ikonnogo dela v imperatorskoy Rossii* (Icon and Devotion: Studies of Icon Production in Imperial Russia) was published in Moscow in 1995. For this first translated version with its modified sub-title, it has been substantially revised and edited by the author and myself working in close collaboration. The second of its original three sections ('History of the Craft', most of which dealt with the minutiae of icon production in the Vladimir Province during the 19th century) has been eliminated as being of less interest to the general reader or art historian than the rest of the volume, though a good deal of its material has in fact been redistributed to other chapters. Further extensive reworking of the text has led, it is hoped, to a more streamlined book, accessible to a readership that does not necessarily have the same cultural reference points at its fingertips that educated Russians do. The opportunity has been taken to make use of recent scholarship. Explanatory notes (included among the References), chiefly on historical topics, have sometimes been necessary: I have tried to keep these to a minimum. Occasionally I have added a Russian word in brackets for the benefit of those who know the language, or left a culturally specific term untranslated (e.g., *lubok,* a type of Russian popular print): I explain these on first occurrence.

Readers will soon appreciate the great conceptual and stylistic range of Tarasov's work and quoted materials: from semi-literate, essentially medieval religious polemics to the concepts of the *Annales* historians, from theological to art-historical to 'culturological' discourse. It would be idle to pretend this has not posed special problems of translation: given that good English scholarly writing tends more towards the pragmatic and laconic that Russian seems to, I have tried to aim in the direction of simplification, though without omitting any of the author's points, or usurping his (or his quoted authors') style. As an example of the intractability of the translator's task, one may mention that the Russian word *blagochestie* in the book's title means in English both 'devotion' and 'piety' (and both are used as appropriate in the text); by contrast, as readers of chapter Four will discover, two words for the English 'face' (*lik* and *litso*) have had to be distinguished in translation, despite the measure of artificiality that this implies.

For the many biblical quotations I have followed the Authorized Version, with which most English readers have a special familiarity. Names of saints, dedications and titles of icons have led to problems for which perhaps arbitrary solutions have had to be found, unless there is an easily recognizable Western (or Greek) equivalent. Following Orthodox practice, I have referred throughout to the Virgin Mary as the Mother of God, save where the context is unambiguously Western. Her many variant icons often have titles with a place name component: these have usually been transliterated from the Russian adjectival form. The specifically Russian feast day *Pokrov* (often misleadingly rendered as 'Intercession' but implying 'protecting veil') has been left in transliterated form.

We have chosen to use the 'reader-friendly' transliteration system set out (for example) in each of the three volumes of the *Cambridge Companion to Russian Studies*, which has been found in practice to give the English reader a fair idea of pronunciation. 'Soft' and 'hard' signs have not been indicated. Where standardized English forms exist (e.g., Moscow, Archangel, St Sergius, Ivan the Terrible), these have been used; the names 'Alexander' and 'Alexandra' are spelled in English fashion. I have preferred the forms of the names Dimitriy Rostovsky, Simeon Polotsky to the forms 'of Rostov, of Polotsk' respectively. Names of Russian rulers from Peter the Great onwards are rendered in anglicized form. Dates up to 1918 are given in the 'Old Style', i.e., by the Julian calendar (13 days behind the Gregorian in the 20th century).

Many friends and colleagues answered queries on individual points of this translation; my warmest thanks to them all.

Robin Milner-Gulland
University of Sussex, 2002

Introduction

This book is an attempt – never previously undertaken – at a cultural study of the icon in Imperial Russia, linking it closely with older and newer types of devotional piety; hence the title. We know that the 'New Devotion' in 14th-century Western Europe was accompanied by radical changes in the concept of the visual image. Risking some simplification, it can be said that a similar situation came about in mid-17th-century Russia. The reform of the Russian Orthodox Church, begun by Patriarch Nikon (1605–81) and Tsar Aleksey Mikhaylovich (*r.* 1645–76), led to the establishment of a new ritual and a new sign system for the religious image at the Great Moscow Council of the Church in 1666–7. Hitherto, Russian icons had shown the saints making the sign of blessing with two fingers, while the abbreviated name of Christ used the letters 'IC XC'. In icons of the new devotion the name of Christ was abbreviated as 'IИC XC', and three fingers formed the sign of blessing.

These apparently simple changes occurred amid profound shifts in Russian culture and mass consciousness. The new type of icon and the new devotion were the result of the influence of Renaissance ideas at the Russian court. They were also linked with the individualization of religious sensibility, the appearance in Russia of Western, Latinized rhetoric, and, finally, the gradual decay of the icon-painting canon and the replacement of the Byzantine and Old Russian icon by religious painting in the official Church.

Meanwhile, the old type of icon, with the older symbolism, remained closely connected with the popular culture of the Russian Old Ritualists, often known as the Old Believers. They rejected the mid-17th-century

Church reforms and continued to live – as their successors do to this day – according to the established devotional norms. These had been laid down at Church councils during the reign of Ivan the Terrible, above all at the *Stoglav* Council of 1551. (This 'Council of a Hundred Chapters' produced a lengthy document in the form of answers to problems besetting many areas of Church life.) In the later 17th century and early 18th, the chief ideologists of Old Ritualism included such well-known figures in Russian history as the Archpriest Avvakum (1620–82), the deacon Feodor (*d.* 1682) and the Denisov brothers, Andrey (1674–1730) and Semyon (1682–1741).

A fair amount has been written about the connection between the venerated image and religious experience, but most of it in the form of studies of ancient, Byzantine or Old Russian art.[1] Post-Byzantine icon painting has been less fortunate: only now is it beginning to attract attention. This is true too of the Russian icon of the 18th century and later. This situation, I suggest, not only allows, it positively encourages the exploration of fresh topics and perspectives, the more so since they can build on the rather broad theoretical base laid down by published work on the theory and semiotics of the icon, and on the theory of the visual image.[2] Research into the later icon may also broaden our ideas about the everyday practice of icon veneration in earlier times, which as yet is little understood.

A growing interest in problems of *mentalités* makes modern cultural history turn all the more readily to the analysis of spiritual life, to the study of the invariant, stable structures of consciousness, to its deepest layers – to the mentality that reflects the historical experience of a nation. It is here that we can capture the system of 'automatic responses' of the collective mind-set, its images and concepts, which is determined by culture, language, religion and social life, and which is the regulator of behaviour or, so to speak, the *existence-in-the-world* of one or another people. Scholarship in these fields can help us understand the particular nature of icon veneration and the characteristics of mass religiosity.

The icon, as symbol of the Incarnation (the 'heart' of Orthodoxy), was always capable of subtly registering and reflecting the most complex rhythms of historical reality. It is also the case that the icon not only passively reflected, but actively influenced human consciousness, transmitting into the world not only ecclesiastical and devotional impulses but historical ones too. In the Byzantine theory of the image, two major functions of the icon stand out: its pastoral and edificatory purpose and its sanctificatory role.

The first function was explained at the Seventh Ecumenical Council (the Second Council of Nicaea, held in 787), which identified the need to portray the lives of saints in such a way that their labours and deeds should be made known to the people – and to humble people in particular. Thus the belief of the Fathers of the Church that an icon is a 'book for the illiterate' was affirmed. In the resolutions of the Council it was emphasized that, the more that 'with the help of the icons' Jesus Christ, the Mother of God, the angels and the saints

> become the object of our contemplation, so much the more are those who behold these icons moved to the recollection of their prototypes, do they acquire more love for them, are they moved to kiss, to respect and to reverence them, but on no account to render them that true worship which, according to our faith, is proper to the Divine Being alone.[3]

Meanwhile, the Trinitarian dogma and the Eastern Church's teaching on the Holy Spirit, distinct from that of the West, were the precondition in the Orthodox lands for its stress on the possible suffusion of the created world with grace. That was the basis on which the second highly important function of the Orthodox image was established: the sanctification of humanity. Defending the icons of the saints, St John Damascene, a major 8th-century opponent of iconoclasm, underlined their grace-bestowing action on individuals, since the active effect of the Holy Spirit on the living world also corresponded to the presence of grace in the icon.[4] The possibility of an individual's attainment of union with God by means of the aid of the icon becomes one of the chief features of Christian anthropology, which was explained by Byzantine theorists of the image primarily through the Incarnation and the participation of humanity in the divine essence. The Orthodox icon not only could clarify the plan of the Creator but, being 'constructive', could also bring it about. The possibility of sanctification through the icon was always regarded in Orthodox tradition as determined by its representing not the 'nature', but the 'person' of Christ, that is Christ's hypostasis that, passing understanding, unites (according to Chalcedonian dogma) two natures within itself. This transmission through the icon of the hypostasis of 'personality' (and also of the 'personality' of the sanctified human being – the saint) also determined the active effect of the icon on humanity and the 'world'. Hence the icon could occupy its own very special space within the history of consciousness and culture, while the people's attitudes to the icon could include historically formed stereotypes capable of casting light both on the shaped and the unconscious historical experience.

From this starting-point my task was to use primary sources to demonstrate the peculiarities of the Russian ontology of the icon – in other words to attempt to see the 'life', the existence of the icon in the *longue durée* (or 'Great Time') of Russian consciousness. This way of posing the problem has effectively excluded any aesthetic evaluation of the icon, or rather it has shifted aesthetic criteria to a secondary level and replaced them with the scrutiny of religious sensibilities and patterns of consciousness within the general lines of Russian cultural development. Thus in *Icon and Devotion* the reader will not find exhaustive descriptions of iconography, or of the various styles and 'schools' of Russian icon painting of and since the 18th century. Nor will the reader find any finished picture of the evolution of Old Russian painting or of the development of its traditions. Instead of a chronological account of the history of icon painting in Imperial Russia, the reader will discover a rather mosaic-like picture formed from distinct subjects, stories, descriptions, disruptions and typologies that show various temporary characteristics, which in their totality are subordinated to my construction of a typological cultural model.

This model's purpose is related to an evident feature or theme of Russian life – the fact that a huge number of icons are to be found in its cultural–historical space. The model should explain how behind this theme (or state of affairs), which initially seems devoid of significance, there exists a deep and complex but entirely real field of study. This involves one particular, historically defined configuration of ideas and common concepts that comes to the fore: that of 'Holy Russia' and 'Moscow, the Third Rome', which of course keeps its pre-eminence in Russian history for centuries, and exercises direct and indirect influence both on the fate of Russian culture in general, and on the special nature of Russian icon painting and icon devotion in particular.

Various scholars have explored the consequences on Russia's history of the conception of 'Moscow, the Third Rome' and the ideal image of 'Holy Russia'.[5] Basing itself on the state and religious paradigm of Byzantium, the notion of the Muscovite tsardom as a specially charismatic 'empire' with messianic aspirations – the last of the 'sacred empires' in whose image could be seen a 'realized' eschatology – predetermined the dominance of deep religious and emotional ideas in the development of the Russian consciousness. At a certain point in the formation of the popular mentality, a particular assortment of utopian values, images and signs was assimilated, and this lived on in spite of all subsequent historical change. Already in the world view of the abbot of Pskov monastery, the Elder Filofey, the concept of the final stage of the universal 'transmission of Imperial power' (*translatio imperii*) and the discovery by Rus of special charisma emerged as the chief foundation of his cultural conception. The famous eschatological quality of his idea revealed itself thus:

> So know, thou lover of God and of Christ, that all the Christian kingdoms have come to an end and have been united into the single tsardom of our ruler, according the prophetic books, and that this is the Tsardom of Russia: for two Romes have fallen, while the third stands, and a fourth there cannot be.

This *fullness of time*, a sort of end of history, in which the image of the eschatological Heavenly Kingdom of Christ on earth is, in effect, already visible, is founded equally on the opposition holy/most holy and on the stark juxtaposition of the sacred Russian empire to the 'unbelief' of the rest of the world (to which, because of that alone, salvation was denied):

> Unbelief is as water; see, chosen one of God, how all the Christian kingdoms have been drowned by the faithless ones, and how only the single Tsardom of our one ruler stands by the grace of God.[6]

Hence it is evidently of the greatest importance that in Muscovite Russia the universal and fundamental mental construct of *translatio imperii*, developed in the early Middle Ages, was burdened with more-or-less unique historical circumstances. This collective religious feeling was not only accepted, but taken over with ease: it was being incorporated into the remarkable religious enthusiasm that accompanied the Reformation, some of which opposed icon veneration, and also against the background of the conquest of the Balkan Orthodox world by the Muslim Turks, the 'faithless ones'. Following the Byzantine model, Muscovite Russia began to conceive of itself as no more or less than the unique and God-chosen state, possessor both of the chief symbols of sacred power and of the main single symbol of Orthodox faith – the icon. The concept of 'tsardom' (i.e., 'empire'), traditional in Imperial theology, acquired the character of the utopian concept of Holy Russia, or metaphorically speaking of Russia as a 'Great Icon', whose vast geographical space had to be saturated through and through with holiness. This value system lived and moved within the *longue durée* of the history of consciousness, spreading over those depths where, as followers of the Annales school of history conceive, super-slow movements of ideas and speculative constructs take place, where the kernel of the collective unconscious is formed, in which archetypal ideas are self-generating. Embracing the most varied, sometimes quite incompatible, forms, these super-slow movements perpetually emerge as if 'in dialogue' with factual history ('Little Time') breaking through culture's surface, revealing themselves thereby as a powerful organizer of new cultural structures and phenomena.

It was on such a wave of cultural disturbance that the religious culture of the 'Old Belief' developed: a period of 'long duration' in the concept of the Muscovite Tsardom's acceptance as an empire of special charisma turned out to be subject to the powerful action of events. The active working-out in Muscovite Russia of the idea of 'sacred empire' and of the link between holiness and ethno-cultural space became, in Imperial Russia, a sharp polarization of religious experience, which gave birth to the peculiarities – unique in modern times – of icon veneration and of the way icons formed part of popular culture. The attitude of everyday consciousness towards the icon entered into a complex inner relationship with the ideal model of 'Holy Russia' and world consciousness generally, since the common 'religious storehouse' of collective purposes and system of feelings was also the foundation on which both various types of devotion and the various sign-systems of the venerated image would arise. On a theoretical plane we here encounter, incidentally, the concept of 'great time' (explored by Mikhail Bakhtin) within cultural history.

The spiritual moment of dislocation connected with the early 16th-century struggle between the Josephites (*styazhateli*, 'Possessors'), who believed it appropriate that monasteries enrich themselves as landowners, and their more ascetic opponents, the Non-Possessors, has of course given rise to a vast literature. Most specialists have come to the conclusion that the victory of the adherents of Joseph of Volokolamsk over the followers of Nil Sorsky led to the consolidation in the Russian church of a certain ritualized severity and confessionalism. However, perhaps only Georgiy Florovsky clearly discerned the inner link between the innovativeness of the Josephites in the matter of icons, and changes in mass religious sensibilities and in attitudes to the icons. The argument between the high-ranking civil servant Ivan Viskovatiy and the Metropolitan Makariy in 1553 concerning religious painting was described by Florovsky as 'a collision of religious–aesthetic orientations: between traditional hieratic realism and symbolism nourished by the excited religious imagination'. Viskovatiy's standpoint, that 'it is not proper to revere the image beyond truth', was rejected the moment that the religious masses themselves were drawn into the internal quarrel between the Josephites and the Non-Possessors, whereupon there was a polarization within the common people.[7] In other words, the affirmation in the 16th century of the 'Josephite' regulated devotion, with its excessively developed ritualism and orientation towards an external cult aesthetic, led to an attitude to the icon that was characterized by heightened emotionalism while containing within itself a formal show of piety, whereby the numerical quantity of icons was often linked with authenticity of devotion. Developing Florovsky's thoughts, Leonid Uspensky wrote about the age of the Council of a Hundred Chapters, the *Stoglav*:

> In parallel with the switch of spiritual life to an externalized regulated piety there takes place a switch towards externality in art too. The dogmatic content of an image begins to lose its dominant significance and is no longer always sensed as fundamental. The enthusiasm for good appearance and good order typical of Josephism stimulate quantity at the expense of quality.[8]

Thus we can infer that in Muscovite Russia the icon was drawn into the ontological context of the construction of a 'tsardom' of unique charisma, and took up a special place in the system of Russian popular culture and in the sacralization of the profane sphere. The icon as religious symbol always displays a mystical connection of the earthly with the heavenly: it is a sign of the higher world in the lower. Hence its elevated role within the universal cultural opposition sacred/worldly worked in the direction of the primary understanding in the Old Russian tradition of the sphere of the sacred as the sphere of culture; while the profane was frequently treated with contempt. The vast quantity of icons in Russia that revealed signs of the heavenly world in the earthly aimed not only to 'reflect' sacred history but actively to influence the collective consciousness: over the centuries there arose a conviction of the ubiquity of the image of Christ on Russian soil, that is to say in the idea that Russia was under divine protection, was a land 'chosen by God'. The history of Russian icon production turned out to be closely linked with the development of the theory of 'Moscow the Third Rome' and with the formation in the unconscious historical experience of an artificially constructed and speculative model of 'Holy Russia'.

In order to demonstrate the general dependence of icon production in Imperial Russia on collective religiosity, I have focused my attention not so much on 'high' culture – the religious painting of the Imperial Academy of Arts – but rather on lower, everyday culture, and more specifically on the well-known popular icons of 'Suzdalian painting' from Palekh, Mstyora and Kholuy. I hope to convince the reader that in the 18th and 19th centuries these three villages were the leading centres of large-scale icon-painting in the Orthodox world. Once upon a time they were part of the Suzdal principality (thereafter they fell within the Vladimir governership), but the adjective 'Suzdalian' was attached to them and became their general name.[9]

The level of dissemination of Suzdal icons within the Empire can hardly be compared with the popular dissemination of icons from any other workshops. It is enough to mention that, according to statistics from the mid- and later 19th century, in the single village of Kholuy between 1.5 and 2 million icons were produced per year. These incredible amounts are not some exceptional historical case: what explains them is their connection with the peculiarities of Russian devotion and the utopian models that remained alive for centuries in the mass consciousness. Communicating a particular ontological closeness to the Godhead, these millions of icons made the space surrounding a person resemble a kind of 'icon', the image of a 'realized' eschatology of 'Holy Russia'.

Since *Icon and Devotion* is the very first attempt at a comprehensive cultural–historical approach to this complicated and uninvestigated subject-matter, its aim is not so much to answer questions as to pose them as clearly as possible, by bringing into the scholarly realm new documentary and illustrative materials, most of them published here for the first time. In juxtaposing these with 'older', doubtless generally known, materials, I trust that the latter will seem all the more resonant.

This has also determined the book's structure. Each of its two parts is devoted to a single theme, which, even if discursive, is internally connected with the main problem. In Part One, general questions of the history of religious sensibilities and of the veneration of icons are discussed, chiefly on the level of everyday culture.

But while I describe and analyse facts taken from the most varied sources, I have attempted to delineate them through the outlines of 'great' history, pinpointing their meaning in the context of the model to which I have already referred. The history of Imperial Russia is traditionally taken to begin with the foundation of the northern capital, St Petersburg, in 1703, and to end with the abdication of Nicholas II on 15 March 1917. However, so as to observe the invariant structures of consciousness, it has proved essential to take the history of culture in its most varied temporal forms, that is, to use time as a 'means of observation'. To put it in another way, I chose a method that would provide not only a description of monuments, but also the juxtaposition of experiences, a perpetual comparison, sometimes even prioritizing an examination of 'one's own' and 'others'. What seems ordinary to us is seen by others in quite another light.

The history of icon painting is inseparable from the history of icon veneration; thus between these two histories there must be some sort of invisible but very real and extensive common ground on which the meeting of ideas and feelings with everyday life, with actual reality, takes place. In fact, the analysis of these contacts deals with problems of icon production, of the development of the unusually complex structure of the icon-painting industry, embracing the shape of everyday life and the work of the icon producers, the mechanisms of trade, and the types of images designed for prayer. In Palekh, Mstyora and Kholuy, icons were painted that answered to the generally accepted norms both of the official cult and of the Old Belief. This universality of the Suzdal industry, its close connection with popular religious life, enables us to examine the icon business of Imperial Russia in close-up, and to find points of contact between the super-slow movements of ordinary forms of existence, drawn into the current with the kind of history that can be termed 'eventful', i.e., implying quicker rhythms and changes.

The religious and moral systems of devotion determined not only the place of icons and their production in worship, but also the particularities of their artistic language, their subject-matter and iconographic themes. In this sense the sign system of the venerated image faithfully reflected both changes in religious philosophy and the general orientation of one or other types of culture. For that reason, as I analyze the working principles of icon-painting craftsmen and the artistic life of the icon, I have tried not to separate it from the universal mechanisms of 'low' culture, or of the peculiarities of religious sensibility and the 'rules of faith'.

In the Imperial Russian period, the art of the icon developed primarily on the lower level of popular craft culture; it was the sort of mass craft industry typical of modern times, precisely that 'low-level cultural store' (*gesunkenes Kulturgut*) that German ethnography had identified by the beginning of the 20th century as a genetic result of the separation of culture into learned and profane spheres at the end of the Middle Ages. Thus, as I examine the laws and mechanisms of the formation of the Russian icon-painting craft from the 18th century to the early 20th, I have tried to emphasize their universal significance for the world of Orthodox culture that Ricardo Picchio named *Slavia Orthodoxa*, a concept he developed in the 1950s to describe the common cultural elements of all Slav peoples of Orthodox faith.

Beyond that, the typological model I have set up often comes into direct conflict with ordinary Christian culture and its urge towards unity and autonomy from subjective systems of devotion. Since it was important for me at this point to see the unity of such processes within the Christian world, elements of the compositional structure of faces, landscapes, etc., have been examined not from the point of view of the evolution and formation of styles, but from that of the universal laws of the aesthetics of craft-based art – sometimes obviously, sometimes not, undergoing the effect of changes in religious psychology and in a people's mapping of the world. Hence arises the unavoidable comparison between 'high' and 'low' art: the presence within culture of a 'high' and 'low' level dictates a dialectical approach in any examination of the influence of the 'learned' on the 'profane'. With all this in mind, and without in any way pretending to any universal or unconditional quality in my observations, comparisons or conclusions (it is clear that reality is always more complicated than any model), I have none the less tried to show that the artistic structure of the mass-produced craft icon could reflect profound and historically determined collective values, something particularly evident in any consideration of the fate of the national culture as a whole.

The publication of this book in English owes much to the cooperation of several British scholars, in the first place Professor Robin Cormack and Professor Stephen Bann, to whom I am deeply indebted. My special thanks to Professor Robin Milner-Gulland, who undertook the difficult task of translating it into English and editing it. I also wish to thank Gordon Lankton and Alexander Tumanov for their sincere interest in, and support for, this translation. I am most grateful to friends and colleagues for advice and comments they made both during the writing of the book and after its completion: Gerold Vzdornov, Ludmila Sofronova, Boris Uspensky, Larisa Tananayeva and Anatoliy Turilov. My final thanks are to my photographer in Moscow, Victor Solomatin, and to the staff at Reaktion Books.

PART ONE

The Icon and the World

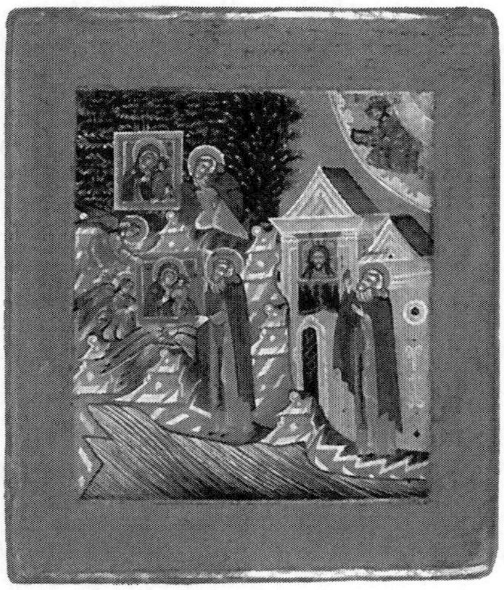

Who coverest thyself with light as with a garment:
who stretchest out the heavens like a curtain . . .
Psalm 104:2

The sky is the Lord's incorruptible raiment.
The world is an incorruptible raiment.
Russian folk saying

Previous page: 1. *Appearance of the Icon of the Mother of God to Avraamiy of Galich*, end of the 17th century or early 18th. Kolomenskoye Historical and Architectural Museum-Preserve, Moscow.

CHAPTER ONE

Venerated Image:
The Sacred in the Everyday

Icons are so ordered that everything depicted in them is presented in its own ontology. Their makers took much trouble to distort the phenomenal world profoundly with a special reverse perspectival scheme, whereby parallel lines are represented as diverging from, rather than converging on, a distant vanishing-point beyond the picture space.[1] This perspective subjects everything within the spatial-temporal rectangle – the icon's 'mirror'– to the laws of the sacred. But we should note that when a person surrounds him- or herself with icons in the quite literal sense, a reverse mirror effect can easily arise: reality itself can be subordinated in one's consciousness to the sacral mode, and so can appear more authentic than it is.

The Russian world had always diligently saturated itself with signs of holiness; interpenetrating, the real and semiotic levels 'worked' in a certain direction: that of liberation from the earthly and imitation of the heavenly. The deep-rooted mental construct 'Holy Russia' was the major influence in Moscow's well-known desire to become a home-bred Byzantium: the reliability of the higher providential purpose of the Moscow tsardom as the last sacred empire was often linked with nothing less than the ubiquitous earthly presence of heavenly powers. For that reason, from the very start of the construction of this empire the icon was a founding element of the Muscovite way of life, one that left deep traces in the subsequent history of religious sensibilities.

The Burden of Numbers

The quantity of icons in Russia never ceased to amaze observers from other lands – even Orthodox lands. The Archdeacon Paul of Aleppo, for example, an East Christian visitor to Moscow, has left us a mass of interesting information. In his memoir, *The Journey of Patriarch Makarios of Antioch to Russia in the Mid-17th Century*, he noted that 'In each house there is a countless multitude of icons, adorned with gold, silver and precious stones, and not only within houses, but also at all doors, even at house-gates, and this is true not only of Boyars, but of peasants in the villages, since their love and faith towards the icons is very great.'[2] This sacralization, at every social level, of the Russian world through icons existed for centuries. The interior space (the house) and the exterior space (the world) were often constructed as if they made up one sacred space, a Great Icon, called on to symbolize no more nor less than Holy Russia, the special protection of Rus by heavenly powers, the ubiquity of Christ's image in it.

The house is one of the main symbolic manifestations of Sophia, the Wisdom of God. Holy Wisdom establishes harmony first of all in the world of the home: its primary function is 'home-making'. Hence in the Christian apprehension the home was always associated with the well-ordered and settled world, fenced in from 'chaos'. Meanwhile the word 'paradise' acquired a special modality: people wished not only to contemplate this 'paradise', but to sense it everywhere, starting with the home – humanity's microcosm. Thus in the mid-16th-century volume *Domostroy* ('Book of Household Management') by Silvester, a priest at the Annunciation Cathedral in the Moscow Kremlin, we read that in the actual domestic microcosm only an ideal orderliness is admissable. He compares the Russian household with paradise itself as a little model of the universe. In this connection *Domostroy* recommended placing icons in every room – a practice that Paul of Aleppo found suprising. As we read there,

> Each Christian must, in all the rooms, hang by seniority holy images, adorning them beautifully, and place light-holders in which candles are to be lit during prayers in front of the holy images, and are then extinguished after the service, are covered with

> a curtain for the sake of cleanliness from dust, for correct order and for their preservation.[3]

A century later Paul of Aleppo recorded that

> In each Russian cell there is an icon screen with images, and not only within, but also outside, above the door, even above the staircase door, for such is the custom among the Muscovites, that they hang icons on all doors of their houses, their cellars, their kitchens and their store-room.[4]

The 'main corner' of a Russian peasant house was also the 'High Jerusalem', the 'window to Heaven', the 'image of the other world'. But in the houses of those who had the opportunity, or were sufficiently rich, the 'main corner' was turned into a domestic church – a 'prayer-place' or oratory. Again it is Paul of Aleppo who first gives us a detailed description of it, later followed up by the 19th-century Russian historian I. Zabelin. As Paul says, 'In each of their houses there is a marvellous, elegant church, and each person boasts to others of its beauty and its outer and inner paintings.'[5] This domestic 'High Jerusalem' was almost totally covered in icons. According to Zabelin:

> One wall of it [i.e., the oratory] was completely occupied by the iconstasis in several tiers, whereon icons were set in the likeness of church iconstases, starting with the Deisis, or icons of the Saviour, the Mother of God and John the Baptist, constituting so to speak the foundation of domestic iconostases.[6]

What we are faced with, in other words, is the Russian 'high iconostasis', a distinctive 'symbol' of Muscovite devotion (illus. 2). But what is an iconostasis from the theological point of view? It acts both as the framing for the altar-space and as a window into the world of heavenly beings. We know that somewhere around 1400 the Byzantine templon (an openwork altar-rail) was transformed in Rus into a continuous wall of icons. This wall separates the congregation from observing the action of the liturgy: people do not see the mystery of the Eucharist, as they do in a Catholic church. Their gaze is directed only towards the iconostasis – the symbolic image of

2. Iconostasis of Annunciation Cathedral, Moscow Kremlin.

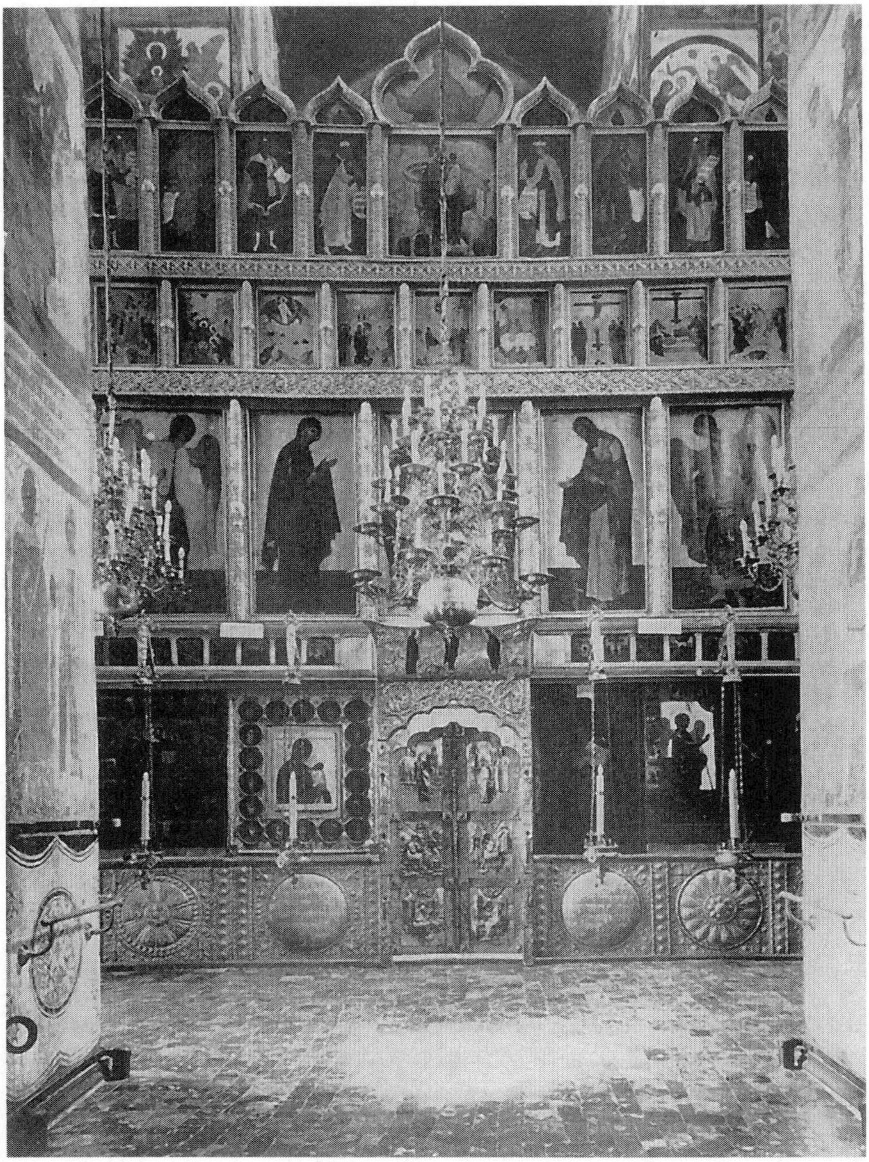

the economy of salvation, linked with Christ and the Mother of God. Hence the Russian high iconostasis was also perceived as no less than the 'window on Heaven', about which Pavel Florensky authoritatively wrote almost a century ago.[7]

But the frame of a window always concentrates attention, always brings the object close to the viewer. This means we have a definite basis for regarding the evolution of the iconostasis in the context of the individualization of religious sensibility and personal veneration.[8] The Russian high iconostasis brings the icon and the world together; it exalts the significance of the image in the salvation of humankind; and it is the sacralization of the world by means of the icon.

By the second half of the 16th century, multi-tiered iconostases were appearing in Rus, and not only in the churches, but in homes as well. These so-called 'domestic iconostases' were in the form of folding panels. Their iconographic programme could contain a series of local icons, a full Deisis, tiers of the feast days, prophets and patriarchs, though these tiers were not always present. People took folding iconostases with them on long journeys and on military expeditions. These domestic iconostases gave the impression of a scaled-down church iconostasis (illus. 3), and thus testified to fundamental changes in the system of religious sensibilities. Their type is that of an *Andachtsbild* – that is, a personal image for meditation of the kind that spread over Western Europe within the system of the 'New Devotion' in the 14th century. When opened up, Russian folding icons, like an *Andachtsbild*, could look like the cross-section of a place of worship;

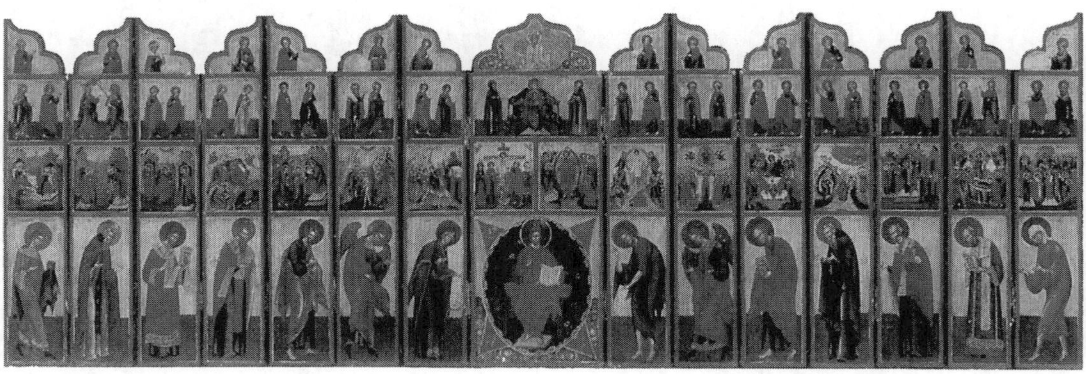

3. Folding icon with 15 scenes representing an iconostasis, 19th century. State Museum of the History of Religion, St Petersburg.

when folded they resembled its portal, or the 'royal gates' in an iconostasis. Thus people could see before them the 'door' to a place of worship, open it and find themselves at once in a world of angels and saints;[9] there they could be alone and face-to-face with God. This apparently simple

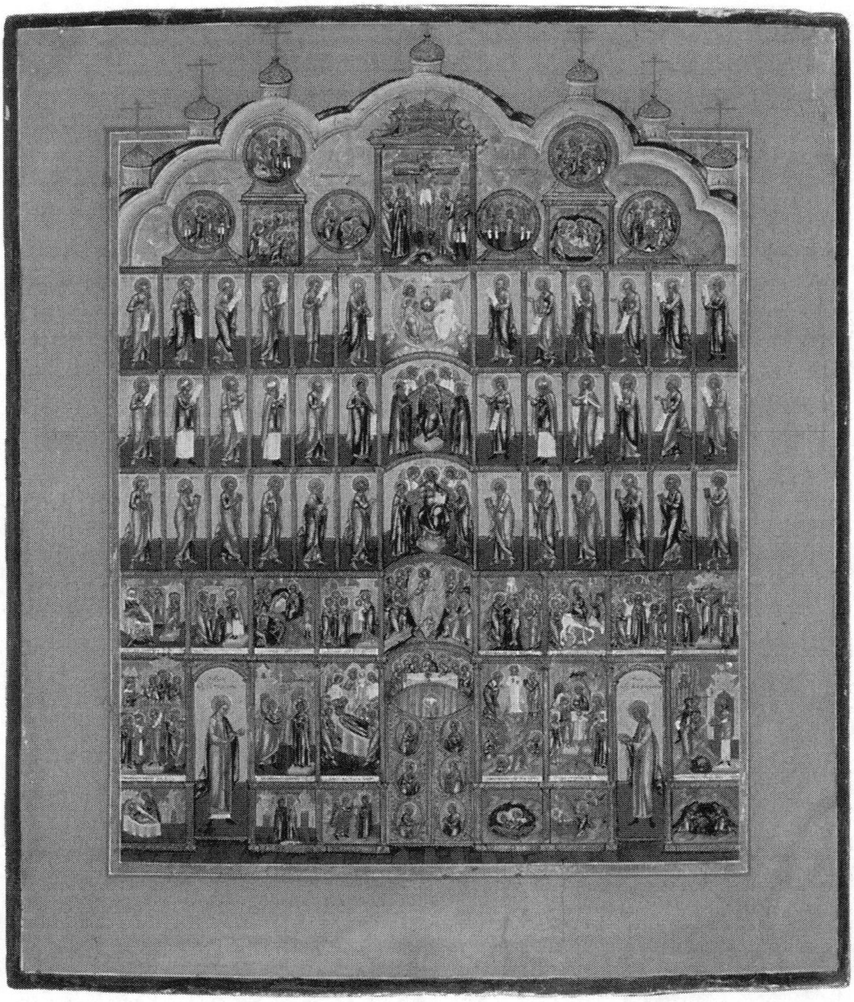

4. *Iconostasis*, first half of the 19th century. Kolomenskoye Historical and Architectural Museum-Preserve, Moscow.

mechanical operation put formerly inconceivable opportunities into the hands of mere mortals – the revelation and internalization of sanctity. Earlier, such 'playing' with the sacred space would have been largely limited to the Church; but in the 16th and 17th centuries, it was moving into the home.

Thus the mental reduction of the distance between God and the world led to the demand for personal possession of a multi-tiered iconostasis, or rather of its scaled-down model. So the appearance of this model in the

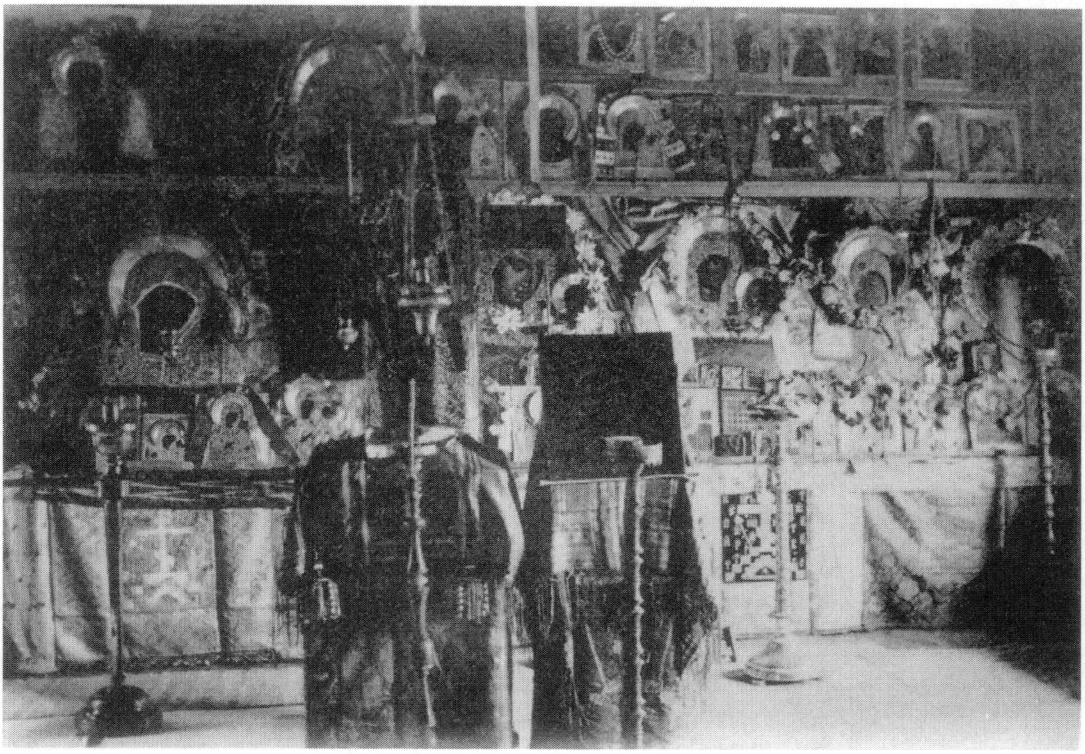

home was an important sign of the sacralization of inner space. People entering a domestic place of worship had to feel that they were almost in Paradise (see illus. 5). Immediately before their eyes was a large, high iconostasis, and on the walls its smaller model and icons within shrines. Moreover, in Russia in the 17th, 18th and 19th centuries, the representation of a high iconostasis on a single board transformed it into a personal prayer image (illus. 4).

5. The Old Ritualist oratory (*molennaja*), late-19th-century photograph. Private collection. Moscow.

The individual segments of the sanctified space of the oratory were united by the Holy Word – oral and written. Orally it resounded at the time of prayer, while in written form it was inscribed on a special board set into the frame and located on the wall beside the icons. Such 'prayers' on boards were often written for Tsar Aleksey Mihkhaylovich by court artists and writers, for example Ivan Saltanov and Polikarp Fomin.

The piety of the last Russian tsar, Nicholas II (1866–1918), and his empress, Alexandra Fyodorovna, is well known. At the beginning of the 20th century there was a huge quantity of icons in the Imperial chambers and oratories. As in the 17th-century 'Golden Age' of Muscovite piety, icons almost entirely covered the walls of rooms. Thus the 'Plan of the Locations of Images and Icons in the Former Bedchambers of their Imperial Highnesses in the Great Kremlin Palace' indicates 40 icons in the Emperor's bedroom alone, though we have every reason to believe that not all are listed, since some of them have such high sequential numbers (133, 134, etc.). Icons hung on both sides of the bed; overall, images of the Mother of God (the Smolensk, Iviron, Feodorov, Jerusalem and Vladimir variants) predominated, and there were also many Russian saints, above all those canonized at councils in Ivan the Terrible's time: the Moscow Metropolitans Aleksiy and Peter, various princes, Sergius of Radonezh and Kirill of Beloozero, Vasiliy the Blessed, Savva Storozhevsky and many others.[10]

A modern reconstruction of the Empress Alexandra's bedroom in the Alexander Palace at Tsarskoye Selo near St Petersburg is consistent with this document (illus. 6). A wall of icons that staggers the imagination has been transferred from a church into a secular building – losing its unified, elegant and dogmatic conception in the process. Instead we have a programme of personal devotion, based on the idea of intercession and on just the same mystical juxtaposition of Heaven and earth. In this way the age of Nicholas II gives a considerable insight into the earlier period of Tsar Aleksey Mikhaylovich, as it does into Russian history as a whole. It is no accident that the mid-17th century was then regarded, under the influence of the historian P. P. Milyukov, as the period of the 'fullest flowering of national ideals'. The choice of saints, the huge quantity of icons, and particularly their 'tapestry-like' location on the walls of the Imperial chambers, exemplified that special attention to the icon with which the official theocratic utopia of the last tsar was saturated.

In the 16th and 17th centuries the mental construct of 'Holy Russia' or of Rus as Great Icon had both a temporal and a spatial dimension. The temporal dimension presupposed mythic time – the eternal existence of the Muscovite tsardom – and the spatial the cosmological closeness of heaven and earth. By *c.* 1900 the topos 'Holy Russia' (as presenting the culture with a particular set of values, images and signs) was also linked with the model of an ideal autocracy in two different dimensions. On the one hand 'Holy Russia' was understood as an ideal, a historical model of Russia. On the other hand it was taken in the context of the Slavophile myth to be an individual cultural-historical type, a special 'civilization' that by its nature was opposed to the West, i.e., a sort of 'anti-Europe'.[11]

The contamination one with another of these ideal images of Holy Russia in the religious renaissance under Nicholas II explains much. This renaissance was a matter of strengthening the weakened connexion between monarch and people. However, it is important to emphasize that, in this political context, the accent was placed on a metaphysical link, bringing politics and metaphysics close together.

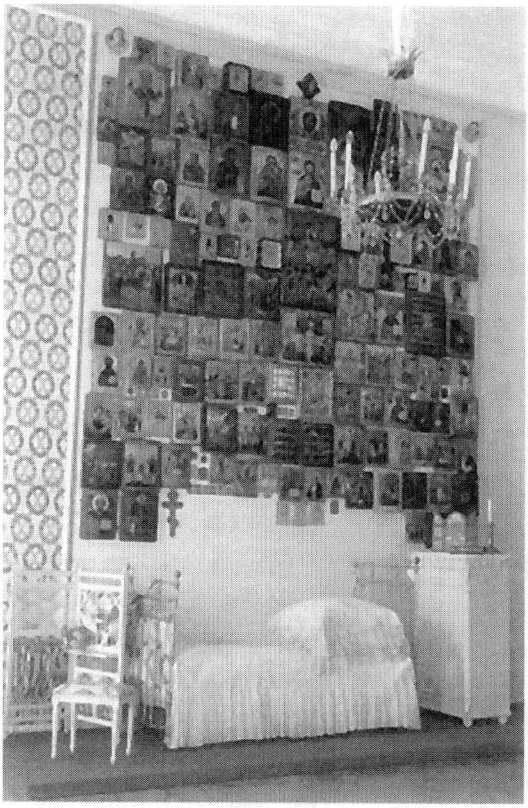

6. The Bedroom (reconstructed) of Empress Alexandra Fydorovna at the Alexander Palace in Tsarskoye Selo as it was in the early 20th century.

The official Russian religious art of the 18th and 19th centuries had broken with the Byzantine and Old Russian tradition; but at the beginning of the 20th century it turned to that tradition anew. The Orthodox icon always represented a link between two worlds. Once again symbol coincided with meaning. So that the symbol might once again acquire forcefulness and function, it was essential to revive the medieval icon-painting canon.[12] The revival of the traditional icon indicated a turning to national sources in the realm of religious experience. Only then could the small icons within the 'Great Icon' again symbolize God's favour towards the Russian lands, since from ancient times the external space was no less sacralized than the internal. Millions of icons, thousands of churches and hundreds of monasteries daily reminded people over the course of many centuries of the universal presence of the image of Christ in Holy Russia.

The well-known Russian publicist and economist V. P. Bezobrazov has testified that, in the mid-19th century, at every crossroads scattered among the fields and the forests of Vladimir region one would chance on a chapel or a timber post bearing an icon, for 'here there is an incalculable multitude of such posts'.[13] To put icons in the trunks of old trees was a distinctive feature of Russian piety: such images, secretively hidden away from human eyes in the forest depths, seemed naturally to sanctify the wild space. But they also sanctified 'cultural' space – gates, streets, the walls of houses, of fortresses and of strongpoints in towns and villages. Here, as travellers observed, icons were placed at the most 'honoured' points. On the doors of churches, town gates, on streets and in market-places – everywhere Sigismund Herberstein, Antonio Possevino, Johan Pernstein and Adam Olearius saw icons, marvelling at their number and at the special respect paid to them.[14]

As the Middle Ages waned, both in the West and in Russia, church interiors changed. Several altars (up to three, normally) would often be constructed, with the aim of acquiring as much grace as possible for the believers. In this context the Church of the Pokrov (the 'Protecting Veil') – best known today as 'St Basil's' – on the Moat in Moscow is unique: its nine altars symbolize the acquisition and concentration of God's favour in a single spot. It is no accident that a sacred name is attached to it: 'The Jerusalem' or 'New Jerusalem', as the same foreign visitors testify. Crucially, its doors were open day and night, presuming the endless dispensation of grace.[15] Since such a building was as much a holy image as an icon was, its very name was an aspect of its sacredness for the believer. Given the believers' opposition between 'the holy and the most holy', believers would discern beyond the name 'New Jerusalem' the authentic, more real reality, in particular that which had been revealed to the author of the Apocalypse: 'And I, John, saw the holy city, New Jerusalem, coming down from God out of heaven, prepared as a bride for her husband. And I heard a great voice out of heaven saying, Behold, the tabernacle of God is with men, and he will dwell with them, and they shall be his people, and God himself shall be with them, and be their God' (Revelation 21: 2–3). For exterior space a church or monastery was a 'higher' sign of holiness than a mere small icon. The number and magnificence of churches and monasteries in Muscovite

Russia testified to the same ubiquity of the image of Christ in the Russian land. People saw a concentration of holiness in the quantity of churches and monasteries, and in the 16th century rumours were current that Moscow contained 5,300 churches, monasteries and chapels.[16] Other versions made the number 1,500 churches and monasteries with up to 10,000 monks.[17] 'In the Kremlin and the city there are very many churches, chapels and monasteries; within and without the walls there are counted more than 2,000' (illus. 7).[18] Hence naturally the quantity of churches was invariably a subject of pride in popular tales as late as the 19th century.[19]

No less telling a feature distinguished the roads that stretched to every corner of the 'tsardom' from its centre: 'All the roads abound with churches, and wheresoever anyone may travel, he can stop to attend a service at a church close by.' Bell-ringing in particular was an indicator of Muscovite piety. Nothing so excited foreign observers as the full pealing of bells on the eve of feast days or Sunday, for 'the earth trembled and the thunderous sound of bells rose to the heavens'.[20]

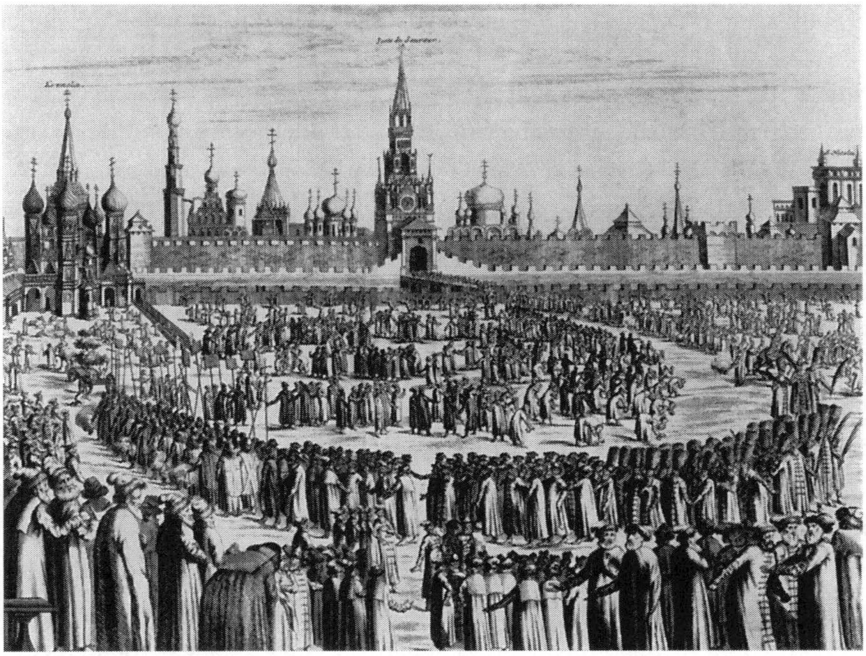

7. 'The Moscow Kremlin: Palm Sunday Ceremony', from *Voyage du* [sic] *Adam Olearius* (Paris, 1727).

The reforms of Peter the Great were, of course, in strong contrast to the outward grandeur and brilliance of Muscovite Russia. On the upper cultural levels a different logic determined the model to be followed: the orientation towards Byzantium was replaced by an orientation towards the First Rome. 'Of two possible paths – the capital as place of concentrated holiness and the capital in the shadow of Imperial Rome – Peter chose the latter.'[21] The reforms meant that the construction of a new church required official permission not only from the higher spiritual authorities but from the ruler too. In the process, attention began to be paid to the number of parochial households, to their ability to sustain a parish, and also (this is very telling) to the distance separating churches.[22] The same applied to monasteries. The space of Rus, which had become Imperial Russia, was undergoing secularizing processes while it was becoming even more sacralized within the cultural milieu of the Old Belief, with many people continuing to live according to the rules of Muscovite devotion.

In greater contrast to the splendour of Holy Russia was the Orthodox 'Orient'. The remainder of the world of 'Slavia Orthodoxa' in the post-Byzantine period was experiencing not the 'burden of numbers' of holy objects, but rather a siege mentality arising from the need to survive within the space of the Muslim world: the Ottoman empire was hostile to Christianity, which invariably convinced the Russian mind of the exceptional purity of the Russian Orthodox faith and of its chief token – its icons. Pictures of ravaged monasteries and churches succeeded the once brilliant cultural–historical landscape of the former Byzantine lands. From the 16th century, minarets – signs of the victory of Islam over Christianity– dominated this cultural–historical space. Islam forbade not only tall Christian churches, but even tall houses, 'sign of an arrogance that was hateful to it'.[23] Not surprisingly, the impoverishment of Balkan church life continually affronted Russian travellers and scholars. Many facts testify to the destruction of places of worship and desecration of holy sites, their 'deconcentration'. We should remember that, for the believer, the place of worship is not only a 'house of prayer', but a model of the universe. Thus the massive destruction and desecration of places of worship was fraught with major structural changes in consciousness. Behind the changes in the architectural landscape there was a transformation in 'architectural thinking'.

The well-known Russian historian and publicist Alexander Gilferding, who visited Herzegovina, Bosnia and Serbia in 1857, left us a description of the typical interior of a Balkan village church:

> In one of the villages . . . we saw what passes for a village church in Herzegovina. It is a little stone chamber which could easily be fitted within an ordinary room in one of our houses. A bare partition of boards takes the place of an iconostasis; there are no royal doors in it; a bare slab of stone on a plinth serves as an altar. The church contains no cross, no image, no books , no vessels: all these objects are kept in the local villagers' houses and are brought to the church on days when services are to be held; if anything had been left in the church then the Muslims would inevitably have seized it; earlier churches had to stand open, without locked doors . . . [24]

In his *Journey through Macedonia* (1900), Nikodim Kondakov recollected the one-time royal wealth of the churches and monasteries around Skopje, which had been built in the age of Serbia's political independence and flowering. In his own time, however, all these rich churches had the appearance of 'sad ruins'.[25]

Even in Constantinople Russian scholars in the 19th century estimated that by the end of the 16th century, only 26 churches – very impoverished ones – remained. Arkhangelsky wrote that in the former capital of the Byzantine empire, some of the churches were turned into mosques, while others were closed. At the end of the 17th century, only 22 churches remained, but even these were hardly distinguishable from poor dwellings. In many towns and villages Christian places of worship underwent the same fate. 'After this it does not come as a surprise',

> that in the whole expanse of Bulgaria and Rumelia travellers would find places of Christian worship in such reduced circumstances that they could not be distinguished from simple barns. And what would be inside them? A single iconostasis which in its impoverishment scarcely bore witness to the building's dedication to prayer

> and inwardness. Many churches, as travellers testified, not only lacked the necessary church vessels, but even the sacred books.[26]

All this tells us that the culture of icons in the Balkans differed greatly from the situation in Russia. This contrast can also be observed on the level of their actual production process. Here the 'burden of numbers' provides a context that is equally interesting.

We should not forget that the world of icon production had a special culture of its own that always displayed a certain sensitivity towards, and propensity for, emotionalism. This restless world reacted swiftly to changes in religious sensibilities, in the orientation of official and unofficial piety, and also to social circumstances in the broadest sense. As the Middle Ages turned into the modern period, the demand for prayer images rose sharply in both Catholic Western and Orthodox Eastern Europe.

The struggle for purity of popular devotion, the orientation towards personal revelation and the values of early Christianity were common both to the Reformation and the Catholic Counter-Reformation. Scholars even define the 16th and 17th centuries as a period of 'second Christianization' in Europe, distinguished by stricter norms of faith than those of the Middle Ages. After the Council of Trent in 1545–63, when the Western Church formulated its Counter-Reformation doctrine, art was allocated a prominent role in the process of this 'Christianization', just as it was in the drive to reform the Catholic Church.[27] More attention was now given to the significance of the icon in the matter of human salvation, both in Catholicism and Orthodoxy. In this connexion Philippe Ariès aptly notes that in a Catholic painting of the period in the church of Perthuis an angel is bearing up to Heaven a soul represented as a child carrying a small image.[28] It is no accident either that Catholic authors at the time of the active dissemination of Protestant ideas used to emphasize the piety of Russian venerators of icons. Luther's irreconcilable opponent Johann Fabri commented on this in his *The Religion of the Muscovites who Live Close to the Icy Ocean* (Basle, 1562).[29] The 'strictness and modesty' of the Russian icon painters was also noted by the Jesuit Antonio Possevino, who tried without success to convert Ivan the Terrible to Catholicism.

Following the Council of Trent, Greek Orthodox craftsmen working in Catholic lands began to accept commissions from Catholics no less than from the Orthodox, for Cretan icons were the most highly prized in the Catholic world.[30] Cretan masters were particularly successful at imaging the torments of martyrs, as well as in an archaizing, more severe, artistic language of proto-Renaissance Madonnas. One 17th-century Italian writer was astonished to discover that there was not a single Catholic church in Messina – and he counted 108 of them – that did not contain a Greek icon of Mary.[31] The mass output of Greek workshops on the Mediterranean islands and in Venice during the 17th and 18th centuries penetrated into the Catholic churches, monasteries and houses of Loreto, Fabriano, Palermo, Syracuse and other Italian towns. But it was also directed towards the Orthodox inhabitants of Dalmatia, Thrace, countless Central European towns, and indeed the whole Orthodox East, where, for example, many Cretan icons were venerated as wonder-working.

Over and above the dynamics of the icon-painting trade there could always be discerned the Church's concern for zealousness in faith and purity in popular piety, underpinned by questions of the very aesthetics of that piety. This was true in modern times everywhere from Cairo to the Russian North, from Venice to Irkutsk. But it is interesting that the developmental graphs of mass icon production in the Graeco-Slavonic East invariably took the form of a parabola, while the graph of growth in Russia remained more or less constant. It is not hard to deduce that such rising and falling graphs were the consequence of both global and historically less-significant impulses that at times derived entirely from what went on at upper and lower levels of local cultures.

In Russia the icon business made use of state protection, and at certain moments was itself an important sphere of state politics; in those parts of the Orthodox world that were under the Ottoman empire and Catholic governments, by contrast, its marginality was clear for all to see, and presupposed great vulnerability and sensitivity. A characteristic example is the 'explosion' of icon-production on Crete in its period of Venetian rule and its decline with the island's capture by the Turks in 1669. There is an analogy in the rise of icon production in Serbia when the Patriarchate of Peć was established in 1346, followed again by decline and disintegration after the Great Emigration of 1690 that followed the Turkish reprisals. The national revivals in the Balkans would again lead to a resumption of activity, especially in those areas where circumstances had earlier been less favourable, for example Bulgaria. The interrelation of these declines and revivals is the best demonstration of the integration of the Christian world as a whole. As with any large-scale phenomenon, however, it consists of particular and discrete elements. The production of icons in both Muscovite and Imperial Russia clearly stands out in the Christian world as having its own special agenda that differed fundamentally from the impulses that nourished, for example, the dynamics of Greek icon production in Crete, in the Ionian islands, in Venice or in the rustic craft centres of the Balkans. The unique history of icon production in three Russian villages – Palekh, Mstyora and Kholuy – confirms this. Behind the routine configurations of their everyday activity stood the philosophical constructs and refinements I have already noted.

Within these centres of icon painting the millions of icons that once sanctified the vastness of Holy Russia were made. If we mark on a map all the places where 17th- and 18th-century icons were painted in, say, the Vladimir-Suzdal province alone, we see that they were painted absolutely everywhere: in towns large and small, in monasteries, in villages and in hamlets. Only short distances separate Vyazniki, Shuya, Gorokhovets, Vladimir, Bogolyubovo, Suzdal, Pereyaslavl-Zalessky, Murom, Yuryev and, finally, the major centres of icon painting in Imperial Russia: Palekh, Mstyora and Kholuy (see illus. 8). This map is important testimony to a cultural explosion: from the time of Ivan the Terrible icon production entered a 50- to 70-year-long spell of heightened activity and became a massive operation. The density of these little icon-realms, crowded together on the map, interestingly reflects the saturation of the world of Russia with images, its sacralization through icons and churches. Indeed, Russia in the 17th century reminds one of the situation in Byzantium on the eve of iconoclasm.[32]

As astonishing as is the quantity of icons that were generated is the number of craftsmen who worked in Palekh, Mstyora and Kholuy (illus. 9), all three of which were known from the mid-17th century. Iosif Vladimirov mentions them in his aesthetic tract *The Missive of one Iosif, a Painter, to the Tsar's Painter and Most Wise Delineator, Simon Fyodorovich* (1660–66).

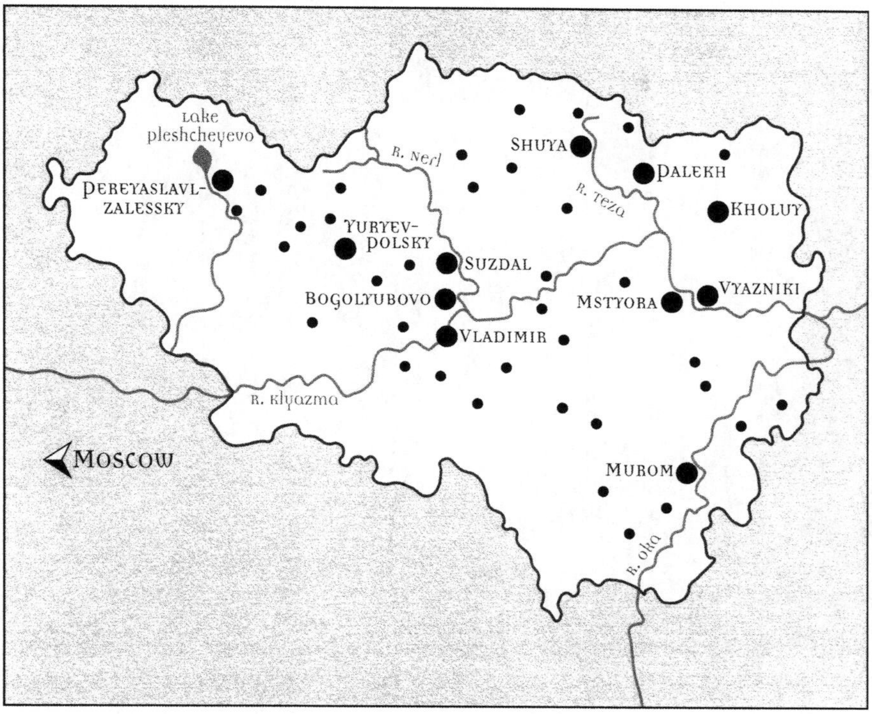

8. Vladimir Province, showing 17th- and 18th-century centres of icon production.

I shall have more to say on this work later, but here wish to note those 'hundreds' and 'thousands' of Palekh and Kholuy icons that the famous master compared to 'wood shavings in a bonfire'. In his opinion their sheer 'burden of quantity' eclipsed their quality (illus. 50).[33]

Among the archives of the Suzdal spiritual consistory is an early list (1752) of icon painters in Kholuy. Compiled in connection with a Government enquiry into the icon-painting business at the village, it contains 350 names, although there is every reason to believe that the list is incomplete. At that time painters were required to put their name on icons to confirm their awareness of the decrees that forbade the making of Old Ritualist icons, but many refused to do so.[34] By way of comparison we may note that, according to M. Chatzidakis's data, for the 18th century as a whole, around 350 icon painters were at work in Greece.[35]

At the beginning of the 19th century no less a figure than Goethe became interested in the icons of Palekh, Mstyora and Kholuy. In 1812 he contacted the Empress Mariya Fyodorovna for information on these three unusual

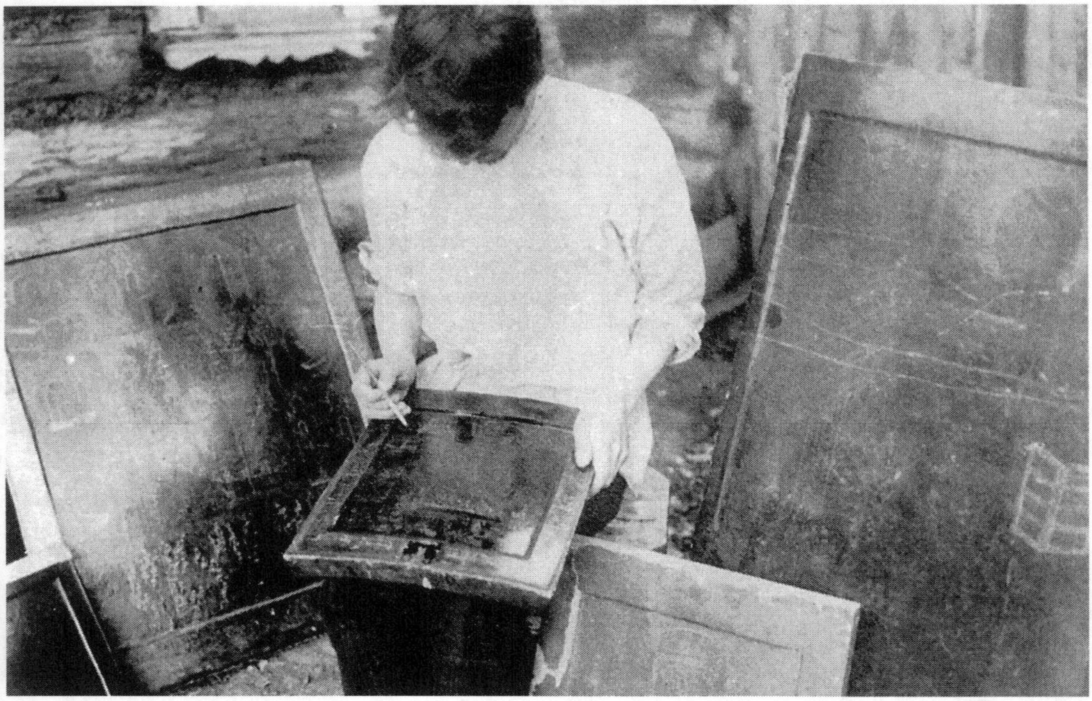

9. An Old-Style icon-painter in Mstyora, late 19th century or early 20th. Archive of Vladimir-Suzdal State Historical and Architectural Museum-Preserve, Vladimir.

places. In answer, A. N. Suponev, the Governor of Vladimir, explained that 700 people lived in Kholuy, and all without exception were involved in icon painting. In Palekh the same trade involved 600 people. There were slightly fewer icon painters in Mstyora.[36] In the 18th century, and particularly in the 19th, the large number of icon-painting workshops in all three villages had spawned numerous collateral industries. The Suzdalian icon business was a complicated labyrinth. For example, whole villages near to Palekh, Mstyora and Kholuy prepared brushes, shrines and boards of wood for icons. Simultaneously, old boards with erased or darkened paint surfaces were collected throughout Russia, and fresh icons were painted on them. The scale of this industry can well be judged by information contained in a local paper of 1879. In that year more than 28,000 old boards gathered from every part of Russia were deposited in Mstyora alone.[37] No industry of this sort appears to have existed either in the Balkans or in the Orthodox East. In the course of its artistic and economic development over several centuries, the icon trade in Palekh, Mstyora and Kholuy continually renewed itself, and by degrees came to dominate the whole of Russia.

From the figures given in statistical articles by 19th-century Russian scholars such as I. A. Golyshev, K. Tikhonravov, P. Leontyev and others, it seems certain that in no other place or period was icon production so massive. Tikhonravov testified that certain craftsmen, painting the whole image apart from the face(s), were able to turn out 600 items a week, while other craftsmen would paint the same number of saintly countenances.[38] Various statistical tables of the same period give similar data, and augment this picture of a startling dynamism with descriptions of the detailed breakdown of the production process and explanations for the remarkable cheapness of icons, which implies not only the universal demand for them, but their ease of preparation and acquisition.

All this makes the figures involved more plausible: by the mid-19th century, icon production in Kholuy alone had reached 1.5 to two million items per year.[39] These data, incidentally, are frequently reinforced. Statistical accounts of the time used to state that almost no one in Kholuy was capable of ploughing or sowing seed: 'except at the time of four major fairs, old and young alike were taken up with the painting of images that are sold throughout Russia, in part by *ofeni* [pedlars] to the number of 1.5 to 2 million images'.[40] Half a century later, V. T. Georgievsky established that a small icon-painting workshop of five or six workers could produce from 100 to 300 'mass market' icons *per day* (illus. 185, 187, 190).[41] Incidentally, a typical example of just such an icon is held by the Society of Antiquaries of London, an early 18th-century Kholuy image of the Mother of God as Life-Giving Spring.[42]

This is the background to what appears to be the unique world of the Russian trade in icons. Evidently in no other place and at no other time was there such a number of rural icon merchants or such a remarkably complicated network of trade routes as in Russia. Swarms of 'Suzdalian' merchants rise up before our eyes like tiny specks of some great history. The leading figure in all this was the Suzdalian *ofenya*, a peripatetic retailer. The village icon painters worked in order to 'keep body and soul together', so smart-minded 'helpers' – merchants and agents – were needed for the market-place. These two commercial roles came together in the person of the *ofenya* and figured thus in the world of Suzdalian icon production, which from its origins and in its massive growth was inseparable from the *ofenya*'s activity.

The number of *ofenya* settlements that had long encircled Palekh, Mstyora and Kholuy corresponded to the number of icon painters in Rus and to the demands of Russian piety for icons. In the last quarter of the 19th century alone (and this was a time when the level of *ofenya* trade began to decline) there were more than 150. And if we take into account that just one region adjacent to the icon-painting centres had a population of 4,200, out of whom, according to the statistics, the majority in the past were *ofeni*,[43] one can imagine the scale of both production and commerce in 'Suzdalian' icons. The master craftsman and the itinerant salesman peddling his products went hand-in-hand.

Fernand Braudel has observed that the itinerant merchant was always to be found where there was a 'gap' in the market economy – that is, an absence of developed mechanisms for trade. Filling such gaps, itinerant salesmen appeared ubiquitously in the 17th and 18th centuries, acquiring a long list of names. In French they were called *colporteur, port-balle*, in English 'hawker', 'huckster', 'pedlar', etc. In Bulgarian their name came from the Turkish *sergi*: *sergidziya*, as in Serbo-Croat it was *torbar*, derived from the Turkish *torba*, meaning bag.[44] In Russian, such a list could easily be made much longer: *khodebshchiki, kantyuzhniki, kartinshchiki, korobeyniki, knigonosky, farisei, masyki, obeztilniki* and finally *ofeni, ofeni-ikonshchiki* and *ofeni-starinshchiki*. From this it can be seen that the icon peddlars had many colleagues in commerce: not only icons were sold. But it was evidently only in Russia that such retail commerce was so closely bound up with the business of icons and popular religious life.

This connection meant that the pedlar acquired special nicknames, special habits and behavioural culture, special appearance and even special jargon. The choice of nicknames for the icon-selling *ofeni* always demonstrated the vast geographical scope of their trade. In Little Russia they were called *varyagi* (i.e., 'Viking merchants'), in White Russia *mayaki*, in the Russian North *torgovany*, in Siberia *vyaznikovtsy* and *suzdaly*, etc.[45]

The techniques of the *ofenya's* trade were always closely related to the religious life of the people. Rules of behaviour, customs and linguistic jargon were the condition and consequence of the semi-legitimate distribution of Palekh, Mstyora and Kholuy icons among the Russian Old Ritualists. In everyday life the *ofeni* were perceived as a self-contained caste. In 1843 the *Vladimir Province Gazette* informed readers that in the Suzdal region

> active and efficient businessmen, known everywhere by the name of *ofeni*, live and travel thence throughout the length and breadth of Russia. These small traders make up a special commercial caste, even possessing their own language of conversation, whether it be artificially devised or something preserved by them from former generations.[46]

No doubt the basic function of the icon-pedlars' jargon was to conceal the processes of trading in Old Ritualist images: this trade was equated in the minds of officialdom with propaganda for the schismatics.

The *ofeni* went everywhere, and this remained the case into the 19th century. Hence the spread of territory where icons from Palekh, Mstyora and Kholuy can be found is incomparably greater than the distribution area of icons from any other icon-painting centres. They and their likes covered Holy Russia with those millions of icons that once sacralized its boundless expanses.

The Details of Ritual

The sacred space of Russia as 'Great Icon' was created not through the image alone, but by sacralized word and gesture. Communing through prayer with an icon, a person would partake of holiness, of the divine condition. The 'word' and the 'ritual' were an indissoluble whole. They constituted the language of everyday religious culture, and to the believer they were God-inspired: the confession of faith is to this day understood as the following of Christ and fulfilment of his commandments. A phrase from the kontakion of the *Triumph of Orthodoxy* – 'but confessing salvation through deed and word we conceive of this' – clearly conveyed the chief principles of the salvational economy and the huge significance of word and ritual in prayer before the icon. As one scholar has explained, 'only in ritual can one attain experience of the integrity of existence and the integrity of knowledge about it, understood as a blessing and referring to the idea of the divine as bearer of this blessing'.[47] When in church (that is, when within the sacralized space of a 'great icon'), an individual was meant to be more strict with him- or herself, more inwardly collected. 'Strictness' is an important word for anyone who has been in contact with Russian religious life, but this 'strictness' is hard to describe and is best left to eye-witnesses.

'I shall now speak about the characteristic feature of pious behaviour which manifests itself in the strict carrying out of church rituals', wrote B. P. Bezobrazov.[48] 'Nothing had altered in people's attitudes to the church', noted another 19th-century observer of the way of life of tradesmen and craftsmen; 'just as strict order was observed as in the past'.[49] Similar observations were made in the 16th, 17th and 18th centuries. A mass of interesting testimony survives on the stringent and frequent habit of prayer among Russian people, both within a church and outside it. As Paul of Aleppo observed, on entering a church Russians prayed at length before the icons,

> since among them one cannot pray otherwise than in front of an icon, fixing one's gaze on it: that is to say they really do prostrate themselves before it, and do not pray just anyhow, as we do.[50]

This heartfelt prayer before an icon in church has, as it were, a double context for Paul: strictness of worship and strictness of the tsardom. In his observations they are constantly linked: orderliness in the place of worship is as though copied in orderliness in the world, although the latter inevitably brings its own correctives into this strictness. 'We marvelled at the procedures in their churches', he wrote. Marvelled at what, precisely? 'Know then that the communion service in this country is performed with full reverence, fear and respect (to the sacred place).'[51]

'Reverence', 'fear', 'respect': these are the words most often used when people speak of the liturgy. Reverence is heard in the very voice with which 'the ecclesiastical prayer is pronounced: the priest utters the versicle and the deacon utters the response not in a loud voice, but full of reverence'. This, too, is how the choristers sing.

> In particular when the bishop would lay hands on the priest his voice would be lowered so that only those at the altar might hear it:

that is just how the deacon too would utter the responses. Such is their custom; we too acquired it from them.

Reverence was also apparent in the way that on the eve of each feast day and on its morning the priest began the service and went out to cense the congregation wearing a chasuble (that is, in full vestments), not disrobing until the end of the service. The Archdeacon of Damascus also saw particular reverence in how the names of the Patriarch and the tsar's family were uttered. He took pains to calculate that in the response they sang 'Lord, have mercy' around 100 times, and 'each time the deacon, on making the response and going to the altar, thrice made a bow before the cross and kissed it; the priest made bows equally'.[52] The church service reflects in outward ritual forms not only the inner content of religion, but also the religious disposition of the human soul: after all, in worship even the lowliest receives God's favour. The Archdeacon makes the interesting remark that, in mid-17th-century Moscow, there was no distinction between the rank of monasteries and that of ordinary churches: before the psalm at vespers they always sang 'Holy Lord' in the monastic way.

Bowing and making the sign of the cross are symbolic gestures by which a person would express humility before God and special ardour in prayer. Describing the manner of public prayer, Paul noted that

> in church they stand as motionless as rocks, and all with uncovered heads, from priests and powerful men to the common people. They finish crossing themselves with *a blow* [my italics] of the fingers against the forehead and shoulders in truth, at which point they make a bow, and do not merely make scrawling gestures as we do.

In descriptions of this bowing the word 'beat' is often used: 'From the beginning of the service to its end they never stop their bows, beating them out one after another.' Particularly surprising for Patriarch Makariy and his son was the behaviour of children. They precisely copied that of the adults (at times even exceeding them in agility), since 'they were nourished with the milk of faith and devotion'; 'as we beheld all that was going on, we were astonished not at the adults, but at the young folk, seeing them make the sign of the cross in Muscovite fashion'.[53]

The 'Muscovite fashion' of bowing was carried out in a special way. Paul of Aleppo, well versed in the practice of ecclesiastical ritual, never ceased to marvel at it. The pictures he draws convey a lively sense of that zeal in faith which in daily life came close to excess. On entering a church, both adults and children at once made several deep bows to the ground and greeted all those present east and west, north and south. In this process the children were even more animated than the adults. They greeted people out on the street with the same enthusiasm. Visitors witnessed how not only simple folk, but the well-to-do and nobility prostrated themselves, kneeling in the dust in their expensive kaftans of finest Angora wool or in clothes with broad collars sewn liberally with gold thread and buttons of precious materials. 'This is the habit they all have, even among the poor.'[54] We may note that later, according to the Old Believers', the gradual rejection within the reformed church of prostrations to the ground would be associated with nothing less than the 'Lutheran' and 'Calvinist' heresies: 'those Latins, Lutherans and Calvinists have all rejected prostrations to the ground in their services. Similarly the Great Russian bishops of our day have all abolished bowing down to the ground'.[55]

Symbolic gestures relating to icons always hinted at the hidden reality of the covenant with God and at trust in his mercy. One of the main ones was the kissing of icons. The custom had the authority of the Fathers of the Church, and to elucidate its essence John Damascene cited St Leontios, Bishop of Cyprus:

> And just as Jacob, having received from the brothers of Joseph, after they had sold him, the blood-stained coat of many colours, kissed the coat with weeping and laid it out in front of his eyes – not weeping for the clothing, of course, but considering that through it he was kissing Joseph and holding him in his arms – so we Christians, bodily kissing the icon of Christ, or of an Apostle, or of a martyr, consider in our souls that we kiss Christ himself or his martyr.[56]

Obtaining grace in prayerful contact with the sacred, the believer seemed to sojourn in the divine realm that surrounded all his or her human existence. Thus the motif of tears could be explained together with the motifs of fear and love. As Johan Huizinga has written, 'devotion involves a certain softening of the heart in which brief outbursts of weeping can easily take place'.[57] In the Middle Ages this was indeed the case, and not only in the West. The 'gift of tears' is mentioned as early as the 7th century in the work of John Climacus, abbot of the monastery of St Catherine on Sinai. Weeping was also unfailingly a presupposition of the Muscovite system of devotion. In his prescriptive words on the icon in his *Domostroy*, Silvester did not fail to mention that it was always proper to render respect to the images 'with tears and weeping, and making confession with saddened heart to beg the remission of sins'.[58] Later, at the end of the 18th century, weeping and tears would prevail in the congregation of the 'self-baptizers', a sect within the Priestless Old Believers,[59] who administered the sacrament of baptism to themselves: this 'detail' of their ritual was counterposed by them to communal singing.[60] The flow of tears as one of the most widespread miracles associated with icons of the Mother of God was interpreted in the post-Reformation era as the Virgin Mary's tears for human frailties: 'She weeps with her icon for our sins, griefs and disasters', as Andrey Denisov explained.[61]

Tears always accompanied an emotive attitude to a sacred object, while the kissing of an icon itself symbolized complex feelings of mixed fear and hope, although sometimes it also became a simple habit in icon reverence. According to Paul of Aleppo, in the reign of Aleksey Mikhaylovich the faithful made physical contact with icons in church only once a year – on the first Sunday of Lent, the feast of the Triumph of Orthodoxy, which had been established in honour of the victory over iconoclasm (843) and was particularly respected in Muscovite Russia. The fact that the majority of Russians touched the icons only on that day testified to a particular reverence in their attitude to the services held on that feast day. The synodic texts of the Triumph of Orthodoxy orientated a person to the worship of Christ not only by word but by image, summoning him or her to create and renew their similitude to God. Contact with icons on this day in particular implied fidelity to the image and steadfastess in its veneration. It is no accident that the last paragraph of the synodic texts pronounced 'eternal memory' to those who demonstrated their deeds 'in the confirmation of truth' through pictures, i.e., icons.

No less symbolic was contact with a church icon on another feast day, that of the Image Not Made by Hands of the Lord Jesus Christ (16 August). According to Church tradition, the first icon of Christ appeared in his lifetime. The Image or Saviour Not Made by Hands was the foundation of Christian icon painting: the face of Christ imprinted miraculously on a cloth became a most important testimony to the Incarnation and the basis of icons produced by the uncreated energies of God, and showed the possibility of miraculous creation.On that feast day, all who came to the place of worship took in the words of the service, bidding them to prostrate themselves before 'the image not made by hand, shining brighter than the sun ' and to beg for 'enlightment' from the icon of Christ, which was the necessary condition for entry into the heavenly kingdom. If the Apostles were led by Christ himself into Jerusalem, then his image could lead mere mortals into Jerusalem too: 'We praise thee, Lover of humankind, beholding thine image and seeing thy gaze: give, O Saviour, to thy slaves through this unhindered entry to Eden' (canticle, 16 August). At the beginning of the 18th century the Danish ambassador J. Juel observed this zealous contact with the icon. Finding himself (while on some business connected with Peter the Great) right inside a church, he noted that when worshippers touched the images of saints and Apostles, 'the Russians kiss them right on the lips and faces, while on images of the Mother of God and the Saviour they kissed only hands and feet'.[62]

If we leave the place of worship for the outside 'world', we shall discover the same 'strictness' lasting through centuries, though with one essential difference: much more often it sinks into a sea of everyday prejudices that coexist with the generally accepted norms of devotion. If we were to believe the observations of the same Paul of Aleppo, we might conclude that the strictness of the 'Josephite' model of devotion could be explained by the character of the tsardom, by the profound emotional imperative of its spirituality. 'Note that strictness in this vast kingdom is very great', says Paul more than once, and eventually comes to the unexpected conclusion that 'if Greeks had possessed the same strictness as the Muscovites, then they would have continued to rule themselves to this day'.[63] Strictness was poured into everything that touched on the pious life; indeed it characterized holiness, at the opposite pole to which were laughter and gaiety: 'God is our witness that we conducted ourselves among them as if we were dead to the world, refusing all pleasures, joys and jokes, in the highest state of morality, though because we had to rather than by choice.'[64] In the tsardom of Muscovy (the 'Third Rome'), strictness was a guarantee of continuing grace – the basis of state power. Thus people preserved such strictness; they even kept watch on it.

Paul forewarns those who prepare to go into the 'land of the Muscovites': that they must forget jokes, laughter and informality; the world under the sign of universal sacredness excludes them. More than that,

> the Muscovites place overseers with the bishops and in monasteries and watch all who come here, day and night, through cracks in the door, observing whether they constantly exercise themselves in humility, silence, fasting and prayer or else carouse, amuse themselves with games, tell jokes, make mock and quarrel'.[65]

Strictness also manifests itself in an excessively zealous attitude towards God. Johann Pernstein, the ambassador of the Holy Roman Emperor, Maximilian II, wrote in his report that the Muscovites do not embark on a single undertaking without invoking the name of the Most Holy and Indivisible Trinity 'with such enthusiasm and piety that you would find it hard to believe'.[66] Numerous travellers of the 16th, 17th and 18th centuries have described the ritual of brief and repeated prayer in front of an icon, both on the streets and at home, and its solemn character for the lay person. The secularizing processes of those centuries hardly touched on this level. This is how the merchants on the south bank of the Moscow River (Zamoskvorechie) went to and from work every day as late as the mid-19th century:

> The merchants mostly lived in their own houses, and it was the custom to attach copper crucifixes or some icon or other above the gateway to the houses. The merchant would go out of his gate, bare his head and begin to cross himself; reaching his shop, he would climb down from his carriage and again crossed himself to the icon – and the icons, as I have said, were hung at every line of merchandise.

> On stopping work in the evenings and shutting up his shop, the merchant, with his assistants and stewards around him, again crossed himself to the icon, after which he bowed in three directions, as if temporarily bidding farewell to those places where he spent the larger part of his life. Old Muscovites in general, on passing by churches, on foot or in a vehicle, would stop and cross themselves.[67]

As a result of their 'great love' toward icons, as Paul of Aleppo noted, Russians would not pray without having an icon or the domes of a church in view, even distantly – 'such is their faith'. At home or in church, praying to an icon, they would turn and incline their heads in all four directions. A disciplined 'squadron of warriors' might go past, but as soon as they saw an icon, they would all take off their caps, turn to the image and pray, despite the bitter cold.[68] When walking along the street, Juel could not help noticing that Russians had the habit of frequently crossing themselves, and 'before the images on the houses or gates', they 'always bow and cross themselves many times'.[69]

Just such an observation had been made half a century before: 'Every time they see an icon they stop and pray to it with great reverence; if perchance one of them might even pass by 100 icons in a single hour, he would stop and pray to each unhurriedly. Not only the men follow this custom, but also the women and children.'[70] Adam Olearius for his part noted that the Russians cross themselves and pray not only to icons, but to crosses set up on churches, and 'for that reason you continually meet Russians in prayer on the streets'.[71] As he observed, every oathtaking involved ritual contact with an icon (illus. 10). No kind of grief could prevent the explosion of devotion in front of an image. Those who were accompanying a corpse to burial turned to the icon fixed above the door, made the sign of the cross, beat their breasts and prostrated themselves on the ground, weeping and groaning.[72]

The habit of pronouncing a brief and frequent prayer before an icon was very deep-seated. The short schema 'Lord, have mercy' conveyed a perpetual turning to God for help, a daily formula for a certain attitude to the world. In this prayer a person was as if momentarily dead to anything base or worldly and unenlightened: the frequently repeated prayer 'narrowed' the gap between the earthly and the heavenly. On entry into any house the first thing that a believer would look for was an image. The model for this behaviour was given in the *Nomocanon* (*Kormchaya*) of the 16th century, underlining the particular nature of reverenced images: 'Entering a house and leaving it, we bow to and venerate the first-formed substance, just as our forefathers bade us, for this is the sign of believers'.[73] Sigismund Herberstein reported that in each Russian house and dwelling-place, icons of the saints, 'drawn or cast in metal', stand always at the most 'honoured' place, 'and when one visits another, then on entering the dwelling place, he immediately bares his head and looks about him to find where the image is. On seeing it he twice makes the sign of the cross and, lowering his head, says 'Lord, have mercy'.[74] Johann Pernstein records almost the same: 'In their houses they adhere to their habits of prayer in similar fashion: thus for example on entering or leaving a house they always kneel three times before the representation of the Crucifixion or before the icon

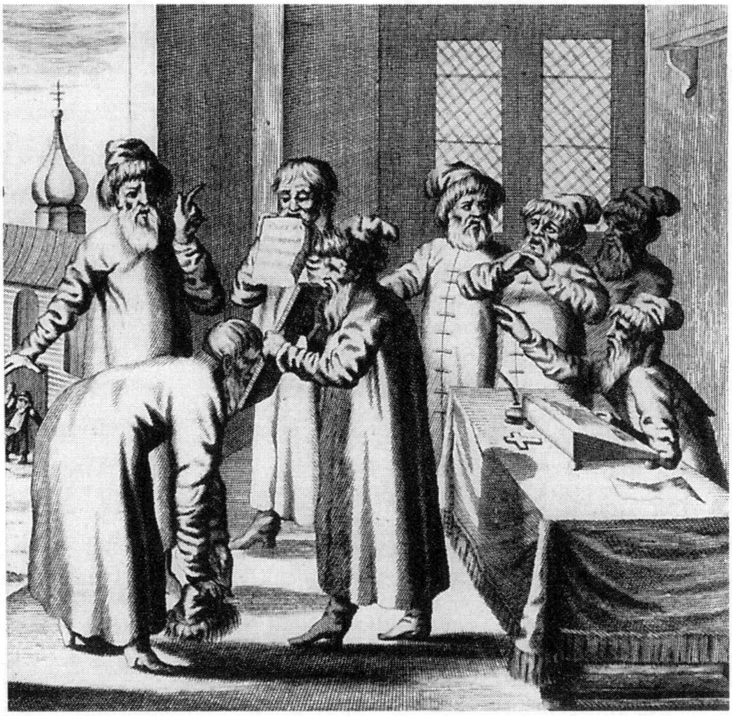

10. 'The Oath of the Muscovites', from *Voyage du Adam Olearius* (Paris, 1727).

of the Holy Virgin as a sign of respect, and they perpetually keep lighted candles in every room, or by every store, marking themselves with the sign of the cross and repeating up to three times the usual "Lord, have mercy". Only after the completion of this ritual do they begin to converse with those in the house; they do the same as they bid farewell to their hosts'.[75] A hundred and fifty years go by, and nothing has changed. The Dutch Protestant artist, ethnographer and writer Cornelius de Bruyn was genuinely amazed at the custom of first turning to the venerated image, then to a person. As a Protestant he strove to attain proximity to God without the intermediary of rituals and symbols; he had no need of the image of the religious 'sym-bolism of hope'. For that reason a reverential attitude to the icon at the beginning of the 18th century seemed to him 'strange'. On entering a room the Russian would not say a word, but would look for the representation of 'any Saint there might be, one of whom would always be in every room. Searching it out, they would make three inclinations before it, covering themselves with the sign of the cross and pronouncing "Lord, have mercy"or else "peace be to the house and all who dwell therein", again crossing themselves,and only after this greeting the householders and holding conversation with them.' This behaviour seemed even odder when visits were made by foreigners, who bowed before the first picture that caught their eye, 'out of alarm lest they fail to render to God the respect appropriate to him'.[76] And only the Orthodox understood this strange custom as authentic veneration.[77]

All these features of strict piety in church and out were supplemented in day-to-day life by a mass of prejudices, superstitions and conventions that revealed the heathen layers of consciousness. We know that in Christian culture concrete expressiveness was attributed to the word itself. Because of this, reverence towards an icon excluded the utterance of those words that, it might seem, lowered the dignity of an image. They never spoke of 'buying' an icon, rather of 'exchanging' it. 'In other places the pious folk also never spoke of buying church candles, oil, etc., rather of exchanging'.[78] More testimony about these kinds of 'minor oddities' was provided by the physician to Tsar Aleksey Mikhaylovich, the Englishman Samuel Collins. Apparently, when icons were spoken about, the words that were chosen for use were as decorous as possible. The icon painters themselves would not usually sell icons, but got rid of them to stallholders or travelling icon salesmen. The foreigner was of course surprised at how in the buying and selling of icons the verb 'buy' was altered: how an image could be only 'exchanged'. But sometimes an exchange really did take place: the old obliterated image would be taken to an icon-stall, where it would be left and 'exchange money' would be put down. In this situation of purchase/exchange any words at all might seem superfluous or hurtful, and sometimes they were completely replaced by silence: if the proffered sum for a merchant seemed too little, he would silently push the money away, and the purchaser would add to it silently, and so on till the sum seemed adequate.[79]

A no less curious custom was described by Paul of Aleppo. After a husband and wife had spent the night together, they could not only not make contact with the icons in a church, but could not touch them on an icon-stall, as he himself witnessed. A priest had to read over them a special prayer unknown to archdeacon Paul, or his father, the Patriarch Makariy.[80]

A careful attitude towards holy objects was part of the system of state guardianship and control of the icon and the icon business: thus not only the Church, but also the government took part in upholding well-defined norms of devotion. The *Domostroy*'s ideal precepts were repeated in post-Petrine Imperial edicts. The *Domostroy* prescribed making contact with icons 'only with a clear conscience', setting the images out by seniority (first of all, those most revered), covering the icons 'with a curtain for the sake of cleanliness and against dust, for strict orderliness and for preservation'.[81] A decree of Elisabeth's reign (10 May 1744) 'On the keeping of holy icons in their houses by the populace in cleanliness' developed these precepts. The Synod expressed its worries on the subject of non-observance in peasant houses of 'ecclesiastical piety'. In this connection priests were instructed to ensure that the populace kept the holy icons in their houses in all cleanliness, frequently washing and dusting them.[82]

The place where the icon is set is no matter of indifference for the pious consciousness. After all, it is at this spot within sacred space that (as Mircea Eliade pointed out) the hierophany – the revelation of the Deity – takes place. 'As you stand before the icon of the Saviour, stand as if before the Lord Jesus Christ himself'; so wrote the well-known Russian spiritual writer and saint Ignatiy Bryanchaninov in the 19th century.[83]

Because of this, the placing and rules for the setting up of the icon within the system of its veneration were regulated by strict ritual. For example, to take an icon out of a church and set it in a different place was not so simple. In 1825 the inhabitants of Kolomna requested the episcopal authorities to let them 'in their diligence' take the icon of the Don Mother of God out of the Church of the Elevation of the Cross and place it above the gate of the Saviour Tower of the city, where it formerly stood within a white limestone frame. The Kolomna Church authorities instructed the consistory to 'give an opinion' on the matter, and the latter decided 'to refuse permission to the citizens of Kolomna for not having produced worthy reasons for transferring the holy icon, but to let them place another icon over the gateway'. However, the Moscow Metropolitan Filaret Drozdov (1783–1867) imposed an order whereby he nevertheless permitted the original icon to be removed from the church on condition that a copy of it should be put in its place, 'so that there should not be an empty space and a discrepancy with the inventory'.[84]

In the popular didactic Church literature of the 19th century, the placing of an icon often constituted a special topic, in which the norms of devotion would be aired in accessible form. In one of the 'Trinity Pages' of the end of the 19th century is the following incident from the life of the 18th-century Russian saint Joasaph of Belgorod. In 1794, before setting out on an inspection tour of the diocese, the holy man had a dream. On entering one of the churches to be inspected he saw an icon of the Mother of God lying on a heap of dung, and heard her miraculous voice: 'See what the functionaries of this place of worship have done with my visage. My image is intended as a source of grace for this country, and they have cast it into dung.' Greatly disconcerted by this dream, the holy man began to carry out his inspection with particular care. Imagine his surprise when, entering the porch of the Church of the Ascension in the town of Izyum, he saw a large icon of the Mother of God serving as a partition behind which was the church coal-heap. Thereupon he threw himself to the ground before the icon and uttered out loud the prayer 'O Queen of Heaven! Forgive the negligence of thine unworthy servants: they know not what they do!' The tale ends with the information that since that time the icon in question has always stood in a niche behind the left-hand choir.[85]

In the formation of Russian sacred space, the motif of movement with the icon played a special part. In a letter to the Emperor of Byzantium, Leo III the Isaurian (717–741), Pope Gregory II noted that no Christian and God-loving person would set out on a journey and complete it without an icon: 'Thus do all virtuous and godly people behave.'[86] For that reason Russian people took icons with them always and everywhere, whether setting out for the wars or going to the nearest little town. Cornelius de Bruyn asserted that in Moscow there was the conviction that if a person did not have his personal icon with him he could not manage to pray in the proper manner.[87]

Icons were carried on religious processions on Church feast days or solemn occasions of the arrival or departure of official and non-official lay and Church people. The numerous solemn mass processions with icons, which took place not only in the Middle Ages but in the modern period, had a bewitching and uplifting effect on the common people. After all, from time immemorial the miraculous powers of holy relics, affirming the power of Christ and the saints, were attributed to portable icons. Hans the Dane was evidently struck by the exalted piety and brilliance of one of the Orthodox feast days in the 16th century, where he saw how fifteen priests in rich garments 'carried splendid great images with excellently depicted saints on them, adorned with pearls and gold and precious stones'.[88]

In older traditional societies, intensity of feeling and affective reactions were generally widespread. Hence processions with portable icons were very common in Byzantium. Among the best known were those in Constantinople with the icon of the Hodigitria, revered as the palladium of the Byzantine Empire.[89] Thanks to Russian pilgrims, this and other processions became well known at home.[90] In Russia there had long been two types of such processions: those that took place every year on predetermined days, and 'special' ones. Examples of the first type are processions with a cross around churches in Holy Week; at Epiphany to bless the water; another on 1 August (Old Style) from the main churches of a town again to bless the water, following the example of Constantinople, where on this day three main holy items were venerated: the life-giving Cross, the miraculous image of Christ by the source, and the icon of the Hodigitria. As well as these there existed a multitude of processions with icons in honour of both ecclesiastical and state events: in commemoration of liberation from an enemy invasion, the foundation of churches, even processions out in the fields for communal prayers requesting to be spared drought. The 19th-century Russian ethnographer and writer Sergiy Maksimov had this to say about the latter: 'Church processions consist of a throng stretching over half a mile, and in the course of one summer it would be hard to put a number to these processions with local icons, circumambulations of fields and prayer services in them'.[91]

From the 16th century to the 19th, iconic images depicting such mass processions become widespread. The 19th-century icon known as *Meeting with the Icon of the Vladimir Mother of God* expresses a mood of general religious inspiration and veneration as the images are carried along (illus. 11). The person who stood in front of this icon in prayer was supposed to experience the same feelings. The icon shows the meeting with the Vladimir Mother of God that was being transported from Vladimir to Moscow so as to protect the city from the invasion of the Tatar Temir Aksak in 1395. After Moscow had been miraculously spared, a feast day for the Vladimir icon and a procession to the Sretensky Monastery were initiated. As with the Constantinople Hodigitria icon, the Vladimir Mother of God was carried on processions and prayers were made before it – right up to the early 20th century. Ilya Repin's well-known picture,

11. *Meeting with the Icon of the Vladimir Mother of God*, 19th century. Kolomenskoye Historical and Architectural Museum-Preserve, Moscow.

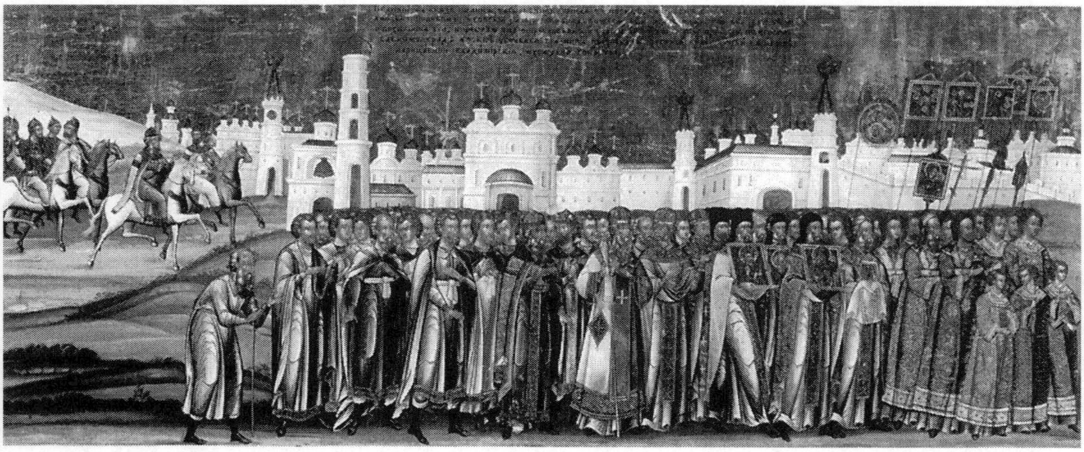

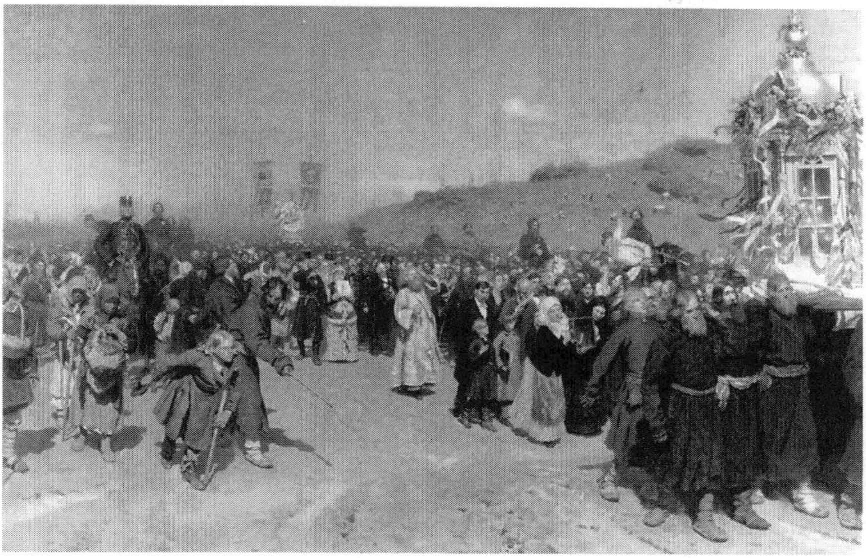

12. Ilya Repin, *Religious Procession in Kursk Province* (1880–83). State Tretyakov Gallery, Moscow.

13. K. Savitsky, *Meeting with the Icon* (1878). State Tretyakov Gallery, Moscow.

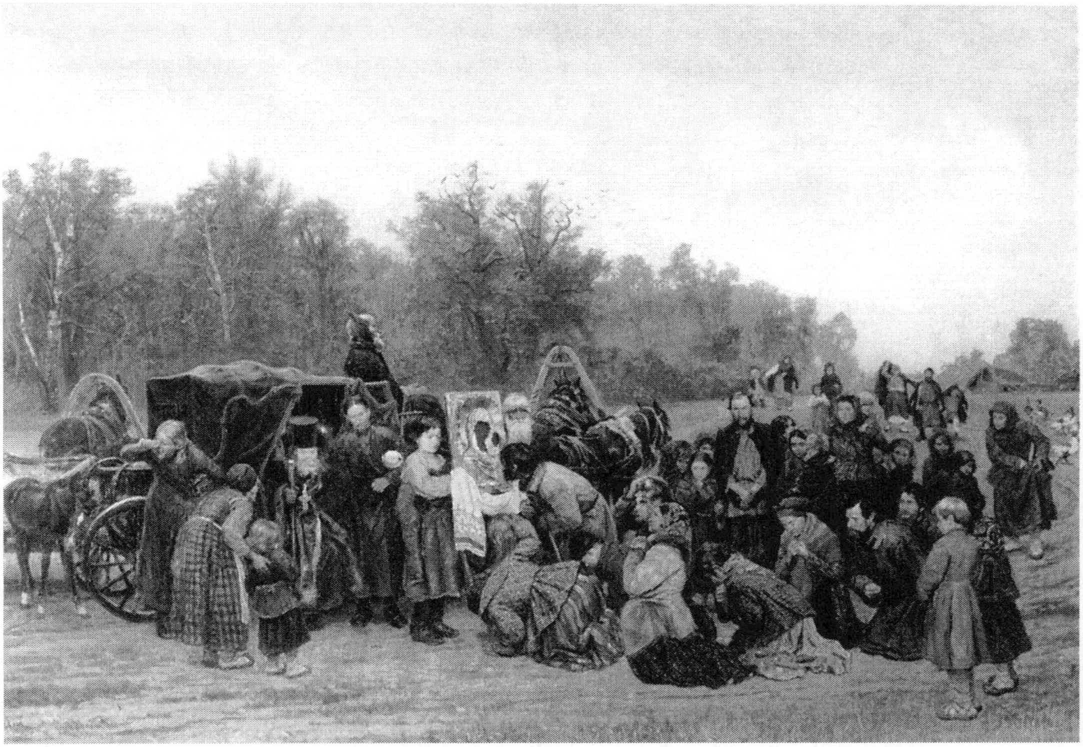

Religious Procession in Kursk Province (1880–83), shows us a more complex sensibility and piety: by no means all are so struck, which at first sight might be explained by secularization and degeneration of belief (illus. 12). However, the overall emotional tension of the scene conveys the 'old spirit' to us. We are similarly persuaded by Konstantin Savitsky's *Meeting with the Icon* (illus. 13). The simple people's general reverence towards the portable icon knows no temporal limits. Significantly, Peter the Great's ban on religious processions with icons (subsequently renewed) encouraged the people to speak openly of his iconoclasm.

Processing with an icon was always seen as carrying the 'banner' of faith, a declaration of its ideas and symbols. Though Alexander III's decree of 3 May 1883 at last allowed the Old Believers to set up crosses and icons over doorways, the 'public carrying of icons', mass perambulations with icons and religious processions remained strictly forbidden to them. Simultaneously, the Church authorities tried to keep close watch on icons that had been placed in wayside chapels, on wayside posts and within trees. The sacralization of 'wayfaring space' presupposed a system of increased control, since everything was intensified within the zone of movement. While on the road from Moscow to Klin, Metropolitan Filaret (Drozdov) noted in certain villages that there were chapels 'of recent construction', consisting of a shrine on a post with icons. The Consistory was deputed to find out from local priests and lay people how long ago these chapels were built, by whom, with what kind of permission, who looks after them, and, finally, whether any profits accrue from them, and if there were, then by whom and to what end were they used.[92]

Icons and beggars constitute an interesting topic, connected on the one hand with the motif of carrying an icon, and on the other with a typical feature of old Russian devotion: almsgiving. The beggar with an icon in his or her hands or held to the chest was always surrounded by a special understanding of the precept of charity, expressed above all in the duty to give alms and to love the victims of misfortune. The icon had to move a person to good works, in particular to give to beggars. The Church took continual care that people should obey the rules of charity. In a sermon inspired by the arrival in town of the miracle working icon of the Abalatskaya Mother of God, a certain priest at the end of the 19th century commanded his flock: 'Christian people, the Queen of Heaven has come to you, clothe yourselves if only for today in deeds of charity: help the poor, give to the beggar, comfort the grieving, forgive your enemy and make peace with all.'[93]

We know that Luther and the Protestants, scrutinizing the Catholic doctrine of 'deserts', rejected devoutness in giving alms to the needy as 'good works' in God's sight. In answer to this, both in the Catholic post-Tridentine West and in Rus, offerings to the Church, philanthropy and almsgiving become very important elements in the system of new rules of belief. In Muscovite Russia beggars began to be showered as never before with signs of heightened attention. They were given money, clothing and food. Around churches and monasteries there began to form special 'parties' of unregistered beggars, who had their own demarcated places, rules of conduct and internal hierarchy. Describing the everyday culture of behaviour of the Moscow merchants, Adam Olearius recounted that, every day as they went to their shops, they would without fail buy a few loaves to hand out to the beggars at the nearest church. Peter the Great launched a war against the system of almsgiving and the army of beggars in the Protestant spirit; it was reflected in the *Pronouncement about the Monastic Calling* (1724) by Feofan Prokopovich (1687–1736), the chief ideologist of the Petrine church reforms, whose ideas corresponded with the well-known views of Luther, who regarded monasticism as a kind of egotism and contempt of worldly obligations. Proclaiming common equality in the sight of God, Luther rejected Thomas Aquinas's concept that impoverished monks occupied the position of major earthly intercessors before God, thus justifying the system of almsgiving. As an internal echo of Protestant ideas, Peter's innovations concerning monasticism and the monasteries also presupposed a Protestant tinge in his strict measures against the 'realm' of the beggars. With time the strictness of these measures was to be reduced. In particular, up to the beginning of the 20th century, the Church bothered only to ensure that an icon in the 'zone of beggars' should not be located at the boundary between devotion and knavery, and that perambulations with icons should correspond to Church rules. In fact, attempts to regulate processions with sacred images and solicitation for alms had been made as long ago as the *Stoglav*. A special chapter (no. 74) was dedicated to this:

> There wander through the world, through towns and streets, and through households, through villages and through hamlets, monks and nuns, and wandering bands, and women, and other lay people who walk with sacred icons and wander about. Certain ones too from the confusion of dreams and the temptation of devils bethink themselves to prophesy and collect money for building, and others beg for expiation of sins and walk through market-places with icons in unseemly fashion.

With a reference to the 'Tsar's command', the Council approved a resolution

> to announce in the market-places that all such persons should not walk with the holy icons . . . And if any such after the Tsar's command should begin again to wander in unseemly fashion with holy icons, then the icons should be taken away from them and placed in holy churches, while they themselves should be expelled from the towns.[94]

But evidently this mobility was not curtailed, and from time to time it clearly had the tendency to reach a violent pitch. Otherwise there could hardly have appeared among the decrees of the Moscow Metropolitan Filaret Drozdov a resolution 'On Processions with Icons and the Disruption of Good Order'. In 1816 the Consistory received a complaint that every year during Holy Week the peasants walked about the villages with icons taken from the church, and went around with these icons not only without permission, but clearly disrupting 'decency and good order'. An impression of such common ways of behaviour can be gained, perhaps, from Vasiliy Perov's *Village Procession with the Cross at Easter* (illus. 14), which shows us that, despite the authorities' order to local priests ('to keep the strictest observation that in the procession with icons at Easter there should be no disorders and unsuitable conduct' according to Metropolitan Filaret's documents), this kind of perambulation had by no means been stopped. Peasant processions with icons without permission and the indecencies and irregularities associated with them had not ceased.[95] Everyday culture continually revealed its inclination to distort the strictness of devotion through excessive secular enthusiasm.

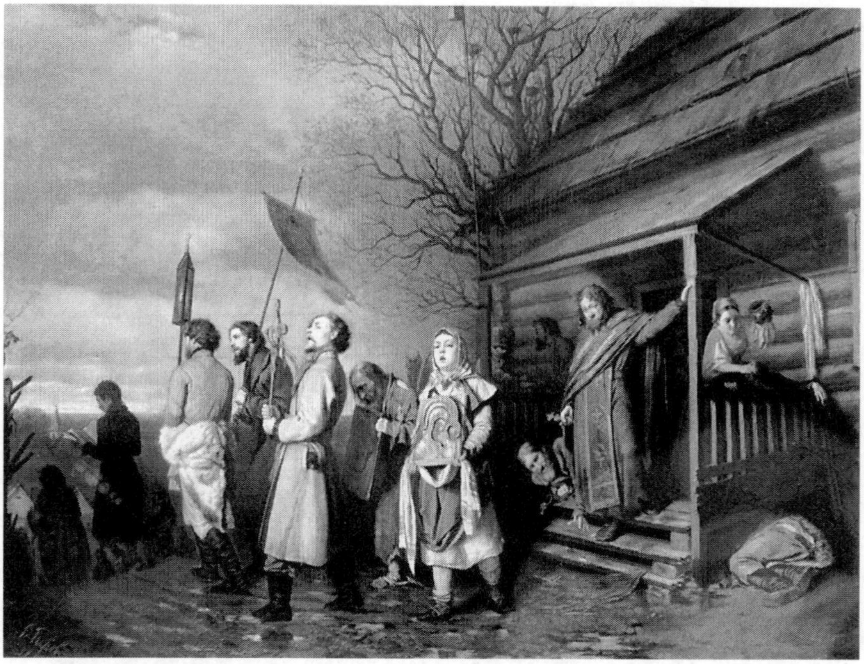

14. V. G. Perov, *Village Procession with the Cross at Easter* (1861). State Tretyakov Gallery, Moscow.

In the transfiguration of humanity, the ritual of prayer in front of an 'icon with Life' (a 'hagiological' or 'Vita' icon) is a special case insofar as it is a kind of 'icon within an icon'. The rhetorical structure of this kind of icon draws the spectator's attention away from communication to code. Such icons appeared as early as the 11th century, intended, as experts think, originally for tombs, serving as places of veneration of a saint. Pictures of the life of a saint instructed and edified the pilgrims. Some of the earliest such icons – of St Nicholas, and one of Basil of Caesarea – are so regarded. They later become personal images for prayer. In the post-Byzantine period they are commonest in Serbia and Russia.[96] In hagiological images of the saints there appeared, first of all, the didactic function of the icon, which was enhanced by its moral and edificatory aspect. Illustrating as they do the feats that, as it were, transfigure a person, such icons addressed themselves not only to the heart, but to the reason.

Let us look at a hagiological icon of St Serafim of Sarov (Prokhor Moshnin, 1759–1833) from the early 20th century, one among tens or hundreds of thousands disseminated among the people (illus. 15). We at

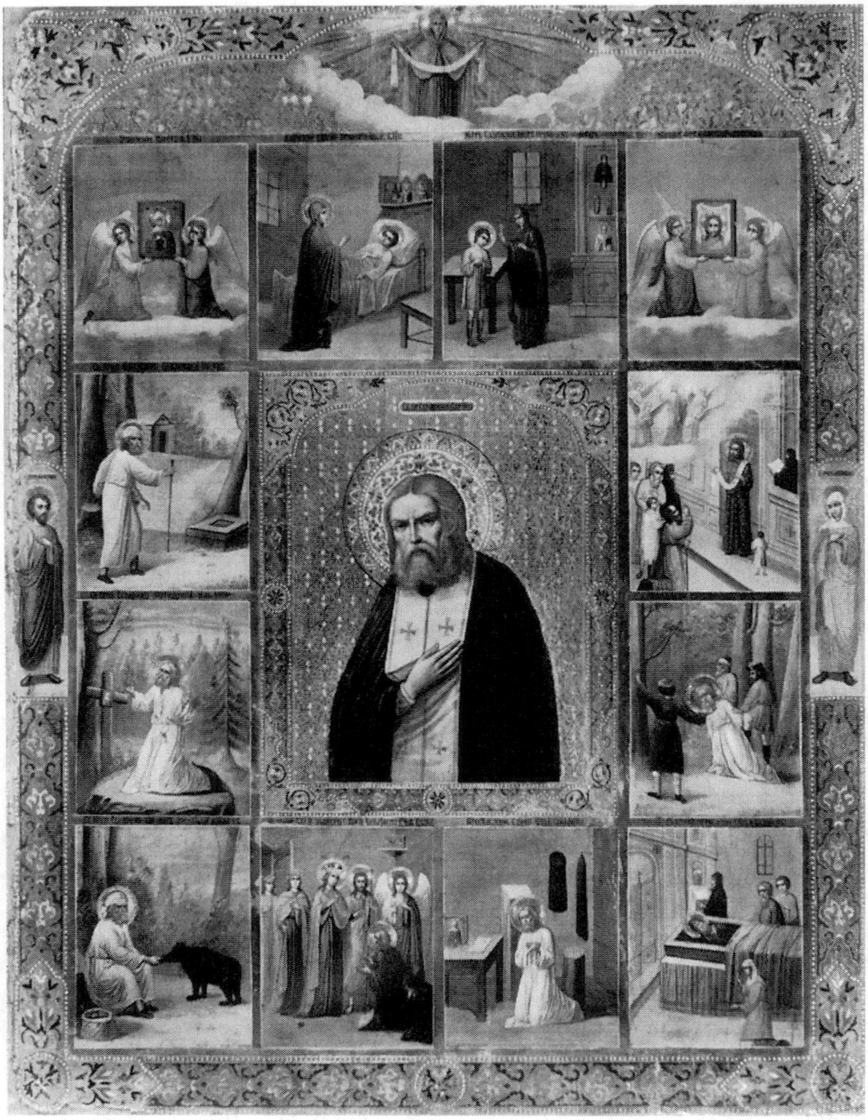

15. *Serafim of Sarov with Life*, early 20th century. Andrey Rublyov Central Museum of Old Russian Art, Moscow.

once notice that the personality of the blessed Serafim is one of the most significant in the history of Russian sanctity, on a par with such saints as Feodosiy of the Caves Monastery, Sergius of Radonezh and Tikhon of Zadonsk. The mysticism of the world of St Serafim is usually considered to belong to the spiritual tradition of Hesychasm or 'holy silence', which since the 14th century had first developed in Byzantine – and then in Russian – monasticism (see Reference 139). First of all representing a method of inner, or 'mental', prayer, this tradition constitutes a highly important area of Orthodox spiri-tual practice, to no small extent both shaping the mentality and constituting a profoundly specific area of the Orthodox world outlook. The interpretation and reflection of this tradition in hagiological icons present a special interest from the point of view of its collective understanding and of everyday devotion.

The central element of this hagiological icon is a 'portrait' of the saint: his icon, i.e., the deified condition of his person. According to the classical iconic composition, the surrounding scenes should present the historical path by which he rose to be a Christian hero, scenes of his feats and the successive stages by which he approached sanctity. We notice, incidentally, that on seven out of the twelve surrounding panels, *icons are depicted*. More than that, two of the most important of these scenes – the first and fourth in the top row – are devoted to illustrating icons themselves. These icons are the ones that St Serafim had in his cell, the 'Tenderness' Mother of God, and the image of the Saviour Not Made by Hands, representing the 'first icon' and directing the mind towards the divine origin of icon-making. This insistent repetition of 'the icon within the icon' introduces a quite special emotional tonality into the narrative.

The location of the icons themselves in historical time, as conveyed in these scenes, causes the praying person to apprehend it in closer connection with sacred time than the traditional formula of description and depiction of double-layered time in the image of a saint's life presents. Following through these scenes' historical, domestic and spatial–temporal details, localizing the earthly path of the saint within history, the praying person begins to understand the internalization of the Holy Spirit, which 'poor Serafim' invoked, in a quite special way. Possessing only one icon, the saint himself, as we know, reached this state by the path of 'mental activity'. The importunate communication of a stream of divine grace through the sheer quantity of icons most likely presumed a path of return: from the outer to the inner. One is further convinced of that by the depiction of icons in the other accompanying scenes: in those of the appearance of the Mother of God to the saint, of the parental blessing, of the death and extreme unction of the saint, in which it would be hard not to feel the durability of the well-known Muscovite tradition of the proper furnishing of space with signs of holiness.

The illness of the young Prokhor and his miraculous recovery, according to an early Life of the saint compiled by the hieromonk Ioasaf, who was the novice Ioann at the Sarov monastery, is directly connected with the icon of the Mother of God and her appearance to him in a dream. Soon after this appearance, during a procession with a miracle-working icon of the 'Mother of God of the Sign' from Kursk to the Korennaya Pustyn, rain suddenly began to fall and the procession was forced to go through the courtyard of the Moshnin house onto another street. Agafya, Prokhor's mother, hastily brought out her sick son and pressed him against the icon, whereupon he was cured. The miraculous cure is, of course, one of the most enduring motifs of Byzantine and Russian hagiography. In the Life of Serafim it comes in several forms: the Mother of God with the apostles Peter and John appears to the saint during his second illness and says to him 'This one is of our line.' The icon carries a separate scene devoted to the visit made by the Mother of God to St Serafim on 25 March 1831, one year and ten months before his death. It was his 'twelfth revelation from God', and lasted over an hour. The iconography of this revelation recalls the well-known Russian icon 'The Appearance of the Mother of God to Sergius of Radonezh' ('Sergius' Vision'). For the worshipper, there must have been a mystical connection between the two topics. This was reinforced by a literary episode from the Life, according to which, having a particular attachment to Sergius of Radonezh, the elder entrusted an enamelled icon of 'Sergius' Vision' to one of the monks with the words 'Place this image upon me when I die and put it in the grave with me.'

It is noteworthy that in the icons of 'The Righteous Death of the Blessed Serafim', widely disseminated at the beginning of the 20th century, three more images besides the Mother of God belonging to the saint are often depicted: 'Sergius' Vision', the 'Saviour Not Made by Hands' and the 'Mother of God of Kazan', although (I must repeat) many witnesses testified that there was nothing in the Saint's cell but one icon with a lamp burning in front of it, some firewood beside the stove (which remained unlit), and a tree-stump that served as a seat. In addition, two further subjects must be

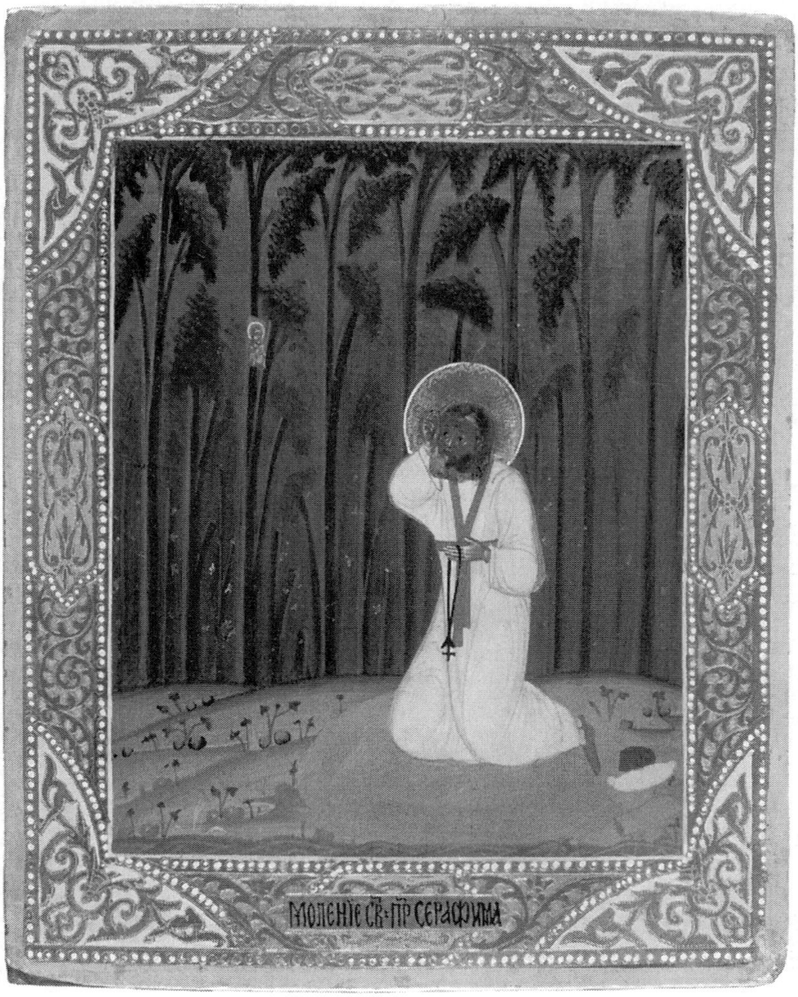

16. *St Serafim of Sarov at Prayer on a Rock*. Mstyora or Kholuy. Beginning of 20th century 22.5 x 13.5. Andrey Rublyov Central Museum of Old Russian Art, Moscow.

mentioned: 'St Serafim of Sarov at Prayer on a Rock' and 'The Robbers' Attack on St Serafim' (illus. 16, 17). The fact that these two were put out in their hundreds of thousands from the village of Kholuy as independent images for prayer is indicative of their attractiveness for popular devotion.

In our icon of his life, no posthumous miracles of St Serafim are presented to us, of the kind that in the Middle Ages would always extend the period of the saint's activity, as for example in images of the lives of three great miracle-workers, saints George, Demetrios and Nicholas. Posthumous

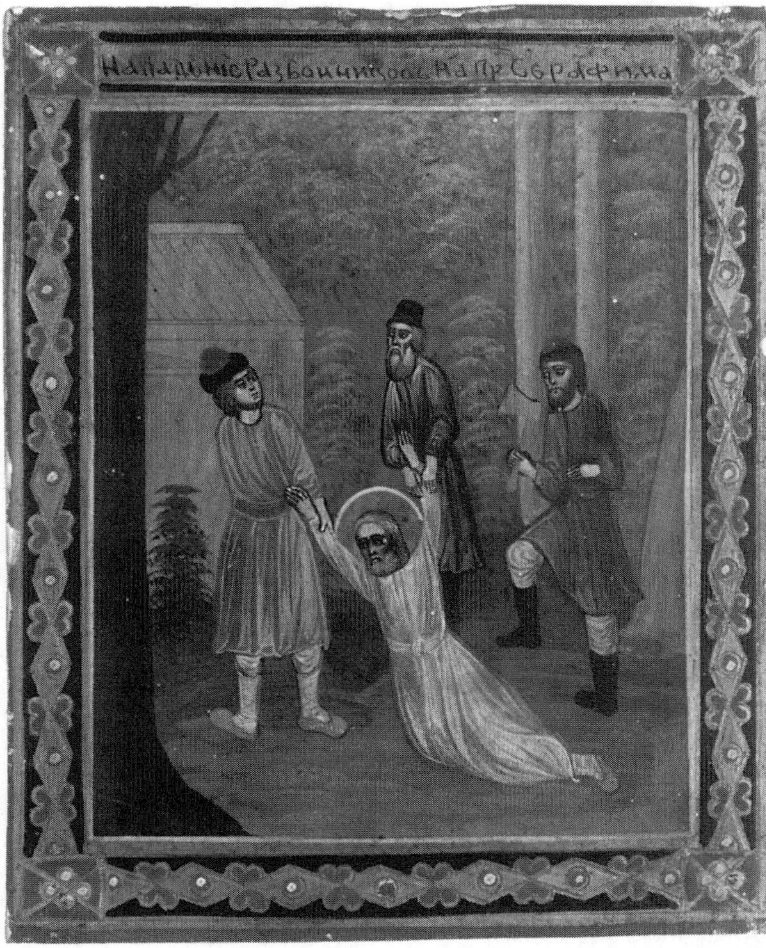

17. *The Robbers' Attack on St Serafim of Sarov*, early 20th century, Kholuy Art Museum, Kholuy.

miracles allowed viewers more easily to identify these saints as heavenly forces and as agents who linked the earthly with the disembodied worlds. In the hagiological icon of St Serafim, this link is constructed as if through an 'icon within an icon'. But the popularity of the two individual iconic scenes mentioned above indicates their considerable weight in understanding the kenosis of the saint and the particular emotional colouring of the ladder of spiritual ascent for an ascetic. These subjects clearly mark within the hagiological icon two major indicators of sainthood: the difficult spiritual feat of the hermit, impressing the imagination as a superhuman effort; and what a well-known specialist in Russian sanctity (Georgiy Fedotov) called 'voluntary abasement'.

In the autumn of 1794, with the blessing of his superior, the thirteen-year-old monk Serafim isolated himself in a timber cell five *versts* (three miles) from the monastery. In the depths of the forest, many parts of which undergo 'semiotic transformations' (St Serafim gave them sacred names – Golgotha, Jerusalem, Gethsemane, the Brook Kedron, Nazareth), the ascete marked out a zone that became hyper-sacred in the course of his toil in Christ: it was hallowed by his feat of standing on a rock for 1,000 days and nights in prayer before his icon. The superhuman severity and harshness of the feat was what still attracted the attention of popular religiosity at the beginning of the 20th century. The ideal of the stylite saints, characteristic of early Christian monasticism and eremitism, admired by early medieval ascetics, had been revived.

The second theme leads us into the area of one of the most puzzling and extremely durable motifs of the Russian religious experience: its attraction towards innocent victimhood, suffering and renunciation, which Fedotov capaciously formulated thus: 'worldly fall – heavenly rise'. Love for martyrs, for the innocently slain victims who in no way glorified themselves, particularly young people – Boris and Gleb (illus. 18), Artemiy Verkolskiy, the Tsarevich Dimitriy (illus. 120), etc. – is a complex variant within this perpetual Russian attraction towards voluntary abasement, connected with profound suffering and not only a simultaneous general forgiveness, but often also with a prayer of intercession for one's tormentors.[97]

The Life by Ioasaf recounts that one autumn, three peasants, 'aroused by malice and enmity', arrived at the hermitage to threaten Serafim and demand money. Though physically very strong, the saint renounced his natural strength and chose the path of sacrifice: putting aside his axe and humbly folding his arms, he answered them: 'Do what you need'. One of the villains struck him in the mouth with the back of the axe-head, knocking out several teeth and covering his face with blood; another hit him on the head; then all three knocked him over and beat him until they reckoned he was dead. Bursting into his cell, the robbers went through everything, but found nothing *except the icon*. They ran off in terror. The saint lay there for eight days, and only a fresh visitation by the Mother of God cured

18. *SS Boris and Gleb*, after 1908, workshop of M. O. and G. O. Chirikov. State Museum of the History of Religion, St Petersburg.

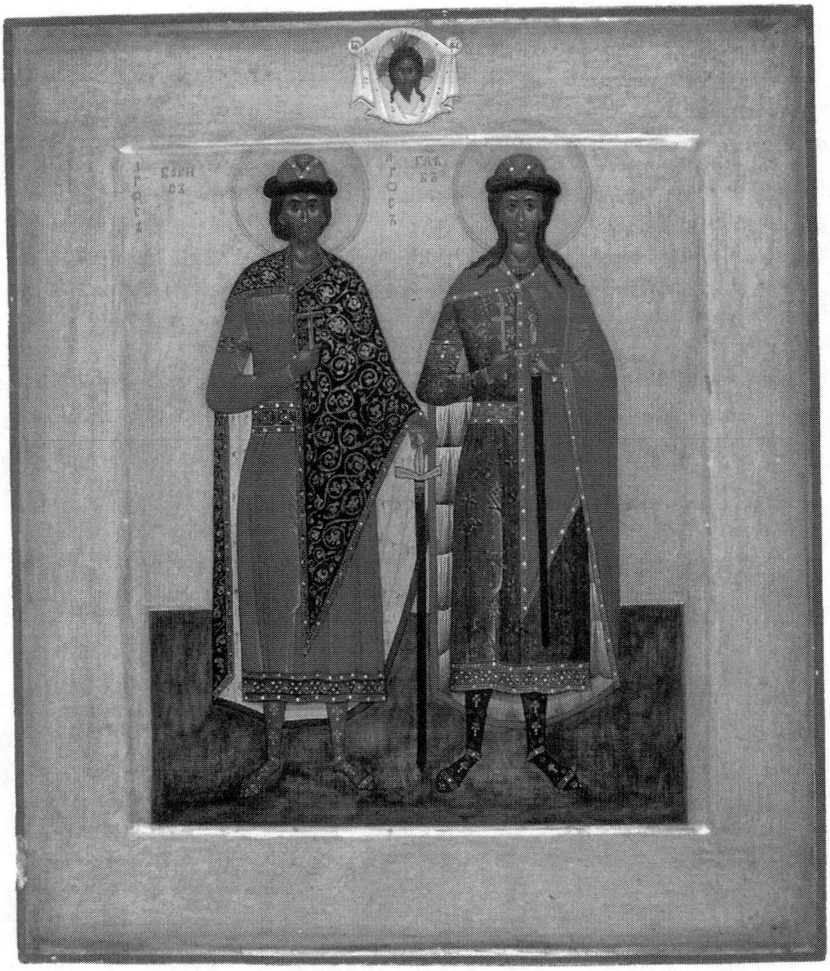

him, though he remained bent-backed for the rest of his life: that is precisely how he is represented on icons (illus. 19).

After all this comes not only forgiveness, but strong and heartfelt intercession before the superior of the monastery for the wrongdoers, who had been quickly discovered: the blessed Serafim threatens that if his tormentors are not forgiven, he will quit the monastery for ever. Later, one of the robbers even joins Serafim's monastery. Thus the special popular veneration for the icon scenes of 'The Robbers' Attack on the Blessed Serafim' becomes

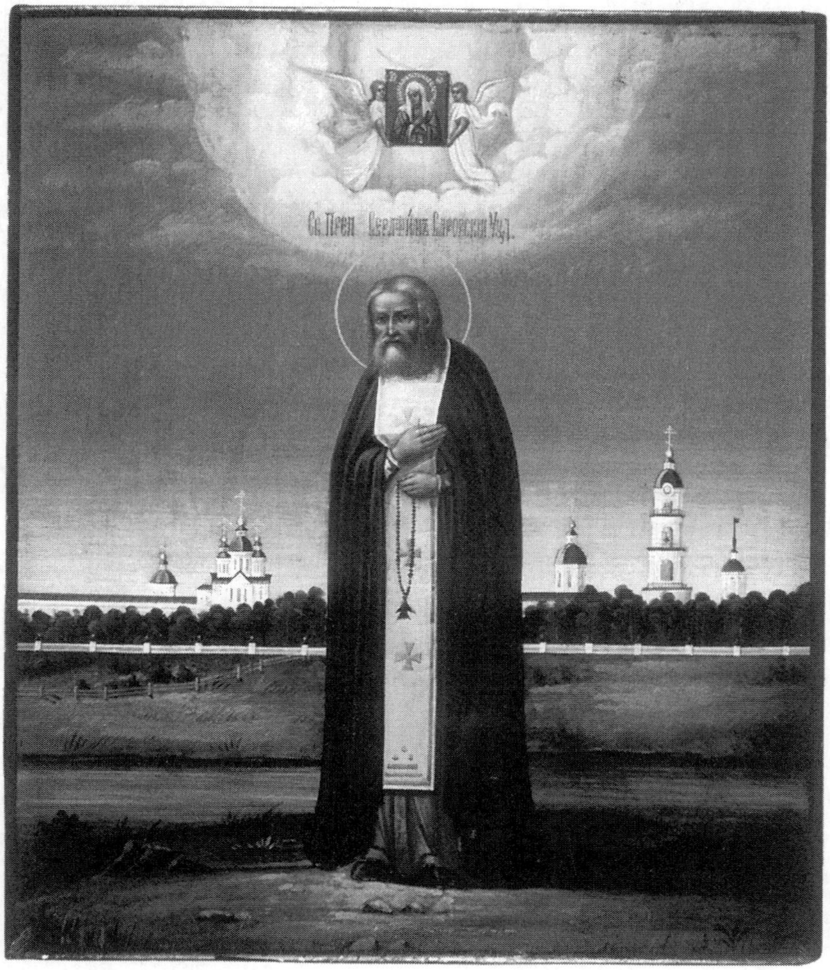

19. *St Serafim of Sarov*, early 20th century. State Museum of the History of Religion, St Petersburg.

typologically similar to the wide distribution in the 17th, 18th and 19th centuries of icons of Boris and Gleb (11th-century princes martyred by their brother), the Tsarevich Dimitriy, the youth Artemiy Verkolsky and other martyrs. The same motif is reinforced by popular enthusiasm for favourite spiritual verses,[98] in which pity towards innocent sufferers is voiced. Thus the posthumous miracles that Yegoriy (St George), Mikola (St Nicholas) and Demetrios of Salonika accomplish tell of the freeing of young men and women: Yelisava from the serpent, two young Russian prisoners who had been captured by the Tatar Mamay, and the youth Vasiliy, a Muslim captive. Equally, Aleksey the Man of God and Ioasaf the Tsarevich were renowned not for their miracle-working powers or for their special position in the heavenly hierarchy, but precisely because of their pitiable fates. Fedotov was convinced that innocent sufferings constituted the main subject-matter of the spiritual verses: there was 'some kind of rapture, some kind of sweet sadness in this description of the abasement of the innocent . . .'.[99]

The motif of voluntary abasement continued also to develop in the teachings of holy men of modern times, who devote special attention to the great New Testament idea of humility, raising it to the plane of a religious 'common exile'. The fact that they appear in a special selection of moral and edificatory teachings for a mass audience in the early 20th century can testify indirectly to their actualization in the would-be religious renaissance under Nicholas II mentioned earlier. The iconic image of the pathetically bent back of 'pitiful Serafim' (illus. 19) visibly symbolized that ideal of 'holy Russia' that people often attempted to relate inwardly to the Orthodox utopianism of the last Russian emperor. 'We must thank those who offend and revile us without cause, since they are our benefactors: with their abuse they assist us to earn crowns from our Saviour and Lord' (words from the hermit Ioann Sezenovsky). Or as the Abbess Antoniya of Kashin taught: 'Be ready for any harsh words, abuse, contempt and thou shalt acquire grace. Be guilty without guilt, fallen without falling, and remember the Saviour who put himself in the place of those without the law.' To a question from one of the monks as to which spiritual feats are particularly acceptable to God, Vonifatiy, abbot of the Feofaniev skete in Kiev, answered that in his opinion there are three 'of great value before God'. In the first place when a person, fallen into an abyss and subject to temptations, accepts them thankfully. Second, when a person attempts to keep his good deeds 'hidden away' from others and remain pure before God, unmotivated by vanity. Third, and finally, 'when someone dwells in obedience to his or her spiritual father and renounces all personal desires'. But so as to preserve the spiritual content of these feats, he went on to say, we must bear offences from others peaceably, and 'train ourselves in such a disposition of the spirit, as if they did not touch upon us personally'.

The motif of an egotistical aspect of sanctity, of an inadequate fight for 'the world' and its sanctification, stands in a complicated relationship with all this.[100] The 'aestheticization' of the world through icons did not yet mean its 'acculturation'. What might the lay person sense in the words of the monk Afanasiy who, as was emphasized in the same anthology of teachings, loved to distance himself from conversations with worldly people, saying 'I shall not answer for them to God, but shall be ceaselessly tormented on my own behalf'? Afanasiy did not like 'useless' conversations with the monastic brothers. One of them, who was well acquainted with Tula, where the elder had been born, began to speak to him about the form of the town: how many new buildings, streets and squares had been constructed in it. The hermit looked at his interlocutor and said: 'It were better, brother, to tell me if many boards will be needed for my coffin and how high a mound of earth will be raised above my remains.' 'With whom is a conversation better and pleasanter, with humans or with angels? Of course with angels', reasoned the monk German; however, the senior monk Zosima expressed the same idea thus: 'When you do not see and do not hear and have no dealings with the world that has gone astray, then indeed will you find peace and your mind strive naturally towards God'.[101]

Thus the ritual of prayer before an icon can carry complex cultural–historical baggage. Gesture, word and iconography reveal a unity of the language of religious culture to which the flow of events was not always subject.

Miracles

Nothing was so enthralling in the everyday life of an ordinary person as a miracle occasioned by an icon. It seemed that the holiness and wonder-working power of images penetrated right through the sinful world, while from the 17th century through to the 19th, waves of secularization faded out helplessly in the face of tradition and durability. The first miracle to proceed from an icon was the healing from leprosy of Abgar, king of Edessa, to whom Christ himself sent his Image Not Made by Hands (illus. 89). The believer could learn about this by reading the legend of the taking of the Image Not Made by Hands from Edessa to Constantinople in the

20. V. P. Guryanov, *Iverskaya Mother of God*, 1898, Moscow. Private collection, Moscow.

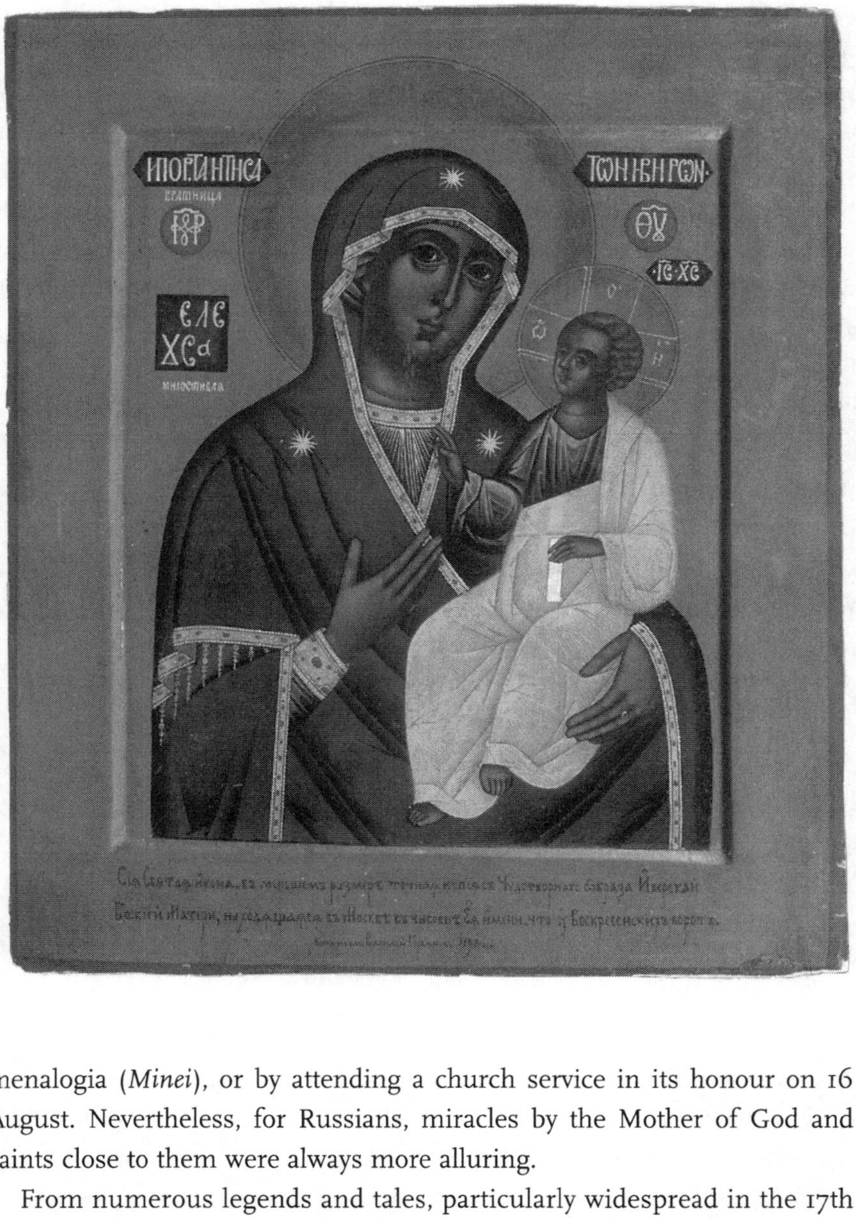

menalogia (*Minei*), or by attending a church service in its honour on 16 August. Nevertheless, for Russians, miracles by the Mother of God and saints close to them were always more alluring.

From numerous legends and tales, particularly widespread in the 17th century, a Russian would clarify any striking or supernatural phenomena. Thus for example from the 'Tale About the Holy Wonder-working Icons of the Mother of God, How and Where they Appeared', in a book by a Russian Old Ritualist writer of around 1700, S. F. Mokhovikov, Russians could specifically find out that the image of the Iverskaya Mother of God had been 'struck in the face by a lance and blood came forth' (illus. 20); that in the case of the Częstochowa image 'the face and throat were cut: blood came forth marvellously from both places'; while the Rudnevskaya icon was 'struck in the face with a whip: two scars, and blood came forth for all to see'. Icons of the Mother of God might remain unconsumed in a fire. In the case of the Vangaliyskaya image, her face miraculously failed to burn in a fire, though 'her depicted garment was burnt'. Icons of the Mother of God could reward the pious person with money, or else with relics of the saints. The Pecherskaya icon gave the icon painters money, relics of saints and also an image. A certain elder received 'a quantity of gold' from the Solunskaya icon, while on another icon Christ could 'receive' bread. But of course there were also other miracles, no less surprising and able to operate on the mind: no-one could doubt that on the Pesidiyskaya icon a lily had grown from the hand of the Mother of God, while from her right hand on the Tolgskaya icon, holy oil had come forth; holy oil came forth too 'out of the head of the Pimenovskaya Mother of God'.[102]

As well as miracles of these kinds, icons revealed themselves continually and ubiquitously. Paul of Aleppo mentioned one of these revelations: an icon had been covered in earth in a ruined house. It appeared in the dreams of an 'important official' three times in a single night. He dug it up at precisely the spot that had been indicated, and subsequently placed it in a monastery.[103] Right up to the early 20th century, traditional theology periodically attempted to clarify the character of miracles emanating from icons. The Protestant concept of the fundamental autonomy of the natural order of course excluded the miracle as representing divine interference with that order. As early as the second half of the 16th century, the Catholic and Orthodox worlds responded by paying renewed attention to miracles, both on the level of learned theology and on that of oral culture. The well-known iconoclastic acts in the age of the Reformation in the West gave rise to numerous legends about 'weeping' images and about the retributions and instant punishments that God would visit upon the defilers of holy things.

Most often, and most easily, a bolt of lightning and instant paralysis (the so-called *contrapasso* motif) could be despatched on such people. There were also numerous legends (transferred in the 17th century to Muscovite Rus)

21. Fire in the church and the preservation of the icon 'Feodorovskaya Mother of God with Miracles', first half of the 18th century.

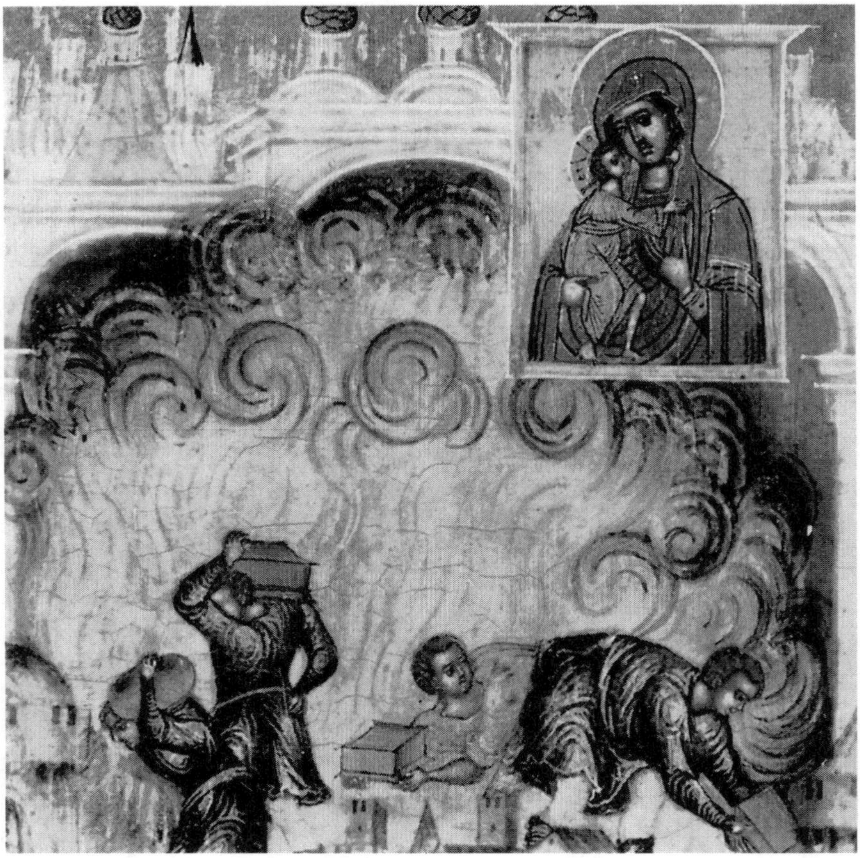

about the miraculous 'self-defence' of images against iconoclastic acts: icons would burn but not be consumed (illus. 21), blows from a sword would cause them no harm, etc. It is interesting that even the Lutherans created legends according to which depictions of Luther were not consumed by fire. Typologically similar folkloric inventions affected even the Calvinists, who spread rumours that 'God has many times struck carved crucifixes with lightning.'[104] Thus, at the beginning of modern times, the world was still living within a dense atmosphere of mass belief in miracles, prophecies and relics; it lived in a perpetual atmosphere of miracle, which in defiance of confessional boundaries did not vanish from the collective consciousness up to the 20th century.

The Russian religious philosopher Yevgeniy Trubetskoy saw in the revealed wonder-working icon 'the healing power of beauty'.[105] However, this conception of theurgic art does not always apply to the complex everyday world with its own rules of life. The inclination of the common people's mentality towards the miraculous is one of these: 'It is rare for any of our villages not to have a wonder-working icon.'[106] The firm belief within the Russian collective consciousness in the icon's active effect on the world was nowhere more clearly revealed than in its wonder-working capacity. After all a miracle is an act, and an act that changes something. The Church often had to call a halt to this alluring devotional sensibility: any such discovery of an icon in an unexpected place could be taken as a revelation. Thus it was in the 16th century, and also in the 19th. On 10 June 1831 someone placed an image of the Holy Trinity at the window of the Nikolskaya Church in Moscow's Podkopayi district, and already by 5 a.m. a mass of people, growing hour by hour, was observed gathering around it. This meant an official had to put the icon in the adjacent Nativity Church. However, that evening 'many begged a priest to carry out a service before this icon', which he could not do without permission from the authorities. The decision of Metropolitan Filaret (Drozdov) reflected the authorities' strictness towards such events. So that it could be 'most reliably observed', the image had to be placed in the cathedral church of the Chudov Monastery in the Moscow Kremlin; no less then twice a month the monks were obliged to report all information about the 'latest events' concerning the icon.[107] Judging by other decisions Filaret made, this practice of verifying the wonder-working power of an icon through the sanctity of the Chudov Monastery was considered normal.

Once removed from a church and set up in some private house, an icon could quite easily become the object of special veneration. It seemed as if popular religiosity was looking for just such an opportunity. On 10 December 1825, the Archpriest Ivan Grigoryev reported to Metropolitan Filaret that an image of the 'Old Korsunskaya Mother of God', which he had taken out of the church of John the Baptist in the village of Parskoye in the Shuya District of Vladimir Province, had been set up in the house of the Moscow merchant Vasiliy Udaltsov. 'A multitude of people of various callings with hysteria and afflictions' began to converge on the icon for prayer. In such cases the spiritual authorities could forbid the cult, confiscate the icon and return it to its church, or on the contrary could facilitate its veneration. All depended on a whole series of circumstances, among which the origin of the icon was considered one of the most important. In this case they took a tried and tested path: the icon was sent to the Chudov Monastery.[108]

The Church also kept an eye on the dissemination among the people of rumours about the miracle-working power of 'revealed' icons. During the 18th and 19th centuries, the local spiritual authorities were obliged as soon as possible to report cases of the discovery of images, not only to the Consistory but to the Senate. Thus while digging a well, the peasant Afanasiy Gavrilov from the village of Yaganov discovered an icon of St Nicholas. The local priest Pyotr Kharitonov immediately put in a report about this find to the rural dean of the local district. The latter informed Moscow and received these instructions: 'Investigate the occurrence and present the icon to a monastery with a cathedral for examination.'[109]

We also have a well-known 19th-century episode of a wonder-working icon in the Berlyukovo Hermitage (not far from Suzdal), about which popular rumours appeared even in the religious journals in the capital. The treasurer of the hermitage informed the Metropolitan that a soldier's wife, Tatyana Kuznetsova, had asked for prayers to be said before an icon of the Saviour located in the monastery's bakery. She maintained that she had seen this icon in a dream and had been told that if she were to pray in front of it she would be cured of her illness 'in the head and in the eyes'. The monks took the icon into the church and held a service of prayer. Immediately the rumour went around that the woman had been cured. People went to the icon in large numbers, while individual monks began to hold prayer services to order without the knowledge of the senior authorities. On receiving a report about this from the monk Gennadiy, the Metropolitan Filaret decided that 'for better examination the icon should be left in the church, and if people should gather there, it is commanded that each week it is to be reported to me what follows'.[110]

What motives were dominant in regulating the actual practice of icon veneration? Of course the official Church sometimes sought out compromises – something confirmed by the case of the veneration of icons and relics of the innocent victim Vasiliy of Mangazeya,[111] whose cult seemed dubious to the spiritual leadership. The general famine of 1803 in the town of Turukhansk was linked by the people with God's wrath at the removal from the church of the icons of the holy martyr Vasiliy of Mangazeya, which had been in the Trinity Monastery there, and the concealment of his relics. In this connection the Church authorities made concessions, instructing the local abbot to 'raise up the image and tomb again'.[112]

There is some interesting material in Dmitriy Sosnin's *On the Holy Wonder-working Icons and the Christian Church* (1833), from which it emerges that the Church often had to adapt itself to the popular mentality. It is not so hard, for example, to find both in ancient Rus and Imperial Russia the conviction that all icons are wonder-working. Initially Sosnin attempted to elucidate the way miracles happened. First, miracles could be witnessed in the rare appearances of icons of the Saviour, the Mother of God and the saints. As a rule they occurred in wild places, such as deep forests, in the ashes of a fire, and so on. In Sosnin's opinion these icons were painted mostly by unknown, but without a doubt, 'pure and holy' hands. Second, there were the signs that would accompany such appearences, for example, an unusual light or miraculous voice. Among miraculous signs, Sosnin also included the 'self-preservation' of an icon at the time of a fire or the collapse of a church dedicated to it. Third, and last, wonder-working icons poured forth on people the gifts of grace, which in most cases led to the healing of illnesses.[113] Sosnin put forward two main arguments against the superstitious apprehension of miracle. The first was that in wonder-working icons, God visibly reveals his presence, and that cannot be a permanent or frequent matter. Error in this is rather dangerous, 'since if we were to meet the unmediated armament of God's power everywhere, this fact alone would reduce our respect for it, and easily thereafter for the very Activist'. The second argument was that miracles cannot originate from all the icons with which a devoted people adorn churches and their own homes, since in that case there would have to be a ceaseless flow of miracles in the world, sanctified as it is by the uncountable multitude of icons.[114]

By focusing primarily on his criterion of the 'weakening of the authority of God', Sosnin – from the point of view of traditional Orthodox theology – omitted a very important point: miracles cannot be regarded as normal in the life of a church, whose practice of worship is defined by one single miracle, the Incarnation of God. In contradistinction to this, fundamental attention was devoted to explaining the wonder-working power of the icon as the pouring forth of a stream of divine grace. Taking the division between the Old and New Testaments as between traditional religions of Law and Grace, he demonstrated that there should be immeasurably more miracles in the Church of the New Testament, since with Christ's coming into the world 'a stream of divine grace poured down from Heaven'. From this was derived a characteristic equation within the popular consciousness: the more wonder-working icons there were in the world, the more grace there was in it, and vice-versa. In the same way as the compromise of the synodal Church with the widespread belief that all relics of the saints are incorruptible seems somewhat risky, to make one's belief in the wonder-working power of icons depend on belief in Christ's own miracles has turned out to be equally incautious.

The kind of common 'religious store' of collective attitudes and system of sensibilities that was established in the 16th and 17th centuries was linked with the peculiarities of the construction of an especially charismatic Muscovite Tsardom, and would invariably have an effect on sacred spaces in Imperial Russia. It was also always subject to various kinds of influence. The tendency towards unification of the culture of the Christian world seems gradually to have brought elements of foreign origin into this store – for example numerous tales about the Mother of God that arose in the post-Tridentine West, Catholic and Protestant iconographic schemes, various kinds of edificatory parables and elements from cycles of Lives of the saints. Universal predispositions of the popular mentality also replenished the same store. Everything was part of the complex dynamic of a broad swathe of problems, within which the phenomenon of miracle originating from the icon, and the artistic structure of the icon itself, seemed to reflect what was determined within Russian devotion by its actual subjective experience. In the context of the theory of 'Moscow the Third Rome', the cult of the icon of the Vladimir Mother of God acquired special significance in the system of religious sensibilities from the end of the 16th century. The Vladimir icon was taken in Muscovite Rus as the semiotic equivalent of the famous Constantinopolitan icon of the Hodigitria – the palladium of Byzantium.

The Dormition Cathedral of the Moscow Kremlin (1472–9) inherited the glory of Rome and Constantinople, Kiev and Vladimir. In the 16th and 17th centuries it was filled with sacred objects from across the Christian world, and thus as it were took the place of Santa Sophia of Constantinople. It also became the new 'home' of the Mother of God, since the chief holy object in the Byzantine Empire – the Hodigitria icon – had 'abandoned' Constantinople, conquered by the Turks in 1453, and had 'transferred itself' to Rus. Hence the icon of the Vladimir Mother of God was taken as the sole authentic icon by St Luke. It became the palladium of Muscovy and of Imperial Russia, often equated in the popular consciousness to the 'home' of the Mother of God. This was reflected in a well-known popular saying: 'Holy Russia is the Mother of God's house.' Church tradition ascribed to Luke the creation of three icons of the Mother of God after Pentecost: images of the 'Tenderness' and 'Hodigitria (Showing-the-Way)' types, and also of the Mother of God without the Child. Enveloped as they were with the Evangelist's authority, copies of these icons were supposed to possess special wonder-working power, since they reproduced the genuine features of the Mother of God, as the holy Evangelist witnessed them; and (in words she spoke to Luke) the Mother of God not only approved her icon, but also communicated to it a special power of grace. In the texts on holy personages read out in Orthodox churches, it is as if the moment of distributing special powers of grace with the help of direct speech from the Mother of God is granted not only to the icon painted by St Luke himself, but to all subsequent copies of it.

The sacralization over the course of centuries of the inner and outer space of Rus through icons was linked with the name of the Mother of God. Her icon invariably entered into the peasant 'domestic church', together with the Saviour and St Nicholas. The major church of the Tsardom – the great Dormition Cathedral of the Moscow Kremlin, whose model was copied semantically in a multitude of large and small settlements – was dedicated to the Mother of God. To her revealed icons were also dedicated a vast number of monasteries, churches and chapels within them. The acquisition of grace was realized at altars dedicated to her, including at the 'church of all churches', the Cathedral of the Pokrov[115] on the Moat (i.e., 'St Basil's') dedicated to an exclusively Russian feast of the Mother of God. In the light of our problem it should be underlined that in the cult of the

Mother of God, the Russian Orthodox Church always primarily honoured the first person to achieve divine status, that is, the final goal that Christ placed before the fallen world, leaving it his icon.

In the traditional theology of the post-medieval world, the link between the Mother of God and the illumination of the created world has put Mariological problems at the centre of the greatest disagreements between Orthodoxy, Catholicism and Protestantism. The Protestant development of the idea '*sola fide*' (by faith alone) led to a denial of the cult of the Mother of God, the saints and miracles; this at once called forth a reactive response both in the Catholic West and the Orthodox East. After the Council of Trent (1545–69), the cult of the Virgin Mary in modern Catholic devotion sometimes began to put the veneration of Christ himself in the shade. In Western Europe an enormous quantity of altar images of the Virgin appear, as also of places of worship dedicated to her. If in Protestant theology and the Protestant way of life the forms of human apprehension of God became ever more abstract, in Catholic and Orthodox lands they became even more 'concrete', though these two ways also substantially diverged. The development both by the reformers and also by many Roman Catholic theologians of the conception of a fallen creation and teachings on primal sinfulness (*natura totaliter corrupta, massa damnatur*) led to the dogma of the 'Immaculate Conception', known already from the 16th century to the 18th in Spain, Italy and other countries, and ultimately sanctioned by Catholic Rome in 1854. From the Orthodox point of view this dogma led only to a belittling of the glory of the Mother of God, since it did not coincide with the Orthodox teaching on redemption. In opposition to the Catholics and Protestants, in the 16th and 17th centuries the Russian Church emphasized the liturgy and the idea of the mediation and intercession of the Mother of God. In future the development of the Orthodox concept of Divine Wisdom and the illumination of the created world became intricately interwoven in Rus with the state mythologeme, which was actually at once reflected in ecclesiastical–liturgical practice and in the veneration of icons of the Mother of God, as well as in their diversity.

The Russian liturgical calendar in modern times has interestingly reflected the connection between the Mother of God and the concept of *the sanctity of the surrounding world*: the beginning of the Church year was marked by the Feast of her Nativity, while it ended with the Dormition, in which death was experienced in an already disembodied state. It is interesting that approximately from the 17th century, this cycle began to be sanctified with the celebration of icons of the Holy Wisdom. The Nativity was sometimes connected with the Holy Wisdom icon in its Kievan version, while the Dormition was connected with its Novgorod version.

An apocalyptic meaning was attached to the Kievan image of Holy Wisdom, since it was linked with the Heavenly Church, with whose incarnation on earth the liturgical year began (illus. 22). The Novgorod iconography of Holy Wisdom, by contrast, contained images both of the Mother of God and of Christ, and referred to the symbolic experience of the pre-terrestrial cosmos (see illus. 65). Hence its link with the feast of the Dormition was expressed in a service for the icon of Holy Wisdom, in which fragments of the Dormition service were used, where it was stressed that this icon 'was painted for the Feast of the Dormition of the Most Holy Mother of God, inasmuch as She is the Church inspired by Wisdom and the Divine Word, known as Sophia'. Here again we recall the consonance in the Russian experience between Sophia and the Mother of God. In contrast to the Byzantine tradition, the dedication of the Santa Sophia Cathedrals in Kiev and Novgorod was linked not with the Word (*Logos*) but with the Mother of God. From the correlation of Holy Wisdom and Mother of God over many centuries, a belief in the potential sanctity of matter, the base of all creation, was derived, as also in the summons to mankind to participate in the ultimate transfiguration of the world.

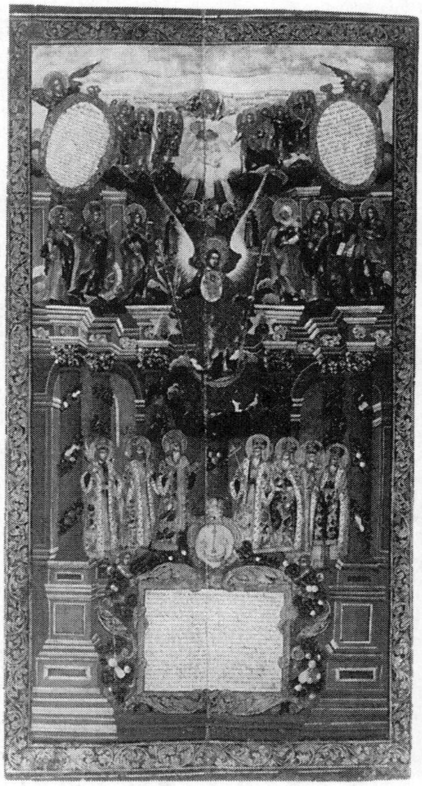

22. *'Wisdom hath Builded her House'*, second half of the 18th century. Local History Museum, Totma.

The particular liturgical significance of the icon of the Mother of God was also reflected in the Russian 'high' iconostasis: to the right of the royal doors is located the image of the Saviour, to the left that of the Mother of God. Pavel Florensky noted that almost half the prayers in church services were directed to the Mother of God. In the Russian Orthodox church calendar there are about 260 of her icons celebrated in the liturgy, while in the so-called Sergius Menologion (*Mineya*) there are up to 700.

No less a quantity of texts both for church and domestic use corresponded with the huge number of icons of the Mother of God in the 18th and 19th centuries. The canons, akathists, troparia and feast day services were augmented by elaborate folkloric inventions, apocryphal tales and stories about visions and icons of the Mother of God. Thus the highly popular folk apocrypha 'The Mother of God's Visit to the Place of Torment' and her 'Dream' were included – as and when needed – in the Lectionaries (*Chetyi – Minei*), Prologia and Triodia. The theme was developed just as intensively in the Lives of saints and in chronicles, as also in popular booklets for the common people in the later 19th century and early 20th. We should note that if, as these Lives indicate, the Mother of God manifested herself to Russian saints, then these manifestations were at once reflected in images for prayer, which attained huge popularity, as in the case of

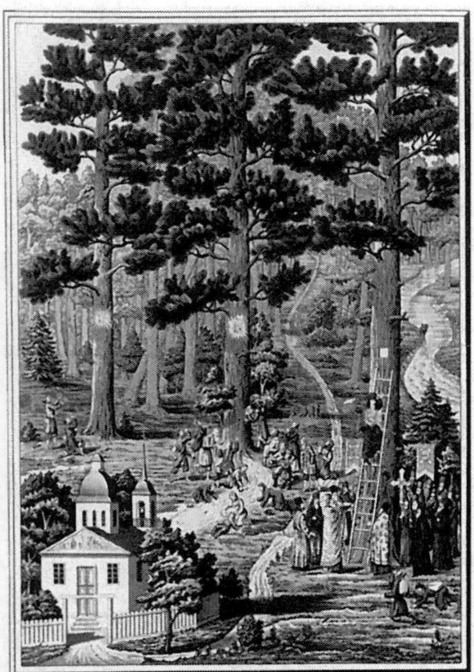

23. *Appearance of the Wonder-working 'Pustynno-Glinskaya' icon of the Nativity of the Most Holy Mother of God*, late 19th- or early 20th-century lithograph. Russian State Library, Moscow.

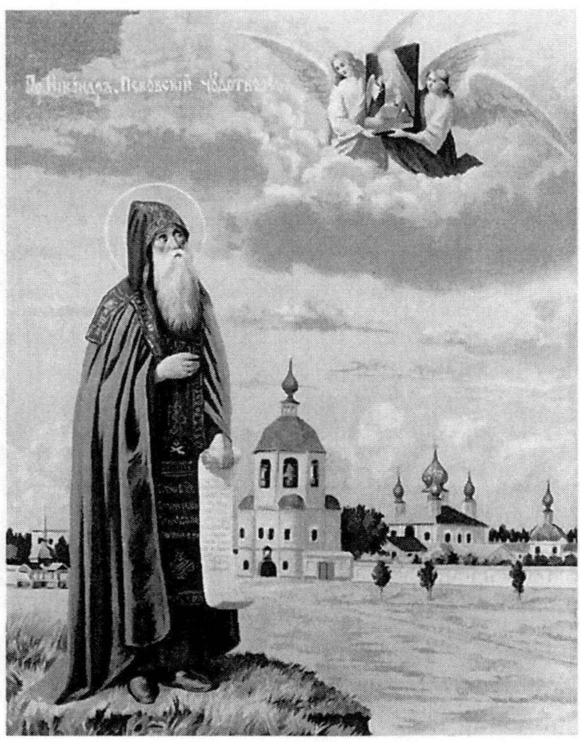

24. *Nikandr of Pskov, Wonder-worker*, late 19th or early 20th century, coloured lithograph. Russian State Library, Moscow.

'The Vision of Sergius' or 'The Manifestation of the Mother of God to Serafim of Sarov'. Frequently the miraculous revelation itself was described in a way that derived directly from the icon: in the words of the Life of the Blessed Martiriy Zelenetsky the Mother of God manifested herself just as she was depicted on the icon in his cell. Here one cannot help but be reminded of Florensky's observation that it was precisely from icons that saints most often descended to appear to people in prayer.[116] Gilbert Dagron calls this 'the topos of recognition of the saint', well-known to Byzantine hagiography.[117]

Nowhere other than in Imperial Russia will we find such a dissemination in the 18th and 19th centuries of icons, miniatures and religious paintings for the common people on which icons are depicted (illus. 23, 24). Nowhere else were images of Lives and small icons for prayer, with large numbers of the heavenly host depicted on them, so widespread and popular; finally, nowhere else did the people so venerate icons on which the saints were represented in prayer before the image of the Mother of God, or little icons intended for pilgrims on which might be depicted a saint with the monastery he or she founded, and almost always, too, a picture of the wonder-working icon to which a church or chapel in this monastery was dedicated. All of these were peculiarities of Russian piety, the expression of a special popular reverence towards the image and an important aspect of the popular cult of the saints.

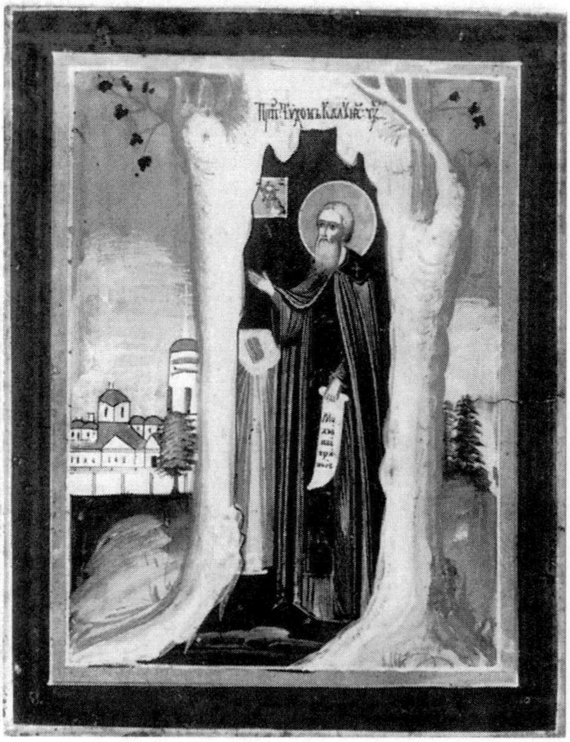

25. *St Tikhon of Kaluga*, second half of the 19th century. Andrey Rublyov Central Museum of Old Russian Art, Moscow.

In this preference for incorporating an icon into the sacred space of another icon, the special significance of the image in the economy of salvation was reflected. Here are just a few examples. St Tikhon of Kaluga was invariably depicted by Russian icon painters standing in prayer before an icon of the Saviour (illus. 25), sometimes within the trunk of a tree, in which the saint hid himself and where two icons are located – of Christ, and the Mother of God. St Pafnutiy of Borovsk is occasionally represented in prayer before an image of the Mother of God. On frequently encountered small popular icons, St Nikodim of Kozhozero holds an icon of the Mother of God in front of him. St Adrian of Poshekhonye is shown on the background of a monastery or river, while to the right of him there is an icon of the Mother of God or the Dormition in a tree (illus. 26, 27). St Vasiliy, Bishop of Murom, was depicted both in prayer images and in miniatures holding an icon of the Mother of God (illus. 28). Finally, Avraamiy of Galich is also invariably represented with her image in his hands on numerous icons from the later 16th century to the 19th (illus. 1, 29, 30).

All the earthly actions of Avraamiy of Galich, whose Life was written by the abbot of the Chukhloma monastery Protasiy in the mid-16th century, were centred on the appearance of a wonder-working icon of the Mother of God to him. On the saint's hagiological icons the believer could examine, from one scene to another, a gripping tale with details of his everyday labour in Christ: first Sergius tonsures Avraamiy and the latter goes into

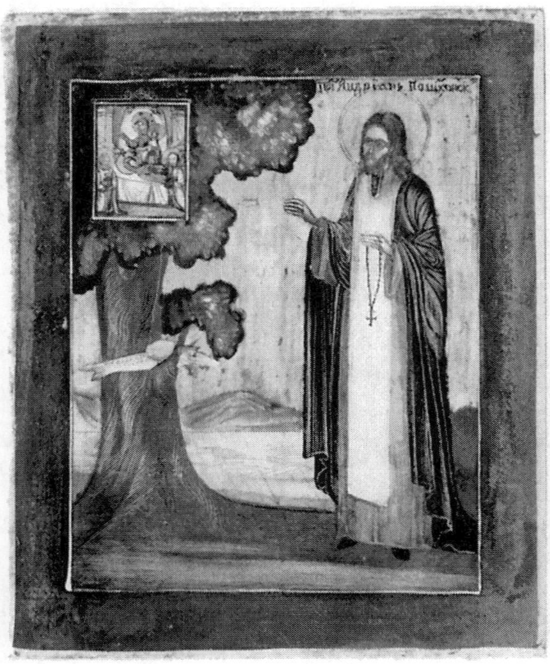

26. *Adrian of Poshekhonye*, second half of the 19th century. Andrey Rublyov Central Museum of Old Russian Art, Moscow.

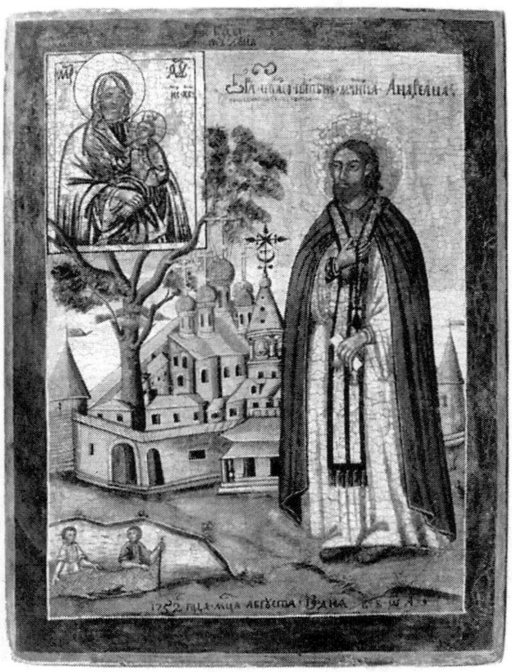

27. *Adrian of Poshekhonye*, 1752. Collection of N. and S. Vorobyov, Moscow.

the wilderness; when Avraamiy reaches the land of Galich, while praying on the shore of the lake, he hears a voice bidding him to climb a hill on which there stands an icon of the Mother of God; on top of the hill the blessed one is astonished by an unusual light coming from the icon that is in the branches of a tree; after Avraamiy's prayers the icon detaches itself from the tree and descends into his hands; as in a multitude of similar cases, he builds a small wooden church on the site of the revelation of the icon and establishes his cell there; at the request of the Prince of Galich, Dmitriy Fyodorovich, the saint carries the wonder-working image in a boat across the lake to Galich (the scene of the Prince's meeting with the icon should impress the viewer with its solemnity: in front of the icon there is a prayer service as the people congregate); finally, the saint establishes a monastery at the site of the revelation of the icon with funds donated by the Prince and the citizens of Galich, while he himself goes away to Lake Chukhloma. On two icons of Avraamiy of Galich from the later 17th century to the early 18th in the Kolomenskoye museum, there are a separate representations of the saint's miraculous discovery of the wonder-working icon (illus. 1, 30).

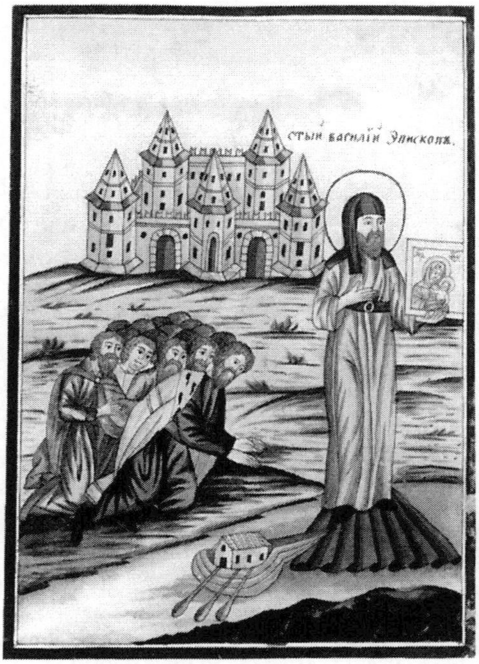

28. *St Vasiliy, Bishop of Murom, Walks on the Water*, a 19th-century miniature. Private collection, Moscow.

A focus on the idea of the salvatory service of a saint connected with a miracle emanating from an icon of the Mother of God becomes, from the 16th century, one of the most stable hagiographic and iconographic motifs. In the next century it was developed further on the basis of the penetration into Russian culture of many tales about the Mother of God of Western origin. These found their reflection in various printed materials, such as *The New Heaven, Created with New Stars, That is to Say the Most Blessed Virgin Mary with Her Miracles* (Lvov, 1665) by the rector of the Kievan Mogila college, Ioannikiy Golyatovsky; *The Much-valued Pearl* (Chernigov, 1646) by Kirill Trankvillion Stavrovetsky; *The Imagined Paradise, in which are Many Blooms* (Iversky Monastery, 1658–9); and *The Bedewed Fleece* (Chernigov,

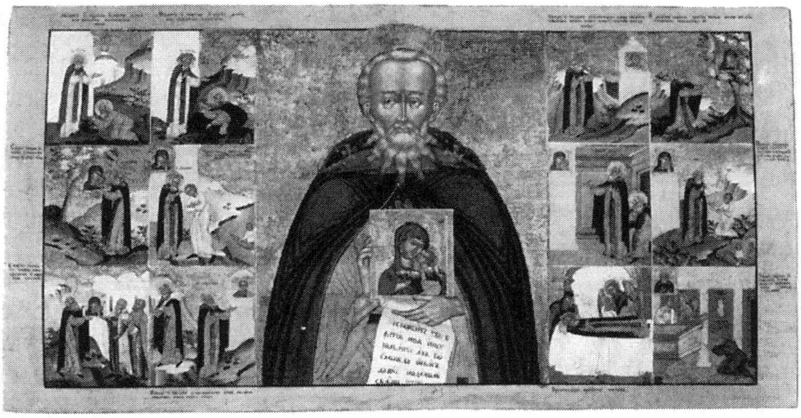

29. *Avraamiy of Galich with Life*, 18th century. Andrey Rublyov Central Museum of Old Russian Art, Moscow.

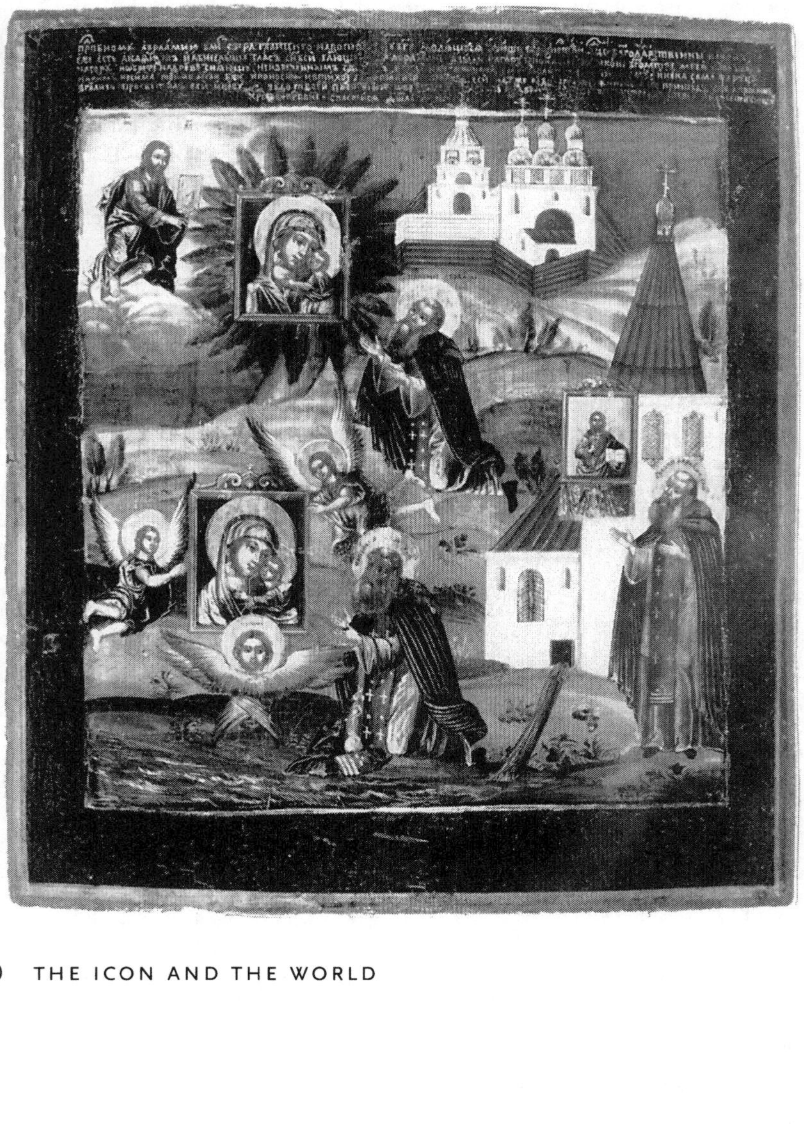

30. *Appearance of the Icon of the Mother of God to Avraamiy of Galich*, second half of the 17th century. Kolomenskoye Historical and Architectural Museum-Preserve, Moscow.

31. *Mother of God of the Sign, with Narrative*, 18th century. Kolomenskoye Historical and Architectural Museum-Preserve, Moscow.

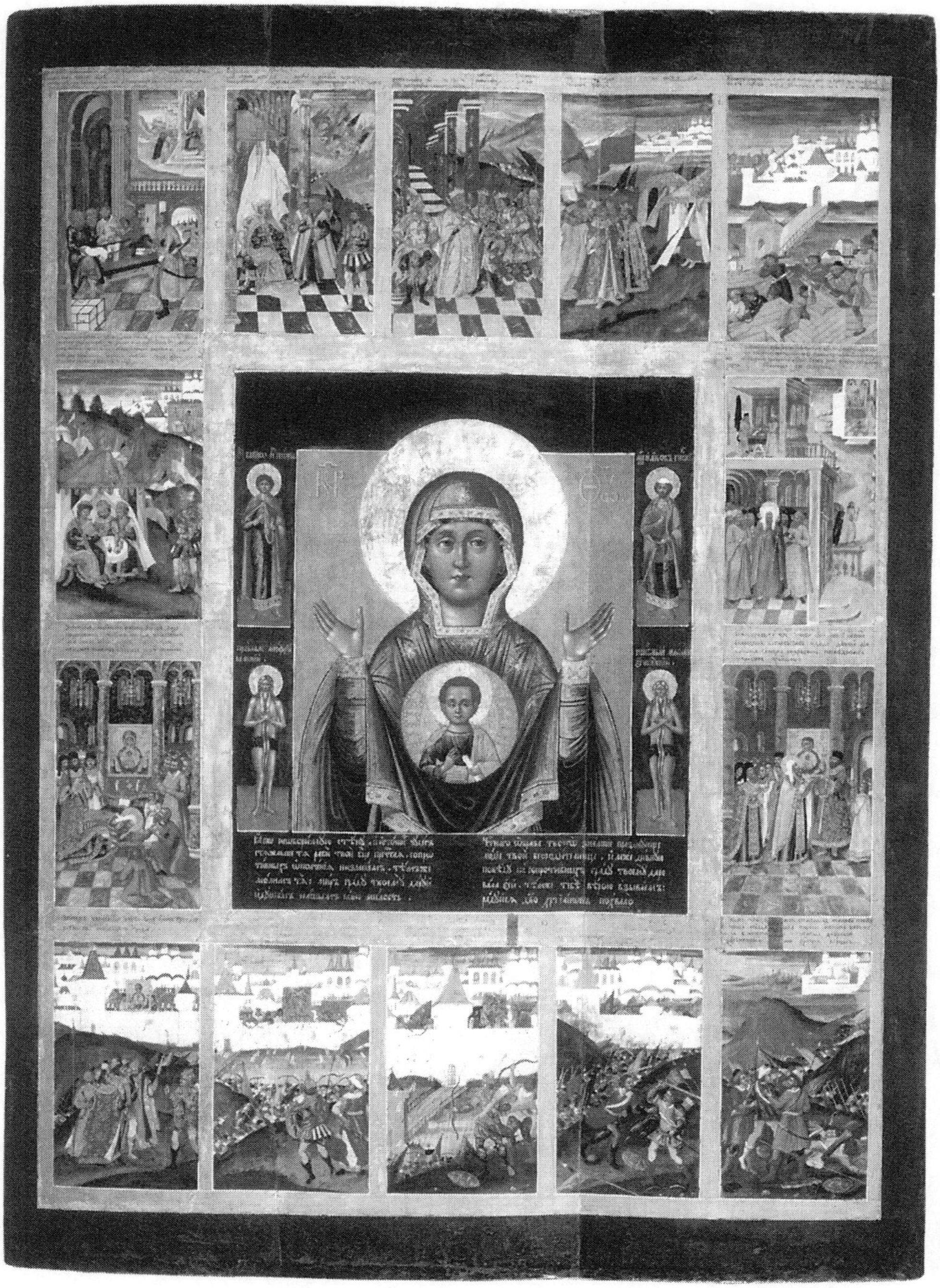

1683) by the well-known Russian saint and author Dimitriy Rostovsky, and also in several other printed and manuscript works. They were immediately reflected in popular religious pictures and in icons.

The well-known Old Russian icons of the Vladimir and the Feodorovskaya Mother of God, the icon of the Mother of God of the Sign with scenes of miracles, and many others, show the charismatic quality of the Russian land. In the 17th to 19th centuries these icons were disseminated in a huge quantity of copies and variants, remindful of how full Russia was of sanctity and miracles (illus. 31; see also illus. 157, 158). In this connection, all the 'icons within icons' that I have mentioned are not only semiotic realia: the depiction of a depiction always carries a heightened degree of conventionality.[118] Hence representations of icons within icons would convince a person of the sacredness of the surrounding world, as if in a 'snap-shot' image of history on the boundless expanses of 'Holy Russia'.

The additional layer in the collective mentality represented by Peter the Great's ecclesiastical ideas would scarcely touch upon the already well-established unalterable systems of representation. Like his methods of fighting popular superstition and 'dematerialized miracles', Peter's ideas merely reflected the growing complexity of those minds that represented upper-class culture: secularization mixed in with rationalism, currents of Protestantism, and the 'burden' of governmental purposes. Beyond the miracles, people began to discern the previously concealed ignorance of the populace and the self-interest of the clergy. The wonder-working quality of icons often becomes the subject of mockery. The medieval link between Muscovite devotion and the miracles wrought by icons is regarded sceptically. It is significant that miracles begin to be unmasked by rationalistic means, and in the process there are attempts to make the results of this unmasking widely known. The new picture of the world is saturated with rationalistic thinking, keen to give an explanation for everything on a materialistic basis and to exclude from consciousness the 'incomprehensible remainder'.

If Dmitriy Merezhkovsky is to be believed, false miracles were discerned by Peter the Great everywhere, but the main fact is that he dealt with them like a 'great technician'. In an impoverished church in the Peterburgskaya Quarter of St Petersburg, an icon of the Mother of God that put forth tears and supposedly foretold great misfortunes for the new capital was discovered. Peter went straight to the church, inspected the image and discovered the deception: at the back of the icon he found little brass screws that secured two small wooden boards between which 'Grecian sponges' and springs had been set. Removing these boards, the Emperor showed how the icon 'wept': if one gently pressed them, the sponges, saturated with water, gave out 'tears' that trickled through scarcely visible openings in the eyes of the Mother of God.[119] This amusing tale can well be compared with F. Poulson's mention of an ancient statue whose restorers discovered it contained a device through which a real person could speak on the statue's behalf.[120] One can only guess at the authenticity of this story, but it is vital to note that a miracle connected with the indication of the lack of grace in the new Imperial capital should be perfectly capable of being unmasked by a method that earlier could not even have been contemplated.

So as to further Peter's reforms and to make popular devotion healthy, a series of decrees was issued with the aim of rooting out 'everything superfluous, not essential for salvation, wholly self-interested, invented by hypocrites and a false temptation for the common people'. So that false miracles should not be invented, severe punishments were instituted, such as permanent forced labour on the galleys with preliminary slitting of the nostrils. That meant that becoming convinced of a miracle would often mean going through a legal investigation.[121] During ordination bishops swore an oath that in their diocese 'there should be no superstition and cults that are hateful to God'. The same applied to priests.[122] As one scholar wrote, the 18th century, with its harsh persecution of all who 'proclaimed new miracles', was no time for a new miracle to find witnesses to its authenticity.[123] In the 18th century the number of miraculous incidents and revelations of icons of the Mother of God was much reduced: in 1714 there was the miracle of the Kargopol-Kazan Mother of God icon; in 1737 the miracle of the Feodorovskaya Mother of God icon connected with the Cossack leader Ilovaysky; in 1739 the revelation of the Akhtyrskaya Mother of God; in 1748 the Kaluga Mother of God icon was revealed in the village of Tinkovo near Kaluga. After this last event the heavenly powers 'absented themselves' from the imperial Russian lands for nearly 80 years, up to the famous miraculous manifestations from the fresco of the

Pecherskaya Mother of God in the archbishops' palace at Yaroslavl in 1823.[124]

To put it another way, when we speak of miracles we not only enter into a secret and compact world of that which is imagined or revealed by God, but also into the world of earthly passions. It was not, of course, just a matter of the severity of the Petrine and subsequent edicts. What was important was that at a certain moment a 'false' miracle from an icon was recognized by the hierarchy as a fact that threatened the state: they began fighting against 'false' miracles not by methods of persuasion but by those of punishment. In all this the factor of Old Believer devotion was not as marginal as it might appear. In the 18th century, in the opinion of the powers that be, it was indeed the Old Believers who disseminated rumours that 'many a candle has been extinguished, and the miracles have ceased'.[125]

Meanwhile, the religious sensibility of the masses was inseparable from archetypal thinking and from the universal peculiarites of popular Christianity. Here the predispositions of oral, 'cold' culture, which always left more space for highly coloured fantasies and contaminations in comparison with literary culture, had a stake in the game. It is generally acknowledged that in the popular consciousness the Orthodox religion was contaminated with relics of paganism, and that on the level of everyday existence this lent the Christian system of images a special coloration. In the system of standard rituals there could be seen an indissoluble fusion, a sort of particular Orthodox practice in comparison with conventional religion. As modern scholars have demonstrated, paganism transformed itself within the Christian model of the world and became an integral part of it. Elements of it can be found, for example, in the the concept of an all-powerful King of Heaven, Jesus Christ, of the heavenly and earthly hierarchy, and finally in the ethics of salvation in general.

The cult of icons in the popular milieu always contained elements with which the Church strove to do battle: the people called icons 'gods', in which it is hard not to discern a relic of a pagan mindset and the complex configuration of popular spiritual life. Worship of the image was always capable of transgressing the proper boundary of veneration and 'true worship' proclaimed at the Seventh Ecumenical Council. Much is clarified by studying the 'Sophia orientation' of Russian popular religiosity, uninterruptedly connecting the earthly and incorporeal worlds. In popular consciousness the cult of the Mother of God, in harmony with the cult of Sophia, the Divine Wisdom, was simultaneously contaminated with the cult of Nature and of 'mother damp earth'. Thus if in icons of Christ people saw first and foremost a stern Judge and Heavenly King (to which the predominantly widespread image of Christ Pantocrator – Ruler of All – bore witness), then in icons of the Mother of God they saw a defender, a sufferer and intercessor for the sinful world before God. Miracles from icons of the Mother of God were by far the warmest and closest to the heart. In popular consciousness it was as if they ranked first among all the various 'saving', 'helping' and 'healing' miracles that were expected from icons of the saints. From this came the unchanging requirement among the common people to include the icon of the Mother of God in the rhythms of their working lives and of their everyday cares.

Cases from popular Mariology of the attribution of one or another function to icons of the Mother of God are practically too many to count. Here is just one very widespread example. At the Feast of the Annunciation (7 April), the icon of the 'Annunciation to the Mother of God' participated in the ritual of blessing the grain to be sown. It was set in a tub of grain and prayers were said to the miraculously conceiving Mother of God, trying thus to influence the fertility of mother earth. Almost every type of her image was associated with one or another function, about which the icon painters, carefully noting such information in the iconic pattern-books, were well aware. Thus they knew that one should pray before an icon of the Burning Bush for protection from fires. A touching scene of such a prayer can be seen in *Fire* by N. S. Matveyev (illus. 32). People prayed to the Kazanskaya icon for 'recovery of sight in blinded eyes'; to the Feodorovskaya for relief in childbirth; for 'preservation of the health of infants' to the Tikhvinskaya Mother of God. People prayed to the Hodigitria icon as they set off on long journeys, for Hodegitria is 'She who shows the way'. In recent times it was also the object of prayers for those wishing to become icon painters, during which the words addressed by the Mother of God to St Luke were repeated.[126]

The fusion of the principles of written culture and popular mentality that took place at the end of the Middle Ages was reflected in the popularity of large prayer images and popular printed pictures showing liturgically

32. N. S. Matveyev, *Fire*, 1891. State Museum of the History of Religion, St Petersburg.

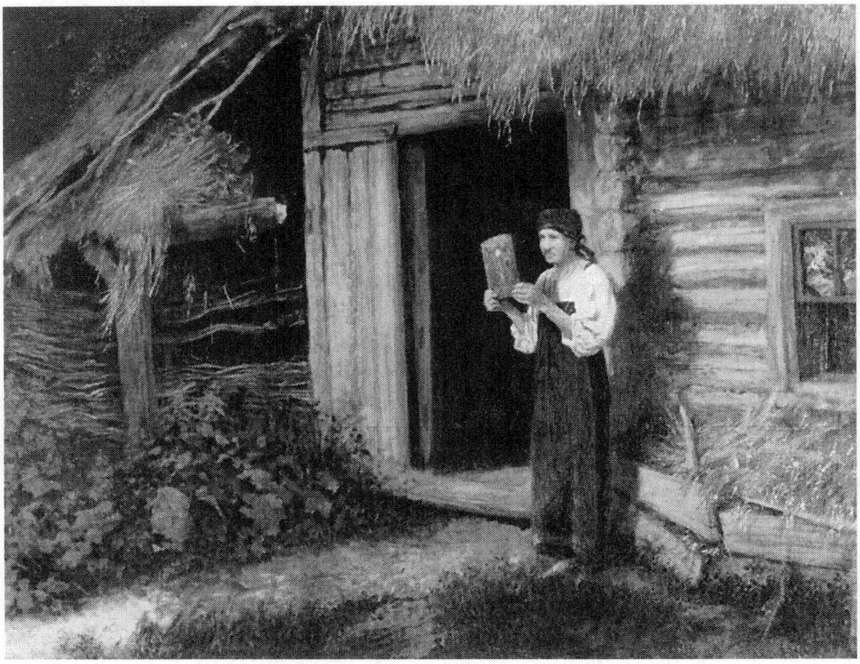

honoured icons of the Mother of God (up to 130 or more), which as Dmitriy Rovinsky observed were distributed in vast quantities in the villages right up to the early 20th century.[127] The depiction of icons of the Mother of God could also often be found on the frames of large altar images of the 18th and 19th centuries. It seems that the people passionately wished to see not a heavenly, but an actual earthly presence of the Mother of God. A no less typical echo of the veneration of her icon is the assertion, met with in spiritual verses, that Christ himself could have painted her countenance:

> And I myself, mother, shall descend from heaven
> I myself shall take your soul out of you,
> Shall inter your relics with the angels,
> With the cherubim and with the glorious seraphim;
> I shall delineate your features on an icon,
> Shall place it in God's church behind the altar.[128]

In connection with all this the people gave the Russian land a special name – 'House of the Mother of God' – in which is seen too the main function of Sophia, Holy Wisdom, with her embodied aim of saving the people: 'house-management' ('economy').

The 'specialization' of saints, their veneration as patrons of one or another craft (illus. 33), presents a common set of features in both Catholic and Orthodox piety from the end of the Middle Ages and the beginning of the modern period. But the active, 'constructive' impulse of the icon always

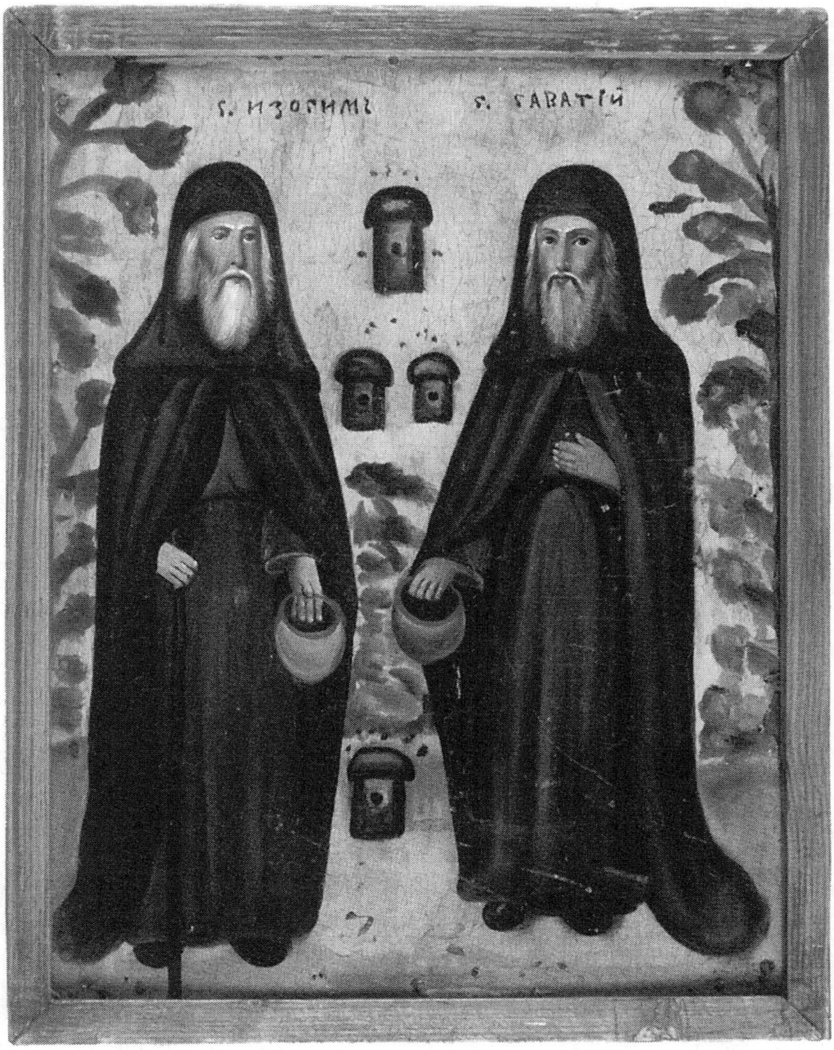

33. *Zosima and Savvatiy of Solovki as Patrons of Beekeeping*, 18th-century north Russia. State Museum of the History of Religion, St Petersburg.

conveyed a special ontological proximity of the divine to everyday religious sensibility. The visual code of sanctity laid a particular kind of emotional dominant upon it. The artistic structure of the icon reflected this dominant to no less a degree than the ritual of ordinary life did.

The problem of the specialization of 'village' saints and of contamination with pagan concepts has been well studied: it turns out to reflect archetypal, and hence universal, experiences of the popular religious consciousness. However, in explaining the national aesthetics of devotion, it is important to note that, apparently, there was nowhere else to match Russia in the 18th or 19th centuries for the widespread dissemination of 'healer' icons, on which were depicted a whole multitude of saints, who, as the people believed, would help in the cure of various illnesses, and who received a characteristic name: 'A narrative-icon, telling by which saints what cures in grace are given by God' (illus. 34). The universal urge of late Catholic and Orthodox popular religiosity to enlist the 'collective support' of the Heavenly Host in the system of Russian devotion is characteristically echoed in the icon.

The 'healer' consists of icons within an icon, that is, the quintessence of the curative functions of the prayer image, of belief in its capacity for providing a defence against disasters and illnesses. The large rectangle – the 'mirror' of the icon – has been broken up into smaller rectangles, each of which is filled with one or several saints with dates when they are remembered liturgically and with corresponding explanatory texts about their healing function. In prayer before such an icon, a person's consciousness would simultaneously engage with a whole system of well-known miracles. A personal prayer image of this type would, as it were, concentrate grace; it would serve as a kind of facilitation for the descent of God's mercy and for receiving a reply from the saints to prayerful requests for their indulgence.

The modern emphasis on personal piety has evidently had various effects on different religious systems of behaviour. If, for example, in Calvinism the descent of grace depended on one being among the chosen, on systematic self-control and on firmness of faith, in Orthodoxy the idea of personal devotion was closely related to the development of the concept of intercession. Further evidence about this is provided in particular by the frequency of

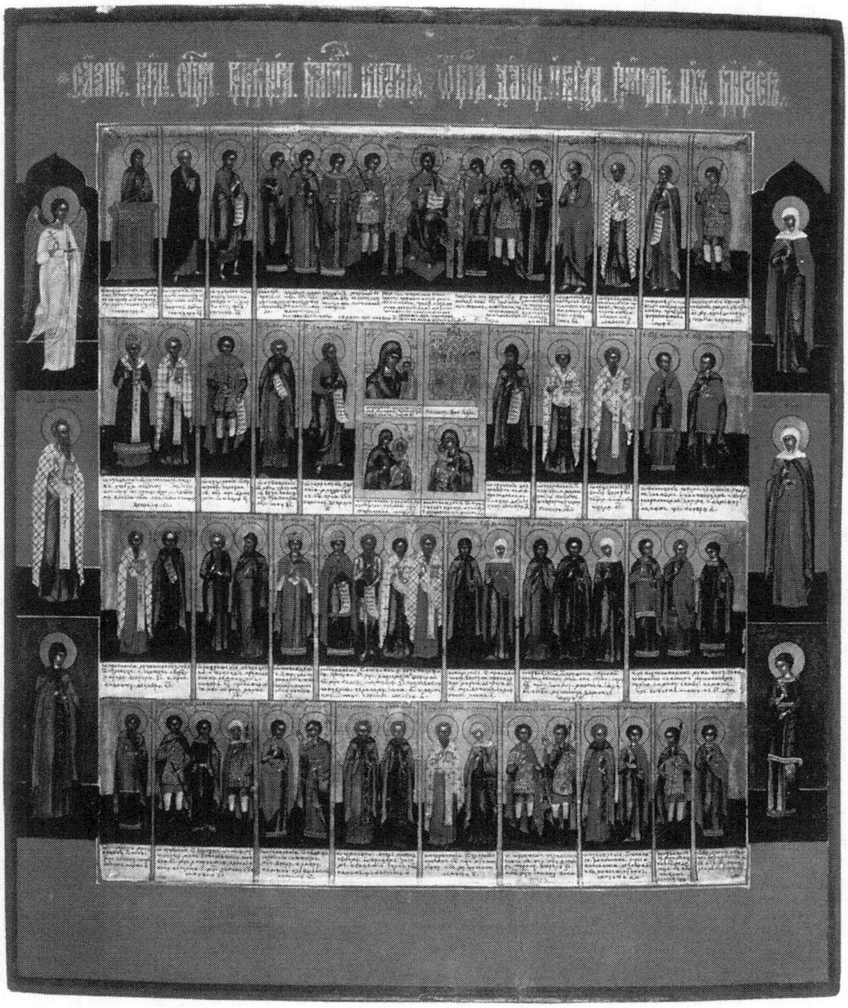

34. *A narrative–icon, telling by which saints what cures in grace are given by God,* second half of the 19th century. State Museum of the History of Religion, St Petersburg.

short or long texts about 'healer' icons encountered in icon pattern-books of the 18th and 19th centuries.

Thus for a cure from 'illness of the eyes', people prayed not only to the Kazan Mother of God but also to the martyr Menas and Longinus the Centurion; for pain in the head to John the Baptist, for toothache to St Antipas, and for fever to St Martha. Romanos the Wonder-worker should help avoid barrenness; Barbara the Great Martyr, St Haralambos and St Onouphrios, to avoid sudden death. Certain saints had the power to influence

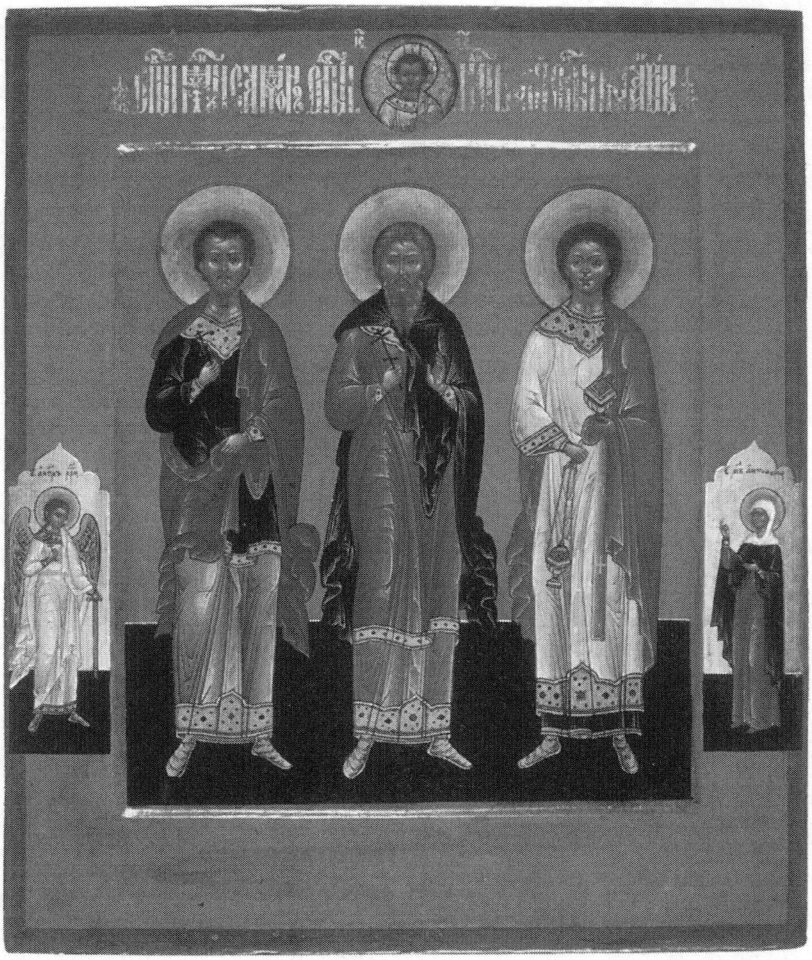

35. *Guriy, Samon and Aviv*, second half of the 19th century, Mstyora. State Museum of the History of Religion, St Petersburg.

human relationships: if a husband should 'be seized by hatred towards his wife', who had done nothing wrong, people prayed to saints Guriy, Samon and Aviv and asked for their icon (illus. 35); even nowadays they are considered protectors of the family. The saints could influence human fates not only in the earthly, but also in the heavenly world: those who had died without repentance could be freed from eternal torment by saints Nifont and Marof, who were also capable of defending people from 'evil spirits'. The latter caused no small agitation, since they led simple mortals into temptation. There was a special 'system' for this eventuality. To be spared from addictive drunkenness one prayed to the icon of St Boniface, or else to St Moses Murin; from love of money ('gold enchantment') to saints Cyprian and Ustinya; St Martimian should spare one from 'the passion of lechery'. If people lacked the mental skills 'for the acquisition of book-learning' they would direct their prayers to saints Cosmas and Damian, while they could pray to St John the Evangelist so as to learn icon painting (illus.36). The saints were capable of anything, even 'the discovery of stolen objects and of escaped slaves' (St John the Warrior).[129]

The everyday reception of such a 'text' implied not only a style of popular thought-processes. Beyond the 'text' there always stood a distinct architecture of religious awareness. This context also facilitates our understanding of the unusual popularity from the 18th century to the early 20th of the icon of 'The Resurrection and Descent into Hell with Feastdays', in which a hagiological composition was used (illus. 37). The central part of the icon is occupied, as a rule, by the Resurrection of Christ – the major

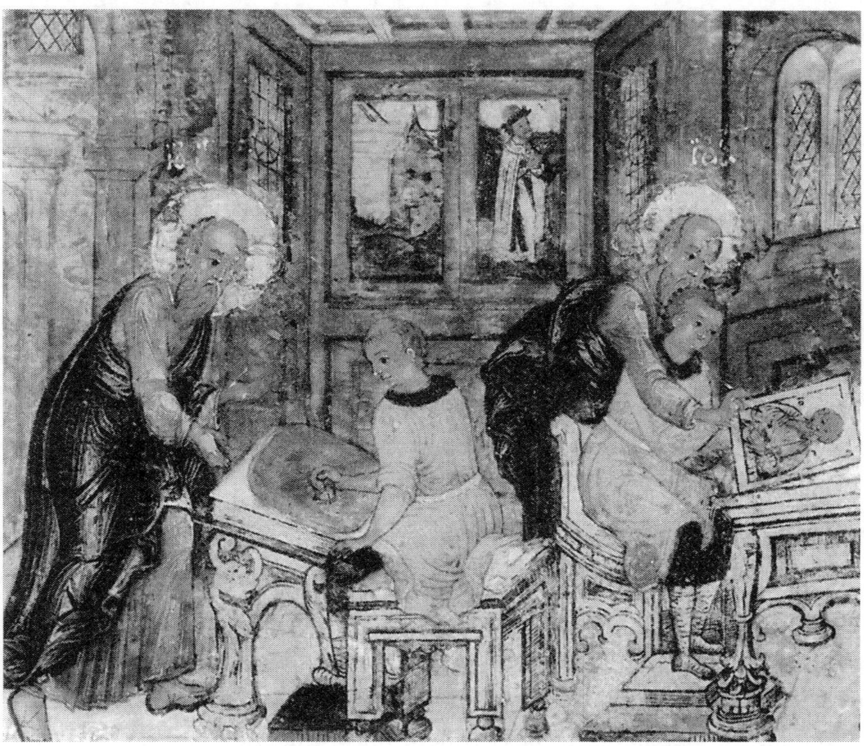

36. 'St John the Divine Instructs a Pupil in Icon Painting', a scene from the Kostroma icon *St John the Divine, with his Deeds*, 1680s. Kostroma Historic Museum-Preserve in the Ipatyev Monastery.

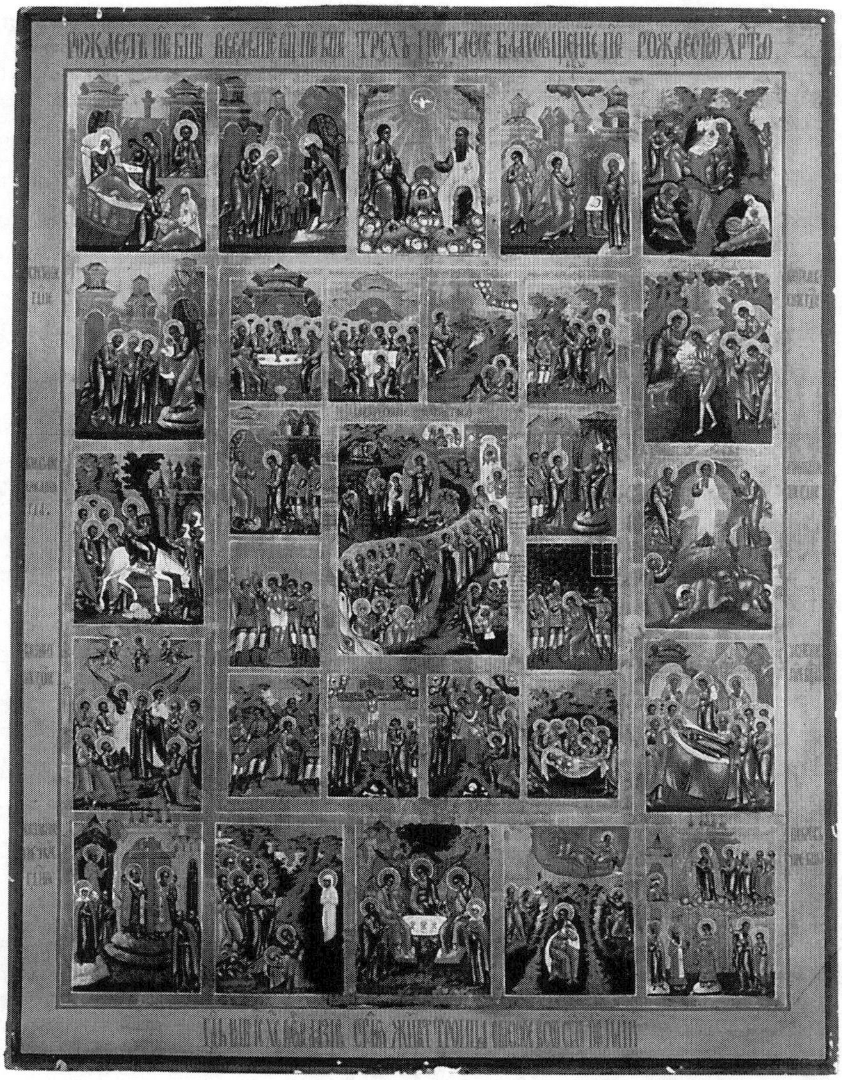

37. *Resurrection and Descent into Hell, with Passion Scenes and Feast Days*, 19th century, Kholuy. Kholuy Art Museum, Kholuy.

Orthodox feast. The fact that Orthodoxy has given it first place, in distinction to the Catholic choice of Christmas, is a sign of pre-eminent attention to the dogma of the Resurrection. The central part, as an 'icon within the icon', perpetually reminded the praying person of this. Around the centre are panels showing the twelve most significant Orthodox feasts: the Nativity of Christ, the Baptism, the Purification, the Annunciation, the Entry into

Jerusalem, the Ascension, the Trinity, the Transfiguration, the Nativity of the Mother of God, the Elevation of the Cross, the Presentation in the Temple, the Dormition (note that the number of feasts can be greater). The order of these scenes most often accords with the beginning and ending of the liturgical year, thus starting with the Nativity of the Mother of God and finishing with the Dormition. In this way the theme of the Mother of God turns out here too to be internally dominant. Since the seasonal aspect of rituals was preserved in the Orthodox Church, all these feast days were seen by the people as timed to coincide with the cycles of nature: the beginnings and ends of agricultural tasks. Hence the ordinary prayer before the icon of 'The Resurrection and Descent into Hell with Feasts' served to convince a person not just of Christian dogmatic truths, but also of the presence of God in the world of creation, in daily toil and in the ineffable miracle of the constant working of grace.

Alongside all of this, the common people's sense of the miraculous could easily turn into an ambivalence or worse. If, for example, in the West one might often come across a superstitious veneration for relics, in Russia it would be directed towards icons. Thus (as Adam Olearius relates), during a fire in Novgorod in 1611, a certain pious man, desperate to save his house, began zealously praying before the icon of Nikola. But when his prayer brought no result, in his disappointment he hurled the icon into the fire, crying 'If you do not want to help us, then help yourself and put it out!'[130] In the Time of Troubles at the beginning of the 17th century, some Smolensk peasants fled from the Poles into deep forest. When the latter nevertheless came upon them and seized their possessions, they hung icons upside down in the trees, and began to blaspheme, saying 'We make prayers to you, but you do not save us from Lithuania.'[131]

It has become normal to connect the understanding of such symbolic inversions with the *topos* of the 'world upside down' and the Bakhtinian carnival tradition. Such phenomena recall the medieval 'rituals of dishonour' and the practice of punishment in effigy, when in the period of the 'great dispute over grace' public 'punishments' of works of religious art were organized. Thus in Saxony in 1524 a representation of St Francis was suspended from a gallows; a year earlier, a sculpture of St Jan. We know too about mockery and punishments in effigy of leaders of the Reformation, for example the public burning of a portrait of Zwingli.[132] Such 'anti-behaviour' could also have magic functions, could take the role of 'a natural' condition for active intercourse with the other world.[133] However, we should note that here once again we are dealing with archetypal mental constructs, which in the history of mentalities know of no national, confessional or even sometimes temporal boundaries. The facts about iconoclasm that David Freedberg adduces also testify to this.[134]

The passionate thirst for the miraculous and for divine grace was also manifested in the decoration of icons. Possibly nowhere else did the aesthetic of 'Josephite' piety and the 'materiality' of ritual display itself more than in the splendour of the ecclesiastical cult and the magnificence of the images. In the mid-16th century the lateral margins of the icons get narrower: icons begin to be set up side by side in a row, leading at once to a larger quantity of them. Simultaneously they begin to be covered more and more often with glittering cladding or frames (*oklady*).

The decoration of holy images is a universal cultural mode: the link between holiness and splendour or brilliance is a characteristic of many religious traditions. Hence the image of a glittering world, derived from gold, silver and precious stones, constitutes a most important spiritual symbol (illus. 38). But the 'cold' religiosity of the Protestants clearly stoked up this urge towards the semantics of splendour among the Orthodox and Catholics. In the autumn of the Middle Ages, the bewitching saturation of devotion with bright materials would appear to have reached its limits. During the reign of Aleksey Mikhaylovich, the Russian 'beautified church' was to become an analogue to the Catholic religious–aesthetic concept of *Ecclesia ornata*; the Patriarch Nikon introduced into his 'Tables' (*Skrizhal*[135]) the dictum of Simeon of Thessaloniki: 'Beauty and grandeur in a place of worship indicate that Christ is the splendid bridegroom, and the Church his splendid bride', which once again reminds us of the cultural interconnectedness of the Christian world.

Splendour and luminosity were always bound closely together in the Christian consciousness with a view of the world as an icon. The Russian popular proverb of the 19th century, 'The world is the incorruptible raiment

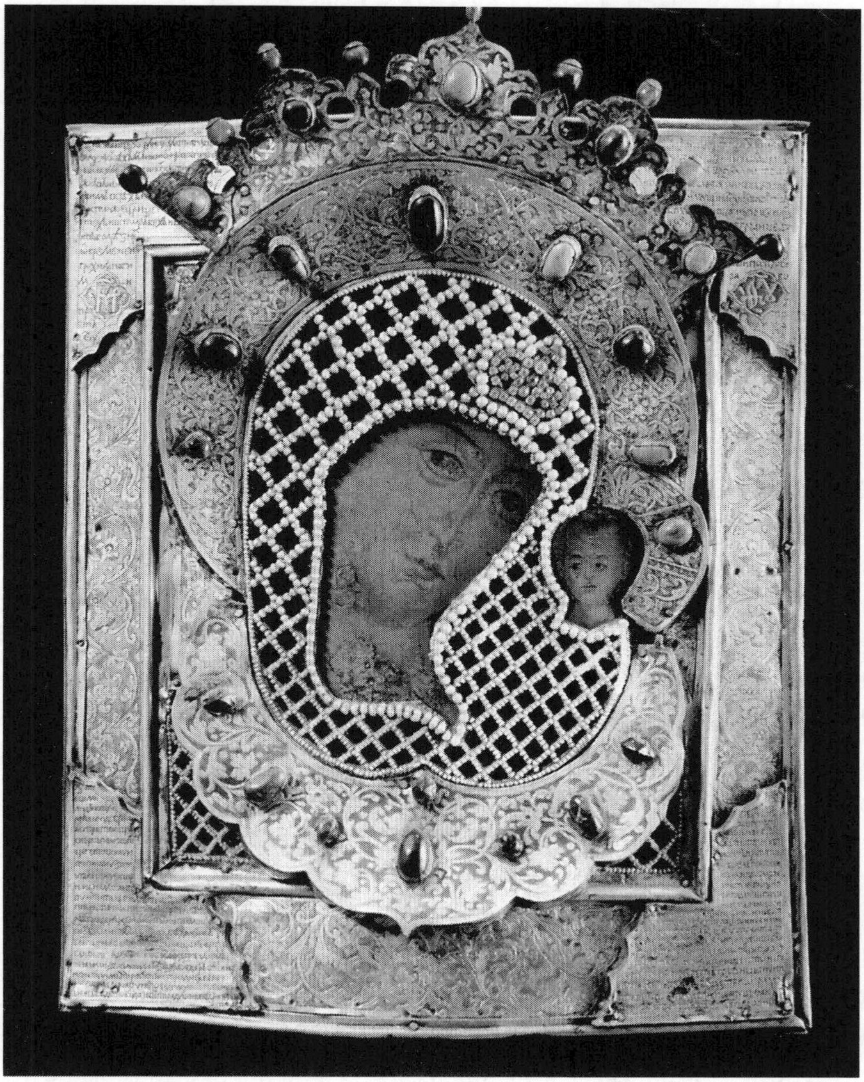

38. Decorated icon of Kazan Mother of God, 17th century. State Tretyakov Gallery, Moscow.

of the Lord',[136] presupposed nothing less than an image of the world whose ontology is rooted in the activity of the Holy Spirit. The world as 'incorruptible raiment' is an unusually spacious metaphor, conveying from one point of view an understanding of the world as filled with 'goodness' (*blagost*), and from another an understanding of the world as a simulacrum of the primal image, of the world as some kind of an 'icon' that is not identical with God, but rather with his 'raiment', his 'shining shadow'. For that reason an excessive saturation of the sacred sphere with light would always sensitively reflect the ethics and aesthetics of salvation. Here the popular love for all that was 'colourfully heathen' encountered the official Imperial predilection for luxury and sumptuousness in cult matters. As a consequence, 'enthusiasm for silver cladding' within mass religiosity would eventually be raised to a degree that would presuppose a special emotional mode of apprehending the higher and the lower worlds. In the 19th century this would remain to a considerable degree the same as in the 16th and 17th centuries.

Paul of Aleppo, who had travelled widely in the Orthodox East, was frequently struck by the splendour and radiance of the Muscovite tsardom. But sacral splendour would always attract the attention of the Russian observer too. In the ornamentation of a wonder-working icon, the acquisition of divine favour took on special meaning. An essential aspect of this was that making copies of wonder-working icons often presupposed copying the cladding and applied decoration too. Thus around 1514 a copy was made of the wonder-working Vladimir Mother of God icon from the Moscow Kremlin Dormition Cathedral. On its margins was an imitation of the golden casing made for the icon at Metropolitan Fotiy's command. It still stands in the Dormition Cathedral in place of its prototype.

In 19th-century Church politics we sometimes come across 'very indicative' cultural phenomena. The priest, lesser clergy and churchwarden of the Church of the Trinity on the Arbat in Moscow sent a request to the Metropolitan Filaret (Drozdov) for permission to order some new icons and two silver frames with gilding. 'I was naked and ye clothed Me', answered the Metropolitan, 'and let these words not be forgotten in some chance thought of zeal for silver icon frames. If there should be those showing diligence enough to have silver icon-frames made, in gratitude for God's blessing, then bring this to their zealous attention, as has been the ancient custom.'[137]

It sometimes happened that parishioners were deprived of their own locally venerated icon. The parishioners of the village of Luzhki in the Zvenigorod district were left without the icon of the Blessed Alexander Svirsky, whom they specially honoured, at the whim of the local landowner

Aleksey Politkovsky. By his command the icon was transferred to the Anosin convent. Since the icon had been adorned by the parishioners with a silver cladding eight pounds in weight, a lawsuit ensued, which by the decision of the Church authorities went against the pious parishioners. They received the answer that their silver cladding was 'a sacrifice to God and hence no longer their own property'.[138] Those who had lost their icon could scarcely have been content with this. Valuable adornments had by the mid-19th century long become signs of wealth and prestige too in the uncontainable urge for splendour. That means that in the adornment of the icon (as a method of acquiring grace), everyday vanity was often present: just that to which the well-established popular name for icons – 'God's charity'– refers.

All this can be seen as starting from the rejection of the views of the 'Non-Possessors'. The Russian saint Nil Sorsky (1433–1508) had been hostile to excessive splendour: silver icon-frames were not needed for the Hesychast's 'mental activity'.[139] In contradiction to this, Muscovite devotion concentrated attention on the luminous saturation of Muscovite Rus – the 'Great Icon' whose religious–emotional dominant would so clearly manifest itself in the culture of the Old Belief. In particular, in the well-known *Russian Vineyard* by the Old Ritualist author Semyon Denisov (1682–1741), Rus is compared with a 'second heaven', a kind of 'icon'. As did the space of an icon, the space of Rus concentrated light above all: 'splendid Russia shining forth with the all-splendid light of piety, for so all-luminous is the greatly brilliant light of Orthodoxy'. Incidentally, this space has truly cosmic dimensions – it is boundless, thanks to the grace 'poured out' on it: 'for the Russian land has been, as regards its boundaries, greatly abundant with grace, as regards its lands, mightily rich in Orthodoxy, from sea to sea, from its rivers to the ends of the universe, all of it stretching out in splendour'. The whole structure of this sacred space was held together with 'right belief', concentrated in the grandeur of Russian churches and monasteries, whose image is drawn towards the starry heavens, is wonderful and shines. The author himself gazes on, and impels the reader to see, nothing less than the marvellous luxuriance of this 'iconic' Rus, that is to say the realized image of splendour, which 'most brilliantly shines, obedient to the light of the righteous sun of Christ'. 'Behold' – he writes – 'the all-encompassing splendour, see the ecclesiastical grandeur, and also behold the all-saving goodness of the monasteries, and also turn thine eyes to the heaven-like beauty of the coenobium, and how great it is and how great also the heaven, spread out with bright stars, like wonderful pearls, like *greatly-valuable precious stones* with which it most marvellously adorns itself: so greatly extended and all-encompassing is Russia, with its fine monasteries and magnificent places of God's worship: as finely adorned, as richly set out as if it were even worthy to be named a *second Heaven*' (my italics).[140]

The Petrine Baroque culture for its part brought as a corrective to this only the antithesis of a Greek-type culture (lofty–lowly) and the introduction into the 'brilliant' sacred sphere of a greater dose of worldliness. By Catherine II's time, certain Church leaders, for the greater luxuriance of their services, invited along hairdressers who would curl the hair not only of the choir but of the subdeacons, following current fashion,[141] while in the 19th century both N. S. Leskov and D. A. Rovinsky, while visiting monasteries, saw cells that, in the words of Leskov's diary, resembled 'boudoirs'.[142]

It remains to say that the attitude of the Petrine government to miracles was rather strangely connected with its attitude to the decoration of icons. Whereas the unmasking of false miracles was accompanied by stern punishments, the removal of brilliant valuables from icons was brought into the system of officially sanctioned confiscations. Decrees of the Synod noted that among offerings to icons there were many ancient and finely wrought objects, such as old coins, precious stones and a multitude of rare artefacts, and instructed 'knowledgeable' people to go around the monasteries.[143] These confiscations were part of the history of Peter's methods of fighting superstitions. But they remained in the popular memory as iconoclastic acts, contrasting with the special nature of the Muscovite 'holy way of life'.

CHAPTER TWO

Dispute about Signs, Dispute about Faith

Attempts have been made to explain the specific qualities of the Muscovite Tsardom and how the aims of its culture are connected with the idea of the ubiquitous presence of the icon in Russia. But so far there has been little understanding of how the huge quantity of icons that sanctified the extent of the empire was to find itself at a single moment mystically disembodied. Patriarch Nikon's liturgical reform (in the mid-17th century) presupposed, as well as everything else, a change in the two most important categories of sacred symbol – 'likeness' and 'name'. For Muscovite consciousness this meant no less than a denial of faith and destruction of their picture of the world.

It is enough to recollect just two major events to sense the dynamics of this truly semiotic revolution. In 1652 Nikon was elected Patriarch. After the Church Council of 1654 he sent off to the Constantinopolitan Patriarch Paisiy his famous 26 questions concerning ritual and the mistakes that had crept into the Russian Church service books. Two years later his 'Tables' (*Skrizhal*) appeared, according to which the Greek archiepiscopal staff, new garments for those officiating, new forms of liturgical vessels and so on would be introduced. At a gathering of the Russian archbishops in the same year, a curse was laid on the two-fingered sign of the Cross that had been affirmed at the *Stoglav* council – that is, on what for an Orthodox Christian was one on the chief signs of his or her covenant with God and a major symbol of everyday piety. For ordinary folk, how they put three fingers together symbolized the Holy Trinity, while the two that were extended symbolized the divine and human natures of Christ. Last, at the Great

Moscow Council of 1666–7, the New Ritual system was finally introduced, the Old Believers were anathematized and the view of the older icon as an image of false likeness was affirmed.

On old Russian icons the abbreviated name of Christ was rendered IC XC, while saints made the sign of blessing with two fingers. We can find the same sigla for Christ on the famous mosaic in the central lunette of the narthex in St Sophia in Constantinople, and also on many Byzantine icons. On Russian icons of the new devotional type from the mid-17th century to the early 20th, the sigla for Christ was indicated by the letters IИC XC, while the two-fingered sign of blessing was replaced by three fingers. The new type of official Russian icon also included all the symbolic forms of the New Ritual – the Catholic version of the Crucifixion, new vestments for the clergy, a different form of archbishop's staff, etc., all of which corresponded with contemporary Greek Church usage. Without exception they were rejected by the Russian Old Ritualists.

The Ambivalence of Symbols

Since it is a symbol of the Incarnation, as it were the 'heart' of Orthodoxy, the prayer-image attracted to itself the whole drama of struggle, and at the same time reflected it like a mirror. We should note that in the Christian system of comprehending the world, religious signs and symbols are by their nature ambivalent. They demand choice or differentiation, insofar as they can be only true or false. The possibility of the reversal or non-identity of signs was always related in religious consciousness with the understanding of the true and the false paths of salvation.

Nikon's reforms and his turning towards a contemporary Greek model of devotion meant, for the Old Believers, the 'end' of the Muscovite holy empire (the 'Third Rome') and the end of the purity of Muscovite Orthodoxy, which had to a large degree defined itself earlier in contrast with the 'Hagarene captivity'[1] of the former Byzantine world. Since the time of Mehmet II (who conquered Constantinople in 1453), the terms 'Caesar' and 'Rum' had established themselves among the titles of the Ottoman sultans: that is to say 'Eastern Roman Emperor', 'Emperor of the Romaioi'. The

Roman or Byzantine heritage was also reflected in the Turkish state emblem of a crescent moon with a star, which had earlier been the crest of Constantinople. The first Rome had traditionally been saved by the geese whose cries had warned the guards of the enemy's approach. The second Rome, Constantinople, was once saved thanks to the moon: unexpectedly appearing one night through a rift in the cloud-cover, it had highlighted enemy soldiers creeping towards the defences. Established by one of the branches of the Seljuk Turks in Anatolia, the 'Roman' sultanate derived its name too from the Arabized form of the root of the word *Roma*, as did the name of individual Byzantine Greeks (Rum = Roman).

Even the signs of Greek holiness turned out to be ambivalent: the Byzantine 'symphonia' ('harmony' between Church and state), having ceased to exist within the Empire, prolonged its existence in an inverted semiotic space. In 1453, almost immediately after the fall of Constantinople, there took place, as in former times, the solemn ceremony of induction of a new Ecumenical Patriarch, as laid down by the Byzantine order of consecration. The patriarchal insignia were handed over by the Byzantine emperor, a role taken this time by Mehmet II: the Patriarch Gennadios Scholarios recognized the Sultan as his overlord, while the Sultan for his part repeated word for word the Byzantine formula of consecration, presenting the insignia to the Patriarch and pronouncing the words: 'The Holy Trinity, which has given me the Imperial title, gives thee the Patriarchal title of New Rome.' Together with the symbols of office, Mehmet II gave Patriarch Gennadios unlimited civil power over all Christian subjects of the Porte, and in 1572 the Patriarch of Constantinople was proclaimed 'Rumilet Bashti' – spiritual head of all Christians in the Ottoman empire. In the Ottoman Islamic realm from that moment on, the power of the Greek higher clergy extended not just to the Church and ritual life, but to a considerable extent over the communal existence of the Orthodox peoples.

From the viewpoint of Moscow one could also observe the 'converted' names of the centres of Byzantine sanctity. Let us again recall that for the Christian consciousness face and name were the two most important categories of religious symbol as locations of a certain divine presence. The loss of one of them meant its loss as a symbol (whether in respect of an icon or place of worship) of divine grace. Mehmet II's promise that the conversion of Christian churches into mosques would not be permitted was to remain a dead letter. The main holy sites of Constantinople (hence of the 'whole' Orthodox world) were turned into mosques: the churches of St Sophia, the Holy Apostles, the Pantocrator, St Theodore the Studite and others. They all received 'converted' names (for example, 'Ayasofya').

In Muscovite Rus the observed spatial symmetry involved first and foremost an opposition between its own reception of 'Roman' sacred symbols and their illegal, military acquisition as 'spoils of war' by the Muslims (the chief sign of Byzantine imperial power – the double-headed eagle – had already been adopted under Ivan III via the intermediary of the heraldic eagle of the Holy Roman Empire). Moscow's right to them was not subject to earthly laws. Hence up to the time of Peter the Great (who captured Azov in 1696) it was considered by no means obligatory to fight for these signs. As early as in the writings of Filofey (*c.* 1465–1542),[2] we can find an almost complete formulation of the titling of the Moscow grand prince as tsar and autocrat. The acquisition of the title of the Byzantine emperors – 'Caesar' (implying Christian overlord) – symbolized the inheritance by Moscow of the 'sacred imperium' and the sacral unification in Russian statehood of the fullness of power. On this basis (as has been demonstrated earlier) was developed the concept of a special charisma not only of the Russian tsars but also of the patriarchs, who were established in 1589. But on the same ideological basis Muscovite Russia, on acquiring the main symbols of sacred authority, began to consider itself also to be the 'last', unique and divinely chosen state possessor of the main symbol of Orthodoxy, the icon, and more precisely of its special charisma. In the atmosphere of the Reformation, which rejected icon veneration in several variants, and with the 'converted' signs of Christian holiness in the Orthodox East, Muscovite devotion surrounded the icon with a special kind of aura. The concept of the special charisma of the Russian icon was brought into the area of concern not only of the Church but of the ruler, and a heightened attentiveness resulted.

If the *Stoglav* Council of 1551 indeed had a 'reformative' role, then in the first instance that was related to a concern about the purity of grace in an image. In his response to the Council (chapter 5, question 3), Ivan IV emphasized that it was proper to have a great care for icons. Answering the Tsar's own question, the Council composed what without exaggeration must be its most poetic and linguistically elevated chapter. At its very beginning the icon was singled out in the renovated system of devotion: 'Let it happen that in the capital city of Moscow and in all the towns by the Tsar's advice that the Metropolitan, the archbishops and the bishops should care for the multiform Church dignities and *most of all for the holy icons* and for painters and for other Church ranks according to the holy rules . . .' (my italics).[3]

The sign system of ritual affirmed by the *Stoglav*, as also the sacral title on an icon of Christ abbreviated as 'IC XC' and crossing oneself with two fingers, as shown on icons, was apprehended by the masses exclusively in the context of the acquisition and safeguarding by the Muscovite tsardom – the 'Third Rome' – of the genuine signs of Christianity.

The reform of the Russian Church in the mid-17th century turned everything upside down. Those sacred symbols that were once understood as authentic began to display a new ambivalence within the Muscovite 'sacred imperium', but now against the background of the schism within European Christianity: it communicated an extra excitement to mass religiosity, while it communicated to the religious symbols that heightened 'sensibility' which (unlike in the High Middle Ages), 'ceases to be subsidiary and subordinated, but forces itself into a leading place and demands autonomy for itself'.[4] It is no accident that precisely at that time, and in particular in post-Tridentine Catholicism, interest in the sacred monogram increased: the sacred monogram began to be wrapped around with a certain heightened religious and emotional agitation that sprang up everywhere. Against its background, the refusal of Patriarch Nikon and Tsar Aleksey Mikhaylovich to retain the old symbols induced in the collective belief-system a deep conviction of the gracelessness both of the 'world' of Muscovite Russia and of its new icons. A clear illustration of this ambivalence of symbols, the depth of its effect on mass emotions and religiosity, can be found in the paired Old Believer picture icons, widespread among the Priestless (*Bezpopovtsy*) from no later than the start of the 18th century and to be encountered up to the early 20th (illus. 39, 40). Each of the comparative, paired icons consists of two pictures, reflecting each other with a symmetrical depiction of the signs of the Old and New Rituals: three-fingered and

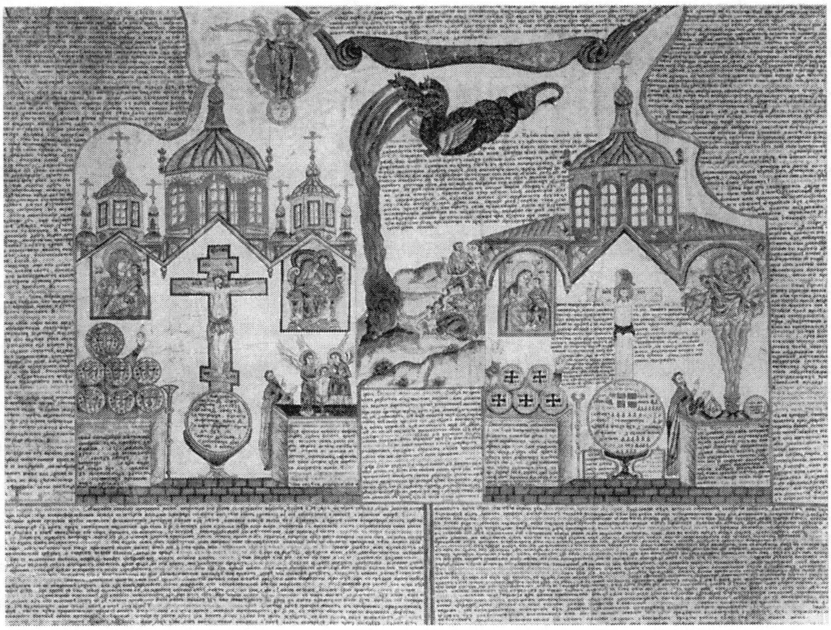

39. Illustrated manuscript comparing the symbols of the Old and New Rituals, second half of the 19th century. State Historical Museum, Moscow.

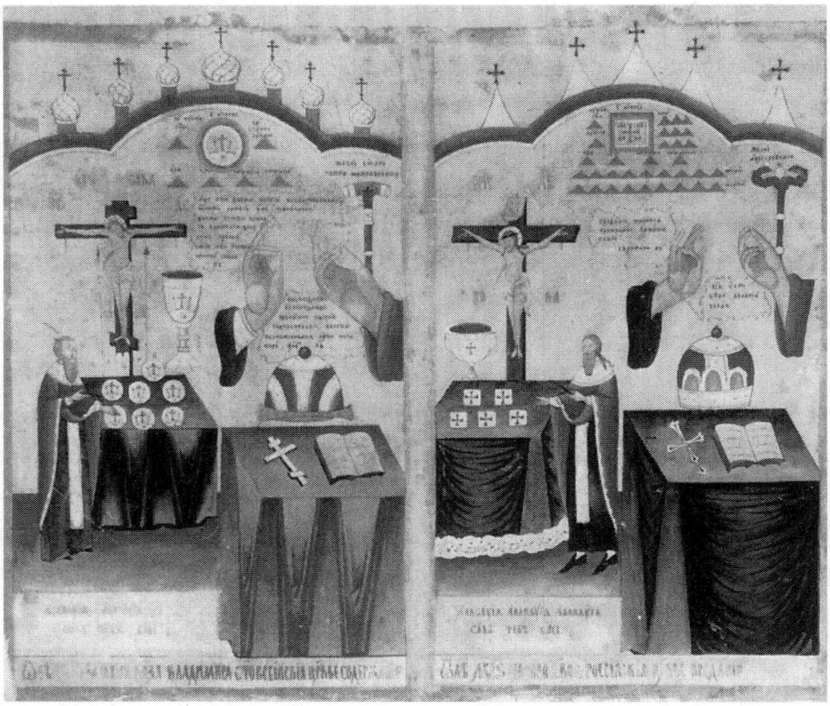

40. Illustrated comparison of the symbols of the Old and New Rituals, late 18th century or first half of the 19th. State Museum of the History of Religion, St Petersburg.

two-fingered signs of the Cross; old and new formulae of blessing; eight-ended and four-ended altar crosses; two types of Crucifixion; the new in Western style (with the 'drooping' body of Christ and 'IИC XC' inscribed instead of 'IC XC'); two kinds of archbishop's staff. On these paired icons it can also be seen that the Old Believers cast doubt upon the soteriological meaning not only of the depicted symbol, but of the Eucharist symbol, in as much as they also constrastively opposed attributes of the liturgy – wafers of a circular and square (new) form, altars, Eucharist vessels and 'perambulations' of the priest around the altar. Since after Nikon's reforms of the liturgy the Church ceased, in the eyes of the Old Believers, to possess the authentic signs that were the keys to the Heavenly Kingdom, the Eucharist itself could no longer be taken to be the transubstantiation of Christ's own body.

In the hagiological icon of St Serafim of Sarov we saw sacred didactics on the level of the sanctification of a human being operating; these picture icons by contrast are directed towards rational apprehension: the rationalization and individuation of post-medieval religious sensibility is interestingly reflected in them. They show a typically Baroque didactic approach and method of organizing the 'text'– contrast and mirror symbolism. As far back as in Pseudo-Dionysios[5] we can find the comparison of the structure of the world to a system of mirrors reflecting the divine light. However, in the Baroque age the idea of the mirror significantly transformed the category of the comparison. The Baroque mirror could easily operate not only with authentic, but also false similitudes. Thus in displaying evident ambivalence, the old and the new sets of symbols on Old Believer paired icons are reflected one in the other. They reverse themselves, as it were, so as to demonstrate to the believer that the one is just the shadow of the other, a shadow inviting false assumptions. Icons of this kind permitted one to think only in strong antitheses. 'Playfulness' could come in only at the level of irony, as is clearly visible on an example of one such comparative icon of the 19th century, whose part representing the new rite carries the following text:

> These are the dissensions that the modern-day schismatics cause us in Russia: about the three-fingered or two-fingered sign of the

Cross, about four or eight-ended crosses, about double or triple hallelujahs, about the number of wafers, about shaving of beards and the painting of icons and innumerable other matters, all of which are things of only middling import, not defined by the word of God, totally unnecessary for salvation, for free Christian choice.[6]

From the very beginning of the Nikonian reforms and the correction of service books, the sign system of the prayer image, hallowed by Muscovite tradition, served the Old Believers as proof of the authenticity of their devotion. For centuries the icon had been closely bound up with the liturgy in Russia,[7] so it is no mere accident that the start of the 'new Nikonite faith', according to Semyon Denisov, took place when Patriarch Nikon 'first ordered the image of the Annunciation to the Most Holy Mother of God to be painted in an unusual and novel manner, as the Most Holy Virgin having the infant complete within her'.[8] In the later Old Believer text 'The Tale of our Hierarch Nikon', this depiction of the Annunciation was called 'The Nikonite Sophistry' (illus. 41).[9]

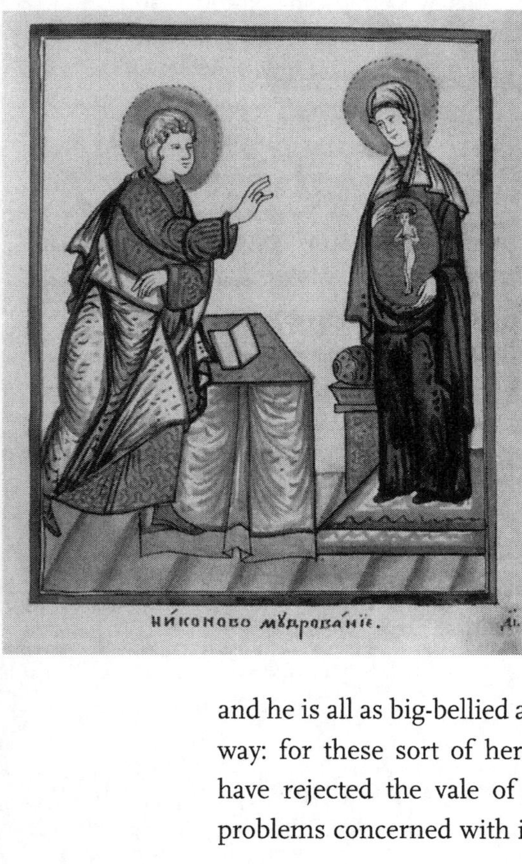

41. 'Nikonite Sophistry', a miniature from *The Tale of our Hierarch Nikon*, early 20th century. Library of the Academy of Sciences, St Petersburg.

Since the defenders of the Old Devotion resolved the problem of the new likeness and the new name of the official icon monosemantically in the context of the faith, they related the new sign content of the image both to iconoclasm and also to the 'Latin' and Lutheran faiths. We find the new type of Russian icon identified with heresy and the 'German' faith in Avvakum: 'they paint the image of the Saviour Emmanuel: the face is rounded, the mouth is bright red, the hair is curly, the arms and muscles are plump . . . and he is all as big-bellied as a German . . . and all of it is painted in a fleshly way: for these sort of heretics have come to love fleshly corpulence and have rejected the vale of tears'.[10] A more substantial elucidation of the problems concerned with icons is to be found in the 'Pomorian Answers',[11] a specially authoritative work among the Old Believers. Speaking of the question of the likeness of an image, the monks of Solovki affirmed that the icon painters who followed the new piety paint icons not according to the ancient Greek and Russian wonder-working images, but out of their own imagination: 'they make the appearance of the flesh of the Saviour and Christ and other saints plump; and in other depictions make them unlike the ancient holy icons'. So as to emphasize their correctness, the authors referred to the saints' asceticism and the mortification of the flesh they had seen depicted in old icons.

The authenticity of the names of the icons was demonstrated in just the same way (in the annotations to the Seventh Ecumenical Council icons are 'by their names full of holiness and grace'). The new sigla for Christ 'IИC XC' was not sacred in the eyes of the Old Believers, for it was nowhere to be found on the ancient holy images. This monogram was taken from modern Greek books, infected, as they thought, with 'Latin' and 'iconoclast' heresies. The symbolism of the old finger position for making the sign of the Cross was shown in the 'Pomorian Answers' to be a Trinitarian dogma. Commenting on the *Kirillova kniga* ('Cyril's Book', 1644), the New Ritualists considered that they had established that the fourth finger signified the hypostasis of God as the Word. Keeping in mind the resolution of the *Stoglav* about icons of the Holy Trinity, the authors of the 'Answers' explained that it was not written there that one should form this hypostasis with this finger. It was just as when in icon painting three figures are represented in the image of the Holy Trinity: the Church has not told us to write on it which is the Father, which the Son and which the Holy Spirit, but to write the general designation 'Holy Trinity'. Here, too, can be found the basis of the two-fingered sign of the Cross and the way to inscribe the name of Christ by their representation on old Greek and Slavonic images. It is worth noting that this fully accorded with historical reality.[12]

After the Great Moscow Council (1666–7), the official Church ordered the correction of the two-fingered sign of the Cross and of the title 'IC XC' on old icons.[13] In connection with this particular 'sensitivity' of the sign, the formal organization of pages of manuscripts of the 'Pomorian Answers' is noteworthy. For greater visual explicitness, the scribes would often copy into the margins of the 'Pomorian Answers' the right hand of Christ and the

Mother of God, from famous wonder-working icons, raised in blessing. The intensified emotional apprehension of the sacred abbreviation and of the two-fingered sign of the Cross on a wonder-working icon excluded any further kinds of argument (illus. 42). A person could read, consider and learn that at the time of Maksim, Metropolitan of Kiev and Vladimir, the image of the Fedotievskaya Mother of God was revealed near Ryazan: 'it shows to such a person the hand in blessing using two fingers'.[14]

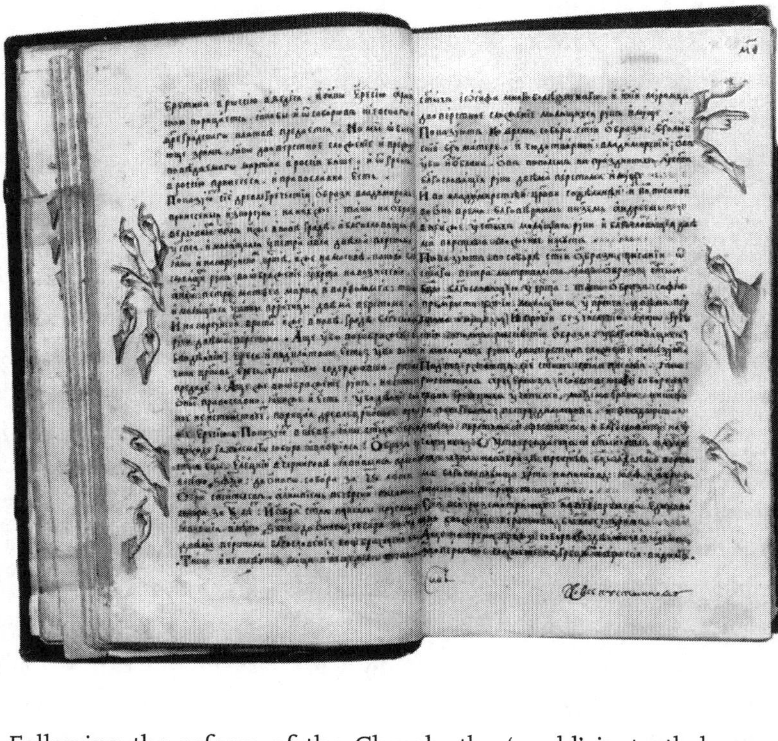

42. 'The Pomorian Answers', a manuscript volume with marginal drawings, 1723. Russian State Library, Moscow.

Following the reform of the Church, the 'world' in truth began to be perceived in terms of damnation and salvation (illus. 43). The anathemas pronounced on the Old Believers at the Great Moscow Council met with answering curses directed not only at the Church hierarchy, but towards those icon painters who corrected the holy symbols on the old icons. 'If anybody should paint on the sacred images of prayer right hands in a pinched position, by the heretic tradition, let him be cursed'; 'if anyone should paint an image of the holy Fathers making a blessing with the right hand incorrectly according to the heretic tradition let him be cursed'; these things can be found in several Old Believer anthologies of writings.[15] It is worth noting that equivalent popular printed icons often featured the opposite in the form of 'Nikon's legacy', for example 'I curse those who do not make a sign with the first three fingers, but make the sign with the index and middle finger projecting'. (If one is to trust the Old Believer icon painter Grigoriy Yakovlev, who converted to the official Church, Old Believer icon painters themselves often corrected the right hands of saints in blessing on icons.)[16] After all this there came to be a deep-rooted conviction in the collective consciousness of the authenticity of the two-fingered sign of the Cross on icons for prayer, something that can be judged by the observation in one of the main newspapers in 1873:

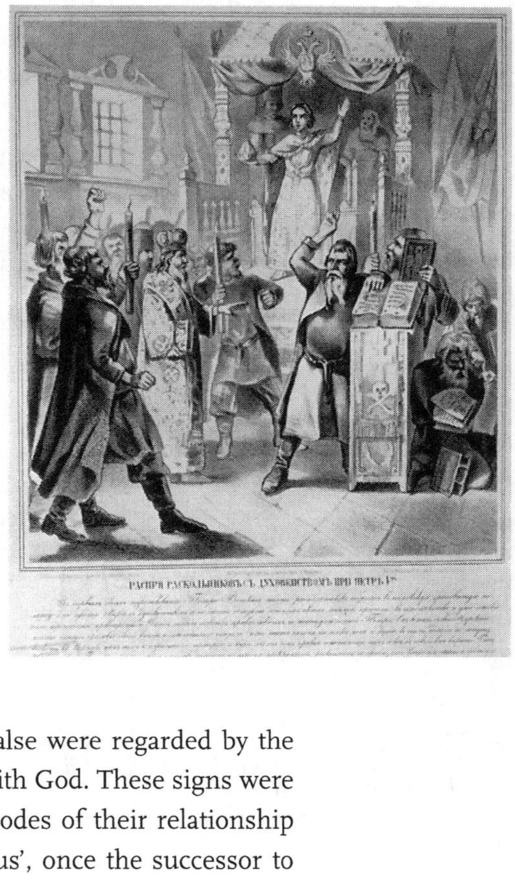

43. *Dispute of the Schismatics and the Clergy in Peter I's Reign*, 1863, lithograph. State Museum of the History of Religion, St Petersburg.

> Ask, for example, of a common man, even if he is not a schismatic, why he prays with two fingers put together? Without giving the matter lengthy thought he will tell you: that is how our grandfathers and great-grandfathers prayed, that is what they taught us, and they taught us to pray in this way because it was laid down by God – and he will show you an icon where the hand in prayer or blessing is depicted with the two-fingered sign.[17]

Symbols that the New Ritualists designated as false were regarded by the common people as a most enduring convenant with God. These signs were often in addition regarded as one of the chief modes of their relationship to the earthly world: to the expanses of 'Holy Rus', once the successor to Byzantium, and to mankind itself.

As late as the 17th century in Muscovite Rus, for a man to shave his beard and moustache was unequivocally linked with the 'Papist heresy'. The 'Imprecation against Beard-Shaving', included in the 'Service Book' under Patriarch Filaret (1619–33), emphasized that it was the iconoclast Emperor Copronymos[18] who initiated this 'spiritually destructive' and heretical custom. Thereafter all the Roman Popes wallowed in it. In the following two centuries the Old Believers simply elucidated this European fashion as sin and heretical behaviour. The wearing of wigs and shaving of beards, said the 18th-century Old Believer writer Ivan Vasilyev about the New Ritualists, are justified by them in their books, and they do not regard them a sin; their teaching is opposed to the teaching of the apostle Paul and the blessed Chrysostom (St John Chrysostom, 'Golden-mouthed', 347–407, Patriarch of Constantinople and a prolific author).[19] As well as this, shaving of beards was almost always linked with the iconoclastic 'Lutheran' and 'Calvinist' heresy: 'Latins, Lutherans and Calvinists and those of many other tongues shave their beards'.[20]

It is interesting that for non-Russians the essence of the Schism by the time of Peter the Great was reduced to the problems of the sign of the Cross and beard-shaving.[21] Then the Imperial power took on itself the function of supreme corrector of the divine image not just in the icon, but in the very human being (and incidentally, one must not forget the mercantile advantage for the state in this). By a decree of Peter the Great (confirmed again in 1752), Old Believers were obliged to sew copper tokens with the inscription 'The beard is a useless burden – tax has been levied on this beard' onto their clothing (illus. 44). Relations between the state and the individual began to be characterized by a heightened degree of conventionality. According to Synodal documents of 1732, the proper clothes for bearded people and schismatics consisted of a coarse linen bib, a loose tunic and a single-breasted caftan and homespun coat of undyed cloth. It was further laid down 'that those schismatics and bearded men should wear these clothes as prescribed both summer and winter without exception'.[22]

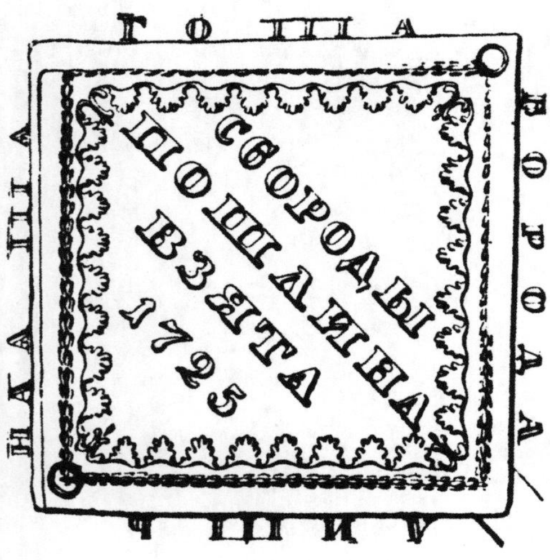

44. Tax levied in 1725 for beard-wearing: a drawing of the token worn on the breast.

If, for the Imperial ideology, shaving one's beard seemed but a 'trifle' (as Feofan Prokopovich and Dimitriy Rostovsky sought to demonstrate in their works), for the common people it was linked with the likeness of God's image in humanity and had a sacred meaning that found its reflection in the iconography of the image, the popular print and the engraving (illus. 45, 46, 47). The unusually large ('spade-shaped') beard seen on 18th- and 19th-century Old Believer icons of St Maksim the Greek, condemned at the Moscow councils of 1525 and 1531 and not canonized by the official Church, is a sort of sign of right belief and a 'banner' against the 'Lutheran' custom of shaving the beard. (It should be noted, however, that the veneration of Maksim the Greek as a saint among the Old Believers arose in the second half of the 17th century and continued into the 18th, after official recognition of his memory by the Moscow Patriarchate. But he was not officially canonized until the Local Council of the Russian Orthodox Church of 6–9 June 1988.) It is characteristic that the 'sign' of the beard often appeared on icons of the saint in a symbolic juxtaposition with his texts about making the sign of the Cross and the twofold alleluia. On 18th- and 19th-century icons, Maksim the Greek often holds an open book displaying the words 'Utter the twofold alleluia . . .' or 'Holding then three fingers together . . .'.

45. *The Barber Wishes to Shave the Schismatic's Beard*, a *lubok* woodcut of the first quarter of the 18th century.

46. *T. T. Trifonov, the Son of an Olonets Merchant, aged 28 years*, a 19th-century lithograph. State Museum of the History of Religion, St Petersburg.

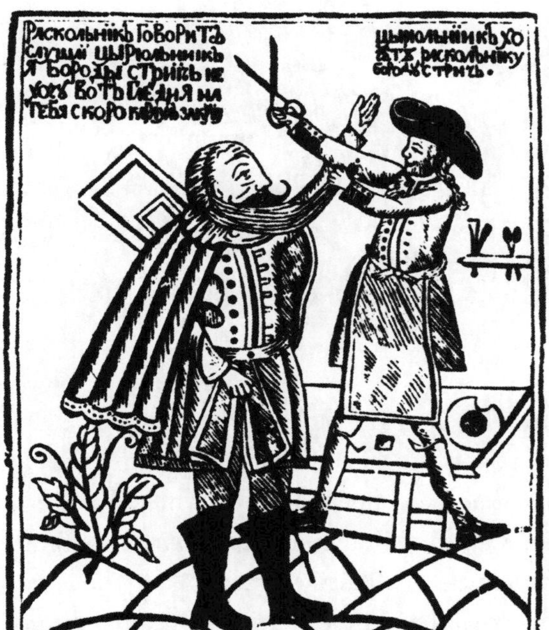

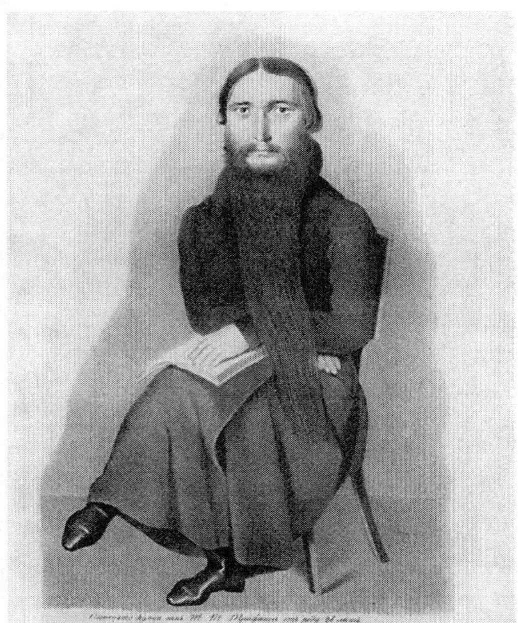

47. *Maksim the Greek*, 18th century. Collection of N. and S. Vorobyov, Moscow.

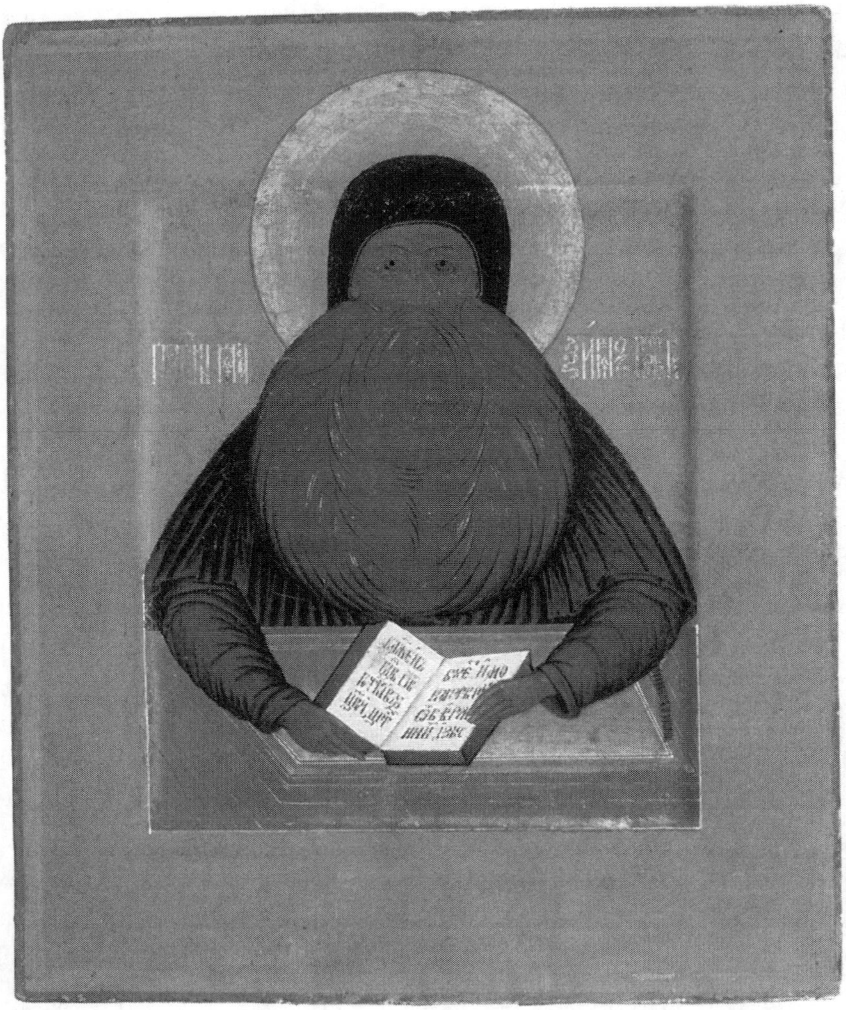

Testimony to this is also provided by S. F. Mokhovikov's story about a miracle brought about by an icon of Maksim the Greek, which recounts events that occurred in 1720. Mokhovikov, an Old Believer who worked as a watchman at the Annunciation Cathedral in the Moscow Kremlin, became the victim of threats from a certain clerk, Mikhail Morsochnikov. The latter, a zealous exponent of the Petrine decree on the shaving of beards, threatened to shave the Old Believer himself. Thereupon Mokhovikov, relying on

Maksim the Greek's intervention, ordered an icon of him from the painter Yevstafiy. However, fearful of the authorities, Yevstafiy depicted Maksim with three, rather than two, fingers forming the gesture of blessing. For this blasphemy he was horribly punished by the saint: his hand became withered immediately.[23]

Presumably it is from this period of Peter the Great's rule that images of Christ and the saints on icons are increasingly taken to be a visual example of the true likeness of a Christian, something the Church contested right up to the end of the 19th century. Thus the Metropolitan Filaret (Drozdov) in his time tried to establish that the icons did not reinforce the *Stoglav*'s ban on shaving beards, but merely bore witness that beard-growing is worthy of approval, since we see it in the saints and in the Saviour himself. He went on to argue that 'the icons do not indicate that shaving of beards is forbidden, but, on the contrary, the icons of the Great Martyrs George and Demetrios tell us that it was the habit even of saints'.[24]

The elder Leontiy (otherwise known as Ioann Lukyanov), travelling on foot to the Orthodox East in 1701–3 with the aim of finding 'proofs' of the authenticity of modern Greek devotion, said subsequently that 'in their houses there are no icons, they have mixed themselves with the Turks in all ways'. This conviction of the lack of grace elsewhere in the world when compared to Muscovite Rus, the conviction of the 'inauthenticity' of its iconic art in connection with the 'confusion' and 'renaming', always conveyed a special coloration to the symbolic thought processes of the Old Believers. A symbol must also be seen as an indication of the existence of collective memory. In this sense the old symbols of the ancient icons were filled with a historically concrete mythology that foreordained a special historically dramatic quality to their reversal. This once again demonstrates that in the medieval Byzantine and Old Russian icon, the sign always strove to coincide with its meaning. Once the relation between sign and meaning became variable, the iconic symbol began to make way for metaphor, and metaphysics for rhetoric.

The Complications of Renaming: A Tract Concerning the New Devotion

The correction of the signs of the old devotion on images for prayer was one of the most complex problems that the defenders of the New Ritual, with Tsar Aleksey at their head, encountered. So as to secure the mass support of the faithful, they attributed to the Old Believers not only a failure to understand the essence of the reforms, but frequently the very same heretical and iconoclast formulae of thought. As a first step by Nikon in his assault on the leaders of the Old Ritualist opposition, he accused one of them, Loggin of Murom, of nothing less than *demeaning the icons* of the Saviour, the Mother of God and the saints. A Church council meeting took place in July 1653 in Moscow. From Loggin's own testimony it emerged that while he was still in Murom, he happened to accuse the wife of an army commander of having much cosmetic white lead on her face. When she objected 'Archpriest, you say bad things about white lead, but without it you cannot even paint images', Loggin answered: 'These compounds are produced by the icon painters, and if the compounds were put on your ugly face, you would not even want it yourself. And let me tell you, the Saviour and the Mother of God are more worthy in themselves than their images.' This was enough to deliver Loggin over to 'strict policing', that is to say, to have him placed under arrest.[25]

The official polemical compositions and decrees of the second half of the 17th century through to the 19th give an important insight into popular religious life. The New Ritualists tried not to speak openly about the connection of the 'Cross made with the hand' and the name of the Saviour with the 'untrue likeness' of the image for prayer. This was particularly so, incidentally, in the early phase of the quarrel. In this regard it is worth pausing over the well-known tract – *The Missive of one Iosif, a Painter, to the Tsar's Painter and Most Wise Delineator Simon Fyodorovich* – by a court icon painter who served under Tsar Aleksey Mikhaylovich, Iosif Vladimirov (see illus. 48), which is usually studied for its aesthetic premises or from the point of view of its anti-Protestant tendentiousness. It is fair to say that Leonid Uspensky, in touching on these aspects of the tract, expressed doubts about the 'wisdom' of its defence of the icon for Russians. 'But to defend, and demonstrate the use of, icons to Orthodox people, especially Russians', he wrote, 'was to push at an open door. At that time in Moscow people erred rather in the direction of an excess of veneration for icons, sometimes to the point of perversion, than of any iconoclast tendencies.'[26] But for *which* icons? Iosif Vladimirov's missive was a *tract about the new piety*, since we can assume that what he was writing about also concerned the *sign system of the new ritual* on images. Like the paired comparative picture icons discussed earlier, the tract by this court painter, written in 1660–66, is typically Baroque in its textual organization, subject as it was to rhetorical rules and the need to convince. But if in the comparative icons the ambivalence of symbols was presented openly and graphically, with Iosif Vladimirov it was deliberately hidden within the opposition between the likeness of a 'good' icon and the likeness of a 'bad' one. The *name* of the icon and the *sign of the Cross* are deliberately nowhere mentioned. Likenesses that are juxtaposed so as to reflect each other reveal a veiled ideologism. On the other hand, such markers of the 'bad' image as 'dimness' (which is opposed to 'light'), 'uniformity', 'unlikeness to the holy personages' and, finally, the love of the common people for 'bad' old icons, at once leads one to suspect that the real subject of discourse is the *renaming of symbols*, that is the very type of an icon with a defined sign symbolism (illus. 49).

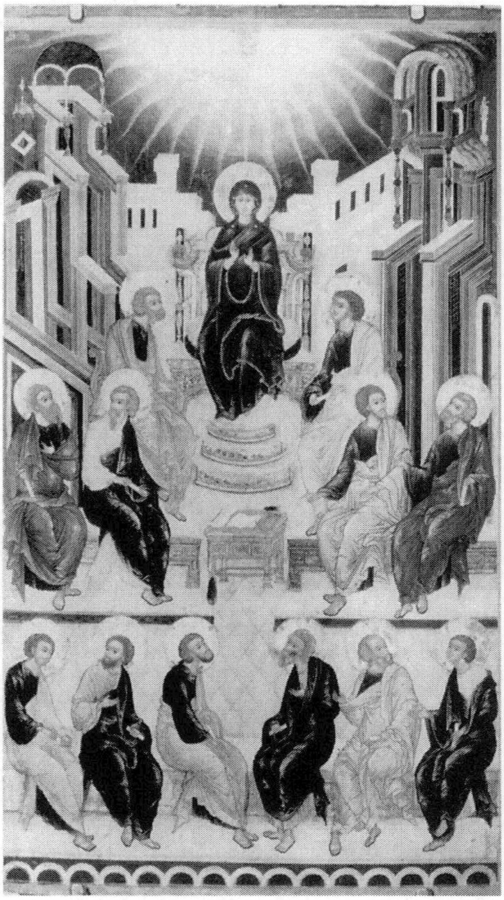

48. Iosif Vladimirov, *Descent of the Holy Ghost*, 1666. Church of the Trinity, Nikitniki, Moscow.

This is confirmed in the first place by a discussion of the 'zeal' of Patriarch Nikon on the subject of 'the painting of the holy icons', and also confirmed by Vladimirov's remarks on the Moscow tradition – on the existence of 'authentic' images only in Muscovite Rus, which was fully consonant with the recognition by the reformers of 'authenticity' not only in modern Greek ritual, but in modern Greek images too. Thus, in the

49. *The Metropolitan Aleksiy, Moscow*, late 17th century. Moscow Kremlin State Museums.

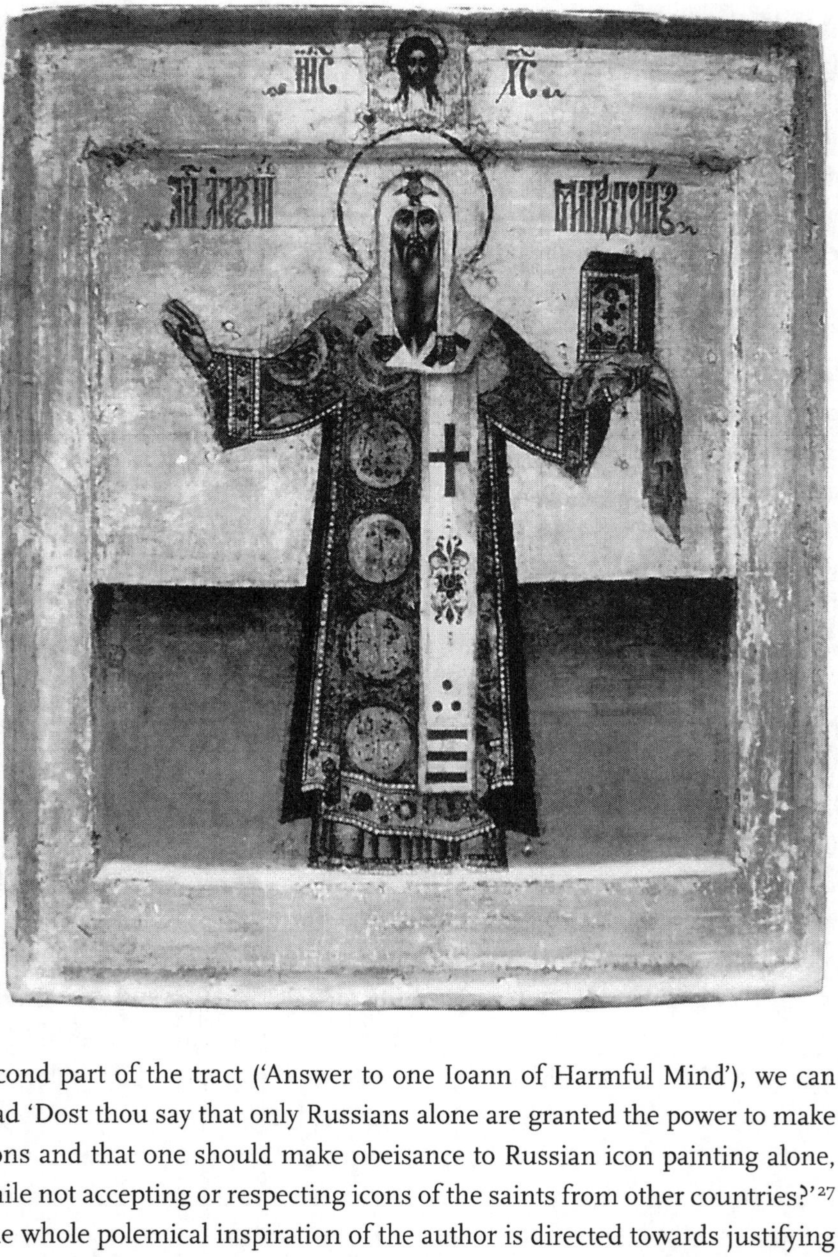

second part of the tract ('Answer to one Ioann of Harmful Mind'), we can read 'Dost thou say that only Russians alone are granted the power to make icons and that one should make obeisance to Russian icon painting alone, while not accepting or respecting icons of the saints from other countries?'[27] The whole polemical inspiration of the author is directed towards justifying the necessity of correcting the 'old' type of Muscovite icon. The 'inauthenticity' of likeness in the old icons was most often explained by the limited skills of the village icon painter. But we should note that it is also explained by 'dissimilarity' with Greek prototypes: 'Many Russian paintings do not correspond with the actual good Greek prototypes, new ones have many differences with the old and *old ones with the new*' (my italics).[28]

The identification of 'dim-looking' old icons with icons that were decrepit allows Iosif Vladimirov to find a justification for their correction and even destruction in the tradition of the Fathers of the Church who, it must be said, really did not forbid the destruction of an old, decayed icon. Both Theodore Studite and John Damascene said the same on this point. Bishop Leontios of Cyprus, too, in contradicting the accusation of the iconoclasts that the iconodules worshipped material objects, spoke of the acceptability of burning old wooden icons: 'We do not bow down to images and icons and figures of the saints as if they were gods. For if we worshipped the wood of an icon as if it were God, then of course we should also worship other trees and we should not burn icons, as often happens when the image is spoilt.'[29] The practices of everyday devotion, and at times the Church itself, often surrounded the moment of destroying an icon with extra rituals. Both in the Orthodox East and Russia it was most often specified that old wooden icons should be used for kindling a fire on which holy oil would be prepared. More often still, the common people were afraid to burn icons: they were set adrift on a waterway, face uppermost, or else they were superstitiously buried in cemeteries; Tsar Aleksey himself pronounced a special blessing on such an occasion. Paul of Aleppo reported that the Tsar ordered the 'incorrect' Western icons, which Patriarch Nikon broke up on the flagstones of a church floor, to be buried in the soil.[30]

Because of this, and without mention of the sign content of the old 'untrue' likeness, Vladimirov stressed the possibility of its destruction as if he were holding forth against superstitions: 'But thou, senselessly, dost not comprehend how not only badly and incorrectly painted icons are worthy to be scraped down, but one should also burn decrepit icons.' Significantly, he refers also to the decree of the *Stoglav* that specified the renovation of icons.[31] It was far harder for Vladimirov to resolve the question of the wonder-working properties of old and 'bad' icons. The authenticity of old likenesses was proved for the Old Believers by their revealed miracles. Thus, in speaking of them, the court painter could point only to the need to paint icons 'with good mastery'.[32] And, finally, there is just one place in the tract where Vladimirov says almost in so many words that a 'badly' painted icon is not the likeness of Christ. Here he saw the danger of substituting a true image with a false one: 'So too is it dangerous to accept all icons of the saints. Not every image or representation suffices for Church acceptance without consideration: but if on examination Christ and the saints are rightly and well painted, then it is acceptable.'[33]

A comparison of Iosif Vladimirov's tract with other writings of the same period reinforces the idea that the reform of devotion in its early stages hesitated to touch the popular prayer image, something that emerges in particular from the Tsar's decree of 1669 that forbade the village icon painters of Kholuy from engaging in the trade of icon production. Probably, then, the very first mention in Vladimirov's tract of the greatest centres of folk icon painting at the time – Palekh, Kholuy and Shuya – is not accidental. It was precisely in those places that the peasants painted prayer images with the old symbolism by the thousand: these are the ones defined as 'dim', 'ill-painted' and 'incorrect' (illus. 50).

When the decree of Tsar Aleksey is analysed it is quite obvious that in its first draft the concept of 'incorrect' icon painting was directly linked with the two-fingered blessing, although in the fair copy that was issued, this type of blessing ('cross made by hand') was not mentioned. In other words, the authorities were evidently scared to make a public announcement about the necessity of correcting the sign system of the old ritual on popular icons. So, in the first draft, the Tsar's decree announced that

> at Moscow and in the towns an order should be promulgated and firmly adhered to that people of clerical or monastic rank, their flock of all ranks, lay people of the male and female sex and children who are growing up, should cross themselves by hand, according to the earlier ancient rules, also according to the tradition of the Holy Fathers and according to the enquiry conducted by the recent holy council, that they should cross themselves with three fingers bent, and henceforth should not cross themselves in an ignorant way.

Straight after that the topic changed to keeping watch on icon painters, about their 'good mastery' which was contrasted with 'incorrect painting'.

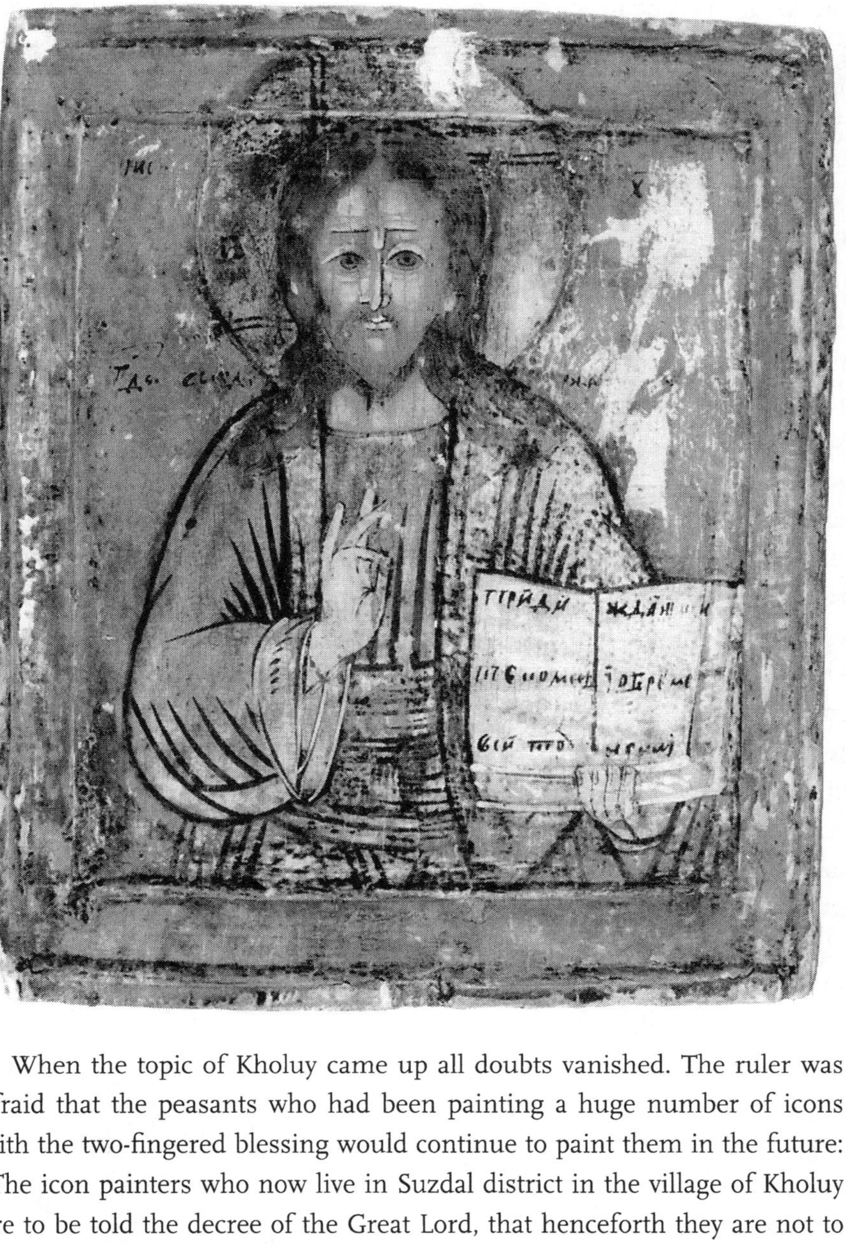

50. *Christ Pantocrator*, a Suzdalian-style icon from the end of the 17th century or the early 18th. Private collection, Moscow.

When the topic of Kholuy came up all doubts vanished. The ruler was afraid that the peasants who had been painting a huge number of icons with the two-fingered blessing would continue to paint them in the future: 'The icon painters who now live in Suzdal district in the village of Kholuy are to be told the decree of the Great Lord, that henceforth they are not to engage in icon painting. And concerning the *Cross* [my italics], they are to be informed of the Great Lord's decree as has been written in this document above.' In this first draft it is not explained why the people of Kholuy are forbidden to paint icons. One can only guess. But we can find a direct explanation in the second draft, and also in the final version. Both texts practically coincide, and there is no longer any mention of the two-fingered Cross in them: 'And furthermore in a certain village of the Suzdal district, which is called the parish of Kholuy, in that same Kholuy the inhabitants, from thoughtless reading of the books of holy writings, make so bold as to paint holy icons without any thoughtfulness or fear.'[34]

In the *Discourse Concerning the Veneration of the Holy Icons* by the famous poet and churchman at the court of Tsar Aleksey Mikhaylovich, Simeon Polotsky (1629–80), the problem of the *name* of the image was posed more openly – evidently because this text was presented to Tsar Aleksey just as the Great Moscow Council was about to begin, and it is possible that it was in fact discussed at that Council. Demanding that the name of Christ be inscribed on icons according to the New Ritual, Polotsky indicated that it was sufficient for the veneration of the images if painters portrayed the human form of Christ 'with a proper inscription', and that there was no ultimate need for a lifelike image. Unlike Iosif Vladimirov, who equated the old sign system of the image with bad painting, Polotsky was more concrete, emphasizing that 'crudely painted icons' do not dishonour the saints: they only show a lack of artistic skill. For him, both an 'artistic' and an 'inartistic' image of Christ 'sufficiently resemble the living face of Christ'. It is well known that Polotsky praised and supported the 'lifelike' quality of those artists who were capable of painting in the *chiaroscuro* manner and introduced perspective techniques, both new at that time. But the essential thing for him was the principle of the *ecclesiastical* manner, even if the icon painters were imperfectly skilled in the art. In full agreement with the reforms that were getting under way, Polotsky also proposed that the village icon painters had either to be forbidden to engage in the craft, or be ordered to take care to paint better. In contrast to Vladimirov, he considered that to destroy icons with the old symbolic system was an iconoclastic activity. It would be appropriate merely to take such icons away from the faithful and correct them.[35]

In official polemical writings of the 18th and 19th centuries, attacks on the old icons as the most important basis of the Old Believers' means of proving the authenticity of the old devotion were to be continued. Thus St Dimitriy Rostovsky (1651–1709) attempted to elucidate the problem of the 'worship' of the icon, about which he wrote: 'We venerate holy icons, kiss them and bow down to them, but we do not idolize them, we do not say that an icon is God.' One of his chief polemical points was that 'the old icon is the sum total of their belief', on which basis he accused the Old Believers of idol worship. Upholding the principle that the old icon cannot serve as a proof of correct belief, he named the 'Brynsk schismatic hermitages' as 'demonic nests', which of course hardly helped to win over the adherents of the old piety.[36]

The problem of the signs on old icons was resolved on a somewhat different level by the Moscow Metropolitan Filaret (Drozdov) (1783–1867), who attempted to show that on ancient icons it was not the two-fingered sign of the Cross that was depicted, but a blessing through the litany of saints. In his opinion, in 'truly ancient' icons, this blessing was sometimes represented skilfully and clearly, and sometimes not altogether distinctly, which allowed the Old Believers to take it as the two-fingered Sign of the Cross. 'Look in the Santa Sophia cathedral in Kiev' – so he addressed the Old Believers – 'at the ancient, and, therefore, completely uncorrected mosaic hands of saints John Chrysostom and Gregory the Wonder-worker raised in blessing: in these one cannot but observe the blessing through the liturgy of saints, among other things because the little finger is shown raised, and not bent.' Thus in the Metropolitan's opinion, people began to represent the two-fingered sign of the Cross on icons only after the *Stoglav* Council, which was, of course, not so.[37]

Because of this the 'new faith' was not very easily established in the popular consciousness. People wanted to believe that those icons in front of which they had habitually prayed were still fully capable of assisting in their salvation. Neither theological subtleties nor arguments about 'authentically' or 'inauthentically' ancient images would carry much conviction. This became all the more so since from Avvakum's time onward, an insistence on salvation through 'simple' and 'unsophisticated' faith became a dominant feature of the old manner of devotion. 'For we have had no knowledge of school, and we have not become acquainted with grammar and rhetoric and philosophy, and we have seen what rhetoric and philosophy are.'[38] This commonplace came at the end of several Old Believer 'question books' about icons; books in which we find reproduced essentially one and the same system of proofs regarding authentic signs, leading to salvation, and false signs, leading to damnation.

CHAPTER THREE

In a World without Grace

An apocalyptic fear of the transformation of the Tsardom of Muscovy into a tsardom without grace, an empire of Satan, is one of the complex aspects of Russian cultural history. At once the question arises of internal analogues to similar processes in Western Europe – the rise of demonology and demon-mania in the Baroque age and the early Enlightenment. But in Russia (as elsewhere) these tendencies had their own distinctive features. A search for one or more causes would only minimize the profundity of the dislocation in mass religious sensibilities that had taken place.

The Schism in the Russian Church apparently for the first time really pinpointed a particular vulnerability in the deep strata of the collective unconscious regarding the external, 'eventful' rhythms of history. Everything would seem to predict that the 'historical models' launched on the ocean of mass consciousness could all too easily sink to the bottom. But just as quickly and unexpectedly, they might be stirred up and collide with the surface ripples of events. It took only for the reformers to touch on the sign-structuring formulae on which this model relied, and an explosion took place with colossal consequences. On the one hand the collective sensibility at once attributed yet more significance to the utopian theme of the 'Third Rome', while on the other it began rapidly to 'disperse itself' in sectarian religiosity and in the systems of devotion characteristic of the modern age, with their reliance on *personal righteousness*.

The religious individualism of the Old Believers was a reflection of general changes in people's sense of themselves. For reformers, the truth of God was chiefly guaranteed by faith: a retreat from the Church took place and the meaning of personal righteousness was heightened. But the Russian philosopher Vladimir Solovyov (1853–1900) had reason to call the 'patriarchal tradition' of the Old Believers a 'Protestantism of local tradition' in comparison with Western Protestantism of 'personal conviction'. In the Russian realm of faith and piety it was not so much 'patriarchal origins' and a 'return to the times of the Apostles' that counted most, rather local Russian customs dating from the time of the *Stoglav*.[1]

This point concealed deep differences within the national religio-psychological systems, within which ritual and icon played totally opposing roles. In Protestantism, icons were rejected as superstitious relics, as symbols that bore no special relation to the revelation of God and the descent of his grace upon the world – indeed, as things that were even harmful or heathen. But during the Schism, icons acquired the function (as Max Weber would have put it) of a strange way of allocating the privilege of salvation. The essence of the situation that had arisen in Russia can be seen in how the icon, without doubt highly important in the cultural and socio-religious value system of the previous period, though these very periods, both on an official or 'surface' level and to a considerable extent in the consciousness of people in that critical age, were sharply opposed to one other. Preserving its link with the initial situation (the system of 'prescribed devotion' and the model of the Third Rome), the icon was introduced into a broader and more intense cultural milieu, which widened its significance yet further. The icon had acquired an ideologically defined framework: its particular cultural– historical space within the utopian system began to emerge.

The Shadow of Antichrist

The idea that Imperial Russia was the kingdom of Antichrist determined many features of the Old Ritualist veneration of icons. One was the refusal to venerate depictions of tsars and emperors in churches and chapels of the old ritual. After the mid-17th century this refusal was in stark contrast with the sacralization of the monarch in official Orthodoxy, whereby the Imperial cult was gradually introduced into the everyday practice of the synodal Church. Without going into detail on the question at this point (I shall return to it), let me simply note that by the beginning of the 19th century the state mythology had penetrated into the sacral sphere of traditional spirituality to such a degree that Alexander I was impelled to try to change the situation. On 5 November 1817 a decree was circulated to all diocesan church leaders, in which the Emperor expressed his doubts about the sacralization of his person:[2] 'On my last progress through the provinces I was forced in some of them, to my regret, to listen in speeches pronounced by members of the clergy to inappropriate praise of myself in terms that would be properly ascribed only to the One God.'[3] As early as the second half of the 17th century, icons carrying representations of royal personages begin to appear in official Orthodox places of worship. One such is the well-known icon of the Vladimir Mother of God ('The Tree of the Russian State') by the court icon painter Simon Ushakov, who depicted the Tsar's family on it.

The alternative Old Ritualist devotion was unshakeable in its conviction that the depictions of tsars and emperors belonged to the category of the satanic and the heathen, which attests to the perception by the Old Ritualists of Russian Europeanized culture as a heathen and, by the same token, satanic culture,[4] and also reveals the stubborn logic of the concept of the 'treachery' of the Orthodox tsar, and through that the apostasy – the 'God-forsakenness' – of Imperial Russia. Thus, in those congregations and sects in which teachings about Antichrist and eschatologism were most active, resistance to the cult of the Emperor was revealed its most extreme forms. As a covert Orthodox observer of the first half of the 19th century noted, the senior priest of the Moscow Preobrazhenskoye Cemetery (of the Old Believers), Semyon Kuzmin, ordered that 'all icons that portray the tsar "even in his ancient clothing" must be placed along the side walls in the chapels so that nobody should ever pray to them: for to bow down to an image bearing a representation of an autocrat, according to . . . Semyon Kuzmin's teaching, is hateful to God'. In the following secret report it was emphasized that the Fedoseyev sect (Fedoseyevtsy) had nourished a hateful feeling towards the ruler, and towards the royal house generally, since the times of Aleksey Mikhaylovich. This 'feeling' led to careful observation of all signs relating to the person of the Emperor: remarks about the coronation ceremony of Nicholas I came into this report. The Fedoseyev sectarians noticed that at the coronation he put on the sacred shoulder mantle, symbol of the patriarchal rank, in this way 'stealing it' and 'subduing the Church'. From this the conclusion was drawn that Nicholas I had unmasked himself as Antichrist.[5] Finally, P. V. Sinitsyn asserted that in a chapel of the Preobrazhenskoye Cemetery there could even be found a picture showing the Emperor as Antichrist.[6]

Beyond all this there stood a complex reality. From the time of Tsar Aleksey the problem of Antichrist had effectively two sides. The deep-rootedness of the motif in the Christian system of understanding the world might always be burdened by the collision of the deep layers of consciousness with 'superficial' events.[7] There had long existed a firm link in the Christian system of ideas between the *idea of the sign* and the *idea of truth*. As we have noted, within this system the sign had to coincide with its meaning. From this point of view, the disloyalty of Tsar Aleksey to the signs of the old ritual could not be regarded otherwise than as an infringement on the faith; and more than that, as a war against Christian belief. On a second level, that of its intersection with the 'eventful' rhythms of history, the idea of the correctness of the Orthodox tsar acquired a further complication with the idea of the special charisma of his person and of the realm as a whole. We can recall the petition from Solovki, in which the monks, attempting to make the Tsar change his mind, addressed him thus: 'thou who art alone the master of the whole universe and watcher over the uncorrupted Christian faith, autocrat, Great Lord and Tsar, *surpassing all others in devotion*, and having gathered all that is pious into thy realm, and calling thy realm the Third Rome of piety, the Muscovite Tsardom' (my italics).[8] The breaking of the 'hyper-durable' bond between sign and meaning, that is to say the renunciation of the old devotion by the tsar's person, brought with it a whole complex of grave consequences. The permanence of formulae and stereotypes always instilled a sense of the durability of the existing world order in the believer.

After all, if the Russian tsar, as living symbol and Christ's deputy on earth, were to renounce his loyalty to the signs of charisma in the Russian lands, that would mean that the power of Antichrist was confirmed in it. For such a dualistic consciousness, any miracles that might now take place in it would be false ones. The possibility of acquiring grace was made considerably harder: it might be altogether reduced to nothing (as, for example, the *netovtsy* – 'Negativists' – thought). In religious symbols, and particularly in the icons, they saw not 'windows into another world' but only hints and signs of the presence of Antichrist: this was all the more so where depictions of Tsar Aleksey and Nikon themselves were concerned (illus. 51). Hence the teachings about Antichrist became deeper-rooted and more variegated in the folk mentality. It was continually aroused by this idea, relating it to a wide circle of objectives. From there too, there emerged a vast corpus of iconic works and polemical texts both within the Old Belief itself and also as a response from the official Church: a variety of long-term historical rhythms were at work.

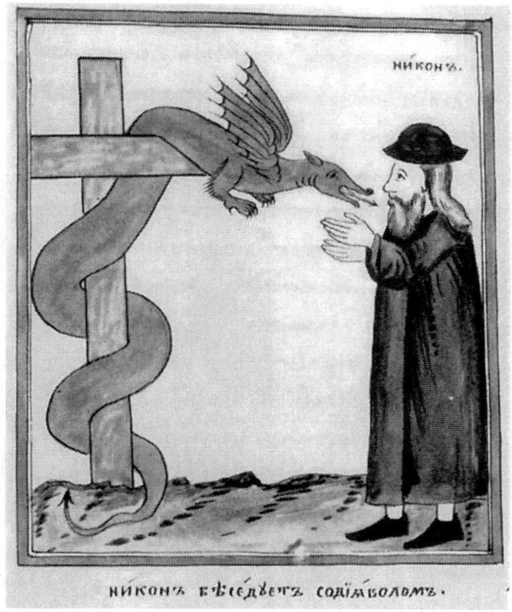

51. 'Nikon Converses with the Devil', a miniature from *The Tale of our Hierarch Nikon*, early 20th century. State Museum of the History of Religion, St Petersburg.

The Schism strongly polarized the collective consciousness. Proponents of reform tended to affirm love of life and the fundamental worth of worldly existence. Its opponents, though, drew conclusions that were in large part hostile to everything earthly and transitory, and remained spiritually deaf to the demands of the new culture and secular system of sensibilities that were evolving. In this context, the strengthening of eschatological apprehensions and a sharp sense of the 'coming end' – of living through 'the last days' – were common to all Old Believers. People retreated to monasteries and hermitages with very different motives from those of early Christian monasticism and eremitism. They went to them so as to evade the eternal atmosphere of perdition that saturated the world of official devotion.

The masses began to live in a passionate expectation of the Last Judgment. From around 1700 more and more small *personal* images of this Last Judgment, as it was envisaged by the account in St Matthew's Gospel, which contains an almost complete vision of the other world, began to appear. The end of time would frequently be before the eyes of every person in daily life: it was portrayed, in detail and scene-by-scene, on a small

52. *Last Judgment*, 19th century. State Museum of the History of Religion, St Petersburg.

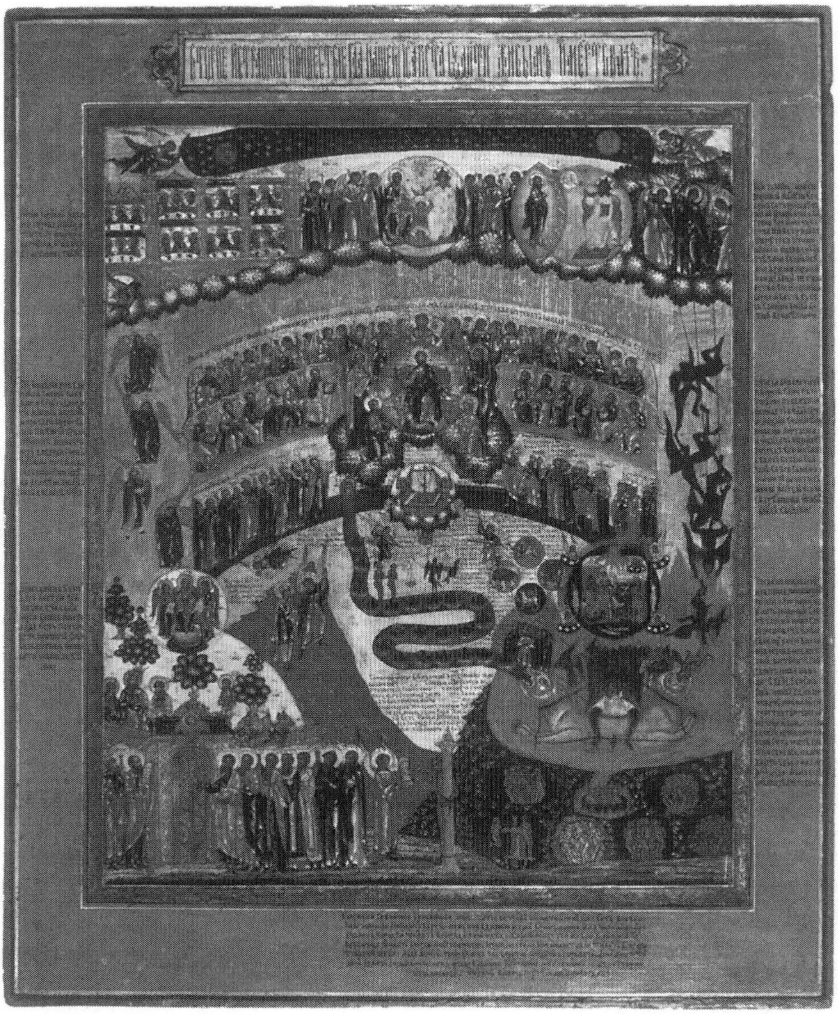

icon (illus. 52). The Weighing of Souls by the Archangel Michael is here linked with the opposition between Heaven and Hell (the righteous are separated from the sinners) and is superimposed on the concept of the Second Coming. The description of the Last Judgment in St Matthew's Gospel (25: 31–3) reads:

> When the Son of Man shall come in his glory, and all the holy angels with him, then shall he sit upon the throne of his glory: And before

him shall be gathered all nations: and he shall separate them one from another, as a shepherd divideth his sheep from his goats: And he shall set the sheep on his right hand but the goats on the left.

Icons that showed the same themes include those of the Resurrection of Christ with Twelve Feasts, the central area of which is occupied by the scene of the Resurrection and the Descent into Hell, and also those of the Almighty: images of the Saviour on the heavenly throne expressed the apocalyptic idea of the end of time as described by St John the Divine (illus. 53). On other icons the throne was not depicted: the Almighty holds an open book showing the words 'Come unto me, all ye that labour and are heavy laden, and I will give you rest. Take my yoke upon you, and learn of me . . . ' (Matthew 11: 28–9). This combination in one prayer image (or two images, standing side by side) of 'major' and 'minor' eschatology (the Last Judgment at the end of history, and immediate judgement after the death of a person) is one of the paradoxes of medieval Christian thinking. As early as the 12th century in the West an iconography had emerged that superimposed a Gospel-based concept of the Last Judgment on an apocalyptic concept of the end of time. It is an essential point, howeer, that in Muscovite Rus all these images of the other world increasingly began *to be concentrated in the everyday microcosm of the human being* at precisely the turn of the 17th century into the 18th. The drama of a heavenly court of judgement had removed itself from the interior space of a church to the 'fine corner' of the peasants' house.

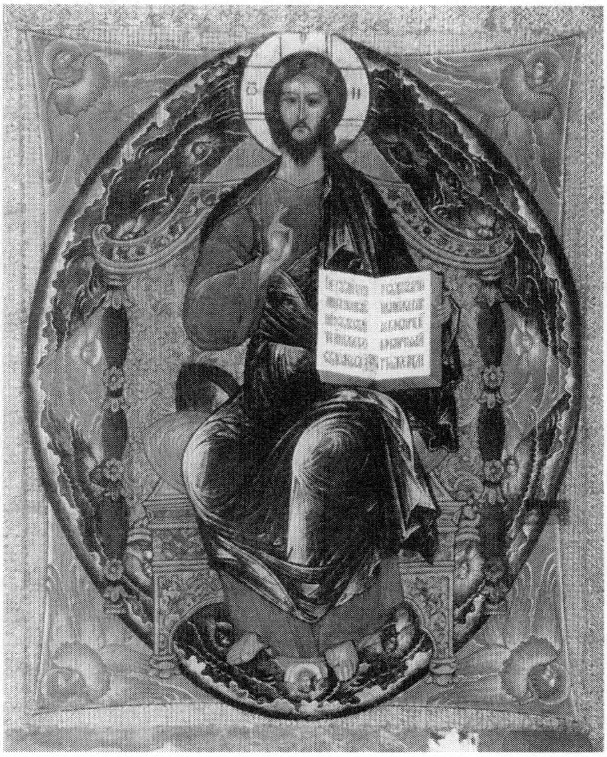

53. *Christ Pantocrator*, late 18th century. State Museum of the History of Religion, St Petersburg.

As the theme of the Last Judgment was actualized, so the cult of the

54. *Guardian Angel*, 18th century. Kolomenskoye Historical and Architectural Museum-Preserve, Moscow.

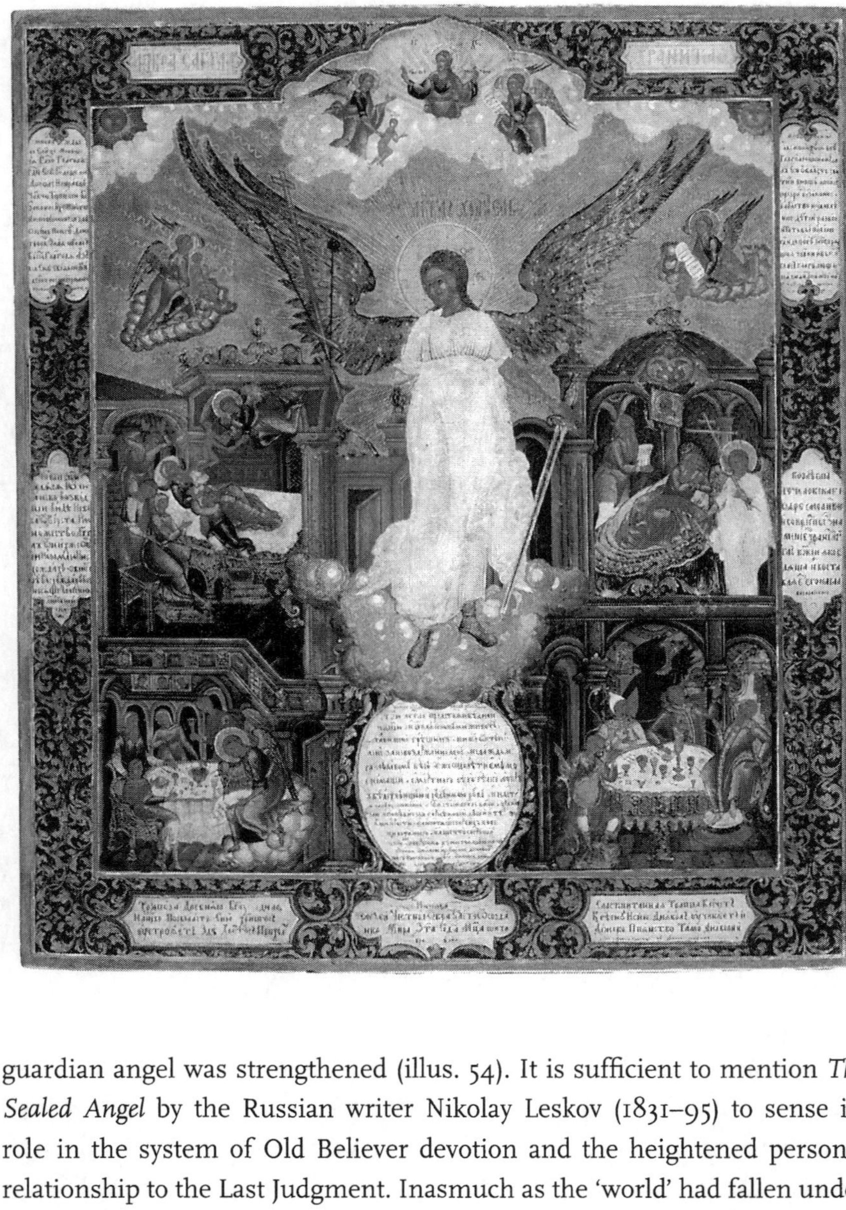

guardian angel was strengthened (illus. 54). It is sufficient to mention *The Sealed Angel* by the Russian writer Nikolay Leskov (1831–95) to sense its role in the system of Old Believer devotion and the heightened personal relationship to the Last Judgment. Inasmuch as the 'world' had fallen under the power of the Devil, had 'gone astray' like a lascivious maiden (the form in which 'the world' was often embodied in Old Believer popular prints: illus. 55), the guardian angel protected the Old Believer from the surrounding world itself. In this the guardian angel was considered not only to watch

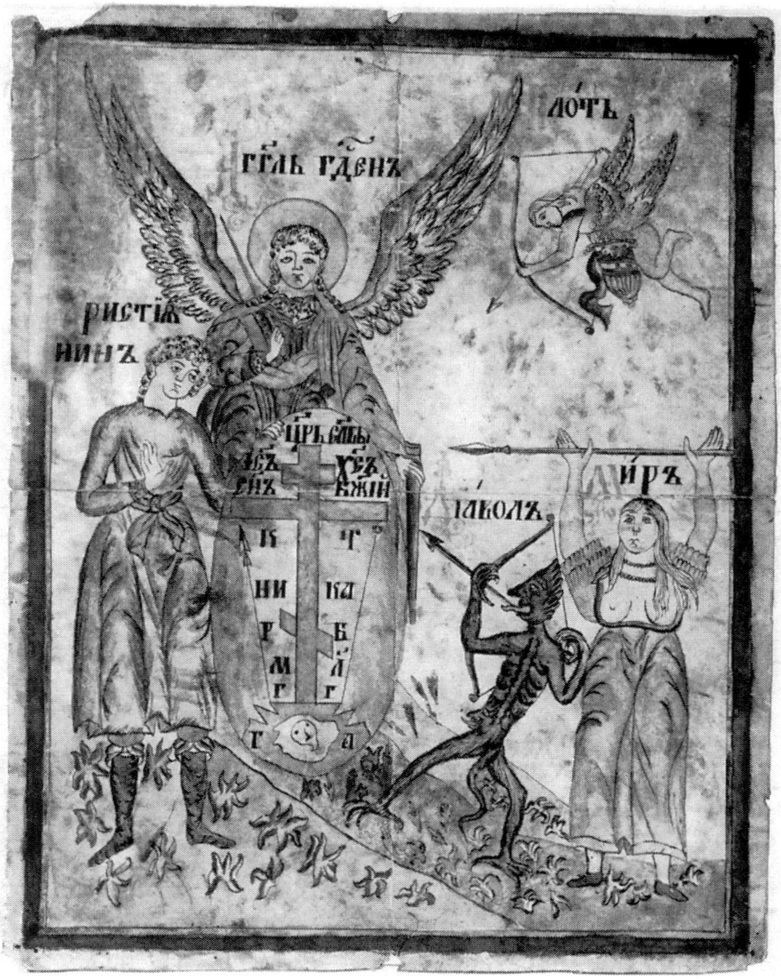

55. *A Christian, a Guardian Angel, a Demon and 'the World'*, late-19th-century drawing. State Historical Museum, Moscow.

over a good death (St Joseph took this role in the West), but also to be the angel who inscribed a person's good deeds – a decisive catalogue at the Last Judgment – onto a special scroll: from the guardian angel the Archangel Michael had to learn about the worldly deeds of an immortal soul.

The theme of ordeals begins to be actively worked out in the illustrated synodic books of the 17th century, and later in separate religious pictures. On an Old Ritualist manuscript *lubok* (popular print or drawing) of *The Death of St Feodora and a Vision of the Ordeals of the Soul* (an illustration of

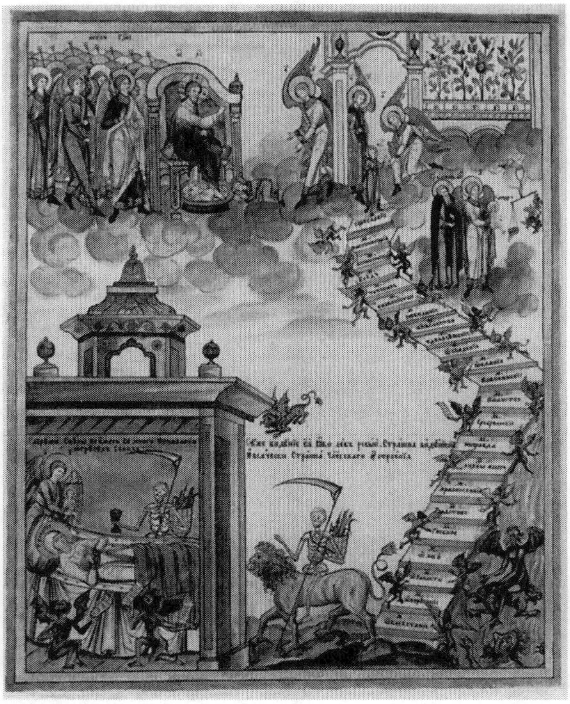

56. *The Death of St Theodora and a Vision of the Ordeals of the Soul*, late-19th-century drawing. State Historical Museum, Moscow.

a subject from the Life of St Basil the New, written by his pupil Grigoriy), the unknown artist depicted a guardian angel by the bed of the saint, receiving her soul (illus. 56). Nearby stands a skeleton, symbolizing the inevitability of death and instilling reflections on the vanity of earthly life, on the necessity of contempt for the world, and there are also envoys of the Devil unrolling a list of human sins. Here too we see the process of the weighing of the saint's soul and the apocalyptic scene of the Last Judgment, in which the blessed soul is already falling at the feet of the Heavenly King. In another *lubok* – *The Fates of the Righteous Person and the Sinner* – the same Baroque device of mirror images is employed as in the Old Ritualist comparative picture icons that we examined earlier. If the emissaries of Antichrist rejoice in the fate of the sinner, then in the fate of the righteous person it is the turn of the guardian angel, adding 'virtue' to the scales of destiny, which overcomes wickedness (illus. 57).

The changing individual consciousness was given over to the new stereotyped images that were adapting themselves to the eschatological feeling of the epoch. The image of hell as a place of eternal torments and sufferings was also characteristic for the Western system of Baroque iconography. In our context, however, the essential point is that the image of a hellish monster was often represented on Old Believer religious pictures as an *independent symbol* (illus. 58). Existing in a single sacral space with prayer icons of the Last Judgment and Resurrection, it was counted on to put the conscience yet more on its guard. Expectation of the 'coming of the end' spilled over into expectation of eschatological vengeance – a heavenly court of judgement headed by Christ at which 'they were judged every man according to their works', and the words of the elders in Revelation (20:13; 11:18)

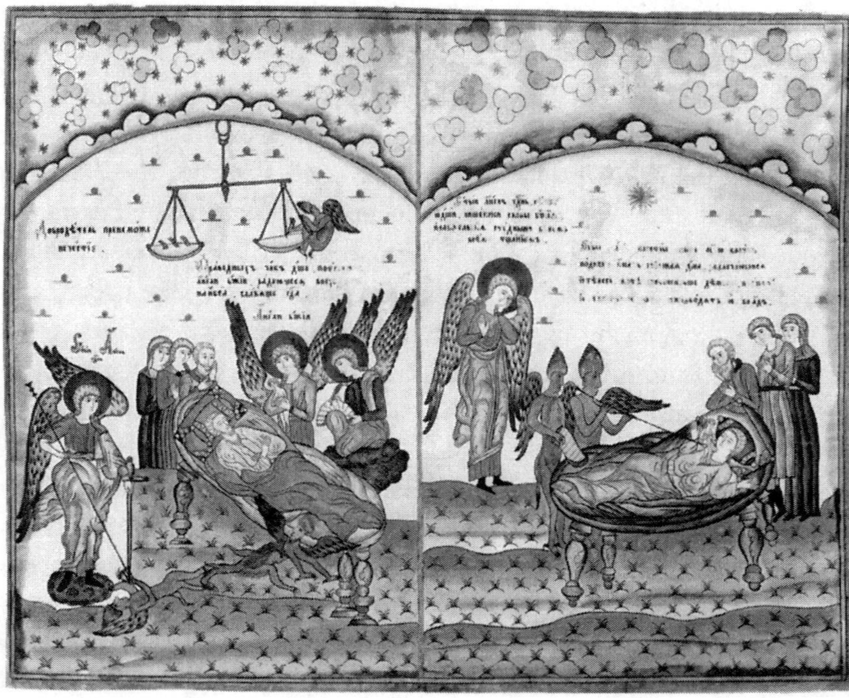

57. *The Fates of the Righteous Person and the Sinner*, end of the 18th century or early 19th. State Historical Museum, Moscow.

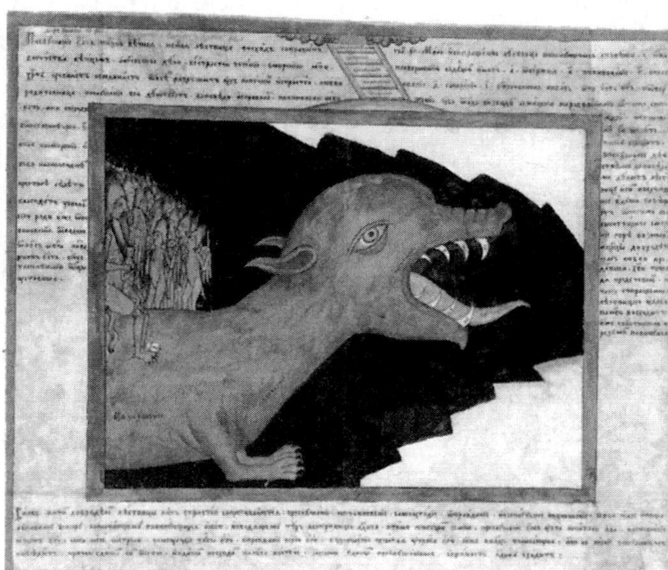

58. *Infernal Monster*, mid-19th-century drawing. State Historical Museum, Moscow.

seemed to be realized: 'and thy wrath is come, and the time of the dead, that they should by judged, and that thou shouldst give reward unto thy servants the prophets, and to the saints, and them that fear thy name, small and great; and shouldest destroy them which destroy the earth'.

On countless Old Ritualist icons of the Lord Almighty, the Heavenly King has, as it were, 'replaced' the Orthodox charismatic tsar on earth ('in the graceless world'), which of course has not reduced the divine dignity of the Last Judgment. The flexibility of the boundary between the natural and the supernatural made this possible. The wide distribution among the people of the icon of the Lord Almighty is analogous to the frequency in the spiritual verses of 'Heavenly Tsar' as an epithet for Christ.[9] If the real world, after all, were to be taken as the kingdom of Satan, it had also to be taken as a *place of torment*, demanding that it should swiftly and justifiably be placed in the dock. It is natural that the idea of the power and incarnation of Antichrist should have become one that captured and polarized the collective consciousness. It also considerably strengthened the egotistical aspect of salvation. As an Orthodox observer at the Preobrazhenskoye Cemetery reported as late as the mid-19th century: 'Their understanding of the Apocalypse convinces the Fedoseyevtsy that Antichrist has already arrived, and they are unshakably certain that their congregations alone will be spared the wrath of God.'[10]

The doctrine that Antichrist had already appeared in the guise of an actual person was maintained by the followers of Kuzma Andreyev at the beginning of the 18th century on the River Kerzhenets, to the east of Nizhniy Novgorod, famous as a centre of Old Belief. Antichrist was identified as Peter I. This way of thinking was strengthened both by the Petrine reforms and by the famous 'All-Jocular Company' gatherings organized by Peter. They were headed by Nikita Zotov, former teacher of the Tsar, with the title of 'Ioannikita, Patriarch of Prezburg, the Yauza and all Kokuy'. The offices of Church dignitaries, deacons, etc., were handed out to members of the 'company': the Tsar himself took the post of 'archdeacon'. In addition there was also a Prince–Pope with his college of cardinals and a Prince–Abbot, in all of which, besides mockery of the patriarchal dignity, scholars have rightly seen an anti-papist tendency revealed in the evident contamination between

Petersburg and the First Rome.[11] For our purposes, though, it is important to note that in the popular consciousness, all these were signs not so much of overt revolutionism, as of removal of the opposition between the sacral and the worldly, and hence of the most incontrovertible transformation of the Orthodox tsar.

In response, the Petrine innovations were parodied in Old Ritualist popular prints, which allegorized and mocked them codedly. The system of images that had embraced Heaven and divine personages was supplemented by a special earthly iconography, in which people were frequently shown awaiting their deserved retribution for terrible sins. Examples of this were *Baba-Yaga Fights with a Crocodile*, *The German Woman Riding on the Old Man*, *The Consecration of a Tax Collector*, *The Old Believer and the Barber* and *The Devil in Rome*. A final example is the famous *Burial of the Cat*, which Dmitry Rovinsky published in six different versions, and one copy of which carried a reference to the date of Peter I's death.[12] People saw an analogy with the period of Iconoclasm (726–843); this was reinforced by Peter's abolition of the Patriarchate (much respected by Old Believers) and his decrees forbidding various iconic subjects, religious processions with icons, etc. At the moment when the Russian harmony of 'tsardom' and 'spiritual authority' was destroyed, it was the *icon* that often came to mind: Peter was seen by the people as Antichrist, since they also saw in him another *iconoclast*.

Most of the 'Priestless' Old Believers envisaged the reign of an Antichrist who was 'of the spirit' and 'invisible'. They were close to those of the Fedoseyevtsy who lived in Poland in the the early 18th century and subsequently in the Vyazovo district and the Vyg hermitages. Feodosiy Vasilyev, founder of the Fedoseyevtsy sect and teacher to the 'Priestless', spoke of the 'spiritual', not of the 'perceptible', appearance of Antichrist in his exhortation of 1701 to hold fast to the Schism. 'Now it is 43 years', he wrote,

> since in our Muscovite realm God's grace and true reading and singing have ceased to be in our churches. Yet do not expect to witness Antichrist in the future with your senses: when Christ appeared on earth, and lived among people, he did not reign perceptibly in the world – thus too will you not apprehend Antichrist through the senses.

The comparison of Antichrist with Christ was made on the basis that the son of perdition might in all ways assimilate himself to the Son of God. In 1707 Feodosiy Vasilyev wrote a rebuttal of the official polemical works *Signs of the coming of Antichrist* by the Metropolitan of Ryazan, Stefan, and *Brief Answer about the Birth of Antichrist* by Metropolitan of Novgorod, Iov, in which the power of Antichrist was already concretized and understood as *deviation from the faith*, in consequence of which Antichrist had appeared in the world and was reigning. To reinforce his conception of deviation, Feodosiy cited the authority of John Chrysostom (*Answer to the Question about Antichrist*), and referred to the symbolic method – popular since the late 17th century – of deciphering the year of the Great Moscow Council (1666) as the apocalyptic number of Satan (1000) and of the Beast (666). By such calculations the Old Believers reckoned the preceding stage in the seizure of the world by the forces of evil had been the Union of Brest (1596),[13] while the sign of Antichrist was the penetration of features of Western Christianity into official Orthodoxy.

As the early teachers of the Old Ritual had also believed, the kingdom of Antichrist for Feodosiy Vasilyev had begun in the West, from which it spread to the East and after 1666 to Russia. 'See how in fulfilment of 1666', he asserted,

> the kingdom of Antichrist had extended itself even to Rus. This can be seen in the first place from the fact that Nikon has brought in heresies of precisely the Latin faith. Such for example are the four-ended cross, the spelling 'Iisus' (Jesus), the litany of saints and in particular the three-fingered crossing of oneself.[14]

The singling out of the three-fingered cross as a chief sign of deviance from the true faith was at once conveyed by the iconography of 'priestless' popular prints, the most widespread of which were illustrations to the homily of John Chrysostom on the sign of the Cross (illus. 59, 60). Including extracts from the *Prolog* (Calendar of Saints' Lives) and from the printed catechism of the Patriarch Filaret, they represented scenes of the layman's prayer before the icon of Christ. The demons and the guardian angel present in the same scene gave visible instruction about sin and virtue. The three-fingered cross was inscribed in the book of sins – 'So who crosses himself

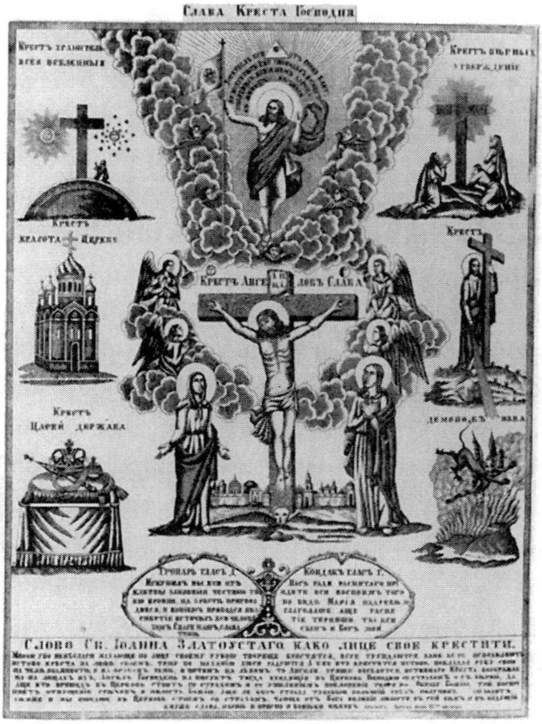

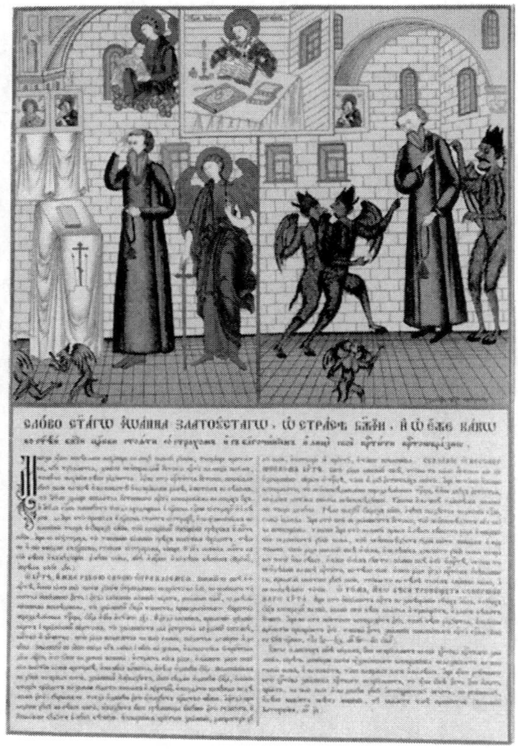

improperly gives the demons pleasure at that gesture' – while the two-fingered sign truly corresponded with the icon of the Saviour.[15] Hence, in the words of an eyewitness, 'all the Old Believer icon painters imitate each other in painting schismatically the name of Jesus and hands with the wrong position of the fingers on all the icons, distributing them as widely as possible'.[16]

59. *Discourse of St John Chrysostom on How to Cross Oneself*, 1875, lithograph. Russian State Library, Moscow.

60. *Discourse of St John Chrysostom on the Fear of God*, late 19th century, coloured lithograph. Russian State Library, Moscow.

Within this whole circle of ideas, questions about the veneration of images were closely linked with those concerning the clergy and the Church, and also about a reduction in the number of sacraments. It was within this relationship of dependence that a distorted veneration of the icon emerged. The strictness of the former Muscovite piety was echoed in the strictness of the sectarians.

In the economy of salvation, the sacraments and sacramentalism played a most important part. From the twelfth century in the West, and soon after in the East as well, the figure of seven major sacraments became established. Through these the invisible grace of God was conveyed to humanity. In holy writ the sacraments had the significance both of hidden mystery, inaccessible even to the angels, and of that divine economy through which the human race would be saved. By the Church's teaching, the sacraments had at least three main features. The first of these was the divinely established nature of the sacrament. Thus three major sacraments – communion, baptism and repentance – had been instituted by Christ himself. The other sacraments (annointing, marriage, laying on of hands, extreme unction) had been mentioned in the New Testament epistles and by the Fathers of the Church. A second feature of a sacrament was its visible symbol, to which were assimilated the uncreated divine energies and through which God's blessing on human life was called forth. Their establishment was confirmed by the historical experience of the Church. Finally, the Church regarded a third property of a sacrament to be its transcendentalizing purpose – the capability of grace to engender the image of God in humanity, to cleanse a person from sin. Through sacraments the union of humanity with God was effected anew.

The Protestants' reduction in the number of sacraments, and in particular their attitude to the eucharist, naturally also affected their opinion of the veneration of icons. According to the teaching of both Orthodoxy and Catholicism, Christ is substantively present in the communion bread and wine. The eucharistic image is Christ himself. The acknowledgement of a real divine incarnation in the bread and wine also determined, from the point of view of icon venerators, the possibility of representing Christ on an icon, even though the latter is not Christ himself. The icon is merely the location of a certain presence, since, as John Damascene explained, 'not in every respect is the image wholly similar to the prototype, to that which is represented: but the image is one thing, the representation another, and their distinction is quite clear, even though both of them represent one and the same thing'.[17] Since Zwingli and Calvin cast doubt in principle on the substantial presence of Christ in the eucharist, they were the most consistent enemies of all icons, as also of the cult of the Mother of God and the saints. Luther, for his part, admitted the reality of transubstantiation of the bread and wine. Thus, despite the general downgrading by Lutherans of the significance of religious images, they were nevertheless admitted – in particular the image of the Last Supper, as representing the establishment by Christ of the eucharist, and also of the Crucifixion. However, the reality of transubstantiation was pronounced by Luther to depend on the 'purity' of one's faith in Christ; so the absence of 'unclouded' faith deprived the bread and wine of their grace-bestowing power.

Luther reckoned the sacraments, and particularly the eucharist, to be symbols of the adherence of the believer to the renovated Christian church. They were linked with points of principle, and above all with *sola fide* – the idea of salvation only by faith, which together with his opposition to the theory of freedom of will, formed Luther's argument against the Catholic concept of 'deserts'. Hence a radical re-evaluation of grace took place in Protestantism. If previously grace had been the main consequence of the Church sacraments, now it came to be more closely associated with personal experience of Christ: there was a sharp turn of direction towards individualization.

The foregrounding of the problem of the believer's direct relationship with God, without the mediation of the Church, seems at first sight to bring the ethics of salvation of certain Old Believer congregations and sects close to Protestantism. The idea that some were 'elect', harmonizing with the idea of the inequality of religious charisma, evidently saturated the spiritual climate at the end of the Middle Ages. These ideas formed the basis for new models of piety and behaviour. In Western Protestantism, however, people continued to set up a personal relationship with God – in particular because of the notion of divine predestination – that led also to the 'unmagicking' of the world, which has had such a fundamental effect on the development of European civilization. In contrast to this, the individualization of religious experience within the Old Ritual was conditioned more than anything by the loss of the Church and the 'tsardom' of special charisma. No radical conceptual rethinking of the concepts of grace, of sacraments or, first and foremost, of the eucharistic symbolism can be found in the Old Ritual. Hence the reduction in the number of sacraments (or their complete absence), and the special veneration of icons that arose in connexion with this, were in complex ways connected with ideas of the *gracelessness of the surrounding world.*

Among the 'Priestless', where teachings about Antichrist had their widest circulation, the sacraments were reduced to a minimum (baptism and repentance) or were totally denied ('Negativism'): 'Because of the Devil, Christ's sacraments are not enacted', as we can read in several 'Priestless' compendia of the 18th and 19th centuries.[18] Among the 'Priestists', however, the sense of apocalypse did not attain such extreme forms: they admitted all the sacraments and strove for their proper realization – for example, in searching for a bishop. This variety of Old Ritualist approaches to the ethics of salvation was at once reflected in attitudes to the prayer image. Thus the 'Priestists' admitted icons from 'heterodox' icon painters so long as the ancient pre-Nikonian symbolism was preserved, but among the 'Priestless' strictness was redoubled. Here we encounter some most unexpected manifestations of faith and of icon veneration.

Two subdivisions of the 'Priestless' – the *Spasovo soglasie* (or 'Negativists') at the end of the 17th century and the *Ryabinovsty* in the second half of the 18th – reached the extremity of concern regarding the grace of the image in the popular economy of salvation. Basing themselves on the teaching that Antichrist would 'destroy everything holy' in this world, the *Ryabinovtsy* denied all the sacraments, while the most radical among them denied even icons. The *Ryabinovtsy* could only save themselves through prayer. Their prayer house consisted of four walls painted black, four 'graceless' black oblongs, symbolizing nothingness, emptiness, the absence of grace in the surrounding world. And one sign alone – an eight-ended cross without any representation of the crucified Christ on it – with a short, repeated traditional prayer ('Lord, have mercy!') that we have already encountered, addressed to this cross, were able to assist salvation. In contrast to the prayer places filled with icons of the other Old Believers, and to the former sacralization of the world of Muscovite Rus through icons, we have here a symbolic inversion. Apocalyptic fear had linked up with the consequences of superstitious icon veneration. It is worth noting that, in denying icons, the *Ryabinovtsy* foregrounded the very problem of the 'obscuration' of the image's grace that had first been aired at the *Stoglav* council when it dealt with the question of the depiction of 'tsars and princes and saints and people who are alive' on icons.[19]

Boris Uspensky has noted that the motif of veneration of the Cross without representation of the crucified Christ (on the grounds that Christ was taken down from the Cross) among the *Ryabinovsty* had links with the same veneration of the Crucifixion among certain proponents of Nikon's reforms.[20] In Nikita Dobrynin's denunciation of Stefan, Archbishop of Suzdal, he claimed that Stefan asserted that it was improper that Christians depict 'our Lord God and Saviour Jesus Christ' on the Cross, and that Christians should not paint the Crucifixion. In the light of our problem it is important to emphasize that the 'unobscured' grace of an image was what always disturbed the popular consciousness, and this mental construction was rooted, of course, in the 'sacred way of life' of Muscovite Rus.

In the 16th century a custom still existed whereby each believer possessed his or her own icon in church. Others were not allowed to pray before it, under threat of public penance.[21] In this connection icons were often signed, as we can tell by an 'Annunciation' icon from N. M. Postnikov's collection, displayed in an archaeological exhibition in 1890 in Moscow. On its reverse side it carries the inscription 'Before this image only the Moscow merchant Filip Yeliseyev Bavykin prays.'[22] Because of the danger of 'obscuring' the grace of an icon, it might also be protected from the 'evil eye' of foreigners. Johann Pernstein, as he himself recounts, had to obtain special permission to look at an icon of St Nicholas in a church.[23] Judging by the Archimandrite Pavel, some *Ryabinovtsy* permitted icons in their religious life, and withheld veneration only from certain subjects regarded as 'contaminated', for example, depictions of 'bystanders' or 'historically remembered' figures: the sacred sphere firmly resisted any invasion of the 'worldly'. Thus icons of the Crucifixion were not venerated, since they included depictions of the soldiers attendant at the execution on Golgotha; likewise the sun and the moon. The *Ryabinovtsy* reckoned any such veneration as heathenish. For the same reason they rejected icons of the 'Entry into Jerusalem', on which the Saviour is shown riding an ass: 'An animal must not be venerated.' Finally, particular fear was evoked by icons with representations of 'unclean forces', for example 'The Resurrection of Christ and Descent into Hell', showing an infernal monster, as also by icons of the Last Judgment.[24] It should be noted that a quite different side of sectarian religiosity is seen in the attribution of 'reversed' sacred meaning to some image that was unfamiliar to the people. A. I. Yatsimirsky describes an icon of 'The Pure Soul' in which the 'soul' is represented as 'a most beautified maiden, equal by nature to an angel', which in one of the sects in the Pskov province served as an icon of the Mother of God for 'one Malashka' – a characteristic 'newly revealed Mother of God'.[25]

A consciousness re-aroused by religious fear could display ambivalence at any moment. Michel Foucault noted felicitously that salvation is a binary system: located between life and death, it represents an instrument of transition from evil to good. For this reason the technical aspect of salvation within the popular consciousness was continually subject to an uncertainty that often spilled over into the wish to 'purify' the means of salvation themselves from their evil origin: they beheld moral danger for the future soul there. It is no accident that the depiction of anti-Christian powers on icons was a perpetual topic of concern in Old Believer question books about icons. Examples of their destruction, over-painting or deliberate exclusion from the system of representation are also known. In one of the collections of illustrations of the 'Great Mirror', an unknown pious zealot has cut out all the figures of 'unclean powers'.[26] In one 'Priestless' anthology there can be found a typical question as to whether one can bow down to images of holy personages on which the Devil is also depicted. With reference to the sanctity of ancient icons, the compiler-cum-author answered affirmatively.[27]

Like the *Ryabinovtsy*, the followers of the 'Saviour's Accord' considered that for lay people to accomplish the two sacraments that were accepted by the other 'Priestless' – baptism and repentance – was a blasphemy. Since, as they held, grace had been 'taken up' to heaven, they denied all sacraments and divine worship. This reliance on 'the Saviour's mercy' and their lack of means to acquire grace led to a situation where they began to ascribe the functions of a priest to images on icons: upholders of 'uncompromising negativism' made confession and monastic repentance before icons. In this connnection we should note that certain texts concerning monastic repentance presupposed the perpetual presence of grace only in the person repenting or carrying out an act of prayer himself, which fully accorded with the enhancement of religious individualism and the egotistical aspect of salvation: 'wheresoever thy grace may be, let it surround me, a sinner, all the days and nights and hours, lest I, accursed, might perish as if ashes in the face of the wind'.[28] As P. V. Sinitsyn reported, it was even a rule among members of the *Fedoseyevtsy* to shave the hair from the top of their heads so that grace might descend on them all the more easily.[29]

In the rituals of the 'Melchisedek' sect of the 'Priestless', the icon was endowed with the capability of transubstantiating the holy bread and wine. Since holy orders had terminated for them, as for the other 'Priestless', while the Eucharist continued to be regarded as the main means of union with Christ, members of the sect (flouting the New Testament concept of the eternal priesthood of Christ in descent from Melchisedek) recognized themselves as having 'Melchisedek's priesthood' and invented a particular rite for offering a bloodless sacrifice. As they conceived of it, Melchisedek, king of Salem, on meeting Abraham when the latter was returning from a victorious war against an alliance of four kings (Genesis 14:18; Psalm 110:4), was not made a priest, but brought God a sacrifice of bread and wine. For that reason the 'Melchisedeks' put bread and a goblet of wine *before the icons*; then they prayed, performing the vespers, the nocturne and the matins according to the Rule of the psalter. They did not bless the bread with their hands, since that was permitted to a consecrated priest alone. The sacrament of transubstantiation of the bread and wine (or water) derived exclusively from the power of the icon.[30]

In those congregations of the 'Priestless' where certain sacraments were none the less recognized as essential, the strengthened role of the image in the economy of salvation was expressed through an unusual strictness in its veneration. In their non-acceptance of icons 'desecrated' by the New Ritualists, the eschatological consciousness of the 'Priestless' often reached extremes, sometimes to the point of even burning themselves together with the icons. Thus, in 1693, under Vasiliy Yemelyanov's leadership, 200 Old Believers seized the parish precinct of Pudozh. Inside the church they first of all *cleansed the icons*, after which they began to hold a service. But when 'state representatives' appeared, they locked themselves in and set fire to themselves.[31]

This strictness (bordering at times on obsessiveness) brought discord into the ranks of the 'Priestless'. The 'Filippovtsy' or the 'Old Shore Dwellers' (*Pomortsy*[32]) – followers of the elder Filipp, who with his fellow believers performed the act of self-immolation in a house of prayer in 1743 – refused to pray for the Tsar and differed from other 'Priestless' on the question of

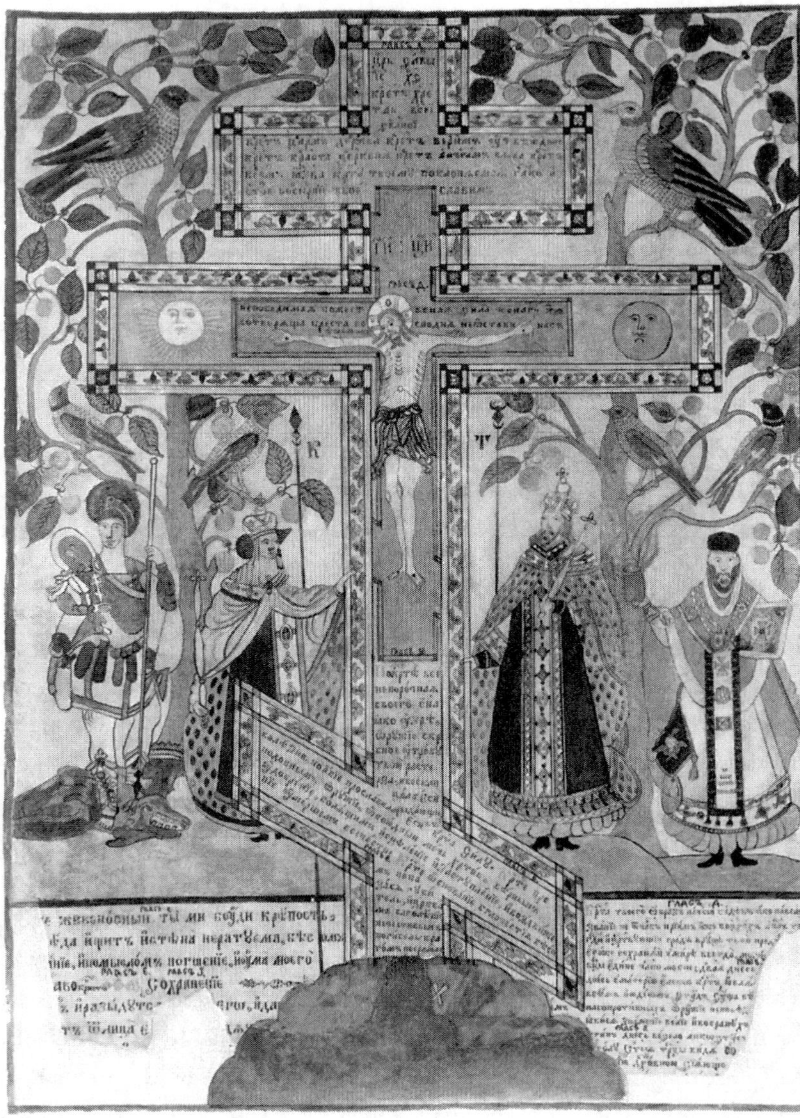

61. *Crucifixion*, late 19th century, drawing. State Historical Museum, Moscow.

acceptance of the sacred monogram 'I.N.Ts.I.' (illus. 61). It was a quarrel on a point of principle, since it was with this inscription that the 'new Nikonian faith' appeared: 'Nikon the Patriarch set up a cross within the Holy Cross Monastery and on it he displayed in Russia for the first time these letters I.N.Ts.I. [И.Н.Ц.И.]; since when on many crosses throughout Russia these letters have been added.' The fact that this inscription came from Little Russia (Ukraine) – it derived from the Latins and entered the Uniate schism on images and in their books, together with baptism by sprinkling, and with the spelling *Iisus* – as well as the fact that in the struggle against the 'new faith', a huge number of zealots of piety were pursued and underwent 'great sufferings' from the Patriarch Nikon – all this put the 'Old Shore Dwellers' in an irreconcilable situation. What is more, in contrast to many other Old Believers, they refused to venerate the icon of the Mother of God, 'Joy of All who Suffer' (illus. 79), because it had appeared in 1688, i.e., after the Patriarch Nikon.[33]

Unlike the 'Filippovtsy', the 'Fedoseyevtsy' preserved the tradition of Feodosiy Vasilyev and venerated the Holy Cross only with the inscription 'I.N.Ts.I.', because of which they were given the nickname 'Inscriptionites' (*Titlovshchina*). Veneration of images with this inscription was confirmed after Feodosiy's death in the 'Polish Articles' of the Fedoseyev Assembly of 1752: 'We must believe in and bow down to the life-giving Cross of Christ with the superscription to the Glory of Jesus Christ reading thus: I.N.Ts.I, or as written on a board I C XC. This alone is to be venerated and worshipped; and whosoever will not bow to this cross must leave the church.'[34] In their veneration of the Crucifixion, the Old Ritualists of the 'Old Shore-Dwellers' congregation parted company with the Priestists. Metal crosses showing the Crucifixion – cast in one of the Priestist centres, the village of Guslitsy near Moscow – had to contain a depiction of the Lord Sabaoth and the Holy Spirit in the form of a dove, with the same four-letter inscription 'I.N.Ts.I.' at the top. This distinguished them from the 'Priestless' cast-metal crucifixes, which permitted at the top only a depiction of the Saviour Not Made By Hands icon and the inscription 'King of Glory, Jesus Christ, Son of God'.

The 'Priestless' had a far stricter attitude than the Priestists toward icons painted not only by the New Ritualists but even by those of other sectarian congregations. Among them the idea developed of purifying metal prayer images with fire, and we can observe concentrated attention towards certain principles concerning icons that had been laid down in old manuscripts of the *Nomocanon*, such as the text 'On how icons that are from the hands of unbelievers are not to be accepted'.[35] To judge by 16th- and 17th-century travellers' reports, this was unswervingly followed in Muscovite Rus.

That the shadow of the Antichrist put them continually on guard is shown by the popularity in their circles of a work by Fyodor the Deacon, *On Recognizing the Temptation of Antichrist*, a text remembered in the 18th and 19th centuries. One of Fyodor's chief ideas was that the Antichrist could appear through 'apostate icons' in which 'dishonour' was mixed with 'piety', which meant that recognizing the latter would be no easy task. Satan would inevitably arrive (or had already done so) and

> seat himself, accursed one, not in a heathen temple, but in God's church, on the holy place, not calling himself an idol, but through blasphemous heresies and all kinds of *apostate icons* [my italics] with corpses, dead human bodies, that is to say with impious people, has summoned those subjugated to his impiety to the destruction of righteousness with torment and godlessness, and brought them to his own worship, while condemning those not subjugated to be delivered to death.

Fear of accidentally encountering an image of the Antichrist was strengthened by the difficulty, or even impossibility, of recognizing it. The 'impiety' of Satan was astonishingly variegated: he weaves together impiety and devotion, and in consequence also 'holy icons with blasphemous images, and to put it briefly every holy place has impiety and foulness close to it, just like that spotted beast the lynx'. To comprehend where 'impiety' and where 'devotion' were located was impossible, since 'to separate hypocrisy from slyness cannot be done, because he has by nature the variegated coat of a beast together with his power, and bears impiety and devotion woven together'.[36] Discussing the 'false prophet of the chronicle', the priest Lazar in his *Tale of the Spiritual Activity of the Most Holy Patriarch Ioasaf* also reminded readers of how the apocalyptic beast of John the Divine could be related to an *icon*: 'he had two horns like a lamb', 'this is the hidden temptation in virtue', 'and if there is an image, it will be called an icon'.[37]

In view of this there is a particular interest in the fact that so-called 'icons of Hell' were disseminated among the Orthodox peasantry, as was reported in both central and local newspapers at the beginning of the 1870s. In 1873 in the village of Stetsovka near the town of Chigirin, the local priest, in blessing a small tinfoil icon brought to him by a peasant, accidentally broke the glass covering it, and thereupon all those present saw below the bent foil an image of a devil with the following inscription: 'Bow down to me for seven years and you will be mine for eternity'. After the local authorities made a check, icons of similar type were discovered in the villages Mordva, Buzhino, Shabelniki, Topilovka, Vereshcheki and other places. On some of them instead of a devil they found, glued to the back of the foil, newspaper caricatures showing a man with a dog's head, a Turk smoking a pipe, and so on.[38] In response to all this, Nikolay Leskov published an interesting article in the newspaper *Russky mir*. He remarked that icons of this kind were widespread, not only in Russia's south-west provinces but 'almost everywhere'. He had either seen them or heard about them from eye-witnesses in the provinces of Penza, Orlov, Poltava and Kharkov, also not far from Moscow. In addition, concealed representations of unclean powers besmirched not just tinfoil icons but also icons painted for the common people, on which a devil would be drawn on the plaster base under the painted surface. There is more: Leskov discovered such depictions only on icons of the New Ritual: 'little demons are met with only on cheap and artless icons in the so-called Frankish style, which not one Old Believer would accept as an icon, and obeisance to which he would consider a sin'. On this basis the article came to the conclusion that the Old Believers intended to tear the people away from bowing down to icons of the new Frankish manner, which they also referred to as 'hellishly-drawn': 'the little demon drawn below on the under-layer of such an icon is, as it were, a stamp, confirming the unquestionable nature of the infernal derivation of the hellishly-drawn icon'.[39] In brief, this was a special game of non-recognition of 'the temptations of Antichrist', of the interweaving of piety and devotion that became increasingly rooted in the mass consciousness.

The Sacralization of the Icon Painter

It was in the context of these habits of mind that the founder of the River Vyg community, Andrey Denisov, developed his principles of the veneration only of those icons that were the work of icon painters of 'the true faith'.

One Old Believer was unable to find in the Holy Scriptures and 'holy books' any appropriate way to test the painters' faith. Neither could she understand why it was forbidden to venerate those icons that, although they might be works by painters who had not taken 'holy baptism', were none the less skilfully executed and 'directed towards the glory of the True God'. To judge by her arguments, the danger of taking a 'heretical' image for an 'authentic' one lay in the illiteracy of the flock. If this Old Believer was unable to write properly, then how could she judge what was 'correct' or 'incorrect' in the complex symbolism of the image? After all, many icons had been painted according to Latin models. The best solution was to test the faith of the painter. In support of this she cited the *Stoglav* and Simeon of Thessaloniki.[40]

The fear of coming across the image of the Antichrist in the world without grace determined the *sacralization of the icon painter*. This older motif is significantly strengthened, and a vast body of texts (in general from the 'Priestless'), including icon painters' pattern-books, bears witness to this.

Max Weber has noted that within Luther's concept of *Beruf* ('calling') is this value judgement: the fulfilment of one's destiny in the framework of one's worldly profession is the highest task of a person's moral life. For all the distinction between 'Protestantism of local tradition' and 'Protestantism of personal conviction', an interesting analogy suggests itself: of all the trades and professions, it was to icon painters alone that the Old Believers set the task of performing a moral and religious undertaking. However, we have to remember that icon painting was understood to be a sacred, not a worldly, profession, and also that the tradition of the Fathers of the Church considered the Holy Fathers to be true icon painters. They were those who saw the world as holy, those to whom were granted the revelations subsequently inherited by the iconographic schemes. The technical execution of the latter was the business of 'wise' craftsmen. It would appear that the peculiarity of the Old Russian tradition lay in the fact that it concentrated attention excessively on the interrelationship between the sanctity of the icon making craft and the model of the craftsman's behaviour.

For the 'Priestless', the world was deprived of grace and holiness. For that reason, if previously the making of icons and church services complemented each other – in traditional consciousness were even at times identified with each other – then after the Schism that portion of service to God, which until then had been allocated to divine worship, was, as it were, transferred to icon production. Thus the determining condition for the grace and sacredness of the image might now be seen (according to Andrey Denisov) not so much in its adherence to the iconic canon, as in the *way of life of the craftsman*. Hence, too, in the post-medieval age there was a particular attentiveness paid to texts that elevated the status of the icon painter and demanded sanctity from him, notably the *Tale of the Holy Icon Painters* (second half of the 17th century), often included in Old Believer icon-painting compendia and question and answer books. What was in it that caught one's eye? Evidently, the main thing was the sanctity of the icon-makers' craft, from which the power of an image to a large degree depended. The icon, delineated by a holy and blessed hand, possessed an unusual power: that of working miracles. Hence the sacralization of the icon painter presupposed 'cooperation with God', both on the level of a divine ontological gift – that of a special calling – and on the ascetic plane, the practical knowledge of summoning the Holy Spirit.

Various motifs were actively developed in this *Tale*: that of the special vocation and election of the icon-painters, the inter-dependence of the sanctity of the craft and the readiness (so important for the Old Believer consciousness) to suffer for the faith, and, finally, the motif of how the wonder-working abilities of icons in the land of Rus were linked with the 'hand in blessing' of the Russian saints. The motif of vocation was traditionally elucidated by the story of St Luke as the icon painter who first drew the image of the Mother of God, and also by the legend of how St Methodius preached, not just by word but by image. According to this story, the reader (whether a mere layman or an icon painter) would come to understand that the power of Methodius's preaching in the Russian lands was completely dependent on his being an icon painter. He had experience in painting images even before his mission with St Cyril, his brother, to the Slavonic countries. Thus when he went to Russia, the first thing Methodius did was to paint an icon, which later turned out to be a decisive factor in St Vladimir's acceptance of the Christian faith: 'He came to the Russian land also and painted . . . an image of the second coming of Christ with figures and the presentation to the righteous of the Kingdom of Heaven and the heavenly dwelling-places. And all were baptized: the Slavs and the Rus and the Bulgars'. (At the time of Peter the Great a strange conviction arose among the upper strata that this image of the Last Judgment was in fact an altarpiece by Hans Memling, *c.* 1473, in the church of St Mary in Danzig; it is known that Peter even wished to acquire it by exchange.)

That icon painting was the business of a chosen few is underlined by the fact that saintly rulers could be painters – a substantial piece of evidence regarding the process whereby the monarchy was sacralized. The Byzantine emperor Manuel Palaiologos (1350–1425), for example, painted many sacred icons, among them the 'Saviour Clad in Gold', showing the Saviour seated on a throne with a book of the Gospels, blessing with his right hand.

Painting images was a feat hallowed as far back as the terrible times of iconoclasm. In the context of the persecution of Old Believers and of decrees against painting icons according to the 'old order', we see the motif of martyrdom for the faith exemplified here. After all, Bishop Lazarous had suffered at the hands of the Emperor Theophilos (829–42), an iconoclast, merely because he had painted an image of St John the Baptist, 'an extremely beautiful one'. Theophilos 'ordered both his hands to be cut off and him to be put in a prison cell and he was there till the Emperor's death and then was freed by the Empress Theodora'. We do not find any martyrs to the faith among the Russian icon painters in the *Tale*. However, there are innocent victims among them, for example Adrian of Poshekhonye, who painted many wonder-working icons. 'Slain by robbers' in his hermitage, Adrian is invariably shown with an icon beside him on his own liturgical icons (illus. 26, 27).

According to the *Tale*, almost all icons painted by Russian saints were considered to be wonder-working. St Peter, Metropolitan of Moscow and all Russia (1305–26), miracle worker, painted many (illus. 62). While he was still abbot of the Spassky Monastery he painted an icon of the Mother of God, which he brought to the holy Metropolitan Maksim. When Maksim died a voice came forth from the image to Peter: the Mother of God herself was giving him her blessing to become the next Metropolitan. Sometimes the term 'wonder-working' is left out, though clearly intended. For example,

Makariy, Metropolitan of Moscow, 'painted many' holy icons. It is related of another saint, Afanasiy, that he painted many wonder-working icons. The same is true of the miracle-working St Feodor, Archbishop of Rostov, nephew of St Sergius of Radonezh. As Archimandrite of the Simonov Monastery in Moscow, he painted a 'wondrous' icon of the blessed Sergius. Russia's acquisition of wonder-working icons is represented by the author of the *Tale* as highly important, and he mentions it several times: 'the reverend father Grigoriy Pechersky, the Kievan icon painter, painted many holy wonder-working icons, which were thus acquired by the land of Russia.' The *Tale* also includes a story from the *Patericon* of the Caves Monastery concerning help given by angels to the Caves' wonder-working icon painter Alimpiy (11th century), who 'assisted him and painted images as if they had been his apprentices'. Finally, the one painter whose icons were all wonder-working was Andrey Rublyov (*c.* 1370–1430), 'the blessed father Andrey of Radonezh'. The author reminds us, with a reference to the *Stoglav*, that icons should be painted 'as Andrey Rublov painted them, and not wholly out of one's imagination'.[41]

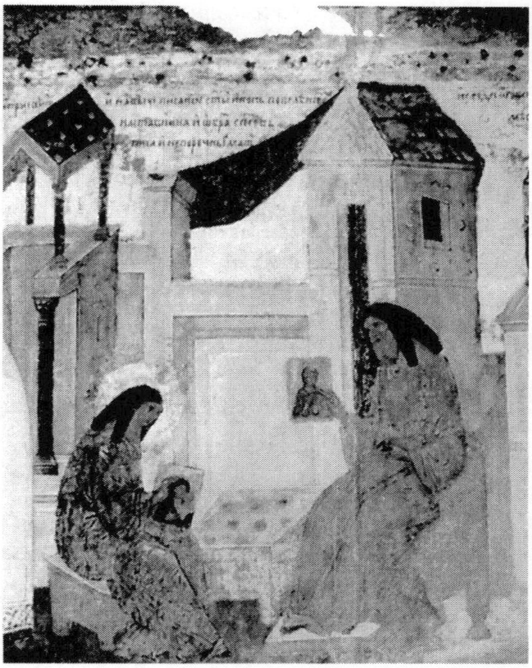

62. 'Peter Brings an Icon he has Painted to the Metropolitan Maksim', a scene from the icon *The Metropolitan Peter with his Life*, 1480s. Moscow Kremlin State Museums.

From the point of view of the sacralization of the icon painter, the text of the *Tale* would be amplified in Old Believer icon pattern-books with a range of other texts, constituting an introductory section of the pattern-book; this was characteristic of the Russian tradition. Throughout the Christian world, religious painters used a variety of models that transmitted a schematic characterization of the saint or holy event, and protected the craftsman from a factually inaccurate conception of the image. Models of the kind existed both in Byzantium and the West. In the Byzantine tradition the requirement to adhere strictly to the ancient models that were 'revealed' to the saints lay at the foundation of all religious art. The composition of a pattern-book from the later Middle Ages can be judged on the basis of the well-known

Hermineia by the monk Dionysios of Fourna, discovered and published by Porfiriy Uspensky.[42] It has been shown that although the manuscript dates from the period 1728–33, it could itself be a compilation of earlier texts, which in their turn were based on still earlier sources.[43] Note that while the *Hermineia* of Dionysios was intended to follow Byzantine medieval traditions, by contrast the well-known tract by the Greek artist Doxaras, *On Painting* (1726), implied a rift with those traditions. These two pattern-books together seem to represent, as it were, the theoretical basis respectively of the old and the new directions in post-Byzantine icon painting in the Greek and Slav East.[44]

In contrast to the Russian pattern-books (they became widespread soon after the *Stoglav* Council), there are no special chapters in the *Hermineia* that develop the theme of the sacred quality of icon making or touch on the problem of the craftsman's own personality. According to the *Hermineia*, the icon painter would preface his labours with a prayer in which, acknowledging his responsibility, he simply requested help from God in his divinely agreeable task:

> Lord God of all things, illumine and make wise the soul, the heart and the mind of thy slave [with such-and-such a name], and guide his hands, that they may sinlessly and skilfully represent thy life and that of thy most pure Mother and of all the saints, to thy glory and for the embellishment and splendour of thy holy church, and so that sins may be forgiven to all who spiritually revere the holy icons and who reverently kiss them, and render veneration to the Prototype. Deliver him from every devilish delusion, that he may prosper within thy commandments, by the prayers of thy most pure Mother, of the glorious holy apostle and evangelist Luke and of all the saints, Amen.[45]

Among the considerable number of Old Believer pattern-books (from the late 17th century to the early 20th) that we have examined, only one contains a prayer that was evidently repeated every day by the painter. He begs for God's mercy in the matter of his salvation: 'Have mercy Lord Jesus on thy slave such-and-such, save him from every hurt, misfortune and sorrow, from all spiritual and bodily sickness, and save him from all enemies visible and invisible and from every sinful temptation. And grant him all his entreaties for salvation and eternal life and do what is beneficial for our souls.[46]

Meanwhile, the same things make continual appearances in a great number of pattern-books and dogmatic theological collections of the 18th, 19th and early 20th centuries: chapters from the written Nomocanon, the *Stoglav* and the *Tale of the Holy Icon Painters*, extracts from the Fathers of the Church. All of these are brought together by one overriding intention – to set the icon painter on the path of truth, to prescribe particular tasks for him not so much in the sphere of his workaday life as in that of his everyday ethic of salvation. It is as if a conceptual model of the righteous life of an icon painter was being set up in the selection of these texts: a life saturated with the motif of the preordained and purposeful quality of his path. The existential determinative aspect of Christian anthropolgy – the concepts of a person's spiritual path, of sin and grace, of prayer and of communion with God – is in this instance developed in its relationship to the painter's professional duties. The compiler of a pattern-book or a compendium is both author and moralizer, listing the requirements of a holy life and warning against 'notions' that would lead the soul of the craftsman to damnation. We should also note that the choice and organization of these texts was in full harmony with the very nature of the Old Believers' intellectual activity, directed as it was above all towards preservation and copying of a defined selection of texts, which they conceived to be fully adequate to penetrate through the graceless world to the summits of religious inspiration and salvation.

The moral code for icon painters was taken as a rule from Chapter 43 of the *Stoglav* and was buttressed by a quotation from the written *Nomocanon*, whose chapter 'A Discourse about Icon Painters and How they Should Be' was copied from Isidore of Pelousion. Their connection cannot be doubted, since the Nomocanon is well known to have been compiled by the Moscow Metropolitan Makariy (1482–1563) just before the *Stoglav* council. This was what 'moral purity', as it was later reproduced in the icon painters' compendia, sounded like:

> It is right for an icon painter to be humble, gentle, reverential, no lover of vain speech or of mockery, not peevish, not envious, not

> drunken, not a robber, not a murderer. And he should preserve to a high degree spiritual and bodily purity, taking the utmost pains, and if he cannot be so totally, then to marry according to the law and enter into wedlock, and to visit spiritual fathers frequently and inform them of everything, and to live by their direction and teaching in fasting and prayer, and in restraint, with humility and without any disgrace and disorderliness.

This moral code was coupled not only with control over the icon painter but also with a demand for its *particular respect*, which was directed towards simple lay folk, towards the spiritual authorities and towards 'powerful people'.[47]

Unlike this text, the *Nomocanon* chapter makes mention of the sanctity of the icon-making craft. According to Isidore of Pelousion, it was right for painter to be pure and to live a spiritual life with good morals, and to adorn himself with humility and gentleness. The icon painter should not be a slanderer, or a blasphemer, or a lecher, or a drunkard, or a swearer, or to have any other such bad habits, since it is commanded that such people should not undertake holy works.

Emphasis on the significance of the life of a craftsman serves to guarantee for the compiler of a pattern-book or compendium the authenticity or falsity of an image. It was with this in view that the text by Feodosiy the Hermit – according to which the verification of an icon by a bishop, a metropolitan or a patriarch meant first of all the verification of the icon painter's behaviour – was most often reproduced: 'whether the icon is a proper representation is witnessed by his life'.[48] It was no accident that the 'moral purity' of the icon craftsman should be given first place. The demand for a certain moral standard had already been elaborated by the Byzantine Fathers of the Church. But we discover an important difference in the Byzantine tradition: it connected and harmoniously coupled the 'moral purity' of the craftsman with the quality of wisdom. We should again recall the words of the prayer from the *Hermineia*: 'Illumine and make wise the soul, the heart and the reason of thy slave', as also the well-known utterance of Basil the Great (329–79) about the icon-painter's 'flowers of wisdom' that allow them to claim victory over the word: 'Arise now before me, ye glorious painters

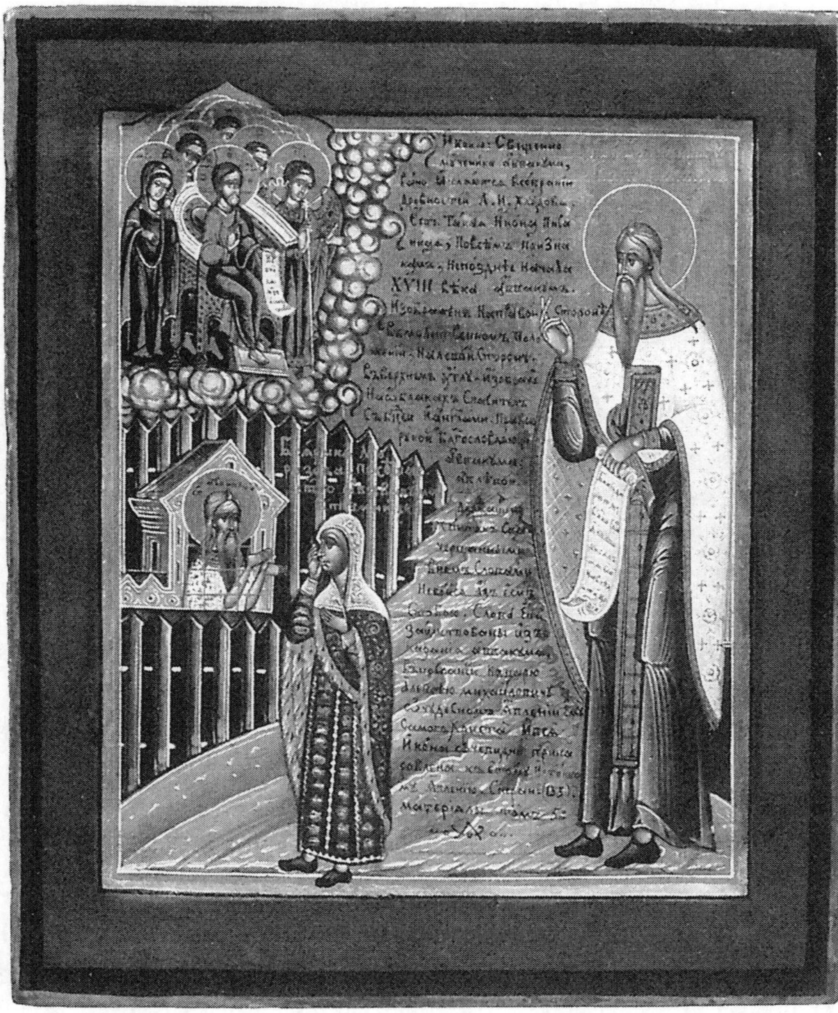

63. *Archpriest Avvakum*, early 20th century. State Russian Museum, St Petersburg.

of zealous rewards. Amplify this imperfect description of the military man with your art. Illumine with the flowers of your wisdom the crowned head inadequately presented by me. May I be vanquished by your depiction of the martyr's valorous deeds.'[49]

By contrast, the Old Believer version of the Russian tradition does not develop the linkage of 'moral purity' with wisdom. The first teachers within the Old Belief, in particular Avvakum (illus. 68), used their authority to exclude 'learning' from their system of salvation as a false and useless value.

Thus it was attracted by the Church Fathers' ideas – reduced to the simplest of schemes – on the apprehension of God without the aid of reason; in brief, by 'simple faith'. Furthermore, the appearance of Ukrainian scholars and theologians amid the proponents of the Nikonian reforms, and the 'captivity' of the official Church by Western theology in the next two centuries, served only to strengthen this hostility towards learning, since all this was simply regarded as the intrusion of 'Latinism' into Orthodoxy and as 'muddying the springs'.

Instead of wisdom, the theme of 'moral purity' was alone elaborated as appropriate to the context of true religion and as a confessional norm. Hence there arose among the 'Priestless' a special attentiveness to the topics of drunkenness and lasciviousness, while the icon painter's dedication to his task and service to his calling were raised to the level of ethical maxims. It also determined the ethical and aesthetic tone of his devotion. The particular respect in which the Fedoseyevtsy held celibate icon painters bore witness to a tendency for the monastic model of behaviour to infiltrate the system for laymen. The attitude of a monkish icon painter towards sexuality was interdependent with the 'grace-bearing' quality of his images. The status of a painter was almost equated with the status of the head of a Fedoseyev religious community. In a decree of the Uglich Congress of 1827 that forbade the Fedoseyevtsy to employ young women to work for them, priors of communities and icon painters were specially singled out: 'Priors and icon painters are not to receive disgraceful persons in their cells, and also young persons of the female sex are not to be hired as workers by any Christians and are not to live in the same cell, and those who do not obey this are to be chastized lovingly, while those who refuse to submit are to be sundered from the Church.'[50] It is known that the Fedoseyevtsy taught that entering into wedlock meant 'perpetual fornication'. By contrast, the 'marrying Priestless', distinguishing themselves from the Fedoseyevtsy, maintained 'that virginity is not a universal commandment and that according to our Saviour's words not all can accommodate it, and thus too to preach universal virginity is contrary to the Lord's Gospel'. Within the Fedoseyev sect the 'marryers' could not worship in the same prayer house or before the same icons as did the 'non-marryers'.[51]

This attitude to sex was closely linked with an attitude towards the body and the world. Asceticism and a monastic degree of strictness in the piety of the 'Priestless' were manifest in their refusal to take meals not only with New Ritualists, but with members of other sects, since, as they supposed, this leads to the weakening of faith among believers.[52] These qualities also emerged in relation to fasts. Asceticism, being a practical teaching on acquiring the gifts of the Holy Spirit and cooperating in God's work, had long demanded moderation and always presented dangers in the case of 'self-motivated' spiritual feats. The Russian Church observed both one-day and prolonged fasts. But wilfully to increase their number with additional fasts was to risk excessive and stupefying mortification of the flesh. The strict, and somehow exceptional, attitude of the Fedseyevtsy towards fasting was a feature that astonished outside observers in the 18th and 19th centuries.[53] It is also worth noting that to some extent it echoed the 'impermissible' aspects of Muscovite devotion, about which Paul of Aleppo (despite all his admiration for it) wrote in the 17th century: 'to all that is contained in the rule, the canons and the decrees of the typicon, the Russians have added ceaseless fasts, unwavering attendance at church services, ceaseless bowing down to the ground even on Saturdays and Sundays, even though all this is impermissible'.[54] On the evidence of the 'spiritual verses', the observance of holy days had a tendency to expand: to the Wednesday and Friday fasts, Monday was sometimes added. This incidentally is confirmed by the decrees of the 'Priestless' councils, laying down that 'on Wednesday and Friday there is no butter or oil to be eaten, and also on Monday one must fast'.[55]

The theme of drunkenness and lechery straightforwardly outlined the sphere of sin within the consciousness of the Old Believer – a sphere that simultaneously included ambivalence and laughter. Numerous 'Priestless' manuscript illustrations to texts that condemned drunkenness stood in contrast to the popular literature of the 17th century and early 18th with its Baroque universalization of laughter and the comic. Specialists have noted that the specific quality of parodies dating from the Baroque period (*Homage to the Tavern*) consisted in their combining confessional utterances with drunken chatter and the attributes of Church ritual with real-life tavern scenes. Drunkenness could simultaneously both be condemned (*Tale of Misery–Luckless–Plight*) and have its own rights: *The Tale of the Reveller* upheld the right of the drunken hero to posthumous recompense.[56]

The fundamental seriousness and strictness of the Old Believer's religious consciousness considered this sort of thing as inadmissable: everyday behaviour was endowed with an extreme religious tonality. The *Stoglav* forbade drunkards and lechers from painting icons. In the 'Priestless' commentary on the 43rd chapter of the *Stoglav*, these behavioural signs were now taken to signal an icon painter of another faith, i.e., a 'Nikonian', a 'Latin' or 'Armenian', and were measured against a confessional norm. The author of one of these commentaries, who followed Andrey Denisov in warning against apparently 'correct' icons that were painted by 'lovers of innovation', reasoned that since in the conciliar *Stoglav* it was commanded to paint holy icons, and the holy council defines a painter as honourable and abstemious, those who are not abstemious and are drunkards are to be totally banned. The holy church must be vigilant in such matters, and avoid acquiring icons painted by persons not enlightened by true belief, and whose vision the evil spirit has obscured; 'Latins, Nikonians, Armenians and many more burdened by the temptation of dishonour are of this kind'.[57]

Authoritative texts were consciously selected with the aim of demonstrating that the icon could not possess the divine impulse if it was painted by heterodox icon painters. The quotation most often used comes from an instruction by St Isidore to Eusebius of Pelousion that makes up a chapter of the 16th-century Nomocanon 'On icons: that these painted by the hands of unbelievers should not be accepted, and that holy icons should not be given into the hands of unbelievers.'[58] In this redaction of the text we encounter the idea that even antiquity and accuracy do not guarantee the grace of an image if it has been copied by the hand of an 'unbelieving' icon painter:

> If by any chance one should be discovered in our Greek or Russian Orthodox lands that is ancient, and it shall have been devised after the Church schism, particularly if by a Greek from Italy, and even if the making of the icon is skilfully conceived according to the prototype, it is wrong to make obeisance to it, for it will have been devised by the hands of unbelievers, even if it follows the prototype, for their conscience does not serve purity . . .

And when the text goes on to forbid the painting of icons to unbelievers and foreigners, who are furthermore called unrighteous and 'pagan Armenians', the reader of the manuscript of the compendium would mentally relate these words to the 'Nikonians'.

Contacts with the external world were strictly limited for Fedoseyevite icon painters. Decrees of the Fedoseyevite councils forbade them to take on lay workers.[59] They wished the painter to have a status equivalent to that of the priest – i.e., one whose activity could substitute for conducting divine services. Hence this close attention to the authority of Feodosiy the Hermit, who compared the work of the priest and the painter on the basis of the derivation of the iconic craft from the hand of the holy apostle Luke. As Feodosiy thought, icon painters inspired by the Holy Spirit are linked in their worthiness with priests. He also considered that similar ideals of conduct, particularly in respect of their degree of freedom, united priest and painter. The painter did not have the right to serve or work wherever he wanted. He could only be in one service – the service of God.[60]

The system of behavioural norms was interwoven with a system of prohibitions that strengthened the severity of this demand for true religiosity. The ideal of moral purity implied a prohibition on an 'unbecoming way of life'. This, though, was related not only to matters like drunkenness or lechery, but the ban on painting icons also applied to those who did not have God's special gift for it. Here too the Nomocanon and *Stoglav* gave support: 'And even though a person should lead a good spiritual life, if he is incapable of designing holy icons beautifully, such a person should not be permitted to paint holy icons, but should earn his nourishment by some other craft.'[61] A person chosen by God to paint images must not deviate from this preordained path. If an icon painter turned to painting 'wordly things', that was regarded as a sin and a mockery because of the sacredness of the icon-making task.

The system of prohibitions aimed towards the icon painter's imitation of monastic behaviour also touched on at least two major questions that reflected aspects of the 'long Middle Ages'. These were the sins of pride and acquisitiveness. In communal (coenobitic) monasteries, where the monks were not allowed their own possessions, these two sins – which St Sergius of Radonezh and his successors put in prime of place – were overcome and redeemed. The sins of pride and cupidity were contrasted by Johan Huizinga as sins of former and of modern times. In the Middle Ages pride was considered 'the mother of all vices', constituting 'inflated individualism', in a world in which salvation could only be attained within and through the social group.[62] But in modern times a new concept of personality led to a gentler attitude toward pride and self-love.

The network of personal links and obligations within an Old Believer community, and the codification of its daily life in the context of the preservation of the medieval doctrine of 'contempt for the world', actualized the problem of collective salvation. Like certain ascetically orientated Protestant sects, the 'Priestless' brought in the institutions of novitiate and mentorship. The stricter the rules of everyday behaviour, demanding (as, for example, among the Fedoseyevtsy and the Filippovtsy) incontestable obedience from the members of the community to the superior and to the principles of monastic life, the more significant the sin of pride appeared to be. Any manifestation of 'individuality' closed off the road to salvation. In one of the Old Believer icon painting copy-books of the mid-19th century, a master craftsman made a handwritten note that placed pride at the forefront of the sins: 'Four things there are and if a person has one of them he will not have peace and God will not accept his prayer: 1. Pride. 2. Rancour. 3. Censoriousness. 4. If he has no love, that person will not receive salvation from God.'[63]

Among the 'Priestless' the sin of avarice (at any rate in respect of icon painters) was considered no less important. The inclusion in the 16th-century Nomocanon by Metropolitan Makariy of a text on the sinfulness of an icon painter who demands a high price for his labours can be reckoned to reflect the general opinion of the period. But from the time of Peter the Great, the 'world deprived of God' certainly did not want to renounce its worldly rewards. Disposing of wealth began to be seen as the palpable form of worldly aristocratic luxury and extravagance – something that in the traditional mind-set was perceived as no more and no less than the work of a devil-monarch. Wealth as the source of evil and sin was given much space in the Synodic and the novellae of *The Great Mirror*, a popular work among Old Believers. The same subject often provided material for *lubki* (popular prints) among the Old Ritualists. They also recalled the life of the legendary wonder-worker and icon painter St Alimpiy, who conversed with angels and who divided the money he had earned into three parts: with one portion he bought pigments, another he gave to the poor, and the third he donated to the monastery; meanwhile, he laboured 'day and night, without giving himself repose'.[64] It is of interest that according to his Life, Alimpiy's pigments had miraculous powers: the holy painter healed a leper by smearing his wounds with the paints he used for icons.

In this connection, the icon-painting copy-books included a chapter from the Nomocanon 'On How the Holy Icons are Not to be Acquired for a Price in Silver', in which the pious life of the icon painter presupposed a monastic style of behaviour and adherence to the example of 'the ancient godly and wise artists'. A lay icon painter was obliged to demand for his labours only enough to cover essentials – food, clothing and the purchase of pigments. It is noteworthy that this system of non-acquisitiveness with regard to the icon had for a long time had a double implication in Rus: the purchaser of an icon was also obliged to part with wealth. By a curious convention the purchase of an icon meant in such a case entering into a game that had a serious character: it was a question of the charitable rules of almsgiving and of the obligation to spend money in a sacred cause. This was discussed in the chapter 'On How an Artist Must not be Impoverished'.

Incidentally, to give 'everything' for an icon was a feature of Old Russian devotion. One of the first to cast doubt on it was Iosif Vladimirov, who accused rich people buying icons of 'haggling much as if over buying a slave and talking much about money'. But this royal painter clearly identified 'costly painting' with images from the New Ritual. It was not, of course, a matter of niggardliness, but of the fact that many people of the time (as he also says) still 'kept faith in bad icons' (that is, those using the old symbols). In many tales of the period about wonder-working icons of the Mother of God could be heard an appeal for people to give 'everything' for an icon, and naturally this appeal found its spiritual echo: in Aleksey's reign it is clear that people spent freely on icons. (Incidentally, the same was often true in the West: as we know, Vincenzo Gonzaga, Duke of Mantua, gave up a Margravate for a Madonna by Raphael.) It is interesting that in the late 19th century, the motif of money sacrificed for an icon found, quite literally, its material embodiment in the well-known image of the Mother of God, 'Joy of all Those who Suffer, with Coins'. On 22 July 1888, as a result of a lightning strike on the chapel of a glass factory not far from St Petersburg, coins that had been placed in a bowl for offerings had adhered to the miraculously preserved image of the Mother of God. After that miraculous event, copper coins were not only drawn on, but often actually stuck onto icons of the Mother of God. Once introduced into the sacred space of the icon, such coins became the corporeal symbols of the cult of almsgiving, sanctified by God. However, as has already been noted, certain Old Believer congregations (the 'Old Shore-Dwellers') did not venerate the Mother of God 'Joy of all Those who Suffer' on the grounds that it had first appeared in 1688, that is, after Patriarch Nikon, whereas among certain members of the 'Wanderers' sect (the 'Moneyless'), 'unrighteous' coins were condemned as bearers of the visage of the Emperor – an 'apostate' and Antichrist. The words of the Gospel, 'go thy way, sell whatsoever thou hast, and give to the poor, and thou shalt have treasure in Heaven: and come, take up the Cross and follow me' (Mark 10:21) could be taken literally by the fevered eschatological consciousness, transferring them immediately to their actual situation and system of behaviour. For the 'Moneyless', wandering through the world with copper crosses hanging from their chests, buying icons from an 'honourable artist' had no place in their system.

Icon-painters' copy-books and manuscript anthologies give us a good opportunity also to follow the development of the idea of the icon-painter as 'warrior of God'. The idea took root that the creation of images was equally a human and a divine process, that the icon painter created an image just as God had created the world and humankind in his image. This symbolism of ideas can be found in a succession of notes and marginalia by icon painters in the pages of copy-books. The relation of word and image is a complex theological problem to which the craftsman gave much thought, judging by the quotation one of them made from the start of St John's Gospel ('In the beginning was the Word, and the Word was with God, and the Word was God') in a copy-book. Thereafter, the symbolism of the creation of an image corresponds to the creation of mankind by God. Straight after the beginning of St John's Gospel, and before an exposition of the compositional range of pigments and technical devices required to 'reveal' an image, we can read a note about the 'composition' of a human being: 'Question: of what was the first human on earth created? Answer: From earth, in such and such quantities. Answer: First of all of earth, second of the sea, third of the sun.'

Interestingly, such day-to-day notes, written in margins and on the reverse sides of pages, lend the icon painter's copy-book the air of a diary of intimate jottings. Thus on a page with a Gospel text we find in small script: '1847, June 25th, there died Pyotr Ivanov, once one of the good icon painters', while on the reverse of the page that contained the prayer of the icon painter (given earlier) we find an all too prosaic note about how to tackle bed-bugs; for this bracken is essential: 'gather bracken, boil it in water, wash the house with that water, bed-bugs will stop, has been tested.'[65] The demands of the everyday world pressed in continually.

The task of those more experienced persons for whom it was important to direct the master not only to 'create' the image of God with paints, but through his imitation of Christ, was quite another matter: that meant to become his likeness, a saint. For this reason, information about practical methods of attaining the Holy Spirit were also presented to readers of the introductory section of pattern-books. The icon painter, like any human being, according to St John Damascene, is a third type of image: he 'is created by God in his likeness'.[66] Therefore he carries the divine image within himself in the sense of an ontological gift, while he is God's likeness in the sense of his potential, his capacity for spiritual perfection. That the craftsman was reminded of this by the Father of the Church's text on the relationship of image and prototype is no accident either. A person's veneration of an icon and the creation of an icon by a craftsman were both brought about by its 'nature', i.e., by the image and likeness of God, which are 'within' it: 'all people are obliged by its nature always to bow down to it' (the image of Christ), 'and not because of legitimate tradition, but inasmuch as God first created mankind in his image'. This idea is an essential component of the thought of, for example, the compiler of the introductory section of S. T. Bolshakov's pattern-book in order to show the natural quality of obeisance not only to God himself, but of the veneration of his likenesses, that is the saints, the example of whose behaviour had always to be present in the consciousness of the icon painter who recalled the words of the Apostle Paul: 'Be ye followers of me, even as I also am to Christ'.[67] Andrey Rublyov was considered an uncanonized saint immediately after his death (he was eventually canonized in June 1988), and for centuries not only his icons, but also the very image of the holy monk Andrey – whose memory was maintained in the liturgical calendar – were exemplary to the Old Believers.

The Theology of the People

The danger of obscuring the grace of the image continually nourished a distinctive folk theology of the icon among the Old Believers. Popular fantasy, inventions and ideas extracted from the apocryphal texts and spiritual verses were curiously combined in it with quotations from the Scriptures, decrees of the Church councils and ideas from the Fathers of the Church. During the 18th and 19th centuries, 'question-books' about icons were as a rule included in general manuscript anthologies of edificatory essays, stories and saints' lives. They can give us an interesting insight into just what might disturb the popular consciousness in icon veneration, what topics needed explanation or were puzzling to ordinary people. A conviction of the 'gracelessness' of the Empire caused them to put the most varied questions to themselves. The official theology of the icon and official bans on one subject or another had a significant influence on them.

'Given the isolated state of the Russian clergy, the role of theological education has no analogies in any other country. Without a clear understanding of this a full picture of Russian church life in the Imperial epoch is impossible', as the historian of the Russian church Nikolay Zernov wrote.[68] The Old Believers' conviction that official theology was 'infected with Latinism' was (it must be noted) fully in accord with reality. The first seminaries appeared in Russia at the start of the 18th century. Since they represented an aspect of Peter the Great's plans to transform the country according to a European pattern, the seminaries were alien to the authentic traditions of Orthodoxy. Up to the early 19th century, teaching in them was conducted in Latin; the instructors and pupils used Catholic or Protestant teaching materials. Catholic doctrine was criticized during this period through the arguments of Protestant theologians, while so as to condemn Protestant iconoclasm, Catholic arguments were often used. Specialists affirm that *The Rock of Faith*, written at the beginning of the 18th century by Stefan Yavorsky (1658–1722) in response to the heretical iconoclasm of Dmitriy Tveritinov (1667–1741), contained several borrowings of this kind.[69]

The famous Synod decrees of 6 April and 21 May 1722 can also be considered a response to iconoclastic heresy and 'popular superstitions'. A whole series of icons judged to be 'hostile to nature, to history and to truth itself' were forbidden. Although the resolutions cited the Great Moscow Council (1666–7), there was not the least hint of any kind of theological grounding in the Synodal decrees. However the very form and character of the argumentation in the official decrees contained many 'popular' concepts.[70] Thus in banning the canonical 'Nativity' icon they revealed a typically 'popular' concern for the purity of the image: because it was inadmissible to portray 'extraneous' figures (among whom Salome was counted) on icons, the subject itself – 'the image of the Mother of God suffering at the Nativity of the Son of God and the women with her' – was forbidden. Another ban was placed on 'the image of Floros and Lavros with horses and grooms known under invented names'. Among images 'contrary to nature' they included the icon of the martyr St Christopher 'with a dog's head', as also the icon of the 'Three Handed Mother of God' because she had three 'natural' hands painted on her. The ban on representations of God the Father, contained in the 43rd chapter of the Great Moscow Council, was the basis for putting a whole range of icons, widespread at the time not only among the people but in churches, on the forbidden list. Among them were *Shestodnev* ('six days') – 'the image of the six days of universal creation by God, in which God the Father is depicted reposing on cushions'; *Otechestvo* ('fatherhood') – 'the image of the Lord Sabaoth in the form of a very old man and of the only-born Son of God within him and between them the Holy Spirit in the form of a dove'; finally, the 'Annunciation with God the Father, breathing forth from his mouth'.[71]

Religious culture at grass roots level always reacted sensitively to that which was happening in the upper echelons. In this process, themes and 'tasks' at the 'bottom' could not avoid being simplified and schematized:

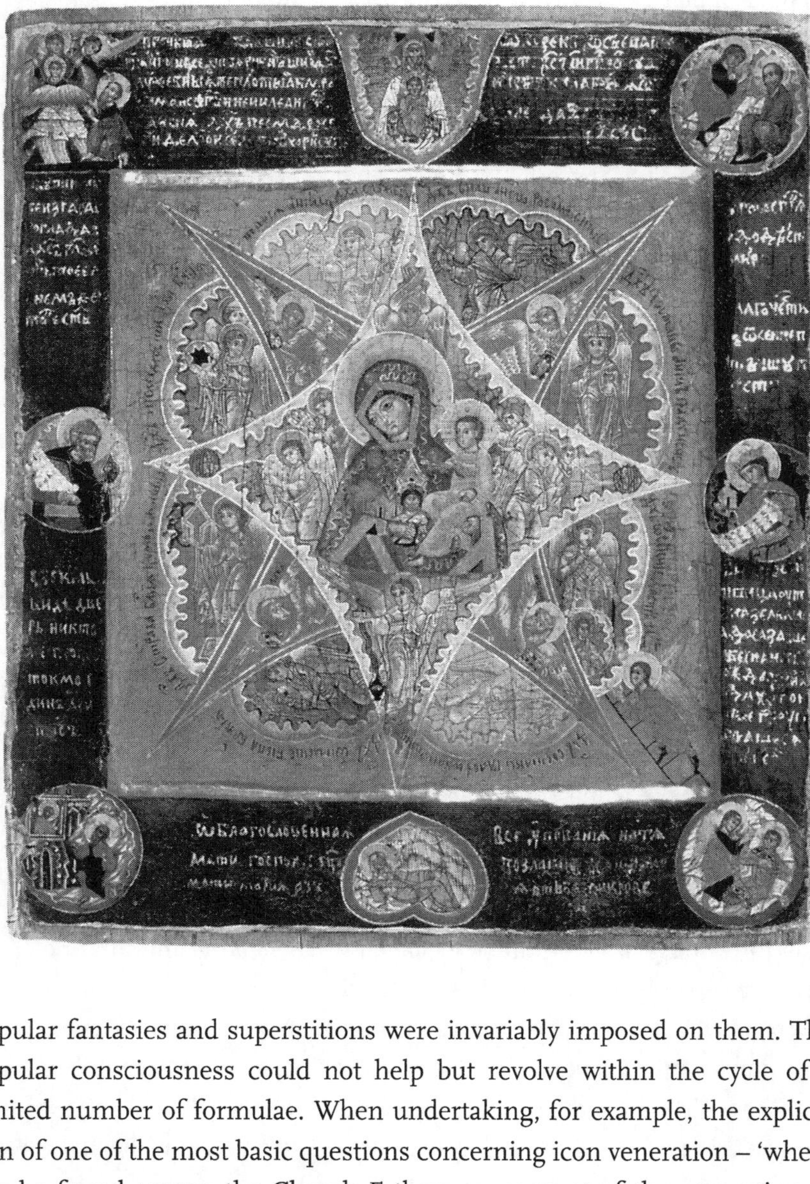

64. *Mother of God as the Burning Bush*, second half of the 17th century. Kolomenskoye Historical and Architectural Museum-Preserve, Moscow.

popular fantasies and superstitions were invariably imposed on them. The popular consciousness could not help but revolve within the cycle of a limited number of formulae. When undertaking, for example, the explication of one of the most basic questions concerning icon veneration – 'where can be found among the Church Fathers an account of the veneration of holy icons, and how it is not proper to worship them?' – a firm belief in the identical nature of the 'Nikonian' and Lutheran faiths was sufficient for an 'Old Shore-Dweller' author. Recollecting from the decrees of the Seventh Ecumenical Council not the boundaries between veneration and worship

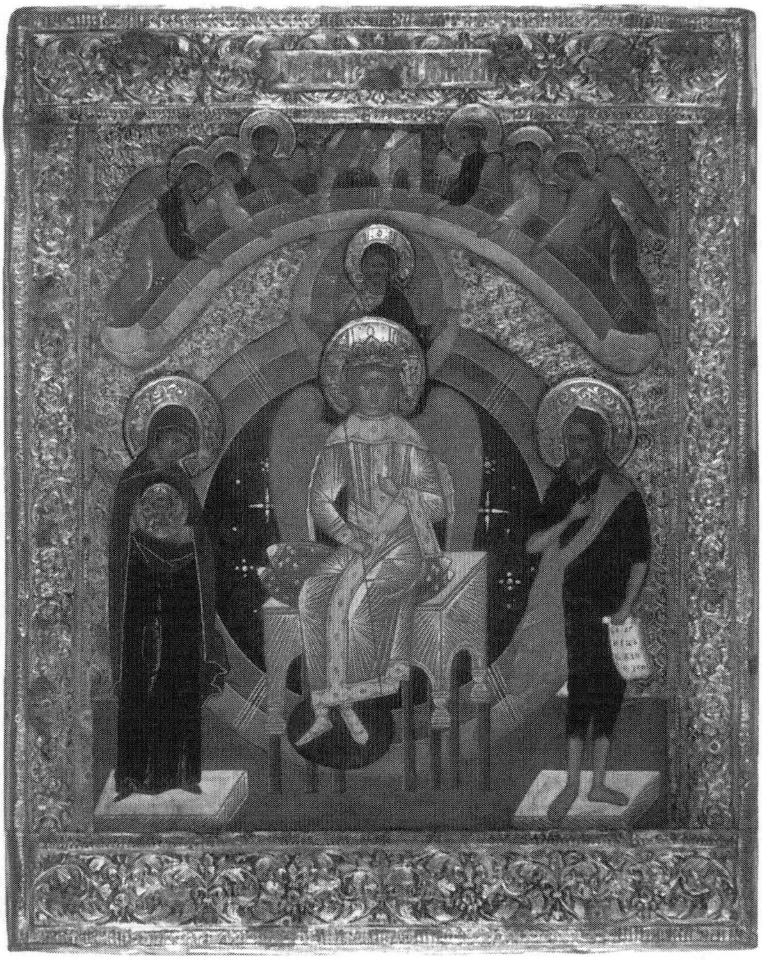

65. *Sophia, Wisdom of God*, 19th century. State Museum of the History of Religion, St Petersburg.

(an icon can be venerated but only God can be worshipped), but only that the image of Christ should be depicted within God's churches, on holy vessels, vestments, walls and panels, this Old Believer came to the conclusion that the Lutheran teaching is not to bow down to icons but only that it is right to honour them.[72]

Other icons forbidden by the 1722 Synod, the 'Mother of God of the Burning Bush' and 'Sophia, Wisdom of God' ('in the form of a certain maiden') would become a component of popular theology for nearly 200 years (illus. 64, 65). The particular popularity of the 'Burning Bush' can provisionally be associated with its popular acceptance as a defence against the elements – fire and thunder. The icon appears in the same aspect in the service dedicated to it, established in 1680 and celebrated on the 4 September – the day devoted to the Prophet Moses. When a new iconography of the 'Burning Bush', now filled with symbolic and allegorical details, appeared in the second half of the 17th century, it impelled the Old Believers to elucidate this subject more than any others.

The character of the questions and answers in one of the most widely disseminated Old Believer textbooks – the *Alphabetical Book on the Burning Bush,* which first appeared at the beginning of the 18th century – was effectively unchanged until the end of the 19th century. This *Alphabetical Book* provided a typical popular elucidation of the icon's symbols, with insignificant variants in different compendia. The question that had caused more arguments than any other, ever since Patriarch Nikon's time, read as follows: 'Wherefore is the Most Holy Mother of God depicted in glory, holding on her arm a child three years of age, while turning her face away from him, and clasping another child to her lap with her arms?' The image of an interior child, as the author–compiler explained, symbolized the birth of Christ from the Father, 'before all ages of the Mother of God'; while the child on her arm tells of the nativity of God the Father from a virgin. The three-year-old age of Christ symbolized the three persons of the Godhead.[73]

Often however explications of icons of the 'Burning Bush' and 'Sophia the Divine Wisdom' led only to warnings. In particular a 'Filippovite' author of the late 18th or early 19th century cautioned that, although these icons take their origin from the holy ecumenical councils, even in antiquity there were some icon painters who designed them according to their own sensuous ideas and lusts, and this of course increased the danger of confusion between a 'genuine' and a 'false' image.[74]

It is possible that the official ban on the icon of the Annunciation 'with God the Father, breathing forth from his mouth' was reflected in its unusual elucidation as the triumph of divine principles over the forces of Antichrist. Since the popular mentality was always watchful for the presence in an image of evil forces that might cause harm to the Mother of God, the greatest attention was focused on her. Thus the well towards which the Mother of God was going, and beside which she was receiving the Archangel's message, symbolized, according to one anonymous 18th-century author, 'the life of this world', while two eagles represented two angels: the red one was a guardian angel, the dark-blue one an angel of the Devil. The central figure in this explanatory system was that of a lion: 'and the lion beheld an enemy and roared at the pure maiden before the Annunciation and when it saw the angel of the Lord it lay down like a cat.'[75] In the same compendium the location of the image of the Mother of God behind the altar is explained by analogy with the apocryphas and spiritual songs: 'For before all the Most Holy Mother of God was brought in and set upon the altar.'[76] Georgiy Fedotov has noted that in the popular consciousness, the Mother of God 'lives' in her icon beyond the altar, and that this is an enduring concept in folk poetry. Both a worshipper and a hostile person are capable of locating the Mother of God on the image behind the altar: in a poem about the siege of the Solovki Monastery, one of the Tsar's commanders shoots into the church at the icon of the Mother of God: 'So did the commander wound God's Mother on the altar . . .'.[77]

The traditional Old Believer reliance on the *Stoglav*, and those traditions of Muscovite ancient ways that they particularly respected, could be sensed in other commentaries. Since the Synod decree of 21 May 1722 expressly forbade carved icons in churches, an anonymous Filippovite author of the time particularly specified the veneration of cast metal or carved wooden images, the more so since they were rejected by adherents of some other sects on the basis of a missive from the Patriarch Ioakim (1674), which maintained that the Holy Fathers 'had not commanded that icons should be carved on wood, in the round like real people'.[78] In this instance the entire theological argument came down to an assertion of the antiquity of such images, which could be found as far back as the low-relief figuration on the gates of Santa Sophia of Novgorod and of the great Dormition Cathedral in the Moscow Kremlin.[79]

Far greater arguments were provoked among the common people by questions as to whether the invisible heavenly powers could be represented: these were touched on in the resolutions of councils and in official explanatory texts of the 16th and 17th centuries. After the Great Moscow Council we can observe a stricter attitude in Church literature to 'historical truth' and to deviations from dogma. Thus the monk Yevfimiy responded sharply to the fact that icon painters depicted 'the Most Holy Mother of God in royal clothing and having wings', while John the Baptist was depicted with wings as if one of the angels. Although, as he said, the word 'angel' meant also 'messenger' and was appropriate to the Forerunner (Baptist), none the less his depiction with wings contradicted historical truth: in his lifetime he was not one possessing wings.[80] In opposition to this, the 'Priestless' explained the acceptability of representations of angels with reference to visions and apparitions: 'For angels are by nature bodiless, invisible, and they are spirits not circumscribed by place: in this they have a resemblance to their Creator'; they are depicted in their essence or by their apparition.[81] Hence they venerated the icon of John the Baptist the Angel of the Wilderness: on his death John was an angel and came down winged and proclaimed joy to all.[82]

Similar doubts were provoked by the question of representing God the Father. Though the 43rd chapter of the Great Moscow Council said that 'henceforth the image of the Lord Sabaoth is not to be depicted' and that God the Father had not been seen by anyone in the flesh, the ban soon came to be disregarded in the (official) New Ritualist Church (illus. 66 and see illus. 165). The frequency of the icon of God the Father showing the new symbols led to continual arguments among the Old Believers: this is confirmed by our discovery in the archives of duplicated material relating to the Old Believer congress of 1904 in the village of Gorodets. A certain Grigoriy Tokarev and a priest, Father Afanasiy, 'disturbed' the inhabitants of the village by casting doubt on the sanctity of cast copper folding icons made by the 'Shore Dwellers', on which was depicted the New Testament Trinity. We should remember that Old Ritualist copper icons had been cast since the first quarter of the 18th century at the 'Priestless' settlement on the River Vyg, and in the second half of the 18th century and throughout the 19th these served as matrices for casting various types of images for both 'Priestists' and 'Priestless' in the village of Guslitsy, near Moscow and elswhere.[83] For this reason their iconography scarcely changed, though (to judge from documents) it was periodically disputed.

The Gorodets congress included Old Believers from the provinces of Kostroma and Nizhniy Novgorod with Terentiy Khudoshin from Saratov presiding as spiritual father. In his short statement, the permissibility of

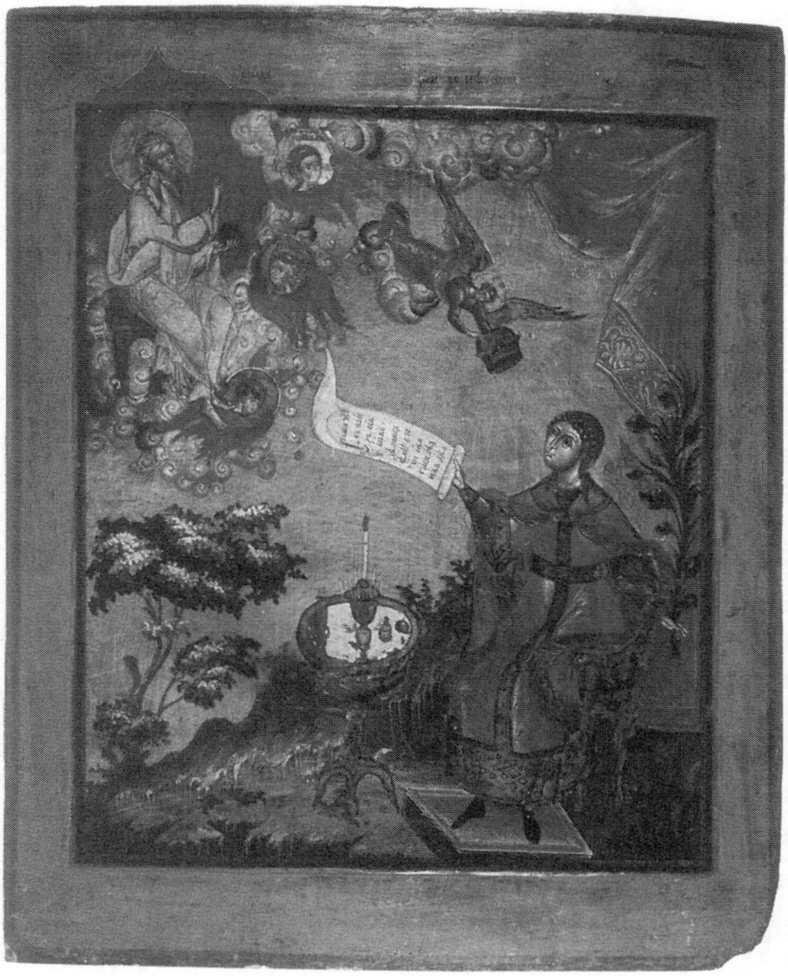

66. *The Heavenly Kingdom*, first half of the 19th century. State Museum of the History of Religion, St Petersburg.

representing God the Father was supported in traditional manner by the same arguments as Metropolitan Makariy had used in his dispute with Viskovatiy in the mid-16th century. Actually, no doubt to carry more conviction, only the sixth element of the 'Symbol of the Faith' was adduced in the village congress's resolution:

> We Christians of the shore-dweller congregation, inhabitants of the village of Gorodets, have assembled in the house of prayer and have debated the holy icons and their representation of the sacred image

> on cast copper icon-leaves and other holy icons – drawn in the understanding of the Symbol of Faith 'Ascending to the heavens and seated at the right hand of the Father'. Thus, so that henceforth none from our brotherhood should need to cogitate on this holy icon, this icon should be left immediately in the house of prayer in God's service and there should be no more argument henceforth. And any who may stir up dissensions and arguments on this holy icon should be expelled from the congregation, for the peace of the Church.[84]

As we analyze these various documents we may involuntarily recall the question of the incorporeity of angels raised in the period of Byzantine iconoclasm (726–843). The iconoclasts pronounced that the form of the angels cannot be delineated. In response, the Patriarch Nikiphoros declared that people represent the incorporeal angels because they passionately wish to behold them. Evidently, actualizations of the Old Testament desire to see God came to the surface more than once in history. It had its own peculiarities in Imperial Russia. The low level of the official theology of the icon could not help but strengthen the 'simple faith' within whose system the icon always occupied a special place.

The Synod's prohibitions were rarely equipped with theological reasoning, being almost wholly concerned with official confiscations and the destruction of Old Believer icons, which brought a quite new feature into both popular theology and the veneration of the image. We can conditionally name it a 'halo of martyrdom' around the Old Believer icon. After the Great Moscow Council, a vast number of icons carrying the old symbols were repainted. The motif of suffering and of innocent subjection to contumely, quite a complex one in the Russian experience, thus acquired additional profundity. The visual code that reflected and supported it began to include, as well as the traditional images of martyrs, a huge quantity of destroyed and repainted icons. The fact that popular consciousness attributed to these pictures not only miracles, but sufferings equal to Christ's own, emerges from the same dogmatic–theological compendia of the 18th and 19th centuries. It is not accidental that they are continually beset by the problem of whether icons that predated Patriarch Nikon could work miracles.

One of the anonymous 'Priestless' writers of the end of the 18th century significantly constructed his reply on a comparison of the graceless world of Imperial Russia with the whole remaining Christian world, including both the Second and the First Romes (in the second half of the 17th century, Deacon Fyodor, who enjoyed special respect among the Old Ritualists, had written on the same matter).[85] Living far away, he was unsure whether miracles came from icons for the 'perverted' (i.e., unbelieving) people in Rome, Tsargrad (Constantinople), Jerusalem and Russia itself. Admitting that in certain places there were wonder-working icons that had not been overpainted, he significantly attributed the 'halo of martyrdom' to all the ancient images in the land of Rus.[86]

This notion was strengthened by official decrees on the public burning of icons representing the first martyrs of Old Ritualist piety – which, incidentally, had its analogies in punishments *in effigie* (discussed on pages 113–14) at the time of the Reformation. Thus, at the instance of the Moscow investigatory office for schismatic affairs, the Synod approved a decision to burn an icon of the Archpriest Avvakum that was venerated by the Moscow Old Ritualists, at the same time specifying that before the conflagration the faces of Christ and angels should be scraped off the icon.[87]

The burning of Old Ritualist icons was mentally linked with the burning of Old Ritualist books as portrayed in miniatures of the 18th and 19th centuries. The manuscript 'Catalogue of the Library of the Old Ritualist Church' by Pavel Lyubopytny (1829) from Ye. V. Barsov's collection contains on the first page a miniature equipped with characteristic symbols: on a sacrificial altar is a disordered pile of Old Ritualist books with a flame nearby. Before the altar, standing on a crescent moon, is the Mother of God, towards whom a ray of light carrying the words 'The Gates of Hell shall not Prevail' reaches down from Heaven. The altar itself is inscribed 'Victory over Hell' (illus. 67).[88]

In this connection one can recall the *Tale of Our Hierarch Nikon* that was widely disseminated among the Old Believers in the 19th and early 20th centuries. The illustration 'Nikon Smashes the Holy Icons' accompanied the account by Paul of Aleppo of how Patriarch Nikon broke up Frankish icons by smashing them against the flagstones of the cathedral floor on the

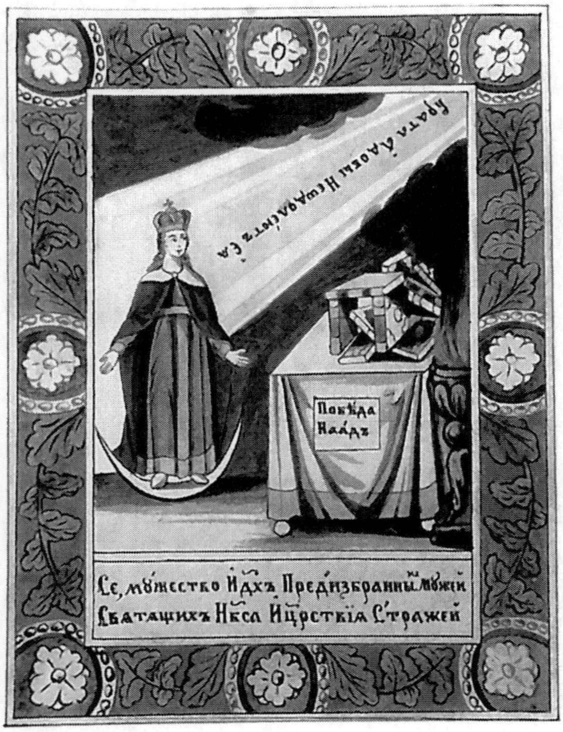

67. 'Mother of God', a miniature from Pavel Lyubopytny's *Catalogue of the Library of the Old Ritualist Church*, 1829. Russian State Library, Moscow.

Feast of the Triumph of Orthodoxy (illus. 68). The particular emotional tonality of these actual events was strengthened by the supposition of their prime significance in the rift between the Patriarch and Tsar Aleksey Mikhaylovich: 'Through these actions by Nikon, worthy of great horror, the Tsar and all the boyars began to grow cold towards Nikon.' In the context of outrages committed against icons there are depictions of an eight-pointed cross in place of an inner sole in Nikon's boot ('Nikonian feet'), of a Crucifixion image beneath Nikon's bed and so on.[89]

These pictures were amplified and elucidated in various kinds of manuscript texts. One tale whose presence could be to some extent perceived in the context of sufferings for the icon as the main symbol of the old faith was 'And which Holy Names who have Suffered for Icons', included in the anti-heretical volume of S. F Mokhovikov. But the imagination might be stirred even more strongly by handcrafted popular prints (*lubki*) of horrifying scenes of executions. Two such prints, entitled *The Terrible Execution of Captain Vasiliy Levin for Making the Sign of the Cross and for the Ancient Tradition* (illus. 69) and *The Execution of Colonel Nemchinov*, were inserted as an addendum into an illustrated copy of the 'Tale of Our Hierarch Nikon' from F. A. Kalinkin's collection. Extensive writings bear witness to the fact that the persons illustrated were ascribed the status of modern martyrs. The first picture carries the inscription: 'In 1722 in Petersburg there took place the terrible execution of Captain Vasiliy Levin, who underwent terrible insupportable sufferings in extreme old age for not accepting *the new books and new icons* and for being a supporter of the two-fingered sign of the Cross, and a propagator of holy antiquity' (my italics). The second miniature is elucidated by a story of how in Tobolsk in 1722 Colonel Nemchinov, when

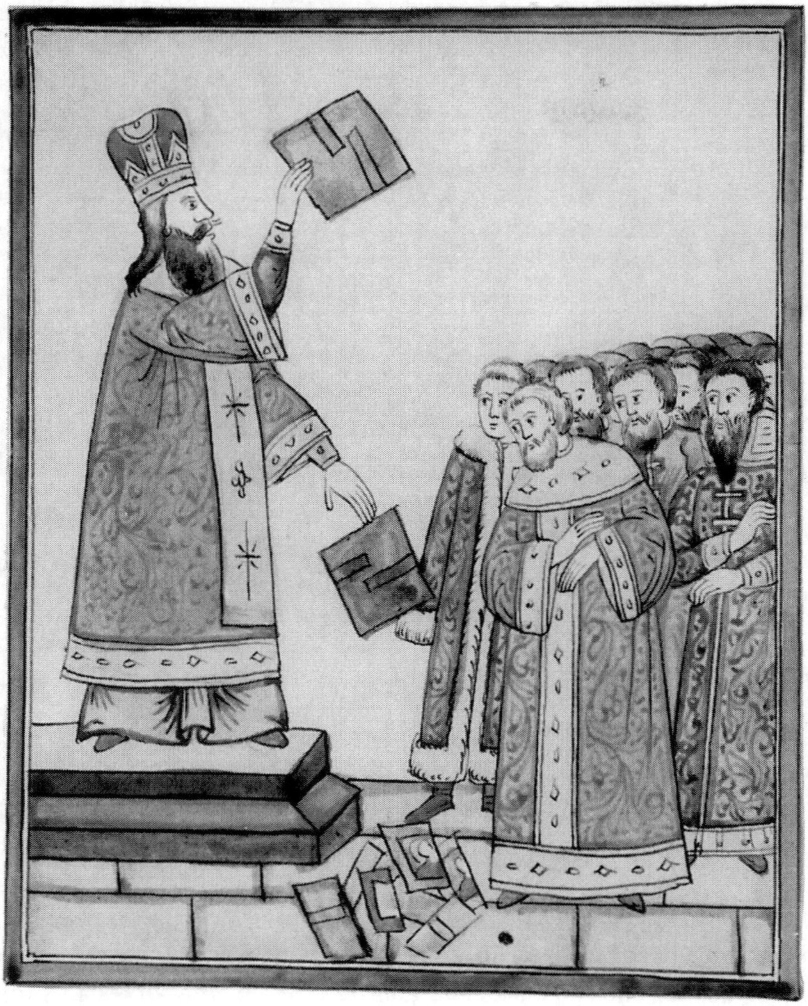

68. 'Nikon Smashes the Holy Icons on the Flagstones of the Church Floor', a miniature from *The Tale of our Hierarch Nikon*, early 20th century. Library of the Academy of Sciences, St Petersburg.

presenting himself to make the oath of allegiance, would not renounce the two-fingered sign of the Cross. 'For this they cut off Nemchinov's head, and his body was stuck on stakes in various places so as to frighten others. This has been copied from the archive of the Preobrazhensky office of the secret chancellery.'[90] The well-known picture 'Depiction of the Vengeance Wrought by the Officer Meshcherinov on the Participants in the Solovki Rebellion of 1668–1676'[91] can be put in the same category.

Here we can recall how motifs of martyrdom in post-Tridentine Catholic

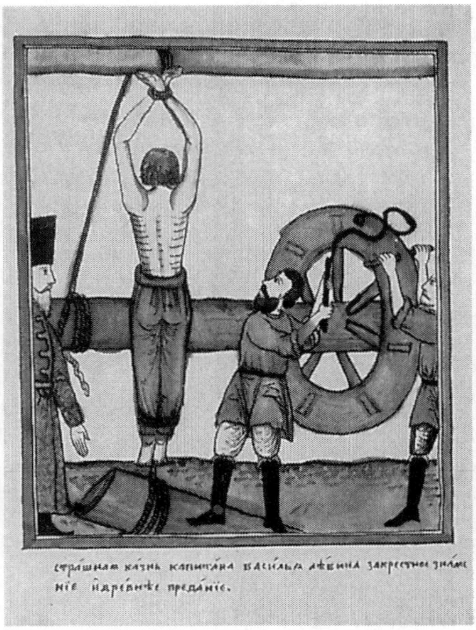

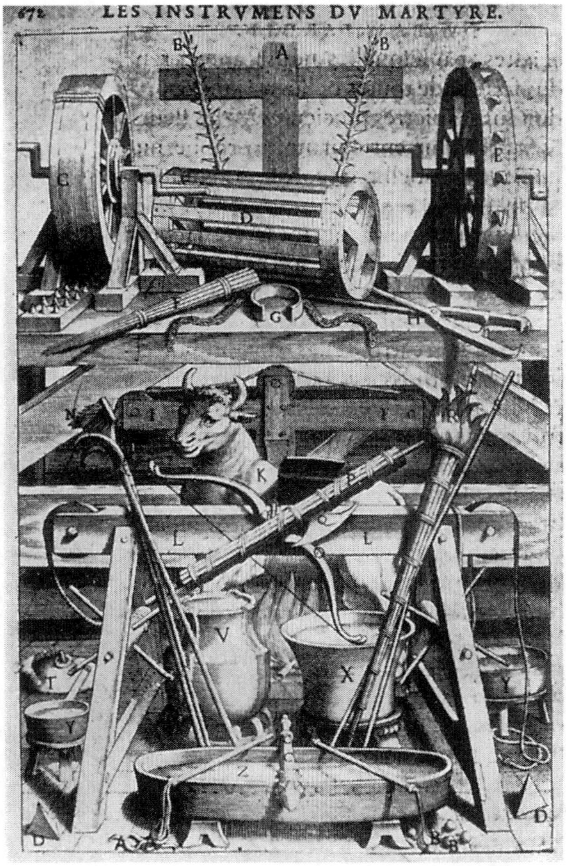

69. *The Terrible Execution of Captain Vasiliy Levin for Making the Sign of the Cross and for the Ancient Tradition*, early 20th century, drawing. Library of the Academy of Sciences, St Petersburg.

70. *Instruments of Martyrdom*, late 16th century or early 17th, engraving.

iconography were realized in connection with the heightened cult of Christian saints and in response to their rejection by the Protestants (illus. 70).[92] From the second half of the 16th century this iconography began actively to penetrate into the world of Eastern Christianity, where it found 'favourable soil' in connexion with the Orthodox resistance to Islam. In the Balkans icons began to be painted, Lives to be written and churches to be dedicated in honour of such recent martyrs to the faith as St John the New and Nikola the New. The former had been burnt alive in Sofia on 11 February 1515 for refusing an Ottoman judge's command that he renounce Christianity; the latter had been condemned to death by stoning, also in Sofia, in 1555 for refusing to convert to Islam. Balkan painting of the 17th to

19th centuries gave particular prominence (in comparison with Russia) to such subjects as 'The Forty Martyrs of Sebaste' and to the Life of St Haralambos, with illustrations of his torments. Similarly in Bulgarian icon painting of the 19th century, we encounter the holy warrior St Menas on horseback with scenes of martyrdom to which the icon of the holy warriors George, Theodoros, Eustaphios and Dimitrios, combating various evil forces, is appended.

Of the peculiar tonalities that characterize these apparently similar themes, the plight of the modern Russian Old Believer martyrs seems perhaps the hardest of all, since their sufferings were wrought not by 'outsiders', but by Russians. The linked Muscovite concepts of sacredness and of ethno-cultural space were converted in Imperial Russia into an acute polarization of religious experience. The icon and 'the world' had entered into a complex relationship, that shows us the excessively fractured rhythms of a whole massive layer of consciousness and culture. In the face of eternal damnation there always lurked in 'the world' a sense of uncertainty and disquiet.

PART TWO

The Icon and Popular Culture

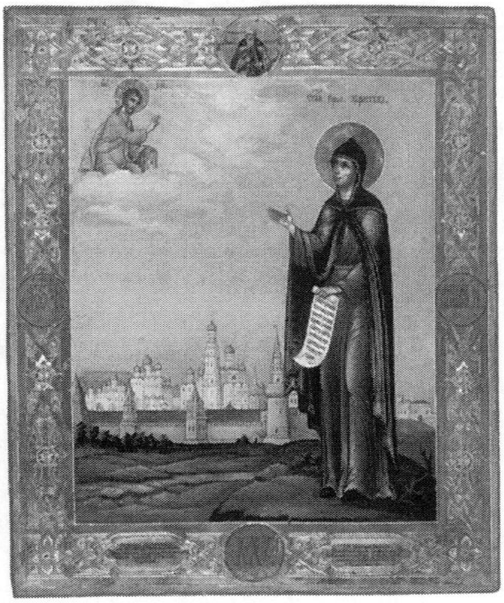

An icon can be of high or not-so-high quality, but a genuine apprehension of otherworldliness, a genuine spiritual experience invariably constitutes its foundation.
Pavel Florensky[1]

Previous page: 71. I. Pankryshev, *St Paraskeva*, 1889, Mstyora. State Museum of the History of Religion, St Petersburg.

At all periods the collective practice of religion has demanded a corresponding system of understanding and communication. We have already attempted to demonstrate how this dependence manifests itself not only in the area of the norms of devotion. Both devotion and icons were bound up with historically well-defined signs, with a special type of Orthodox vocabulary. As we shall show, in modern times the communicative function of religious images was much complicated as a result of cultural experiences. If subjective religious experience revealed a tendency to become delimited and individualized, culture at the same period showed exactly the opposite tendency – a striving for unity and an urge to understand the self as part of a whole. It is the artistic language of the post-medieval Russian icon that can tell us how these two tendencies could nonetheless make contact.

The existence in Imperial Russia of a great number of different iconic types speaks not only of the complexity of the Russian religious experience, but also of the development of the art of the icon at this period primarily on the level of lower, popular craft culture. From the second half of the 16th century the aim of the official Orthodox and Catholic churches to strengthen popular religiosity coincided with the demarcation and broadening of the sphere of mass religious art. The formerly integrated religious artistic culture began gradually to become stratified into areas of official and lower, mass art. General processes of secularization and the strengthening of the popular impulse in the socio-political and cultural life of society created an ideological foundation for the flourishing of the lower forms of religious art both in the Catholic West and the Orthodox East.

P. P. Muratov once wrote: 'In its sense of style Russian painting holds a leading place among other kinds of art. In each of its types as well as high achievements there are poor and mediocre objects that come close to being mere craftwork. But it is a matter for deep amazement that even these poor and mediocre objects do not depart from the general style of the type as a whole. We cannot encounter such stylistic strength either in modern art or even in that of the Renaissance.'[2] By singling out the 'stylistic strength' of 'poor' craft icons, Muratov noted an aspect of a many sided and complex totality that was important, but not the most important one. The chief internal impulse towards expression of form on the craft level of culture consisted in precisely the opposite principle, that of the continual instability and erosion of the boundaries of this very 'stylistic strength'.

P. G. Bogatyryov and Roman Jakobson also drew attention to the universality of the laws governing the poetics of popular craft art. Noting the folkloric role of the 'debased cultural store' (*gesunkenes Kulturgut*) established by German ethnographers, they upheld the concept of the 'perpetual interaction between so-called 'high' art and the art of the people'.[3] In this context, B. R. Vipper's observations (made in the 1930s) on the formation of local national styles through the interaction of genetically diverse forms of art are particularly useful. Vipper described complex 'low-level' phenomena with the help of the concept of 'rusticalization': this would usually appear when traditions and elements of style migrated either from one nation to another, of from one to another social group; it was just in such situations that forms of art would always be generalized and simplified, their typical features enhanced.[4]

Thereafter, the concept of the appearance at the beginning of the modern period of a 'marginal' artistic stratum and the fluctuating nature of its boundaries were investigated in a whole series of Russian language studies, which considerably widened and concretized the evolution of its artistic structure and the imminent laws that governed the forms it took. With this in mind the conditional term of 'the primitive' was brought into scholarly use for this stratum.[5] The phenomena relating to it were a kind of materialized boundary, a relationship between high art and folkore.

The 'stylistic strength' that Muratov noted was linked with the religious function of the icon. However, the universal laws governing the forms that the craftsman gave an icon were superior to mere subjective religiosity. At 'marginal' levels artistic forms could 'freeze up' and 'harden', but they were also continually on the move: at this point there took place both a 'lowering' and a 'primitivization' of the models of high art and equally an interaction with folk art. The master craftsman was not just a copyist but also showed himself to be a kind of creator of forms: 'the transformation of work belonging to so-called monumental art into the so-called primitive is also a creative act. A creative approach is manifest here both in the selection of the work that is appropriated and in its adaptation to other kinds of techniques.'[6] Hence we can speak of the attachment of the ordinary craftsman's artistic consciousness to the intellectual background of his epoch and of the predominant influence of one or another type of culture upon him.

Significant attention has been paid by modern scholars to questions of the poetics of Mannerism and the 'low-level Baroque', and scholarly concepts such as 'the primitive', the 'vernacular' and 'popular Mannerism', have been derived from analyzing structurally complex low-level artistic forms.[7] It is a matter of deeply encoded categories of popular artistic consciousness, allowing us to tease out links and parallels with apparently long-gone periods of cultural history. In this context the well-known proposition of Arnold Hauser that the 16th century is closer in spirit to our own times than to all succeeding centuries remains relevant.[8]

As we all know, classic Mannerism of the 16th century in Europe preceded Baroque art. Historians have made it into a defined period and given it a variety of names. Mannerism was an art of the upper elite, with a tendency towards high finish, perfection of form and intellectualism. The term *maniera*, according to John Shearman, presupposed stylization and a rupture with naturalism: art – so the Mannerists believed – should serve the cause of correcting nature.[9] Incidentally, arising as it did at the end of the Middle Ages, Mannerism opened up rules for the creation of forms that have largely corresponded to the peculiarities of artistic thinking in the modern period generally – more precisely, the artistic thinking of lower social strata and groupings. 'Play' with traditional forms and appreciation of ancient art in its mythologizing aspect seemed to resonate with the formal features of popular craft art and lower-level modifications of high art; all these phenomena permit scholars to attach the concept 'Mannerism' to them, although, of course, more in a metaphorical than a precise sense. Mannerism was a style open on all sides, including 'unofficial' popular culture. Moreover one can cautiously say that at a certain stage the principles of Mannerism met and intertwined with the artistic principles of the Baroque, which was much assisted by the latter's inclination toward 'mass culture', towards the popularization of its religious and aesthetic ideas. Hence in the low level normative poetics of the 17th century to the 19th, we can observe the most unexpected and paradoxical transformations of, for example, such very important categories of Mannerist and Baroque artistic thinking as ornament and frame (illus. 72, 73). In this connexion I. A. Golyshev (1838–96), a specialist in Russian popular culture, significantly commented on the subject of popular miniatures in Russian synodics of the 17th century, that 'in frames, ornaments and individual letters we may note a strong loyalty to assiduous execution, showing that total enthusiasm and effort, sparing neither time nor labour, was applied to this craft'.[10] In other words, *ornament* and *frame* were transformed into deeply encoded categories of the artistic consciousness of the popular craftsman. His work, both from the point of view of what it borrowed and its general inclination toward quotation, displayed itself primarily in *ornamentalism*; it was toward this that his 'enthusiasm' was primarily attracted, a sort of 'ornamentalism' of his habit of thought.[11]

72. *Nativity of Christ*, first half of the 19th century. Kolomenskoye Historical and Architectural Museum-Preserve, Moscow.

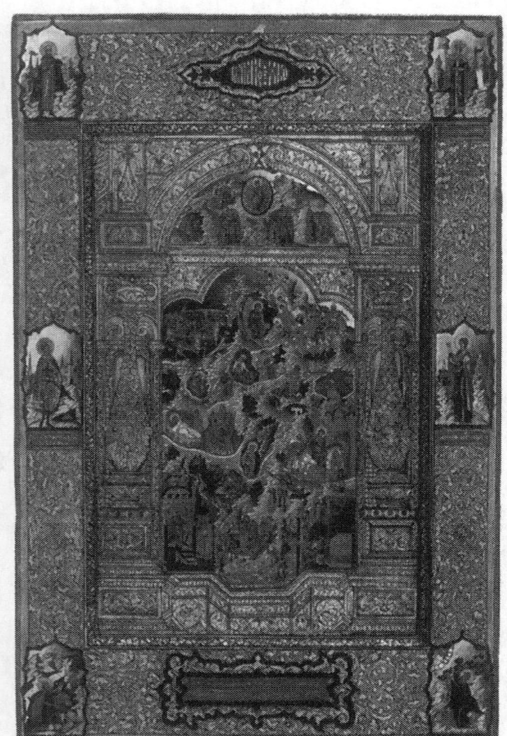

At the same time one must also take into account that Muscovite Rus, which transformed itself at the beginning of the 18th century into Imperial Russia, was a special kind of cultural–historical space in comparison with Western Europe. Here the absence of 'classical' Renaissance forms, and the longer process of the division of culture into a learned and a lowly sphere, conditioned the acquisition of Mannerist

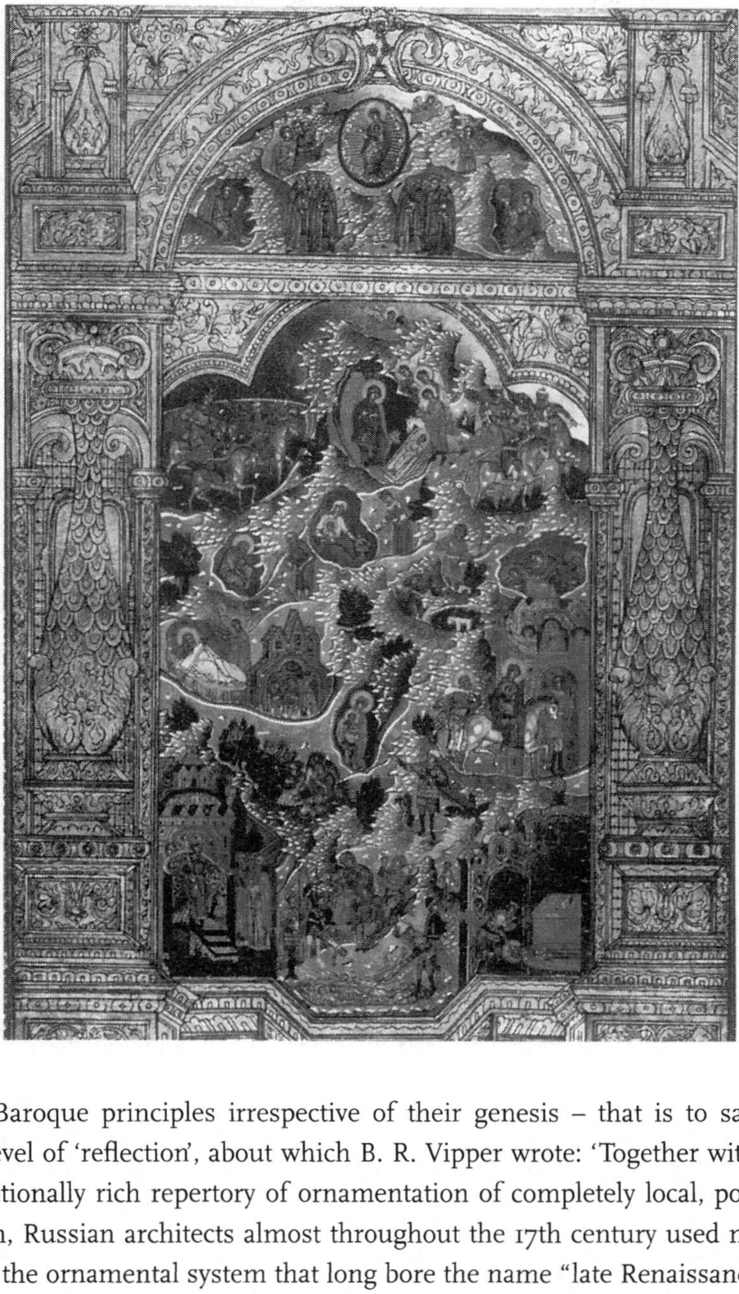

73. Detail of illus. 72.

and Baroque principles irrespective of their genesis – that is to say, on the level of 'reflection', about which B. R. Vipper wrote: 'Together with the exceptionally rich repertory of ornamentation of completely local, popular origin, Russian architects almost throughout the 17th century used motifs from the ornamental system that long bore the name "late Renaissance" or "Northern Renaissance", and which nowadays is usually related to the Mannerist style'.[12] In the process of their adoption, these form-creating principles acquired a particular semantic colouring. This relates to what was nationally specific about making a new picture of the world, about the appearance of a new attitude towards the human being, the growing role of secular art, and, finally, to a longer development of the medieval artistic tradition, of which Old Believer icon production was part.

Popular craft icon painting of the 18th century through to the early 20th presents us with a huge corpus of material, remarkably complex in its artistic language and structure of religious feeling. So as to get an overview of this material from the viewpoint of the internal mechanisms of popular culture, it has been conditionally divided into three groups. In the first are the 'Frankish' and 'painterly' icons that most closely correspond to the devotion of the new ritual. Their mixed artistic language and active violation of the canon allow the formative mechanisms of low-level craft products to be most clearly observed. The second group contains traditional, mostly Old Believer, icon painting, in which we observe loyalty to the medieval canon and the development of the post-Byzantine tradition right up to the beginning of the 20th century. The third group contains the cheap Suzdalian 'commercial' icons for the common people, so-called 'primitives'. These allow us not only to trace the interaction of tradition with folk art, but also to glimpse the predispositions of Russian piety overall – that is, the 'experience' of which Florensky also wrote. From this point of view it is significant that the sign system of the icon penetrated the sign system of Russian popular culture as a whole; the over-abundant saturation of the Russian cultural–historical space with icons and the special role of icons in popular devotion could not help but manifest themselves on the level of the forms created in mass secular art: that is, on the plane of the popular craftsman's stereotypal artistic thinking.

CHAPTER FOUR

East and West

The 'Frankish' and 'painterly' icons of the 18th, 19th and early 20th centuries include many transitional types and variants influenced by phenomena that had been appearing in Russian court art since the mid-17th century, when Western art began to influence Russian icon painting. Craftsmen always relied on a conspectus of source material for their ideas and compositions, as V. P. Bezobrazov discovered in Safonov's Palekh workshop in 1861, where 'one can find systematic collections of pictures in various styles and a store of classic foreign works on the subject of painting'.[1] In the archives of the Safonov workshop, still located in Palekh, are interesting exemplars that Palekh icon painters used in the second half of the 19th century and the early 20th. There are individual prints from various editions of the Bible, including Piscator's (1650, 1674), Weigel's (1680) and Schnorr's (1850s); reproductions of works by Italian and Northern Renaissance masters – Michelangelo, Leonardo, Raphael, Cranach, etc. – torn from illustrated books and from the journals *Starye gody*, *Apollon* and *Zolotoye runo*. Photographs and reproductions of 19th-century Western religious painting by F. Ittenbach, G. Sinkel, A. Noak, E. Gebhardt, A. Schaeffer, E. Bendemann and G. Pfanschmidt comprised a special category (illus. 74, 75). Not only Western, but Russian academic models were frequently copied, from reproductions of the wall paintings (mid-19th century) in the Cathedral of Christ the Saviour in Moscow, to Lazovsky's album containing photographs of wall paintings and icons by V. M. Vasnetsov and M. V. Nesterov (1880s) in the St Vladimir Cathedral, Kiev. In the archives of the Belousov workshop there are numerous

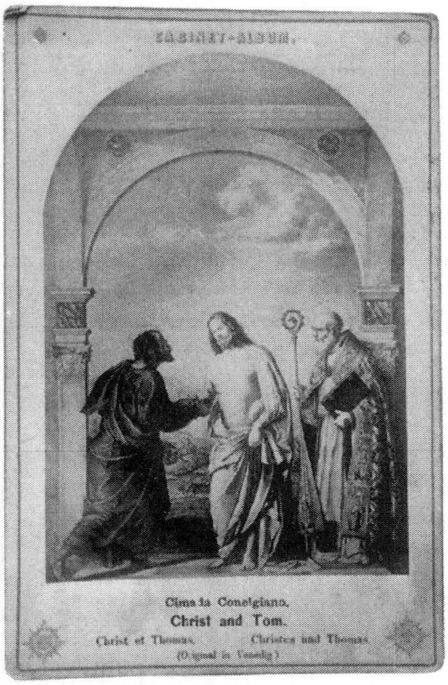

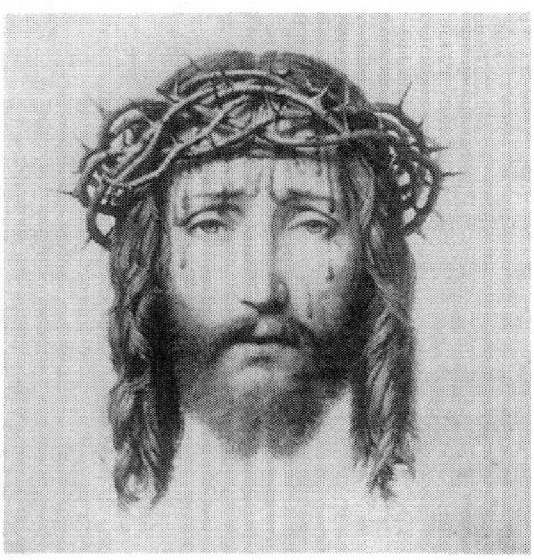

74. C. Conegliano, *Christ with St Thomas*. Exemplary photograph from N. M. Safonov's icon-painting workshop in Palekh. Archive of L. Bakanov, Palekh.

75. F. Ittenbach, *St Veronica's Veil*. Exemplary photograph from N. M. Safonov's icon-painting workshop in Palekh. Archive of L. Bakanov, Palekh.

photographs of icons by P. M. Sokolov and other academicians whose paintings – judging by later Palekh icons – were particularly valued and carefully copied (illus. 76). Finally, Russian and Western examples of ornament formed a special category. Well-known publications of these by G. Gagarin (1887), F. Solntsev (1849–53), V. Stasov (1872–87), V. Butovsky (1873) and N. Simakov (1882) were joined by German journals such as *Dekorative Vorbilder* and illustrated pages in the series *Ornamentenschatz. Vorlage* and *Vorlagen für Ornament-malerei. Motive aller Stylarten von der Antike bis zur neuesten Zeit.*

It is important to add that analogies to examples of this kind are easily found in the Balkan lands, underlining the universality of the principles governing the forms of modern Orthodox icon painting. Consider the sources of the famous 19th-century Bulgarian icon painter Zakhariy Zograf, who carefully put together his own book of exemplars, glueing into it prints after paintings by Raphael, Dürer, Rubens, Cranach and Rembrandt, as well as original prints and copies by Jacques Callot, Lebrun, Jan Breughel, Salvator Rosa and many other Italian, French, Dutch and German artists.[2]

All these examples tell us about the lively transference into Orthodox iconic space of Western Catholic and Protestant imagery; the popular craftsmen of the 18th and 19th centuries unknowingly copied Mannerist rules. Jacques Bousquet aptly called Mannerism 'a market-place of permissiveness', Max Dvořák 'a conception of all-embracing limitlessness',[3] while John Shearman described it as a style 'knowing no bounds, for the ideas constituting its basis are almost all ideas from other ages, only taken to their limits'.[4] Even so, later craft culture simplified, translated and transformed the Mannerist symbolism it inherited.

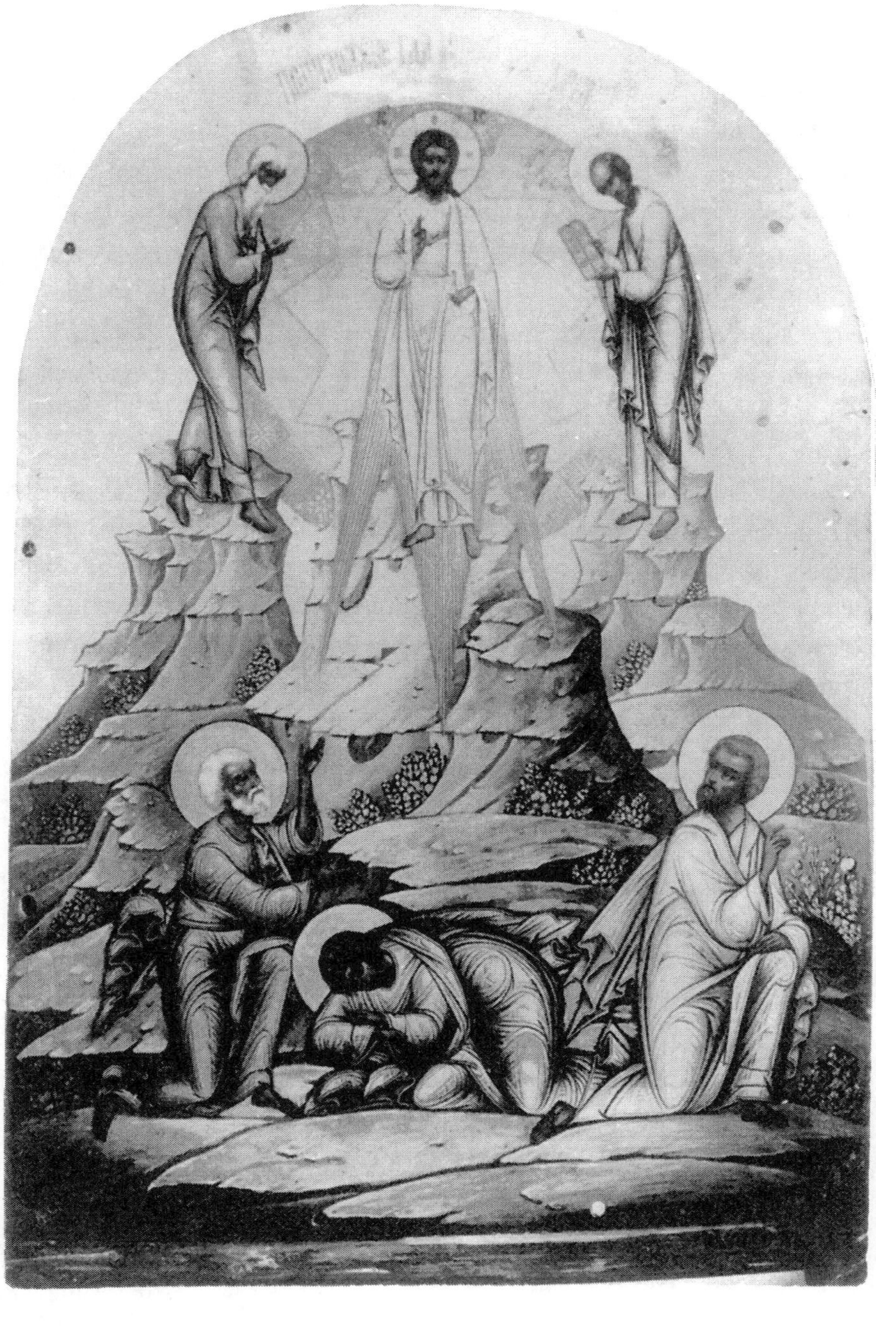

76. P. M. Sokolov, *Transfiguration*, 1900. Photograph from the archive of the Belousov workshop in Palekh. Author's archive, Moscow.

In the field of religious art, both the Council of Trent in the West and the *Stoglav* Council in Muscovite Rus put didactic tasks first, as was demanded in an 'age of heretics' – a time of exceptional religious agitation and the intensification of confessional clashes. The decrees of the Councils reflected (as I have noted before) the search for ways of renewing and strengthening Church life in the face of the Lutheran threat. These decrees particularly reflected the peculiarities of Catholic and Orthodox concepts of the icon too.

The strengthening of the soteriological significance of the prayer image in 'post-Tridentine' Catholic piety took place in the context of a different world outlook from that of Muscovy. In the West the process clearly took place in parallel with the continuing development of the tradition of scholasticism, which presupposed the apprehension of God first of all through reason. The Mannerist and Baroque Catholic image, relying on individual religious experiences and feelings, always found itself as if overshadowed by the objective of rationalistic explanation of divine authenticity, which had been elevated to a dogma at the Council of Trent. The image was orientated towards rhetoric rather than metaphysics. The latter strengthened an already strict policing of religious painting: this led to a renewed scrutiny of certain elements of its artistic structure, based on a reworking of the idea of personal revelation. However, prayer images continued to be regarded in traditional manner as 'decorations for churches' or 'Bibles for simple people', since (from the point of view of traditional Orthodox theology) the dogmatic basis of their interpretation – *filioque* as the point of departure from Catholic trinitarian doctrine – persisted. According to this, the Holy Spirit is sent into the world by the Father and the Son; for that reason, even within the Trinity itself the Holy Spirit (as hypostasis) issues from the Father and the Son. Hence, according to Catholic trinitarian doctrine, the plan of the divine economy had been shifted onto the temporal plane of inter-trinitarian existence. As various scholars have shown, this involved a reduction in the significance of the icon in the matter of the sanctification of humanity on its path towards apprehension of the Divinity: God is rather to be apprehended through reason.

Hence Catholic art of the 16th and 17th centuries in its struggle with Protestant ideas followed in the wake of theology, which opened up new meaningful possibilities in it. Art defended mysteries, and first of all the mystery of the eucharist and penitence: the Last Supper of the apostles and the penitent saints Peter and Mary Magdalene become the subject of a huge number of religious pictures. It also defended the Church of Rome and the cult of saints: the throne of St Peter, the image of the Virgin Mary and numerous scenes of martyrs for the faith, who had suffered for their loyalty to Catholic Rome in England, Germany, Asia, Africa and America, became its favourite themes. Catholic art became saturated with a special emotional agitation, in thrall to apocalyptic inclinations and motifs: at particular moments the collective religiosity was concentrated on the theme of the Last Judgment. Finally, it was theology that impelled artists to address themselves again and again to images of the Holy Family, St Joseph and the Guardian Angel.[5]

In Muscovite Rus, partly in response to Protestant teachings, the prayer image acquired a fundamental historic 'mission', based on both the Byzantine theory of the icon and on the pattern of state–Church relations: the icon was brought into the construction of a 'tsardom' of special charisma. Because of its sanctificatory impulse, the prayer image was destined not only to 'reflect' sacred history, as in the West, but also actively to influence and to change historical reality. The absence in this context of a developed tradition of scholastic theology ensured that from that period onwards it was precisely within the icon that the contemplative work of the Russian religious consciousness was undertaken with greater vigour than ever. This was at once reflected in the mobility and liveliness of prayer-image iconography of the mid-16th century to 17th, and particularly in its reworking of a whole complex of Western ideas and motifs sharing a common significance with Roman Catholicism. An abundance of new hagiological icons of saints appeared. In small images that would fit a lectern, painters begin energetically to develop an eschatological and ecclesiological thematics in which the basic dogmas of Christianity were to be newly illuminated. The 'pictorial scholasticism' in which

77. S. Pulzone, *'Immaculata' Virgin, Angels, Saints and Donor*, last quarter of the 16th century.

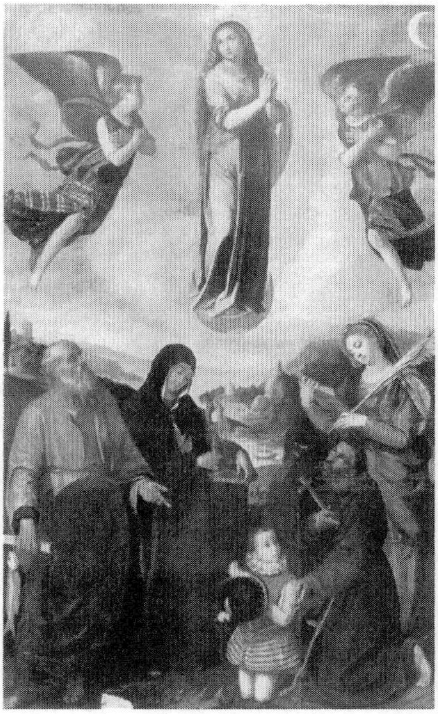

Viskovatiy had rightly seen the influence of 'Latin sophistication' – though he was condemned by the Metropolitan Makariy and his followers as an 'enemy' of the Greek tradition – is here communicated as Orthodox iconography. We should remember that in the mid-16th century, craftsmen from Pskov and Novgorod were making new icons for the domestic church of the Russian Tsar: the Annunciation Cathedral of the Moscow Kremlin. They seem to have been responsible for scenes that have in common an affirmation of the New Testament Church: 'The Trinity in Deeds', 'The Restoration of the Church of the Resurrection' (i.e., the Holy Sepulchre in Jerusalem) and 'The Elevation of the Cross of Our Lord'; the eschatological theme was expressed in the icon 'The Last Judgment according to the Vision and Prophecy of Daniel'; other subjects included 'I Believe', 'Praise the Lord in the Heavens', 'Sophia the Wisdom of God', 'Thou Art Forever the Priest in the Line of Melchisedek', 'In Thee Rejoiceth', 'What shall We bring Thee, O Christ', and others; finally, the well-known 'Four-part' icon (see illus. 166), in which scholars have often noted borrowings from Western iconography.[6] The development of this subject matter, and particularly the 'Four-Part' icon, testified simultaneously to a qualitatively new approach to the spiritual content of the prayer image, which now began to be considered not only as a reflection of the divine archetype, but even more as an explication of theological constructs. F. I. Buslayev called the new 16th-century icons 'theologically didactic', while N. P. Kondakov considered their thematic development in Suzdalian icon painting of the 18th and 19th centuries to be 'the historical input of the Russian common people into the art of Christianity'.[7]

With this as background, it is essential again to emphasize that the widening – both in the West and in Rus – of the sphere of popular craft art actively promoted complex iconographic displacements and stylistic influences. Soon after the Council of Trent, a new type of Catholic painting appeared in the West: *Arte Sacra*. Its spiritual content and intellectual conception are usually linked by scholars with the ideas of the Jesuits, and in particular with the 'Spiritual Exercises' of St Ignatius Loyola. Just as with a small prayer icon in Muscovite Rus, an enormous quantity of religious images on the pictorial model of *Arte Sacra* are reproduced before and after 1600. Their huge circulation (like, incidentally, the mass distribution of

Catholic and Protestant prints) 'washed away' the confessional boundaries of cultures: a strong tendency to mutual influence emerged. One of the chief compositional elements of *Arte Sacra* pictures was an image of the kneeling donor located in its sacral space (something that had also been encountered earlier in Western art). The same can also be observed in Catholic and Protestant funerary images, on which we can often observe one or several kneeling human figures, represented in prayer before a depiction of the Crucifixion.[8]

In Muscovite Russia this and other motifs would be reworked within the framework of the icon-painters'canon: 'Eastern' and 'Western' would be in unstable equilibrium. The representation of the kneeling donor, already familiar from the Byzantine tradition, would receive a particular emotional content and meaning in the new Orthodox iconography under the influence of the general thought patterns of the age.

A multitude of new iconographic types depicting lay people or saints kneeling in front of the Mother of God or Christ appear at the end of the 16th century and continue into the 17th: this is simultaneously assisted by the development of themes of visions and miracles, the genre of saints' lives, and particularly themes concerning the Mother of God, all common to Orthodoxy and Catholicism. Hence, in the image called 'Unexpected Joy', for example, we see a repentant robber prostrate before a wonder-working icon of the Mother of God (see illus. 201); or we see crowds of suffering lay people in icons of the Mother of God as 'life-giving Spring'; or on 17th-century icons of the 'Saviour Enthroned', saints Zosima and Savvatiy of Solovki, prostrate at the foot of the throne, begin to be depicted. We may guess that the iconography of Mary as the 'Mother of God of the Sun' and 'Joy of All who Suffer' (after 1688) was partly inspired by Catholic iconography of the Virgin 'Immaculata' in allegories of the Immaculate Conception, as worked out in Western painting in the 16th centuryto the first half of the 17th, that is, long before this dogma received the official sanction of the Roman Catholic church (as mentioned in chapter One) in 1854 (illus. 77, 78, 79). Spanish and Italian artists depicted the Virgin standing on clouds, the moon or the terrestrial sphere (signifying worldly transitoriness trampled beneath her feet), with hands joined in prayer, sometimes accompanied by an angel or one or more figures kneeling before

78. *Mother of God of the Sun with Prototypes*, 18th century. Kolomenskoye Historical and Architectural Museum-Preserve, Moscow.

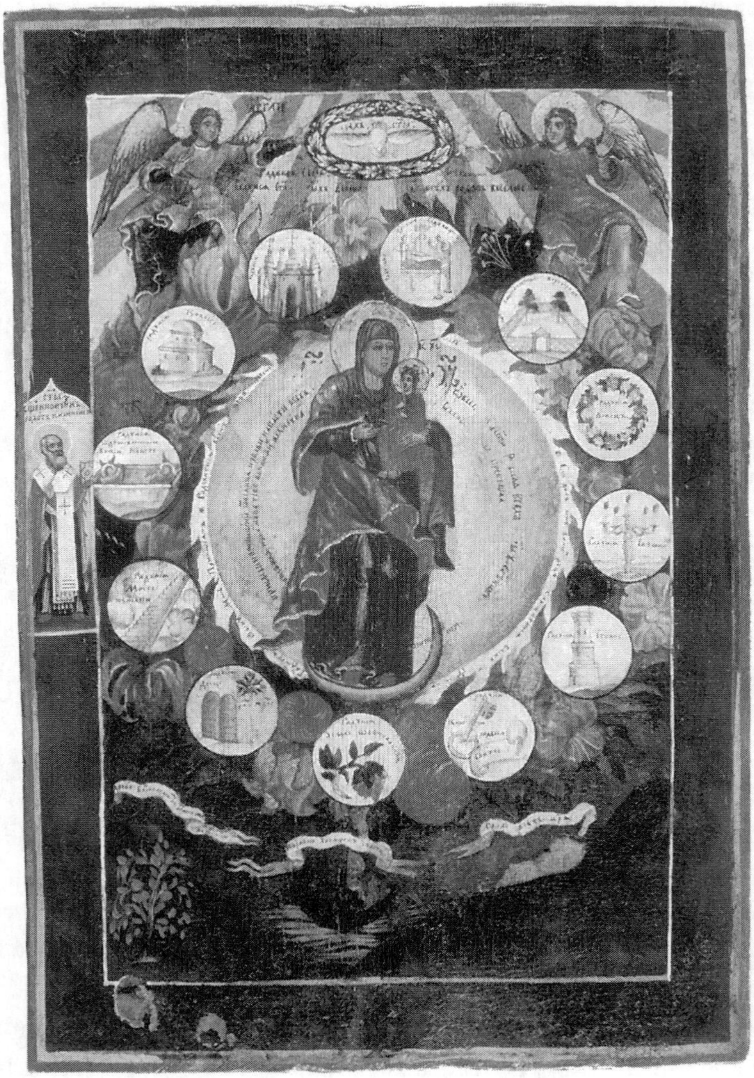

her. The evolution of the canonical iconic type of the Mother of God as 'Joy of All who Suffer' can be followed in an early-18th-century icon from the Kolomenskoye Museum, Moscow: the icon is gradually transformed into a characteristic Western-style image on a religious theme (illus. 79, 80).

In the 18th and 19th centuries, when the medieval canon was finally destroyed in official icon painting, Catholic and Protestant iconographies were already openly being quoted. A clear example of this is the icon of the 'Adoration of the Magi', by the Tver painter Maksim Kultepin, where we find the concept of the Nativity that developed in 'post-Tridentine' religious art (illus. 81). In the Middle Ages attention was focused on conveying the unity of the Holy Family, on the quiet, unnoticed arrival of Christ in the world; by contrast, as the modern age dawned, emotional tension and subtlety were transferred to the moment when Christ is first recognized by humanity: that is to say that the scene of the Nativity is merged with that of the Adoration of the Magi.[9] In acknowledgement of this merging, the late-medieval Orthodox iconography of the Nativity disappeared under the influence of Western art: the Nativity came to be shown as the Adoration of the Magi.[10]

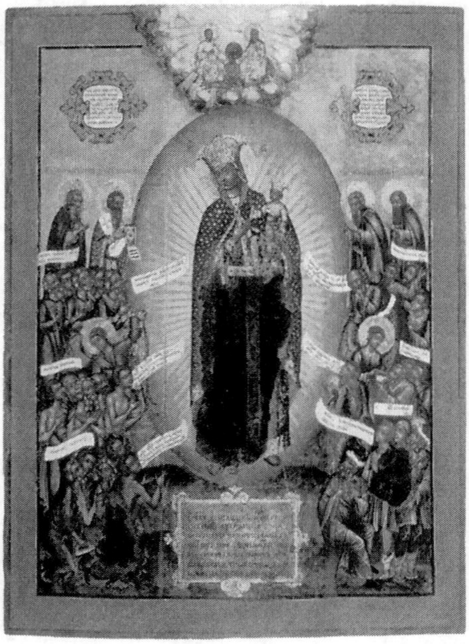

79. *Mother of God, Joy of All who Suffer*, early 18th century. State Tretyakov Gallery, Moscow.

At the same time a whole series of iconographic subjects appeared that are variants of Western European imagery: the 'Veneration of the Mother of God', the 'Prayer over the Chalice', the image of Christ in blessing with a sphere (the Catholic 'Salvator Mundi', 'Saviour of the World'), iconic variants of Raphael's pictures of *The Madonna Enthroned* and *The Archangel Michael* (see illus. 125); Guido Reni's *Christ Wearing the Crown of Thorns* and *The Archangel Michael*; copies of German, French and Italian 19th-century painting (individual examples of which I mentioned earlier); and many others too.

In Russian art of the 17th to 19th centuries the *dark background* also appears. This background, combined with scenes of martyrdom and miracles, is a semiotic indication of Catholic *Arte Sacra* painting;[11] it is often encountered in Western funerary works. As well as the strengthening of a visionary effect in the painting, this blackness as a sign of death, of 'nothingness', strengthened the dramatic quality of the sufferings of Christian martyrs in Catholic religious painting.[12] The appearance of a dark background on icons by the royal painters of the Armoury workshop under Tsar Aleksey Mikhaylovich essentially bore the same semiotic load. A grey

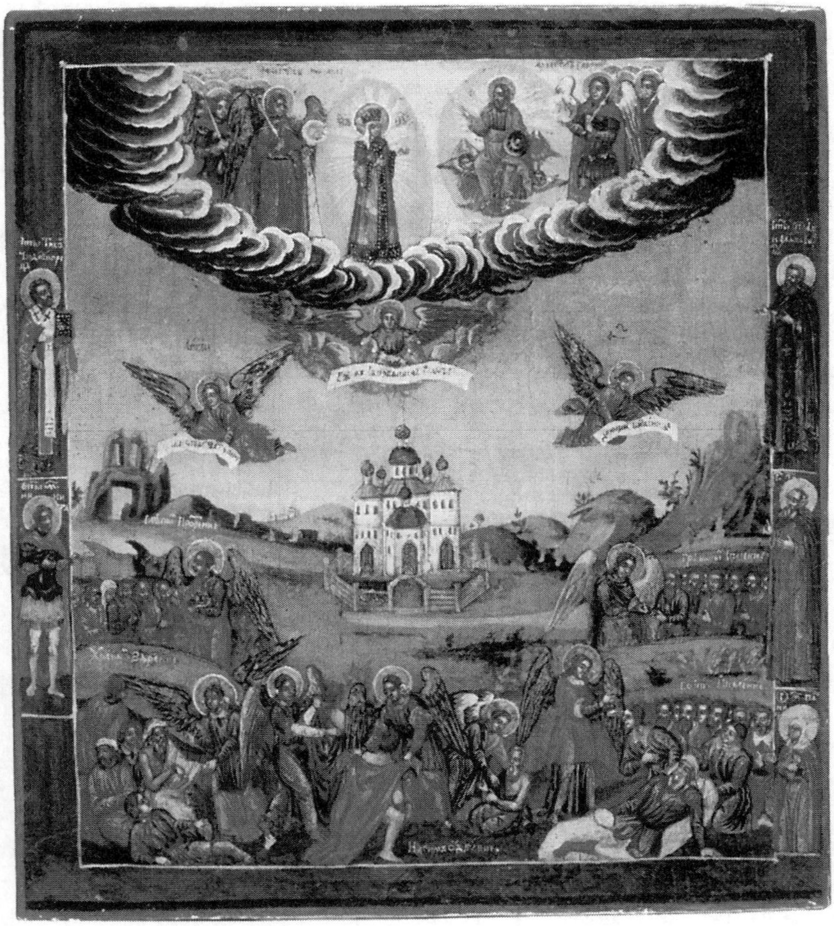

80. *Mother of God 'Joy of All who Suffer'*, early 18th century. Kolomenskoye Historical and Architectural Museum-Preserve, Moscow.

81. Maksim Kultepin, *Adoration of the Magi*, 1844, Tver. State Museum of the History of Religion, St Petersburg.

background can be seen on the 'Crucifixion' icon by Fyodor Zubov from the Chapel of the Holy Wisdom in the Smolensk Cathedral of the Novodevichy Convent, as though the symbolism of the traditional Orthodox image was gradually being destroyed (the background in an icon is a symbol of the divine illumination). Under the influence of the modern Catholic artistic tendency towards sensory illusion,[13] the Mother of God and St John are depicted as grief stricken and tearful. On the icon of the 'Crucifixion with Bystanders' from the iconostasis of the Moscow Kremlin Archangel Cathedral, executed by the Tsar's painters Dorofey Zolotaryov, Fyodor Zubov and Mikhail Milyutin in 1681, a *dark background* is already present.

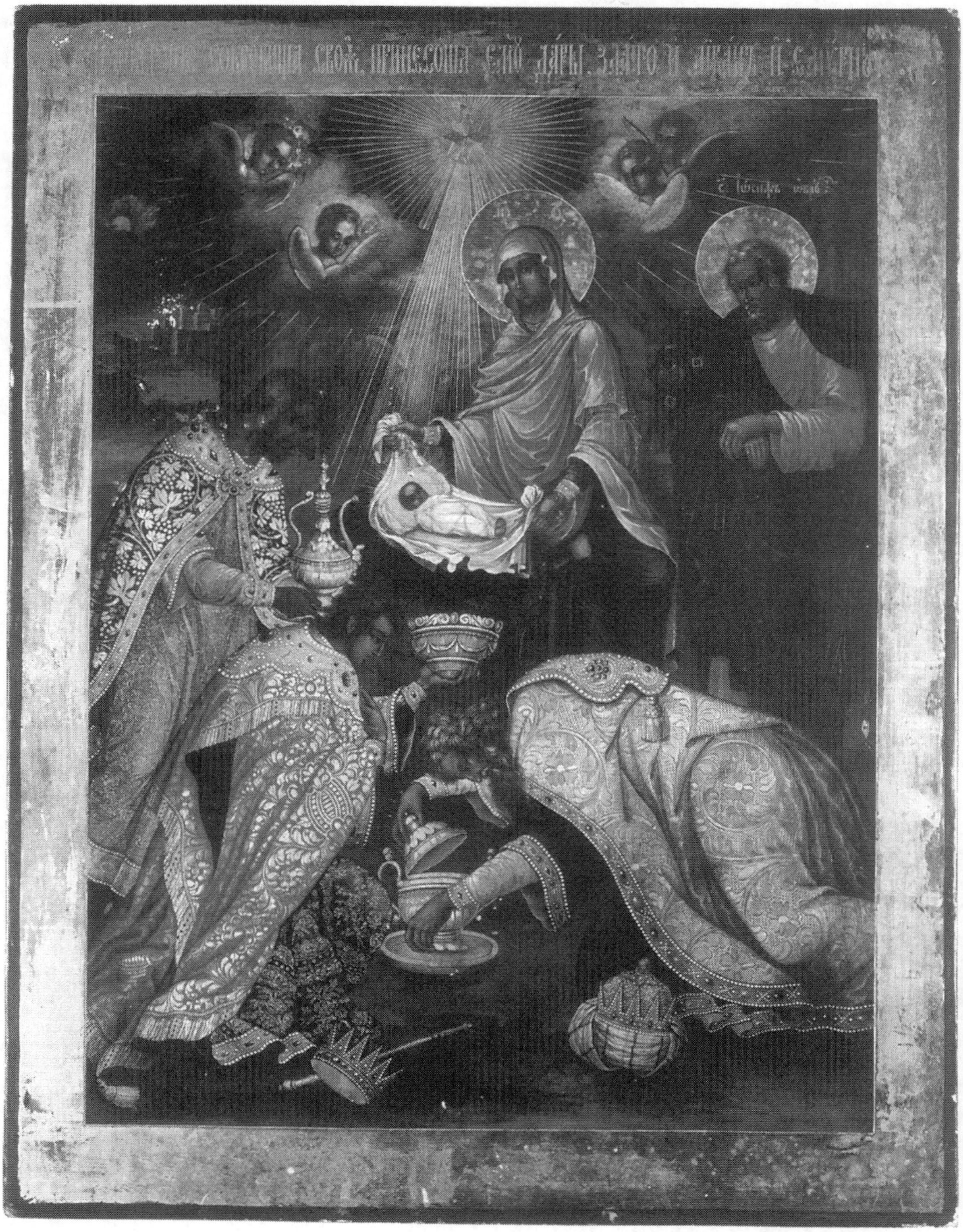

This background is encountered in Russian icons up to the 19th century, as Kultepin's icon of the 'Adoration of the Magi' confirms.

In a reverse process, Orthodox craftsmen's art also had an iconic influence on Catholic imagery. Catholic *Arte Sacra* became somewhat closer to the Orthodox icon in its ideas. Its symbolic impulse was strengthened, and the new Catholic iconography began to exclude unorthodox elements imported from Renaissance culture.

What happened was that, as a result of the new attentiveness of Catholic devotion towards the icon, Orthodox Greek craftsmen, settled in areas where Catholic culture held sway (Crete, Venice, southern Italy, the Ionian Islands, etc.), had to undertake Catholic commissions. And we can see that Greek workshops in these areas – where Eastern Orthodox and Catholic art worlds first met – were evidently the first to rework the Mannerist models. Thus the famous 16th-century Greek icon painters F. Batas and M. Damaskinos not only undertook commissions to copy Parmigianino for the Catholic Church, but introduced elements of the Catholic painterly system into their icons long before the Armoury Palace painters under Tsar Aleksey,[14] and longer still before the Suzdal craftsmen. Scholars have noted borrowings from Greek icon painters in Bassano, Raimondi and Corta. The painter F. Poulakis actively used Sadeler's engravings, while E. Zan reworked the image system of Tintoretto, Crivelli and the same Raimondi.[15]

82. *Descent from the Cross*, 19th century. Palekh Art Museum, Palekh.

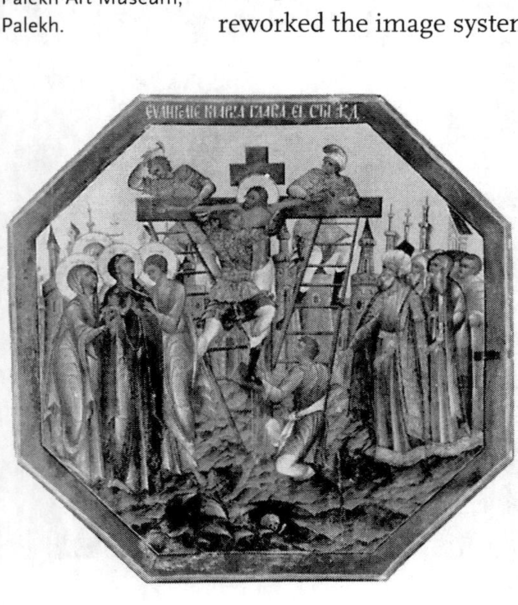

Here, then, was where, in the 17th century, mass circulation of that which had been achieved on the upper levels of Catholic culture took place. Hence, presumably, came the initial impulses towards the influence of the Orthodox icon on the 'post-Tridentine' Catholic image. It is hardly accidental that such icon painters worked in the 'Greek' or 'Italian' style according to their commission; double-sided icons, one side of which was painted according to the Orthodox canon, the other in the style of Italian 'post-Tridentine' art, were sometimes encountered.

All these mutual influences tell us that the changes in human self-consciousness that took place in the 17th century also found corresponding mechanisms within artistic thinking. In the sphere of popular craft art of subsequent centuries we find these mechanisms working through symbols that were devised in Rus precisely in the Baroque age. Changes in the forms of the boards on which icons are painted – to be found as late as the early 20th century – demonstrate this well.

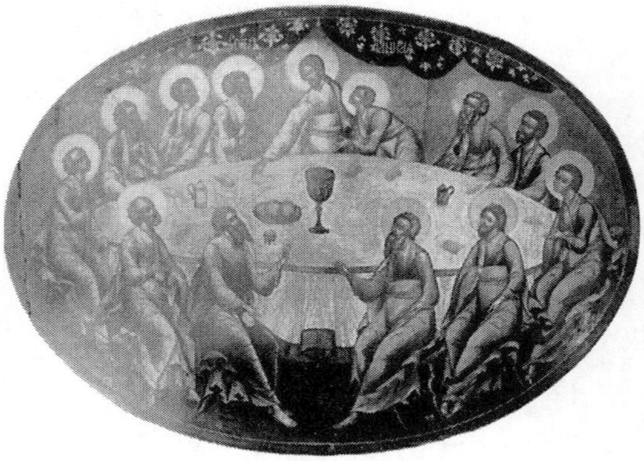

83. *The Last Supper*, 19th century. Palekh Art Museum, Palekh.

If in the medieval period a strictly rectangular board was chosen, from the beginning of the modern age a board could take the form of 'simple' but capacious and multivalent symbols – a cross, an oval, a star or a shrine (*kovcheg*). Florensky considered such graphic form to be the constructive sign of a symbol, since he was convinced that concepts 'abandoned by us as a heritage from bygone cultural epochs and now spontaneously reappearing' could be expressed through 'ideographic signs'.[16] In the 19th century, craftsmen from Palekh painted icons for iconostases in the very same forms that had arisen during the Baroque period. Thus the Deposition from the Cross could be painted on an octagonal board, i.e., a star (illus. 82). The icon of the Last Supper could have an oval form (illus. 83). The appearance of such forms in the 17th century tells us first of all about the general orientation of Baroque culture towards symbolization, while their resurgence right up to the 20th century underlines the 'mobility' of Baroque symbols on a line passing vertically through several cultural–historical strata.

The models of the Palekh icon painters, as we saw earlier, show convincingly that in the second half of the 19th century (unlike in the 'transitional period') 'old' symbols could 'enter into dialogue' with any cultural type. Sometimes preserving their role as 'fixed points', as stable and capacious signs organizing the space of the artistic texts, the symbols were able to transform themselves and function in relation to the most varied cultural orientations, whether 18th-century classicism or 19th-century Romanticism and Realism. What assisted the symbols to become mobile was in essence nothing other than the rhetorical formulae of the popular craftsman's artistic manner of thinking.

A clear example of this is the icon of the 'Fiery Ascension of the Prophet Elijah' by the Palekh craftsman V. A. Khokhlov. A biblical illustration, 'Elijah Fed by Ravens' by Julius Schnorr (1860) served as the model (illus. 84, 85). Employing individual compositional solutions and forms from it, Khokhlov constructed a primitivized version of his image. He retained the pose and gestures of Elijah's figure, as well as the general outlines of the mountains and the rocks on which the prophet sits, also making use of additional details and devices that were thoroughly familiar to him. The complex perspectival system with the well-elaborated landscape is simplified down to ordinary hillocks, with a touch of 'iconicity' on the right-hand side of the stream; the previously luxuriant vegetation is conveyed by a few modest plants. Declining to tackle the academic rendering of garment folds, Khokhlov simplified them clumsily. In addition, following the demands of Orthodox iconography for this prayer image, the figure of Elisha (absent in Schnorr's picture) was introduced, as was the chariot that is to carry the prophet away: these were borrowed from another engraving, 'The Ascension of Elijah', in the same Bible (illus. 86).

'In the workshops of middling painters instead of an iconic illustrated pattern-book you will invariably come across the drawings of Schnorr and Overbeck'; so wrote 'Izograf' ('Icon Painter') in 1882, and evidently he was entirely correct. This was how the mechanisms of 'simplification' and 'generalization' worked at the beginning of the 20th century, but with due qualifications they worked similarly in the 17th, 18th, and 19th centuries. The well-known Palekh icon by Ilya Balyakin 'Do not Grieve for Me, Mother' of 1769 (in the Palekh State Art Museum), deriving from a print by Lebrun, is distinguished by a higher degree of mastery and a more precise knowledge of Baroque forms, but it is based on the same universal aesthetic norms as those expressed in its own way by a Vladimir newspaper in the first half of the 19th century: 'Having before their eyes a sufficiency of images of good recent art, the craftsmen soften the ancient character of their painting and admit into their work the latest innovations as far as their understanding permits.'[17]

To examine the genesis and durability of the mechanisms of this kind of

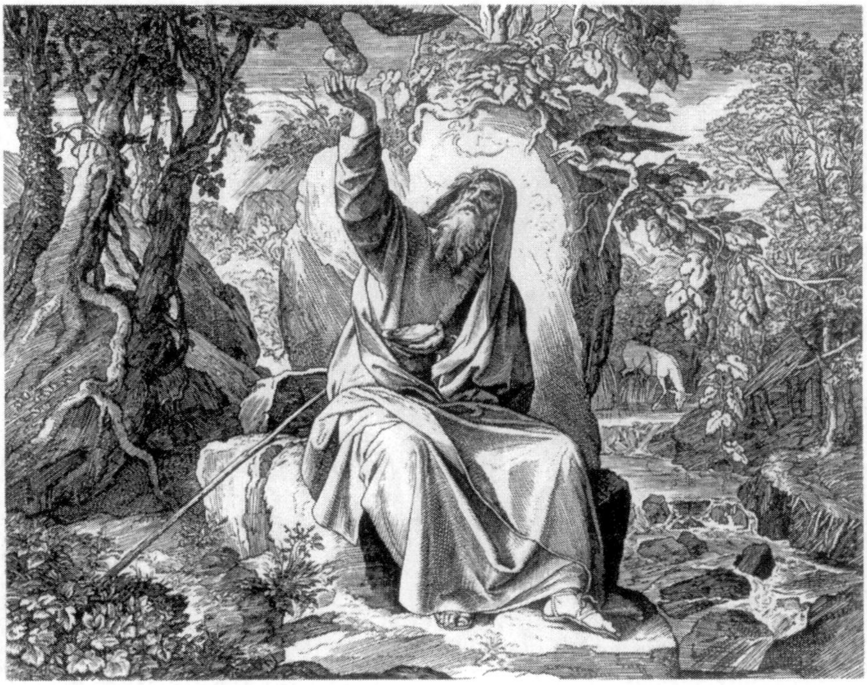

84. 'Elijah Fed by Ravens', engraving from *The Bible in Illustrations by Julius Schnorr von Karlsfeld*, 1860.

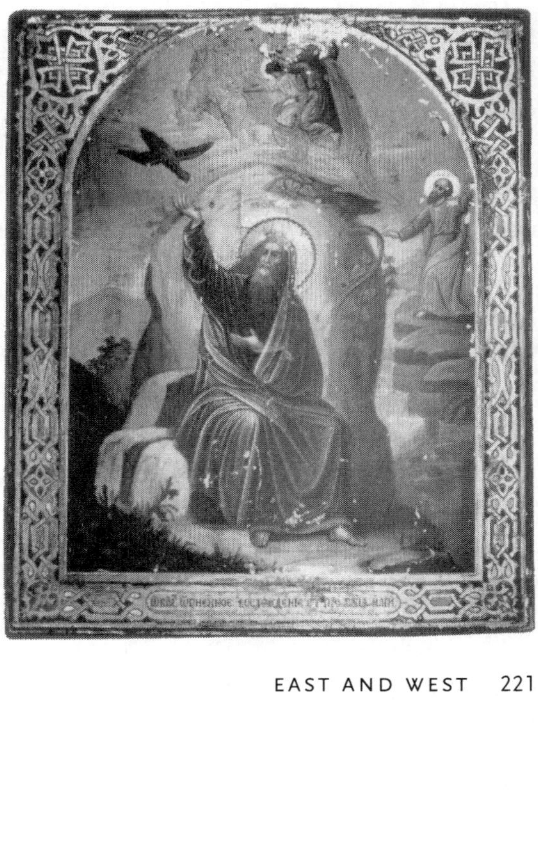

85. V. A. Khokhlov, *The Fiery Ascension of the Prophet Elijah* early 20th century, Palekh. Khokhlov family collection, Palekh.

86. 'Ascension of the Prophet Elijah', engraving from *The Bible in Illustrations by Julius Schnorr von Karlsfeld*, 1860.

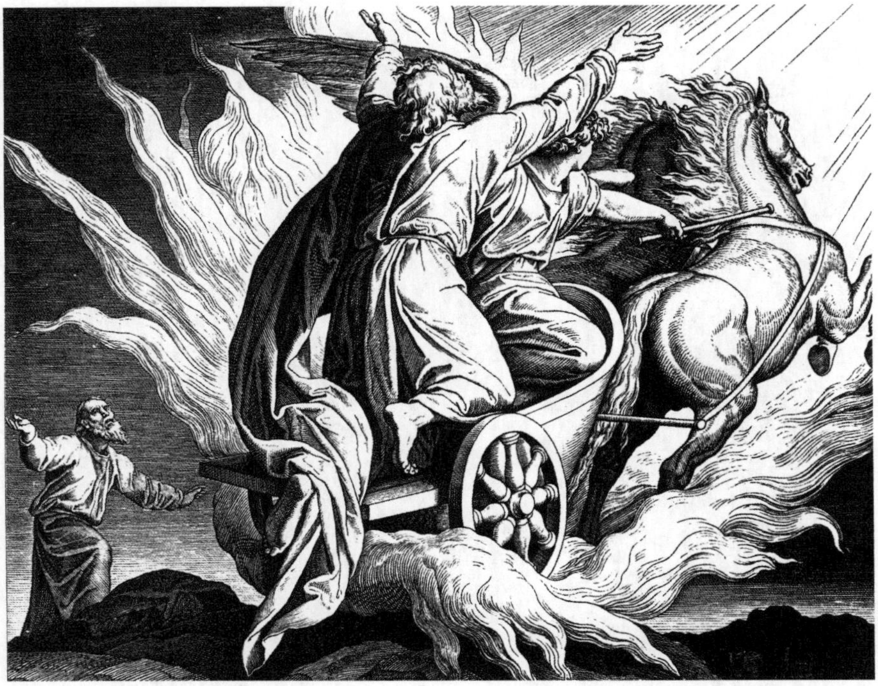

text construction, we may usefully take an example of a most eclectic nature: an interesting icon of the craftsman Ivan Afanasyev, 'The Wonder-working Grand Princes of Vladimir' (1814) from N. M. Postnikov's collection (illus. 87). What we have here is essentially the entire gamut of signs of the New Ritualist 'Frankish' prayer image, dispersed on a semantic level into the capacious system of shapes and signs that constitute meaning: faces, landscape, inscriptions, heraldry and saintly attributes. Their peculiar treatment (when compared with the medieval tradition) betrays in this Suzdalian craft-worker a follower of that Frankish 'painterly' and 'luminous' manner that began to be propagated by the Armoury Chamber school (led by Simon Ushakov) with the introduction of the new norms of devotion. Whereas in the medieval Russian icon, symbol strove to coincide with meaning, in icons by Simon Ushakov and other Baroque period icon painters, metaphors of comparison and commentary on symbols are foregrounded. They are based on Western-style rules of rhetoric that penetrated into 17th-century Russia via Poland and the Ukraine.

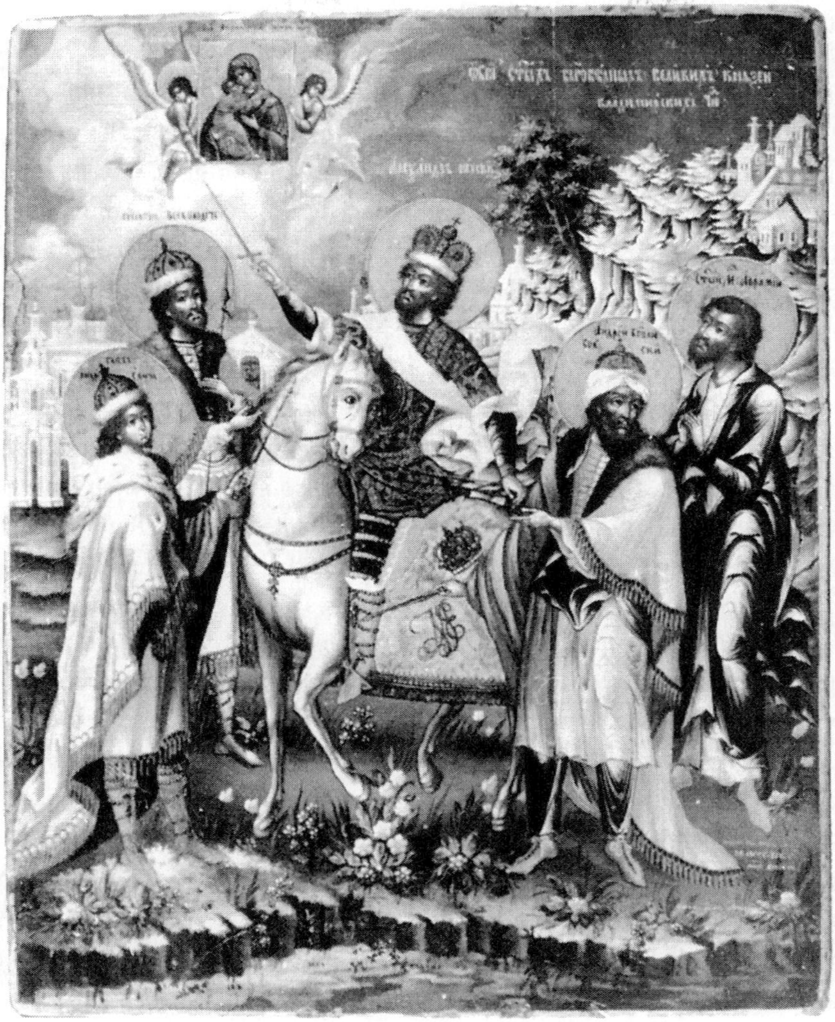

87. I. Afanasyev, *The Wonder-working Grand Princes of Vladimir: Gleb, Georgiy, Alexander Nevsky, Andrey Bogolyubsky and the martyr St Avraamiy*, 1814, Kholuy. State Russian Museum, St Petersburg.

Saturated with state symbolism, heraldry and emblematics, the Frankish icons by the royal icon painters reflected, interestingly for their time, the way Russian culture was penetrated by the ideas of the state and the spirit of recently born absolutism. In subsequent centuries all this would be inherited by the low-level craftsman's art. In the act of sanctifying the human being through such icons, the cultural–historical codes of the Baroque, with their particular emblematizing of thought, their didacticism and their rationalism, were already being realized.

Face and Countenance[18]

The human countenance is the centre of meaning in the icon. This is how it was understood by the Byzantine theology of the image that allowed only the most generalized, schematic resemblance to the original into its representational system. The severity and emaciation of a saint's countenance corresponded to the medieval vision of the world, to its asceticism and to its comprehension of the special role and place of humanity in the divine order, and finally to its understanding of the path by which it might be saved with the aid of the icon of Christ himself.

The icon by Ivan Afanasyev mentioned above is first of all notable in that the images depicted in it stand on the boundary line between *face* and *countenance*, which in Russia was first explored by icon painters of the Baroque period, and which those of earlier ages had treated quite differently. This gave the frontier between art and life, which had always defined the nature of a culture, a new weight of meaning.

Let us examine an icon of 1885, 'The Assembly of the Archangel Michael with selected Saints', in this light. In a cartouche on its lower border there is the inscription 'In memory of the martyrdom of the Emperor Alexander II Nikolayevich [assassinated in 1881] and in honour of the most august family of the happily now-reigning Emperor Alexander III Aleksandrovich'. On the left end of the board an explanation has been added (doubtless in the painter's hand): 'Depiction of the Emperor Alexander III. A. N. Artamonov.' It is most likely that this indicated the wishes of the patron, and assumed that the *countenance* of Alexander Nevsky – the 13th-century name saint and protector of the 'happily now reigning' Alexander III – should be given *the real features* of the Emperor's own face.

The devices employed by Ivan Afanasyev direct us towards the Baroque symbolism of the mirror and the poetics of the enigma, as some earlier examples can convincingly show. Thus the Baroque symbol of the mirror in the portrait of Tsar Fyodor Alekseyevich (1686) was an enigmatic demonstration of his 'divine origin': above the standing figure is depicted the *countenance* of the 'Saviour Not Made by Hands' with features of the *face* of Tsar Aleksey Mikhaylovich, that is of Fyodor's *father* (see illus. 138). Depictions of name saints with facial features of the Tsar or members of his circle began to appear more and more from the late 17th century. Scholars have noted that the countenances on certain icons in the church of the Pokrov at Fili, near Moscow, are taken from members of the Naryshkin family.[19] On an engraving by Innokentiy Shirsky of 1683 that was used in Lazar Baranovich's book *Jesus Christ, Blessing and Truth*, the Muscovite regent Sofya Alekseyevna (half-sister of Peter the Great, and effective ruler during Peter's minority, 1682–9) was depicted in the form of the woman of the Apocalypse with flowing hair and eagle's wings, protecting the young Tsars Ivan IV and Peter.[20] L. Tarasevich depicted Fyodor Shaklovitiy in the form of the Great Martyr Theodore Stratilates.[21] As we earlier mentioned, Catherine II commanded that she should be represented in the image of St Catherine on the iconostasis she presented to the Dormition Cathedral in Vladimir. 'Low-level' craftsmen's variants of the image of St Catherine with individual features of the Empress's face quickly became wide-spread from the end of the 18th century. Finally, we should not forget the Old Believer in Leskov's story *The Sealed Angel*, who complained that 'modern artists have begun to show the Archangel Michael as Prince Potemkin of Tauris'.

Clearly, low-level craft culture actively developed artistic devices that had arisen at some previous point, thus introducing specific feelings and mind-sets into the religious experience. The gradual transformation of the medieval countenance into the individualized human face is a symptom of serious changes in the system of values, since it was always linked with the problem of the relation between the sacral and the worldly within culture. Thus the 'transitional nature' of forms and the appearance of human facial features on saintly countenances by Cimabue and Duccio were linked with the start of radical changes in the history of Western civilization, and specifically with the change of relationship between the sacral and the worldly; Jacques Le Goff has seen in this the main tendency in the historical evolution of the West from *c.* 1200. In the medieval system of values the world was apprehended as an order of things imposed on humankind from outside. Medieval dualism presupposed the distancing of God from creation. The Early Middle Ages voiced contempt for the body, which was regarded (following Pope Gregory I, 'the Great', 590–604) as an 'abominable covering for the soul'. From the 12th century to the 13th, as Le Goff has seen it, everything changed: the body was gradually becoming 'the acknowledged form of each animated being'. Moreover, the artistic reflection of 'the beauty of the flesh', which might proclaim the beauty of the soul, clearly took place in parallel with changes in the concept of sainthood. Gradually, the saintliness of a life as lived became recognized as having priority over the quantity and glamour of miracles. To be saved, a person came more and more to rely on those values he or she had created in the world.[22]

Thus at this first turning-point of Western European Christian civilization the sacral image was already quick to reflect the breakdown in the relation between the sacred and the worldly: the increase in individual features of the countenance conveyed the approaching transformations in world view. From the 'transitional' forms of Cimabue and Duccio to the reforms of Giotto and the art of the Italian Renaissance was a mere step. 'Nature is the model, the ancients are the school': this famous artistic principle enunciated by Vasari meant the death of the Byzantine canon (the *maniera graeca*[23]) that was simultaneously associated with the medieval value system. The human face and its 'unworldly' beauty would become the subject of depiction on the basis of the unification of Christian dogma with Aristotelianism (Thomas Aquinas) and the experience of one of the most popular 13th-century Italian saints – Francis of Assisi. The depiction of the human face in the sacral image testifies to E. Garen's observation: 'The beginning of the new age found its most vivid embodiment in Italy and was characterized by two motifs: a turning towards the world of antiquity, towards classical learning, and the proclamation that one epoch of human history – the medieval age – had ended.'[24]

88. *The Saviour*, mid-16th century, Moscow. State Tretyakov Gallery, Moscow.

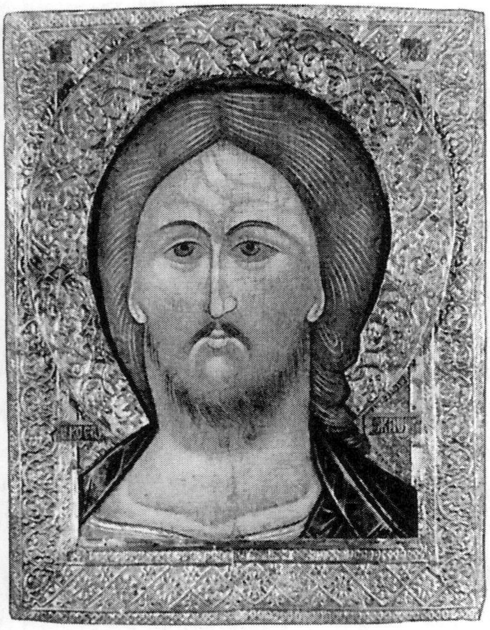

In this light the appearance in works by the Tsar's painters in the 17th century of iconic countenances that bordered on depictions of the human face could not but reflect significant changes in concepts of saintliness, of humanity, and of their place in the order of creation (illus. 88, 89, 90). In the medieval world view, the icon painter's copybook (i.e., the medieval canon) could admit the individualization of a saint's countenance, but would limit it to general characteristics. As Buslayev noted, these characteristics could have been established from recollections by contemporaries of the saint or from visions in dreams. They might also have been formed on the basis of a posthumous portrait made by an icon painter from the saint's relics. Icons of 15th-, 16th- and 17th-century Russian saints 'were normally made on the occasion of their deaths, drawing on memory and sometimes even on eyewitness accounts'.[25] Iconic portraits, in the words of G. D. Filimonov, 'never went against the overall character of the relics: they served as affirmation that this notable member of the elect would be honoured by the Orthodox in precisely his or her heavenly form'.[26] Thus, portrait features on countenances in the Middle Ages invariably showed signs of the priority of heavenly over earthly existence. It is no accident that 'individualization' of countenances first displayed itself in sacral representations above tombs. These include, for example, the paintings of the Archangel Cathedral in the Moscow Kremlin. As Buslayev argued, on tomb icons 'reality was obliged

89. School of Simon Ushakov, *The Saviour Not Made by Hands*, last quarter of the 17th century. State Tretyakov Gallery, Moscow.

90. I. P. Safonov, M. I. Nefedov, *St John the Divine in Silent Contemplation*, early 20th century. Palekh Art Museum, Palekh.

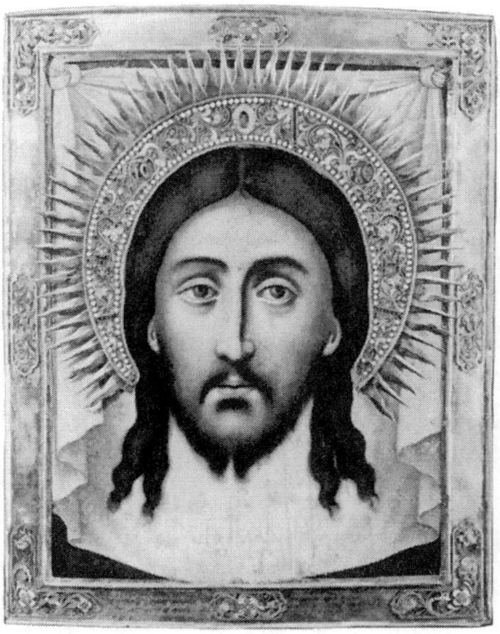

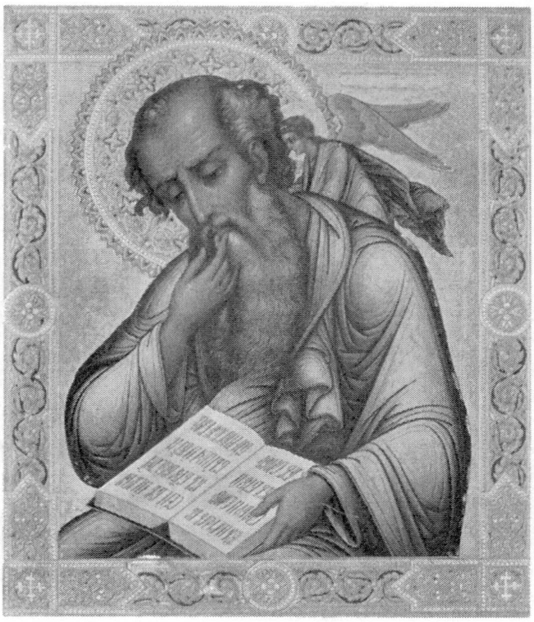

to lose all the individual details of the portrait; it had to conceal itself from the eyes of the icon painter beneath the veil of death'.[27]

The icon painters of the Armoury Chamber, led by Simon Ushakov, began from a fundamentally new conception of human sainthood. In their demand for 'the distinguishing of holy personages' there was concealed a new attitude of the Baroque age towards human personality, as well as a new comprehension of the worldly and of the value of earthly life on the road to the Kingdom of Heaven. 'Take heed, sir, and think about how dark can be the images of the saints who followed in the steps of Christ's teachings', wrote Iosif Vladimirov, attempting to win over adherents of the old canon. Authentic sainthood began more and more to be associated with 'the falling of light', with illumination of the flesh, with joy and happiness, despite the mortification of the flesh in the saint's lifetime:

> And if in the Lives of many saints it is recounted how they humbled themselves with fasting and prostration and went about without washing their faces, can it not be that after their deaths they are not bathed in light from places of illumination and find repose from such pains in delight and inexpressible joy?

The countenances of the saints began all the more readily to acquire individual features in the light of the concept that human kind 'is not created according to a single visage'. As if in response to the Protestant accusation that icon venerators depict all their saints identically, Iosif Vladimirov said that saints, like ordinary people, had in life to be distinguishable, to possess 'their own likeness'.[28]

Hence the *illumined countenance,* artistically on the borderline with the human face, was becoming persuasive testimony to the variety of life of the divine creation, while the medieval canon ('the single visage') began to be associated with the absence of 'one's own likeness' in a person and with ignorance: the concept of 'personality' becomes substantially transformed and reconfigured at the brink of the modern age. The Middle Ages had an ontological understanding of the word 'personality', since it potentially carried within it the divine image: Jesus Christ, 'the divine person with two natures', the Godly and the human. In modern times the word 'personality' begins to be regarded no longer ontologically, but psychologically, and 'personality' is more and more seen as spiritual individuality; people begin to understand the word 'personality' in the first place not as the 'image' of God, but (in Iosif Vladimirov's words) as 'one's own likeness', that is as self-awareness – that image or conception of oneself that an individual might extract from his or her personal history, or more specifically, destiny.

In the Baroque period the problem of how to strengthen the effect of art on religious feelings became prominent, since the Baroque Renaissance and its brand of humanism were fixated on what was individual. In the Baroque theoreticians' comprehension of sainthood, of humanity and of the surrounding world, the accent was placed on *universality*. Hence the worldly and the sacral achieved a new balance: the element of worldliness in the Baroque cultural system was increased, but only to the degree that was needed for the reflection of the *divine impulse* in human nature and in the surrounding world to be as graphically attested as could be. We should again remind ourselves that the Byzantine theorists of the image considered that the possibility of the sanctification of humankind through the icon was conditioned by the latter's depiction not of the 'nature', but of the 'personality' of Christ – his hypostasis that, passing all understanding, united two natures in itself. The medieval canon too conveyed 'personality', in correspondence with the medieval understanding of the role and place of humanity in the divine creation. In the conceptual world of Baroque icon painting, the prayer image could possess sanctificatory power only when, in conveying the 'personality' of Christ, it simultaneously *reminded* humanity that a person not only carries God's image within him or herself, but also possesses a personal 'face'. Christ continues to be the basis and meaning of human personality, of any kind of individuality – however the construction of this personality had begun to depend more on individual features and qualities. As a result God began to be depicted with a 'human face', and thus began to be thought of more and more on a *personal* level, made inwardly close to the individual.

The well-known Baroque cultural orientation towards symbolization and metaphor reached the point that the Tsar's icon painters put forward the new 'countenance' of Christ as a symbol of the 'face', and the 'face' as a symbol of the 'countenance'. This, evidently, was chief semantic content of the new 'light-filled' countenance of Christ that Simon Ushakov produced in the image of the *Great Hierarch* (1657) and in images of the 'Saviour not Made by Hands' (1660–70; see illus. 89), to which the synthesis of various kinds of art – cultivated by Baroque aesthetics – could correspond. Hence, too, a notion was lodged in the religious consciousness whereby a saint after whom a person was named, and whose intercessor before God he or she might be, could perfectly well have that same person's face. It is also evident that it was no accident that this concept was first applied in respect of representations of the Tsar – this fully corresponded with the ideology and spirit of emergent Russian absolutism. The mutually reflecting, as if 'interchangeable', countenance of Christ and face of the Tsar reminded people of the divinely established nature of autocratic power.

The Baroque striving for universality presupposed bringing into play an unusually broad set of means of artistic expression – quite sufficient for craft icon painting of subsequent centuries. 'The Baroque drew absolutely everything into its own space: life as a whole as well as the experience of previous cultural–historical ages, and it immediately transformed everything and fused it together (standard craftsmen's tricks of the trade symbolized high-status materials; antique heroes became attributes of Jesus Christ). The Baroque concealed its purloined material, hid it behind other forms: it preferred everything to be shifted.'[29] In the context of this 'totalizing' Baroque symbolism, this enthusiasm for symbolization both of the earthly and the heavenly world, the symbol of the mirror acquired special meaning. We should also note that the principles of synthesis in the arts, as too of mimesis and mirror reflection, become universal principles in the Baroque age despite all the confessional differences between cultures.

We can easily understand that the iconic countenances discussed above that bear features of Alexander III's face have a 'mirroring' quality: they show a kind of reflected Baroque symbolism. The symbol of the mirror, one of the most important of the Baroque age, passes freely through a variety of cultural epochs, as if in confirmation of Yuri Lotman's words that 'a symbol never belongs to one single synchronous cultural stratum – it always cuts its way through any stratum on a vertical axis, coming from the past, departing into the future'.[30]

In speaking of the ambivalent nature of Christian symbols, we have already noted that the symbolism of the Baroque mirror significantly transformed the Byzantine category of likeness through its ability to reflect 'shades', that is through its universality and capacity to show the object from various sides. It is important to emphasize here that Baroque artists regarded the principle of universal reflection as divinely inspired, 'established by divine wisdom': this principle permitted the mystery of the heavenly imprint on the earthly creation to be conveyed. As Simon Ushakov wrote in his aesthetic tract,

> Not only the Lord God himself is the creator of representations, but also everything that exists [in nature] that we can see possesses the secret and the marvellous power of this art. Every thing that stands before a mirror receives its reflection in it thanks to the wonderful way it is fashioned by God's great wisdom . . . Exactly the same [reflections] of various things [we can see] in water, on marble and on other well-polished objects, in which images are drawn instantaneously and without the application of any labour. Can it not be God and the nature of things that teach us the art of painting icons?[31]

In other words, a sacral meaning was given to the symbol of the mirror. The human face reflected in the 'mirror' of the icon bore a heavenly and an earthly imprint simultaneously: sainthood and deification were apprehended by analogy with the earthly as well as the heavenly.

Meanwhile symbols, embodying cultural memory, could transform themselves and alter their nature under the influence of the general cultural orientation. Thus the age of the Enlightenment demanded 'naturalness'. 'The whole spirit of 18th-century culture was orientated not only towards reason, but also towards common sense, *bon sens*, from which viewpoint the symbolic and ritualistic aspects of previous ages were associated with prejudice and with the "obscurantism" that it was the Enlightenment's duty to change.'[32] It was in this context that countenances on the icons of the official Church began in the 18th century to select features conveying 'naturalness': psychologism was heightened in them, and a more precise physiognomy of the human face appeared (illus. 91, 92). Humanity lost, as it were, the symbolic quality it characteristically possessed in the Baroque age, and was included in the rational and 'natural' order of things.

If the Baroque and Romanticism came out in favour of symbolism and

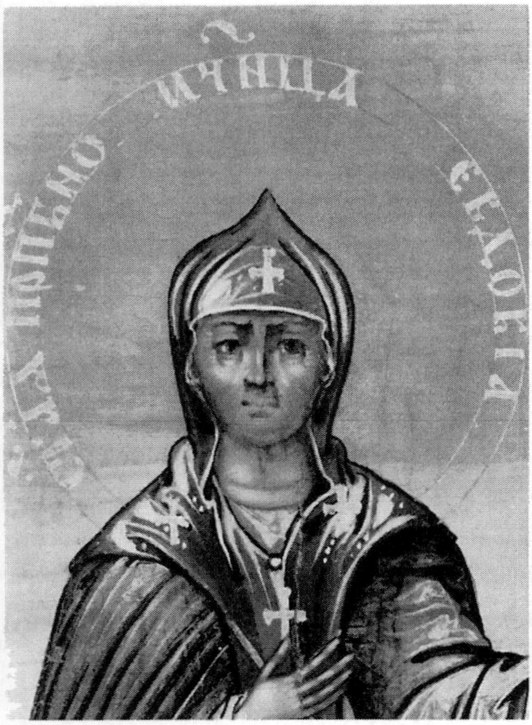

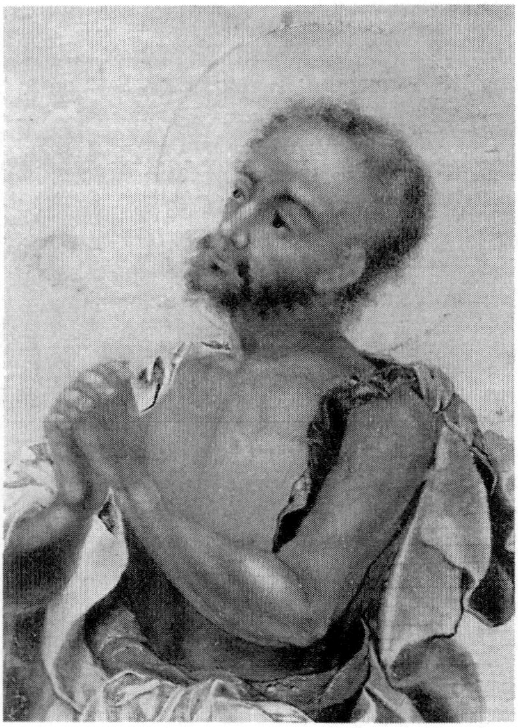

91. *St Yevdokiya*, a detail from a late-18th-century icon. Kolomenskoye Historical and Architectural Museum-Preserve, Moscow.

92. Prokopiy of Ustyug, a detail from the 18th-century icon *Prokopiy of Ustyug, Holy Fool in Christ* (illus. 151). Kolomenskoye Historical and Architectural Museum-Preserve, Moscow.

severance from life (metaphor was dominant), the 19th century – the age of realism – upheld lifelike qualities. In icons of the New Ritual, saints' countenances began more and more often to be rendered in oil paint. To attain a 'light-enhanced' effect, Baroque masters used a mixed oil and tempera technique with many layers of glaze that they had acquired from Dutch artists. Ecclesiastical oil painting of the 19th and early 20th centuries already carried the stamp of the 'age of realism': the countenances of saints had become reminiscent of human faces on non-religious pictures (illus. 93).

Landscape

In Ivan Afanasyev's icon of the 'Wonder-working Grand Princes of Vladimir', the Baroque landscape is distinguished by the unconcealed eclecticism typical of late popular craft art (see illus. 87). We can find in it

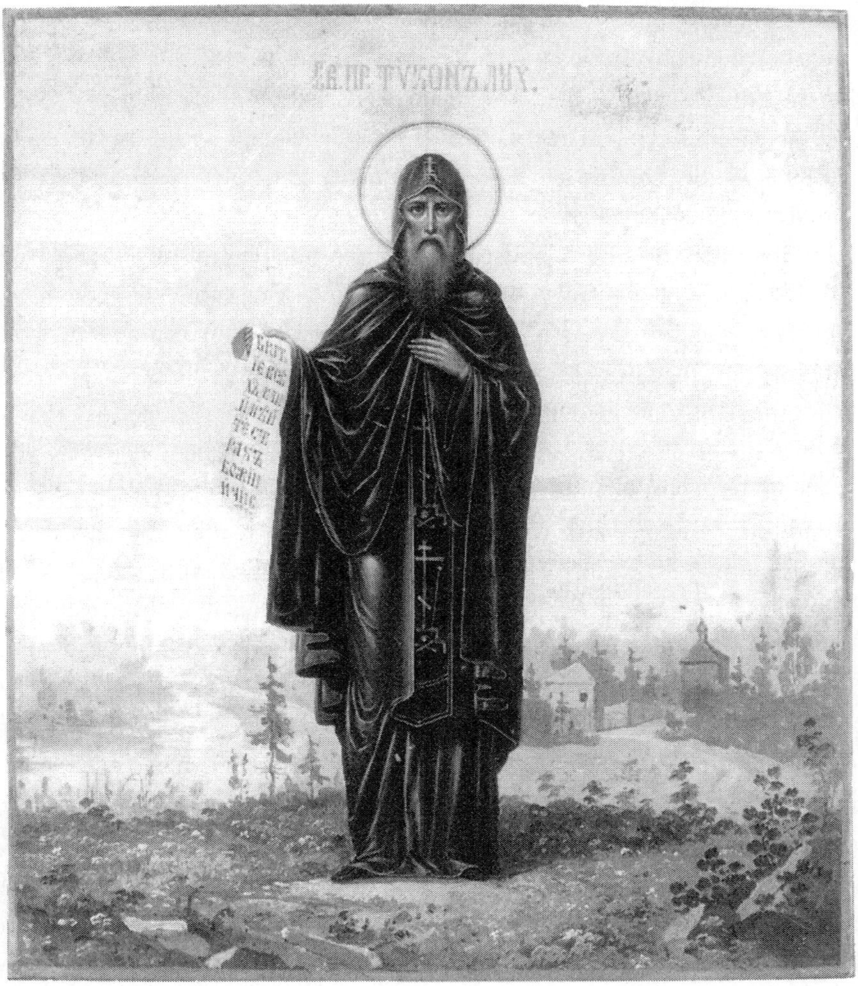

93. *St Tikhon of Lukhov*, early 20th century. Palekh Art Museum, Palekh.

a Baroque church – representing the Vladimir Dormition Cathedral – together with Romantic pseudo-Gothic structures and the large tree that is so often encountered in Baroque icons of the 17th century. The systematic perspective and the architecture of the Dormition Cathedral bell-tower, with its hint of realism, fit awkwardly with the typically iconic slab-topped hillocks, which the craftsman clearly borrowed from traditional Palekh icons of the 18th and 19th centuries. In the foreground there is a spring, an ancient symbol of life: most likely the painter saw a similar one on mass-circulation prints. The extension of the zone of landscape, the latter's role in structuring the icon and the co-existence in it of the realistic and the unrealistic, testify that the village icon painter had inherited those spatial–temporal laws of the icon that were developed by the same Tsar's painters in the context of Baroque cultural principles and concurrent changes in consciousness.

In the medieval canon, landscape is of marginal significance compared with the figure of the saint. Reverse perspective corresponded to dualistic habits of thought: the natural world was schematically apprehended on principle as 'insignificant' and of no value. In prayer images up to the mid-17th century, an ancient system of slab-like forms symbolized the earth, while bunches of herbs and tufts of grass stood for vegetation (illus. 94).

When they disrupted the stern iconographic canon and brought elements of real-life landscape into the spatial composition of the icon, the Tsar's painters strove to symbolize the natural world, which in a Neo-platonic context was taken as a reflection of the heavenly one. It follows naturally that the *real landscape* around New Jerusalem,[33] once sacralized by the Patriarch Nikon, began to resemble a vast 'Neo-Platonic mirror', symbolically reflecting a sacral and heavenly landscape. It is interesting that a similar 'sacral transformation' of the topography is revealed later in the experience of St Serafim of Sarov, who was to give sacral names to the real landscape (a forest grove), which his religious feats would simultaneously sanctify.

Russian Baroque icon painters began to depict the landscape in such a way that it sometimes occupied the whole picture space of the icon. The prayer images turned into a kind of landscape icon. Icons of the 17th and 18th centuries representing monastic landscapes belong to the same conceptual type (illus. 95, 96). Since space organized according to sacral rules in a monastic way was the image of a vessel of salvation, it proved particularly attractive to Baroque synthetic thinking. The principle of the reflection of the earthly in the heavenly here attained a curious and playful multi-layered quality. It is not accidental that icons themselves are often represented on a background of monastic architecture: the Baroque tendency towards symbolization, metaphor and dissimilarity from life led to a heightened degree of artistic conventionality. On the icon of 'The Mother of God of Bogolyubovo with Zosima and Savvatiy of Solovki in Attendance,

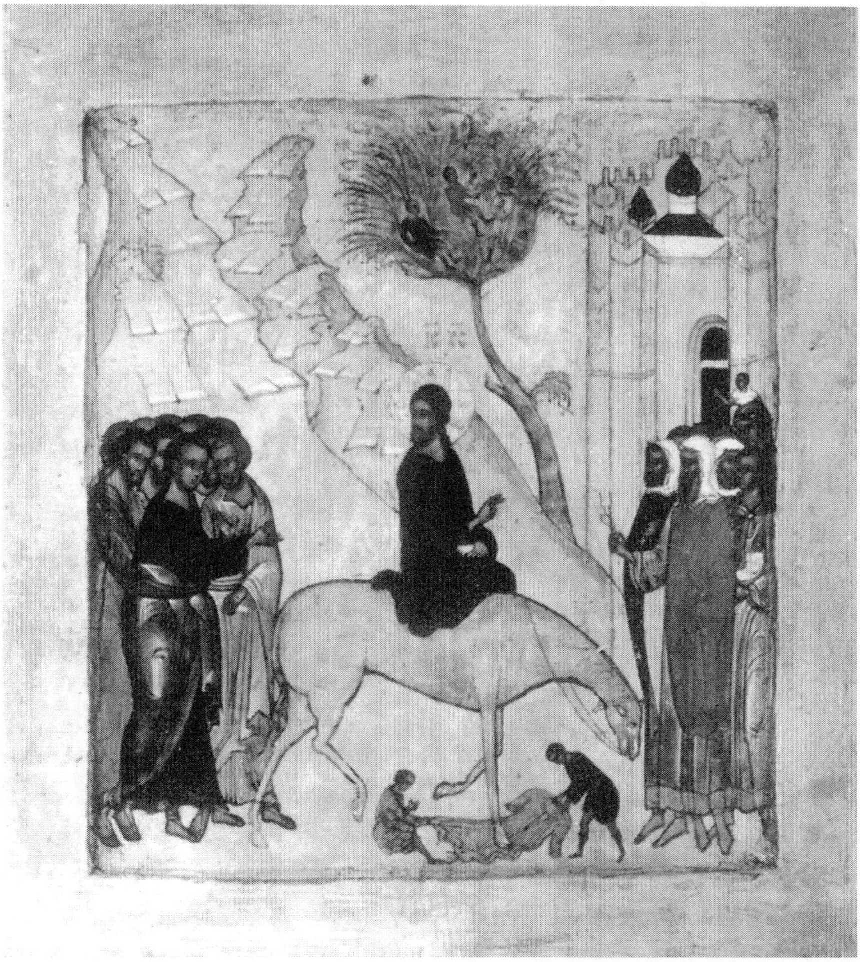

94. *The Entry into Jerusalem*, end of the 15th century. State Tretyakov Gallery, Moscow.

and Scenes of their Life', from the Kolomenskoye Museum, landscape occupies the entire space of the icon, while the scenes from the Life are disposed within a real world that appears to be the reflection of the heavenly world. The icon conveys graphically the harmony of the divine creation, infused with God's purpose of saving humankind: the watery element is intersected by islands on which ordinary troubled life is imbued with the divine providence.

As was the case with the 'metamorphosis' of the countenance into the face, the main precondition for the broadening of the landscape zone in

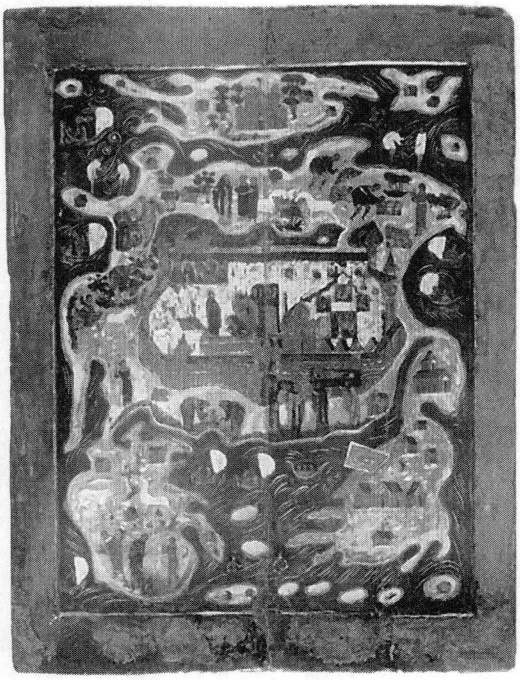

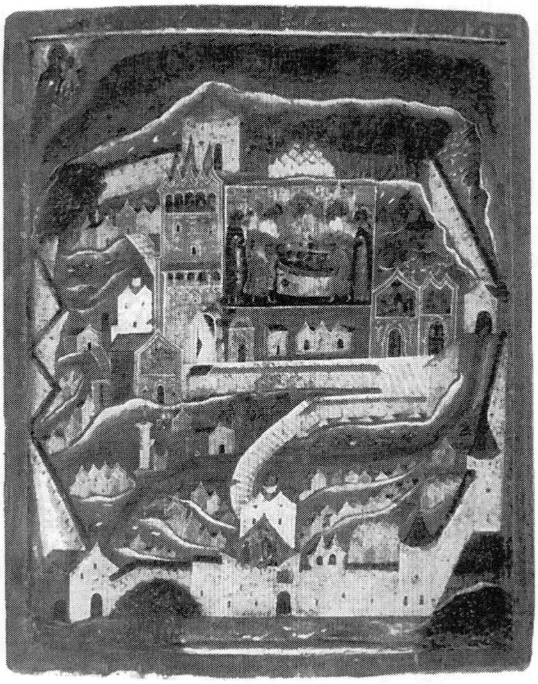

95. *Bogolyubovo Mother of God in the Presence of Zosima and Savvatiy of Solovki, and Scenes of their Life*, mid-17th century. Kolomenskoye Historical and Architectural Museum-Preserve, Moscow.

96. *The Pskov Monastery of the Caves*, end of the 17th century. Kolomenskoye Historical and Architectural Museum-Preserve, Moscow.

the Baroque icon is a new orientation of spiritual life, or rather a new resonance (as compared with the period of the Renaissance) in the concepts of the divine origin of the world and of the renewed sanctification of creation when Christ was incarnated. It is no accident that in Catholic 17th-century images of the Annunciation, the heavens open up:[34] Heaven has begun to be represented as inseparable from earth, while people and angels are no longer contrasted with each other. The presence of the divine impulse in all existence illuminated both the microcosm, i.e., humankind, and the macrocosm: the world surrounding a person was apprehended from a neo-Platonic point of view. People saw it as an expanse filled with a secret symbolism, strewn throughout with enigmas whose solutions promised entry into the Creator's designs. In Western European painting the development of neo-Platonic ideas would become a basis for the emancipation of landscape as an independent genre.[35]

Since earlier the sacral had completely dominated the worldly, the medieval canon and world view also presupposed the full dominance of conceptual space within the icon. The change of relationship between the worldly and the sacred in the Baroque period was at once reflected in the relation of the centre (the figure of a saint or the sacred event) with the periphery (landscape). The sacral centre and the peripheral landscape became necessary for one another at a different level from the latter's subjection to the former: rather that of interaction and mutual attraction, which began to be nourished by the complex Baroque fusion of ideas and symbols of previous ages. Another important condition for the expansion of landscape was the heightened significance in the Baroque age of *personal piety* and of the spiritual enrichment of the subject: hence the tendency towards an individual and subjective apprehension of the icon. The elaborated structure of landscape presupposed a greater participation of the human being in sacred events, and introduced a complex feeling of *shared experience* into the act of prayer. The co-existence of direct and reverse perspective pointed to the sacral worth of earthly actions and to the elevation of their role in the economy of salvation. This co-existence transformed landscape in the new Frankish icons into a kind of 'natural' medium for the activity of holy and of real-life personages and historical events (illus. 97). The peripheral landscape was specially structured so as to be open to dialogue both with the sacral centre (the figure of the saint) and equally with the person participating in the act of prayer. In the theory and practice of European Renaissance art, true perspective assumed an orientation towards a natural model and the active scholarly investigation of the object of representation. The Baroque tendency towards universalism, didacticism and the linking together of various art forms conditioned the co-existence of direct and reverse perspective so as to direct the consciousness of the praying person towards the active apprehension of the sacred image. A fundamentally

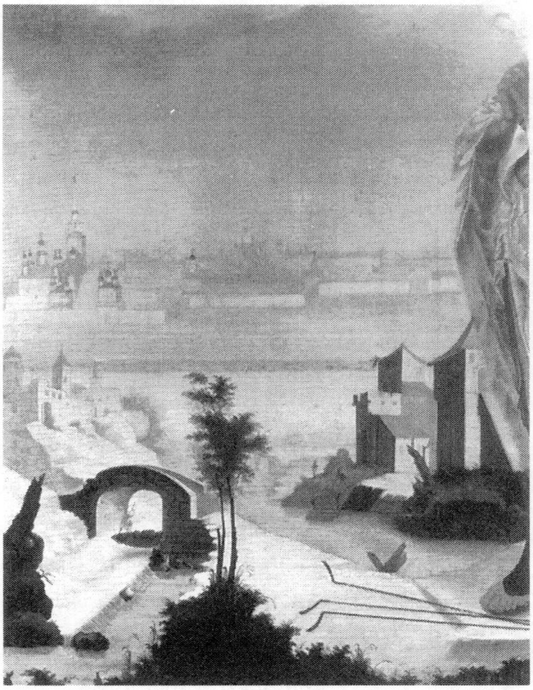

97. A detail from the 18th-century icon *Prokopiy of Ustyug, Holy Fool in Christ* (illus. 151). Kolomenskoye Historical and Architectural Museum-Preserve, Moscow.

discrete and rationalistic investigation of the object of representation was subjected exclusively to spiritual tasks.

A clarification of the way the new study of nature depended on the 'subjectivizing' of spiritual experience in the 16th-century Mannerist age was once given by Max Dvořák. Since it was built on the contrast between antiquity and Christianity, and concerns a common set of European problems, it is fully applicable to our own problem of the extension of the landscape zone in icons. For Dvořák,

> Art, religion and philosophy in the world of antiquity were determined by the objectivization of the surrounding world: they concealed beneath them the urge to link sensory experience with an appropriate structure, with conformity to rules, with harmonization and with the beauty of nature – and to embody it in abstract clarity. The Christian world view by contrast rested upon the subjectivization of the surrounding world as a matter of principle. It discounted sensory phenomena as a factor of little worth, if not a hindrance, since inner illumination of the soul by God and divine revelation was the sole source of truth and the sole value. Thus spiritual ideas and experience, and rational and emotional impulses, come close through theological deduction, and become the starting-point for religion and for all the spiritual connexions with the surrounding world – art included.[36]

From what has been said it is clear that the symbolic structure of landscape began to 'react' as a result of changes in cultural orientation just as it happened with the countenances of saints: landscape could have more inner freedom as sacred periphery.

The self-awareness of culture has always expressed itself through symbols. Thus the inclination of Baroque culture towards metaphor and allegory was reflected in the landscape of the well-known icon of the Azov Mother of God of the early 18th century (an icon that compositionally echoes L. Tarasevich's engraving of the 'Azov Mother of God' on the frontispiece of the *Kievan Caves Monastery Patericon*, Kiev, 1702). In the creation of a 'metaphoric focus' an equal role is here played by both the inscription and the picture. The invented architecture of the towns of Azov and Kizikermen

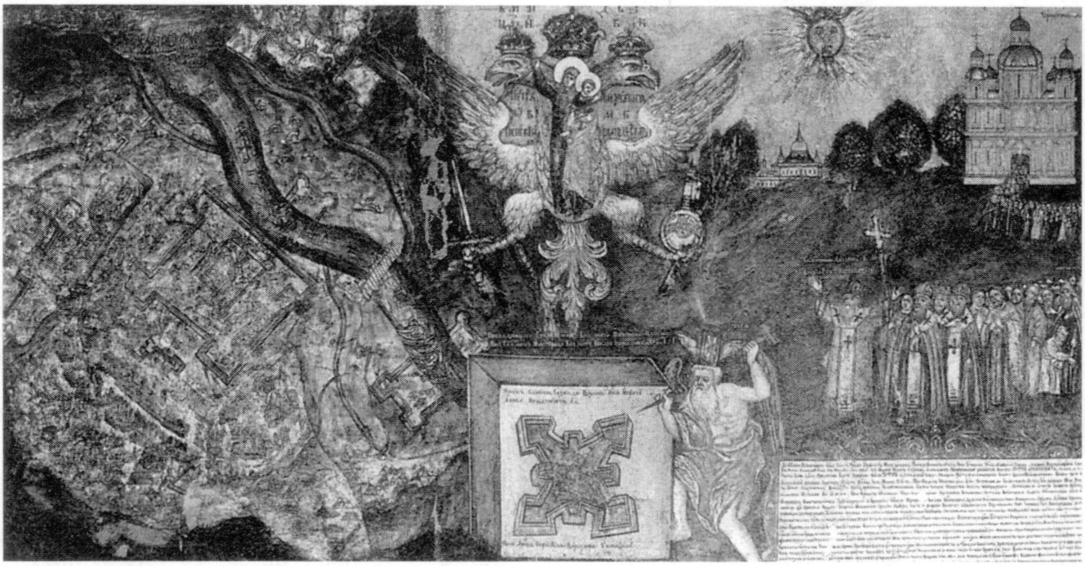

is elucidated with the words 'Babylon [i.e Azov] is fallen, is fallen, that great city. And thou, Capernaum [i.e., Kizikermen], which art exalted to the heavens, shalt be brought down' (Revelation 14:8; Matthew 11:23). This metaphor, equipped with biblical symbolism, ascribes the protection of the heavenly powers to Russia in the struggle with the Moslems (see illus. 133).

98. Detail from the icon *Chernigovskaya-Ilyinskaya Mother of God*, 1696 (illus. 134). State Museum of the History of Religion, St Petersburg.

The same theme is no less interestingly revealed in the allegorical landscape of the 1696 icon of the Chernigov–Ilyinskaya Mother of God On it, a real cartographic plan of Peter I's capture of Azov is depicted, painted in honour of the event in the same year, as well as a map of New Azov, symbolically resting on a stone: we witness the appearance of a specifically scientific interest in nature (illus. 98). The schematic linkage of earthly and transcendental levels received scholarly confirmation, as it were, in the new icons. The reliable topographic precision in representing the area and its architectural structures bore witness to the icon painter's detailed knowledge of the objects of representation and his use of documentary materials. That is to say that he was here treading the fine line between a scholar and a creative craftsman, so displaying his learned qualities in the spirit of the Baroque age.

An allegorical figure in the form of a semi-naked, winged Antique figure of a man is used by the icon painter as a complex symbol for a multi-layered intellectual game. It might represent the arrival of Russia's time (the figure is labelled *chas*, 'time' in Polish) to take over the place of the Polish Commonwealth and the Austrian empire in the struggle with the Ottoman Porte; from Golitsyn's expeditions of 1687 and 1689 and Peter I's capture of Azov in 1696 there commenced a string of Russo-Turkish wars, almost two centuries long, under the banner of liberating Christians and the lands formerly under Byzantine rule. The same male figure might signify the victory, mission and establishment of the Christian Church, since the plan of New Azov, engraved on a stone, is presented as based on a cross-shape – alluding to Constantine the Great's words 'In this sign we shall conquer'. This idea is made particularly convincing by the sun – in the Baroque system, a symbol of Christ – that we see in the heavens. The location together in landscape–space of allegorical and historical levels was a response to the Baroque age, when the former watertight compartmentalization between art and life gradually began to break down.

We constantly encounter such plans in both the 18th and 19th centuries. On the icon by Ivan Afanasyev in the Vladimir Dormition Cathedral, where the wonder-working icon of the Vladimir Mother of God (shown above the figures of the saintly princes) was kept, is juxtaposed with 'fantastical' pseudo-Gothic architectural decor, evidently borrowed from a print (illus. 87). We can see another interesting juxtaposition on an 18th-century icon of the 'holy fool' St Prokopiy of Ustyug (illus. 97). The background is taken up with a panorama of the monastery of St Michael the Archangel in Ustyug, in which we can recognize its two main churches – those of the Presentation and of Michael the Archangel. In the foreground, however, we are given a typical Western European landscape, parts of which the craftsman took from some Italian, German or Dutch picture of the 17th or 18th century. This fantastical Western landscape may be no less than a complex symbol of antiquity, 'secondarily mythologized' in the 18th century, that already in the early Baroque period had begun to serve as an inexhaustible source of material for constructing complex symbolism to demonstrate the truths of Christianity. In this landscape we can discern the 18th-century icon painter's conception of what Antique, Roman landscape might be (see, too, illus. 99).

Throughout the 18th century to the early 20th, allegorical and topographically precise backgrounds were also developed independently, without obviously being imposed. However, the allegorical and realistic symbolism was almost always displayed in accordance with whatever means of rendering artistic material was dominant in one period or another. The 18th-century cultural drive towards rationalism and science, 'documentalism' and 'a mechanistic understanding of matter'[37] often revealed itself in the way the topographically precise landscapes on icons began to bear a more evident imprint of cartography. Icon painters frequently depicted scenes from above, permitting them to present a town, a monastery or a locality as a plan or map. Just such a landscape, reminiscent of a plan and conveying the scheme of a town, a monastery and a river from above, can be seen on an icon of St Feodosiy of Totma (in the Russian Museum) from the end of the 18th century. The Totma Spaso-Sumorin monastery is depicted standing on a headland between two rivers, whose names ('River Kovda' and 'River Pesya Denga') are inscribed as they would be on a map of the period. With cartographic precision, the icon painter also depicted the three main churches in the monastery, dedicated to the Transfiguration, to the Ascension and to St John Chrysostom.[38] A landscape of a similar type, reminiscent of a map, is shown on a 19th-century icon of 'The Miracle from the Icon of the Mother of God of the Sign'; it gives us a fairly exact idea of the circles of town fortifications and number of urban churches in Novgorod at that time (illus. 100). Particularly noteworthy from the compositional point of view are the icons of the 18th and 19th centuries showing St Nil Stolbensky, with his monastery in the background, standing on an island in Lake Seliger and partly on the peninsula of Svetlitsa. It is possible to date the actual icons from the number and character of the monastic buildings and churches. Thus the church

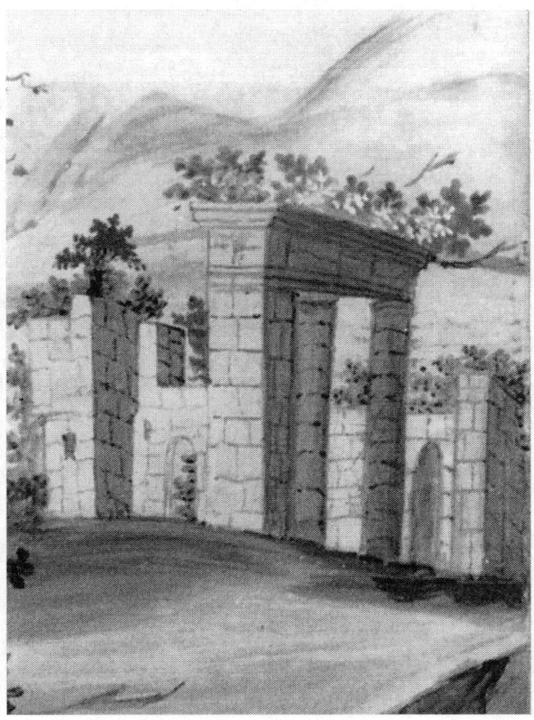

99. A detail from the icon *St Yevdokiya*, end of the 18th century. Kolomenskoye Historical and Architectural Museum-Preserve, Moscow.

dedicated to St John the Baptist built in 1781 on the site of Nil's cave[39] was at once depicted on icons that retained the earlier composition in other respects (see illus. 123).

The urge to give landscape an active role in fashioning religious experience led the Frankish icon painting of the New Ritual towards the development of genre-based art and the inclusion of real-life events in the sacral space of the image. In the early-18th-century icon 'The Mother of God, Joy of All who Suffer', the 'earthly' sphere, unusually extensively developed, calls for greater attention towards the human world, bright and full of contrasts; the Orthodox image is more and more infused with generally accessible edification (see illus. 80). The realistic symbolism of the 19th century, by contrast, directed towards metonymy, brought the forms that had become characteristic of the times into landscape. Reckoning on an intentionalistic consciousness, the 'structures of everyday life' might also sometimes acquire a hint of allegory, as a result of which the prayer image would become an illustration of personal piety.

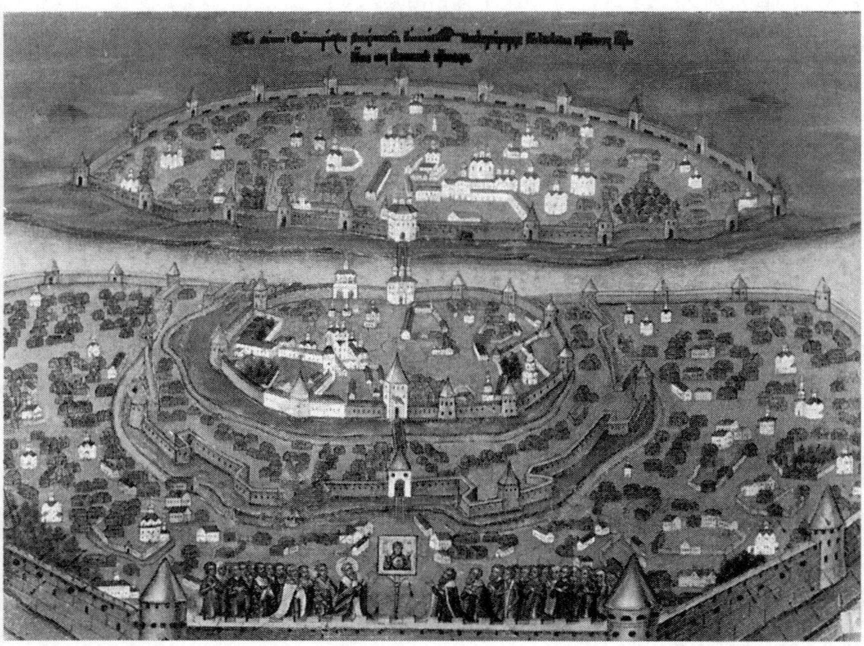

100. A detail from the icon *Miracle from the Icon of the 'Sign' ('View of Ancient Novgorod')*, 19th century. Kolomenskoye Historical and Architectural Museum-Preserve, Moscow.

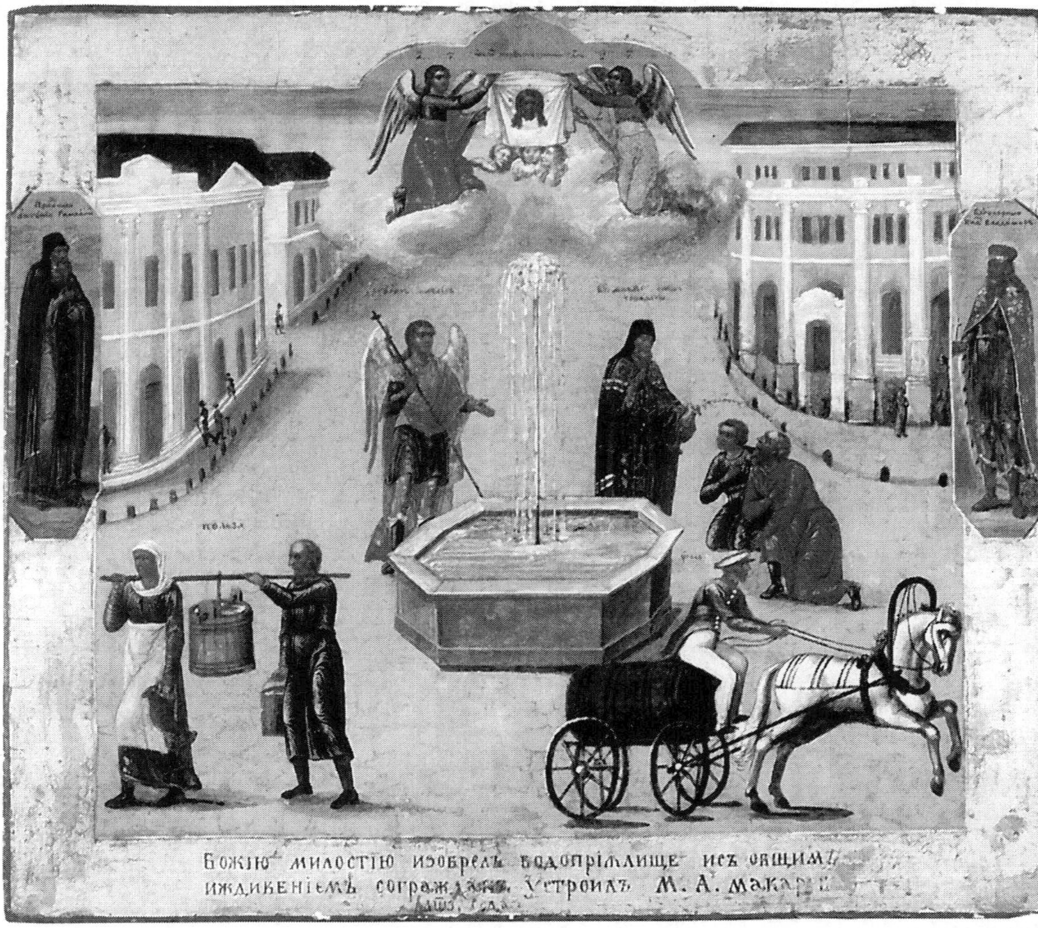

We begin to meet icons that convey messages about the charitable worldly deeds of the patron. Thus, in 1837, the Kaluga merchant M. A. Makarov had an icon made in connection with his construction of a new water supply system in the town (illus. 101). On its lower margin there is an inscription telling us about the personal piety of the donor: 'By God's grace M. A. Makarov discovered a water supply and with common funding from his fellow citizens built it, 1837.' We should note that the name of the prayer image, located on the lower margin, tells us on the one hand about the influence of the picture's signatory, and on the other about the pious 'self-abasement' of the patron. In the centre of the composition the painter

101. *'By God's grace . . .'*, 1837, Kaluga. State Museum of the History of Religion, St Petersburg.

placed a well – one of the favourite Renaissance symbols of life. Disposed around it are the figures of the Archangel Michael, a holy man and townsfolk, conveying the earthly meaning of the merchant's charitable deed: water might 'quench thirst', 'extinguish fire' and generally be of use. This earthly action is presented before a background consisting of the real main buildings and streets of the town, thus localizing the symbolism of the scene in a concrete historical space. Icons of this type bore witness to the affirmation of a new, more individualistic religious psychology, which without doubt could be considered a common flag-bearer of the modern period.

Landscapes with genre scenes of earthly actions are encountered in all the Eastern Orthodox lands in the 18th and 19th centuries. At the end of the 19th century A. Dmitrievsky described the numerous icons of the Burning Bush, doubtless made in the monastery of St Catherine on Sinai, and whose lower part contained a depiction of the monastery together with its adjoining garden and a perspective view of the Rahi valley. As Dmitrievsky noted, 'the representation is so carefully done that one could actually take it as a portrait made from nature'. This landscape 'from nature' also contained genre scenes, such as the monastic distribution of bread or the defence of the monastery against enemies of Christendom.[40]

The development of the 'Russian national idea' and the realization of the topos of 'Holy Russia' in the late 19th century and early 20th markedly ideologized the historically real landscape in icons by the Suzdalian masters. Realistic symbolization expressed the idea of the protection of the Russian empire by the heavenly powers differently, for example, from how it was done in the late 17th century and early 18th. Lifelikeness, upheld by 19th-century culture, loaded realist symbols with weighty circumstantiality and with the concrete task of presenting a clear embodiment of the official myth. Since the symbol is the real life of the idea itself,[41] realistic views of the Moscow Kremlin as the chief focus of holiness of the Moscow Tsardom, the centre of 'Holy Russia', enjoyed a particularly wide distribution. The orientation of official piety during Nicholas II's time towards the model of Muscovite Russia in the 17th century found its reflection in the background landscape of the icon (illus. 102). An example is the 'Feodorovskaya Mother of God with Name Saints of the Imperial

Household', painted by V. P. Guryanov in 1913, in honour of the 300th anniversary of the Romanov dynasty. In another icon, of the 'Guardian Angel' (1912) by Guryanov, the same kind of landscape expressed the idea of the protection of the Russian empire by heavenly powers: the figure of the angel is depicted with cross and sword against the background of the Moscow Kremlin walls (illus. 103, 104).

On the icon of St Paraskeva (*c.* 1890) by I. Pankryshev, whose workshop in Mstyora, as V. T. Georgievsky put it, 'painted to order only and in every style',[42] the figure of the saint is again portrayed against the background of the Moscow Kremlin. The image was dedicated to Countess P. S. Uvarova,

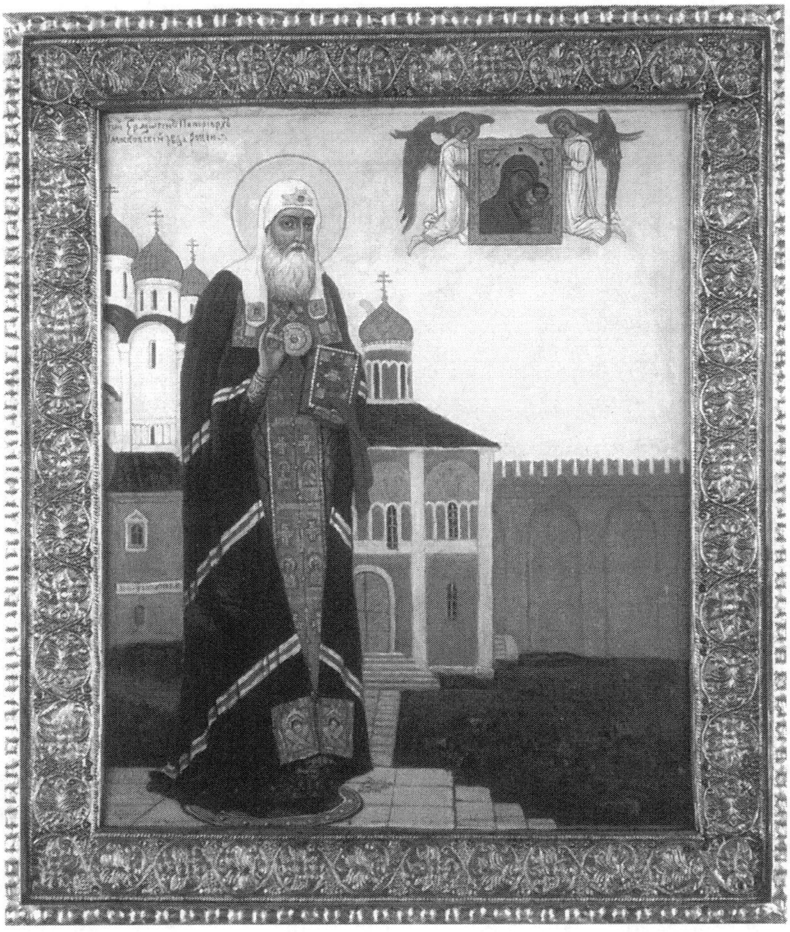

102. *Patriarch Germogen*, early 20th century. State Museum of the History of Religion, St Petersburg.

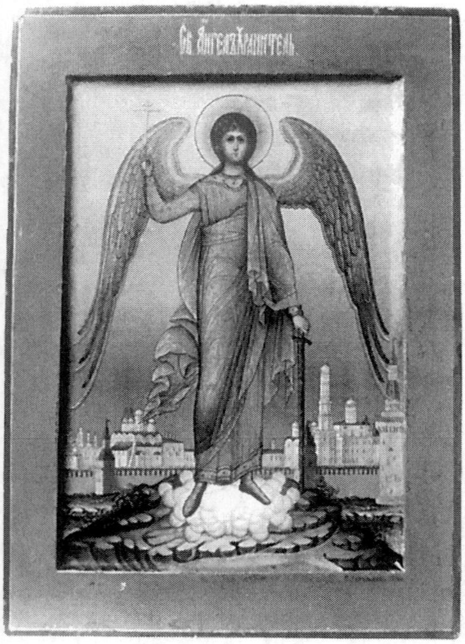

103. V. P. Guryanov, *Guardian Angel*, Moscow, 1912, State Museum of the History of Religion, St Petersburg.

and its landscape was meant to reflect the idea of the protection of the work of the Moscow Imperial Archaeological Society on its 25th anniversary by her own name saint (see illus. 71).

During the second half of the 18th century icons began to be painted in Russia in which the enigmatic quality of Petrine Baroque 'allegorial' landscapes was replaced by a kind of 'ideal landscape',[43] which corresponded to the spirit and fashion of the Enlightenment. Their symbolism developed as if in parallel to the that of topographical realism, and on a lower level reflected no less interestingly the mental background of the times.

The Palekh icon of 'St John the Baptist in the Wilderness' presents us with a typically 'idealistic' (or 'Romantic') landscape, distantly reminiscent in detail of the classical scenes of Claude Lorrain or the then-fashionable canvases of Salvator Rosa. The variety and complexity of *chiaroscuro* effects, the richness of colour and tone, the freedom in location and vegetation, the unexpected effects of perspective – all these were borrowed by the craftsman from secular painting and printmaking that one way or another had come to his notice. As a result the prayer icon was turned into a kind of sacral image of Nature, populated not only by saints but by exotic beings: the new spirit of enquiry that appeared in the 17th and 18th centuries propelled scientific expeditions to distant lands, which furnished examples, descriptions and prints of exotic plants and animals.

In Catherine the Great's reign, 'enlightened devotion' came into fashion. Trying to create a 'natural religion', a 'religion of Reason', the deists of the age of Enlightenment beheld in the harmony of nature proof of a Creator's existence. Since nature was accorded a high aesthetic evaluation in the culture of the age, landscape painting and the art of constructing gardens and parks acquired particular significance. Nature and the landscape garden were construed within the context of the utopian 'natural paradise', while humanity, located in 'wild' landscape, was supposed by this way of thinking

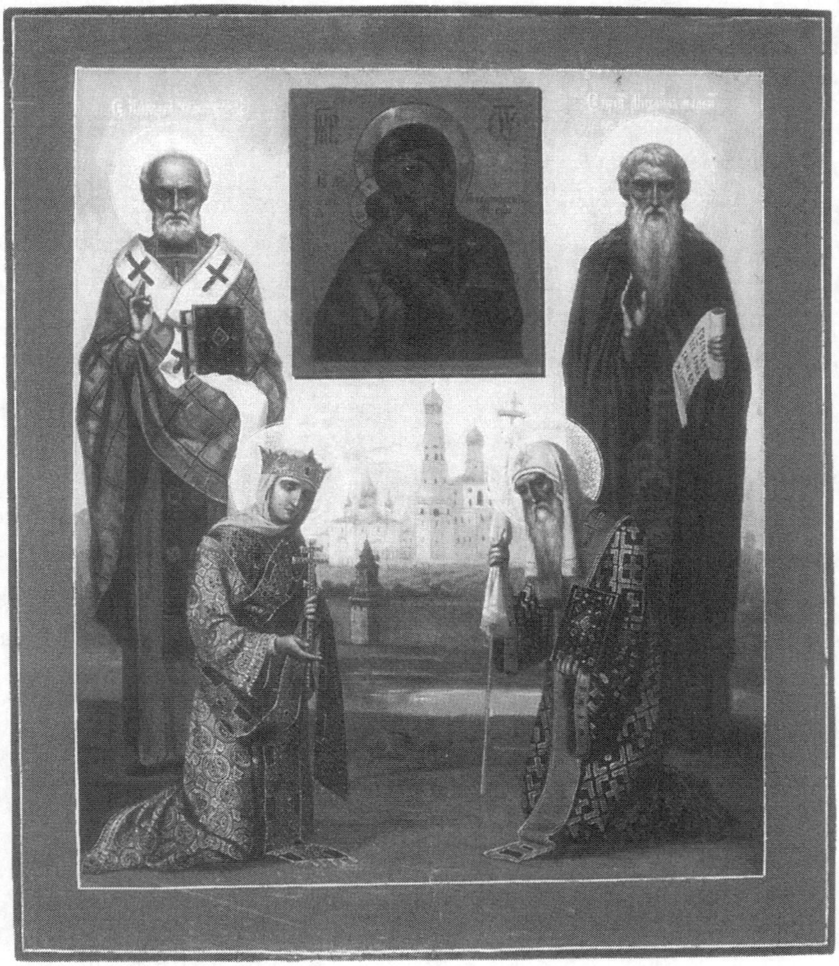

104. V. P. Guryanov, *The Feodorovskaya Mother of God with Name-day Saints of the Imperial House: Nicholas the Wonder-worker, Tsaritsa Alexandra, Metropolitan Aleksey and Michael Malein*, 1913, Moscow. Inscribed on the back: 'This icon was painted for the Church of the Holy Trinity, in commemoration of the 300th anniversary of the blessed rule of the House of Romanov, by the assiduous icon painter V. P. Guryanov. 1913.' State Museum of the History of Religion, St Petersburg.

to seek in its own soul an order that would correspond to the God-given surrounding natural scene. Thus in one Palekh icon the figure of St John the Baptist 'sinks' into the landscape (illus. 105). The same is true of an icon of 'St John the Divine on Patmos' from the second half of the 18th century (illus. 106). It is important to note that the natural landscape in both these icons seems chaotic only at first glance. By the canons of classicism, landscape could not exist without mankind and traces of its activity: the 'mechanistic concept of matter' presupposed the saturation of nature with reason, and its depiction with didactic purpose. Thus, in the depiction, both that of the 'wilderness' in the first icon and of 'Patmos' in the second we can observe Romantic pseudo-Gothic architectural stage scenery, demonstrating that the holy personages' relationship with 'savage and turbulent' nature has been adorned by its intelligent appropriation and organization. Incidentally, these Romantic structures tell us that some components of the Romantic landscape were an inalienable part of the visual art and icon painting of the Enlightenment. In just the same way, as D. S. Likhachov observed, certain Romantic elements in parks 'appeared far earlier than the age of Romanticism itself in literature, and only later were made meaningful for the Romantic era'.[44]

105. *John the Baptist in the Wilderness*, second half of the 18th century. Palekh Art Museum, Palekh.

106. *St John the Divine on Patmos*, second half of 18th century. Palekh Art Museum, Palekh.

107. A.V. Khokhlov, *John the Baptist in the Wilderness*, early 20th century, Palekh. Collection of Khokhlov family, Palekh.

In the artificial garden organized by natural principles in the second half of the 18th century, people often tried also to create a special emotional atmosphere of the simple, virtuous life. They constructed hovels and hermitages in such gardens, symbolizing the quiet, simple life of the pious person living in accord with nature. An interesting reflection of this motif can be seen in the second Palekh icon, 'John the Baptist in the Wilderness', which is an early-20th-century copy of a late-18th-century image. Instead

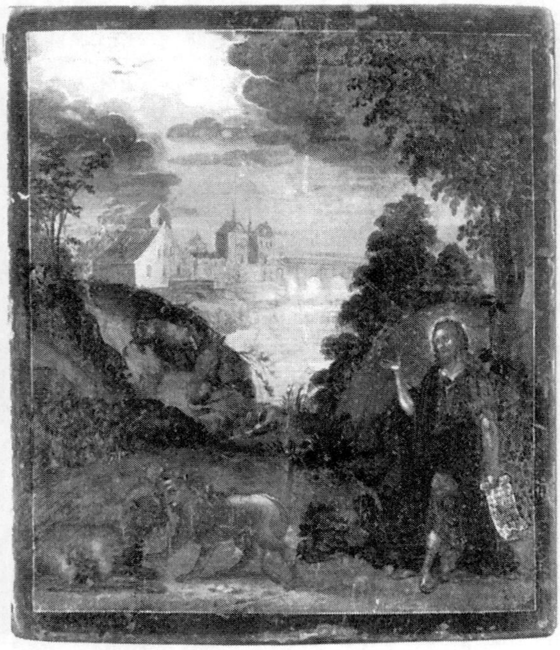

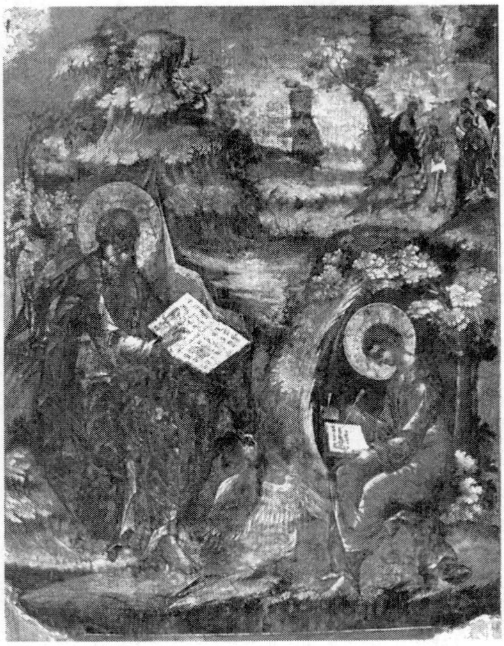

of pseudo-Gothic stage scenery, a hovel appears in it; this conceals itself in a landscape reminiscent of a heavenly paradise that has descended to earth (illus. 107).

In neo-Romantic art the landscape of Palekh icons was to acquire the symbolism characteristic of Russian Art Nouveau; a good example of this is an image of St Tikhon Lukhovskoy from the beginning of the 20th century (see illus. 93). The distant views and 'quiet hermitage' painted in the manner of M. V. Nesterov (1862–1942) convey neo-Romantic moods typical of the Russian religious renaissance. The same neo-Romantic coloration can be discerned in the symbolism of the hermit's hut on hagiological icons and small-scale images of St Serafim of Sarov, a vast quantity of which were produced in Palekh, Mstyora and Kholuy in 1903, on the eve of Serafim's canonization.

Word, Emblem, Heraldry

'In the beginning was the Word, and the Word was with God, and the Word was God. The same was in the beginning with God. All things were made by him; and without him was not anything made that was made. In him was life; and the life was the light of men' (Gospel according to St John, 1, 1–4). These opening words of the Fourth Evangelist established the special relationship between the word and the image in the Christian world view. The word inscribed on an icon always possessed great significance.

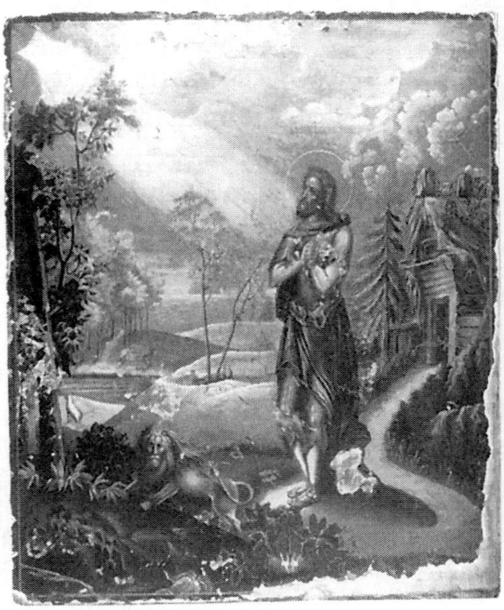

The *title* of Ivan Afanasyev's icon, 'The Wonder-working Grand Princes of Vladimir', is written not in a solemn decorative script (as was normal on old examples) but in semi-uncials. It is significant that from the 18th century, titles of icons in cursive hand begin to be more and more widespread. The titles themselves are increasingly included in the picture. This new symbolic linking of the word, its graphic qualities and the sacral representation created a new semiotic space for the work of art as text. In the medieval tradition, word and picture supplemented each other. It is sufficient to recall Basil the Great's dictum, cited earlier, on the 'additional' power that the image lent the word. In the Baroque icon of the New Ritual this medieval syncretism of the verbal and pictorial categories underwent a significant complication: the picture began to be apprehended actually as united in substance with the words.

The foundation of this unification of word and picture was a new factor within Russian medieval culture: Baroque rhetoric. After its acceptance of Christianity, early Rus adhered, of course, to the rhetorical tradition of Byzantium.[45] However, this tradition, unlike the Latin one, did not facilitate either the development of rhetoric as a scholarly discipline or the creation of textbooks for its study in the East Slav context. Thus both Old Russian literature and icon painting, to put things simply, orientated themselves on examples and not on the rules that generated those examples.[46]

The 17th century, meanwhile, brought a new attitude to rules in themselves. This was connected with the absorption of rhetoric in its Western, Latin variant. Through a Polish cultural medium the Latin rhetorical tradition began to accommodate itself within an East Slav milieu, first of all in the newly founded educational establishments. At first this process of adopting rhetoric as one of the seven liberal arts developed in Ukraine and Belorussia. Courses in rhetoric were given at the Kievan Mogila college, in the 'brotherhood schools' and other educational establishments. Very soon, however, rhetoric as codified for textbook use went beyond the bounds of merely instructional purposes.

As a descriptive system, rhetoric in Russia had a special authority in the cultural context of the period. Rhetoric on the Latin model acquired and maintained a universal significance for the language of Russian culture as a whole right up to the end of the 18th century. We shall only understand the meaning of the changes in the medieval iconic system of representation if we clarify the rhetorical devices and rules of aesthetic thought during that period. The careful description of the devices of invention (*inventio*), arrangement (*dispositio*) and formulation or embellishment (*elocutio*) in works on poetics and rhetoric served as direct instruction for the composition not only of literary texts – sermons, panegyrics, plays, poems – but of visual ones too: icons, portraits, all kinds of pictures and works of art. The Baroque, of course, is a rhetorical type of culture, directed towards the model and rules for its repetition.

The rhetorical teaching on the subject of embellishment (*elocutio*) that embraced all the categories of transformation of ordinary language, of the model that rhetoric proposed, had a special significance here. It included topics such as addition (*adjectio*), subtraction (*detractio*), transposition (*transmutatio*) and substitution (*immutatio*). We may suppose that it was just these categories that exercised a serious influence on the way the role of framing and ornament were treated in the new Baroque icon. Hence it was that framing and ornament acquired a particular semiotic significance at that time. Following the major rhetorical objective of persuasiveness, the religious image began to acquire a multitude of possible framing-structures, thought of as its 'ornament', that is its embellishment (*elocutio*). The very choice of frame, its decoration and conceptualization were subject to the peculiarities of the various rules of rhetoric. Thus in the Baroque period the gradual 'filling up' of the icon with ornament is invariably accompanied by a new symbolic linkage between word and visual representation.

108. Detail from *Feodosiy of Totma*, end of 18th century. Kolomenskoye Historical and Architectural Museum-Preserve, Moscow.

The titles of saints on Baroque icons could be included, interestingly, in the space of the nimbus (halo); they could even be components of the outline of the nimbus itself. Thus the string of words turned into a symbolic boundary between the 'sacral' (the periphery of an icon) and the 'super-sacral', i.e., the nimbus as a concentration of the uncreated divine energies and of grace (illus. 108; see also 91). Incidentally, this framing function of the word could 'mirror itself' in other frame elements. Icons of the 17th to 19th centuries often display margins and internal delimited areas that are almost completely filled with texts. The ornamental text effectively imitated the frame; it served as decorative adornment and it carried aesthetic and functional significance (illus. 109, 164).

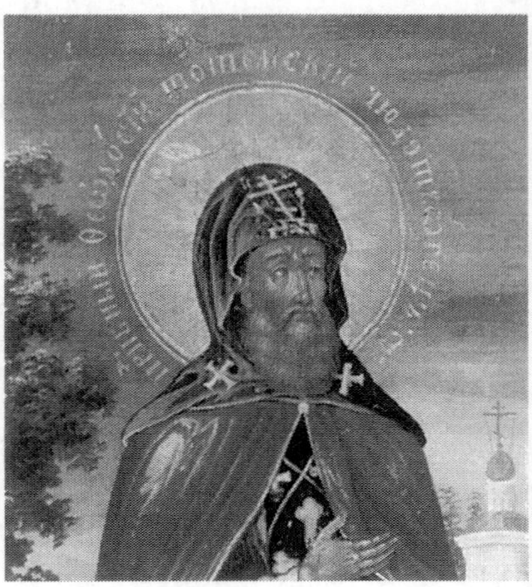

One of the significant demonstrations of an increased rhetorical role of the word is the widespread Baroque motif linking it with the cross – a most archaic symbol, a symbol of the highest sacral values, to which many cultural texts subordinate themselves.[47] The symbol of the cross becomes a most important organizer of artistic texts in the Baroque age: it registers a multi-layered content.

On the New Ritualist icon of 'The Resurrection of Christ', painted in 1722 at Pereyaslavl-Zalessky by a local craftsman, Aleksey Loginov, word and cross appear in an uninterrupted symbolic unity (illus. 110). The verses inscribed on the icon bear witness that the word had here acquired independent significance in the context of a synthesis – typical for Baroque poetics – of different artistic forms: poetry and painting. Here too can be discerned the important Baroque principle of play and enigma, linked with the Baroque concept of the mind as a gift from the Creator – the great divine gift to mankind. The aesthetic principles proclaimed in the Baroque – 'poetry is spoken painting', while 'painting is silent poetry' – spurred on this game of the mind and orientated the devotional consciousness towards the apprehension of a text of an esoteric kind. Such a text would be accessible only to the initiated and to those possessing a key to its proper reading. The enigma could seemingly be deciphered only by people of the 'same faith'.

Loginov's icon is distinguished by a many-layered structure of images that presupposes a slow, gradual reading. Its compositional basis consists of the symbols of cross and circle. The depiction of a cross against the background of the circle conveys a striving for vertical and horizontal symmetry, and here expresses the absolute nature of the redemptive sacrifice of the Saviour. On the vertical axis, in correspondence with the mirror principle of Baroque thinking, within this cross there is another reflected – containing the Crucifixion, Golgotha and the kneeling Mary Magdalene. On the side-arms of the cross the Mother of God and St John the Divine are depicted. On the circular medallion at the centre (which seems to reflect the greater circle), we are given the Resurrection of Christ itself, in a Western version with prostrate Roman warriors. This iconographic type of the Resurrection, connected with Western iconography, chiefly circulated in New Ritualist icon-painting of the 17th to 19th centuries. The centre of the composition is also framed by scenes in medallions illustrating Old and New Testament subjects. 'Earth' in the icon is symbolized by Christ's Descent into Hell.

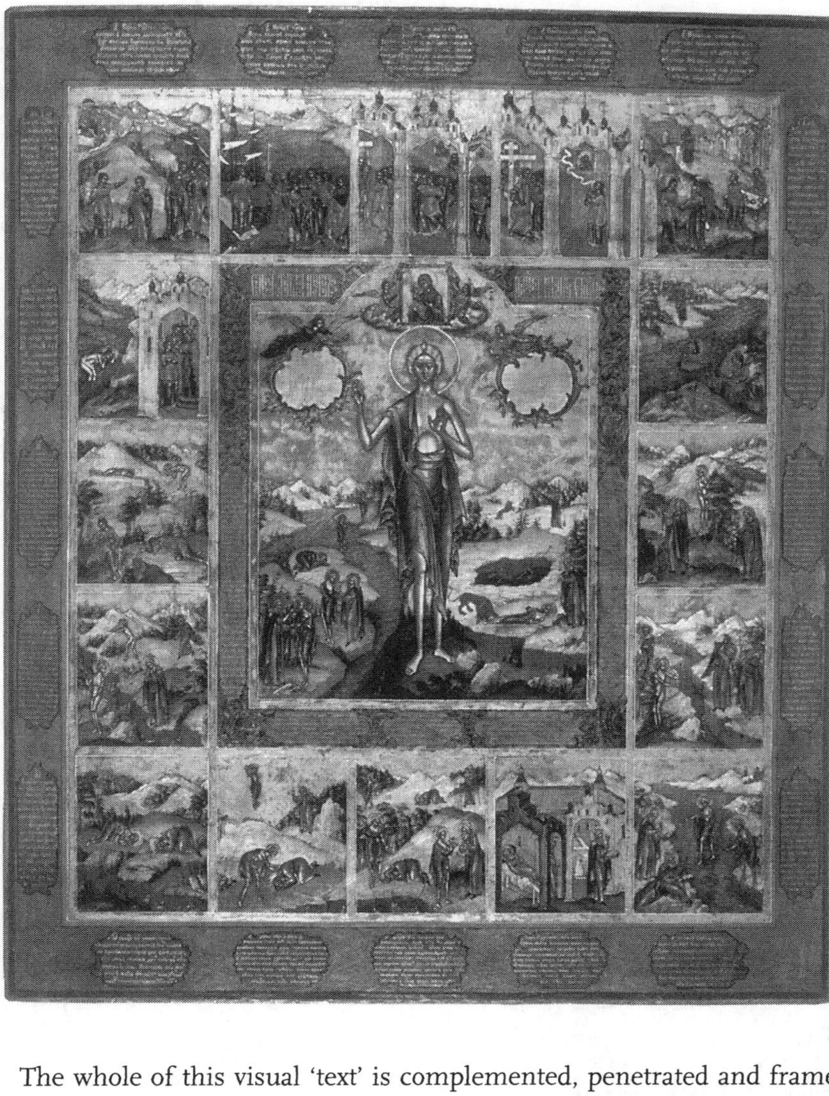

109. I. V. Bogatyryov, *St Mary of Egypt with Life*, 1804, Urals, Nevyansk. State Museum of the History of Religion, St Petersburg.

The whole of this visual 'text' is complemented, penetrated and framed by the titles and verses written on the scrolls. It is as if an emotional, religious and semantic code for the decipherment of complex layers of symbolism were concealed in them. Thus the order in which one would logically read the verses echoes the correct order for the performance of the liturgy from the official Orthodox Church's point of view. The painter has given the key to reading the verses on the four scrolls held up by angels that frame the central image of the Resurrection. This word (in Russian, *voskresenie*) has to be read syllable by syllable as it is split up on the four scrolls: *vo–skre–se–nie*. As for the order in which these syllabic components are arranged, it corresponds to the direction a priest takes walking round the altar at the moment of communion according to the New Rite: that is, against the motion of the sun, in contrast with the Old Rite – 'going sunwise', with the sun (illus. 111).

Following this key, the believer would begin to read the verses, arranged as a poetic equivalent to sun-rays. In Baroque emblematics, as I noted earlier, the sun traditionally symbolized Christ (just as the moon symbolized the Mother of God). Related as they were to the pictorial aspect of poetry (*picta – poesis*), such poetic graphemes were widespread in the Baroque period in both high and low culture.[48] Poetic graphemes in the form of allegorical figures of the sun, an eagle, a star, a heart, etc., were produced by Simeon of Polotsk and by many other Baroque poets. It was the pattern of the sun that was selected by Aleksey Loginov for his icon: as the icon painter himself puts it, the rows of letters arranged to represent sun-rays lead 'in brightness amid the paths of the Cross'.

110. Aleksey Loginov, *Resurrection of Christ*, 1721. State Museum of the History of Religion, St Petersburg.

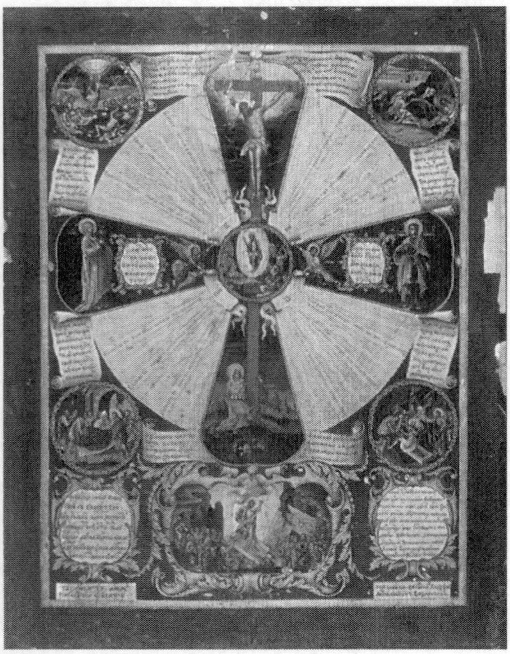

In each of the sun-segments formed by the intersection of the large cross's arms there are three lines of poetry. In the upper left segment the universal meaning of the redemptive sacrifice is expressed in verse (with a few lacunae): (1) The Saviour Jesus has arisen for the sake of the most blessed truth; (2) And through resurrection having reanimated us in saintliness . . . ; (3) In truth Son of God, Blessed Ruler of the Angels. Thereafter, the theme of glorification by the heavenly hierarchy of the miracle that has been enacted is developed: (1) The archangels in heaven make their praise of the holiness of Christ; (2) And in the same way they glorify the holy . . . ; (3) While the cherubim God's holiness ineffably . . . . Then the human race praises the Resurrection: (1) Human beings praise the

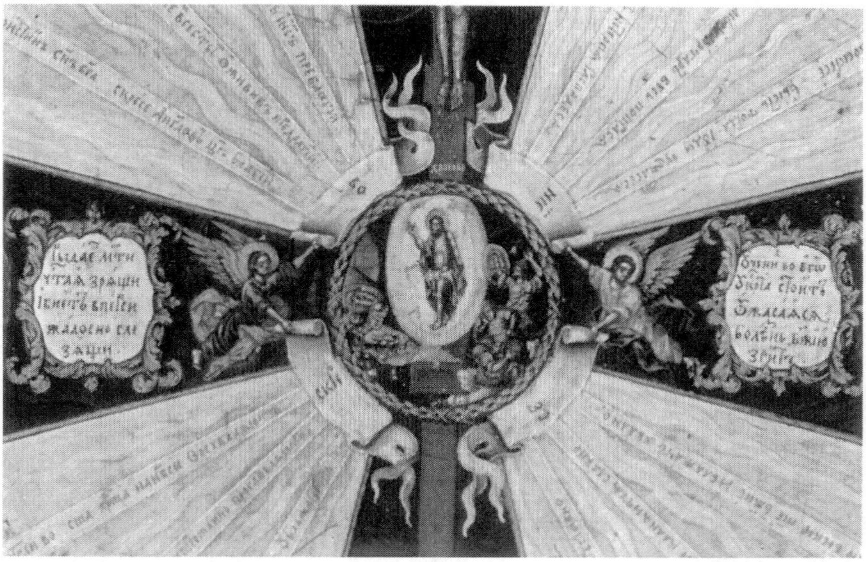

111. Detail from the *Resurrection of Christ* (illus. 110).

Resurrection honestly and wholeheartedly; (2) For it is glorious to praise the Resurrection of God; (3) They magnify God's Resurrection and give praiseful blessings. Finally, in the last segment of the grapheme in verse, the theme of the victory of the risen Christ and of vengeance on the forces of darkness is developed: (1) When He was resurrected then Judas hanged himself; (2) At the Lord's Resurrection all Tartarus was cast down; (3) Learning of the Resurrection the Devil was routed in despair.

As is clear, the craftsman also simultaneously encoded a definite hierarchy of the 'heavenly 'and the 'earthly' into this sequence for reading the verses. Thus the emblematic aspect of graphic poetry was adapted not only to the didactic purpose of acquainting believers with the New Ritual but also to the particular significance for Orthodoxy of the act of Resurrection. The art of the icon painter seems focused on the decipherment of the multivalent quality and the 'secret' sense of the text. It was related also to the entertaining and playful elements that were revealed in the unbroken continuity of the verse lines on the scrolls and the pictures in the medallions. By symbolically coupling these lines and pictures the icon painter both strengthened the didactic aspect of the prayer image and plugged the human mind, as it were, into religious experience. The strengthening of the role of reason in religious experience would, of course, become one of the main nerves of Baroque culture. In this connection, in the lower-right-hand corner, the craftsman wrote in his verse 'introduction' to the iconic text as a whole (illus. 112):

> The image . . . of Christ's Resurrection has been composed in verses. And we display them between the paths of the cross shining . . . This has been written not with contrivance, but for people to reflect on, for the solace of the assiduous. And from the scrolls you will learn the accomplishment of the words in which in the text the Resurrection is inscribed.

From this it is clear that all the playfulness was imbued with an extremely serious character. This accent on didacticism and the demonstration of deep mystical content of New Ritualist symbols welded together the artistic text. All the semantic symbolical layers in the icon have turned out to be strictly determined and interrelated.

The *topmost* scroll, which seems to crown the entire scene, is divided into two thematic parts. The verses, a stylization of the Gospel text, are here set out as if to mirror each other, and are deliberately attached respectively to the beginning and end of the poetic grapheme. The part to the left relates to the cosmic significance of the Resurrection and adheres to the heavenly aspect of the grapheme:

> When Christ was raised up on the cross
> Then were all the creatures and the earth downcast
> The sun was obscured and the moon . . .
> And the stones also were turned to dust.

The right-hand side by contrast, illustrating the victory of God over the forces of evil, adheres to the earthly:

> The veil of the temple was then rent in twain
> And the Devil was trampled down by the angels
> Through the Cross all are released from their oath
> Who living in the world are consumed by sin.

Demanding thus imaginative capability from the worshipper's mind, the icon painter also distributed the pictures in the medallions and the verses on the scrolls according to a logical scheme. In the upper left and right medallions he presented illustrations of verses on Old Testament themes. The vision of the prophet Ezekiel and the episode in which the prophet Jonah who (the Bible tells us) remained three days and nights in the belly of a whale, calling upon God, was at His command vomited out onto dry land, both demonstrated the Old Testament foundation of Christianity's great miracle:

> Ezekiel sees . . .
> A vision boldly
> And miraculously . . .
> A body alive
> This wonder reveals
> Resurrection
> And is to be for the salvation
> Of all Christians.

And on the opposite scroll there is:

> Jonah by an earthly whale
> Was taken and devoured.
> But after three days
> This man was revealed as saved,
> Foretelling that in three days
> Christ would be resurrected
> Be revealed as entire
> Without any suffering.

Thereafter New Testament scenes of miracles and resurrections performed by Christ are explained:

> 1. In . . . dead
> Christ resurrects
> And re-establishes thereby
> This power,

And by this reveals
His Resurrection
And glorifies those
Who believe in Him.

The four-day
Dead Lazarus
Christ raises up,
Summons from the tomb.
By which raising
It is meant that God
To others who believe
Should be a giver of life.

On . . . having descended into Hell
The Saviour of all,
God and man, Christ the redeemer,
Retrieved all the saints from there
And, bestowing grace, led them into the kingdom,
While he destroyed the copper gates of Hell
And the fastenings of the eternal doors.

All this complex symbolism, informed by Baroque tastes, of course demanded knowledge and preparation from the worshipper. In that sense Aleksey Loginov's icon testifies to the serious significance of the development of Russian religious culture of Patriarch Nikon's reforms. It is a crucial point that the icon was painted by a craftsman from the provinces, not the capital, which speaks well of the level of education of a lowborn person of that period. The verbal message on an icon became an address to human reason and feeling simultaneously: it acquired a special meaning in spiritual life. Nor is there anything accidental in the general passion for poetry: 'The attitude that poetic activity was a form of spiritual, honourable and noble labour partly explains the universal 17th century passion for writing verse, reaching the point of graphomania. Not only professional poets, but any literate people wrote poems'.[49]

Another icon that we can view as belonging to the same typological series is the 'Mystery of the Cross' (*c.* 1814), whose iconography was borrowed from a print of the same title from the mystical work of the German writer Karl von Eckhartshausen and was linked with Masonic culture and symbolism (illus. 113). The symbolic linkage of word and cross here acquires visual transparency not only in connection with the edificatory aspect of the image, but with its deliberate inclusion of secret meanings that corresponded with the mystical orientation of Russian society at the end of the 18th century and early in the 19th.

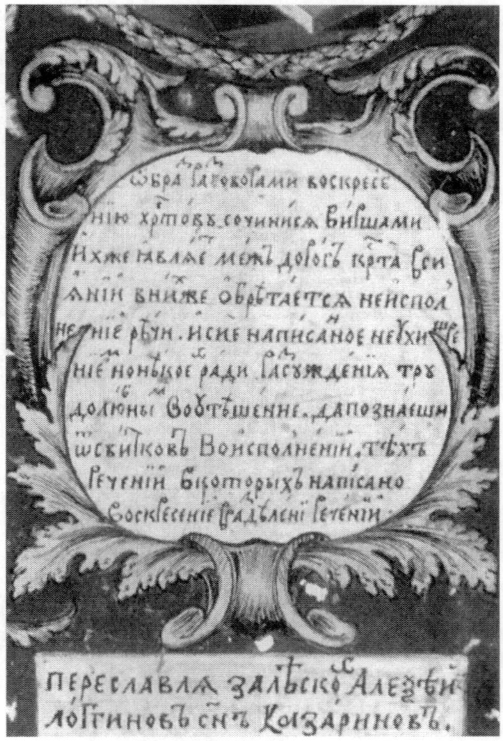

112. Detail from the *Resurrection of Christ* (illus. 110).

Christ carrying the Cross is depicted within a circle. His figure is surrounded by a multitude of crosses that seem to reflect one another – a typical effect of variously angled mirrors. Quotations from the Old Testament prophet Isaiah and the apostle Paul, bordering the circle, open the image up to us. On the inner frame is inscribed: 'But he was wounded for our transgressions and bruised for our iniquities; the chastisement of our peace was upon him, and with his stripes we are healed' (Isaiah 53:5). This Old Testament prophecy is reinforced by a New Testament quotation: 'For even hereunto were ye called: because Christ also suffered for us, leaving us an example, that ye should follow in his steps' (I Peter 2:21).

Within the 'mirrored' part of the icon each of the crosses receives a name that acts as a crucial key for its comprehension: 'Oppression by enemies', 'untruth', 'poverty', 'mockery', 'malice', 'spite', 'thirst', 'contempt', 'rendering evil for good', 'slander', 'unjust punishment', 'ills and humiliations', 'unjust people' – all these represent the 'lawless' aspects and sins of the world, for which Christ would be the redeemer.

Though specialists have often maintained that in Russian Orthodoxy (as distinct from Western Christianity) 'no special attention was fixed on the sufferings of Christ' (G. Fedotov), the theme of the Passion of Christ was

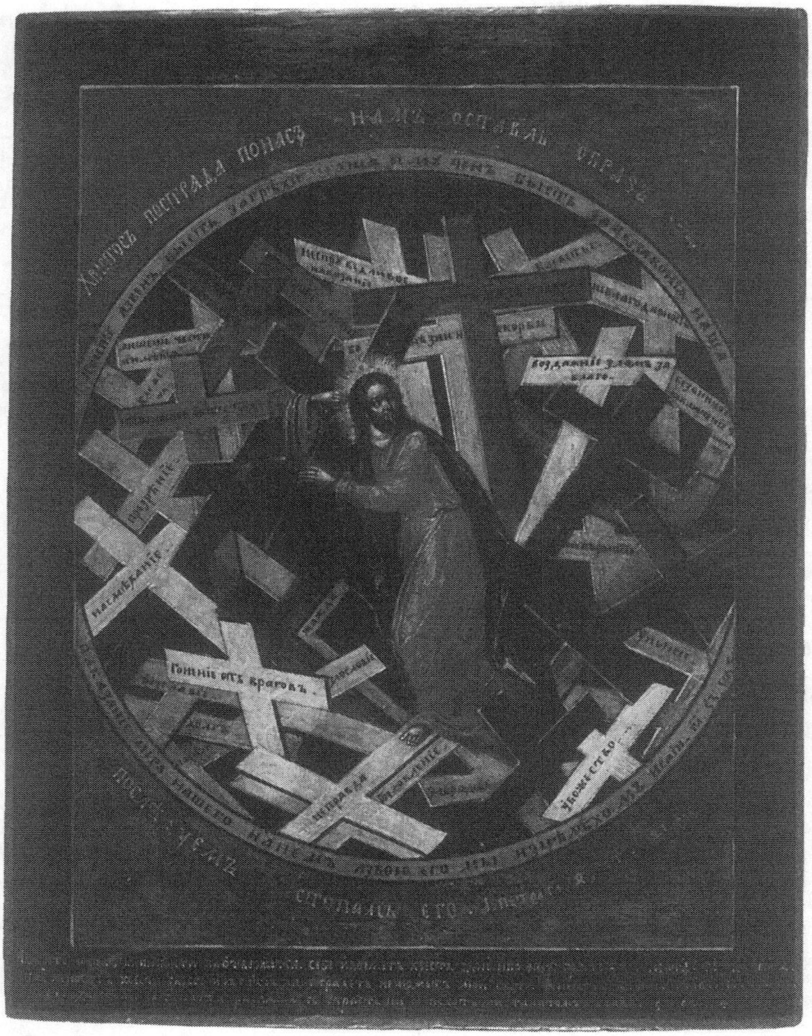

113. *Mystery of the Cross*, *c*. 1814. State Museum of the History of Religion, St Petersburg.

widespread in the mass-produced craft icons of the 18th and 19th centuries. The first icons of a Passion cycle were made by Fyodor Zubov for the iconostasis of the Smolensk Cathedral of the Moscow Novodevichy Convent in 1684, using Western prototypes. They instigated the active development of the subject, exemplified by the 18th-century icon I have just described. In parallel with this the Deisis gradually disappeared from the Baroque iconostasis of the late 17th and 18th centuries: the medieval idea of heavenly intercession for humanity began to be replaced by a reorientation of the believer's consciousness towards the salvatory worth of earthly actions in following the historical path of Christ. Hence we can see representations of the Passion cycle on 18th-century Suzdalian icons of the Resurrection and the Descent into Hell too. They were often arranged in the form of an inner frame for the central element – Christ's Resurrection. They were also included in menologic icons representing the feast days of the year, as also in complex subjects involving the Mother of God (see illus. 37). It is noteworthy that their sequence is in some cases to be followed 'against the sun' (anti-clockwise), i.e., in the same direction as priests would take around the altar according to the New Ritual, as used in the symbolic structure of Aleksey Loginov's icon.

The greater dependence of iconic representation on the word during the Baroque age gave birth to illustrative icons in which themes of edificatory parables as well as of visions and complex allegorical homilies were developed. In particular, certain icons that were quite widely distributed before and after 1700 can be put in this category: 'The Parable of the Rich Man' (illus. 114), 'The Parable of the Blind Man and the Lame Man', 'The Debate Between Life and Death', 'Monastic Purity', 'The Fates of the Righteous Person and the Sinner' (illus. 115), 'The Vision of the Sexton Tarasiy', 'The Vision of Yevlogiy', 'The Ship of Faith', 'Christ and the Bride', 'The Healing of the Blind Man', 'The Parable of Lazarus the Beggar' and some others (illus. 116). In this urge towards illustrativeness we perceive precisely that internal dependence of visual representation on the word that was to have a lengthy domination in the icons of the low-level Baroque. A characteristic example of this is provided by an 18th-century icon, 'The Labyrinth' (illus. 117).

An unknown icon painter selected the labyrinth as a suitable form for his didactic purposes. The magic square and the labyrinthine circle as examples of 'many-pathed tablet' (Simeon Polotsky) gave people a visual example of a 'way out' of an unrighteous path in life onto the authentic path of salvation. On the icon a mortal human being is shown inside the labyrinth. To either side of the latter, right and left, the same person is shown dying. On one side his soul is being received by a guardian angel, on the other by an angel of Satan. At the top is depicted the wall of Paradise with Christ seated on a throne; the angel bears up the soul of the righteous.

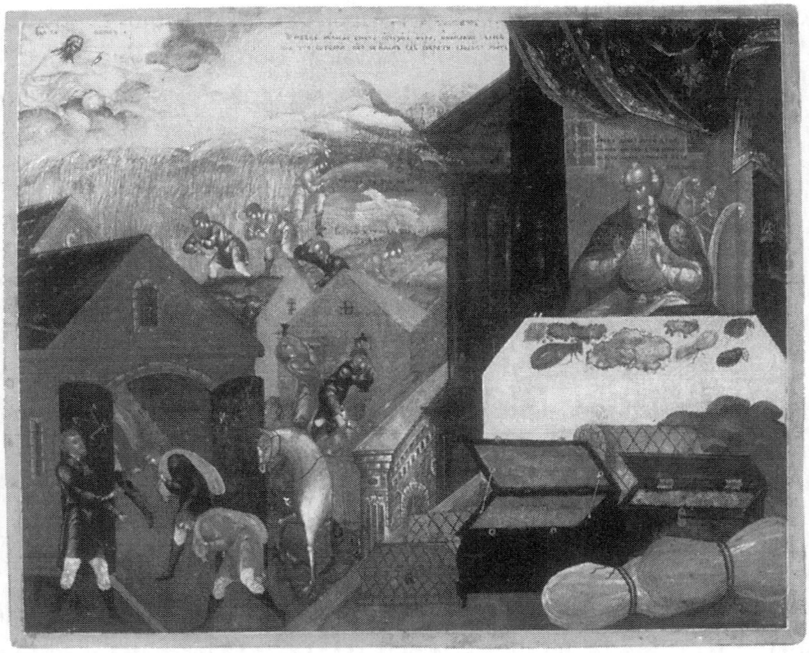

114. *The Parable of the Rich Man*, 18th century. Kolomenskoye Historical and Architectural Museum-Preserve, Moscow.

Below is depicted fiery Gehenna, which is the destination of the person's soul if, in traversing the labyrinth, he goes by dangerous paths. In correspondence with the significance of the word in the Baroque system of thought, these paths are provided with names and depicted according to a system of symbolic colour-opposition, in black on a red background: they are Envy, Slander, Murder, Lechery, Drunkenness, Pride, Vanity, Despondency, Wrath, Cupidity, Greed and Gluttony.

The labyrinth is a favourite motif of Baroque emblematics. In using the emblem of the labyrinth, an icon painter was able to put forward the subject-matter of personal devotion in its complex connection with abstract speculation and concretely visible signs. In brief, we have here an emblematism of artistic thought that is characteristic and ubiquitous in Baroque culture. Its 'hidden' and 'peripatetic' symbolism can be seen in icons up to the early 20th century.

The visual legibility of the artistic text was always linked with emblematics. A work saturated with emblems, whether print, funereal image, portrait or

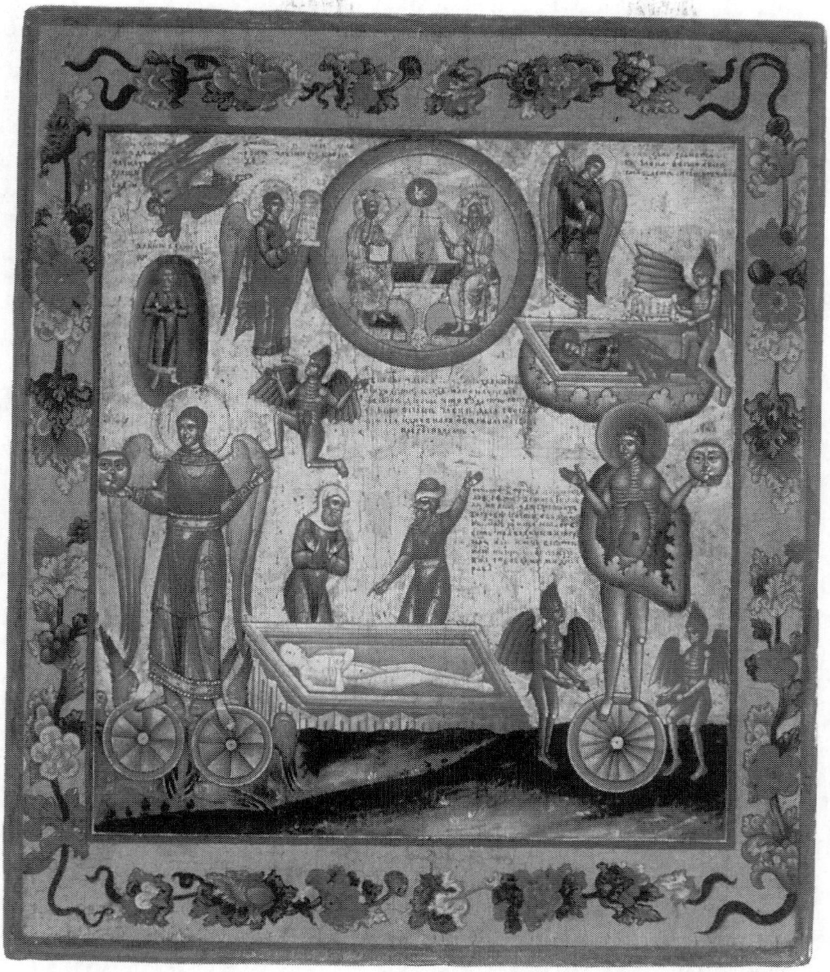

115. *The Fates of the Righteous Person and the Sinner*, 18th century. State Museum of the History of Religion, St Petersburg.

icon, would invariably fall into components that made sense only in the context of the unity and integrity of the whole composition.

The classic emblem consisted of a triad: device (*inscriptio, motto*), picture (*pictura, icon*) and signature or epigram in verse (*subscriptio*). From the second half of the 16th century this traditional tripartite form, containing a symbolic drawing and a symbolic verbal device, put its stamp on an unusually broad range of Catholic and Protestant works of art. The influence of emblem poetics on the Russian icon was distinctly felt in the second half of the 17th century, while in Russian and Balkan craft icon painting of the

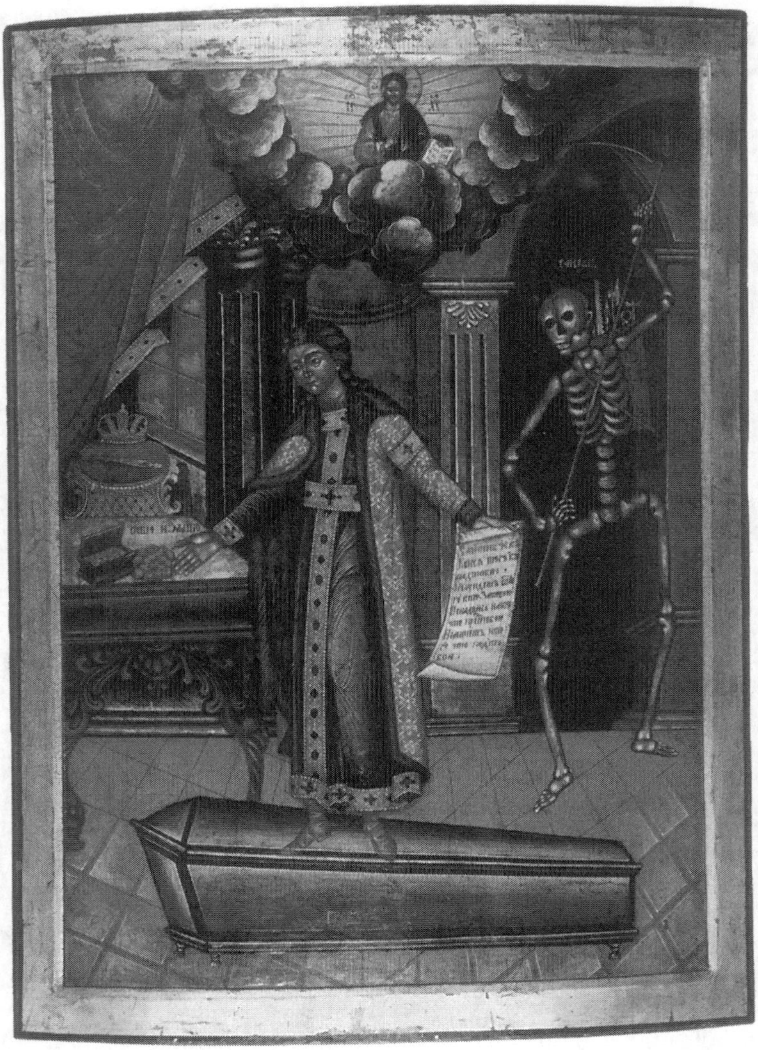

116. *'Mortal Man, Fear What is Above You'*, early 18th century. Kolomenskoye Historical and Architectural Museum-Preserve, Moscow.

18th century and early 19th it had already been transformed into a deeply encoded phenomenon.

If, for example, we juxtapose a classic emblem from Alciato's compendium *Emblematum Liber*, a Protestant epitaph image by the master craftsman J. Twenger (1586) from the church at Żurawin, and the synodal Orthodox icon of the Tsarevich Dimitriy[50] with scenes of his Life (1745), we can clearly see a transference of the classic symbolic triad that is typical

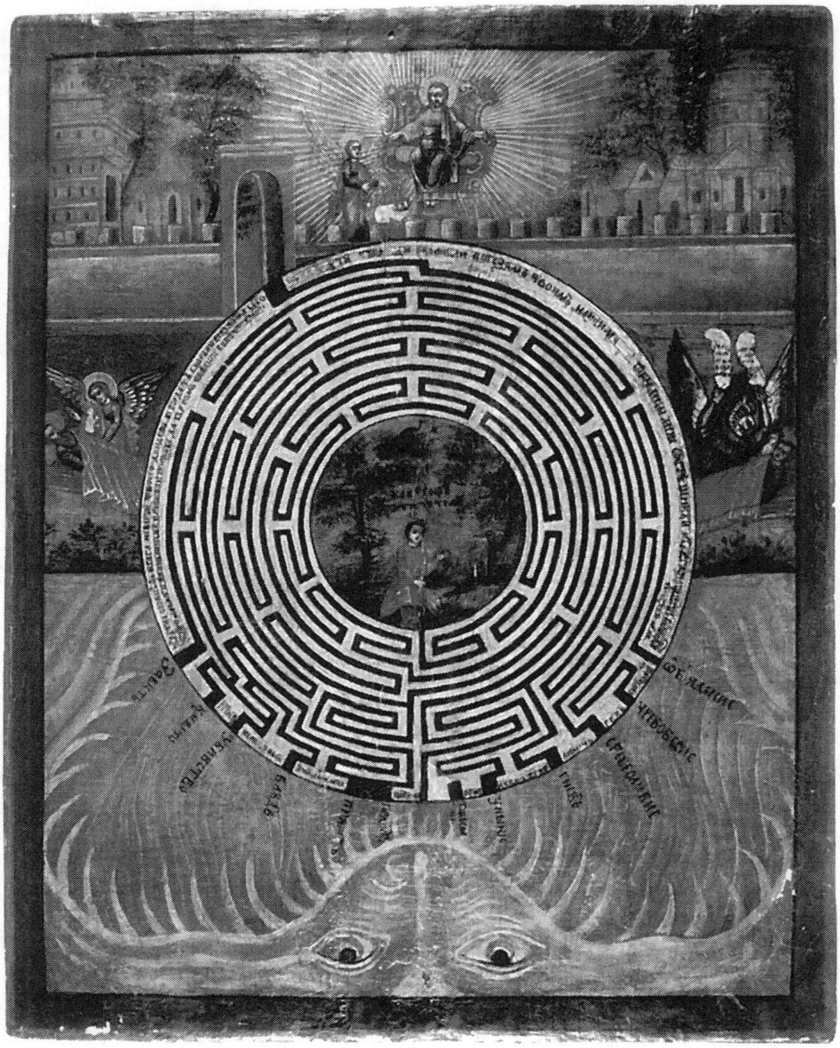

117. *Labyrinth*, 18th century. State Museum of the History of Religion, St Petersburg.

of the emblematic mentality. In the last two instances the picture is located between the title of the image and the extensive text that takes the place of the verse signature of the emblem, i.e., its explication (illus. 118, 119, 120).

The same thing is exemplified if we juxtapose Western European and Russian engraved portraits, or the Catholic and the Russian religious folk print and icon. Over the personage's image is located his name, while below

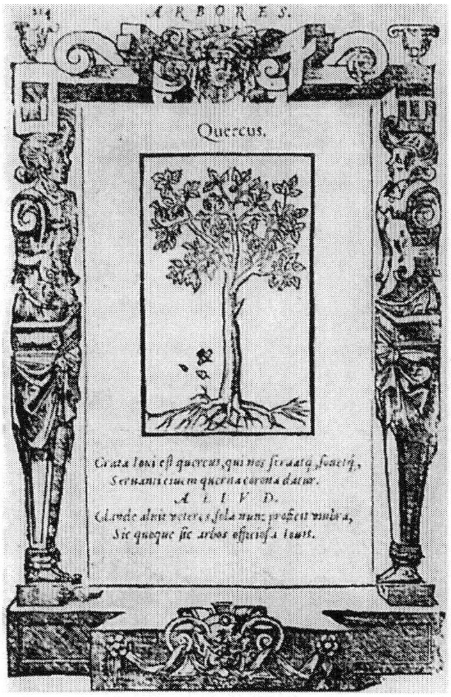

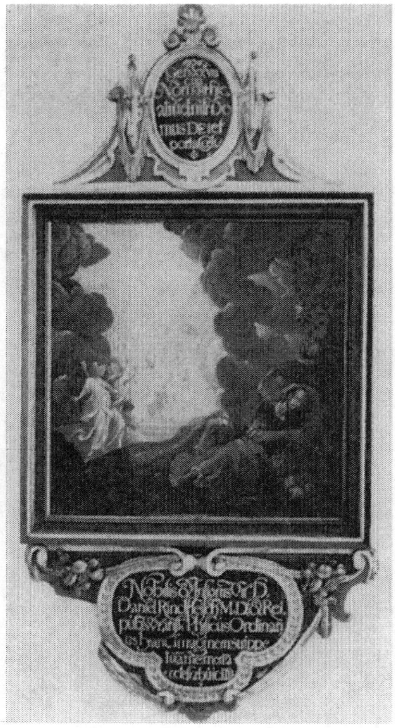

118. 'Quercus', an emblem featuring the oak from Andrea Alciato's *Emblematum liber* (Lyon, 1550).

119. J. Twenger, Epitaph for Daniel Rindfleisch with a scene of Jacob's Dream, 1596.

it is a more extensive text with panegyric content in the case of a worldly picture, and a sacral sense in the case of an icon (illus. 121, 122, 123). On an icon of the Holy Tsarevich Dimitriy with his Life, directly dependent on Western funerary images (even to its imitation of an outlined frame and fretwork cartouches) we see that its title – 'Image of the Holy and Faithful Tsarevich Dimitriy' – is given above the picture. This picture ('icon') illustrates the Tsarevich's innocent death, while the text of the troparion (in the 'fifth tone' of the Orthodox chant), given in a cartouche below the image, explains the sacral meaning of the event that has occurred and its significance for the Church (illus. 120).

The construction of the emblem is even more clearly visible in the icon 'St Aleksiy, Metropolitan of Moscow and the Blessed Sergius of Radonezh' (illus. 124). In a cartouche frame above the picture we find the icon's equivalent to an heraldic 'device':

> Holy Aleksiy entrusts Sergius with his office:
> But the latter refuses to accept it.

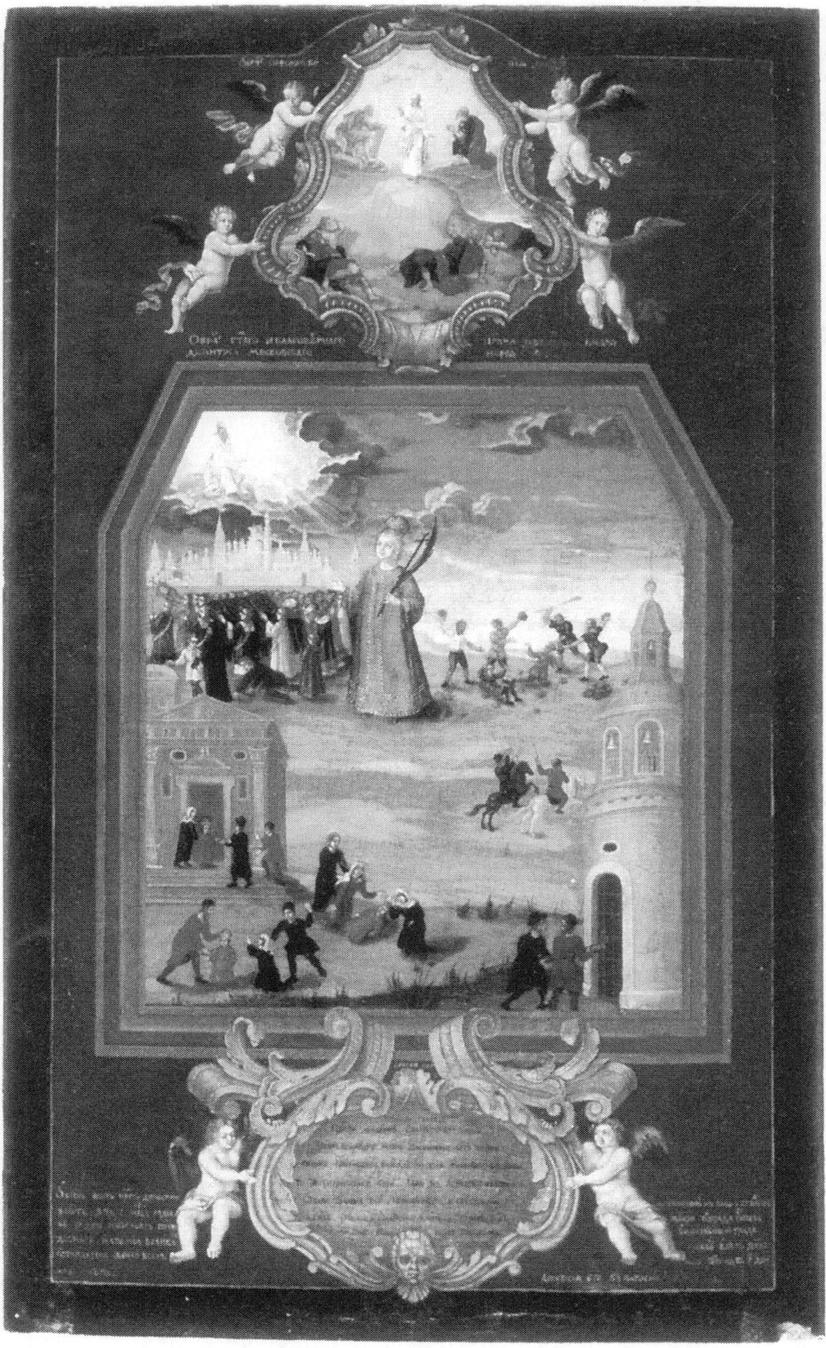

120. *Tsarevich Dimitriy with Life*, 1745. State Museum of the History of Religion, St Petersburg.

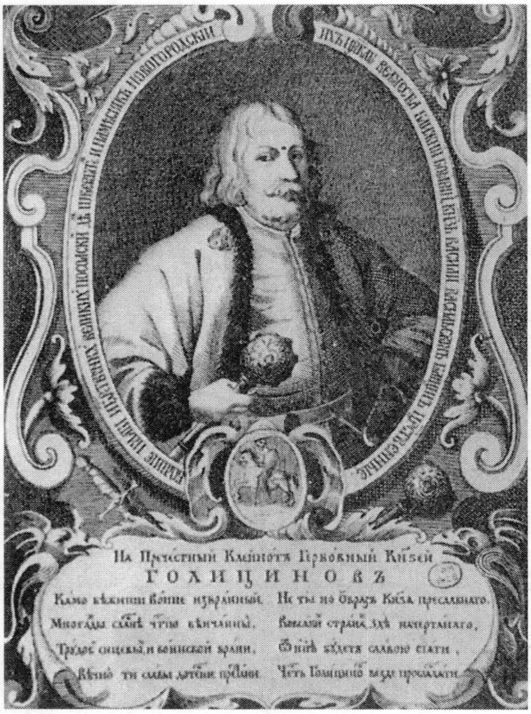

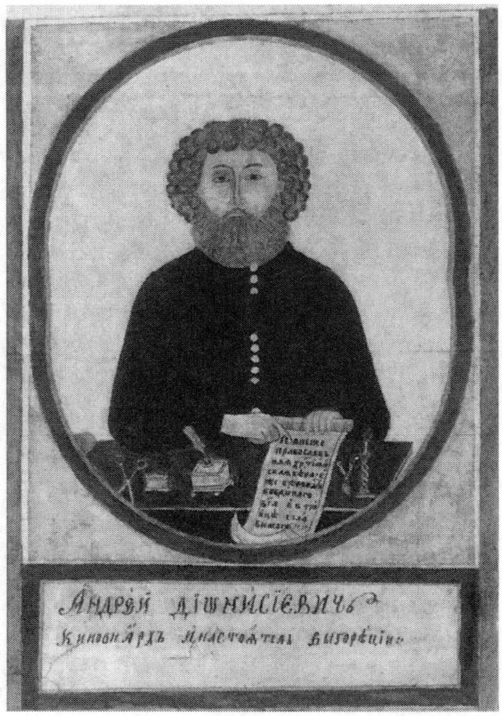

121. A. Tarasevich, *V. V. Golitsyn*, late 1680s, engraving. State Hermitage, St Petersburg.

122. Andrey Denisov, religious picture, a late 18th- or early 19th-century drawing. State Museum of the History of Religion, St Petersburg.

Below, on an unfurled scroll, the viewer will already have read a conclusion in verse to the very picture showing the saints:

> One contends with the other,
> And each performs a wondrous feat,
> But which is the victor?
> Both the righteous holy man
> And Sergius are triumphant:
> To the Lord's will both of them agree.

In this way the altered construction of the emblem constituted the basis for a huge number of works not only (I should emphasize) by official, but also by Old Ritualist icon painters. From the second half of the 17th century right up to the early 20th century, the representation of any Christian hero or sacred event might be located between the title (the name) of an icon and its explicatory 'signature' text in a special frame below (for example, the

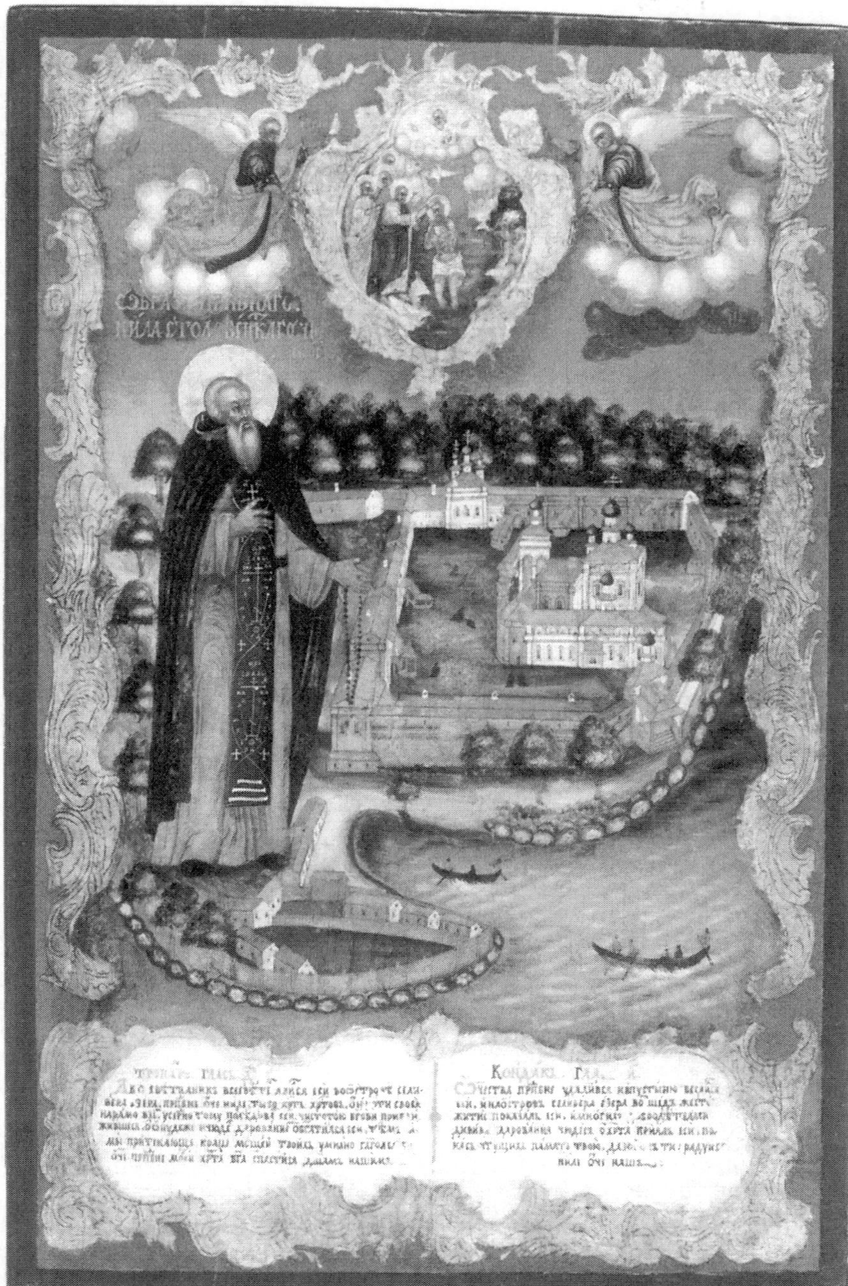

123. *Nil Stolbensky*, 1740s. Kolomenskoye Historical and Architectural Museum-Preserve, Moscow.

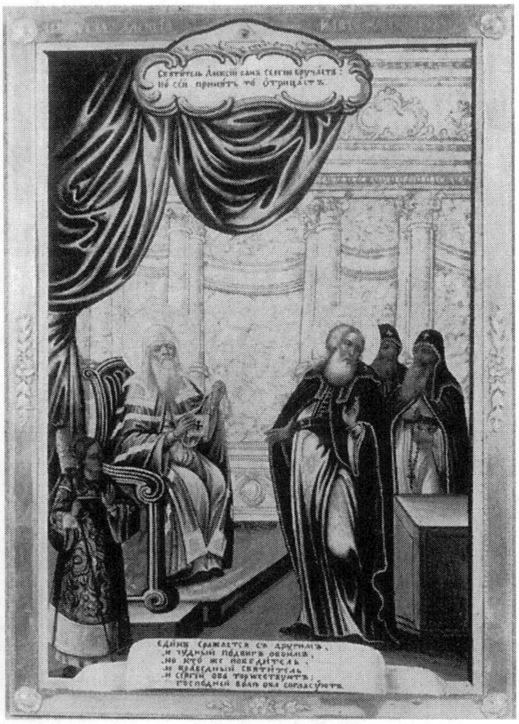

124. *Metropolitan Aleksiy of Moscow and the Blessed Sergius of Radonezh*, 1801. State Tretyakov Gallery, Moscow.

text of a troparion). With the passing of time this symbolic structure underwent various changes, but the fundamental meaning remained unchanged – the text framed the picture and at the same time revealed its meaning.

On such icons as 'The Archangel Michael, Commander of the Lord's Avenging Hosts', 'The Mother of God of the Sign and the Archangel Michael with Texts Glorifying the Mother of God and Praying to the Archangel for Help', 'The Deposition of the Relics of St Mitrofan, Metropolitan of Voronezh' and the Western 'Epitaph of Nicolas Utman (1565)', we see characteristic transformations of the emblem: above the image the names of the icons (often in a frame) are located, while below them, also in frames of various kinds on a white background, there are extensive texts, explicating the new rhetoricized foundation of the icon (illus. 152–8).

The form of the frames assumed a particular semantic load: it had to draw the worshipper's attention not only to the picture but also the word, to its very lettering. It is no accident that, just as in antiquity, when the Middle Ages were coming to an end there arose a particular delight in the monogram, which could convey a sacral meaning through the linking of certain letters. At the same time both a new attraction towards the ideographic conveyance of a sign structure, and a special sensitivity and essential expressivity in the way the very letters were produced are reflected in the particular aesthetic formation of the linkage: the sigil of Christ more and more often was shaded with gold, which helped the lettering to carry the conviction and weightiness of a precious object. Hence the form of the additional frame itself, as a new compositional element of the icon, first of all showed that the abbreviated name of Christ or the Mother of God had acquired its own frame on the icon, analogous as it were to the frame of the picture. This made word and picture equal as far as sacral semantic weight was concerned.

In this context the form known as the cartouche gained a special role in the composition of the new Baroque icons. A cartouche meant a decorative frame in the shape of a half-opened scroll, a shield or an ornamental garland. In European Mannerist and Baroque art, cartouches are encountered everywhere. They were used as the decoration of facades of buildings and window-frames; they enclosed book titles as well as artistic, graphic and heraldic motifs. The cartouche in that period became the universal framing structure, one that would long outlive its epoch and has lasted indeed to the present day.

In Russian icons of the second half of the 17th century and into the 18th, the cartouche in the form of a mysteriously unfurled scroll symbolized a book, and served as a signal for how the picture should be apprehended. From that time on it became one of the most widespread devices for framing the titles of icons, various texts on them and often the picture itself. The form of the cartouche testified to the fact that the framing of texts and depictions had started to orientate itself towards metaphor and the symbolism of comparison. In this sense the cartouche always aimed at broadening context, at 'encasing' the symbol in a stream of meanings.[51]

The task of the cartouche was to elucidate the symbol through a choice of significations, to relate frame and depiction in a symbolic unity, to perceive the world as the integrated Divine Creation. A frame in cartouche form immediately included the symbol in the play of commentary and caused it to glitter with varied meanings. Precisely through its 'oddity' the cartouche drew special attention to the symbol: it attracted the sensibilities and opened the eyes to the profound mysteries of the Word. Hence the cartouche could occupy an important place in the composition of the prayer image, as is exemplified in the icon 'The Saviour Not Made by Hands, and Narrative Scenes' (illus. 129). This icon is a typical rhetorical structure in the 'frame within frame' manner – consisting, in fact, of several frames. The traditional smooth margins of the medieval icon are unexpectedly 'disrupted' at the top by a golden rectangular cartouche in the form of a half-displayed scroll carrying the text. This causes the viewer's attention to

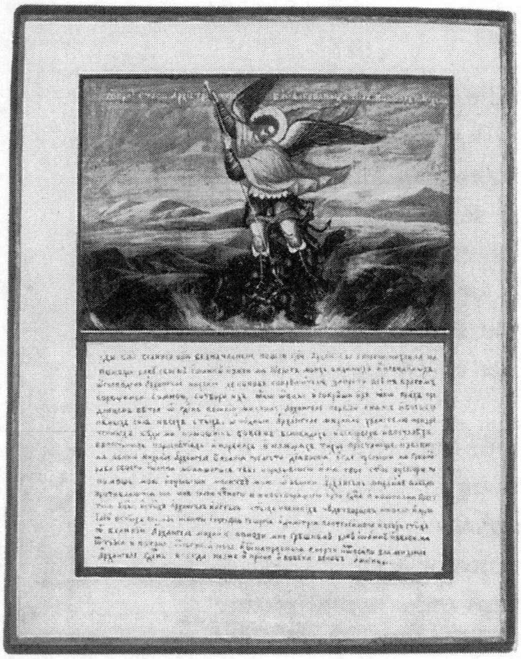

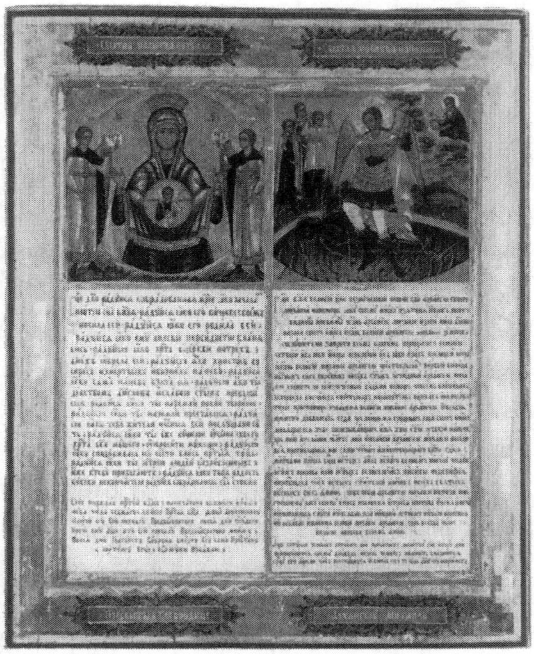

125. *The Archangel Michael, Commander of the Lord's Avenging Hosts*, late 18th century or early 19th. Private collection, Moscow.

126. *The Mother of God of the Sign and the Archangel Michael, with Texts Glorifying the Mother of God and Praying to the Archangel for Help*, mid-19th century. Private collection, Moscow.

switch from participation onto the code, as is appropriate in a rhetoricized structure.

The cartouche itself emerges as this encoding device: it serves as a signal not only to what it surrounds, but to itself, to its own form. Thus in the centre of the icon the viewer beholds a cartouche that occupies practically the whole space of the icon. It continues and complicates the play of meanings. Subjected to this rhetorical strategy, the cartouche as it were 'opens itself up' here: it resembles an imperial throne on which the Lord Pantocrator can be seated. As if to confirm this, individual details of the cartouche as frame transform themselves into individual elements of a throne. In the upper part of the frame we see the semi-circular back of the throne with two angels seated beside it; they are holding laurel branches and mirrors with narrative scenes. The similarity of the frame to a throne is also emphasized by its golden colour.

Further on this rhetorical additional element of the cartouche is gradually dissolved within its usual elements, consisting of curlicues and laurel foliage. Within the cartouche we see two more angels. They stand on clouds

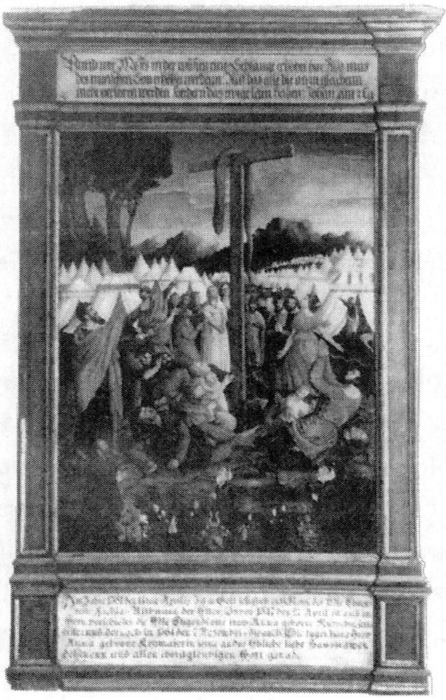

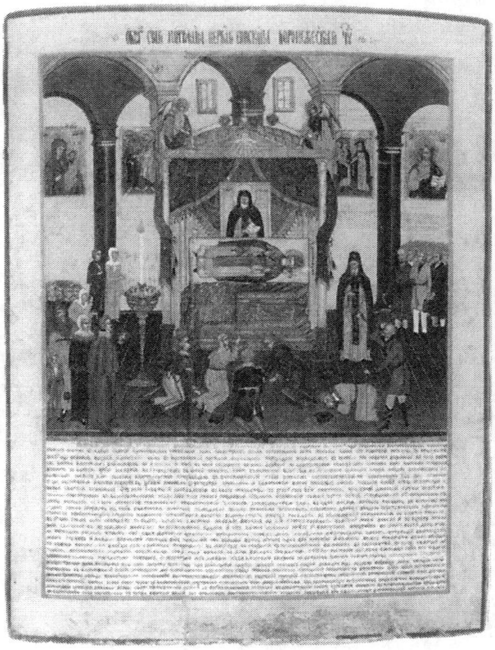

and hold a kerchief carrying the image of the Saviour Not Made by Hands in one hand, a coronet in the other. Beneath them the earth is displayed, with a narrative scene of the arrival of the Image Not Made by Hands in Edessa. Thus the cartouche with elements of an imperial throne is the key to understanding the idea of the real substitution of Christ's coming by his icon, the Image Not Made by Hands. This close connection of the cartouche with the picture is visibly amplified by its indissoluble link with the Word. The interior space of the cartouche is bordered by a small detached frame with a narrative text. Seraphim link it with the cartouche itself and with the background of the icon, as if to lower the whole composition down to earth. Here we see city walls and churches, the craftsman's signature and a text on the white half-displayed scroll.

127. Epitaph of Nicholas Utmann, enclosing an image of the Brazen Serpent, 1565.

128. *The Deposition of the Relics of St Mitrofan, Metropolitan of Voronezh*, 1832–40, Voronezh. Private collection, Moscow.

From the mid-17th century the rhetorical structure of 'frame within frame' becomes one of the chief devices in modern Russian icon painting. It brought varied shades of meaning into the icon. This was achieved by the forms of the frames themselves, their placing, and equally by the peculiarities of the depictions and texts within them. Thus, on an icon of

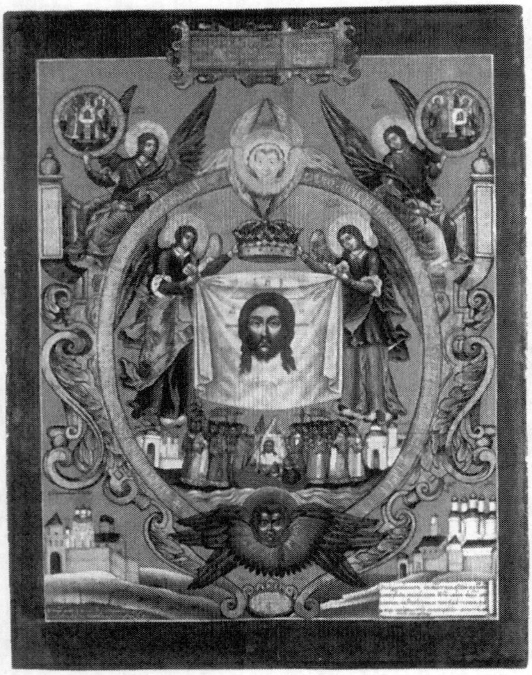

129. *Saviour Not Made by Hands and Narrative Scenes*, 1706. State Tretyakov Gallery, Moscow.

St Nil Stolbensky from the Kolomenskoye Museum, the background to the cartouche is white, while black and cinnabar-red letters are used together in the text of the troparion and kontakion (illus. 123). But often the background to 'enclosures' is in bright red, while the written text uses gold or white lettering (illus. 130).

On icons of the 18th and 19th centuries, the text of a troparion, kontakion or a prayer was often replaced by one or another dedication. From the 18th century a strong tradition was also established of locating the name of the emperor in the lower cartouche – this was linked with the intrusion of panegyrical emotion into icons of the New Ritual. The text quoted earlier that dedicates the icon to the martyr's death of Alexander II was included in this way. In a cartouche with a white background there is the text of the blessing from the Synod on the occasion of the wedding of Pyotr Fyodorovich (Peter III) and Catherine (subsequently 'the Great') on an icon of 1745 of the 'Marriage in Cana' –an icon that, incidentally, reminds us more of a Dutch genre picture than of a prayer image.[52] Finally, there is a text on an icon of the end of the 19th century by I. Pankryshev ('Guardian Angel with SS Olga and Akepsim'), whose text also points towards the special 'emblematic' quality of the frame with the name of the emperor inside it: 'To the Tsar and Tsaritsa, their Imperial Majesties, in commemoration of the birth of the first-born to Her Highness the Princess Olga on 3 November 1895' (illus. 131).

When words and letters were replaced in the 'enclosure' by a picture, say a landscape, the latter (in accordance with the emblematic principle of thought) took on a special semantic load. Thus on the icon of various saints painted by the same I. Pankryshev in memory of the archaeological work of I. A. Golyshev (Museum of the History of Religion, St Petersburg) there is a representation of the Moscow Kremlin within an oval frame below. The text of the dedication was placed on a white ribbon underneath; in an analogous extended white frame beside it is the craftsman's signature: 'This icon was painted in the workshop of Iosif Pankryshev, in the village of Mstyora, Vyazniki District, Vladimir Province'. Hence landscape, dedication and signature were coupled together in a particular emblematic manner, reminding us of the role the emblem once played in the spiritual culture of the Baroque.

130. *Archangel Michael with his Deeds*, first half of the 18th century. Rostov and Yaroslavl Architectural-Historical Museum Preserve, Yaroslavl.

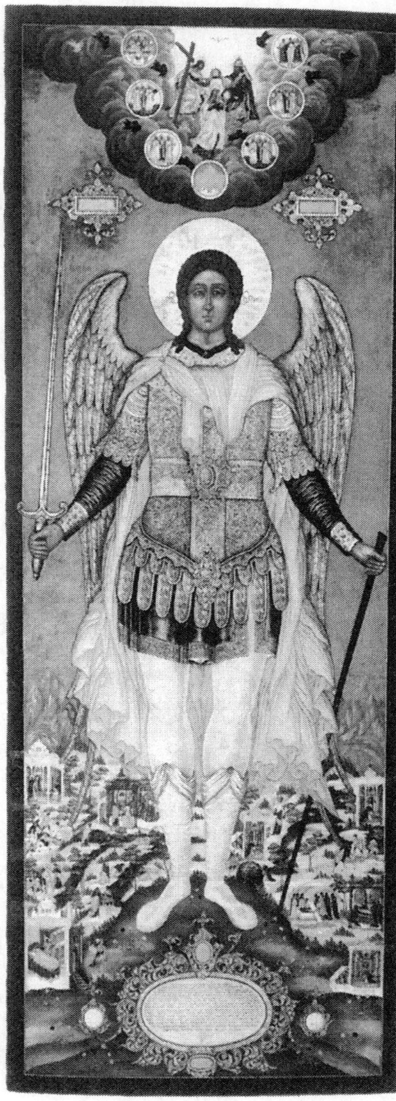

The special language of the emblem, in which word and picture stood in an indissoluble symbolic unity, could help in the resolution of the task that proponents of the new piety, in Russia as in the West, confronted in the second half of the 16th century and after – the re-education of human beings who had been 'corrupted' by the Renaissance. And since in the struggle for humankind the emblem could appeal not only to feelings, but to reason, the emblematic principle of thought was close to the problem of how to strengthen the rationalistic effect of religious art. The role of the icon in 'constructing' humanity, traditional in the Orthodox lands, turned out to be in harmony with general tendencies of the Baroque age. In the new official type of icon not only was there an attempt to express concepts of the abundance of the divine creation characteristic of the Baroque, but also to strengthen its *didactic* impulse through an appropriate language. The instigators of the new Frankish manner of icon painting also put the idea of an emblematic and symbolic synthesis of the arts at the service of this didacticism.

The traditional form of the emblem outlined above gave rise to a complex system of semantic relationships. The author of *Iconology* (1593), Cesare Ripa, founded this system on Aristotelian logic and rhetoric. On this subject Gombrich notes 'Ripa himself has tried in his Preface to explain the principles underlying this method of visual definitions. As a cook or caterer at the

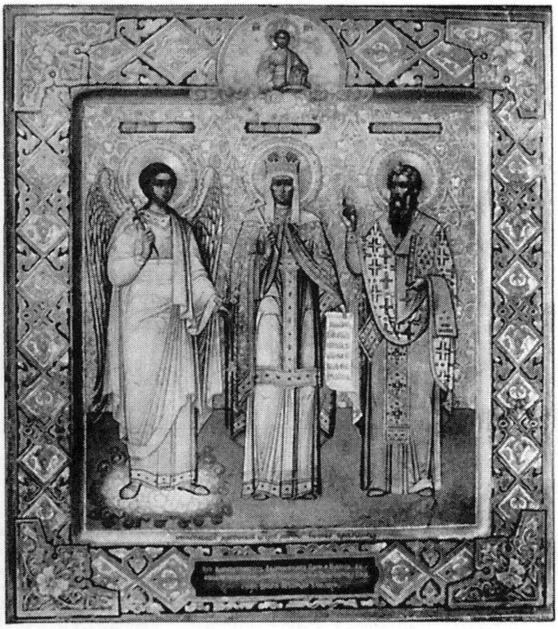

131. I. Pankryshev, *The Guardian Angel with SS Olga and Akepsim*, 1895, Mystora. State Museum of the History of Religion, St Petersburg.

courts of the mighty he was not a trained thinker, but he does his best to bring his method within the orbit of Aristotelian Logic and Rhetoric. From the Logic he derives the technique of definition, from the Rhetoric the theory of metaphor.'[53]

As J. Białostocki has suggested, the new (in comparison with the Middle Ages) emblematic principle of linking picture and text could have been initiated by the special role of Holy Scripture and the divine word in Protestant doctrine. Luther's demand that fragments of Holy Scripture should be included in epitaph images was to have an immediate influence on Protestant art, which later would be saturated by the spirit of the emblem.[54] It is typical that in the Baroque period the emblem becomes the usual means for the artistic embodiment of a world picture.[55] In the Catholic world, reforming Jesuits and theorists of 'post-Tridentine' Catholic devotion and art began to attribute particular significance to this way of artistic thinking. They were the authors of popular collections of emblems that reached Russia in the 17th century. The Academy founded in Kiev by Peter Mogila, Orthodox Metropolitan of Kiev in 1632–47, on the model of Jesuit colleges, devoted considerable attention to the theory and practice of emblematic art in its teaching programme. Thus people in 17th-century Russia were well acquainted with one of the most widely distributed books in Europe, Alciato's *Emblematum Liber*, one of the emblems from which I compared with the icon 'Tsarevich Dimitriy with his Life', and also with Ripa's *Iconology*. As well as this the library of Simeon and Silvestr Medvedev contained three books of *Symbols and Emblems* by I. Camerarius, the *Polyhistoria of Symbols* and *Egyptian Symbolism* by N. Kossen, and others.[56] These books that had reached the cultural elite were without doubt available to the icon painters of the Armoury Chamber, as also were various Western European didactic compendia of engraved portraits that were known as *icones*.

In this way the emblem entered into the sign system of the icon, simultaneously embracing the most varied areas of spiritual life – theology and sermon, literature and theatre, and also the art of portraiture.

Thanks to the art of icons and religious pictures, emblematics became widely ensconced in the religious experience of the 18th and 19th centuries (see illus. 78). In 1743 there appeared an illustrated publication called *Spiritual Emblemat* (sic), a small book consisting of 40 pictures engraved by Ivan Lyubetsky. 'This *Emblemat*', as D. A. Rovinsky explained, 'contains various admonitions: how to live dutifully in this world so as to be saved in the life to come, with its admonitions equipped with allegories and emblems'.[57]

Yuriy Lotman observed that the Baroque 'consciously strove for the folklorization of its ideas'. It is indeed the case that popular craft art reproduced and gave wide distribution to that which had been created, and that which was being forgotten, up above. The art of the emblem was in its time put to the service of confirming the absolutist ideology of Peter the Great: the first Russian collected volume of emblems, *Symbols and Emblemata*, was published in Amsterdam in 1705 at his personal command. And throughout the 18th century, and at least for the first half of the 19th, the emblematic tradition stayed alive in the popular craft milieu: in 1788 a collection was published in Russia of *Selected Symbols and Emblems* by N. Maksimovich-Ambodik that was augmented with new emblems. Thus emblematics introduced official state ideology too into the mass consciousness.

It was certainly not by accident that a heraldic sign found its way into Ivan Afanasyev's icon of 1814 (see illus. 87). The heraldic device represented on the saddle-cloth of Alexander Nevsky's steed was genetically linked with the way that new Frankish icons were equipped with imperial emblematics. The representation of the crest of Russia – a two-headed eagle with the attributes of power, sceptre and orb – was already in the reign of Aleksey Mikhaylovich beginning to be widely used in court painting and poetry. Symbolic verse graphemes in the form of a crest were included by Simeon Polotsky in his long poem 'The Russian Eagle'. A two-headed eagle is depicted on the title page of the book *Sword of the Spirit*.[58] The two-headed eagle appears on engraved portraits of members of the Tsar's family and court circles, as also on everyday objects – vessels, clothes, etc. (illus. 132). The inclusion of heraldic emblematics in a sacral image on the one hand ideologized it, responding to the spirit of absolutism, and on the other served the task of glorifying the imperial person and with it the Russian state. Bringing a panegyric content into the icon, the two-headed eagle, as it were, united in people's consciousness the traditional values of Orthodoxy with belief in the mission of the 'Third Rome' with its ideology of absolutism. The two-headed eagle 'descends' to the level of popular icon painting in the 18th and 19th centuries from official images of the late 17th and early 18th centuries, whose content was linked with the struggle against Islam and for the liberation of Azov.

On the early-18th-century icon of the Azov Mother of God, the two-headed eagle in fact is the 'frame' for the Mother of God symbolizing the power of empire (illus. 133). The gesture of the Mother of God, placed in front of the crest, is not only an indication of her defending and blessing the Empire, but also of the 'sign' or 'banner' (*znamya*), presupposing a war on behalf of the Faith.

The inscriptions on the icon reinforce both the motifs of divine blessing on this war and of the Faith's invincible might. This is also symbolized by the depiction of St George the Victorious and by arrow-like lightning shafts that emerge from the heraldic orb and strike down crescent moons – symbols of Islam – on the architectural backdrop of Azov. V. Borin observed that the under-drawing of an icon of the Azov Mother of God from the late 17th century showed St George with the portrait-features of V. V. Golitsyn, who led the expeditions of 1687 and 1689 against the Crimean Tartars. On the icon of the Chernigov-Ilyinskaya Mother of God of 1696, the Azov Mother of God is depicted below, on the background that was described earlier of an allegorical landscape with a map of an already conquered Azov (illus. 134). The Christ-Child blesses an inscription set between the wings of a heraldic eagle: 'Peter Alekseyevich Russian Autocrat' – thus appropriating for the Emperor the glory of victory and of a wise head of state. It is noteworthy that on the same icon the imperial crest is also depicted in a cartouche in the top-right corner – that is to say, where the abbreviated name of the Mother of God might earlier have been located.

On popular craft icons the depiction of a crest is most often encountered

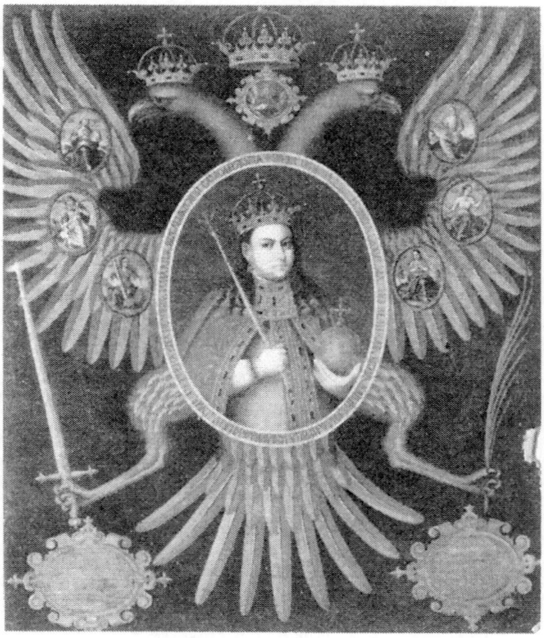

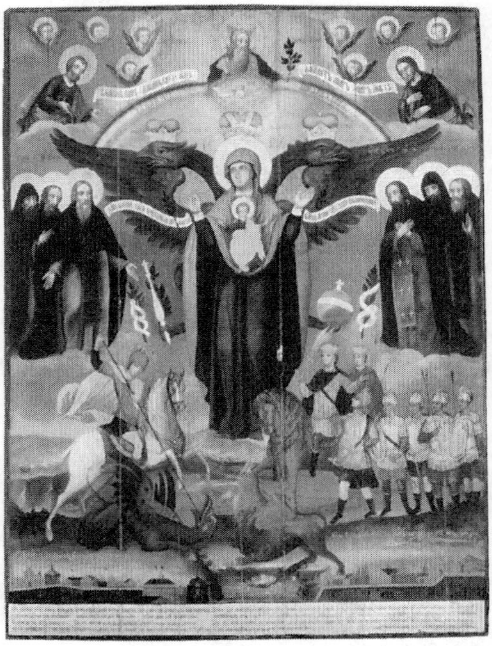

132. *The Muscovite Regent, Sofya Alekseyevna*, 1680s. State Russian Museum, St Petersburg.

133. *Azovskaya Mother of God*, early 18th century. State Historical Museum, Moscow.

in the middle of the bottom margin. Thus on the icon of the 'Akhtyrskaya Mother of God' from the collection of H. Villamo, the emblem of the two-headed eagle is indeed located in a circle on the bottom margin, and seemingly 'disrupts' the inscription: 'Depiction of the Wonder-working Akhtyrskaya Icon, that Appeared in 1732 on the Second Day of July'.[59] Imperial heraldry is here symbolically connected with the event of the icon's appearance, thus indicating the special grace bestowed on the Empire.

Since the towers of the Moscow Kremlin were adorned with two-headed eagles as far back as the reign of Aleksey Mikhaylovich, crests started to be depicted on architectural backdrops of Moscow's holy places in icons. There is a document that testifies how this continually troubled the consciences of Old Believers: 'A Descriptive Tract in Defence of the Two-headed Eagle on Icons and Other Objects', dated 1865. To demonstrate the legitimacy of reverencing icons containing the emblematics of the crest, the author of this tract made much of the antiquity of the emblem's origin: 'it was sent to Russia from the pious Greek emperors'. Therefore 'this eagle is to be found even in the pictures on ancient holy icons'. But ordinary folk often failed

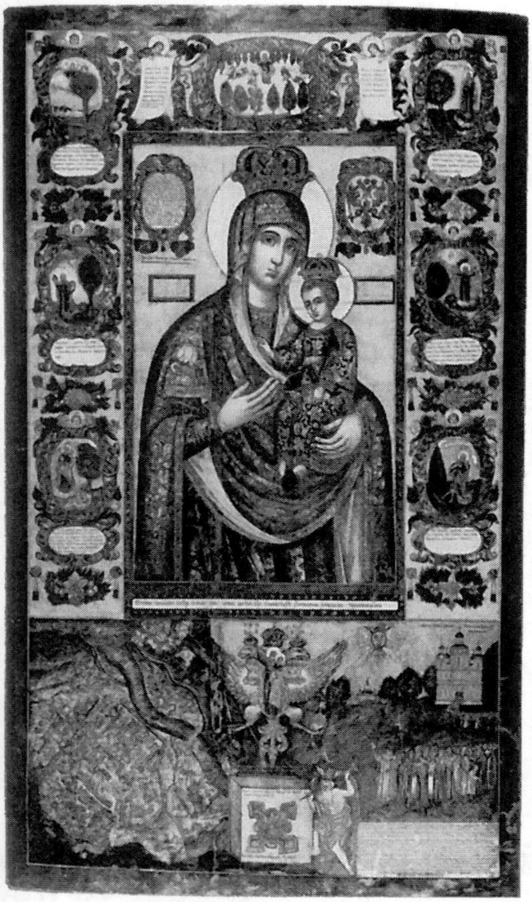

134. *Chernigovskaya-Ilyinskaya Mother of God*, 1696. State Museum of the History of Religion, St Petersburg.

to understand the actual semantics of the crest, in which they discerned 'a bird, of an appearance unfamiliar in nature and never having been seen by anyone living on earth'. Because of this they equated the two-headed eagle with Antichrist: 'unwilling to venerate that image inasmuch as the image, a two-headed eagle, is like Antichrist'. The extensive explications by the unknown author confirm the widespread infusion of Baroque symbolism into the culture of the Old Ritual, which in essence was surreptitiously conveying the same panegyric content into religious sensibilities.[60]

The Portrait Icon

We have already noted that the human face is the meaningful and emotional centre of the prayer image. However, the spiritual sense of an icon is apprehended also through the overall contour and pose, the gestures and the material attributes of holy personages. It is not hard to see that pictures on New Ritualist images from the second half of the 17th century to the early 20th are on the borderline between the icon and the portrait. The icon by Ivan Afanasyev of 'The Wonder-working Grand Princes of Vladimir' contains clearly expressed features of the ceremonial portrait, with which there are several points of comparison (see illus. 87). Thus the figure of St Alexander Nevsky is evidently borrowed from a mounted portrait of an 18th-century monarch or grandee. St Gleb is represented in a three-quarters pose typical of the ceremonial portrait of the 18th and early 19th centuries, while the ermine cloak on his shoulders as a symbol of monarchical power indicated that the portrait of some Western king or Russian autocrat lies at its origin. The poses and attributes of these saints thus speak of the influence of secular portraiture: the stiffness characterizing the figures corresponds more to the demands of an aristocratic representation than to the intercession and concentratedness of prayer. We can guess that on Russian soil the genesis of such forms was closely bound up with the image of the ruler in Baroque culture, when the Tsar's portrait began to operate in a new symbolic structure of Court ceremonial.

Writing about the origins of the concept of the Byzantine icon as a locus inhabited by a special kind of presence, Andrei Grabar once noted the link between this mental construct and the idea of the role of the Roman Emperor's portrait in official rituals: on a ceremonial level the portrait of the Emperor could take the place of the actual person.[61] The engrained habit of comparing the portrait of the Emperor with an icon was no accident either, of course, in the explanations Basil the Great and St John Damascene give of the nature of the boundary between image and prototype.[62] With the circulation of imperial portraits within the Russian Orthodox Church in the 18th and 19th centuries, such a comparison may well have again proved necessary for mid-19th-century Russian theology. Archimandrite Anatoliy (Martynovsky) commented that 'As portraits of some notable person, for example the Sovereign, would not be taken by even the least educated Christian as worthy of the respect given to the actual person represented on the portrait – so will he not respect the icon as if it were the very object represented on it.'[63]

As we have already observed, it became normal in the art of post-Tridentine Catholicism to put a realistic portrait of the donor into a religious image – something that was undoubtedly a development of an earlier tradition both in the West and in Byzantium. The same could be said of Protestant epitaph images either side of 1600, on which we can see portraits of the deceased's relatives. They might be depicted kneeling and in prayer before an icon or a crucifix. But often they were represented in the lower part of an epitaph image, as if symbolizing 'earthly' requests on behalf of the dead person's soul.[64] All these images were linked with the genesis of portrait art in the West (illus. 135, 136).

The influence of these sign systems on the tradition of Orthodox popular icon painting was felt more strongly at the Western frontiers of the Russian Empire and in the West Slav territories, where there were close contacts between Catholic, Protestant and Orthodox cultures. Here the 'marginal' position of Orthodoxy and the development of icon painting as a low-level craft were determined by the destruction of the canon and a development of donor portraits that brought it close to Catholic and to Protestant art. Speaking of Ukrainian icon painting of the 17th century, Ye. Kuzmin once wrote:

> The habit of placing portraits amid holy persons lasted almost to the middle of the 18th century, when it began to go out of use for political reasons, like everything reminiscent of 'Polish', i.e. Catholic, influence. From this intrusion of the 'world' into sacred subjects is was only one step to complete fusion with them. And that step was taken. Together with icons in which the patron was placed alongside the sacred scene we an often encounter cases where his portrait is fused with the saint's representation itself.[65]

In Russian popular icon-painting we can sense more complex superpositions and transformations than in Ukrainian examples: it discovered a new type of representation of the human figure not in a foreign model, but above all in its own official art. F. Kaempfer has convincingly shown that the locating of donor portraits, in particular of rulers, within the space of the sacred image is one of the most stable motifs in the Byzantine tradition, inherited by Russian art of the 16th century through to the early 18th.[66] Incidentally, it is essential to add that in the 'transitional age' of the Baroque, images of rulers on icons began to carry the stamp of a more complex fusion of state Byzantinism with the common European absolutist ideology of the 17th century, which regarded the persons of absolute monarchs as 'living replicas of God on earth', and not only in Russia.[67]

On the one hand, as in post-Tridentine and in Protestant religious art, 'realistic' portraits of donors began to be made and shown in the new official Muscovite icon painting (illus. 137). The elders of the *Stoglav* Council, led by Metropolitan Makariy, gave a positive answer to Ivan IV's question about whether it was permitted to represent on icons 'tsars and princes and churchmen and people who are still alive'. In the first instance

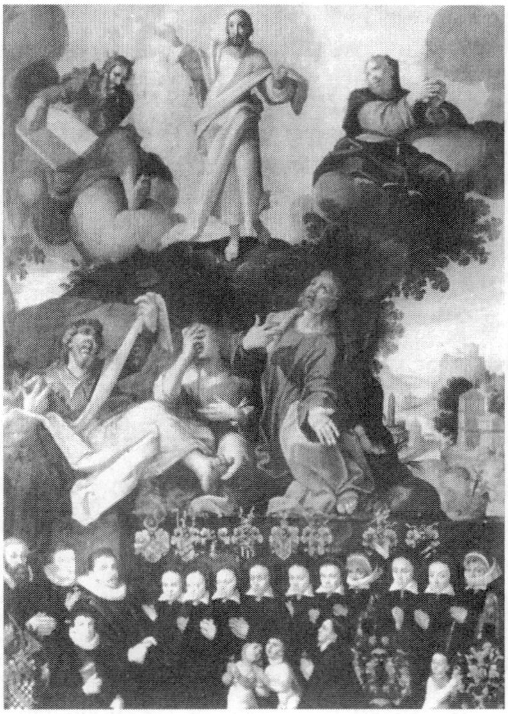

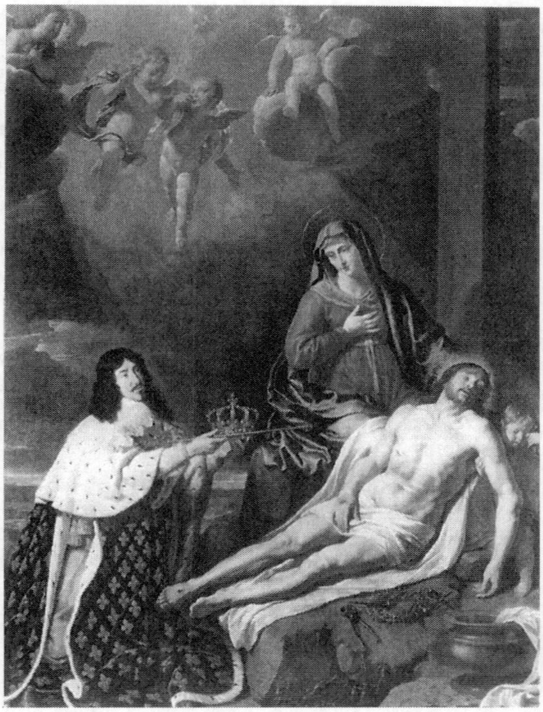

this related to the depiction of rulers on icons with a liturgical theme: experts believe that icons in the Annunciation Cathedral of the Moscow Kremlin (mid-16th century) initiated the tradition of including 'portraits' of patrons who could be identified with actual people in the liturgical processions.[68] Such portraits of the Tsar's circle relied without doubt on the authority of the representations of the Tsar himself: as G. D. Filimonov once wrote, 'the right of representation was transferred from saints to rulers, and then insofar as art emerged from the service of the church this right became a general acquisition'.[69] Thus the depiction of Tsar Aleksiy Mikhaylovich and his family – the Tsaritsa Mariya Ilyinichna with the Tsareviches Aleksey and Fyodor – can be viewed on Simon Ushakov's icon 'The Tree of the Muscovite State' ('Praise to the Vladimir Mother of God', 1668, Tretyakov Gallery). Pictures of Tsar Aleksiy Mikhaylovich, Tsaritsa Mariya Ilyinichna and Patriarch Nikon can also be seen on the icon of the 'Elevation of the Cross' by I. Saltanov, while on an icon of the Azov Mother

135. Epitaph of Peter Honnald with the scene of the Transfiguration. Silesia, 1595.

136. Philippe de Champaigne, *Vow of Louis XIII*, 1638, oil on canvas. Musée des Beaux-Arts de Caen.

of God of the early 18th century there are portraits of Tsars Peter and Ivan on horseback. (Peter and his half-brother Ivan V were officially co-rulers from 1682 until Ivan's death in 1696.) All these images of 'those who are alive' served as if to sacralize the Tsar's person, and thus responded to his special quality of devotion in comparison with that of ordinary mortals. In this connection we may recall the development of the theme of imperial devotion in Byzantine art of the post-Iconoclast period, where representations of the Emperor before Christ, the Mother of God, other saints or the Cross appear. The autocrats needed to have their orthodoxy confirmed by these images, since during the iconoclast period the Byzantine emperors were the leaders of the heresy.[70]

On the other hand, in the new synthesis of the official state ideology and culture, the portrait of the tsar, which was already recognizably different from a donor image on an icon, began simultaneously to carry iconic features. Irrupting into the secular Baroque portrait of the autocrat, features of iconicity were first intended to encourage not only the sacralization but also the glorification of his personage. It was as if the features of the icon subjected themselves to the formation of the official ideology, and hence also to the idea of representation.

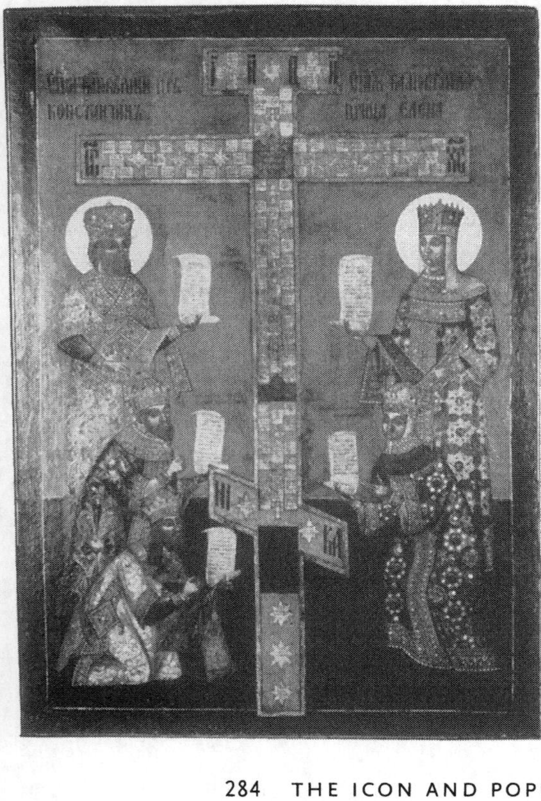

137. Ivan Saltanov, *Adoration of the Cross, with depictions of Tsar Aleksey Mikhaylovich, Tsaritsa Mariya Ilyinichna and Patriarch Nikon*, mid-17th century. Moscow Kremlin State Museums.

Russian popular craft icon painting of the 18th and 19th centuries retained the complex interaction of these two motifs (compare illus. 138 and 139). We are persuaded of this by the previously discussed icon of 1885 from Kholuy 'The Assembly of the Archangel Michael with Selected Saints', on which the name saint was shown by special command with the actual features of Tsar Alexander III. Also interesting in this context is a group of images connected with Alexander II's life and tragic end. The unsuccessful assassination attempt on the Emperor by A. K.

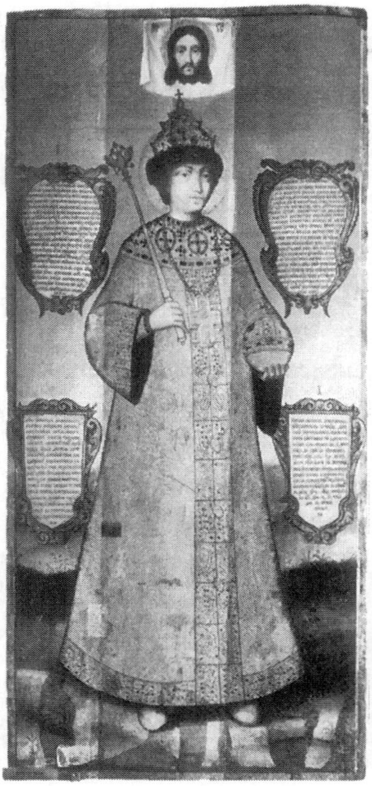

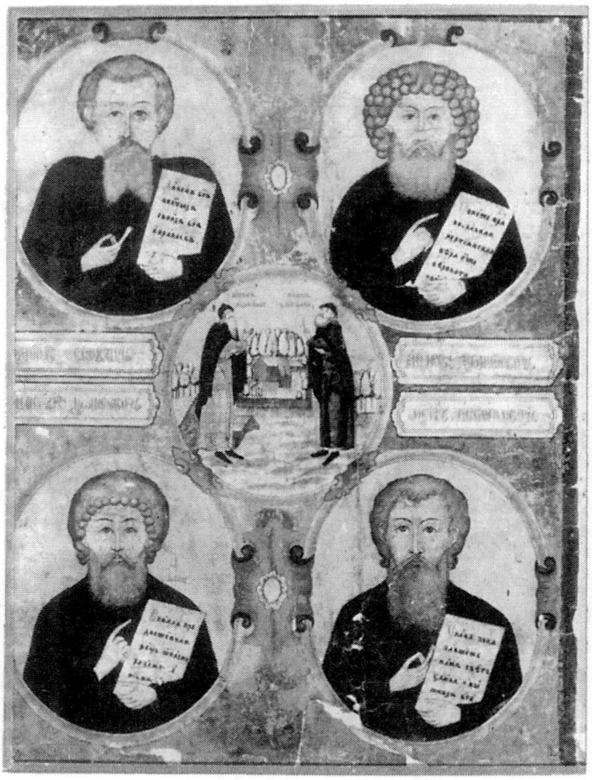

Sokolov on 2 April 1879 was reflected in the picture-icon 'Prayer of Gratitude for the Miraculous Saving of the Life of Alexander II' (formerly in the palace at Tsarskoe Selo). On the reverse side of a Crucifixion from the chapel of the Anichkov Palace, the slain Emperor is depicted lying in his coffin, together with the two bombs thrown at him, and also the explosion itself on the Catherine Canal in St Petersburg on 1 March 1881 (illus. 140).

Thus the tradition of state Byzantinism, still vigorous in comparison with Western lands, took on a strange new twist in 17th-century Muscovite Rus, both as concerned the establishment of the sign system of the secular portrait with its relation to the icon, and as concerned the new type of icon in its relationship with the monarchical portrait. In the tomb-portrait of Tsar Fyodor Alekseyevich, to which I have already referred, the solemn representationalism of the figure is attained primarily through its iconic 'stiffness' and symbolic quality (illus. 138). Baroque emblematism and

138. Ivan Bezmin, *Tsar Fyodor Alekseyevich*, 1686. State Historical Museum, Moscow.

139. *Founders and leaders of Vyg Old Ritualist community: The Monks Korniliy and Vitaliy, Pyotr Prokofyev, Danila Vikulin, Andrey and Semyon Denisov*, end of the 18th century or first half of the 19th, drawing. State Museum of the History of Religion, St Petersburg.

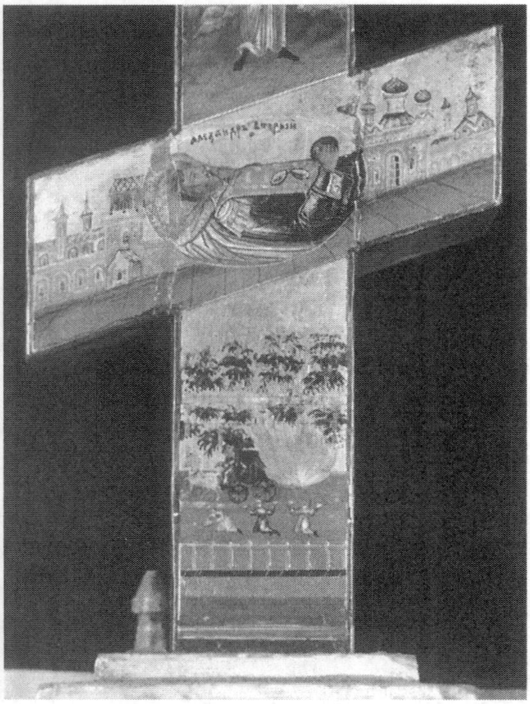

140. Detail from *Crucifix with a Depiction of Emperor Alexander II on his Deathbed and with the Scene of his Murder beside the Catherine Canal in St Petersburg, 1 March 1881*, 1886. State Museum of the History of Religion, St Petersburg.

synthesis of various art forms (in this case of the portrait, the icon and the emblem) was reconceptualized in the context of the medieval sacralization of the monarch, of the adoption of 'Byzantine' sumptuousness by the Russian court and the need to satisfy the absolutist ideology. But in parallel with this, as if in response to the level of formality of court customs and the penetration of state ideology into culture, new icons also began to obey the new norms.

While the representation of a ruling personage was becoming a secular portrait icon during this 'transitional period', the medieval and canonical representation of a saint was turning into an *iconic portrait*. Incidentally, it should be noted that the mechanism (embedded in the Byzantine cultural tradition) for turning the portrait of an emperor into a Christian icon, about which A. Grabar wrote, once again began to operate at this cultural turning-point. And it was not only an assortment of Baroque symbols that took part in this game, but also the awareness of stereotypes that was prolonged through 'Great Time'. The secular portrait began to exercise an active influence on the official Orthodox icon, and hence on the official image of sainthood.

Both ancient and (particularly) modern saints of the Empire acquired the features of important secular figures on prayer images of the New Ritual. In the majority of cases they display sternness and severity. There is an attempt to emphasize influential and aristocratic qualities in sainthood. Christian heroes are endowed with attributes and psychological characteristics different from those of a medieval world view. In the Baroque artistic system, with its urge towards syntheses, one could instantly discover the appropriate languages of the post-Renaissance portrait so as to express the new concepts. Incidentally, these new tendencies in the understanding of sainthood as worldly activity and influence could be linked with thoroughly medieval attitudes when it came to canonizations: thus when saints of the 18th, 19th and early 20th centuries came to be canonized (Dimitriy Rostovsky, Innokentiy of Irkutsk, Mitrofan of Voronezh, etc.), incorruption of their relics and miracles were regarded as the basic criteria of sainthood.[71]

A characteristic example in this context is an icon of Dimitriy Rostovsky – the first saint to be canonized for general church commemoration (in 1757) after the Synod had been established[72] – from the second half of the 18th century (illus. 141). The anonymous icon painter has created a new variant of a prayer image – a sort of *parsuna*-like icon[73] – by analogy with the sort of Western and Eastern European portraits of the 18th century, and possibly with *parsuna* portraits made in Dimitriy's own lifetime, in which the figure was represented next to a bookshelf (illus. 142). The saint is depicted in his full metropolitan's robes, with his staff in his left hand and an open bookcase, furnished with volumes in expensive varicoloured bindings, as a background. The New Testament Trinity is depicted in a luxurious carved frame, facing the saint. This frame could well serve as the frame of a mirror or a Catholic altarpiece. The heavens are rolled back to display Christ seated on a cloud and holding a cross – the symbol of redemption.

Above the saint is a heart, enclosed in a heraldic frame with a mitre and an archbishop's staff. The allegorical symbol of the heart is a major component of the portrait icon. Like the depiction of a mirror, the heart is a favourite motif in Baroque emblematics, and is encountered in many emblem collections. In the Early Middle Ages it symbolized the spiritual impulse, a person's spiritual integrity and love for the Creator.[74] In the Baroque, with its system of artistic personifications worked out on Antique and Renaissance foundations and linked with accounts of the bodily organs, the heart was understood as a symbol of the human soul, and reflected the loftiness, purity and intimacy of the religious disposition.[75]

Thus, together with books, the emblem of the heart conveyed a sense of the dispensation of particular divine grace on the saint and on his holy feat of literary labour. The organization of space in the New Ritualist icon began to acquire great significance for the new image of sanctity. In former icons, space was closed off as a matter of principle: it was subject to rules

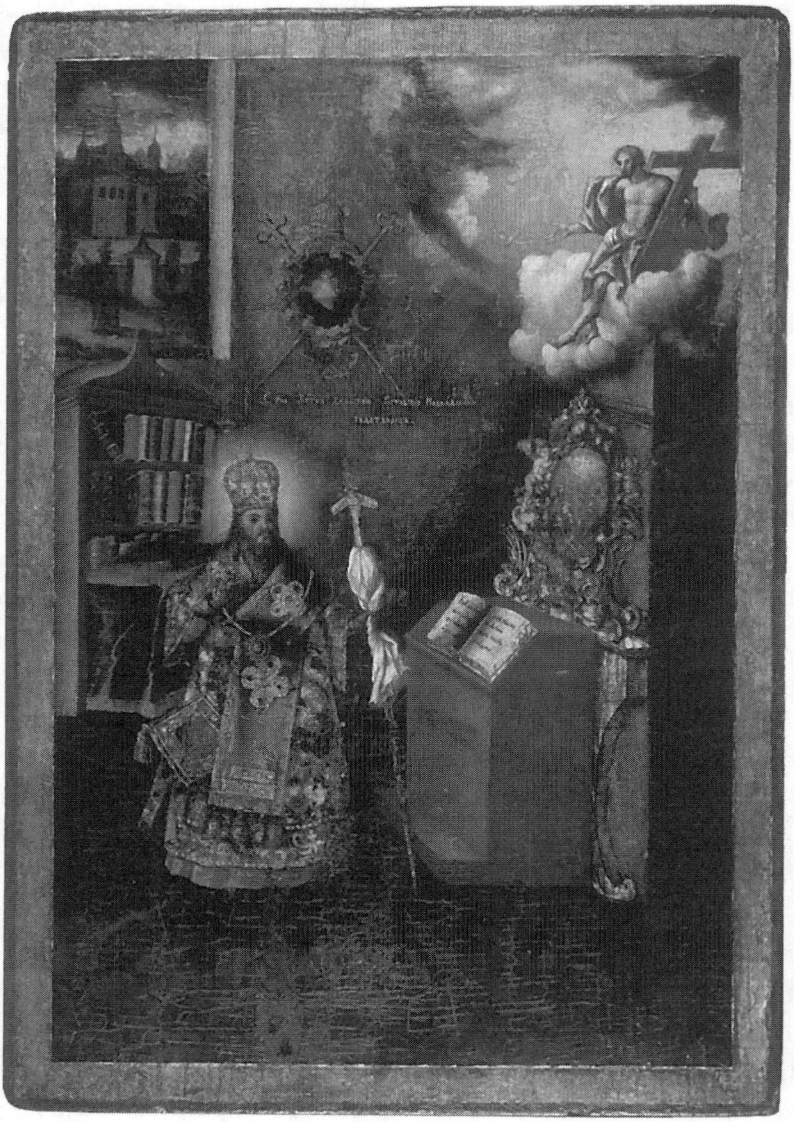

141. *Dimitriy Rostovsky*, second half of 18th century. State Museum of the History of Religion, St Petersburg.

of internal movement and emphasized the 'other-worldliness' of the saint's image. In newer icons space was deliberately constructed as if opened up to the world: this implied a stress on an active rather than passive way of salvation – that is, on the need for an active influence of the saint on the 'world', and hence on the person who was standing before the image in prayer. Thus in Ivan Afanasyev's icon of 'The Wonder-working Grand Princes of Vladimir', spatial openness is conveyed not only through elements of true perspective, but through the three-quarters turn of St Gleb (characteristic of formal portraiture) towards the viewer. It was as if intimate contact were at once set up with the spectator. In Catholic *Arte Sacra* pictures this emotional contact is realized in Western fashion by a more intimate and more free relation to the sacral: the gaze of a three-quarters-turned saint could be directed at the viewer.

An important place in the icon of St Dimitriy Rostovsky is taken by a *veduta*, which reveals a landscape with a monastery. This kind of *veduta*-window can be seen on many other Frankish images of the 18th century: a good example is an icon from the Moscow Kremlin Museums collection, 'The Mother of God who Recompenses the Fallen', reminiscent in its composition of a Catholic Madonna and Child. The *veduta*, which came into Orthodox icons from Western portraits of the 16th and 17th centuries, bore witness to how religious culture had changed its thought processes: its universal devices for opening up the image conveyed the inner urge of European culture for unity (illus. 143).

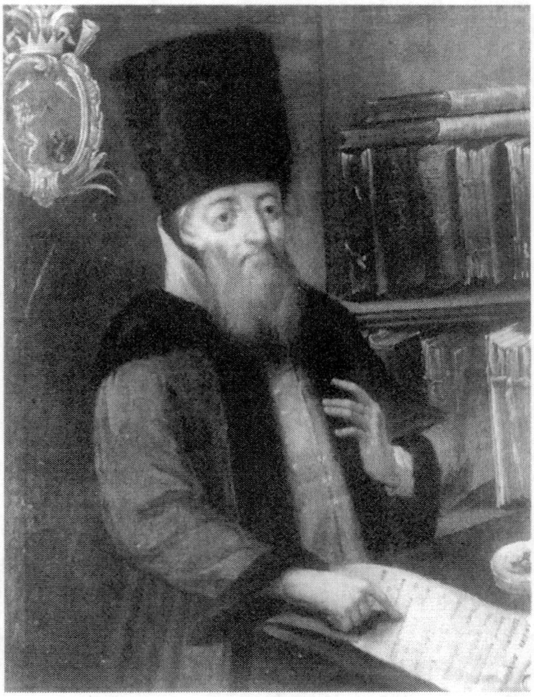

142. *A. L. Ordin-Nashchokin*, late 17th century or early 18th. State Historical Museum, Moscow.

Another image, not previously encountered, showing the new relationship in Frankish icons between a realistic and a metaphysical setting, was that of the curtain (illus. 144, 145). Thanks to their role in the Liturgy, curtains had since ancient times concealed holy objects from the sight of mere mortals. However, in the early Baroque period the Royal Gates of a church lose their former medieval solid and 'closed' qualities; as early as the first quarter of the 18th century Ivan Zarudniy created an altar-screen in the St Petersburg Cathedral of SS Peter and Paul after the manner of Lutheran churches (1722–6). In other words, during this period the role of a curtain-screen as 'celestial gates' was heightened. The fluttering curtain, exposed to the eye, began to evoke the feeling of an indeterminate boundary between the earthly sphere and that of the world to come. In Archbishop Veniamin's *New Tablet*, that for almost a century (from 1801) remained the basis for liturgical practice, is a detailed explication of the curtain:

> Beyond the Royal Gates to the altar is located the curtain-screen, called in Greek *katapetasma*. This is a piece of cloth on strings, either lowered from above or moved from one side to the other. Simeon of Thessaloniki (in his 6th chapter, on the church building) says: 'The curtain-screen, close to the altar, represents the heavenly tabernacle close to God, on which there are the countenances of holy angels and saints who have departed to God. This curtain is called in the statute that which is within, i.e., the inner doorway. And since this same curtain is in certain places lowered down from above, it is further named the heavenly gate or gates, while the gates proper are called the earthly or lower and exterior doorways.'[76]

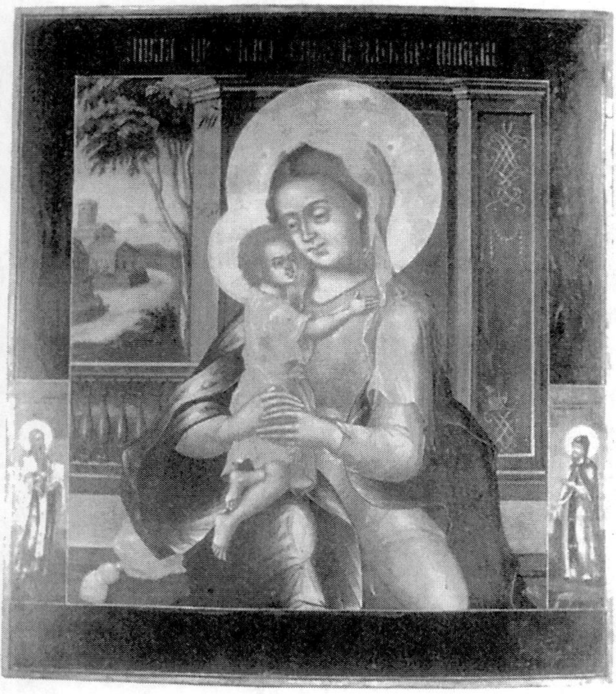

143. *Mother of God who Recompenses the Fallen*, end of the 18th century. Moscow Kremlin State Museums.

The depiction of a curtain on Russian icons of the late 17th century and early 18th possessed a sacral function to conceal or open up the world of divine activity. In this case the picture space of the icon might depend in its construction on the artistic space of a theatrical stage. The billowing curtains shown on the icon allowed the viewer to participate in the world of holy personages, acting in the metaphysical space as if they were theatrical characters. A heavenly wind filled the curtain's ever-moving folds: on the borderline between the worldly and the sacral, everything in its movement was attractive and astonishing for the person in prayer.

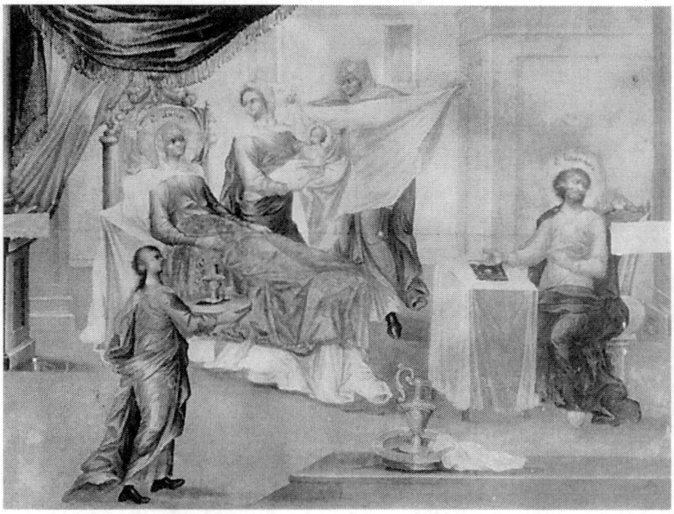

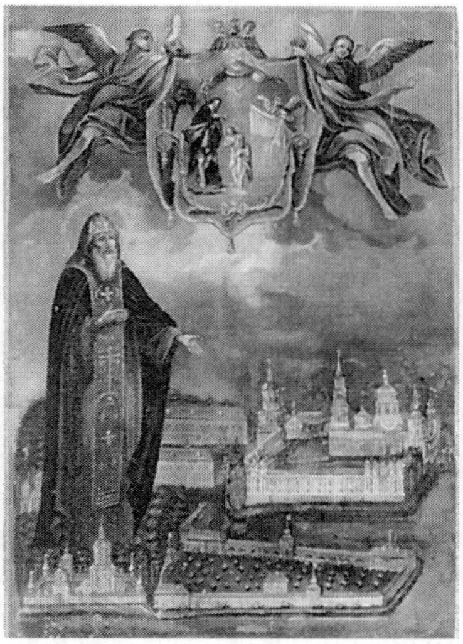

144. *Nativity of the Mother of God*, 18th century. Moscow Kremlin State Museums.

145. *Nil Stolbensky*, 1830s. Kolomenskoye Historical and Architectural Museum-Preserve, Moscow.

The world of objects and the attributes of Christian heroes had a special significance for the revelation of the new image of sanctity on Frankish icons. A heightened semiotic meaning was attributed to the relations between a person and an object. That this meaning is rooted far back in the centuries is witnessed by the way the objects themselves are depicted on icons. In the Baroque period, however, the icon itself began to be regarded as an object, a treasure and a precious thing much more clearly than in the early Middle Ages. As early as in Aleksey Mikhaylovich's reign, icons even acquired a value based on exchange: icons could serve as an equivalent of money.

It is a commonplace that the appearance of the genre of still-life in art is the consequence of a heightened affection for the material world, and more broadly for life itself. By medieval Christian doctrine, love of objects was fit only for condemnation: it signified attachment to the worldly, and distanced the human being from the Creator. The arrival of modern times and the affirmation of a more individualistic psychology meant a change of relations towards objects: the desire arose not only to possess them, but also to contemplate them, love them and commit them to memory (illus. 146). Hence the world of objects in icons of the Baroque period acquired palpable solidity and simultaneously a special symbolic meaningfulness.

146. Tikhon Filatyev. Old Testament Trinity, from Dormition Cathedral, Moscow Kremlin. 1700. Moscow Kremlin State Museums.

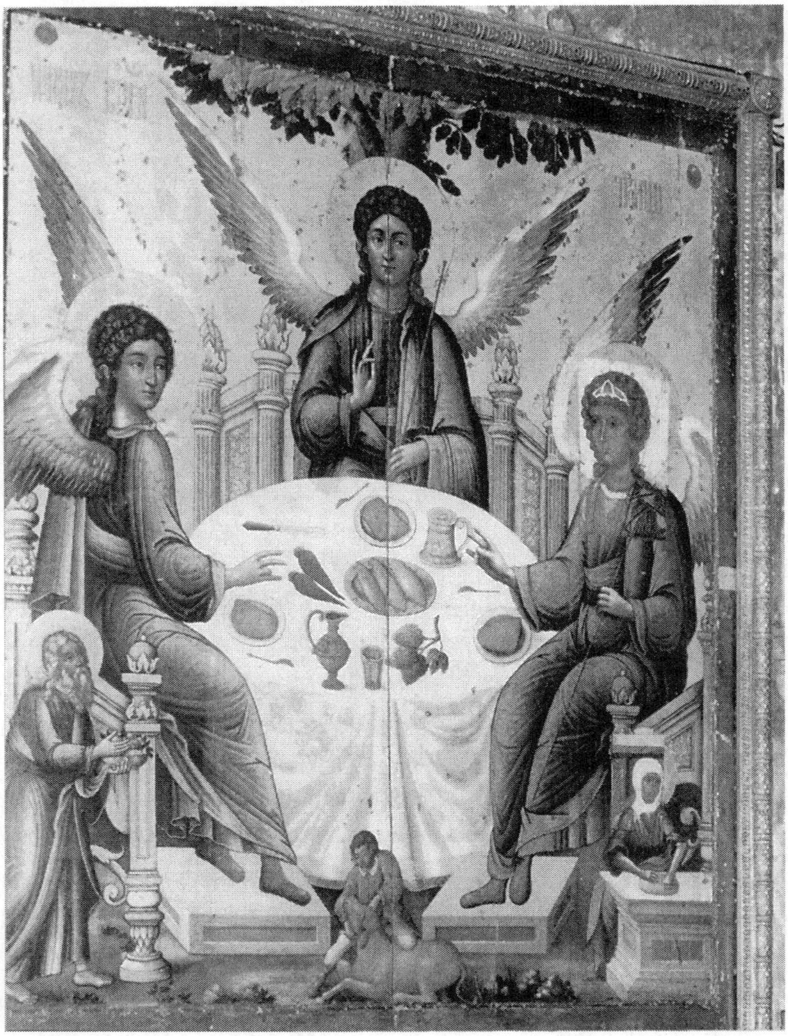

Saints' clothing and its ornamentation, everyday furnishings and elements of an interior, weaponry and finally the very attributes of sainthood – the cross, the wheel, the rod or the holy person's book – all began to be meticulously delineated by the icon painter, with a view to arousing an urge in the spectator to investigate, study and even to desire the world of objects. The sacred was here coming close to the 'everyday': the phenomenal world began to give detailed information about the worldly activity of the Christian hero, about what he did on earth; while he himself endowed the whole image with a special metaphysical dimension.

Thus the mirror, as symbolic organizer of Baroque culture, also interested the icon painter as an object that possessed an alluring aesthetic value connected with its technical nature, its form and its relation to surrounding objects and things. As a symbolic object, the mirror embraced a multilayered content. 'The mirror could appear as a sign of purity, as an attribute of good sense and wisdom (*prudentia*) – one of the cardinal virtues in medieval ethics.'[77] However, with its affirmation of the principle of mimesis, the mirror was also capable of reflecting the world of sacral events and divine beings. Here the mirror took the role of a means for cognition and had gnoseological functions. Hence in many 18th-century icons we see frames depicted that could have served for the framing of mirrors or of pictures. In these icons we see such 'mirrors' reflecting sacral events. Most often they take the place of icons – whose subjects as a rule are connected with the dedication of the chief church of the monastery – above the figure of the saint. These 'mirror' icons have a characteristic carved frame, or sometimes are framed by a billowing curtain that has material solidity (illus. 147; see also illus. 145). Often they are supported by angels. Interestingly, on the icon of St Dimitriy Rostovsky, the heraldic shield too has the form of a carved mirror frame. In it we see a 'reflected' heart – a sign of spiritual purity and religious sincerity in the person depicted. We can undoubtedly take the *veduta* in the icon as a mirror too: it is deliberately counterposed to the icon on the reading-desk that shows the New Testament Trinity and it symbolically reflects a world of reality – that is to say, the monastery in which the saint served as a monk.

147. The appearance and baptism of Christ, in a detail from an icon of Nil Stolbensky, 18th century. Kolomonskoye Historical and Architectural Museum-Preserve, Moscow.

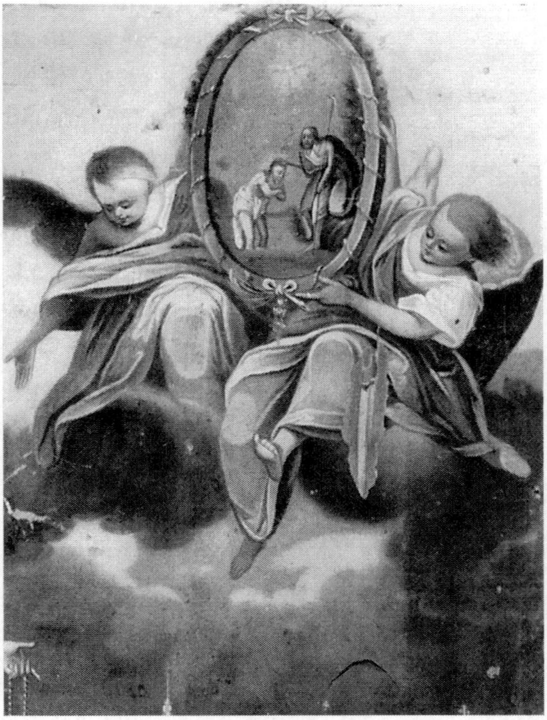

Other 'objects' too become important constructive elements of the sign system in

Frankish icons. On Ivan Afanasyev's Kholuy icon of 'The Wonder-working Grand Princes of Vladimir' there is particular significance in the attributes of royal dignity: the crown on the head of St Alexander Nevsky (repeated together with a crest formed from his initials on the horse-cloth of his steed), the royal ermine cloak that envelops St Gleb, and the royal garments of Georgiy Vsevolodovich and Andrey Bogolyubsky (see illus. 87). All these elements could serve as illustrations to a history of costume. In addition, Alexander Nevsky is shown on horseback with sword in hand, which imbues the whole composition with the idea of sanctity as strength, as the power to exert mighty influence. It is the portrait of a ruler rather than of a saint. The overall outline of St Alexander, and the gestures of SS Gleb, Georgiy Vsevolodovich, Andrey Bogolyubsky and the martyr Avraamiy directed towards him, serve only to emphasize the representative quality of one of the chief saints of the Russian empire. This icon, by the way, can interestingly be compared with the depictions of St George that are widespread in the craftwork art of 19th-century Palekh and whose composition is based on a formal equestrian portrait.

In the icon of St Dimitriy Rostovsky, the most important attribute of the saint is the episcopal library (illus. 141). The depiction of a figure with a bookcase in the background is a feature of post-Renaissance portraiture. In this case it testifies to the significance of literary endeavour in the saint's life, that at once acquires the features of a biography. The holy feat of Dimitriy in the realm of bookish labour found its ritual reflection when the saint was buried: to rest his head in the coffin his manuscript drafts were used, as requested in his will. Thus in the Baroque age, books were allowed to be placed in a coffin at a burial – just as icons could be.[78]

This sacral attitude to the book was in many ways linked with its heightened role in the age's mentality, a context without which the 'multiplicity of meanings of symbols'[79] will always be lost. Following the concepts of Neoplatonism, people sought in books keys to comprehending the secret meanings of the universe. 'The world is a book' was the title of one of the well-known poems by Simeon Polotsky. Hence the book as an object picked up a special semantic colouring: in the Baroque philosophical aesthetic it was interpreted as a repository of words and meanings. In sermons of the time (that were later taken as exemplary), preachers liked to recall the saying of St Basil the Great that 'every object and the variety of created things are as letters and words by which we read the providence and great wisdom of the Creator'.[80]

Keenness to acquire books and a reverential attitude towards the book as a source of wisdom were a common feature of all the main figures of the New Ritualist church in the Baroque period. As Alexander Panchenko observed: 'inveterate life-long bibliophile tastes' were an accompaniment of the creative labours of all those who led the development of Russian culture in its new direction.[81] Among them one can name Simeon Polotsky, Silvestr Medvedev, Karion Istomin, Stefan Yavorsky, Dimitriy Rostovsky, Feofan Prokopovich and many others. Rendering their due to the tastes and fashion of their time, they all had splendid personal libraries.

In the icon of St Dimitriy Rostovsky we can see books depicted as objects with characteristic signs of the jeweller's and bookbinder's art of his time. We can also observe books with coloured edging and rich bindings with buckles on a Greek icon of St Catherine by the well-known 17th-century artist Victor the Cretan (illus. 148), which points towards common features in the self-image of the age.

Russian icons from the end of the 17th century began to display symbolic attributes of bookmaking and literary labour. We can see them on an icon of St John the Divine by Tikhon Filatyev (illus. 149). Attributes of literary labour are also present in a portrait icon of Andrey Denisov from the late 18th century or early 19th. This Old Believer author (who was revered as if a saint) is shown with an ink-pot and pens – such as could have been encountered in the 18th century – in front of him, together with a knife for cutting paper and sharpening pens and a rag to dry the ink (illus. 122). We can easily see that these various attributes

148. Victor the Cretan, *St Catherine*, a 17th-century Cretan icon.

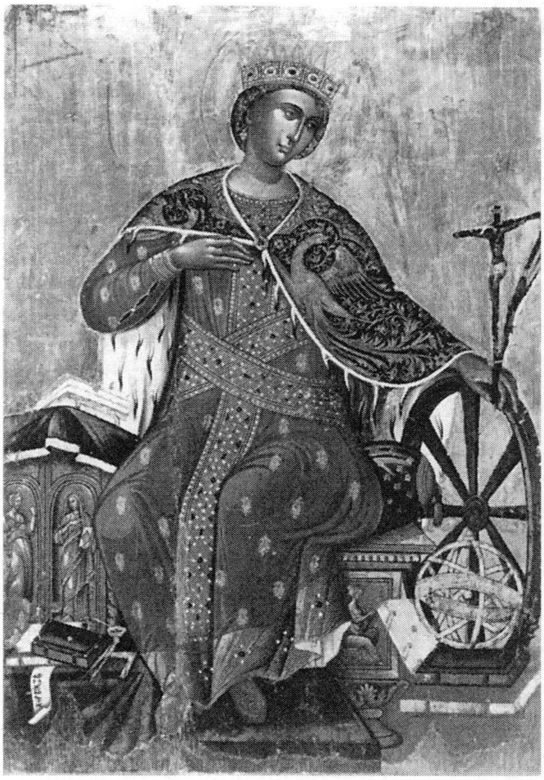

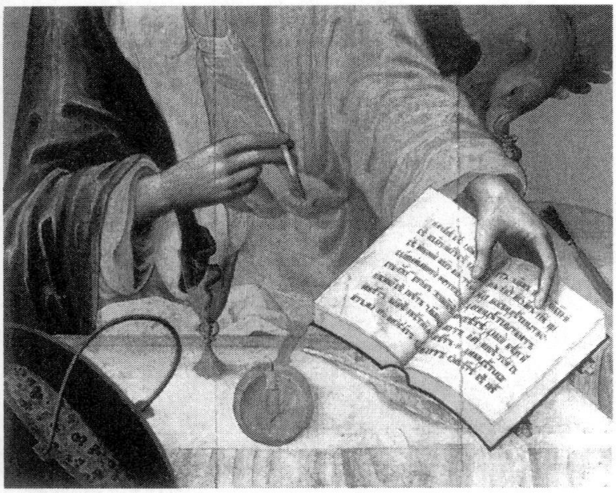

149. Detail from an icon by Tikhon Filatyev, *John the Divine*, 1691. State Tretyakov Gallery, Moscow.

are reminiscent of a still-life within the icon. Just such an early still-life is suggested by the objects related to dining on icons of the 'Old Testament Trinity' by painters from the tsar's workshop, such as Simeon Ushakov and Tikhon Filatyev (illus. 146). That is to say, the semantic foregrounding of certain items took place against a background of heightened status for the object in itself.

In Russian icons of the 18th and 19th centuries, Christ Pantocrator, St Nicholas the Wonder-worker, the Three Hierarchs, St John the Divine and many other figures are almost always depicted with books, whose bindings and coloured edges invariably conveyed that sense of materiality which had tended to appear on icons in connection with changes in the world view of the people.

So as to help create a heroized image, official Orthodox icon painting deliberately borrowed elements of the Antique environment. The semiotic opposition between the Antique and Christian hero was in a certain sense reversed. It is a commonplace that in the Baroque age antiquity served as material for the construction of complex symbolization. Arriving by way of multiple reflections, mytholigized antiquity took on a panegyric function. It was widely adopted in painting, literature, theatre, court etiquette and festivities. Since, though, the religious symbol was also still the 'expression and communication of the mental and spiritual atmosphere of the age',[82] the Antique (and Renaissance) symbolism of the new icons reflected the main changes in the history of religious feeling. It began to be actively used both with a view to the self-assertion of the Christian hero and with the aim of confirming the truths of the Orthodox Church as reformed under Tsar Aleksey.

An interesting example in this context is an icon from the second half of the 17th century in the collection of the Moscow Kremlin museums, 'St John the Warrior' (illus. 150). It is likely that this icon was painted under the influence of the idea of *Ecclesia militans* (the Church Militant), which to some extent accorded with analogous phenomena in West Slav art of the 17th century, particularly the Polish 'Sarmatian Portrait'.[83] The Christian warrior–martyr is presented on the icon in fine shining armour; the background is a perspective 'Dutch' landscape, replacing the view of a military encampment or a field of battle that was normal in knightly portraits of the time. The icon even retains weaponry – signs of military prowess (shield, Roman helmet with plumes, bow and quiver with arrows) – arranged in front of the figure as was characteristic of such portraits.[84] In one hand St John holds a cross, symbol of his martyr's death, while in the other he holds a banner with a four-ended cross and the letters 'IC XC – НИ КА' – the sacral signs of the new liturgy that appeared on sacramental wafers in churches of the New Ritual after Patriarch Nikon's reform. They were always indeed among the objects of the Old Believers' polemical works and picture icons discussed earlier.[85] Hence the banner in the Saint's hand symbolized the heroic struggle for the reformed devotion opposed by the Old Ritualists; its semantic compass was of the deepest in comparison with other portions of the artistic 'text'. In addition it is essential to note the following: if in any form of idealization – unavoidable for conceiving the image in Western European knightly portraits – the depiction of the figure was always accompanied by realistic characteristics, in this icon, by contrast, the 'real' details are symbolic from the start; everything is contained in the interplay of profound religious meanings.

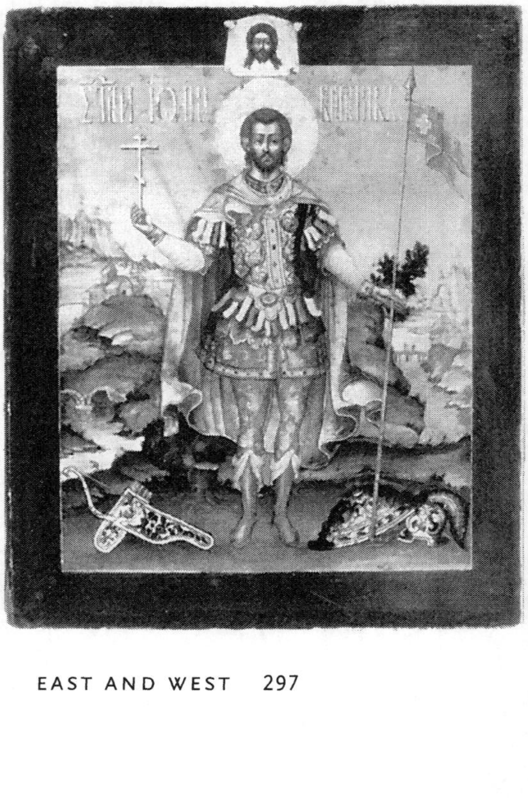

150. *St John the Warrior*, last quarter of the 17th century. Moscow Kremlin State Museums.

We can see the unabashed heroization of a saint's image in the 'antique' manner in an 18th-century icon of Prokopiy of Ustyug (illus. 151). The semi-naked figure of the well-known Russian 'holy fool', clad in a Roman-style cloak, is presented with his hands together in prayer in the Western fashion. The icon painter evidently found his overall

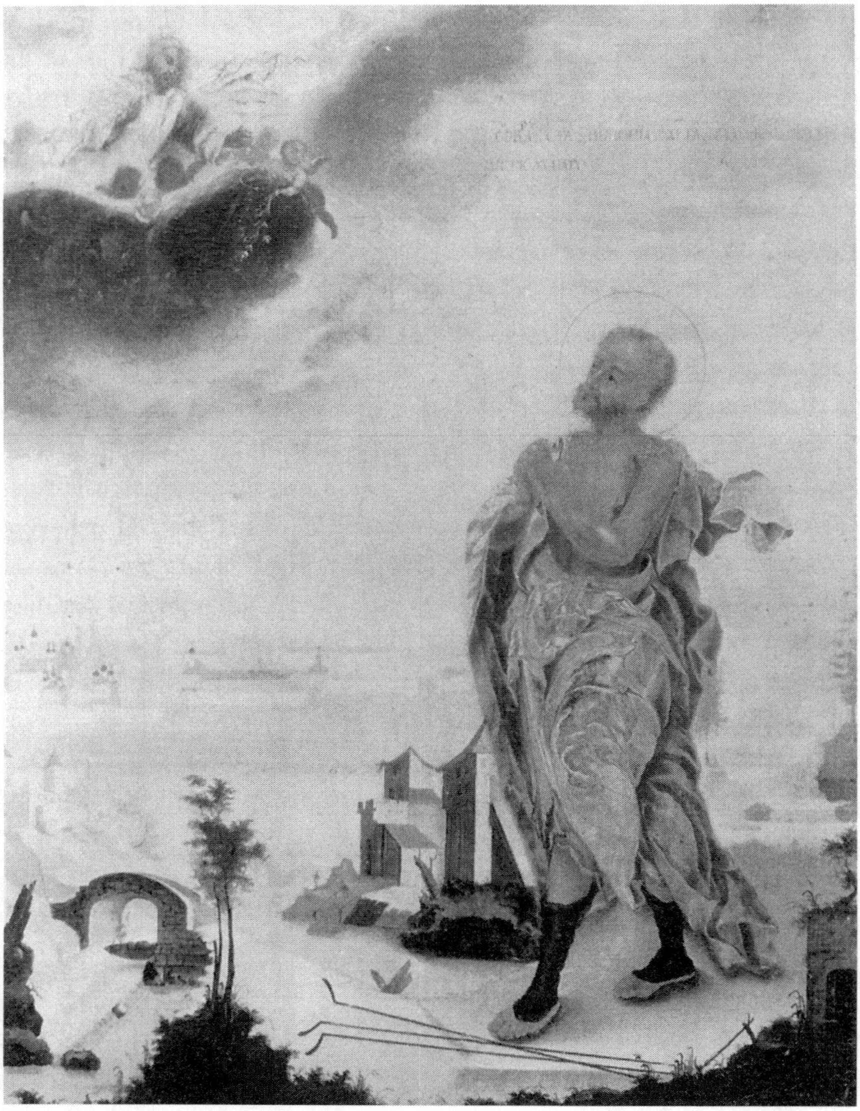

151. *Prokopiy of Ustyug, Holy Fool in Christ*, 18th century. Kolomenskoye Historical and Architectural Museum-Preserve, Moscow.

outline and pose in some 18th-century picture on a mythological subject.

From Peter the Great's time, as I have often already noted, official religiosity became ever more imbued with the complex of ideas of Imperial Rome. Hence the portraits of Russian tsars and grandees, and equally images of saints, were heroized with the aid of what can be called a 'secondary mythologization' of antiquity, which continued to serve as inexhaustible building material for complex symbolic structures. Victor Turner has noted that at the level of sensory perception the complex form of a symbol (as opposed to a simple form: a cross, a circle, etc.) has already passed through a multitude of contrasts, and this narrows down and delimits its mission.[86] The 'puffed-up' Cupids of antiquity that replaced medieval 'disembodied' angels in icons, Antique poses and gestures, details of clothing, Roman ruins and Antique military settings – these were all given a well-defined and, in fact, quite limited function of glorifying Christian figures in the context of the state religious mythology of the time. Each area of culture, of course, set its own 'task' for Antique symbolism, at which point it would begin a new life. It scarcely matters whether the Kholuy icon painter Ivan Afanasyev knew the old legend of the 'Roman' origin of the Vladimir princes. Their images on his icon, heroized according to the taste of the time, are in themselves eloquent of the transformed and 'concealed' state mythological concepts. Low-level culture was always able to retain, and indeed to lay bare, important meanings from past historical periods.

The 19th-century student drawings of Roman body-armour at Kholuy testify that Suzdalian craft icon painting carefully tried to reproduce the characteristics of an Antique environment right up to the turn of the 20th century. Such Roman armour, transformed into primitive scale-like chainmail, can be seen on numerous 'everyday' Mstyora and Kholuy icons of St Alexander Nevsky, St Demetrios of Salonica and St George. The Grand Prince St George of Vladimir, on an icon from the Parilov workshop of the late 19th century or early 20th, is also clothed in a Roman cuirass and cloak. At his sides, against a landscape background, are represented the Vladimir princes Andrey and Gleb, in typical Russian garments from the period of Tsar Aleksey Mikhaylovich. Following neo-Romantic tastes, the Antique setting now agrees with historical truth and is in full accord with 'national' indicators. The religious sensibility is becoming filled with national historical meaning. We have in front of us a primitivized variant of the official art of the Orthodox monarchy of Alexander III or Nicholas II. Christian heroes stand forth in readiness to defend the 'autocracy' and 'Orthodoxy' of still 'Holy' Russia.

All the devices determining form that we have examined in New Ritualist craft icon painting have thus revealed their links both with Baroque culture and post Renaissance painting, as well as with cultural types of previous ages. It now seems worthwhile to demonstrate that the same kind of link can be discovered in icons of the Old Ritual as well. Behind the facade of the post-Byzantine medieval canon, the same symbols and mechanisms of cultural memory were often concealed. In official Orthodox icons, features of the new way of thinking lie, as it were, on the surface, open and visible. In the icon-painting of the Old Ritual, by contrast, we come up against what Ernst Gombrich called their 'elusive meaning'.[87] We are speaking rather of hidden, latent symbolic layerings.

CHAPTER FIVE

The Middle Ages Delayed

Traditional icons and those 'in the old style', as well as the notorious 19th-century Old Believer counterfeit icons, are characteristic examples of the stylization of medieval cultural traditions among the common people and craftsmen of Russia. Their chief spiritual and ideological impulse was Old Believer devotion, which regarded the art of Muscovy in the 16th century and first half of the 17th as an ideal and a model. The explanatory and illustrated icon painter's pattern-book, the compendium of old manuscripts and model drawings, the collection of 'anciently-painted' icons – such were the main 'building materials' with which the Palekh or Mstyora 'craftsman in the old style' worked. A mass of testimony about their selection, preservation and transmission to future generations has survived: 'The whole archaeological subject of icon-painting', wrote N. N. Ushakov, 'is indebted to Palekh for the greater part of its surviving material. It was almost exclusively here that pattern-books were copied, here examples of Russian icon painting were preserved, and here, finally, that traditions and oral information of great importance to the history of icon painting until very recently lived on.'[1] Thus for example F. I. Buslayev, while working on his article 'A 17th-century Redaction of a Pattern-book', used an 18th-century icon painter's pattern-book that belonged to the Palekh painter F. V. Dolotov.[2] It was from Palekh too that there originated the *Comprehensive Explanatory Icon-painting Pattern-book* of the 18th century published by G. D. Filimonov.[3] Simultaneously, Filimonov ordered copies of icons by the 17th-century royal painters for the 'Society for Old Russian Art' from Palekh and Mstyora masters.

Still to this day one can discover old patterns and drawings by Palekh, Mstyora and Kholuy craftsmen in village houses. Many of them retain inscriptions by their owners, dedications to donors and information about their origins. In the Bakanov house in Palekh, where part of the archive of the Safonov workshop was preserved, are 18th- and 19th-century drawings and transfers, some of which were made by the icon painter I. M. Bakanov. Thus, on a version of the Hodigetria Mother of God there is the inscription 'This drawing is taken from an ancient image of the 17th century. Painted by Prokopiy Chirin. By Ivan M. Bakanov.' Many other drawings contain just the name of the owner or donor inscriptions, which testifies to the significance that was attributed in the craftsman's work to such images. Icon pattern-books, transfers and drawings were amplified by collections of ancient icons that were located, as we have seen, in the private collections of icon painters 'in the old style'. Reflecting as they did the aesthetics of Old Believer devotion, all these examples were simultaneously subject to those laws of stylistic formation of low-level craft culture as icons of the New Ritual were: the artistic conception of a master-craftsman worked within the field of superposition and deliberate quotation, as if emphasizing that different ages really can survive one within another.

Concealed Montage

Fragments of artistic 'texts' and numerous reflections of symbols from various periods and from different cultures – these can all be found in Old Ritualist icons, despite the strictness of Old Believer worship. One characteristic example is a Palekh Old Believer icon of the late 18th century: 'Crucifixion with Guardian Angel and Selected Saints in Attendance' (illus. 152).

A strengthening of the personal impulse in the norms of devotion can be seen from the 16th century throughout the whole of Christendom. In this respect the iconography of the Old Believer icon can interestingly be compared with that of Western epitaph imagery, on which beside the Crucifixion a guardian angel and portraits of the deceased person's family and near ones are included (illus. 153). We should remember that the

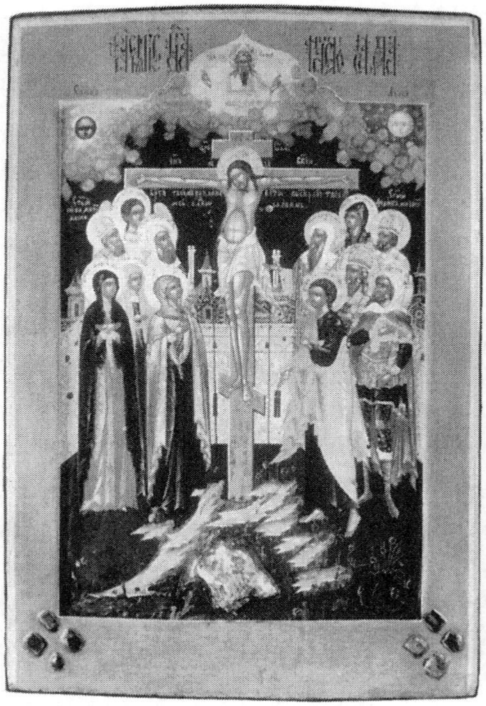

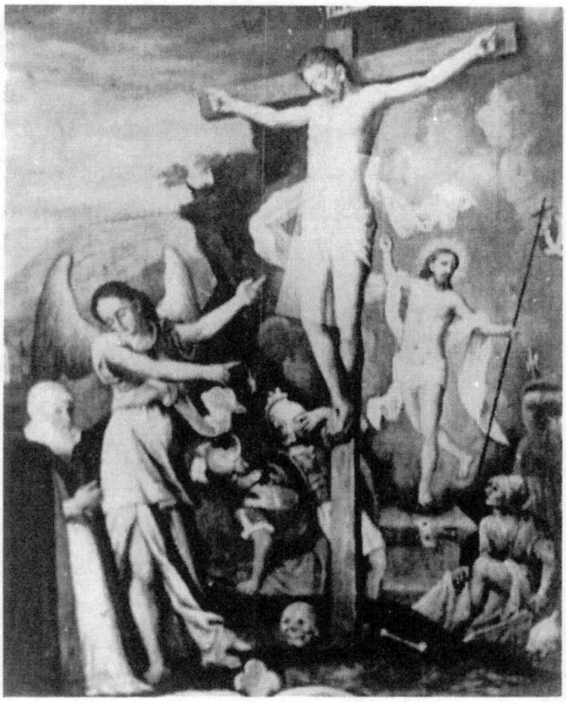

152. *Crucifixion with Guardian Angel and selected Saints*, end of the 18th century, Palekh. State Tretyakov Gallery, Moscow.

153. Crucifixion, Resurrection and Guardian Angel, part of the epitaph, 1582. Church of St Michael, Chrudim, Czech Republic.

'attachment' of Catholic piety to the cult of the guardian angel developed particularly in the age of the 16th-century Wars of Religion, while in the following century Pope Clement X gave this cult official sanction: in Rome and many other places, churches, chapels and altars were dedicated to the guardian angel.[4]

In areas of Eastern Europe bordering on Russia, particularly the Czech lands, epitaph pictures were painted from the second half of the 16th century through to the 1680s. A. Weckwerth and J. Białostocki note the outstanding quality of such images on tomb monuments of former ages. Earlier these images had fulfilled two main function: either they fixed a life portrait of the deceased in a people's memory, or else they correlated the heavenly life of the soul with the perspective of eschatology. Now, however, the conception of an epitaph image became *addressed to the living*: it was meant above all to evoke a sense of prayerful concentration and a supplication beseeching salvation for those who had commissioned it and were depicted in it.[5]

In old Believer icons from Palekh, portraits of actual individuals were replaced by patron saints in accordance with the particular characteristics of Orthodox religious sensibility. Common ground remained only in the schema worked out within the conventional canonical framework, whose wide distribution in Old Believer icon painting was noted (though not explained) by N. Petrov: 'in complex (domestic) icon compositions a guardian angel is normally depicted, and at his sides or next to him a whole multitude of saints'.[6]

On the same icon we also see a deep black background. The Old Believers' choice of a black background for icons, as a sign of death and suffering, evidently corresponded to their religious mood. Internally this choice can be related to the use of a black background in Catholic *Arte Sacra* paintings, where scenes of the martyrdom of Christian saints were depicted. In the context of the 16th-century discovery of the early Christian catacombs in Rome (when, in Mâle's words, 'a different great period of torment was revealed in its most striking aspect'[7]), the colour black in Catholic painting could have a special emotional and semiotic status: it could symbolize the darkness of the catacombs – a space that was hallowed by the feats of the first Christians. Note that after the capture of Constantinople by the Turks in 1453, Santa Sophia ceased to be regarded in Rus as the chief shrine of the Orthodox world. That distinction passed to the Church of the Holy Sepulchre in Jerusalem, whose architectural space included both the site of Golgotha and the Lord's Sepulchre. Hence the black background of the Palekh icon might symbolize too the darkness of the tomb in which Christ was interred and from which he rose again on the third day.

There is yet another interesting detail in the Palekh icon. The cross is set up at Golgotha, the depiction of which (with the traditional head of Adam) has been replaced by an actual small stone brought from the hill in Jerusalem. The two lower margins have eight more little mosaic reliquary stones, brought from the Holy Sepulchre church in Jerusalem, symmetrically set into them at the corners.[8] These material signs of Golgotha also reflected the aesthetic individuality of Old Believer devotion.

Thus the icon itself was as if transformed into the framing of a reliquary, an ancient kind of sacred object. In chapter One it was noted that in Old Ritualist devotion the significance of an ancient icon grew greater in the process of meditation. Now we should note that the significance of its framing – the means by which it was displayed in a given location – also increased in the same context. In the 18th and 19th centuries the early Russian icon with the old symbolism was transferred from the space of the official church to the space of the Old Ritualist domestic prayer place. Here it received the status of a particularly valued reliquary. This is reflected in the appearance of a special type of Old Ritualist icon called an 'insertion' (*vrezok*) in the jargon of Old Believer icon painters. The ancient image was inserted into a new icon and became a component of the new composition. Thus the new icon fulfilled the function of a rhetorical framing to the ancient holy object, as with the Palekh 'Crucifixion' discussed earlier (illus. 154, 155). Incidentally, we have every reason to think that here the Old Ritualist craftsmen followed the same norms of Western Latin Baroque rhetoric as an official Church icon painter. Baroque categories of artistic thinking breathed new life into the very structure of the ancient Byzantine icon.

We know that Byzantium conceived of the icon as a complex sign system with several layers of reception and comprehension. The chief peculiarity of

154. *Zosima and Savvatiy of Solovki with various Saints*, 19th century. Private collection, Moscow.

155. *St John the Divine and the Martyr St Antipas with the Icon of St Nicholas the Wonder-worker*, first half of the 19th century. Kolomenskoye Historical and Architectural Museum-Preserve, Moscow.

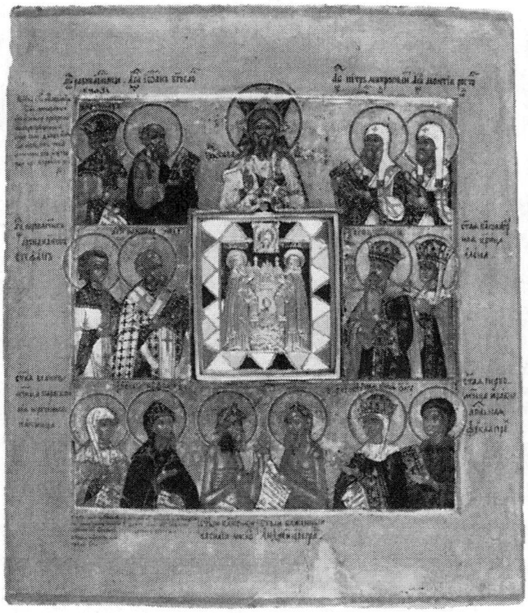

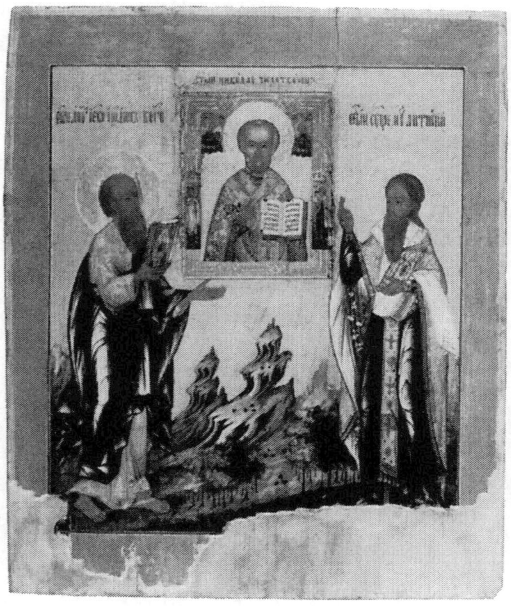

this system was that all these layers existed in a symbolic unity and were subject to their theological and liturgical context. Thus the frame and the picture of a medieval icon were a single symbolic whole. Like the stark wall of a medieval place of worship, the icon frame was conceived as the boundary between two spaces, the sacred and the worldly. The unitary material basis of frame and picture, as well as their common features of decoration, testified that in a medieval person's consciousness this boundary was related more to the sacred space than the worldly.

An icon is painted on one or more boards fastened together by special reinforcing struts. The margins of an icon are produced by the hollowing out of the central area of the icon: in this shallow depression the image itself, be it of Christ, the Mother of God or a saint, is painted. In Russian this framed area of the icon acquired a symbolically significant name, *kovcheg* ('ark' or 'shrine') – thus symbolizing the Ark of the Covenant, a box in which holy objects were stored and concealed from the eyes of the uninitiated (Exodus 25: 1, 17–22; Hebrews 9: 1–5). We also know, however, that with the end of the Middle Ages the frame of an image was transformed from a means of preserving the Divine Countenance into an instrument for its apprehension. This was the essential point in making the distinction between frame and picture that took place in Western Europe during the Renaissance and in Russia during the Baroque period. It was in this context that the *kovcheg* gradually disappeared in the Russian Baroque icon, to be replaced by the *kiot* (icon casing), which resembled the Renaissance window-like frame of a picture. But simultaneously the frame also acquired a special meaning in the composition of an icon – it became an independent focus for art. Since in the Baroque age particular attention was paid to the ancient relics that were so important in securing the Church's authority, in both the Catholic and Orthodox worlds icons and pictures appear within which genuine or imitated ancient wonder-working images are placed, as particularly precious and valued cult objects. Thus the master-craftsman's work itself was essentially transformed into the frame for an ancient image and had its own symbolic and aesthetic function.

The relation between a frame that itself has the status of a work of art and an ancient image that does not aspire to that status was examined by Hans Belting on the basis of a picture by Rubens, the *Madonna of Mercy*

(Chiesa Nova, Rome).[9] In the Orthodox icon, however, such a construct had first and foremost a symbolic significance and a rhetorical aim. It spoke primarily of the fact that the framing of the icon was no longer a medieval box concealing the ancient holy object, rather a picturesque image designed to show it off and inform people about it. The frame brought the holy object closer to the world. That is just the function of numerous Russian icon frames of the later 17th century and the 18th, with the most varied iconographic programmes. Specialist studies have demonstrated that the picturesque late-17th-century or early-18th frame for the 14th-century Mother of God of the Don icon from the Moscow Annunciation Cathedral contained an independent and complex symbolic programme linked with cultural and politico-religious events of the period.[10] An iconic frame might depict the saints who founded the monastery and form the border of an ancient icon with whose appearance their life was connected. An example is 'Avraamiy and Merkuriy of Smolensk' (1723–8), into which the craftsman put a real 16th-century icon of the Hodegitria Mother of God (illus. 156). By contrast, the iconic frame of 'SS John the Evangelist and Antipas' contains not the actual ancient icon of St Nicholas, but merely a copy – even though it too is incised into the board itself (see illus. 155). An iconic frame can also contain a selection of saints who were protectors of a family. In this case Russian icon painters might even insert part of an old prayer image or a small metal icon (see illus. 154).

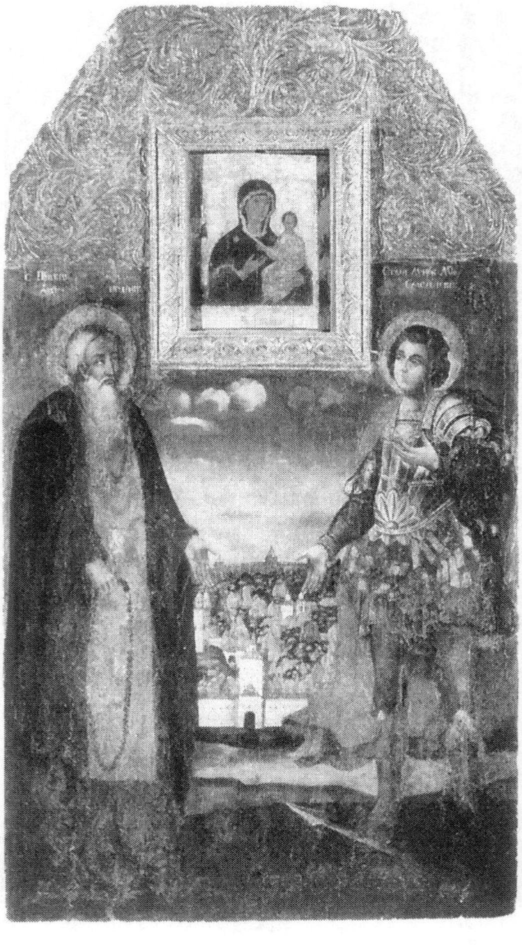

156. Frame: *Avraamiy and Merkuriy of Smolensk* (1723–8); within the frame: the icon *Hodigitria Smolensk Mother of God*, 16th century, Moscow. Belorussian State Museum of Art, Minsk.

Finally, from the second half of the 17th century, iconic frames with compartments carrying narratives about famous wonder-working images – the Saviour Not Made by Hands, the Vladimir, Kazan, Tikhvin Mother of God types, etc. – are widely disseminated (illus. 157, 158). Frames carrying scenes of the Akathist to Christ, the Mother of God and saints appear. They were painted in the 18th century for the official Church in the Baroque style. A characteristic example is a frame carrying the Akathist to the Mother of God painted in 1746 by the master Aleksey Kholmogorets (illus. 159). The luxurious frame contains an extra, inner frame and extensive Akathist texts, that together with small pictures convince the viewer that the ancient Hodegitria image has a special value and significance in the process of salvation. Simultaneously the frame also illustrates the service for the Mother of God. Like a medieval icon casing it is an adornment for an ancient image, an offering by patron and craftsman that will be pleasing to God.

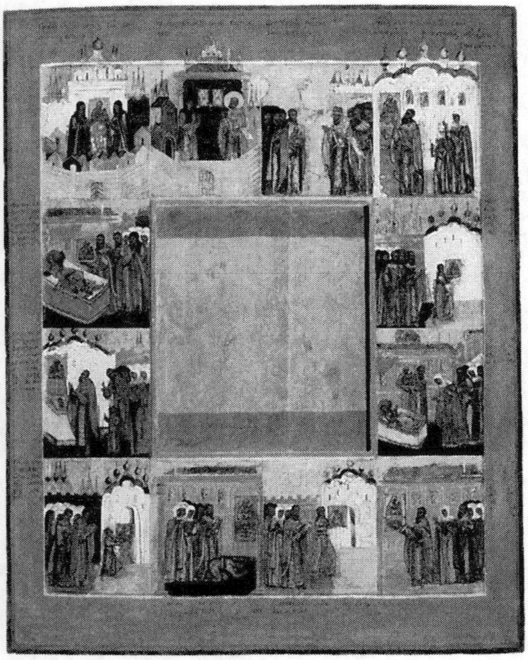

157 Frame displaying the *Narrative of the Mother of God of the 'Seven Lakes'*, last quarter of the 17th century. Andrey Rublyov Museum, Moscow.

158. *Frame with Narrative on the Vladimir Mother of God*, 18th century. Kolomenskoye Historical and Architectural Museum-Preserve, Moscow.

Such frames were made in the 18th and 19th centuries in Palekh and Mstyora (illus. 160). Their style was the choice of the patron, but their structure always embodied a clear rhetorical purpose. This structure was inspired not only by the norms of devotion, but by the rules of Baroque teaching on adornment (*elocutio*). Thus 'transposition' (*transmutatio*) explained that an icon could serve as a 'frame' for another icon, so convincing the viewer of the latter's specially sacred quality. 'Addition' (*adjectio*) demonstrated that the joining together of the old and the new would create a special interplay of meanings. Finally, 'substitution' (*immutatio*) would permit the introduction into this rhetoricized structure of elements of other framings that had not been there before: for example, frames of the title-page of a book or of a window in a wall. The sort of picture frame encountered in Russian Western-type paintings of the period could also enclose an ancient image.

The frequency of such constructs in 18th- and 19th-century Old Ritualist circles clearly represented an echo of Baroque cultural ideas that were superimposed on a medieval consciousness. Testimony to such layering is

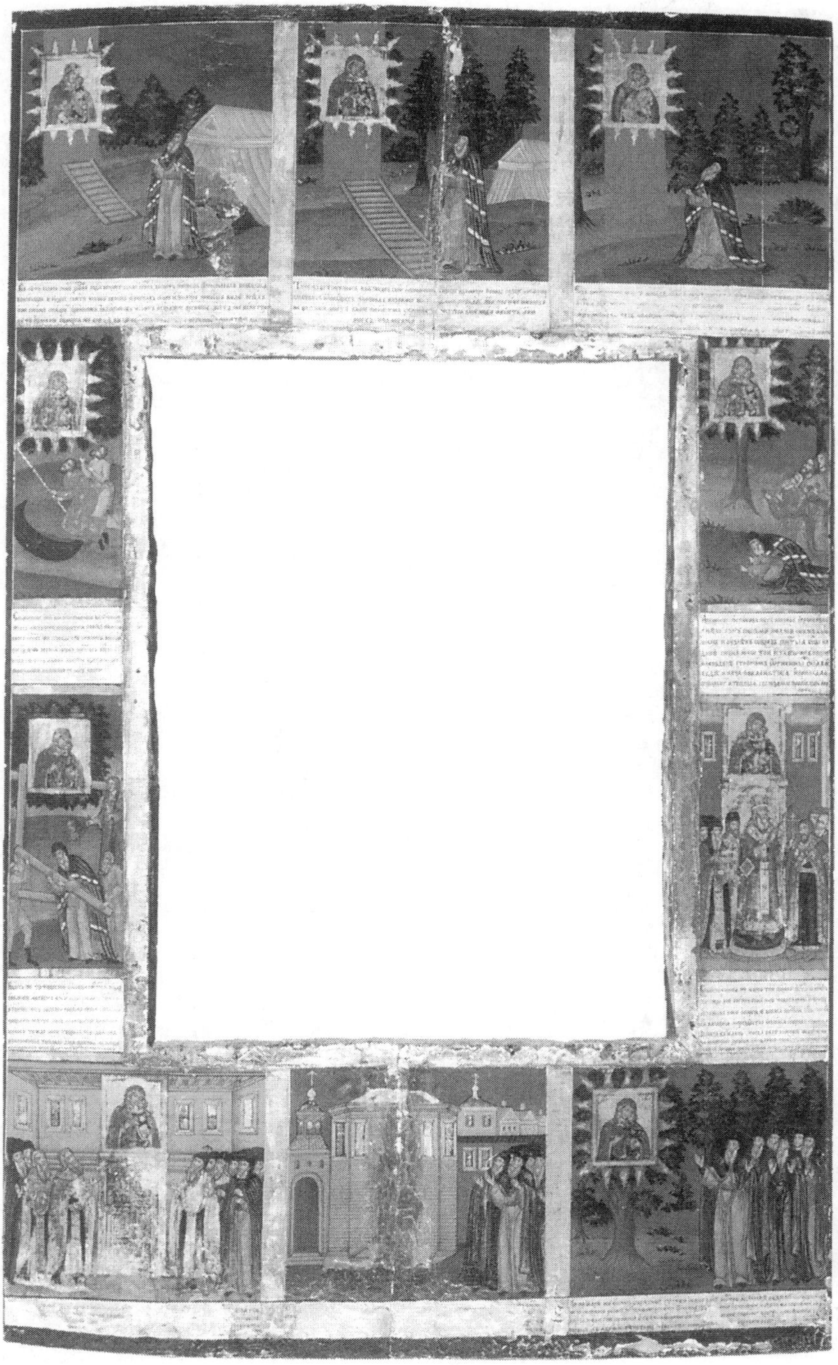

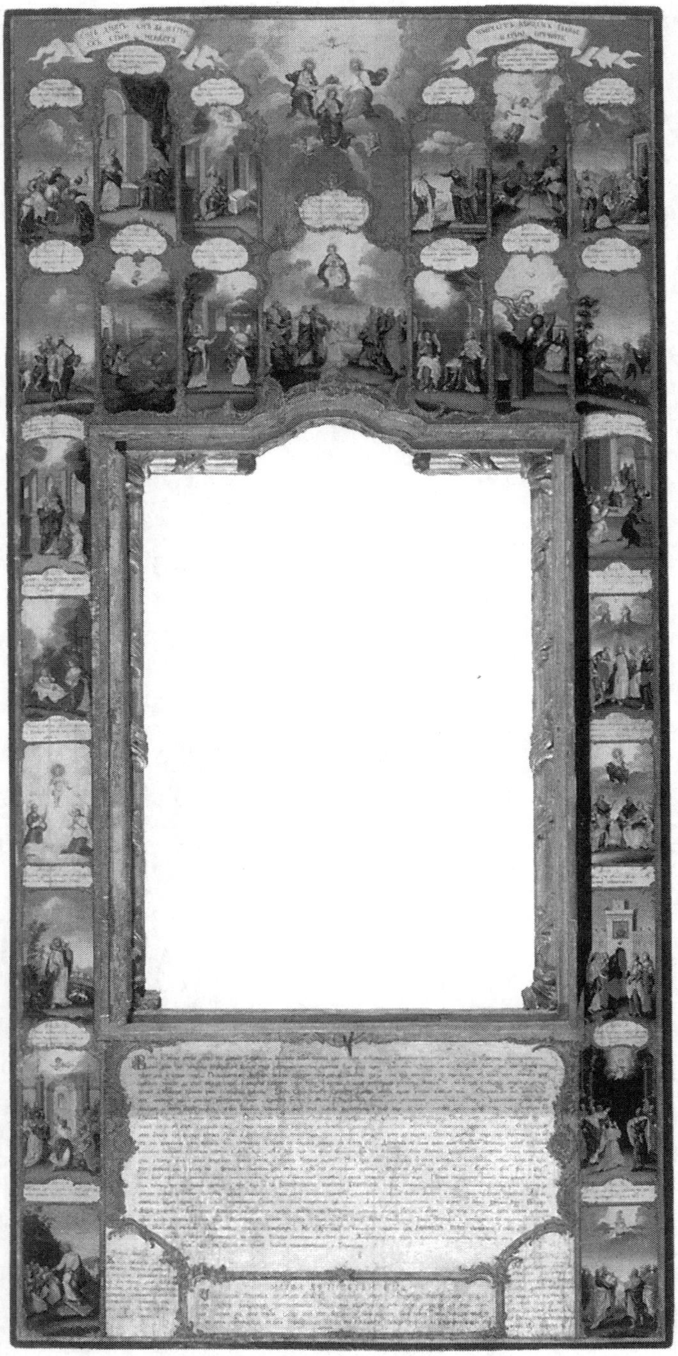

the fact that the *kovcheg* frame of a Palekh Old Ritualist icon contains decoration that corresponds with the Jerusalem reliquary contained within its frame. Thus the frame, despite the broadening of its rhetorical functions, continued to be regarded on the symbolic level as inseparable from the central picture.

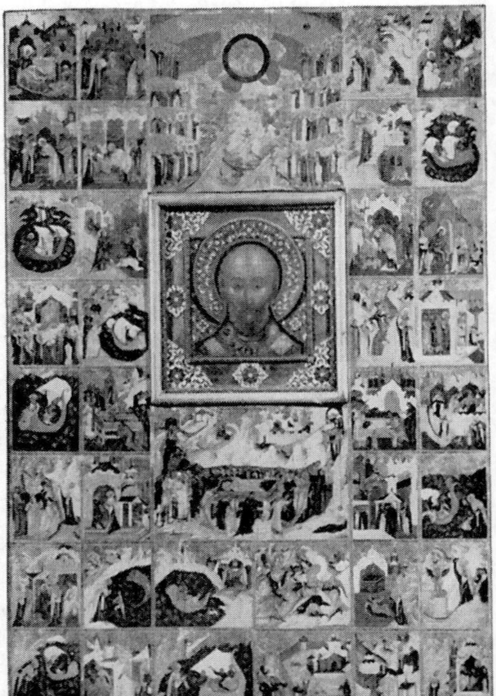

159. Aleksey Kholmogorets, *Frame with Narrative*/Akathist to the Mother of God, 1746. Velikiy Ustyug Museum of History, Architecture and Art.

160. Frame with *Akathist to St Nicholas the Wonder-worker*, mid-18th century. Palekh Art Museum, Palekh.

Writing about the preservation of Old Russian artistic traditions and their development in Suzdalian icon painting, N. P. Kondakov noted a great number of complex narrative subjects, which, unlike Buslayev, he termed not 'theological-didactic' but 'multi-figured' and 'lyrical-symbolic'.[11] These were: 'Symbol of Faith', 'It is Truly Meet', 'Our Father', 'O thou Only Begotten Son', 'Wisdom hath Builded Her a House', 'The Seven Fold Deisis', 'My Soul doth Magnify the Lord', 'How shall we Name Thee?', 'In Thee we Rejoice', 'Praise be to God in the Highest', 'Come all Ye People', 'The Burning Bush', 'The Akathist of the Mother of God', 'I am the Vine' and 'The Church'. As well as these the Palekh, Mstyora and Kholuy icon makers painted such complex subjects as 'Trinity with Deeds', 'Trinity with Entry', 'The Three Hypostases of God', 'Fatherhood', 'Let all that is with Breath Praise the Lord', 'The Six Days', 'The Eye that Does not Slumber', 'Let all Flesh be Silent', 'My Soul doth Magnify', 'New Heaven and Earth', 'The True Vine', 'The Bringing of the Kerchief', 'Now the Heavenly Powers' and a few others (illus. 161, 162, 163).[12]

Kondakov began to collect tracings for all these icons at the end of the 1890s, planning to publish them in the eighth and ninth issues of *Russian Antiquities*, as we can judge by his correspondence with V. T. Georgievsky. In a letter of 7 November 1897 he asked 'can't we get a sketch-book in Palekh or Kholuy of an illustrated pattern-book with drawings of complex icons: "I believe", "It is Truly Meet", "Praise the Lord in the Heavens", "And God Rested", "O Thou Only-Begotten Son", "Come, ye People", "In the Tomb

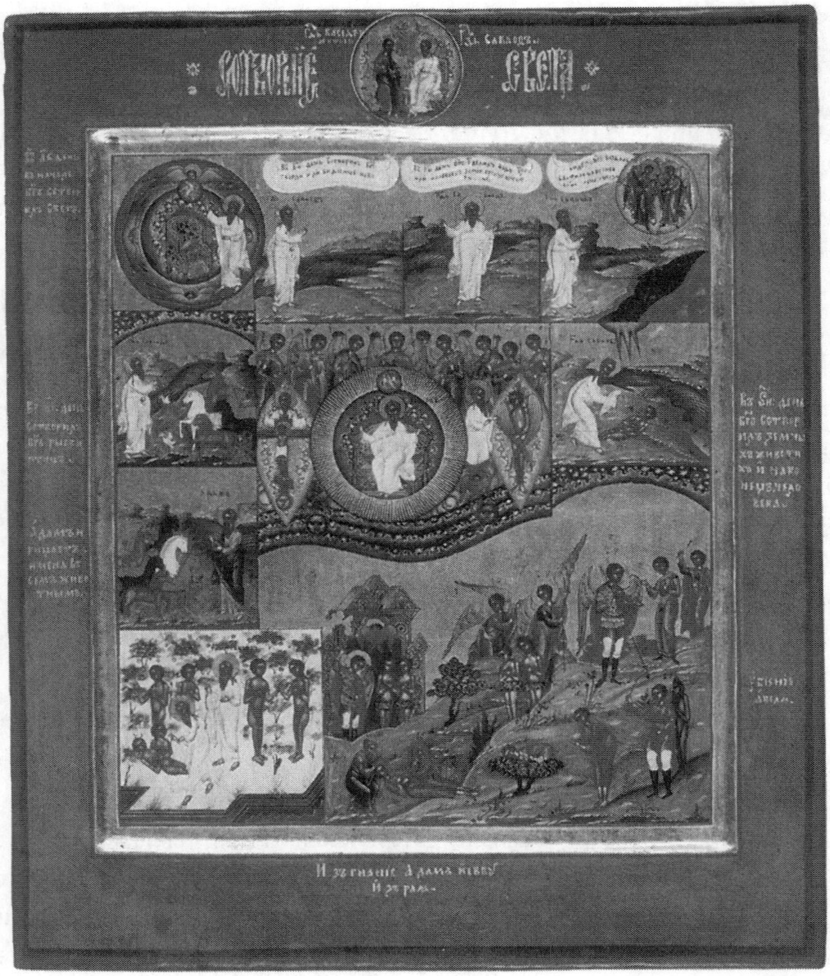

According to the Flesh", etc? I'd be specially interested in drawings, that's to say tracings, of complicated, many-figured compositions of all kinds.'[13] In his next letter Kondakov spoke of the icons themselves ('it'd be good to get even cheap genuine icons of these subjects'), which testifies to his intentions to make a collection of Suzdalian images of this kind.[14]

It is easy to see that in this broad area of iconographic themes the Suzdalian masters inherited that 'painterly scholasticism' that had its origin in Muscovite icon painting of the mid-16th century (illus. 166). The 'theological–didactic' icons of the 18th and 19th centuries, widespread for

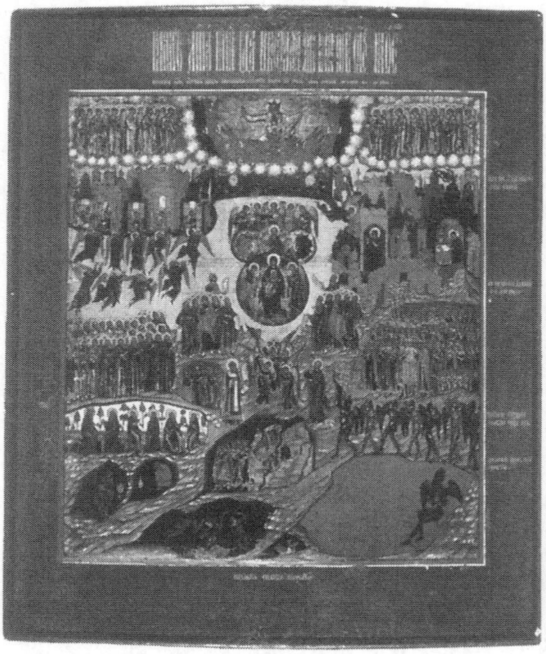

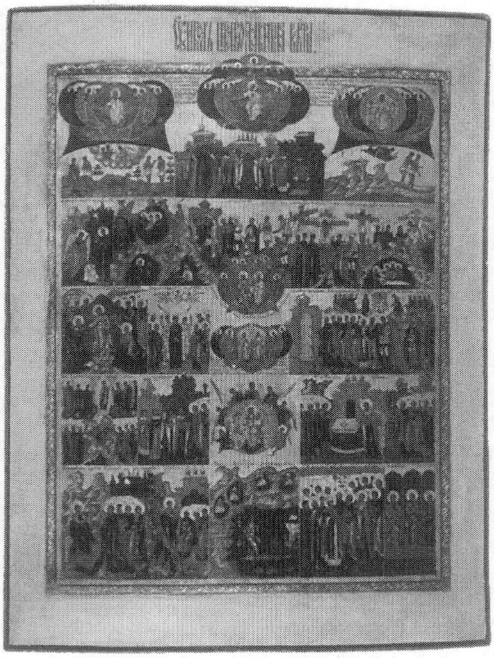

the most part among the Old Ritualists, gave visible witness to the Old Believers' predilection for the Muscovite devotional tradition, sanctified by the authority of the *Stoglav* Council. This was precisely what explains the widespread occurrence in Old Believer icon painting of the 'Four-Part Icon' despite all the 'Latin sophistries' that found their way into it: it consists of 'Come, ye People', 'O thou Only-Begotten Son', 'And God Rested on the Seventh Day', and 'In the Tomb According to the Flesh'. For nearly three centuries the iconography of these subjects remained almost unchanged (illus. 164, 165).

The signs of the times, however, inevitably emerged in them too. But whereas in the iconic frame they became apparent at the level of the very material structure of the icon, in 'multivisaged' icons it was at the level of composition – or the universal rhetorical tabulation – schema that was the basis of the hagiological icon of a saint (illus. 167). It possesses just such a tabulation as its universalized schema to reflect reality. The 'portrait' of the saint is presented at its centre, surrounded by a frame consisting of separate rectangles. In each of these tabulated boxes we find a separate

161. *The Creation of the World*, 19th century. State Museum of the History of Religion, St Petersburg.

162. *'My soul doth magnify the Lord . . .'*, 19th century. State Museum of the History of Religion, St Petersburg.

163. *Symbol of the Faith*, 19th century. State Museum of the History of Religion, St Petersburg.

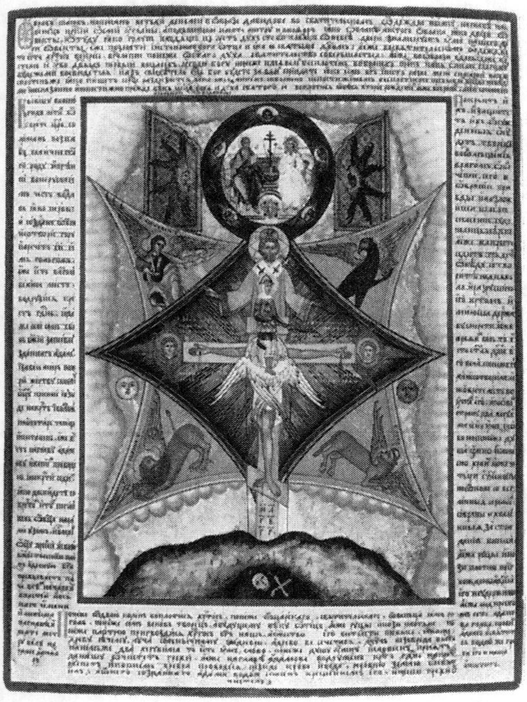

164. *'Thou Art the Hierarch . . .'*, second half of the 19th century. Private collection, Moscow.

scene from the saint's life, appearing not as a unique element of his or her biography but as a token of personality. As a result, the concrete character of the saint would appear as a series of abstract properties enumerated one by one. So what we have is a list of headings – a fundamentally rationalistic attempt to exhaust the subject by enumerating and systematizing all its logical aspects. Hence, naturally, artists in periods noted for rhetoricism never slackened their efforts to cultivate the enumeration of human virtues and vices, of the properties of nature, the world, God and the cosmos. The Russian popular icon painters of the 17th, 18th and 19th centuries could doubtless thank the Hellenistic tradition for this unflagging passion for enumeration: ancient and medieval rhetoric presented them, so as to reflect reality, with a universal scheme of tabulation that they filled up with facts purged of any concreteness – that is to say, with universalized schemas. Yet this idea is only a point of departure: a whole divergent set of possible paths fanned out from it. Thus the passion for enumeration could also reflect changes in the human picture of the world. So a mid-16th-century hagiological icon of St Alexander Svirsky (Dormition Cathedral of the Moscow Kremlin) has a frame with 128 individual cells surrounding the 'portrait' of the saint. In these tabulated cells we find, listed in great detail, abstractly conceived aspects of the saint's life: a previously inconceivable attentiveness towards his earthly path and the worth of his earthly deeds. Earlier hagiological icons limited themselves simply to the chief landmarks of the saint's life. This grandiose frame, constructed on the principle of a rhetorical tabulated schema, tells us above all of the heightening of the didactic purpose of the image in the context of the Church and state politics of the period – a strengthening of the role of the Church and of the Russian saints in the construction of 'Moscow the Third Rome'.

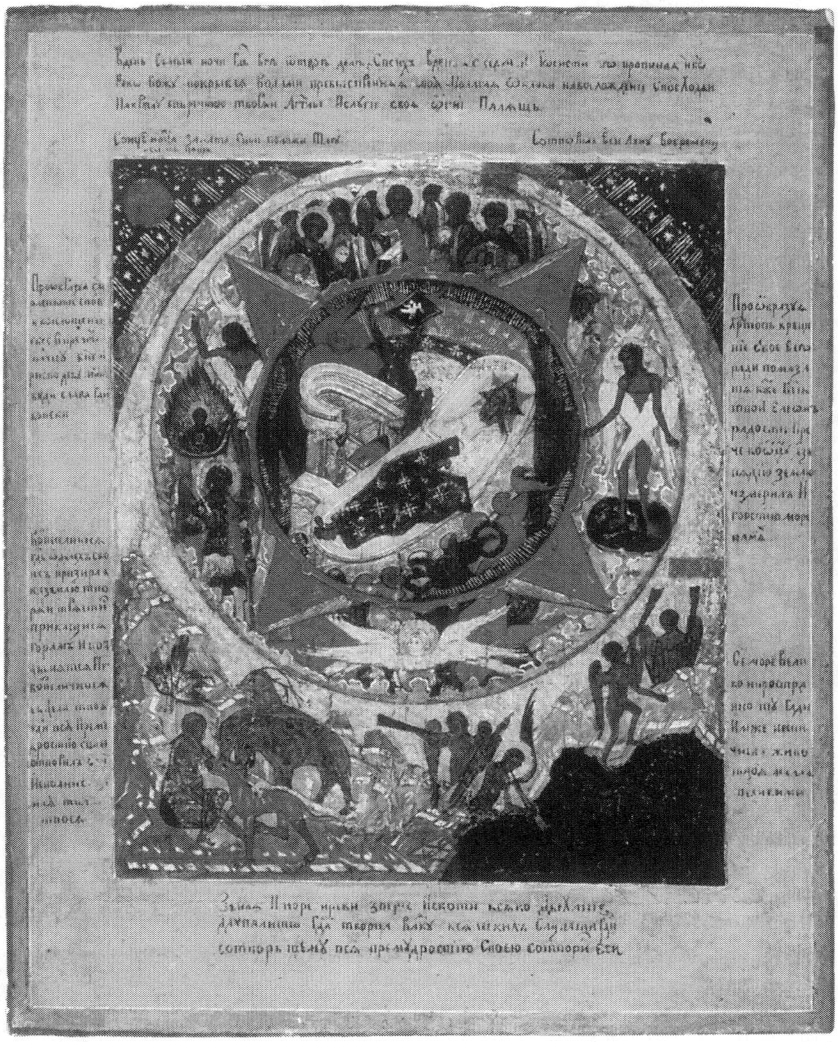

165. *'And God Rested on the Seventh Day'*, second half of the 18th century. State Museum of the History of Religion, St Petersburg.

The strengthening of that illustrative impulse in Muscovite icon painting of the second half of the 16th century was without doubt an echo of the more general mind-set of the age. In the West, immediately after the Council of Trent, various famous commentaries on the Council's decrees concerning religious art and the decoration of Catholic churches and monasteries were published. In the works of John Molanus (1570), Gabriele Pagliotti (1582), Federico Borromeo (1625) and many others, a strengthened

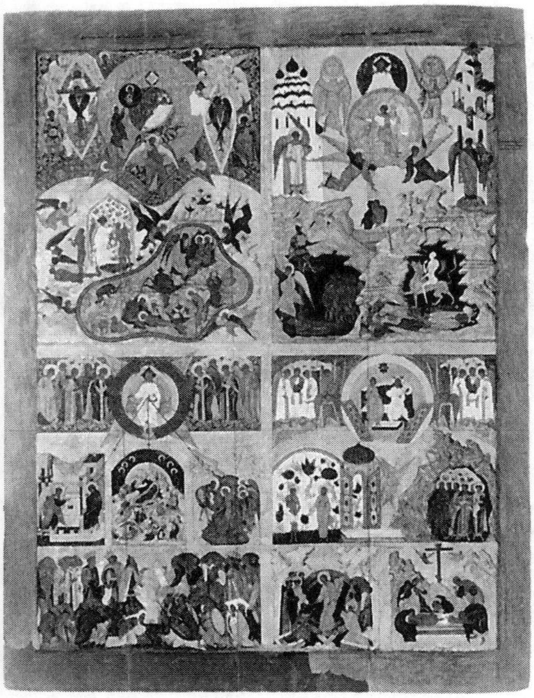

166. 'Four-part' icon from Annunciation Cathedral in Moscow Kremlin, 1547–51. Moscow Kremlin State Museums.

moral and didactic role for religious painting was affirmed. In response to the new doctrines concerning Catholic iconography, practical directions for artists in the most various fields were published, among them the collections of emblems and guidebooks to symbols mentioned earlier.

In this whole context it comes as no surprise that in Muscovite Russia, icon painting copy-books become widely disseminated in the second half of the 16th century.[15] A copy-book is a rhetorical tabulation of all known subjects and saints, based on the same poetics of synchresis as a method of ordering and systematizing the diversity of facts in the actual world. We should remember the test of an icon painting copy-book: every feature of a saintly image ('beard', 'countenance', 'age', 'clothing', 'gesture', etc.) was characterized by juxtaposition with the image of a different saint. The tabulation of a copy-book was merely a bare universalized scheme, but each period filled its compartments up with actual contents. Thus the form of the tabulation itself could not avoid bearing the marks of its time.

So in the second half of the 16th century the tabulation of the icon painting copy-book is saturated anew with the idea of a canon and, more strongly after the *Stoglav* (as in the West) with the heightened didactic impulse of religious art, with its role in the religious education of humanity. Hence, in the symbolic rectangle of the Muscovite icon of the second half of the 16th century, smaller subdivisions become gradually more frequent: the Russian icon was filled with an edificatory intention and the notion of a 'Bible for the simple folk', more characteristic of Western religious art. Muscovite narrative icons counted on a gradual and rationalistic reading; their symbolic level, saturated and complicated with allegorical details, now made a greater appeal to human reason, reflecting a stronger rationalistc apprehension of the world.

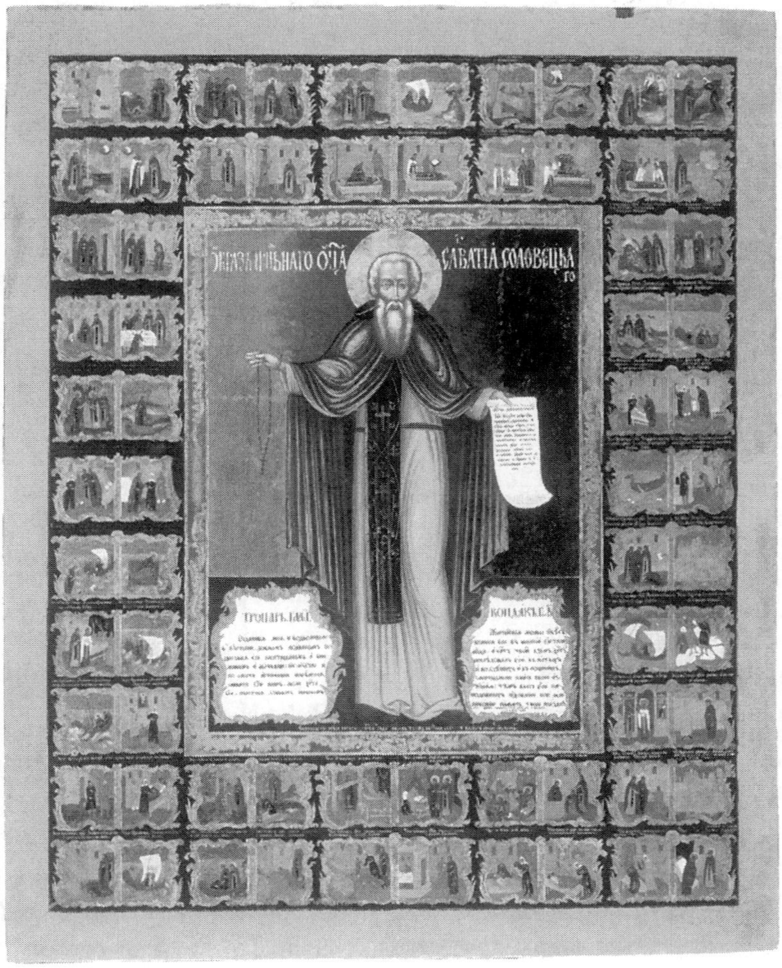

167. *Savvatiy of Solovki with Life*, 18th century. Kolomenskoye Historical and Architectural Museum-Preserve, Moscow.

When the transition to the New Devotion took place under Tsar Aleksey Mihaylovich, Simon Ushakov, on the model of Western European anatomical atlases, planned to make an 'Alphabet of the Arts': a sort of new pattern-book that was to consist of pictures of all the parts of the human figure. At this new stage of the development of the idea of the 'Third Rome' (i.e., the creation of an East Slav Orthodox empire headed by Moscow), through a re-evaluation of the *Stoglav* Council decrees and the enactment of liturgical reforms, the didactic role of the icon was further strengthened. The artistic conceptual principles typical of Baroque poetics – emblematism, particular stress on the word, riddling, etc. – began to interfere in the development of the concept of a new icon composition. The greater interpenetrability of various art forms conditioned the heightened influence of engraving on icon painting. The prayer image tended more and more towards the dry and schematic composition typical of the Western and Russian edificatory picture: a quadrilateral divided into many cells of identical dimensions, as we have seen, a sort of 'tabulation': 'the table was the central element in the learning of the 17th and 18th centuries'.[16] Thus it is no surprise that 17th-century verse from the category of 'artificial poetry' can have a tabulated form: for example the labyrinth verse of Simeon Polotsky, compiled from words that originate in liturgical texts. With its playful and enigmatic qualities, this verse served simultaneously as praise of the Mother of God and instruction for the reader.[17] We see an analogous composition in one of the engravings devoted to the theme of 'the debate of life with death': in separate cells the names of the twelve greatest commandments, instructing the human being on the way of salvation, are located. There are similar schemes in very many other religious pictures and also icons (illus. 168, 169). The universality of the rationalistic tabulation principle in Baroque thought is equally confirmed by the famous *Atlas of Mary*, compiled in 1657 by the Jesuit Wilhelm Humpenberg and containing some 1,200 images of miracles performed by the Virgin Mary.[18]

As early as the second half of the 17th century, icons divided into many cells containing separate subjects, miracle-working images of the Mother of God or figures of saints are increasingly encountered. In Suzdalian centres of art, icons of this kind seem to have appeared in the 18th century, but become specially frequent in the 19th. This is the principle by which icons of the Mother of God, church calendar icons for the year, and also the majority of complex symbolic subjects were painted. We should note that these are all in their own way 'tables', trying to incorporate as many similar representations, united by the idea of praise or edification, as possible within themselves. One organizing principle might be the idea of divine help, for example in 'healing' icons, where saints who might assist in the case of one or another illness (as we saw in chapter One) would be located in separate cells (see illus. 34).

All these examples illustrate the idea of the Ukrainian and Russian

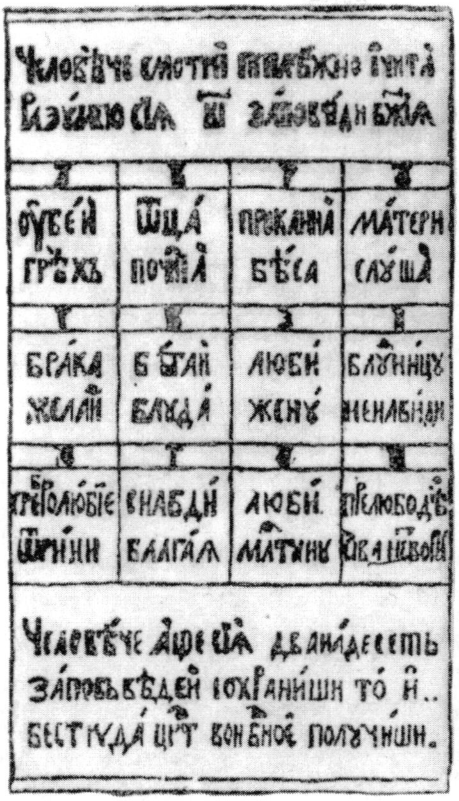

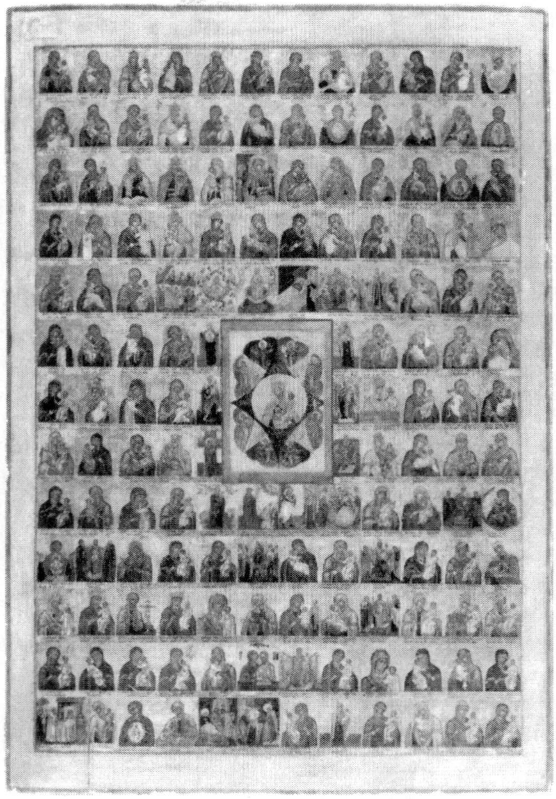

168. *On the Dispute between Life and Death*, 18th-century printed *lubok*.

169. *Mother of God of the Burning Bush with other Mother of God images*, 19th century. Collection of the State Academic Institute of Restoration, Moscow.

Baroque as primarily rhetorical and 'measured', above all following practical aims of spiritual education. The rhetorical impulse of the Baroque was strengthened in Ukraine and Belorussia partially as a result of the task of fighting the Counter-Reformation – a task faced in the 17th century by local printing-houses, 'brotherhood schools' and the Mogila College in Kiev.[19] Here again we may recollect the stylistic and ideological many-sidedness of the Baroque, as a result of which it could adapt itself to popular culture much more simply than could other styles. While adopting popular and medieval traditions, the Baroque simultaneously strove to 'popularize' its ideological and artistic idiosyncrasies. Hence the latter might appear 'in translation' through the course of various cultural–historical periods in the most diverse symbolic guises and forms. The form of the tabulation icon was one of these.

The wide distribution in 18th- and 19th-century Old Ritualist icon painting of narrative-based icons, icons illustrating hymn subjects and 'tabulation' icons on various topics tells us about universal mechanisms of text production within popular craft culture of the post-medieval period. People continued to envision their picture of the world on the basis of the universal rhetoricized scheme of the tabulation icon. An 'ornamental' way of thinking and the desires of patrons both inclined the Palekh or Mstyora craftsman at one moment towards complexity, at another towards simplification of the composition. In 'table' icons a curious 'collage effect' of subjects and symbolic levels might take place. We see this principle of composition in the Old Ritualist icon 'The Crucifixion with Feast Days, Saints, and Images of the Mother of God' by the master Pyotr Shitnikov: the 'Crucifixion' in the central element is framed by depictions of a variety of subjects (illus. 170).

A clear example of the development of the rhetorical principle of tabulation is the 'Resurrection and Descent into Hell with Menologion, Selected Saints and Feastdays' (illus. 171). The icon is executed in the traditional

170. Pyotr Shitnikov, *Crucifixion with Feast Days, various Saints and Mother of God Images*,1873. Private collection, Moscow.

171. *Resurrection and Descent into Hell with Menologion, Selected Saints and Feast Days*, 19th century. State Russian Museum, St Petersburg.

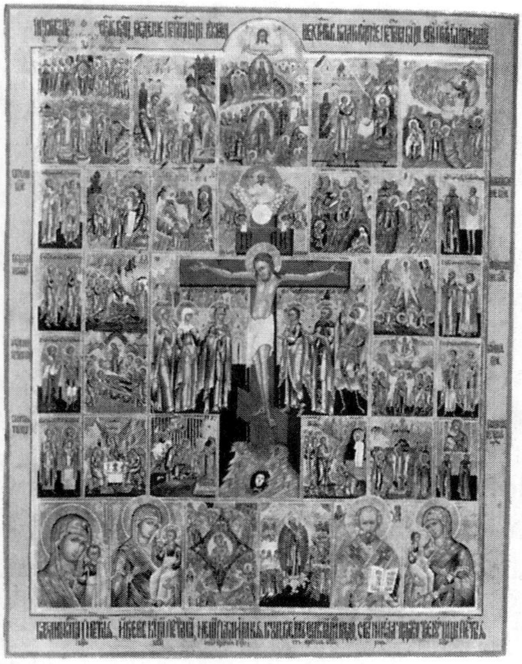

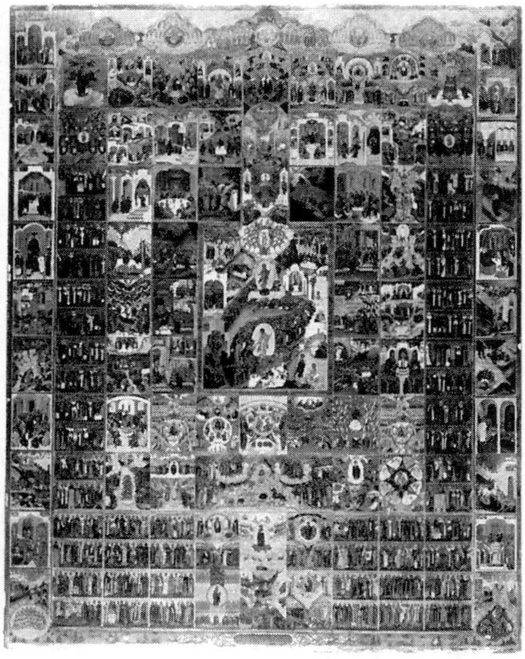

manner of 'small-scale' painting. It graphically illustrates the special function of framing in later craft art. This is a prayer image consisting of a multitude of 'frames', within each of which a distinct theme is elaborated. It all adds up to a tabulation that is over-saturated with information, relying on a well-defined aesthetics of thought and of religious sensibility. Selections and artistic presentation of many well-known subjects reflect the concept of the world as a temple. In connection with the heightened interest in the actual world at the boundary between medieval and modern times, in icon painting ever more attention began to be paid to displaying historical time as opposed to eternal, 'sacral' time. Narratives are now filled with 'earthly deeds'. The temporal–spatial relationships in the icon convey those patterns of thought that live on in the *longue durée* of the history of consciousness.

Practically the whole icon, including the way the lateral margins have been painted, represents 'earth'. 'Heaven' by contrast is presented on the upper margin (or frame) of the icon: it is shown next to the compositions that illustrate the 'Symbol of the Faith'. They are disposed as if they were several tiers of gables, reminiscent of the *kokoshniki* (small gabled roofs) surrounding the base of the drum under the dome of an Old Russian church, giving the whole of the rest of the grandiose composition the quality of symbolizing the earthly Church – whose fundamental event, the 'Resurrection of Christ and Descent into Hell', is located at the centre. The artist frames it with scenes of Christ's passion and of the Twelve Major Feasts, simultaneously putting below them box-like illustrations of text from ecclesiastical chants in honour of Christ and the Mother of God. Depictions of the calendar saints, arranged month by month according to each saint's proper day, are disposed on vertical axes as if to represent the pillars of the earthly Church. Typically, the lateral margins – the icon's frame – are also integral to the overall representation: a magnetic field of creative endeavour for the ornamental conception of the work. For this reason the artist saturated the frame with a further selection of all the feast days known to him that did not come into the Twelve Major Feasts, and also at times scenes from the Lives of the prophets, apostles and martyrs that are quite rare in Suzdalian icon painting. For example, the subject of the 'Forty Martyrs of Sebaste' is more characteristic of Balkan, particularly Bulgarian, icon painting of the 19th century. Interestingly, in the treatment of individual scenes on the frame we see architectural settings and landscapes that show the frankest combination of traditionally canonical and Westernized, Baroque elements. In fact, the frame in craft icon painting always gives greater freedom and opportunity for 'manneristic' playfulness. Even when the icon painter works within the canon, we can find new and unexpected treatment of material on the frame. In this sense the frame as part of the composition is always obliged to comment on the symbol. It lends the picture new meanings and simultaneously links it with surrounding reality.

The dependence of the traditional forms of the Old Ritualist icon from one or another cultural type and general mentality often displayed itself in methods of layering and quotation. We can see the hidden montage of this symbolic polyphony if we compare a late-17th-century Yaroslavl icon 'John the Baptist with his Life' and two late-18th- or early-19th-century Palekh icons, 'John the Baptist with his Life' and 'John the Baptist, Angel of the Wilderness' (illus. 172, 173, 174). In the sign systems of the two Palekh icons we can see two quotations from the pictorial language of the Yaroslavl school of icons that are different in their inner motifs but similar in their external dependence on the artistic mentality of the Baroque. In the first icon the craftsman retained a principle of composition that foregrounded meaningfulness, while adapting it to the demands of his patron, an Old Believer. The other Palekh painter disrupted this principle, developing the landscape theme with accompanying scenes from the Life into a self-sufficient ornamental composition, its inner feeling close to the picturesque icons of the Enlightenment period.

172. *John the Baptist with Life*, end of the 18th century or beginning of the 19th, Palekh; from the Dormition Cathedral in Yaroslavl. State Tretyakov Gallery, Moscow.

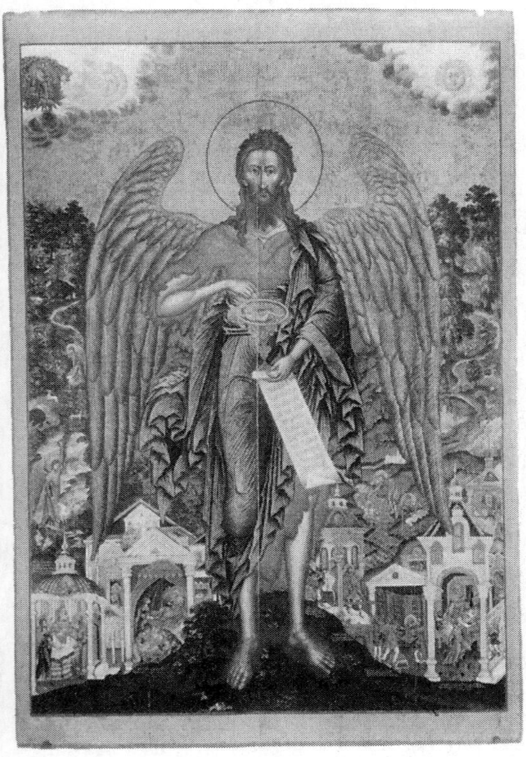

On the Yaroslavl icon the great figure of St John, presented frontally in the centre of the

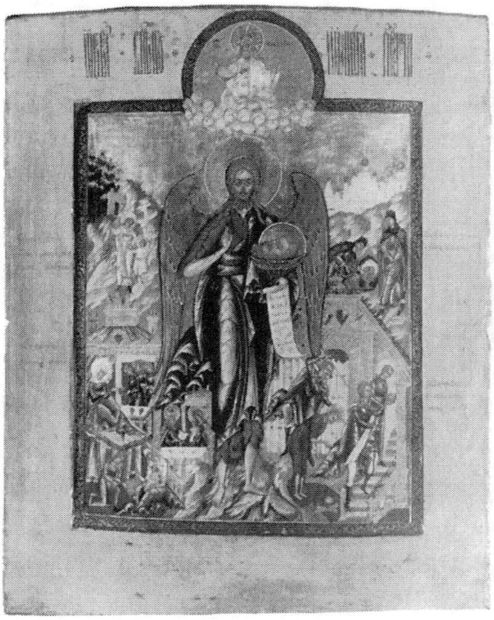

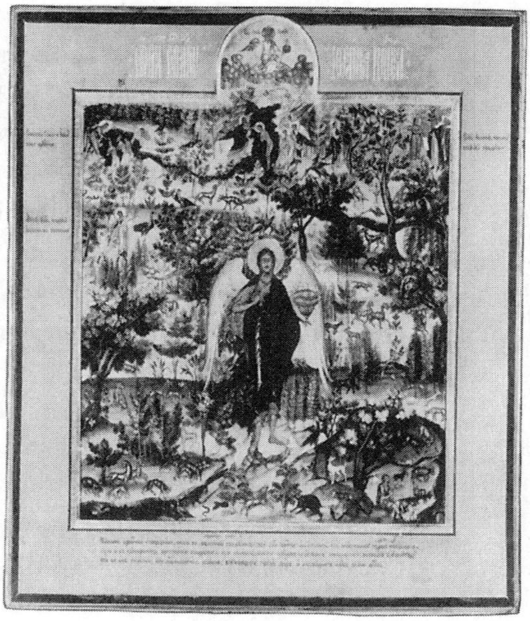

173. *John the Baptist with Life*, end of the 18th century or beginning of the 19th, Palekh. State Tretyakov Gallery, Moscow.

174. *John the Baptist, Angel of the Wilderness*, end of the 18th century or beginning of the 19th, Palekh. State Tretyakov Gallery, Moscow.

composition, its golden wings outspread, shows the well-known Baroque tendency towards representing a saint in accord with contemporary forms of portraiture (illus. 172). Following Baroque concepts, the painter represented the desert (in which St John's life unfolded, from the tale of his being brought up by an angel as a child to his baptism of the people) symbolically, 'in flower', and saturated with the inspirational power of divine wisdom. The remaining scenes of the Life – inscribed into the interior of buildings at the lower corners of the composition – illustrate its narrative quality and detailed, edificatory storytelling. They include the appearance of an angel to Zacharias in the Temple, the Nativity of John, John before Herod, John in prison, Herod's feast and the beheading of John. The architecture, despite its measure of stylization, is rendered with typical Baroque forms and ornamentation. The buildings with their columns, with tent-shaped, double-pitched or domed roofs, with passageways and galleries, contain elements of true perspective.

The Palekh icon 'John the Baptist with his Life' finds a way of representing a huge figure, dominating all around, as if by means of 'double reflection': it comes from the icon of the Yaroslavl school, on which the Moscow

Armoury Chamber school had an influence in turn (illus. 173). We can see the adoption of the same principle in many other well-known Palekh icons: 'Antony the Roman' by Zakhariy Bronin (182);[20] 'The Mother of God, Joy of all who Suffer' (later 18th century or early 19th); the same in Romanov style; 'Isaac of Dalmatia with Life' by M. Arkhipovsky (1833);[21] and finally, in many provincial versions that follow not only the official, but the Old Ritualist tradition of painting.

Guided by the religious function of the icon as the main impulse in forming his style, the creator of the first Palekh icon brought changes first of all into the forms of landscape, the 'Life' scenes and attributive elements. His patron was an Old Ritualist, for whom it was evidently important to emphasize the tragic resonance of the image. For that reason, while John the Baptist in the Yaroslavl icon points his finger towards the sacrificial Child in the eucharistic chalice, in the Palekh icon by contrast the Baptist's already severed head is located in the chalice (the well-known 'severed head' motif, incidentally, had wide currency in art of the 17th and 18th centuries).

The two-fingered sign of the cross of the Baptist's hand is reinforced by the selection of 'Life' scenes on the principle of juxtaposing birth and death. In the composition of the Yaroslavl icon, the master takes only the scenes of the Nativity of John, his upbringing by the angel and the Beheading, adding to them the episode of the discovery of the head of St John the Baptist. Seeking to follow his patron's tastes for concreteness and 'historicism', he alters the symbolism of the architectural forms: he adds in the background depictions of Russian churches with onion domes and eight-ended crosses, absent from the Yaroslavl prototype, thereby at once transferring the Biblical drama to Russian soil. Thus the 'quotation' turns out to be filled with concrete historical content.

In addition, the popular craftsman could disrupt the architectonics of the prototype almost to the point of unrecognizability (illus. 174). The 'quoted' material in the Palekh icon 'John the Baptist, Angel of the Wilderness' presupposes that the peripheral forms of landscape are the key to the work's meaning: against this background the figure of the Baptist is scarcely visible – it 'drowns' within it, as is also the case in New Ritualist icons of the period. Everything seems subjected to the Enlightenment interest in the relation between humanity and nature. The Angel of the Wilderness, making a two-fingered blessing, is placed in a paradise situated on the borderline between the earthly and the heavenly. The closeness of the Creator to the earthly sphere is symbolized in the scene of the Epiphany; we should note that this too is concealed amid 'wild' nature, as is also the case in the relevant portion of the late-18th-century icon 'St John the Divine on Patmos' that we examined earlier. However, from the Yaroslavl icon's selection of 'Life' scenes, the painter took only the tale of the infant St John's being brought up by the angel and the Baptism – to which was added, besides the Epiphany, a scene from Western iconography: 'St John Indicates the approaching Christ'. All the scenes are deliberately hidden away among a great number of beasts and bushy trees. The worshipper's attention is drawn to them only by inscriptions on the margins of the icon. All these mechanisms of 'popular Mannerism' are amplified by the concealed irruption of one of the major Baroque symbolic devices, the emblem, into the artistic space of the icon. While on the upper margin of the icon the traditional title of the prayer image is indicated (in semi-uncials), on the lower margin, by contrast, we see the text of the troparion. This lengthy text, standing out sharply against its light background, is clearly a most important component of the Baroque formation of this image and the way it is to be received. This impression is strengthened by the way the edge of the icon is ornamented in the manner of an engraving, which turns the entire representation into the simulacrum of a book illustration. Such ornament, borrowed from prints on a black, red and golden icon-edge, is one of the typical, characteristic features of Palekh and Mstyora Old Ritualist icons. Thus in the icon under discussion, ornament is executed in the form of scrolls on a wine-coloured edge; in the case of the first 18th-century icon, on a black edge. This decorative framing almost exactly copies the ornament on books and engravings of the 17th and 18th centuries.

Such a frame once again makes us recall such categories of Baroque poetics as transposition (*transmutatio*) and substitution (*immutatio*), which heightened the significance of the frame in the Baroque icon, lending it a play of meanings. They also made icon frames into imitations of books, or of windows or doors into the real world, responding to the same

Renaissance tendencies in mid-17th-century through to early-18th-century Russian culture. Thus in a single icon, a complex and concealed polyphony of texts on various cultural levels emerges.

Myth and Mystification: Self-awareness in the Icon-painting Experience

Modern technical methods of investigation (in particular methods involving magnification in reflected infra-red light) reveal that many icons earlier attributed to the Stroganov school should be dated to the 19th century. Examples of these are certain Stroganov icons from the Russian Museum: 'Selected Saints – Irina, Agafya and Kseniya', 'St Filipp the Metropolitan', 'St John the Warrior' and some others. Specialists have noted that 'so much of the first layer of painting on certain icons traditionally linked with the Stroganov school has been lost that there are no grounds for the attribution, and the work may date only from the time of its restoration'.[22] X-ray photography may also establish that the counterfeiting craftsman has used a mechanical transfer procedure to produce the preliminary drawing, something that (we recall) was characteristic only of late craft icon painting and has no analogies among the authentic Stroganov masters of the early 17th century. That is to say, however precise the imitation was, 'to the point of deception', it cannot conceal the 'work' wrought by internal cultural mechanisms: the counterfeiting master was bound to leave his mark. Hence the icon painters 'in the ancient manner' of Palekh and Mstyora, authors of most of the known imitations and copies of ancient icons, can be rightly considered the chief mystificatory agents both of the old type of devotion and of the romantic interest in its historical past.

It comes as no surprise that in Suzdalian icon production what we encounter is the falsification and stylization chiefly of icons in the Moscow and Stroganov manners, where the Josephite urge for luxury and expensive glitter evidently found their most adequate expression. 'Icons in an excessively delicate style, for example the Stroganov manner' – so wrote Pavel Florensky – 'are of course characteristic of an age that turned its sacred objects into items of luxury, vanity and collectability'.[23] In the mythologized consciousness of the Old Believers the 'Stroganov age' was the Golden Age of Russian Orthodoxy; and it was at that time that the paintwork on the icon itself came to acquire no less precious value than its casing. 'Stroganov icons speak of some more insistent, even though less inspirational, state of prayerfulness', as Igor Grabar remarked.

> This consciousness is expressed in the particular 'preciousness' of their execution. These are not so much representations as most precious objects of religious usage. At the time when for the Novgorod icon painter the basis of the icon was its artistic vision, for a Stroganov painter it was only a matter of decoration, where his devotion could be measured by his long and self-assured labour on subtlety of vision and manual skill.[24]

The enthusiastic response of Paul of Aleppo to Russian icons, so we must assume, concerned precisely this 'Stroganov style'. 'On the subject of iconostases in the land', he said, 'I am incapable of describing them as precisely as I should wish, since they consist of small icons of subtle workmanship, displaying subjects that cause astonishment to the mind.' In another place he noted the attraction of Russian devotion towards the old icon that a century later would begin to inspire the craft of antiquarian-minded Old Believers: 'As concerns their icons and iconostases: they are all of astonishingly fine workmanship, (in frames) of beaten silver with gilding. For the most part icons are decrepit and ancient, for in this land people nurture great faith in old icons.'[25]

The artistic language of the numerous Old Believer counterfeits and stylizations obeyed not only a particular type of Old Ritualist devotion, but a special myth that had arisen that ancient icons were of very great salvatory and aesthetic value. As we know, myth (like symbol) organizes the collective memory while playing an active part in the process of semiotizing cultural experience. Thus, while in the 18th-century Enlightenment a mythologization of Roman history took place on the upper levels, by contrast at the cultural periphery – in the milieu of the Old Ritual – what was mythologized was the history of the Tsardom of Muscovy as possessing special charisma. The period of the *Stoglav* Council and the 17th-century 'golden age' of Russian Orthodoxy in the latter case played the part of a complex symbol that continually provoked and orientated Old Ritualist culture towards symbolization and explication of its mythology. Although mythologism, an immanent property of human consciousness, tended in the Old Ritualist mentality towards closure, the establishment of a mythological canon ('the Middle Ages in arrest') was continually open to the effects of the major currents of belief in one or another cultural period.

We have every reason to believe that the known system of mythic concepts among the icon painters in the old style about Old Russian icon-painting 'schools', 'manners' and 'types of painting' in its greatest development was formed in the Romantic period. It is not by chance that the reinvigoration of neo-Romantic ideas and feelings at the turn of the 20th century gave such a lively stimulus to the 'antiquarian' restoration and straightforward forgery of prayer images, loaded as they already were with commercial notions: the Romantic interest in the national past always presented a convenient territory for the mythologization and mystification of this past.

Old Ritualist counterfeit icons go back in Palekh and Mstyora as far as the first quarter of the 19th century, when I. A. Kovylin founded (at the Preobrazhensky Cemetery in Moscow) a special school for children of Old Ritualists, where they were taught not only to read and write, but 'to copy and counterfeit ancient icons'.[26] It was in the same first quarter of that century that the genre of literary mystifications became particularly popular. Investigating forgeries of Old Russian literary works by A. I. Sulakadzev, I. P. Smirnov reached the conclusion that 'they turn out to be not so much an expression of the author's personal aims as a result of the action of super-personal forces – a consequence of movements that had become common property in the age of early Romanticism'.[27]

From that period the dissemination of Old Ritualist counterfeits and stylizations of Old Russian icons became a rising wave. From the last quarter of the 19th century to the beginning of the 20th, counterfeit icons experienced a new blossoming. In 1900 they were even displayed at the Universal Exhibition in Paris, and before that, in 1890, at the Archaeological Exhibition in Moscow; there they made a particularly distinctive showing in the collection of N. M. Postnikov, who not only collected them enthusiastically but ordered them from Moscow, Mstyora and Palekh 'old style' artists – M. I. Dikarev, M. N. and I. E. Mumrikov, M. I. Tsepkov, A. Zantsev, A. M. and Ya. V. Tyulin and others. At the Moscow exhibition one could see counterfeits 'imitating Stroganov painting', 'Novgorod painting', 'Greek painting', etc. The pious attitude of the patron towards such icons was conveyed by special inscriptions on the back of the icon board, for example: 'This icon of the Korsun Most Holy Mother of God was painted in 1875 at the command of the Moscow merchant Nikolay Mikhaylovich Postnikov by the master Mikhail Ivanovich Dikarev from the settlement of Mstyora.' Eight icons by the famous Moscow 'old-style' painter N. K. Klimov that were exhibited there were accompanied by a characteristic label that reflected a particular interest in this field of icon production: 'Works of the Moscow townsman Nester Klimovich Klimov, a good carpenter for making boards for icons, the first master of the time to excise, suspend on a new board, and correct an ancient icon and to imitate ancient ones.' Klimov mainly imitated Stroganov and Novgorod styles of painting (illus. 175).[28]

Klimov's icon 'Christ Pantocrator' is a typical example of an Old Believer imitation of the Novgorod style. It was displayed at an exhibition of 1890 and has a label for this exhibition stuck onto its lower margin: 'Imitation of Novgorod painting by Nester Klimov. Moscow 1862.' In its construction the icon was, so to speak, a new framing of an ancient icon, in a way its new 'shrine', as I noted earlier in connection with the framing of ancient icons and reliquaries by Old Ritualists. In this instance the craftsman also took an ancient icon and cut a new board out of it. However, unlike the cases where an old image became part of a new composition, Klimov completely obliterated it. He removed the old paint surface and painted it with fresh, but dark, pigments, in accord with the conception current among Old Ritualists of the ancient Novgorodian style.

However, a counterfeit icon could be made with the use of old materials too. Among these may be included the old boards, and the remains of old priming and paint surface on the 'Stroganov' icons listed above in the collection of the Russian Museum, some of which are attributed to Palekh craftsmen. Signs of the 'older text' may also include mechanical damage: worn areas, scratches, dents. The patina of time was enhanced by a suitable choice of artistic style and name – inscriptions that forged a complete sense of unity in the mystificatory craftsman's 'manneristic' game. Invading a

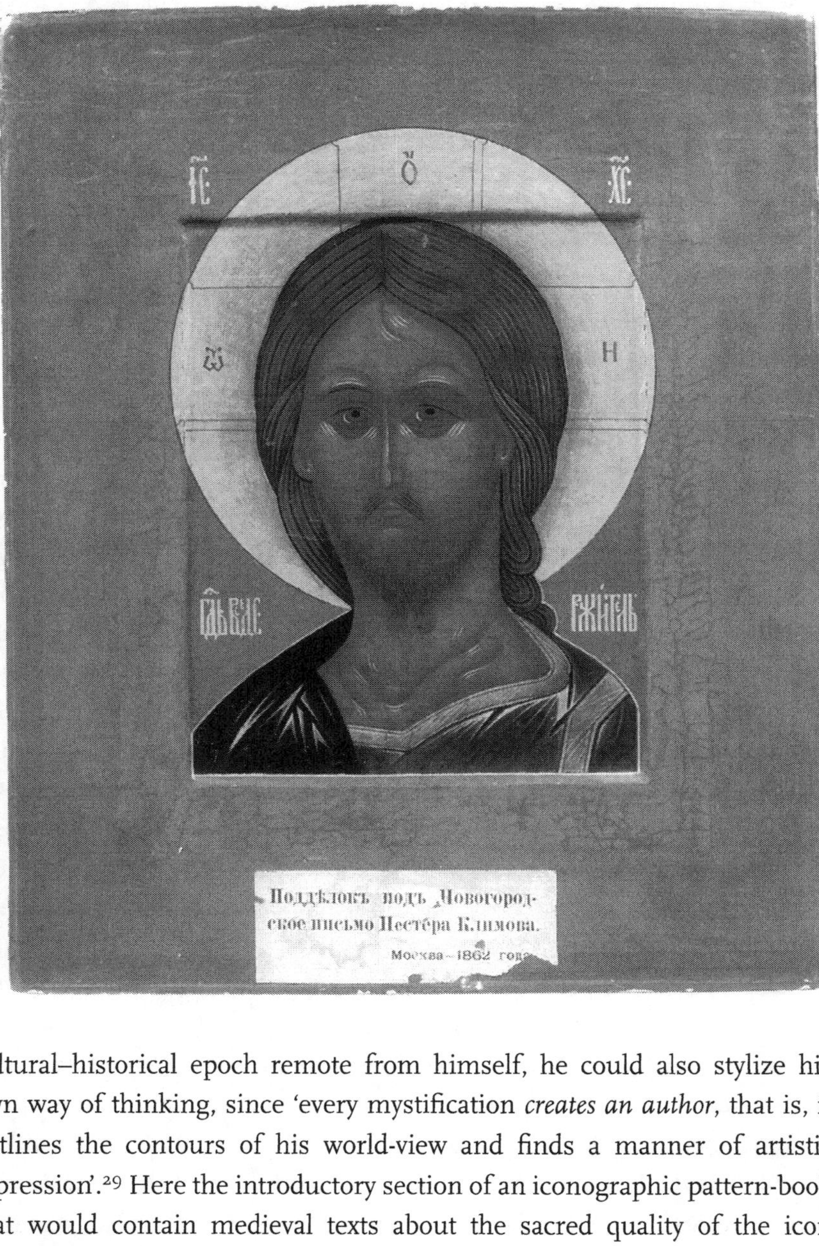

175. Nester Klimov, *Christ Pantocrator*, Moscow, 1862. State Historical Museum, Moscow.

cultural–historical epoch remote from himself, he could also stylize his own way of thinking, since 'every mystification *creates an author,* that is, it outlines the contours of his world-view and finds a manner of artistic expression'.[29] Here the introductory section of an iconographic pattern-book that would contain medieval texts about the sacred quality of the icon painter's trade might give some help to the 'old-style' painter.

An interesting example of a 19th-century imitation of the 'Stroganov' school is the icon 'Fatherhood' from the collection of the Moscow Kremlin museums (illus. 176). Most often, the main authenticizing touch in a counterfeit was the choice of an ancient board: the fundamental material of a representation was accorded a heightened sacred status. Traditionally, the chief holy object of the Muscovite realm – the icon of the Vladimir Mother of God – had been painted by the Evangelist Luke on a board from a table that had belonged to the Holy Family. Icons were also often painted on boards from the coffins of saints, and on boards that had earlier served as altar-tables in churches.[30] Hence an old board from the 17th century was the chief sign of an 'ancient text' in such counterfeiting. It chimed well with the choice of stereotyped devices from Stroganov painting and a new low-relief metal cladding with varicoloured *cloisonné* enamel ornamentation.

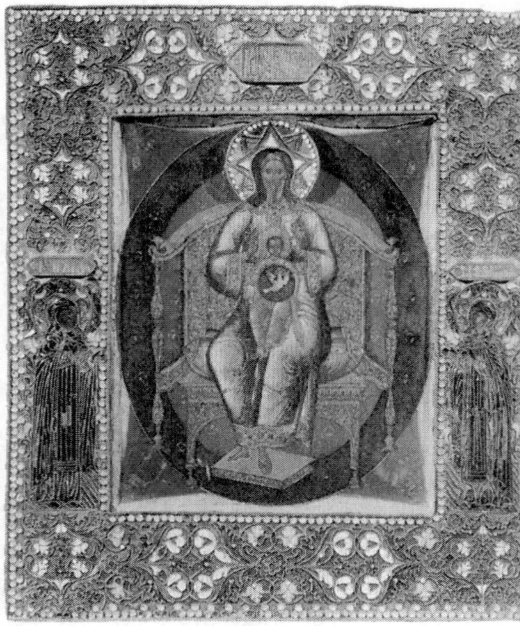

176. *Fatherhood*, 19th century. Moscow Kremlin State Museums.

While following a 17th-century composition, the icon painter concentrated all his efforts on working over the painted surface for a jewel-like effect. The abundance of gold and the imitation of precious stones on the garments of the Lord Sabaoth seem to disagree with the muted luminosity of the multi-coloured enamel of the cladding. The *niello* vegetational ornament of the throne repeats individual elements of the ornament on the cladding, which fuses the language of painting and applied decorative art in a single synthesis. The ideological saturation of the icon and its connection with Old Ritualist devotion cannot be doubted: both hands of the Lord Saboath make a two-fingered archbishop's blessing, whose symbolic quality is strengthened by the depiction on each hand of the abbreviated name of the Saviour: 'IC XC'.

A more complex example of the copying of an ancient manner (here, evidently, Novgorodian) by old-style painters is an icon of the 'Entry into Jerusalem' from the second half of the 19th century or the early 20th in the Kolomenskoye museum (illus. 177). The icon was painted with strict

177. *Entry into Jerusalem*, early 20th century, Moscow. Kolomenskoye Historical and Architectural Museum-Preserve, Moscow.

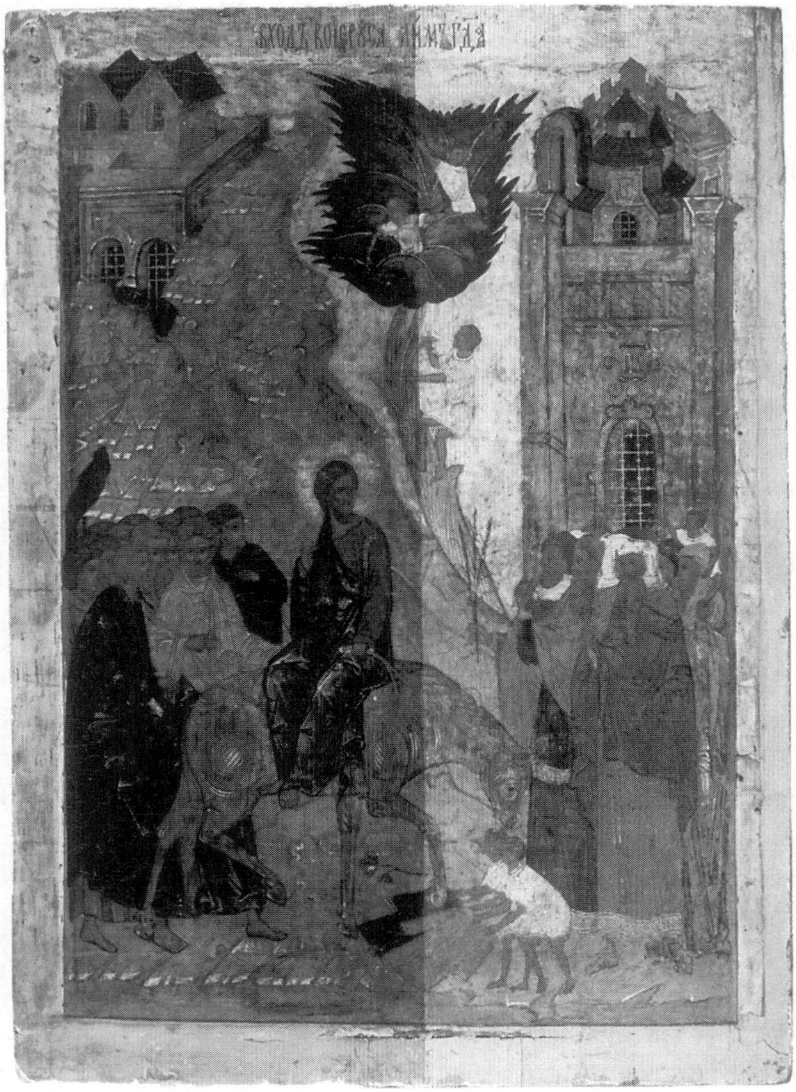

observance of the methods and devices of 15th- and 16th-century painting, while the thick layer of darkened olive oil varnish that covers it testifies to the counterfeiting craftsman's intention to deceive the recipient, to pass off an imitation as the original. It is noteworthy that the icon of the 'Christ Pantocrator' by Nester Klimov (1862), equipped with a label saying 'Imitation of the Novgorod Style', is by comparison with the previous icon merely a stylization. This bears witness to the fact that the definition of the word 'imitation' (*poddelok*) in the 19th century was fairly imprecise: it could mean a fake, an antiquarian restoration, or a stylization.

In Suzdalian icon production, stylizations of older manners presumed a mass of low-level variants, in comparison with which the counterfeiters and the complex stylizations are on the level of 'high' art, in their own way exemplary. Here imitations and mass-circulation stylizations differed both from the points of view of technical mastery and of the level of mystification. In imitations the latter was an objective that was no more than 'inherited' in simplified form by mass production. Everything was reduced to the level of generalized quotations. It is noteworthy that mechanical damage such as would give a worn or pitted appearance was as a rule excluded from ordinary stylizations, but the choice of an old board and dark varnish were almost everywhere obligatory. This is related to the special trade in old boards at Mstyora: they were collected throughout Russia, and each year travelling salesmen brought back tens of thousands of them. On ordinary ancient-style icons it was enough to 'soften', as the painters would say, the painting with dark varnish, so that in the eyes of pious Old Believers among the common people it would glow with the mysterious and muffled brilliance that evoked the alluring luxuriance of the distant Stroganov age. Aimed at simple consumers, the mass production of icons 'in the Stroganov manner' interestingly corresponded with the mythic system of the Old Believer old-style painters, formulated in the late 18th century and the first half of the 19th, about ancient Russian 'styles' and 'manners of painting'.

The Suzdalian icon painters and their Old Believer patrons were mostly convinced that only from the 16th century could one speak of 'genuine' Russian icon painting. They distinguished three major 'manners' within it: the Stroganov, the Muscovite and the Novgorodian. Sometimes they added to these the Ustyug and Frankish styles, occasionally one or two other. 'The names given to the manners of painting alone' – as G. I. Vzdornov notes – 'bear witness to the fact that there was no sort of general principle for classifying icons. They were distinguished either by their relationship to the art of neighbouring lands (Byzantine, Chersonesos – i.e., Crimean, Frankish), or by their place of origin (Novgorod, Moscow, Ustyug,

Siberia, Suzdal), or by their association with certain famous families or the Court (Stroganov, Royal), or by the religious allegiance of their authors (Pomorian).'[31]

All these manners and types of painting had their conventional classifications and subdivisions. Thus the Stroganov manner was divided into three: the first and second Stroganov types, and the third, 'Baronov', type. Siberian painting was considered a continuation of the Baronov type.

The famous work by D. A. Rovinsky, his *Survey of Icon Painting in Russia to the End of the Seventeenth Century*, written almost entirely on the basis of information provided by Old Ritualists, is a reliable foundation for reconstructing the old-style icon painters' mythic system of conceptualizing 'manners' of painting. It is now known that all the Stroganov masters were Court painters and worked in Moscow; only some of their commissions were for the Stroganovs. In the 19th century, however, a myth arose about special Stroganov workshops, whose high quality of icon painting was linked with the exceptional piety of the Stroganov family, since in the 18th century their descendants adhered to the Old Ritual. It was assumed that all genuine Stroganov icons had been painted and preserved in the North. As Rovinsky explained, 'the chief store of Stroganov icons a hundred years ago was in north-eastern European Russia, in Ustyug, Solvychegodsk and other towns. It would doubtless be in vain were one to seek them out in our own times in such places. They have almost all been transferred to Moscow shrines and to the collections of art lovers.'[32] Elsewhere he writes that 'the Stroganovs set up an icon painting school, out of which a great number of icons came over the course of a century; they are notable for the unusual quality of their decoration and constitute major treasures in every amateur's icon collection.' It was the generally received opinion of the time that Stroganov icon painters were 'the first to regard icon painting as an art form and not to trouble themselves only about preserving symbolism and traditions in icon-painting, but also about its beauty of decoration and the variety of its different forms'.[33]

During the first half of the 19th century the myth of the Stroganov school was filled out with a large amount of concrete detail. Imitation of Stroganov, Moscow and Novgorod painting styles stimulated the formation of stereotyped ideas about the devices and particular image-structure characteristic

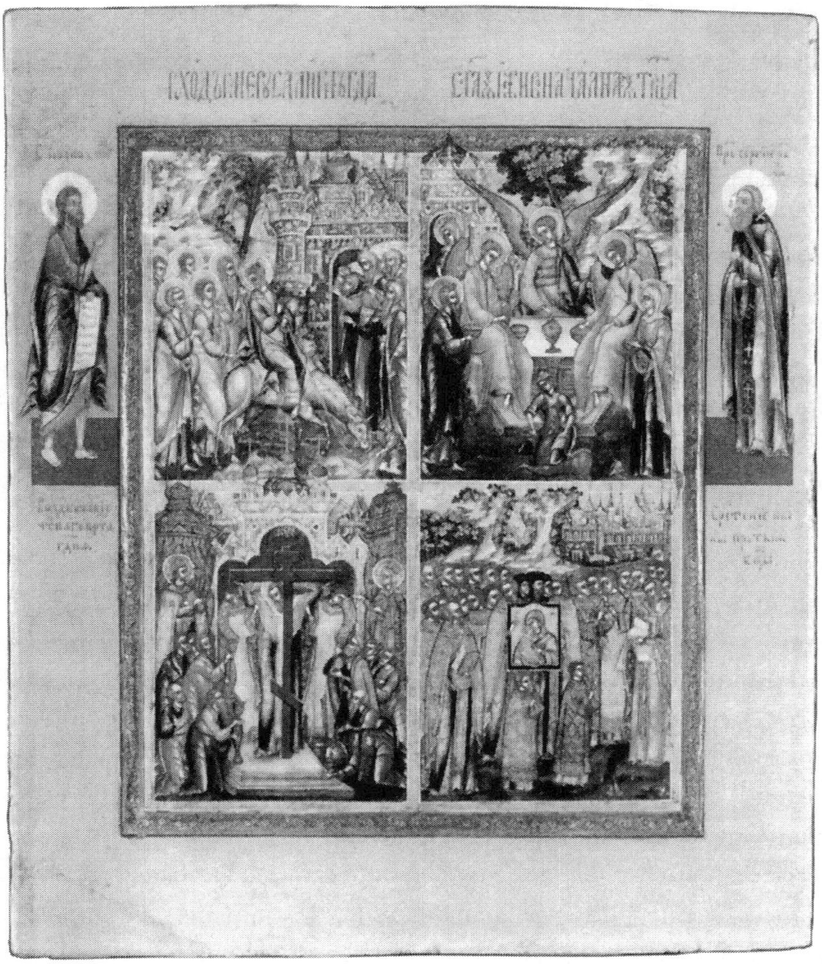

178. 'Four-part' icon: *Entry into Jerusalem, Old Testament Trinity, Elevation of the Cross and Meeting with the Icon of the Vladimir Mother of God, with Saints on the Margins*, second half of the 18th century, Palekh. State Tretyakov Gallery, Moscow.

of each 'manner' (illus. 178). Thus, for example, the old-style painters assumed that the first, 'ancient' Stroganov manner of the 16th century was hardly different from the Novgorod style. Compared with the latter, it merely seemed more complicated: lines, circles and arches in representations of buildings were always drawn not freehand, but with use of a ruler and compass. Faces were painted a dark-green tone, almost without shading, while in the majority of cases garments were marked out with whitened boundaries and black ink lines. They even found analogies to these structural elements in one of the icons ascribed to Andrey Rublyov.

The 'classic' second Stroganov manner always seemed particularly valuable. The distinguishing features of this – so it was considered – were elongated figures '7, 5 to 8, sometimes up to 9 or 10 heads long'. It is interesting that the head of a saint, always considered the centre of meaning and emotion in an Orthodox icon, was regarded by the icon painters as a unit of length for the figure. (It is of interest too, in the context of 'popular Mannerism', to compare these proportions with some of the principles of classic Italian Mannerists, e.g., those put forward by Lomazzo in 1590, who wrote that the finest proportion for the human body was ten times the length of the head.) The countenances would be light-filled and 'of outstanding goodness'. Garments and buildings were seen as endowed with refined and graphic outlines, and shot throughout with gold. Beyond that they invariably considered the buildings 'fabulously beautiful' with 'great embellishments'. The background was, they supposed, sometimes gilded, but more often rendered in the same pigment as the margins. They ascribed the icons of Prokopiy Chirin, Stefan Arefyev, Semyon Borozdin, Ivan Sobol, Istoma Savin, Nikifor Savin and others (whose names were sometimes invented) to the 'classic' Stroganov manner. Around 1900 N. P. Kondakov observed in Venice that local dealers would put imitation signatures on Italo-Greek 17th- and 18th-century icons of 'archaizing' type, making them out to be works of Trecento art.[34] Thus the activity of Palekh and Mstyora old-style painters found its typologically similar analogues. The invented name of a master – i.e., the renaming of the image – emerged as a major feature of the established mythological canon and the game of mystification. It always had a magical effect on the purchaser.

No less of interest when it came to later stylizations was the third Stroganov manner, the 'Baronov', that acquired its name (as I. Bessonov supposed) as late as the 1720s, when the Stroganovs were granted a baronial title. 'In Baronov icons the manner of painting approaches that of Westernized art.'[35] Rovinsky similarly wrote that 'the faces on icons of this kind are entirely luminous . . . Buildings, plants, trees and the landscape generally comprise a major feature of the icon. The light is vivid, The garments of the saints are shot through with gold: trees, plants, buildings, often even hair, are endowed with it.'[36]

In Russian icon production from the second half of the 18th century through to the early 20th, we find a mass of stereotyped embodiments of all these concepts. A background and margins painted in a single colour, together with 'fabulously beautiful' architectural backdrops and landscapes, with saintly figures abundantly decorated with touchings-up in gold – these are all the stereotypical devices of mass production in Palekh and Mstyora in the Stroganov manner. As also seems to be the case in low-level craft culture, these invariants often appeared in unexpected and paradoxical combinations with the peculiarities of other manners and schools. Individual features might well be wildly exaggerated.

An icon of 'St Nicholas the Wonder-worker' by from Palekh by V. A Khokhlov (early 20th century) is a typical example: it has a number of characteristic peculiarities of the Stroganov manner – a glowing gold-tinted nimbus, background and margins of the same colour, a luminous countenance, and also a fairly complex treatment of the saint's garments in contrasted gold and shading (illus. 179). The 'outstanding goodness' of the bright Stroganov countenance has been taken by the craftsman as an opportunity for creating a personal variant.[37] The excessive highlighting of St Nicholas's facial features lend him the appearance more of a figure from popular storytelling than of a mighty Christian hero, and simultaneously fully confirms D. K. Trenyov's observation that old-style painters used bright touches most often in the Stroganov manner, 'though with some odd and noticeable deviations'.[38]

Analogous 'superpositions' can be seen in Suzdalian stylizations of the Moscow and Novgorod manners. A Palekh icon, 'The Mother of God, Joy of All who Suffer' (late 18th century or early 19th), bears not only features of influence from the Yaroslavl school, but also of how this school was understood as being Novgorodian (illus. 180). The yellow ochrous countenance of the Mother of God, and the abundance of this hue in the icon generally, reminds one of the Novgorodian 'yellow-based' manner, into which, according to the Old Believers' and the old-style painters' classification, the majority of Yaroslavl icons fell.

In Rovinsky's view, the 'Novgorod manner' comprised a much broader grouping, and included icons not only from Novgorod and Pskov but from Yaroslavl and other northern towns. The chief repository of such icons was

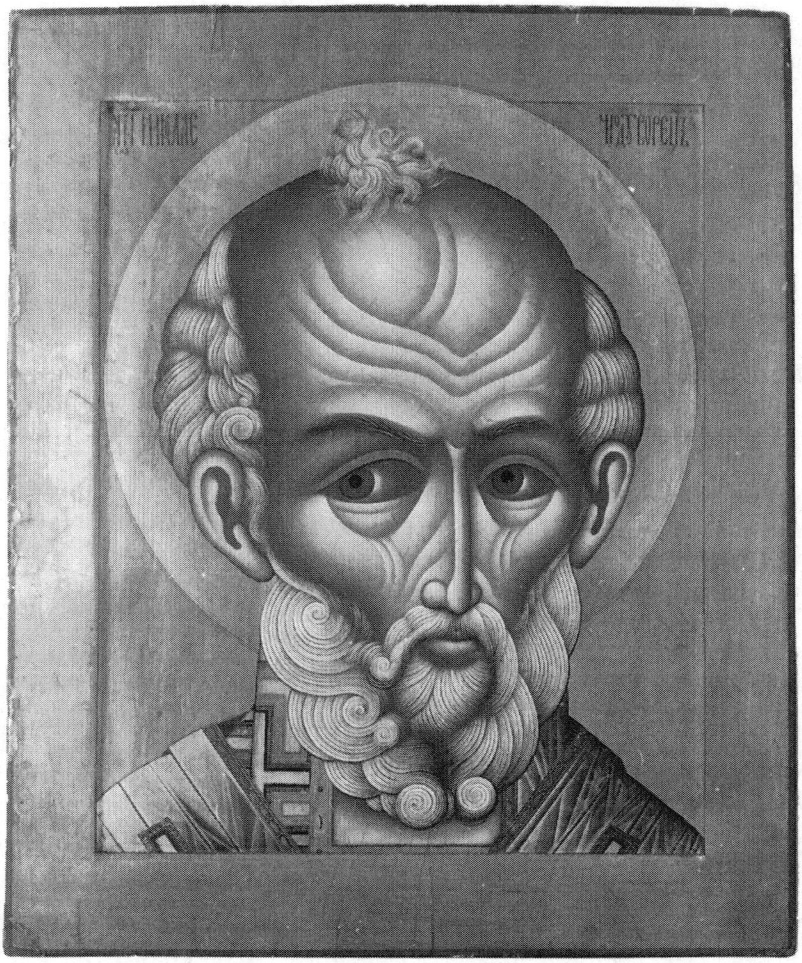

179. V. A. Khokhlov, *St Nicholas the Wonder-worker*, early 20th century. Palekh Art Museum, Palekh.

considered to be Santa Sophia of Novgorod; others were the Yaroslavl churches, with their notable paintings by local 17th-century masters. Distinctive signs of Novgorod icons were taken to be clear-cut drawing with long straight lines and rather shortened figures (by the standards of the icon painters), 7 or 7.5 times the length of the head. Countenances were supposed to be long, noses came down to lips. Garments were in two colours. Thus if a vestment were basically red lake, its folds should be greenish in hue, with thick white and dark lines as well. It was considered that small brushstrokes on countenances, hands and feet were among the

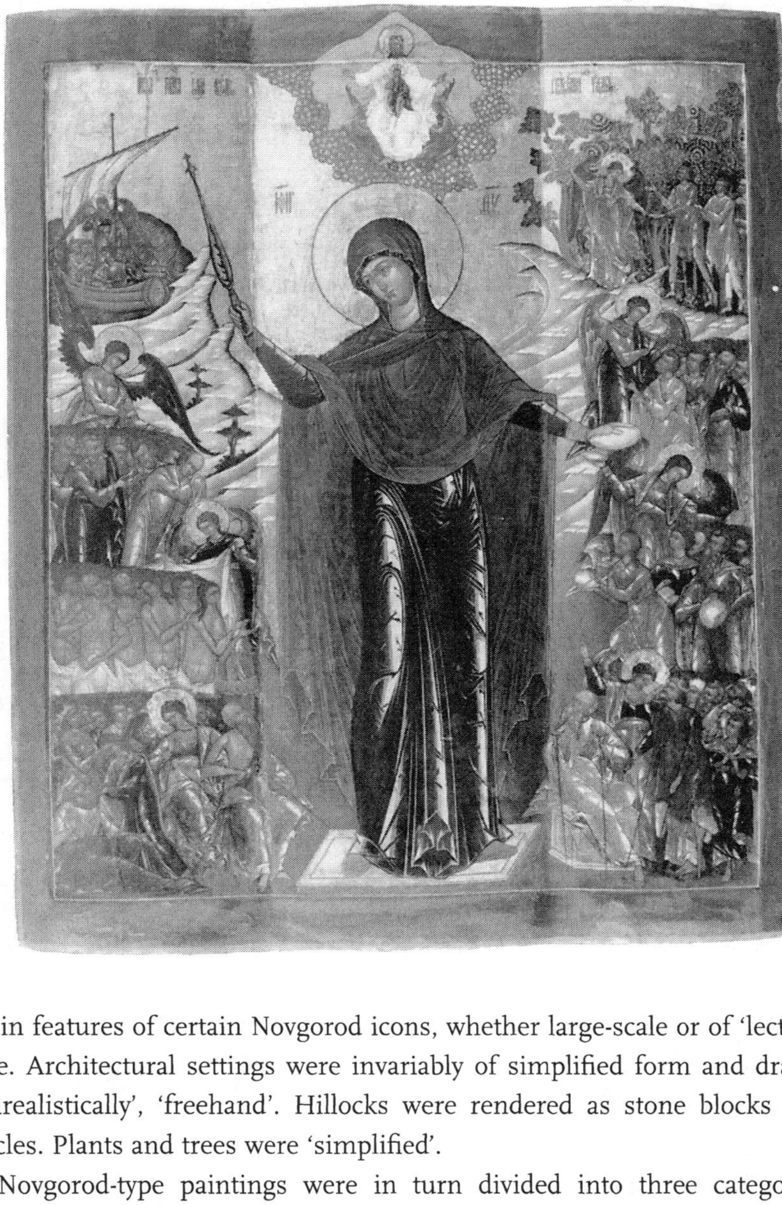

180. *Mother of God, 'Joy of All who Suffer'*, late 18th century or early 19th. Palekh Art Museum, Palekh.

main features of certain Novgorod icons, whether large-scale or of 'lectern' size. Architectural settings were invariably of simplified form and drawn 'unrealistically', 'freehand'. Hillocks were rendered as stone blocks and circles. Plants and trees were 'simplified'.

Novgorod-type paintings were in turn divided into three categories according to the 'coloration', though we can now see blatant contradictions in this categorization. For example, a dark, unshaded face was considered to be a peculiarity that placed images in the first category. 'Shadowless' icons were a transitional stage to the first 'Stroganov manner' (which was once called the 'Ustyug manner'). In the third type of Novgorod painting, so they supposed, ochre should dominate. These – the largest group – were the icons known as 'yellow'. '17th century yellow paintings are exceptionally numerous in Novgorod and Yaroslavl churches', concluded Rovinsky, quoting the words of old-style craftsmen.[39]

As in previous cases, we can see in the Palekh icon 'The Mother of God, Joy of all who Suffer' that Suzdalian stylization did not demand imitation to the point of deception. The figures here are elongated in the way that was accepted as the 'Stroganov manner', though their forms are not marked out in gold. 'Simple' bracken-like plants to the left of the Mother of God are a clear sign of the medieval canon – perhaps still a heritage of the same concept of 'yellow' Novgorod painting. The bushy trees in the top-right corner, however, betray a typical craftsman's synthesis.

To clarify the stylizations of the Moscow manner is yet more complicated. Its features are mingled with elements of Stroganov and Novgorod manners, and true perspective – a sign of Frankish Baroque painting – can be found in them. The old, 'royal' Moscow manner, as Rovinsky wrote, had similarities with the first Stroganov manner, but with sharper markings of shadows and highlights. Buildings are simpler; arches and straight lines are drawn freehand (as with Novgorod painting). Light is almost always vivid. It was supposed that Stroganov icons were technically superior to Moscow ones, but the latter were 'more painterly, folds in garments sometimes delineated the parts of the figures quite successfully, while an attempt to present buildings in perspective can be seen'. The second Moscow manner, by contrast, was supposed to contain icons thought to be from the first half of the 17th century, painted in Moscow but defined as 'completely yellow'.[40] On this basis the school of Makariy, Stroganov icons and the 17th-century Armoury Chamber School were all included in the 'Moscow manner'.

In the first half of the 19th century the concept of the Moscow school was considerably complicated by the myth of Andrey Rublyov[41] and of ancient Byzantine, 'Greek' painting. During the age of Alexander I the idea of the Greek roots of Russian culture became popular. In the historiosophic concepts of the Romantics, the individuality of Russia was perceived in this idea, as was the 'national' character of Russian Orthodoxy: the latter acquired a new designation, the Greco-Russian Faith. 'The Greek faith gives us a special national character': this well-known pronouncement of Alexander Pushkin was fully in accord with the spirit of the time. The orientation of official culture in Nicholas I's age towards 'the native soil' and 'the national idea' would be reflected in the neo-Byzantine ('Greek') style. New Romantic currents at the upper levels of culture were interestingly refracted below in a quickening interest in Andrey Rublyov as the founder of the Old Russian national school of painting.

Among the Old Believers, Rublyov's icons had always been considered wonder-working, but it is from the first half of the 19th century that a heightened interest in them can be detected, stimulating counterfeits and imitations. 'It is a rare amateur who does not attach the name of Rublyov to icons in his collection', Rovinsky noted. We may cautiously assume that it was at that time that the conventional term *Rublyovian icons* appeared, meaning the numerous copies of icons that from their technical execution and iconography could be linked with the name of the most famous Russian icon painter. 'Icons painted in the spirit of Rublyov', Bessonov later explained, 'are called Rublyovian; they are specially well-known among the Old Ritualists'.[42] At around the same time, more and more counterfeit Rublyov icons, bearing the signature of the master, appear. In the old-style icon-painters' workshops, icons in the old 'Moscow manner' underwent antiquarian restoration: 'smoky' washes were applied to the countenances, the whole icon was 'put together', lost fragments of paintwork would be 'reconciled' with new insertions and overpainted in a special technique. This sort of restoration was called 'correcting the icon'.[43] An ancient wooden board and a fake signature of Rublyov completed the mystification in the spirit of the Romantic myth about the deep historical roots of the 'golden age' of Muscovite Orthodoxy.

Simultaneously, popular consciousness began much more readily to attribute a Greek origin to Rublyov's icons. This is confirmed by drawings and tracings of icons of Christ Pantocrator at Palekh. One of the tracings, dating to the time of Nicholas I, contains the inscription 'This original is in the Greek manner: taken in the town of Kresttsy in the summer of the year 1840 on 25 June. Painting by Rublyov' (illus. 181). The craftsman

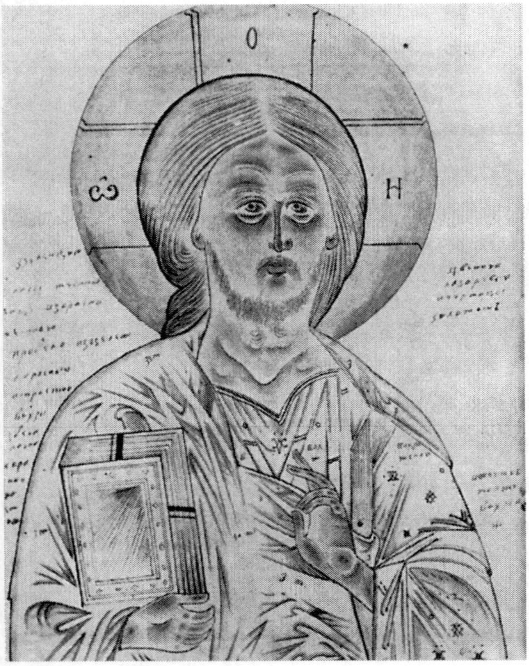

181. *Christ Pantocrator*, 1840, a transfer from Palekh. Archive of L. Bakanov, Palekh.

wrote a detailed 'colour apportionment' of the image by analogy with icon-painting pattern-books: 'greenish tint on the hair', 'facial shading in dark red', 'highlighting of green with red', etc. A drawing of the early 20th century is squared-up (most likely for a classic traditional icon painting in the Palekh instruction workshop set up by the Committee Concerned with Russian Icon Painting). The Rublyovian Christ Pantocrator represented on it is inscribed 'By tradition the work of Andrey Rublyov.'

From these and many other drawings and tracings at Palekh and Mstyora, a huge number of copies of icons of Christ Pantocrator were made in the 19th and early 20th centuries; it is interesting to discover layers of stereotypical concepts about the 'Rublyovian' and ancient 'Greek' manners in them. Thus, if an order were placed for a 'Greek-type' icon, the iconographic scheme of the 'Rublyovian' Saviour would be amplified with stereotypal devices connected with the works of 'ancient' Greek icon painters. A typical example is a Palekh icon of the 19th century, 'Christ Pantocrator' (illus. 182). The Saviour is here depicted in the traditional three-quarters facing pose, with a two-fingered sign of blessing, supporting the open Gospels with his left hand. Its iconography is that of a 'Rublyovian Saviour'. The order book of the Palekh craftsman N. L. Safonov shows that this style also bore the names 'Greek device', 'Greek work' and 'Byzantine work'.[44] The stereotypical idea of Stroganov painting among Suzdalian craftsmen is upheld by the use of the same colour on the margins and as background, and also by the gold lettering on the icon's inscriptions. However, in response to the tastes of an Old Believer patron, the craftsman tried to render the 'sombreness and mysteriousness' that were demanded of 'Greek painting'. The dry, dark coloration of the countenance emphasized its sternness. Sharply defined highlights on the countenance and hands distantly recall the modelling of 17th- and 18th-century Cretan icons. The

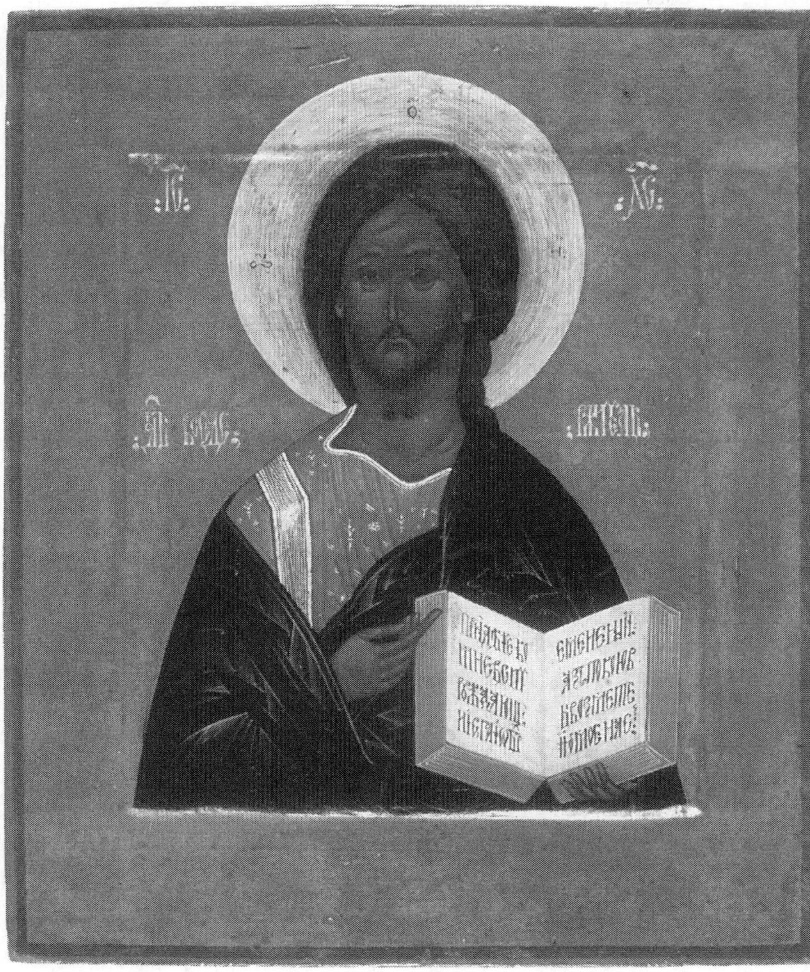

182. *Christ Pantocrator*, 19th century. State Museum of the History of Religion, St Petersburg.

Saviour's tunic is rendered in dark wine-red lines, clumsily indicating its folds. They give us a sense not so much of the craftsman's lack of skill as of his desire to emphasize the 'archaic' quality of the image. The dark brown margins and background lend it an even greater feeling of gloom.

Icons of this kind to some extent confirm remarks by Viktor Lazarev to the effect that the late 'Cretan manner' of the 17th and 18th centuries stood in for 'the whole of Byzantine painting' in the eyes of collectors,[45] as well as observations by Rovinsky. The latter wrote that in churches and Old Ritualist places of prayer, no small quantity of 'Greek' icons were to be found. As they passed from one owner to another, icons could change their names: one and the same image would be called 'Greek' by some, by others 'Novgorodian', by others again 'Muscovite'. He found the reasons for this in the facts that, first, the Old Believers did not like 'simple and poor-quality (even if ancient) painting', to which they also relegated the 'Greek' icon; second, the craftsmen had no authentic Greek icons with which they could compare other icons and determine their manner. Third, 'icons copied from Greek ones were often painted in Moscow or Novgorod, and thus both parties, one naming an icon Greek, the other Novgorodian, would be right, since a Novgorod icon painter had made it after a Greek model'. There was a widespread conviction in the mid-19th century that the coloration of a 'Greek' icon had to be dark, 'harsh' and 'obedient to higher goals'. In Greek countenances they sought 'exhaustion, gloominess and mystery'; sometimes 'in the same icon some noted tenderness, others sternness'.[46] So that the image of the Pantocrator should become 'Rublyovian', people were capable of painting 'in the manner of Andrey Rublyov' in the same iconographic scheme: a countenance worked over with washes ('smokily') would gain a typically Russian softness, while the outlines of clothing would acquire hardness and the glitter of gold.

With their imitations and stylizations of old icons, the art of Russian popular craftsmen reached an unusually high level of 'mannerist' technique in the field of medieval forms and their own kind of skilled scholarship. The special mythological canon of the 'delayed Middle Ages' determined the unique nature of Old Ritualist 'imitation' and 'stylizations': they have no analogue elsewhere in the Orthodox world. The Muscovite Tsardom, that in empirical geographic terms had ceased to exist, thus continued to flourish in the myth of 'Holy Russia' and within a semiotic space that in turn was subject to the influence of one or another cultural period.

CHAPTER SIX

Icons and Popular Art

Unlike the examples we have been examining, Suzdalian mass-circulation icons come into the category of 'primitives' not just from the aesthetic point of view. These images possess a special spirit of folk creativity and their own emotional tuning. Their almost complete anonymity, their choice of subjects, the unusual solutions they arrive at from the point of view of both composition and colour, and, finally, the largely peasant milieu within which they existed – all these factors give cause to speak of the 'folkloric' and archaic vision of the craftsmen who made 'mass circulation' icons. Here the 'primitive' gave visual evidence of its capacity to create artistic values within which the religious tradition might be refracted.

The Aesthetics of Sensibility

In the interpenetration of the sign systems of the primitive icon and the popular religious picture, the Baroque mechanisms of low-level culture came into play. However, it would be hard not to notice that, in contrast to loftier examples of icon painting and engraving, these pictures are characterized by a particular religious aesthetic of sensibility, that in turn quite strongly influences the artistic structure of the primitive image itself.

Popular piety was always and everywhere brightly hued: strong and contrastive manifestations of religious feelings and a pull towards ambivalence were normal in it. In modern times the 'long Middle Ages' were nowhere so clearly revealed as in the sphere of popular religion, with its spirit of folkloric inventiveness. As early as the 17th century, in fact, New Testament images mediated through folk mythologizations became widespread in popular icons and pictures.[1] We need only recall the universally encountered depictions of St George where, in correspondence with the fairytale motif of fighting a dragon, we so often encounter the princess leading the vanquished dragon by a cord.[2]

Vivid and complex emotions found their response in just as vivid colours and sharply defined lines of the rustic images in practically all their cultural and national variants. Even the popular names themselves of Suzdalian mass-circulation icons – 'pretty ones' and 'dark ones' (*krasnushki* and *chernushki*) – imply a particularly emotional tonality concerning the way the common people perceived the earthly and heavenly worlds in exclusively contrastive shades (illus. 190). 'The uninterrupted connection that existed in primitivism between the popular aesthetic and religious content also ensured the long life of rustic imagery.'[3]

There is an interesting characterization of popular taste in the *Vladimir Province Gazette* of 1843, in which the stereotypes of 'high' culture are only slightly modified by 'low' cultural stereotypes:

> The Suzdalian icon manner was at first completely an imitation of the Greek style. Now it is distinguished from the Greek manner generally by the fact that the latter's deficiencies are exaggerated to extremes in it – especially a particular coloration. The distinguishing marks of Suzdalian painting are as follows: much irregularity and unsureness in drawing, as a result of which there is never a natural disposition of things; an excessive angularity of curves and terminations, the absence of flowing lines, without which neither beauty nor naturalness are possible; an absurd treatment of drapery; short figures, and since the craftsmen were ignorant of bodily anatomy, the parts of depicted figures were deprived of any proportionality; finally an excessive variegation of colour. In this respect Suzdalian painting carries the stamp of Russian popular taste, ordering itself how it pleases.[4]

In other words, the archaism of the artistic language responded to an aesthetic of religious experiences. It in turn was subject to that semi-stylized quality that at times ruled in the artistic consciousness of the master craftsman and which found its particular expression in the fact that the icon and the religious picture served as sources for one another. 'Following the religious demands of the people', as Rovinsky wrote, 'the picture provided them with cheap representations of the saints they revered'.[5] The same cheap images were provided for the people by the mass-circulation icon; but of course they had more than cheapness in common.

I. A. Golyshev (1838–96), known as the founder of the first village lithographic workshop in Russia, which produced both religious and secular *lubok*-type pictures,[6] confirmed that in Mstyora, religious *lubok* pictures were included in icon pattern-books. For *lubok* pictures 'icons were provided as originals; just the same thing happened the other way round: picture representations were turned into icons' (illus. 183, 184, 185).[7] Golyshev's lithographic workshop was set up in Mstyora in 1858 and survived to the mid-1880s, when it succumbed to competition from Moscow's chromolithographic firms.[8] A little later there appeared the

183. *Mother of God, 'Rejoice, O maiden . . .'*, 1887, lithograph from I. A. Golyshev's printing-house, Mstyora. Russian State Library, Moscow.

184. *The Giant Bernard Gilly*, second half of the 18th century. State Pushkin Museum of Art, Moscow.

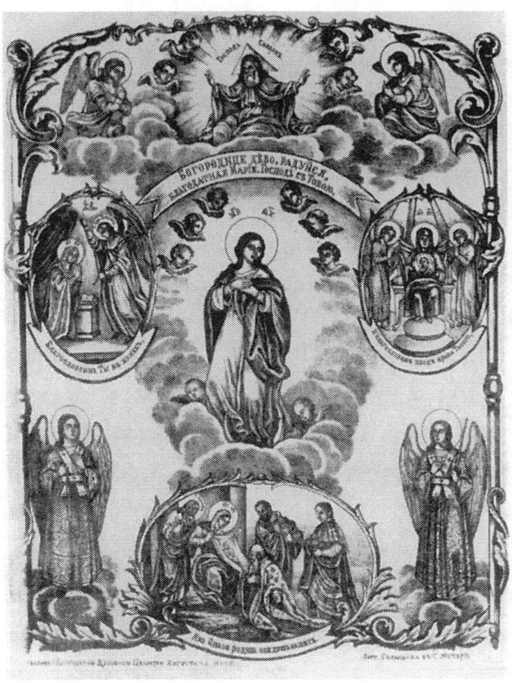

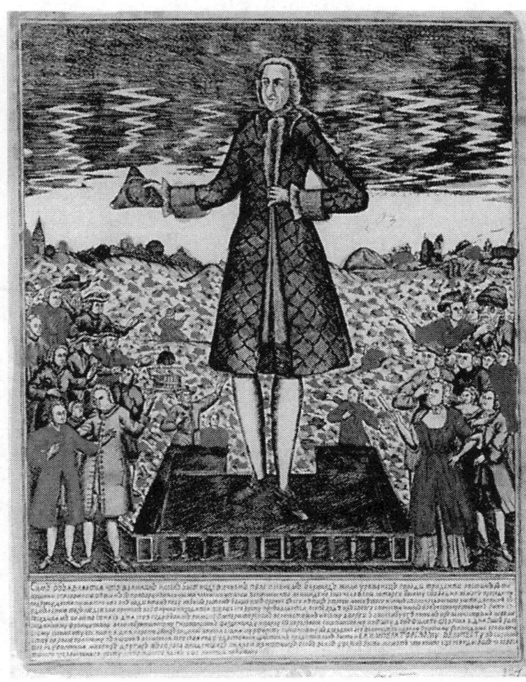

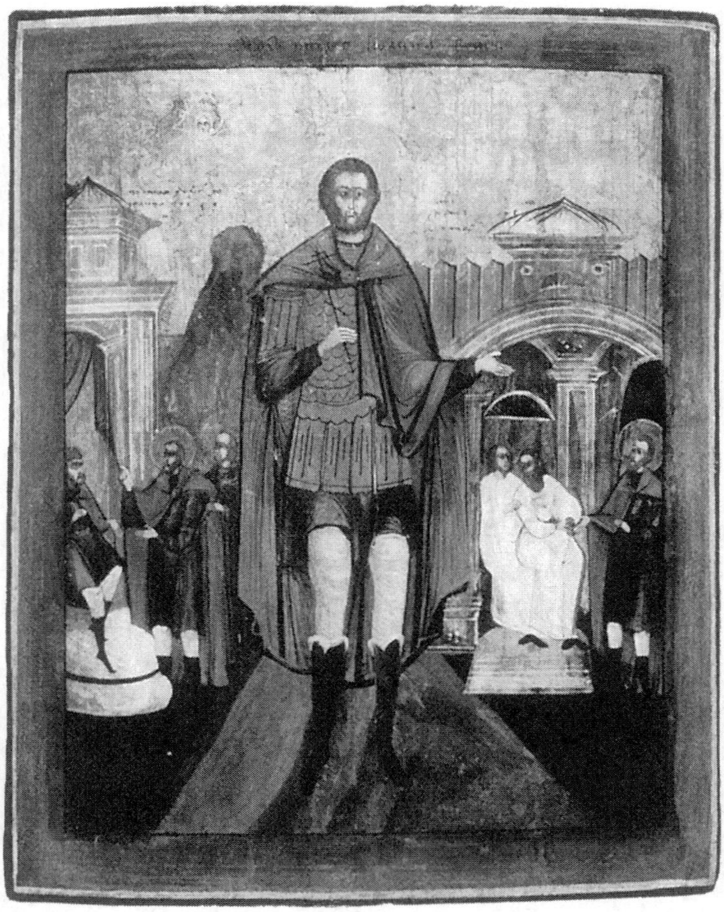
185. *St John the Warrior*, 19th century, Mstyora. Collection of Harry Willamo, Finland.

printing workshop in the village of Bogdanovka in the Kovrov district of Vladimir province, whose founder was the rich *ofenya* (travelling salesman) Ignatiy Akimov-Sorokin.[9] The functioning of print-shops next to icon producers tells us that there was a single cultural–historical space within people's everyday existence and consequently in the production of both popular pictures and icons.

Drawings for the lithographs were on the whole made by local icon painters.[10] According to the statistics for 1874, every subject was printed in the Mstyora workshop in editions of 1,000 to 5,000 copies per year. By 1884 the workshop had 130 lithographic stones with 300 titles and 10 copper plates that had earlier belonged to the Moscow metal-plate printing works of I. Loginov. As prototypes, the local craftsmen also used mass-circulation examples from the Moscow workshops of A. I. Lavrentyeva and P. N. Sharapov. We have evidence that part of what was printed might be orientated towards icon production in the form of a curious, otherwise unknown, Russian folk variant of the Greek Menologion of Basil II (Byzantine Emperor, 972–1025) from the second half of the 19th century; prints for it, made by the village lithographic firm of Prokhorov, have been preserved in a private archive at Palekh. Lithographs with scenes of the martyrdoms of Christian saints were made specially for icon painters: they were printed on transparent paper, from which the image could be conveniently traced for multiple copies. The primitive and clumsy forms betray the hand of a not very skilful village draughtsman. The lithograph carries the inscription: 'From a Greek gospel lectionary of the 10th century' (illus. 186).

Undergoing a certain amount of 'manneristic' reconfiguration, the printed prototypes turned into new exemplars of mass circulation icons, on which ornamented frames and background decorations typical of engravings appeared. We can see these features on many Kholuy and Mstyora

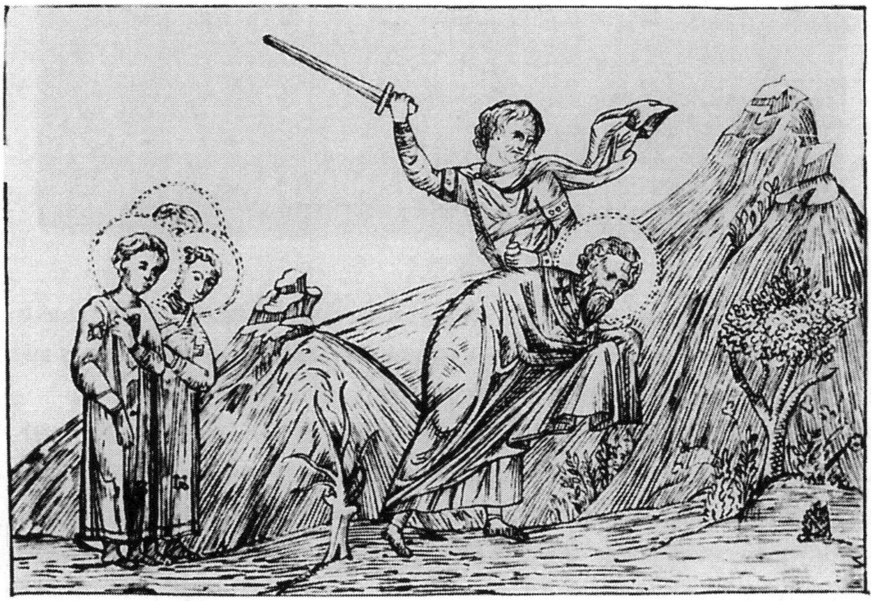

186. Illustration to the Greek Menologion, second half of the 19th century, Prokhorov printing-house. Archive of L. Bakanov, Palekh.

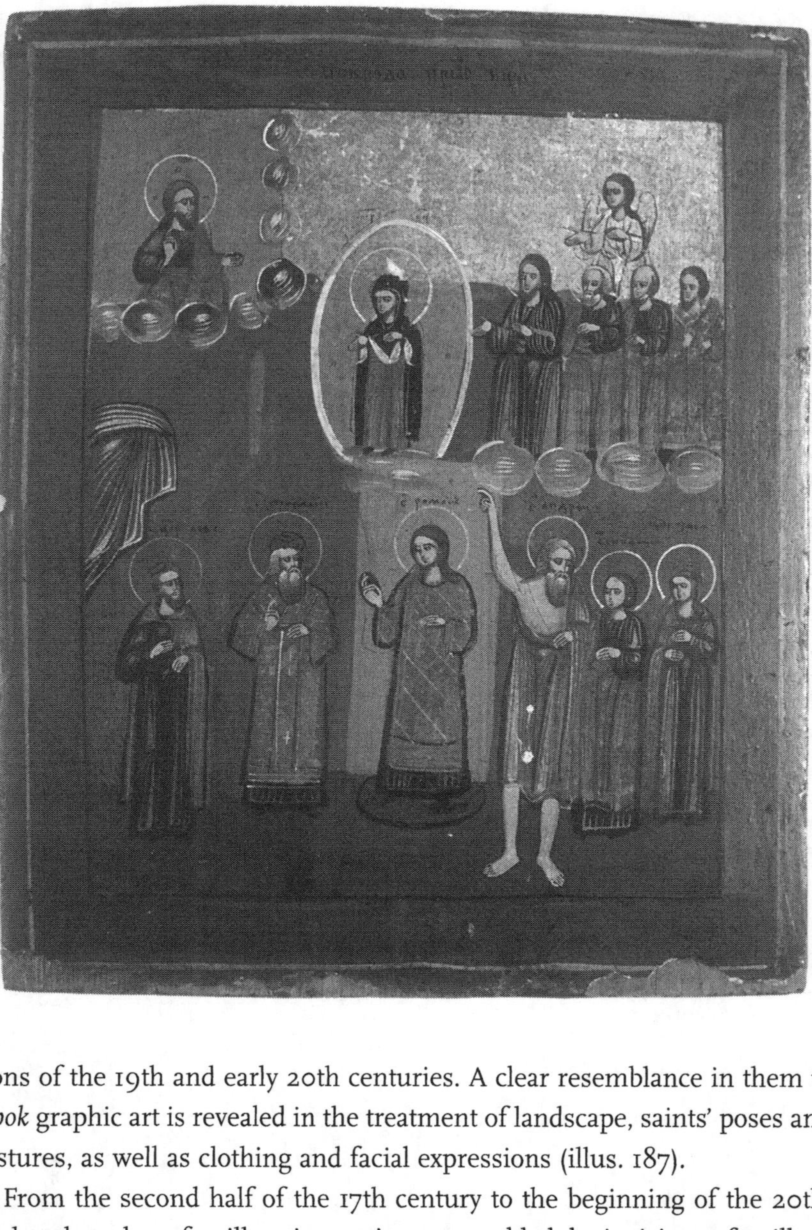

187. *Pokrov*, 19th century, Kholuy. Palekh Art Museum, Palekh.

icons of the 19th and early 20th centuries. A clear resemblance in them to *lubok* graphic art is revealed in the treatment of landscape, saints' poses and gestures, as well as clothing and facial expressions (illus. 187).

From the second half of the 17th century to the beginning of the 20th, the brushstrokes of a village icon painter resembled the incisions of a village engraver's burin. A telling example is a primitive peasant icon of 'The Lord Pantocrator' of the late 17th or early 18th century; here the craftsman painted a typical 'peasant' Saviour with a special emotional tonality. It is either the awesome Judge and Ruler of All, or else the Christ who suffers together with the people, of whose depiction on Russian peasant icons Nikolay Leskov was to say: 'Our simple-souled master understood better than anyone Whom it was necessary to paint . . . As He revealed himself, so He goes, and to us He arrived in the guise of a slave.'[11]

If we imagine the semi-darkness of a peasant's house, where icons of this kind and religious pictures almost always were placed side by side, then we may feel that they were visible to the worshipper only thanks to their simple and capacious symbolism, responsive to archetypes of thought, more precisely to three or four brilliant colours and to bold lines, catching fire and coming to life in the faint illumination of the burning lamp. In brief, we are confronting a stylistic stability before which both time itself and national cultural frontiers are rendered powerless: for the same aesthetic of sensibility can be seen in the primitive icons of Bulgaria, Serbia, Transylvania, or even, say, Syria.

The Spirit of Religious Tradition

The primitive is primitive: however, when we are dealing with 'large-scale repeatability', structural elements of the primitive are fully capable of concealing the spirit of religious tradition within the 'aesthetics of folklore'. Victor Turner's observation about the communicative function of simple (archetypal) symbolic structures is all the more important for us if we take into consideration, first, that the national religious consciousness can reveal its relative stability and fixity only in the most *contrastive shades*, and second, if we take into account the limited scope of its formative texts, among which, as one scholar put it, icon painting is capable of 'the most precise delineation of the sphere of the ideal and the deepest penetration into the mysteries of the religious consciousness . . .'.[12]

The normative nature of its aesthetics, the volume and structural repeatability of the elements of pictorial space in the primitive icon and the popular religious picture clearly determine their capacity to suppress the important meanings of one or another cultural–historical and religious experience.

According to Freud, mistakes in speech or writing reveal the unconscious

188. M. Blinnichev, *Simeon of Verkhoturye*, early 20th century, Kholuy. State Museum of the History of Religion, St Petersburg.

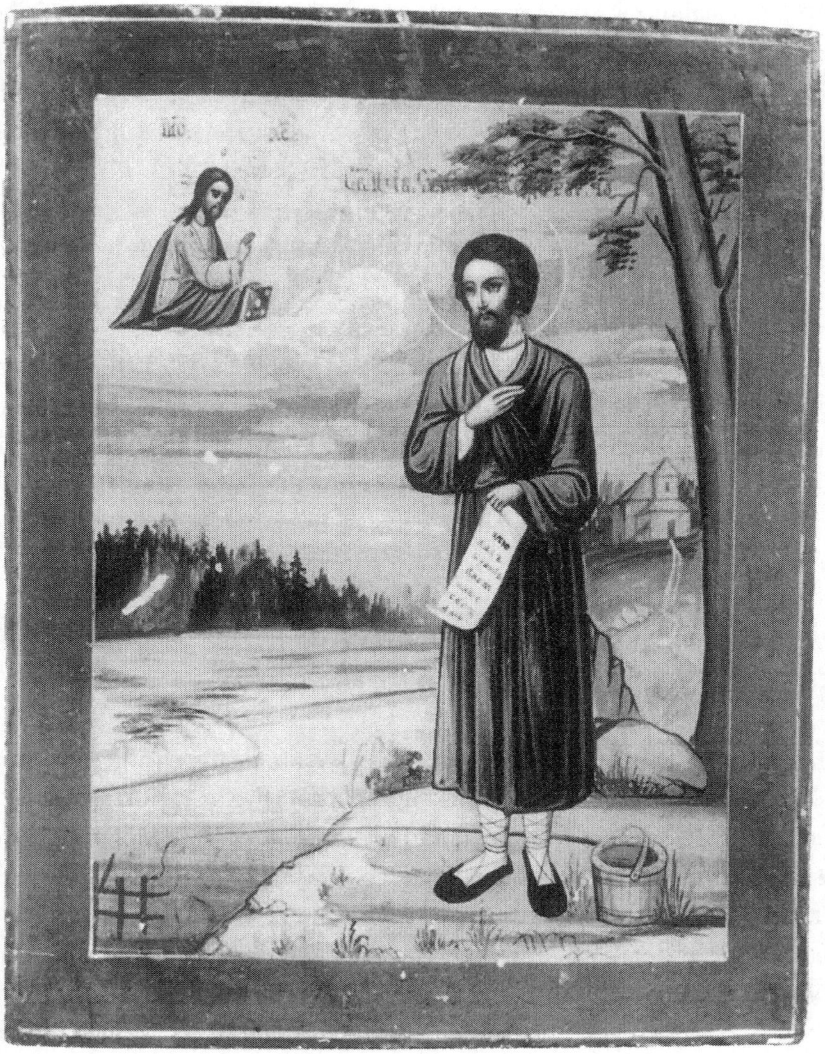

at work. On simple popular icons we can often see mistakes in the inscriptions. For example, on a small 19th-century Kholuy icon the clumsy hand of a scarcely literate peasant has written (without word separation or ligatures) *Fromreveren Nikandr (S 'prepodob Nikandr')*. But in such errors we also find dominant symbols, that seem to be bursting through to the surface from the depths of experience and the collective unconscious. On an icon by the Kholuy master M. Blinnichev of 'St Simeon of Verkhoturye' a New Ritualist abbreviation 'IИC XC' has been put above a head of Christ. However, Christ's hand has, by habit, been painted with a two-fingered sign of blessing (illus. 188). Although the icon had been painted from an official church oleograph on tin made by the firm of Jacquot (*Zhako*), the experience of Old Ritualist icon painting and piety lent it one of its most important signs.

At this point there is no getting away from posing the question of the complex, yet evident reflection of Old Russian traditions as well as of the Old Ritualist religious experience in the Suzdalian mass circulation icon. 'There are almost no peasant houses where you cannot find examples of very recent art' – so wrote a mid-19th-century observer – 'they are all of Suzdalian old-style workmanship'.[13] Taking account of this degree of dissemination of Suzdalian simple popular icons, as also their role in the history of religious sensibility, let us look more closely at their *artistic language,* behind which stood many of the cultural–historical realities that we have discussed.

Sternness and simultaneously *sorrowfulness* of expression in countenances are a typical feature of the Suzdalian 'embellishing' icon (*krasnushka*). A sad and pitiable expression has been given to Christ's countenance in the mass circulation icon of the late 17th- or early-18th-century mentioned earlier (illus. 189). The same expression can be found on innumerable images of the Mother of God. Sadness and emotionality at the sacrifice of the Son can be seen in the 19th-century icon of 'Mother of God of the Passion' (illus. 190).[14] The devices to convey this expression had been absorbed by the Suzdalian craftsmen to the point of automatism, and even with their very fast pace of work occasioned them no trouble.

The figures of saints in mass-circulation Suzdalian images are most often painted in such a way as to create an illusion of other-worldliness and incorporeality, of an interior state of tension. A stereotypical expression of aloofness and reservation is characteristic in these countenances. The figures are elongated, their shoulders sloping, their heads have the small-scale features characteristic of facial concentration. The gaze of the saints seems always directed inward, and sometimes it is as if they possess a secret they do not wish to reveal.

The parsimony and laconic nature of the artistic language, and the

189. Detail from the Suzdalian-style icon *Christ Pantocrator* (illus. 50), end of the 17th century or early 18th. Private collection, Moscow.

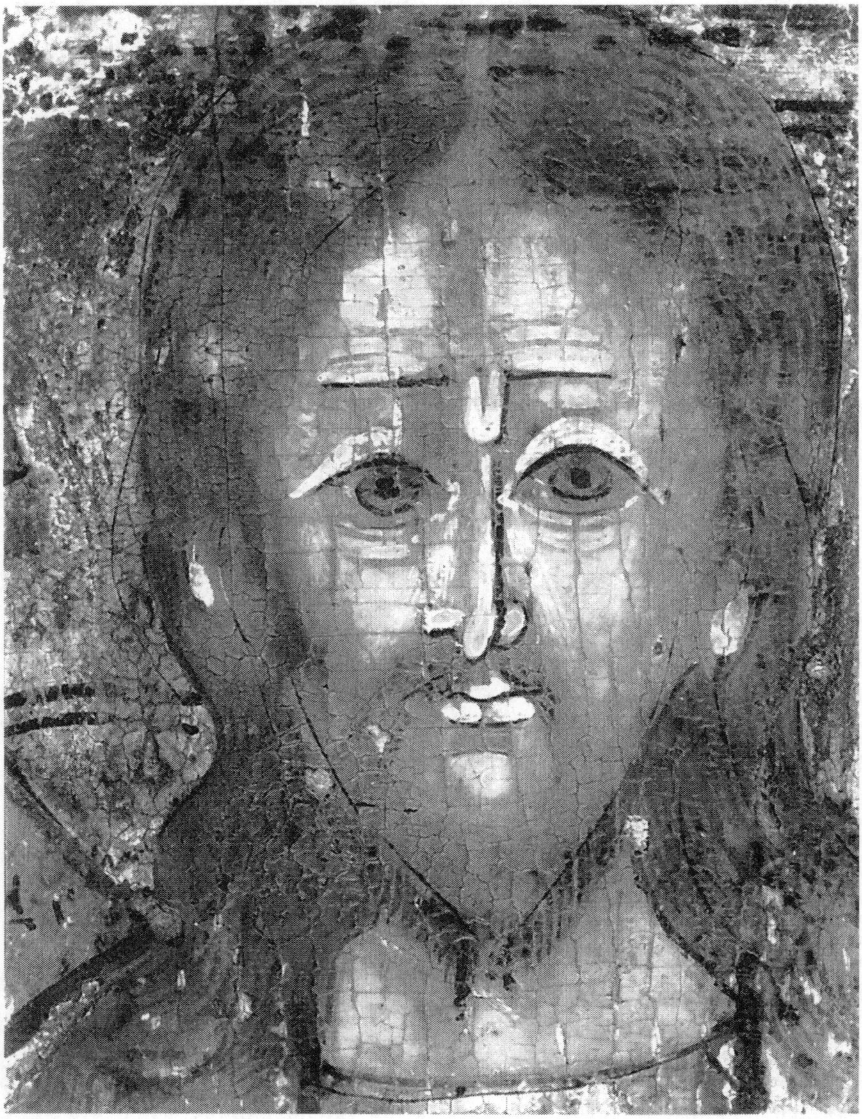

automatism of the studied elements, convey motifs of submissiveness and self-denial, efforts aimed at deepening the self and concentrating spiritual energy, which a few centuries earlier allowed the Old Russian icon to create that special asceticism and internal energy that had always distinguished it from the icons of other countries. This Old Russian asceticism can be tentatively linked with an understanding of sanctity primarily as martyrdom and as trust in another, heavenly, realm, in values that are not of this world.[15] In the circumstances of imperial Russia, this understanding of sainthood not only did not lose its power among the people, but (as was shown earlier) sometimes acquired its most extreme forms within sectarian and Old Ritualist religiosity – which could not but manifest itself in a particular strictness and 'asceticism' of the artistic language of the Old

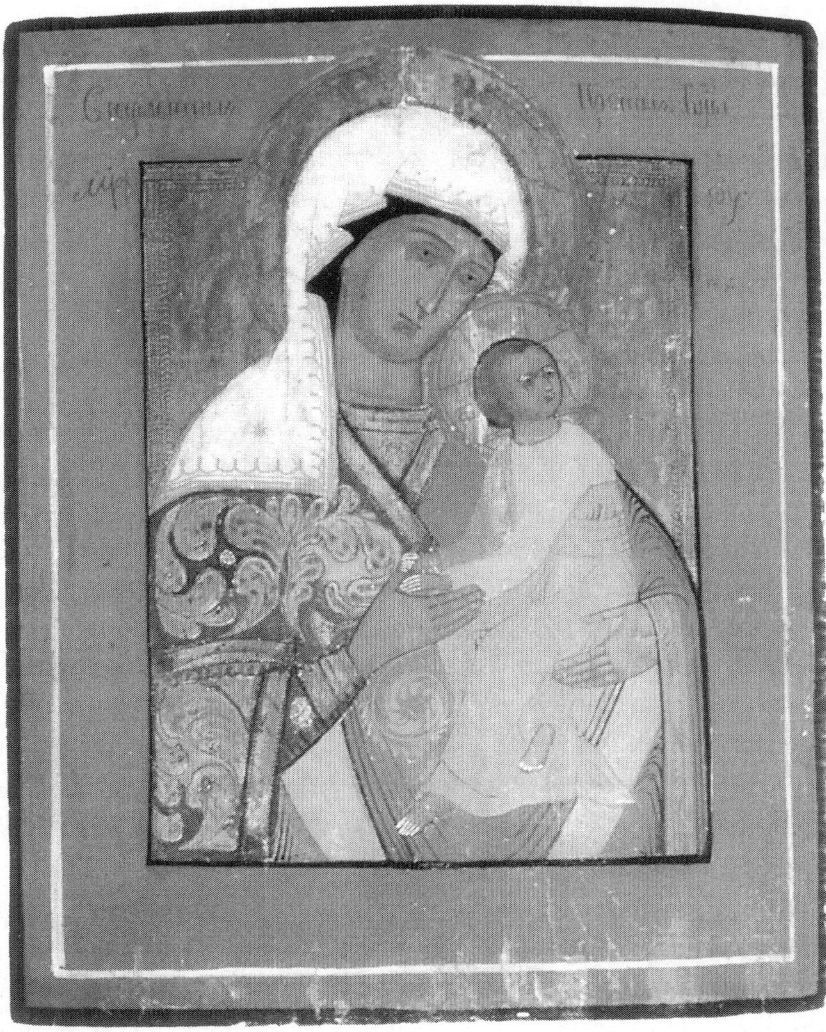

190. *Mother of God of the Passion*, a Suzdalian mass-circulation icon (*krasnushka*), 19th century, Kholuy or Mstyora. Collection of Harry Willamo, Finland.

Ritualist icon. Among the lower cultural strata, 'only those forms are retained that turn out to be culturally advantageous for the given social group', which undergo 'a preliminary collective censorship'.[16]

It is characteristic that the decorative treatment of the frame of Suzdalian 'embellishment' icons did not reduce their internal tension as prayer images (as happened with many Balkan and West Slav variants), but on the contrary enhanced it. The most widespread type of frame of the 'mass circulation' icon had broad orange-red margins (see illus. 131). Most often they went together with either a smooth or an embossed background. A bright red colour on a broad frame is encountered, incidentally, on early Greek icons. Besides its decorative function, it clearly marked out the 'mirror' of the prayer image, making the worshipper concentrate attention on what was portrayed within. But simultaneously, the bright colouring of the frame would also accentuate the frontier between sacral and worldly space, symbolizing the Old Testament Ark of the Covenant. Hence the frame of a Russian popular icon continued to be understood as a medieval means of preserving the Divine Countenance. This is confirmed by the wide popular distribution of icons with a *kovcheg* ('ark' or 'shrine').

One often encounters Suzdalian icons with decorative embossing that imitates a metal casing on the margins and in the background. However, here too, unlike many Balkan icons, the ornament has generally not spoilt the overall mood of worshipful concentratedness. It is subjected to – stifled by – the canonic quality of the figures and the emotional tonality of the countenances, strictly maintained for centuries, through which there often shines that famous Old Ritualist severity and the urge to transform life into the semblence of a divine service. I. A. Golyshev indicated that on images that only cost 'a few pence', colours were slapped on in Mstyora 'any old how'. The same 'lack of order' forcibly struck other observers: 'colours are thrown on in the most varied way possible; few are dark; the predominant colours are red and yellow. Objects do not possess their natural colours: the sky is sometimes painted yellow, the green of trees is greyish.'[17]

Nevertheless, we cannot help noticing that in the Suzdalian mass-circulation icon the colour range as a visual aspect of sanctity possessed a relative stability that is astonishing for 'low-level' types of art. Even in icons 'costing a few pence', the picture space was sometimes treated so that 'light' and shining interrelated generally with a higher impulse, and at this juncture directed their warmth as if inward, into the human heart. On a 19th-century Suzdalian icon, 'The Assembly of the Archangel Michael' (private collection, Moscow), the colours purple and red are applied only to the clothing of Christ Emmanuel and that of the heavenly host, at the same time as the background and haloes are yellow and the heavenly firmament is green: i.e., the colour that comes in the spectrum immediately before those colours that convey the idea of sanctity. Examples to confirm such data could easily be multiplied.

As a point of comparison we can note the way matters of space and colour are resolved in the popular primitive icons of other countries. First, icons with smooth and undecorated margins from the 18th and 19th centuries are scarcely to be found either in the Balkans or the West Slav lands. Margins as a rule are treated as if they were a narrowly outlined carved frame, decorated with multicoloured ornamental folk reliefs, sometimes reminiscent of the frame of a secular picture. The background is often filled either with thick vegetational ornament pressed into the plaster base, or else with flowers and stars. These peculiarities are very characteristic of the 18th- and 19th-century icon painting of Ukraine and Belorussia, Bulgaria and Serbia. They are also found in the icons of Mt Athos, etc. And second, unlike the relatively relaxed compositions of Suzdalian 'embellishment' works, ornamentation in, for example, mass-circulation Transylvanian and Moldavian icons on glass are for the most part orientated towards the maximal control of picture space, towards its filling-up and subjugation. This deflects the tone of prayerful concentratedness in the icon, giving rise to the illusion of a folkloric fairytale cosmos, further enhanced by corresponding colour resolutions. The colours of sanctity are disposed without any strict reference to the divine principle. They seep into the ground, the vegetational ornament, the architectural settings, etc., immediately making the sacred space of the icon both earthbound and fantastical. As a result, other semantic nuances rooted in religious experience are highlighted.

If we fix our attention steadily on the appearance of South Slav, or, say, Transylvanian saints, we can sometimes sense them gazing at ourselves, The gaze of a saint directed on the worshipper can be found as far back as in Greek icons of the 10th and 11th centuries, but it is a particular feature of 'post-Tridentine' Catholic painting. The same device came into several 16th-century frescoes on Mt Athos – this was noted, but not explained by M. Chatzidakis[18] – as also into prayer images in zones of contact between Orthodoxy and Catholicism. The saint's gaze fixed on the viewer presupposed not an interior monologue, but a dialogue: it was directed towards the exaltation of religious experience, essentially alien to the Russian Orthodox tradition. That is why we rarely find the gaze of the saint fixed on us – the spectators – in Russian popular icons.

On the one hand, all this greater 'earthliness' and folkloric quality of Balkan and West Slav icons can be easily explained by the marginal position of Orthodox craftwork in places where Islamic, Catholic or Protestant cultures dominated. When the culture of conquerors is confirmed at the higher cultural levels, the lowlier spheres of popular craftwork become the main factors in a people's creative development. Then the most favourable circumstances for the development of an art of primitive forms arise: the universal mechanisms of primitive style formation with their predilection for low-level Baroque work can be the more active. So can processes involving the interaction of the language of the icon with that of secular and folk art, leading to the swift destruction of the canon, more mobility in the boundary between sacral and worldly space, and, as a result, the saturation of the icon with numerous elements of the real surrounding world.

On the other hand, an intentional awareness, always striving to reconcile the profane with the sacral, could not avoid burdening itself with the very same marginal position in a situation of religious inequality and oppression. Thus the particular world of the Balkans, with its inverted symbols of sacred empire and its crushed national and religious sensibilities, continually created for people a sort of existential situation in which their national and religious values were subject to doubts or completely rejected. So the icon became for Orthodox Balkan peoples (say for Greeks, Bulgarians or Serbs) one of the most important artistic realms of creative effort. Hence in some Balkan icons we can observe a characteristic treatment of space and time, reflecting not only the common European tendency towards maximizing the role of personal piety, but also a certain urge towards the symbolization of national forms – a sort of concealed symbolism. Thus on the frequently encountered 19th-century Bulgarian icons of 'The Fiery Ascent of the Prophet Elijah', the mantle that Elijah leaves to Elisha as a symbol of his prophetic gift is deliberately shown in the form of a Bulgarian cloak, although all the other clothes are those traditionally seen in icons (illus. 191). This motif is invariably linked with the motif of heavenly vengeance on tormentors and oppressors – something, indeed, that emerges from the particularly frequent occurrence in the Balkans of prayer icons of St Demetrios, on which the Prince of Darkness is always shown in the guise of a Turkish warrior. These examples could be multiplied, and their reliability confirmed, if we look at icon painting in different parts of the Balkans.

191. The fiery ascent of the Prophet Elijah, a detail from Zakhariy Tsanov's *Fiery Ascent of the Prophet Elijah and the Holy Warriors, SS George, Theodoros, Eustaphios and Dimitrios, Destroying the Forces of Evil*, 1854.

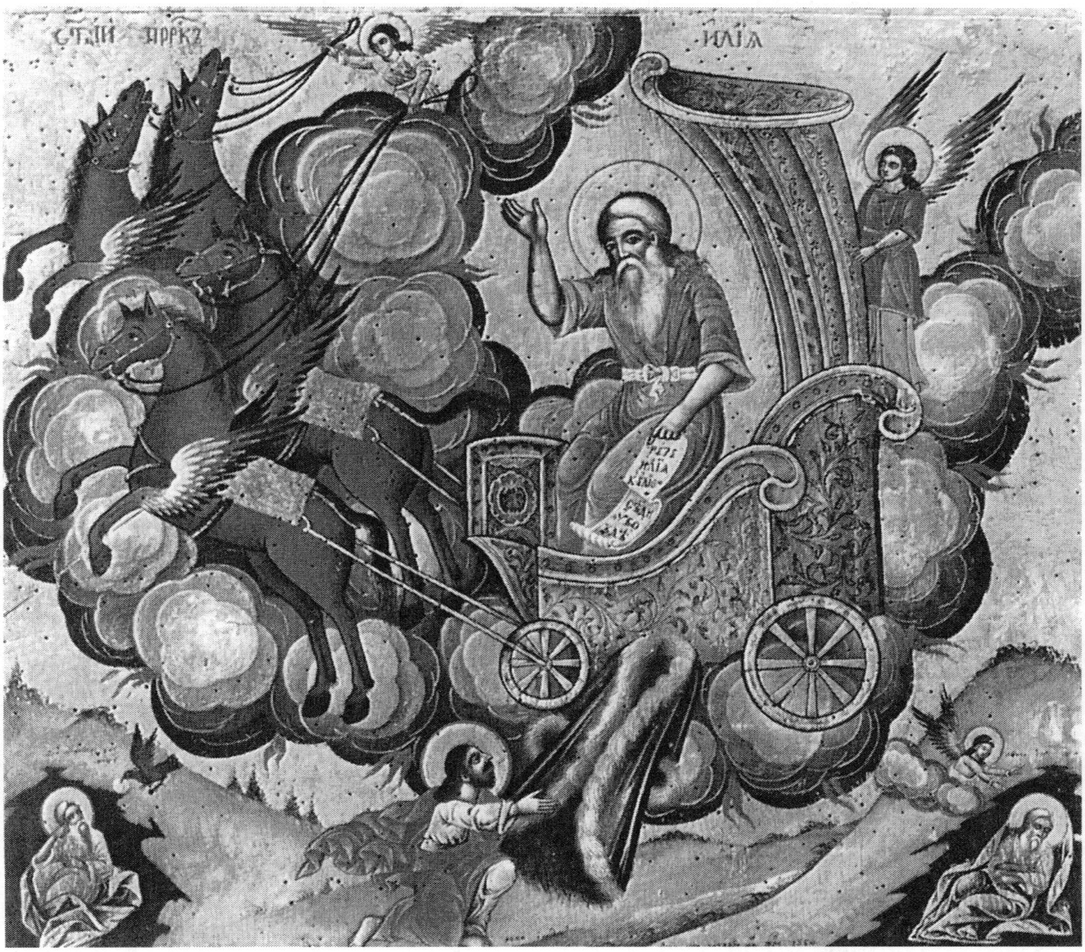

Saturated through and through with 'everydayness', the symbolic structure of the image lent sacred history a more intimate connexion with humanity. Mind and emotions reconfigured the objects of the visible world: they presented themselves as if imbued with inner meaning. The surrounding ethno-cultural space was consciously made to interact with the sphere of grace – in which we can also see that spirit of religious nationalism mentioned earlier in connection with the official religious revival in early-20th-century imperial Russia. It is characteristic that the creation of an independent national Church in Bulgaria and its separation from the Patriarchate of Constantinople (condemned as a heresy called 'Philetism') had a very strong influence on Bulgarian icon painting of the second half of the 19th century and the beginning of the 20th. Symbolization of national attributes and ornamentation in it was immediately enhanced.[19]

If we remain at the level of unconsidered responses and dominant tendencies, we cannot help noticing that the structure of the 'real world' in mass-produced Suzdalian icons is a little different. The particular sacral significance of objects is rather less. We have to take a cautious attitude towards the influence of Old Ritualist religiosity, with its complex inbuilt sense of the world's 'absence of grace' in imperial Russia, its 'abandonment by God' and 'hostility' – in brief, with what was called the scorn of the earthly world on its path to discover the heavenly kingdom. In Old Ritualist icons, as a rule, the symbolization of national forms had a hidden character: it emerged within the framework of the canon and was adorned with the myth of a 'golden age' of Russian Orthodoxy, from which the national attributes (historical costume, architecture, type of countenance, etc.) were acquired mostly by the process of copying late-16th- to early-17th-century icons.

Thus it was not only the religious aesthetic of sensibility, characteristic of all the Orthodox peoples, that was linked with the aesthetics of the primitive image, but also the tradition of devotion that characterized each one of them separately. In the context of historical psychology, that means we can recognize that the icon actively affected humanity and its consciousness.[20] For this reason the peculiarities of its artistic language that I have described were highly diverse in the development of its spiritual vision and value system.

The Projection of Signs: Icon – *Lubok* – the Avant-garde

The languages of the Suzdalian primitive icon and religious popular culture interpenetrated one another; however, the primitive Russian icon and the secular *lubok* had a completely different relationship. Though it exercised a vigorous influence on the secular picture, the icon itself in this instance was very little influenced by it. This observation suggests that, interestingly, the sign system of the icon was projected onto the most varied forms of popular creativity. This layering of signs tells us once again about the special ontology of the Russian icon, its role in the system of popular culture and its place in the way that sacralization embraced the profane sphere. Moreover, the remarkable discovery of this phenomenon by 20th-century Russian avant-garde artists, and the use by exponents of the language of the Russian icon in works produced both before and after the 1917 Revolution, give us the opportunity to witness the ontology of the Russian icon in a light that is somewhat unexpected, but clear enough to reveal profound cultural codes. The peculiarities of the avant-garde aesthetic and its archetypal patterns of thought deliver interesting data into our hands.

Both in the primitivistic paintings of Natalya Goncharova (who, incidentally, continued occasionally to paint icons even after she emigrated to France) and in the works of the 'primitivist' period of Kazimir Malevich (for example, *Reaper*, 1912, *Rye Harvest*, 1912, and *Peasant Women in Church*, 1911) and in Vladimir Tatlin (*Nude*, 1913), elements of the iconic representational system are clearly visible (illus. 192, 193, 194). We see it in the conventionality of depiction and associated deformations, i.e., the concrete devices of the semantic syntax of the icon and its spatial–temporal characteristics: sharp foreshortenings, dynamic poses and a rhythmic quality of movements, reverse perspective, the simultaneous representation of different sides of an object, circularity of form deriving from the summation of the viewer's position, and, finally, a synthesis of the representational and verbal realms.

Just the same elements can easily be found in secular popular pictures. Thus in the 19th-century painting *Dancing Peasant Musician* in the Bakhrushin Theatre Museum, the methods of representation are directly dependent on those of the icon: the countenance is iconic, the folds of the

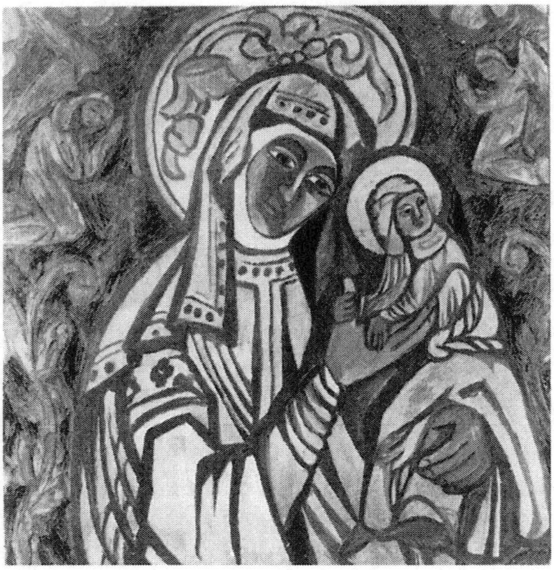

192. N. Goncharova, *Mother of God*, 1905–7.

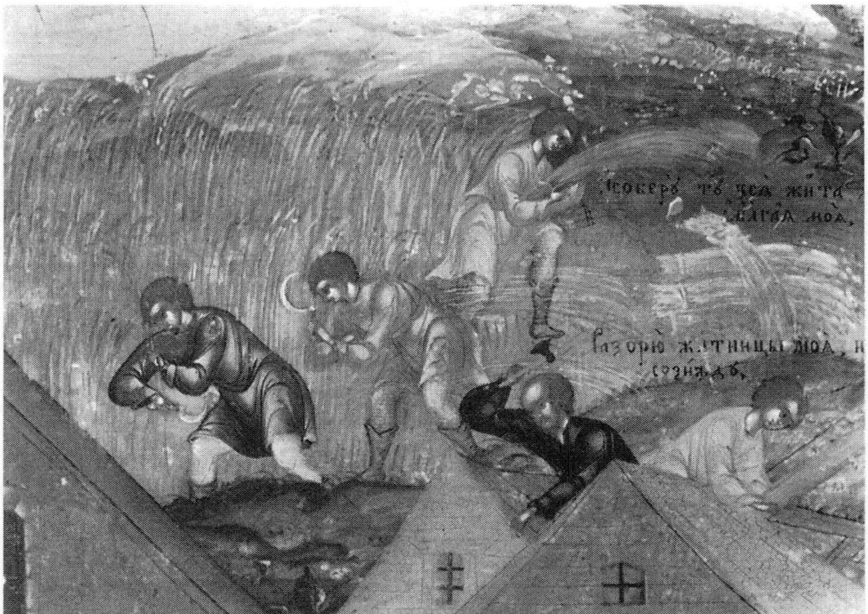

193. A detail from the icon *The Parable of the Rich Man* (illus. 114), 18th century. Kolomenskoye Historical and Architectural Museum-Preserve, Moscow

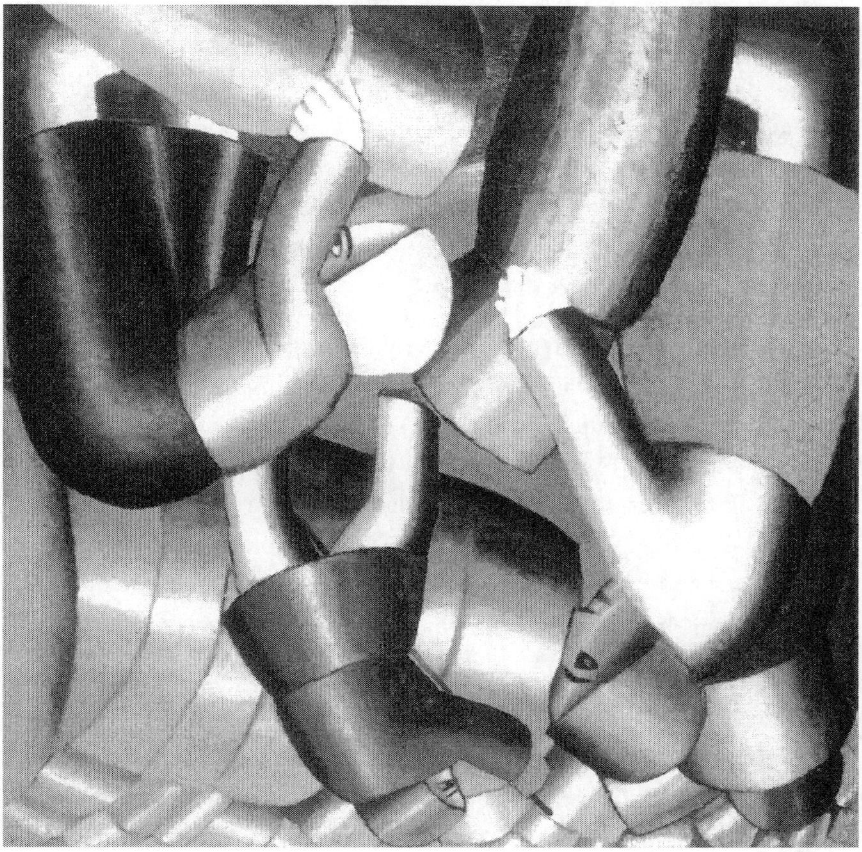

194. Kazimir Malevich, *Harvesting Rye*, 1912. Stedelijk Museum, Amsterdam.

garments are treated iconically too, while the lack of depth and the typically iconic rendering of space with conventional 'sky' and 'earth' scarcely accord with the hat, the musical instrument and the playful intent of the composition (illus. 195).

Its way of conveying time and space, linked with reverse perspective, its symmetry of presentation, its colour, its speculative quality – these are things the peasant *lubok* acquired as a result of that 'burden of quantity' of prayer images that had long sanctified the external and internal space of the world of the Russian village. Hence it is not accidental that (for example) the composition of the well-known *lubok* 'The Giant Bernard Gilly' recalls the composition of the icon 'The Mother of God, Joy of All who Suffer'. Just the same composition is found in a primitive 19th-century icon of

'St John the Warrior' (Mstyora) (illus. 79, 184, 185). In the *lubok* prints 'The Ox did not Wish to be an Ox and became a Butcher', 'Notice of the English Commendants', and many others, the composition of the hagiological icon (Saint with Life) is used (illus. 197, 198).

It was the Russian avant-garde, in turning the primitive into the object of intense formal and structural analysis, who evidently first managed to see the ubiquity of the sign system of the icon in Russian popular craft culture. As Kazimir Malevich wrote:

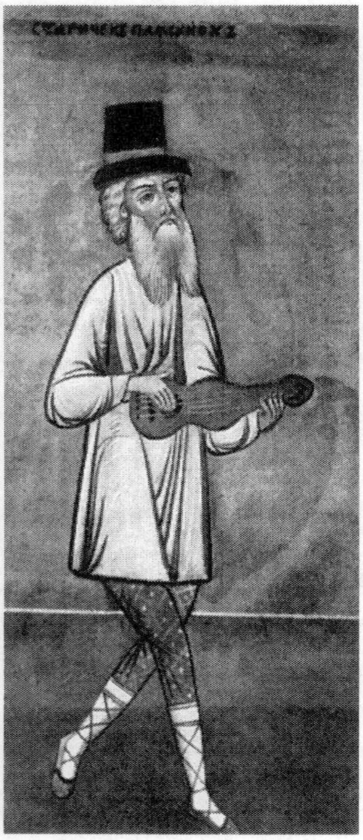

195. *Dancing Peasant Musician*, 19th century. Bakhrushin Theatre Museum, Moscow.

> Icons produced a particularly strong impression on me, despite the straightforward way my feelings towards Nature were nourished. In icons I sensed something remarkable and close to my heart. Then I remembered my childhood: little horses, flowers, cockerels all in primitive paintwork or carved on wood. I sensed some kind of link between peasant art and iconic art: icon painting is the form of higher culture in peasant art.

Malevich underlined the same thought when he said that he 'clearly imagined the whole line of development from the great icon painters' art to the little horses and cockerels on painted walls, spindles and clothes as the line of peasant art', and that, when he started to paint pictures in a primitivistic style, he remained true to this tradition.[21]

It was not only Malevich who saw the connection between peasant and iconic art at the time. Alexander Shevchenko wrote about how the popular *lubok* was a direct 'continuation' of Russian 'spiritually edifying painting', i.e., icons.[22] This was also discussed by Mikhail Larionov and Natalya Goncharova, who then started collecting religious and secular *lubok* prints, as well as the 'constructional material' of peasant icon production itself: icon-painting pattern-books, drawings of individual subjects, traceable drawings, prints and fragments of ornament, and (most likely) actual peasant 'primitives'. Larionov and Goncharova included all this within the concept of *lubok*, and displayed it in March–April 1913 at the 'Target' exhibition. The published catalogue, *Exhibition of Icon Pattern-books and Lubok Prints, Organized by*

M. F. Larionov, speaks of the fairly large collection of *lubok* and icon drawings and tracings belonging to the organizer himself. At the exhibition one could view a large number of Old Ritualist religious pictures – 'The Whore of Babylon', 'Sins Bring Down the Wrath of God on the People', 'The Spiritual Pharmacy', 'The Firm Unshakable Stand of the Christian', 'Remember the Four Last Deaths, the Last Judgment and Heavenly Kingdom', 'On the Coming of Antichrist', 'The Twenty Ordeals', 'The Discourse of St John Chrystostom', 'The Difference Between the Churches', and others. Here too were exhibited many mass-circulation icon-traced drawings: various types of the Mother of God, 'The Saviour', 'Nicholas the Wonder–worker', 'The Prophet Elijah', 'The Image Not Made by Hands', 'The Hospitality of Abraham' (i.e., the Old Testament Trinity), 'The Dormition, 'The Baptism'. We can also encounter subjects that reached the popular milieu from academic religious painting, such as 'The Saviour Expounds the Scriptures in the Temple', 'Christ with the Forerunner', 'Pilate Washes his Hands', 'Christ before Pilate' and others.[23] Finally, there was also a display of the examples of ornament that can be found both on Suzdalian 'embellishment' icons and in Goncharova's pictures (illus. 190, 192).[24]

As we try to reveal the ubiquity of the iconic sign system in popular culture, it is important to emphasize that avant-garde art belongs to those 'borderline' cultural strata in which archetypal signs have great typologizing significance – that is, allow one to judge, with due caution, the types of the culture as a whole. On the formal level the poetics of the avant-garde and of folk art came close to 'ornamentalism', 'to 'manneristic' formulae of text construction and to archetypal ways of thought.

The avant-garde always sought to occupy the territory between art and life, and thus also to work on the profundities of the aesthetic mind-set at the fluctuating boundary between consciousness and the unconscious.[25] This purposeful invasion into the archaic regions of thought, into the unconscious spheres of the human mentality, is illustrated in a well-known passage from Khlebnikov's *Ladomir* ('Harmony–World'), evoking divine beings from diverse cultures:

To the place, to the place where Izanagi
Would read the 'Monagatori' to Perun,
While Eros sat on Shang-ti's knees
And the grey topknot on the balding head
Of God resembles snow . . .[26]

On the gnoseological level, this kind of investigation methodically dismantled any barriers in posing one of the chief problems of avant-garde poetics – the problem of the past. In its quest for signs, for the most essential meanings, the concentrated avant-garde consciousness moved through temporal layers of the cultural memory with the single-mindedness and curiosity of an archaeologist. However, while a real archaeologist would be concerned with the reconstruction of culture, with the search for connections and synthesis, the quest of an avant-garde consciousness rather resembles the experience of 'archaeology as entertainment'. The picture of connections and consequences is rejected by them as something entirely superfluous in the context of the effort of digging out as much as possible of what could attract, entertain, amaze, be interesting or beguiling. Thus the avant-gardist consciousness recombined the experience of traditional culture, since what interested it was not synthesis, but the simple sum of quotations of those archetypal signs of the cultural memory that it so strove to attain. Hence in avant-garde artistic practice there arose 'manneristic' quotations and ornamentalism of thought, at first sight bringing it close to popular craft culture. Incidentally, whereas in the latter these poetic formulae most often did their work unconsciously – on the level of automatism – in avant-garde poetics they were at the conscious level, which for the scholar significantly raises the significance of the use of symbolic elements of the icon in this art.

For an example we can consider an individual symbol in a small watercolour painting, *The Saviour in Majesty* (1910–11) by Goncharova (illus. 196). The raised, rather than bent, forefinger of Christ indicates Goncharova's conscious desire to assimilate her 'icon' to the Catholic (i.e., for the Orthodox, 'alien') sign of devotion. The error of the small primitive Kholuy icon by M. Blinnichev, 'Simeon of Verkhoturye', where the two-fingered sign of blessing is combined with the inscription 'IИC XC' at an unconscious level told us about the special role of the Old Ritualist symbol in popular religious culture (illus. 188). Goncharova's 'error' actually tells us that the avant-garde developed its own relations with God: the old traditional signs of the covenant had been dropped. In the light of all this it is significant that the avant-garde discovered the icon for itself on the wave of historical self-referentiality that swept Russian culture at the beginning of the 20th century. The theme of the icon nourished the spiritual and intellectual atmosphere of the religious renaissance. The widely publicized campaign of activity of the Committee for the Propagation of Russian Icon Painting and the exhibition of Old Russian Art in 1913, timed for the 300th anniversary of the Romanov dynasty, created the conditions for the intellectual elite and society generally to discover the artistic world of the icon.

196. N. Goncharova, *The Saviour in Majesty*, 1910–11, bodycolour.

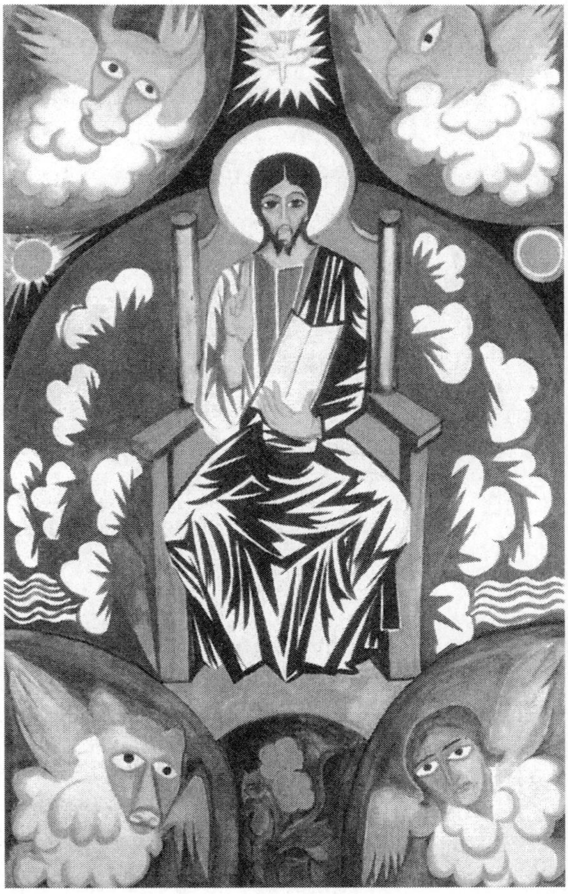

The term *icon* began unexpectedly often to appear in the language of public statements, art criticism, aesthetic declarations and theoretical programmes of the new artistic groupings. The term had become fashionable. The faces in Picasso's paintings, wrote the philosopher Sergey Bulgakov in 1914, 'are alive, and seem to be some kind of wonder-working icons of demonic character, with a mystical power streaming forth from them: look at them too long, and you experience a sort of mystic head-spinning.'[27] Alexander Benois[28] discerned an icon in Malevich's *Black Square*, and in his article on the Futurist exhibition *Zero-One* of 1915 warned about the danger of iconoclasm in the new art: 'The black square in its white setting is not just a joke, not just a rallying-call, not a little chance episode.'[29] In his letter of response to Benois, Malevich himself called his 'square' 'the icon of my times'.[30] Here one may also recall the extravagant reply of Goncharova to numerous remarks about the influence of icons on her, given by Marina Tsvetayeva in her memoirs: 'I'm free to remember a person, so why not an icon? "Forget" is the wrong word, you can't forget things that are already no longer outside you, but within, no longer in the past but in the present. Only perhaps in "forgetting oneself".'

Symbolism, too, paid particular attention to the icon, as did the Russian Art Nouveau tendency. In his article 'What can icons teach us?', M. Voloshin argued that 'Ancient art has risen up before our eyes in all its brightness and fullness. It seems nowadays so brilliant, so contemporary, it gives so many clear and immediate answers to the modern tasks of art, that it not only permits but demands an approach that is not archaeological but aesthetic and immediate.'[31] A. Grishchenko wrote similarly in his well-known work of 1917, *The Russian Icon as a Painterly Art*, based on his paper of 1915, 'How and Why we have Approached the Russian Icon'.

The Russian avant-garde, with its radicalism and extremism, had an approach to the icon that was more that just 'immediate'. Its involvement with the cultural–historical dichotomy of 'Russia and the West', which presented Russian culture with the unremitting temptation to translate aesthetic problems into historiosophical ones, meant that the icon seemed to it not merely a 'way in' to the achievements of French Cubism, but also that final word that might be decisive in its competition with the West. This emerged, for example, from the polemics that arose at the time of the second exhibition of Der Blaue Reiter, the modernist Munich group organized by Kandinsky. It was noticed that the main features distinguishing the Russian from the French avant-garde were 'archaism' and 'synthesis', deriving in particular from Old Russian icons.

The first published manifesto of Pavel Filonov's Analytic Art group,[32] 'The Intimate Workshop of Painters and Draughtsmen: "Made Pictures"' (March 1914) asserted, with a certain amount of avant-gardist shock tactics, that the centre of modern painting had transferred itself to Russia, whose cultural tradition was distinguished by the primitive and the icon: 'We have been the first to discover the new era of art – the age of "made" pictures and "made" drawings, and we are moving the centre of gravity of art to our country . . . that has created unforgettably marvellous churches, handicraft art and icons.'[33] At the same time, the icon, which had become for many a symbol of the national medieval tradition, was perceived in the context of the same sign system as the discoveries of French Cubism. Larionov in particular argued along these lines in the preface to his catalogue, the *Exhibition of Icon Pattern-books and Lubok Prints.*[34]

On the eve of the 1917 Revolution, proclaiming its status 'above culture' and 'demolishing' tradition, the avant-garde bore aloft the sign of the icon as one of the chief tokens of its experiment. After the Revolution, the language of the icon and the *lubok* was widely adopted by leftist (i.e.. experimentalist) artists in agitprop art. The popular aesthetic of religious sensibility appeared in Soviet artefacts of the 1920s in a transformed aspect, but one deeply imbued with the Russian religious experience. The old codes and signs were put to the service of changing the objects of faith in the context of the 'great utopia'. The major oppositions within that experience – 'humorous/serious', 'sacred/worldly' – were transposed and degraded. Having tragically freed the archaic structures of mass consciousness, the Revolution simultaneously brought about a strengthening in the leftist aesthetic consciousness of the nihilistic line of destruction and violence against the old culture, followed by many of those who until recently had been carefully seeking out the signs of sacral tradition.

A comparison of the agitational *lubok* (whose roots were in French Revolutionary art), the primitive icon and the old popular picture tells us first of all about the special function of laughter in the Russian Orthodox tradition, or rather about its lowering, neutralizing role. The removal of the sacred/worldly opposition contained within it one of the superficial reasons for the fairly swift destruction of cultural experience. In V. Lebedev's agitational *lubok* poster 'Uncle Prov' (1920), the composition of a hagiological icon is used. We have already encountered the same composition in the famous 18th-century *lubok* 'The Ox did not Wish to be an Ox and Became a Butcher'. The chief difference between them is that in the old *lubok* the opposition humorous/serious is turned round, while in the agitational *lubok* the same opposition is removed (illus. 197, 198, 199).

Keen to turn his picture into a narrative, the *lubok* craftsman of the 18th century took the scheme of the hagiological icon within which he unveiled

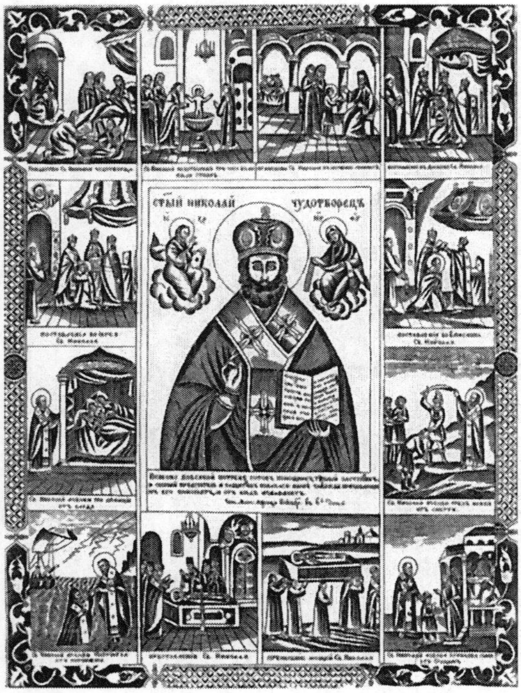

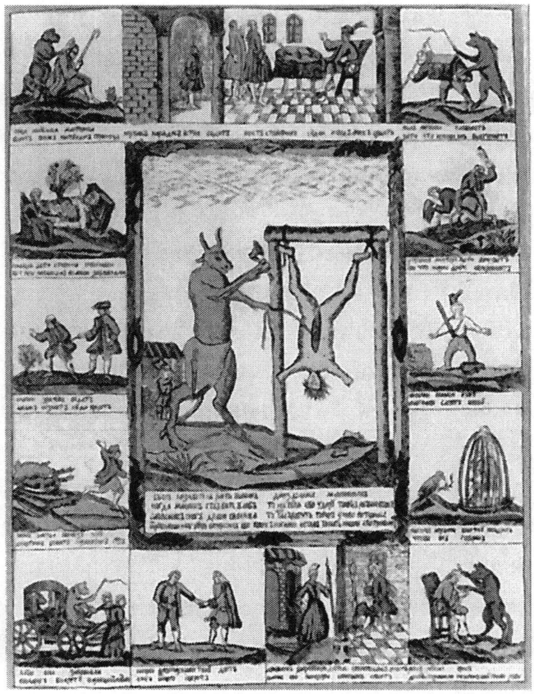

197. *St Nicholas the Wonder-worker with Life*, lithograph produced by Ye. Yakovlev printers, Moscow. Russian State Library, Moscow.

198. *The Ox Did not Wish to be an Ox and Became a Butcher*, mid-18th century, colour-printed *lubok*. State Pushkin Museum of Art, Moscow.

a subject that doubtless went back to the famous picture by Paulus Potter, *The Hunter's Punishment*. The universal rhetorical scheme of 'icon with saint's Life', through which the simple people were accustomed to peruse the stages of the ascent of Christian heroes, had been filled with playful and 'humorous' content. The 'serious' had been turned about and subjected to the playful action characteristic of the world of folk art. Each small picture has a text explaining the scene represented underneath. Reading and examining them all in familiar order, a person would be transported into a special reality that reproduced clownish behaviour. Serious religious experiences connected with the living voice of the hagiological icon retreated to the background. Everything was secondary not to contemplation, but to action, playfulness and laughter. In the central panel of this 'laughter icon' we see the most unusual, 'inverted' scene, while the smaller scenes show subjects linked with it by the logic of absurd situations. The central panel shows the ox 'carving up' the body of the butcher, hung upside-down, with an axe. A verse inscription explains it all:

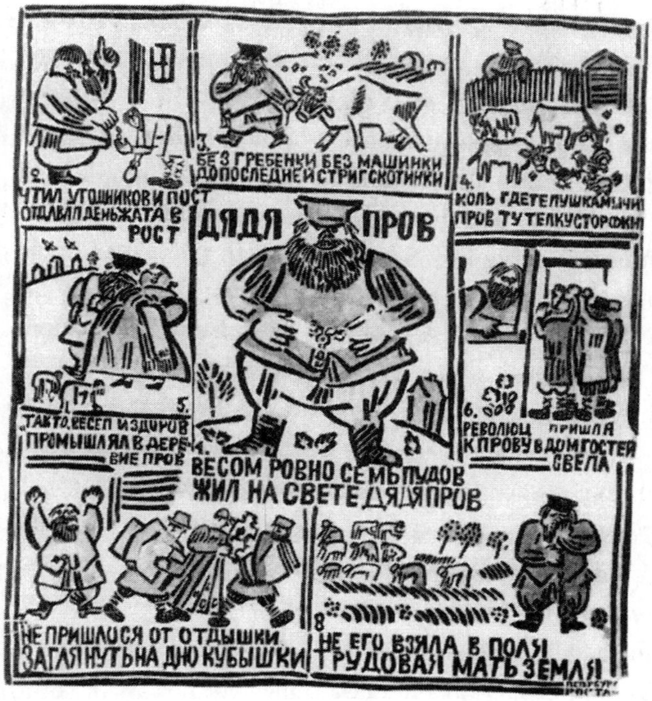

199. V. Lebedev, *'Uncle Prov'*, 1920, poster. State Russian Museum, St Petersburg.

The ox did not wish to be an ox, and made himself a butcher; when the butcher began to strike him on the head, he would not tolerate the blow and poked his horns into his side, and pushed the butcher right off balance, then seized his axe from him, amused himself by cutting off his hands and hung him upside down and started pulling out his guts and innards.

Incidentally this verse inscription is reminiscent of the icon by Aleksey Loginov: it confirms the universality and far-reaching formal principles of the low-level Baroque.

It is significant that his inversion of the 'humorous' (on the level of content) and the 'serious' (on the level of the visual–contemplative schema) – i.e. the so-called 'world upside-down' – is scarcely at all to be found in the Russian primitive mass icon, something that can be confirmed by innumerable icons of 'Suzdalian' type. In other words, if the icon was an active force in relation to folk art (and to the profane realm generally), it revealed itself as firmly closed against the penetration of that playful artistry that characterized the secular *lubok*. That the sign system of the icon should so resist the playful impulse of the picture confirms to some extent Yurij Lotman and Boris Uspensky's concept of the Old Russian 'laughter-world'; they delimited, within the bounds of the Russian tradition, the 'playful' sphere of popular art and the solemn, serious realm of religion, and testify to its continuing reality in modern times.[35] In popular Orthodox culture a relatively narrow area was devoted to laughter: the concept of saintliness generally did not admit laughter or playfulness.[36] The situation of an inverted, 'left-handed' world was understood among the people not as a liberation, rather as ambivalent, inverted sanctity, that is, as a field of activity for the powers of Antichrist. The deep roots of this tradition are attested by the fact that almost everywhere among the East Slavs, as Nikita Tolstoy observed, devilry was associated with laughter, with a Homeric chuckle.[37]

Neither did the Russian tradition permit closeness to the sacral realm of the sort we can observe in Catholic religious art. In Catholic popular prints of the 17th to 20th centuries we can often see the depiction of a person genuflecting in prayer with a request to the Virgin Mary or some saint: that is, the worshipper would be praying before an image on which he or she would be represented. The depiction of a person was like a 'semiotic frame' for the depiction of Christ, the Mother of God or a saint. In this instance, too, it was nothing other than a space within which a distant God and Eros were united (illus. 200). In popular Catholic devotion this motif of bringing the sacral and the worldly together could easily be combined with a mixing of the serious and the humorous. This happens, for example, in popular 19th-century icons from the Banat (in Romania) with etched patterns and paintings on the background of, literally, a mirror. Ordinary people spoke of 'looking into plates'.[38] In such an icon the worshipper could behold him or herself as well as all the surroundings. This 'real world' could invade the prayer image thanks to the special, neutralizing function of laughter in popular Catholic religiosity. For that reason the Western popular picture was linked with both ecclesiastical and carnival culture simultaneously.

For a Russian, by contrast, the conviction that the saints represented on icons would provide prayerful intercession was always sufficient. Incidentally, both the subjects of the icons themselves and the subjects of the religious *lubok* prints reminded people of the necessary distance between themselves and the sacral sphere (see illus. 201). A person would also be reminded of this distancing by the modest place of his or her name saint on a domestic prayer icon – a place on the margin, the periphery, removed from the sacral centre. Hence saints alone could act as a 'semiotic frame' for the Deity, emphasizing the medieval distance between God and the world. The strength of the Russian peasant icon's opposition to the 'laughter–world' and 'playful impulse' is specially indicative if we also take into account that the Russian spiritual *lubok*, actively affecting the icon's artistic system, was of West Russian and Ukrainian origin and was clearly linked with the Catholic tradition. From the latter it might borrow certain iconographic motifs, formal devices and even texts, but not any confusion of the sacral and the worldly.

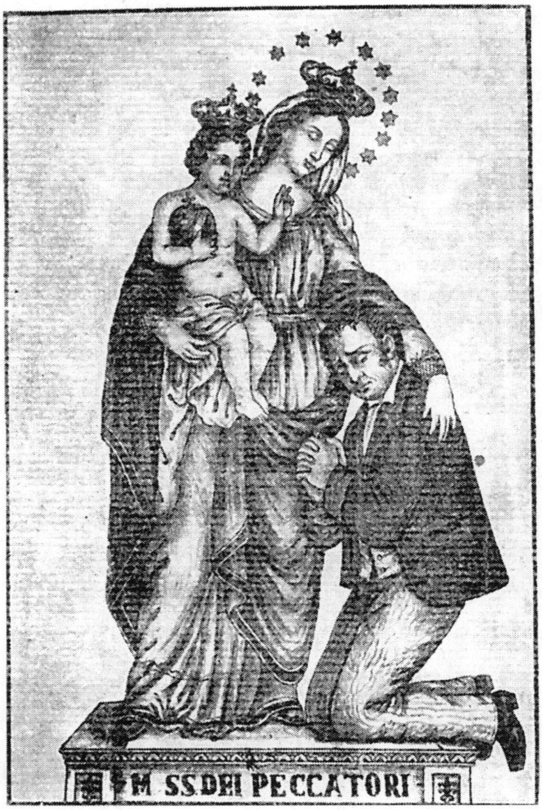

200. *Madonna dei Peccatori (Madonna of Sinners)*, end of the 19th century or early 20th, print from southern Italy.

This closed-off quality of the sacral sphere of the Russian peasant icon is also confirmed by Yuriy Lotman's observation that 'the sharp distinction within the bounds of traditional Orthodox culture between the "playful" sphere of folk art and the serious–solemn area of religion put the Russian popular *lubok* and the icon in distributive opposition within the artistic milieu of Great Russian popular culture, which distinguished it from the Catholic tradition that permitted the fusion of playfulness and religious observance'.[39]

The physical location of the religious and secular *lubok* within the peasants' domestic shrine (the 'fine corner') also relates to the same quality of separateness. As Dimitrij Rovinsky wrote, 'Pictures with spiritual content were mostly stuck up in peasant houses around the walls, following on from the icons, and to some extent supplemented the normal peasant

201. Mother of God 'Unexpected Joy', scene from the four-part icon *Mother of God the Unexpected Joy. Feodorovskaya Mother of God. Nicholas the Wonder-worker and SS Kirik and Ulita*, 19th century. Private collection, Moscow.

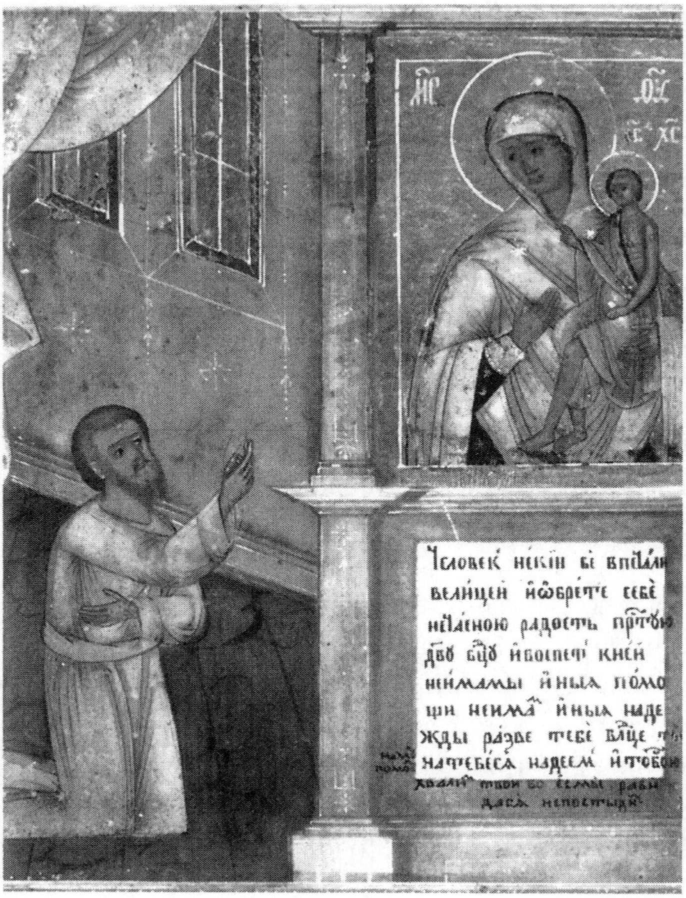

iconostasis.'[40] Secular *lubok* prints, however, were clearly not confused with them: we can judge this from V. P. Bezobrazov's description of the *lubok* collection of the Mstyora coaching inn, consisting exclusively of 'representations of members of the Russian ruling house, various allegories of the torments visited on those guilty of various sins, odd and unusual foreign satires on feminine weaknesses', etc.[41] There were no images of saints among them: they had their own special place.

The removal in the 1920s of the opposition between 'sacral' and 'worldly' in avant-garde and agitprop art presupposed a *change of icons*. In the sign system of the avant-garde the religious symbol lost its mystic content: the sign turned in on itself. Sergey Averintsev gives a precise and capacious elucidation of the resulting structure. Within it the symbol is

> symbolic in an overemphasized, studied way. It carries the sign of its own semiotic quality. It signifies not only what it signifies, but something more besides, namely the idea that has been instilled into the person deciphering the symbol that everything in the world is symbolic. Thus a redoubled 'sign-formation' – paradoxically combining the excesses of abstract schematicism and solid, impenetrable materiality – is cultivated as an independent aesthetic value. From the point of view of the aesthetic norms of the previous century this is reprehensible, from the point of view of the aesthetics of the so–called 20th century avant-garde, on the contrary, it is particularly 'interesting' – however in each case the evaluation really characterizes the person making it.[42]

Unlike the 18th-century popular *lubok* described earlier, the 'saint's Life' iconic composition of Lebedev's agitational *lubok* 'Uncle Prov' is filled with serious rather than humorous content (illus. 199). The sacral scheme is used to introduce Revolutionary ideology into the collective consciousness. For this purpose the deep aesthetic presuppositions of popular devotion, a complex fusion of pagan and Christian elements, were deliberately activated. The *lubok* tells a diverting story about a representative of the 'old world' – a village kulak and moneylender. An opposition of sin and virtue embellishes the edificatory logic of the tale. Among the virtues is one of the most important features of the Socialist utopia – that of physical labour, sanctified, according to the *lubok* text, by the cult of Mother Earth. The sin of wealth and cupidity, personified in Uncle Prov, is 'punished' when 'hard working Mother Earth did not accept him into the fields'. In this purposeful appeal to archetypal ways of thinking, the aesthetic of popular sensibility is welded to a religious tradition that immediately brings to mind unbidden both the connection of the cult of the Mother of God with that of Mother Earth, and also the high value placed on poverty in the Russian 'spiritual verses', which G. Fedotov has discussed.

The removal of the 'sacral/worldly' ('serious/humorous') dichotomy was put on the level of ideology and aesthetics by the new leftist art. Discussing two routes to 'perfection' (that of the Church and that of technical progress, embodied in 'the factory'),Malevich wrote in 1922:

> Both in the superficial and the deeper sense we have identical phenomena in ritualized order, a worshipful attitude, veneration, faith, hope for the future. As the Church has its leaders, has people who depict perfected religious systems, so does the factory training establishment depict its own: the former and the latter both respect and honour their own people. Thus the walls of both are embellished with countenances and portraits by merit and by rank; both in the first and the second there are martyrs or heroes whose names are deemed holy. Thus there is no difference between them.[43]

In the social–aesthetic utopia of Suprematism a nihilistic logic was foregrounded, finding its expression in the icon of the time, the *Black Square*.[44] In the architecture of the new aesthetic thinking, features of authoritarian philosophy clearly came to the fore. Mechanical rationalism, primitive 'educationalism', prophetic pretensions and Nietzscheanism coalesced and poured forth into a rather ponderous form of myth creation, directed against the old culture. The profound connection of the latter with the icon, which had been discovered on the wave of religious rebirth and nationalistic emotions on the eve of the Revolution, determined the fact that the ideology of the *Black Square* was directed against it. 'The icon', wrote Malevich in 1921, 'is preserved in the attic of the skull of the anti-modernists, who now wish to marry it off to contemporaneity, with a dowry of gold and silver garments, stitched by priests. In the garment of a new meaning, one that is not religious (for the bridegroom has gone beyond religions) it is already dying off for the same reason of new meaning.'[45]

In the context of the new myth this inversion of the icon, as a result of which it appears in the 'garment of new meaning' implied on the surface a confirmation of Nietzschean 'nothingness' and the disappearance of the very horizon of meaning. All existence and phenomena together were declared insignificant and without value – thus it is Nothing, 'no longer having a need for God, or God for it'.[46] All this nihilistic logic naturally led the Suprematists to the denial of all forms of God: 'Thus in the end all human meanings leading to the meaning "God" are crowned with meaninglessness, whence God is not meaning, but non-meaning. His meaninglessness must also be viewed at the absolute, final limit as non-objectivity.'[47]

Much of what could be put down to the effects of an over-activated and playful mentality among the avant-garde was on an ontological level quite consciously and rather tragically akin to the costs of the collective experiment. Belief in ritual, hyper-sacralization of the 'earthly' through the visual images of the faith, religious intolerance and antagonism, attraction to salvation by passive routes, and finally the downgraded function of laughter – all this was to be found in the 'Great Time' of the history of Russian consciousness and religious sensibility, and could not help being activated when cultural codes were suddenly relaxed.

I noted earlier that the 17th-century Schism showed seriously for the first time that mythological models like 'The Third Rome' could drop down to the bottom of mass consciousness and equally easily, and quite quickly, become agitated and swim up to the surface. This agitation led to a state in which the mental opposition *icon–world* acquired additional ossification and hardness, with an inner tension. The ordinary consciousness lost at an appropriate historical stage its intermediate, mediating links that guaranteed its equilibrium and protected it from the well-known Russian 'unsteadiness'. Centuries of aestheticization of the Russian world through icons was far from sufficient to preserve this world from quickly losing its cultural configuration and beginning to build anew, diving straight into new collective myths.

The pressing wish to 'aestheticize' the world in the hope of acquiring from reality something special, hyper-real, of artistic status was evidently fated to stay fixed for centuries, so as paradoxically to discover itself in Malevich's artistic movement UNOVIS ('Confirmers of New Art') in its activity of 1919–23. The signs of Suprematism, intended, as the new ideologues said, for the 'transformation in nature' of humanity and the surrounding world, were summoned to give reality the status of a 'deified' (in the inverted sense) condition, the status of being above reality; they were called to make life art. With this intention, Suprematism began to be used as a new adornment of old buildings and objects: its compositions decorated revolutionary anniversary and agitational celebrations, the signs on shops, various types of public transport and food cards. The creation of a 'new utilitarian world of things' – Suprematist architecture, crockery, clothing, etc. – went forward under the banner 'May the overthrow of the old world of art be scored across our hands. Carry the black square as the sign of world economy.' The black square (as the basic 'icon' of UNOVIS) was sewn onto the sleeves of members of the organization. In brief, the cultural space was being informed of a new 'burden of quantity' of new 'icons'. A new world was being created. But as far as the destruction of the old cultural world went, we can note the already familiar superpostition of symbols and their ambivalence.

In a well-known agitational *lubok* by A. Kulikov, 'The Devil Stops Joking When God Sleeps' (illus. 202), we find use of the same two-part Old Ritualist picture icons that I discussed in connection with the ambivalence of Old and New Ritualist symbols (illus. 39, 40), and one of which was exhibited at the Target exhibition under the title 'Difference between the Churches'.[48] Using the formula of the mirror and its true and false images, Kulikov juxtaposed two worlds: one 'old' and 'graceless', over which the Devil makes mock; the other a Communist paradise sanctified by the Lord Sabaoth. Before us we see the typical ideologized function of the popular picture icon, whose ambivalent sacred symbols have been transferred to the plane of confirming the new objects of belief. From one angle, the artist is altering the 'sphere of laughter' of the *lubok*, projecting it onto politics and a new myth. Laughter has lost the naturalness of the 'world upside-down' and has become politically sharper, appropriate only when directed towards 'enemies of the people' and 'old culture', whose value it has put into doubt. From the other angle, the sacral formula 'the true/the false', with its traditionally downgraded function of laughter and religious aesthetic, so close to popular devotion, has been communicated to popular consciousness (compare illus. 203 and 204).

As a result the new myth, far from unexpectedly, received a heightened sacral status, while portraits of the new charismatic leaders replaced icons in the 'fine corner' of a room.[49] Quite soon after 1917, the everyday consciousness began to project this myth onto the traditional prayer icon. An icon in the storeroom of the Museum of the History of Religion in St Petersburg, by the Mstyora hereditary painter V. O. Mumrikov, reflects

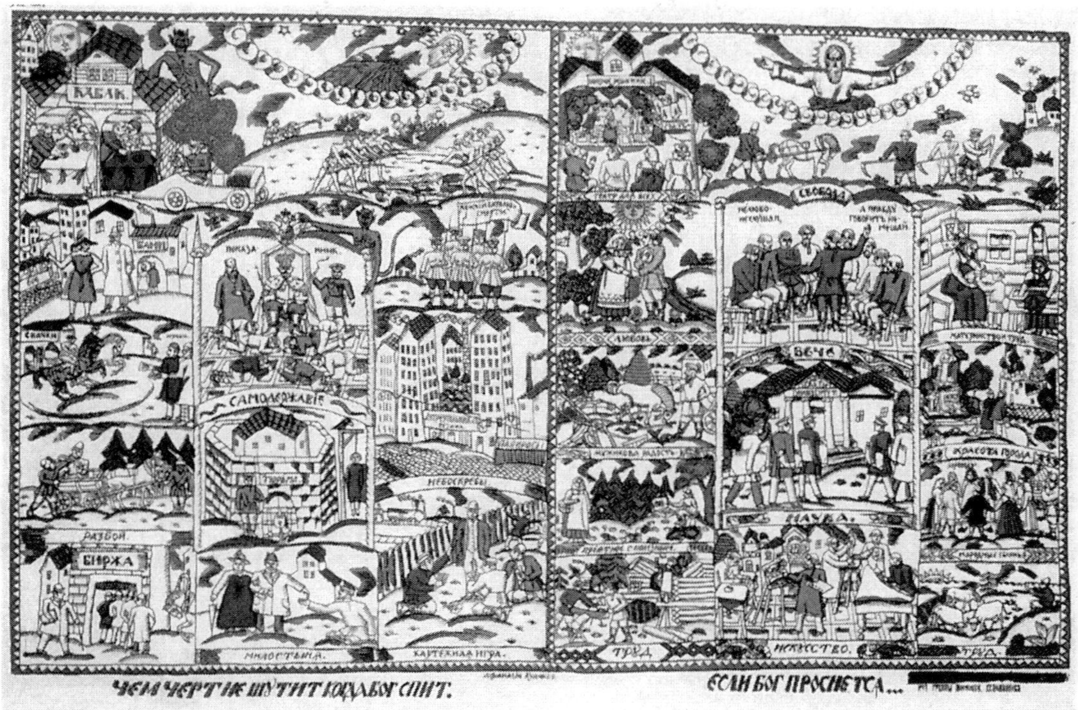

202. Afanasiy Kulikov, *The Devil Stops Joking When God Sleeps*, a *lubok* of 1917.

as if in a mirror the signs of the new ideology, that had reached the village craftsman's consciousness through leftist agitational art. In this context it is interesting to compare the icon with sketches for Suprematist frescoes that their creators intended to 'carry the load of the religious activity of the spirit and the whole utilitarian world of life'.[50] 'Labour will be the ruler of the world' – that was, for example, to be the title of one of the new Suprematist 'icons' made by A. Tseytlin to decorate a tram-car.[51] 'Who does not labour does not eat' was the slogan on the Suprematist tribune of UNOVIS, planned by N. M. Suyetin in 1921. Later, in 1927–9, Suyetin was to make a series of sketches and compositions under the title of 'Suprematist Icons', clearly reflecting the catastrophism of existence and the destruction of human personality, of any individuality: the new 'saints' are deprived of their 'faces', which are replaced by empty geometrical schemes (illus. 205). 'The Physical Labour of the Holy Family' was the title Mumrikov, in the spirit of the times, gave to his genuine prayer image (illus. 206). With its

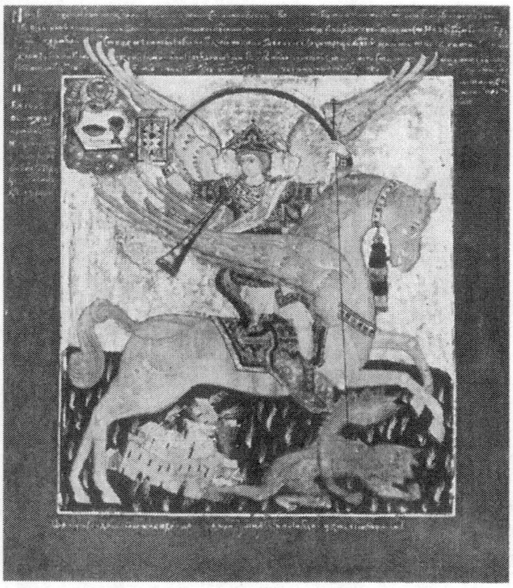

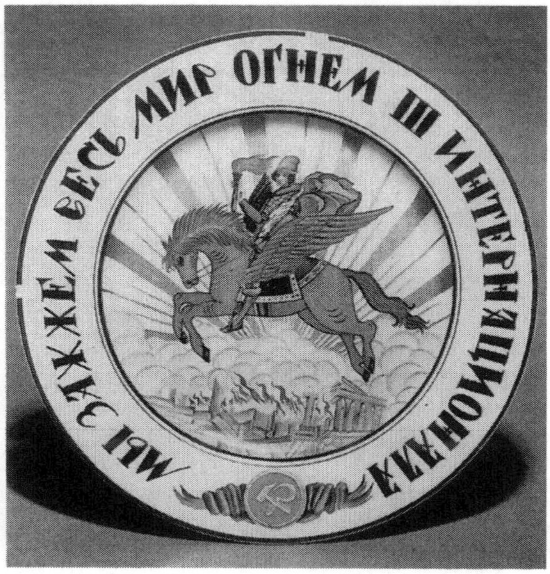

203. *Archangel Michael*, 17th century. State Tretyakov Gallery, Moscow, P. D. Korin's collection.

204. A. R. Golenkina., Agitprop plate: 'We Shall Ignite the Whole World with the Fire of the Third International', 1920. State Historical Museum, Moscow.

205. N. M. Suyetin, *Suprematist Icon*, 1929. Collection of Lev Nussberg, USA.

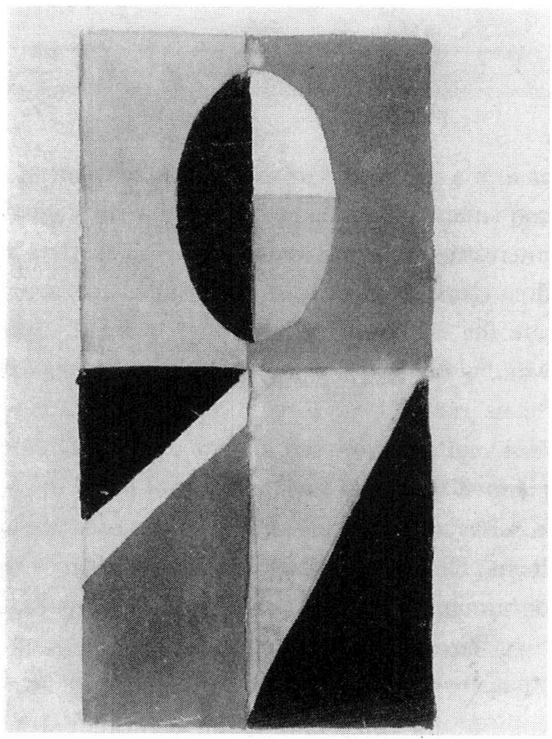

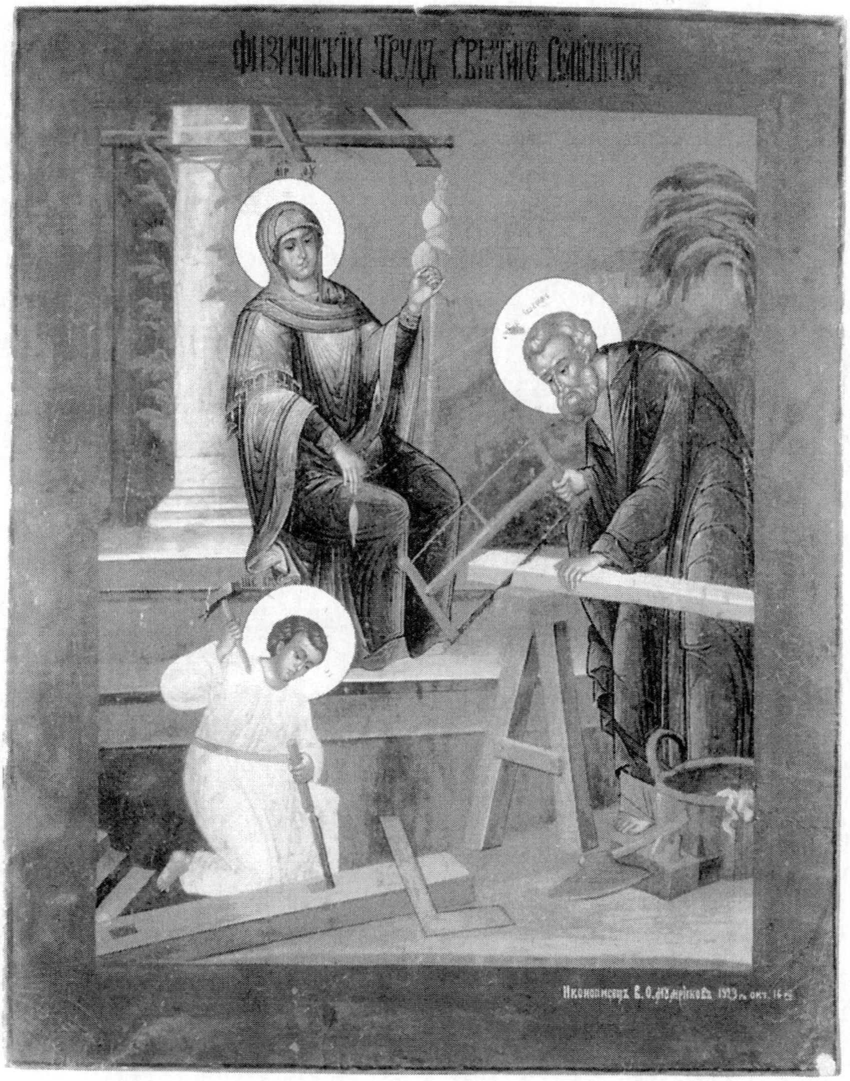

206. *The Physical Labour of the Holy Family*, 1923, Mstyora. State Museum of the History of Religion, St Petersburg.

new kind of title, the icon acquired a complex ideological content. In its countenance are symbolized the attributes of physical labour: the carpenter's tools of St Joseph – saw, set-square and work-bench, modelled by the painter on contemporary local tools. The hammer wielded by the Child Jesus is reminiscent of one of the chief signs of the new Socialist imperium: the heraldic symbol of hammer and sickle. The introduction of Socialist heraldry into the icon immediately gives it the panegyric function that the Russian Imperial crest once lent it at the very beginning of Russian absolutism.

No less interesting and unique is a small icon painted by an anonymous painter soon after the Revolutionary events in Moscow. It is a painted representation of the result of Revolutionary violence directed against the old culture, as its title indicates: 'Copy of the Icon of St Nicholas the Wonder–worker on the Nikolsky Gate of the Moscow Kremlin that suffered Bombardments on 31 October 1917 at the Time of the Revolution' (illus. 207).

In these two icons the signs of historical events are linked with the signs of mythic reality. With an evident internal connection between them, they tell us how a vacuum rather quickly formed in traditional popular culture – only to be equally quickly replenished with new constructs.

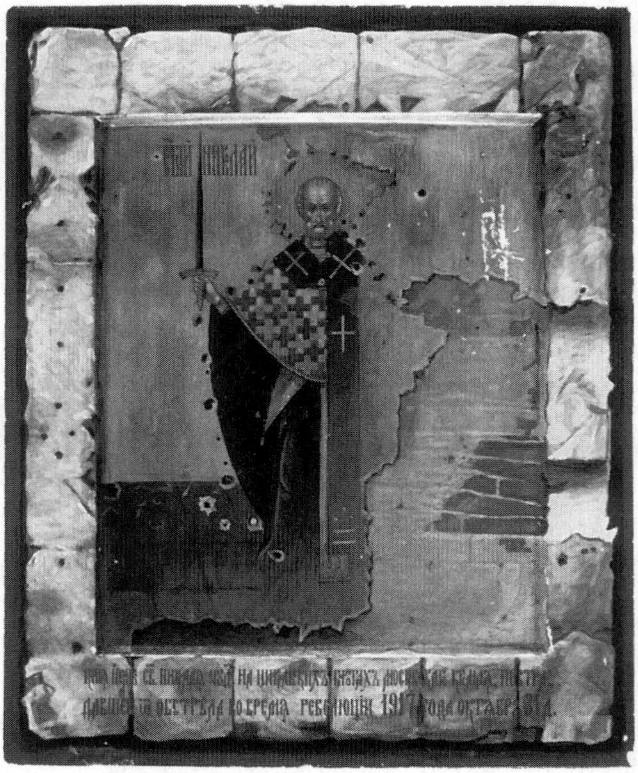

207. Copy of the icon *St Nicholas the Wonder-worker* on the Nikolskaya Tower of the Moscow Kremlin, damaged by Bombardment during the 1917 Revolution, after 1917, Moscow. State Museum of the History of Religion, St Petersburg.

References and Editorial Notes

All additional explanatory editorial notes are signed RM-G.

Abbreviations

BAN Biblioteka Akademii nauk, St Petersburg
DDZ Dnevnye dozornye zapisi o moskovskikh raskolnikakh, Soobshcheny A. A. Titovym. ChOIDR
GMMK Gosudarstvennye muzei Moskovskogo kremlya
GMPI Gosudarstvenniy muzey Palekhskogo iskusstva, pos. Palekh
GRM Gosudarstvenniy Russkiy muzey, St Petersburg
GTG Gosudarstvennaya Tretyakovskaya galereya, Moscow
IRLI Institut russkoy literatury (Pushkinskiy dom), RAN
MV *Moskovskiye vedomosti*
NB MGU Nauchnaya biblioteka im. Gorkogo MGU, Moscow
ODDS *Opisaniye dokumentov i del, khranyashchikhsya v arkhive Svyateyshego pravitelstvuyushchego Sinoda*, St Petersburg
OR Otdel rukopisey
ORKiR Otdel russkikh knig i rukopisey
PLDR Pamyatniki drevney pismennosti i iskusstva, St Petersburg
PSZ Polnoye sobraniye zakonov Rossiyskoy imperii, St Petersburg
PSPR Polnoye sobraniye postanovleniy i rasporyazheniy po vedomstvu pravoslavnogo ispovedaniya Rossiyskoy imperii, St Petersburg
RGB Rossiyskaya gosudarstvennaya biblioteka, Moscow
RM *Russkiy mir*, St Petersburg
SR Sektor rukopisey
VGV *Vladimirskiye gubernskiye vedomosti*, Vladimir
VOGA Vladimirskiy oblastnoy gosudarstvenniy arkhiv, Vladimir

ChOIDR Chteniya v Obshchestve istorii i drevnostey rossiyskikh pri Imp. Moskovskom universitete
MGU Moskovskiy gosudarstvenniy universitet
RAN Russkaya Akademiya nauk

Introduction

1 Kitzinger 1979; Maguire 1981; Dagron 1984; Cormack 1985, 1997; Belting 1994; *Sacred Image* 1995; *The Wonder-working Icon* 1996.
2 Florensky 1985; L. Uspensky 1989; Uspensky and Lossky 1952; Beck 1975; B. Uspensky 1976; Barasch 1992.
3 Acts 1873, p. 593.
4 John Damascene, 1913, pp. 356, 359.
5 Medlin 1952; Kartashev, 1956; Schaeder 1957; Zenkovsky 1970, etc.
6 PLDR, late 15th or early 16th century; 1984, p. 453.
7 Florovsky 1981, pp. 17, 20, 27–28.
8 L. Uspensky 1989, p. 239, and the English translation, L. Uspensky 1991; see also Fedotov 1991 (2), vol. I, p 318.
9 The craftsmen who painted these 'Suzdalian icons' were known as 'Suzdalian God-daubers'. 'Suzdalian sheets' were religious popular prints available from 'Suzdalian *ofeni*' (travelling salesmen).

Part One: The Icon and the World

Chapter One: Venerated Image: The Sacred in the Everyday

1 'Reverse perspective' has been much discussed by specialists in Byzantine and Old Russian art. It is still unclear how systematically or consciously it was employed. RM-G
2 Paul of Aleppo, part 2, p. 32.
3 PLDR, mid-16th century, 1985, p. 77.
4 Paul of Aleppo, part 2, p.150.
5 Paul of Aleppo, part 3, p. 31.
6 Zabelin 1862, pp. 193–4.
7 Florensky 1985.
8 See Walter 1993, pp. 203–24.
9 See Dagron 1984, p. 163.
10 OR GMMK, f. 20, item 5, p. 2.
11 N. Ya. Danilevsky (1822–85).
12 Nicols 1988, Tarasov 2001.
13 Bezobrazov 1861, p. 280.
14 Herberstein 1986, p. 77; Pernstein 1876, p. 5; Rushchinsky 1871, p. 71; Paul of Aleppo, part 2, pp. 109–10.
15 Hans the Dane, 1868, pp. 11–12.
16 Ibid.
17 Varkoch 1875, p. 33.
18 Olearius 1906, p. 324.
19 Maksimov, vol. I, 1907, p. 180.
20 Paul of Aleppo, book 2, p. 150.
21 Lotman, Uspensky 1982, p. 234.
22 Tolstoy 1991, p. 656.
23 Braudel, vol. I, 1986, p. 539.
24 Gilferding 1859, p. 16.
25 Kondakov 1900, p. 181.
26 Arkhangelsky 1885, pp. 48–50.
27 Mâle 1958, pp. 167–70.
28 Ariès 1992, p. 265.
29 Kämpfer 1993, p. 156.
30 Chadzidakis 1976, p. 13.
31 Kondakov 1911, p. 203.
32 See Cormack 1985, p. 124.
33 Ovchinnikova 1964, p. 33.
34 VOGA, f. 560, opus 1, item 108, pp. 43–52, 55–8, 61–2.
35 Chatzidakis 1966, p. 15.
36 Kobeko 1896, p. 3.
37 VGV 1881, no. 8.
38 Tikhonravov 1857, p. 28.
39 Leontyev 1903, p. 35.
40 Shtukenberg 1858, vol. I, p. 21; VGV 1854, no. 20.
41 Georgievsky 1895, March, p. 203; my italics.
42 I am grateful to Robin Milner-Gulland for drawing my attention to this example.
43 Lyadov 1876, pp. 22–3.
44 Braudel, vol. I, 1986, p. 60.
45 Maksimov 1860, p. 220.
46 VGV 1843, no. 21.
47 Toporov 1988, p. 17.
48 Bezobrazov 1861, p. 280.
49 Cited in Kirichenko 1992, p. 177.
50 Paul of Aleppo, part 2, pp. 163–4.
51 Paul of Aleppo, part 2, p. 160.
52 Paul of Aleppo, part 2, pp. 160–63.
53 Paul of Aleppo, part 2, pp. 109, 163–4.
54 Paul of Aleppo, part 2, pp. 96–7.
55 OR BAN, f. 67, item 32, p. 99 reverse.
56 St. John Damascene, 1913, p. 423.
57 Huizinga 1988, p. 210.
58 PLDR, mid-16th century, 1985, p.77.
59 After the mid-17th-century schism in the Russian Church, one part of the Old Believers continued to maintain a priesthood ('Priestists'), while the remainder (the 'Priestless') – probably the majority – maintained that with the apostasy of the bishops no more priests could be ordained. RM-G
60 Pavel 1885, p. 66.
61 OR BAN, F.A. Kalikin, no. 85, p. 12 reverse.52.
62 Juel 1900, p. 227.
63 Paul of Aleppo, part 2, pp. 101, 103.
64 Paul of Aleppo, part 2, p 188.
65 Paul of Aleppo, part 2, p. 101
66 Pernstein 1876, p. 8.
67 Cf. Kirichenko 1992, p. 177.
68 Paul of Aleppo, part 3, pp. 4–5.
69 Juel 1900, p. 87.
70 Paul of Aleppo, part 2, p. 150.
71 Olearius 1906, p. 326.
72 Paul of Aleppo part 2, p. 174.
73 Bolshakov 1903, p. 22.
74 Herberstein 1986, p. 77.
75 Pernstein 1876, p. 5.
76 De Bruyn 1873, p. 69.
77 Paul of Aleppo, part 2, p. 109.
78 Melnikov 1986, p. 460.
79 Collins 1846, p. 9.
80 Paul of Aleppo, Part 2, p. 164.
81 PLDR, mid-16th century, 1985, p. 77.
82 PSPR, 2nd series, vol. II, 1907, no. 619, pp. 98–9.
83 Bryanchaninov 1865, p. 59.
84 Filaret, 1903, vol. I, pp. 488–9.
85 'Trinity Page', Sergiev Posad, 1890, no. 263: 'The particular grace of the Mother of God'.
86 Acts 1873, pp. 44–5.
87 De Bruyn 1873.

88 Hans the Dane, 1868, p. 34.
89 Cf. N. Patterson Ševcenko 1995.
90 Majeska 1984, pp. 36–7, 138–9, 362–6.
91 Maksimov, vol. I, 1907, pp. 15–16.
92 Filaret 1903, vol. II, part 2, no. 3280, p. 186.
93 Grammatin 1893, p. 194.
94 *Stoglav* 1985, pp. 351–2; see also the French translation: M Duchêsne 1920.
95 Filaret 1903, vol. II, part 1, p. 169.
96 Walter 1982, pp. 79–80.
97 See Fedotov 1990, pp. 39–51; Toporov 1987, pp. 221, 243–4; Averintsev 1988, no. 9, pp. 232, 234; see also a comparison of such martydom with the Jesuits' 'third state of humility': Kologrivov 1961, p. 26.
98 'Spiritual poetry' or 'verses' (*dukhovnye stikhi*) are an early genre of Russian anonymous poetry on religious – often apocryphal and folk-coloured – themes. RM-G
99 Fedotov 1991, pp. 80–81.
100 Cf. Toporov 1987, pp. 188, 246.
101 Elders' advice 1913, pp. 343, 613–4, 499, 229, 224, 253.
102 ORKiR NB MGU, Vetko – Starodubskoye sobraniye, sb. S.F. Mokhovikova, pp. 5 reverse – 6 reverse.
103 Paul of Aleppo, part 2, p. 114.
104 Mikhalsky 1989, p. 273.
105 Trubetskoy 1965, p. 54.
106 Maksimov, vol. I, 1907, p. 180.
107 Filaret 1903, vol. II, part 3, pp. 198–9.
108 Filaret 1903, vol. I, pp. 575–6.
109 Filaret 1903, vol. II, part 2, p. 28.
110 Filaret 1903, vol. II, part 2, p. 153.
111 A 17th-century trading town, close to the Arctic Circle on the Ob-Taz estuary, relocated after a fire to Turukhansk. RM-G
112 Golubinksky 1903, p. 462.
113 Sosnin 1833,p. 4; compare VGV, 1841, no. 25, 'On wonder-working icons of the Mother of God in the province'.
114 Sosnin 1833, pp. 66, 65, 13, 4.
115 'Pokrov'(no Western equivalent, though sometimes 'Intercession' is used): a feast and church dedication to the Protecting Veil of the Mother of God, which made a miraculous appearance in 9th-century Constantinople. RM-G
116 Florensky 1985, p 228.
117 Dagron 1996, p. 29.
118 Cf. Lotman 1976, p. 249.
119 Merezhkovsky 1914, p. 48.
120 Cf. F. Poulsen, 'Talking, Weeping, and Bleeding Sculptures: A Chapter of the History of Religous Fraud', *Acta Archaeologica*, XVI (1945), pp. 178–95.
121 ODDS, vol. II, part 2, no. 1031.
122 PSZ, vol. 5, no 2985.
123 Georgievsky 1908, p. 10.
124 Cf. Snessoreva 1891, pp. 321, 296, 415, 235; Poselyanin 1909, pp. 442, 410–14, 558–61, 280.
125 ODDS, vol. II, part 2, no. 1031, p. 309.
126 OR RGB, f. 17, Ye. V. Barsov no. 17. Icon pattern-book, late-18th- or early-19th century, pp. 201–2.
127 Rovinsky 1881–93, Atlas, part 1, preface.
128 Cited in Fedotov 1991, p. 129.
129 OR RGB, f. 17, no 711, icon painting pattern-book, late-18th or early-19th century, pp. 201–2 reverse).
130 Olearius 1906, p. 318.
131 Rushchinsky 1871, p. 79.
132 Mikhalsky 1989, pp. 274–5.
133 Uspensky 1985, p. 328.
134 Freedberg 1991, pp. 378–428.
135 The reference of the title *Skrizhal* is to the 'tables' (or 'tablets') received by Moses on Mt Sinai (Exodus 31:18). The ambitious *Skrizhal*, largely based on a 16th-century Greek text by Ioannes Nathaniel (itself a compendium), spelled out in detail the hierarchical relations within the Church, and between Church and people, that Nikon sought to introduce to Russia. RM-G
136 I. M. Sirot, *Russian Proverbs Deriving from the Bible* (Brussels, 1985), p. 25.
137 Filaret 1903, vol. II, part 3, pp. 28–9.
138 Filaret 1903, vol. II, part 1, pp. 186–7.
139 Hesychasm (literally 'quietism'): a mystical–contemplative doctrine, formulated in the 14th century (and still characteristic of Orthodoxy), whereby an individual, through repeated inner prayer and other disciplines, might attain to apprehension of the Divine Energy. RM-G
140 OR RGB, f. 17, no. 629. S. Denisov Vinograd Rossiysky pp. 2, 3, 4, 5; cf. Bychkov 1992, pp. 407–16.
141 Poselyanin 1905, p. 129.
142 Adaryukov 1921, p. 14.
143 See ODDS, vol. II, part 2, 1878, appendix XI, p. xi.

Chapter Two: Dispute about Signs, Dispute about Faith

1 Hagar, mother of Ishmael (Genesis 16), was considered by medieval Christians as progenitor of the Islamic peoples. RM-G
2 Filofey was the author of a famous missive to Grand Prince Vasiliy III and Tsar Ivan IV. See also p. 27.
3 *Stoglav* 1985, pp. 268, 314.
4 Averintsev 1985, p. 299.
5 An influential Byzantine mystical writer (*c.* AD 500), whose works purported to be by Dionysius the Areopagite, follower of St Paul (Acts 17:34). RM-G
6 OR RGB, f. 17, Ye. V. Barsov, no. 28.
7 See on this subject N. Patterson-Sevcenko 1991, pp. 45–7.
8 OR RGB, f. 17, no. 629, pp. 14 – reverse – 15.
9 OR BAN, f. 67, item 49, p. 51.
10 *Pustozyorkskaya proza* 1989, p. 102.
11 Pomorye: the territory in the vicinity of the White Sea, an Old Believer stronghold: hence *Pomortsy*, 'shore-dwellers'. RM-G
12 OR BAN, f. 67, no. 175, reverse – 172, 223–5.
13 OR BAN, f. 67, no. 175, p. 224.
14 OR BAN, f. 67, no. 175, p. 31 reverse: cf. Barskov 1912, pp. 12–27.
15 OR RGB, f. 344, item 34, pp. 101 – reverse 102.
16 Yakovlev 1888, no. 7, pp. 477–8.
17 RM 1873, no. 211, p. 1.
18 Constantine V 'Copronymos' (i.e., 'Shit-named', supposedly from a regrettable incident at his baptism), Byzantine emperor, 741–75. RM-G
19 OR BAN, f. F.A. Kalinkin, no. 85, 19.
20 OR BAN f. 67, no. 92, p. 64.
21 Juel 1900, p. 72.
22 ODDS, vol. II, part 2, no. 1015, p. 285.
23 RGB, f. 310, no. 338.
24 Filaret 1836, p. 325.
25 Cited from Kartashev 1959, vol. II, p. 152.
26 L. Uspensky 1989, p. 285.
27 Ovchinnikova 1964, pp. 45,
28 Ovchinnikova 1964, p. 25.
29 Cited from Damascene 1913, p. 422; see also p. 383.
30 Paul of Aleppo, part 3, pp. 136–7.
31 Ovchinnikova 1964, p. 56, pp. 25–6.
32 Ovchinnikova 1964, p. 34, see too pp. 36–7.
33 Ovchinnikova 1964, pp. 40–41.
34 Zabelin 1850, pp. 83–5.
35 Bylinin 1985, pp. 288–9.
36 Rostovsky 1855, pp. 13, 9, XIII.
37 Filaret 1836, pp. 322–3.
38 OR RGB f. 17, item 117, p. 175.

Chapter Three: In a World without Grace

1 Solovyov 1966, pp. 251-2.
2 On the 'beatification' of Alexander I after the victory of 1812 against the French, see M. Cherniavsky, *Tsar and People* (New Haven, CT, 1961), chap. 5. RM-G
3 OR GMMK, f. 3, item 5, p. 23.
4 Cf. Zhivov, Uspensky 1984, pp. 219–20.
5 DDZ, ChOIDR, 1885, vol. III, part, p. 54; 1886, vol. I, part V, pp. 133-4.
6 Sinitsyn 1896, p. 21.
7 Cf. Stewart, 1991.
8 Barskov 1912, p. 22.
9 Fedotov 1991, p. 33.
10 DDZ, ChOIDR 1886, book I, part V, p.125.
11 Lotman, Uspensky 1982, p. 242.
12 Rovinsky 1881–1893, Atlas, part I, no. 167.
13 Agreement was reached at Brest-Litovsk between representatives of the Roman Catholic and Orthodox hierarchies of the Polish-Lithuanian Commonwealth to end the Great Schism between the Churches (under the general control of the papacy). It was not accepted by most of the Orthodox laity, and led to the foundation of the so-called 'Uniate' Church. RM-G
14 Smirnov 1909, pp. 163, 165–6, 173–4; see also Irodionov 1890, p. 10.
15 Cf. DDZ, ChOIDR, 1885, vol. III, part V, p. 54.
16 Yakovlev 1888, no. 7, pp. 476–7.
17 Damascene 1913, p. 399.
18 See, for example, OR RGB, f.17, no. 324, p. 41 reverse.
19 *Stoglav* 1985, p. 304.
20 Cf. B. Uspensky, 1976.
21 Rushchinsky 1871, pp. 44–5.
22 Postnikov 1890, p. 22, no 392.
23 Pernstein 1876, p. 3.
24 Pavel 1885, pp. 67–8.
25 Yatsimirsky 1907, pp. 527–8.
26 Derzhavina 1965, p. 104.

27 OR RGB, f. 17, item 117, 1, p. 166.
28 ORKiR NB MGU, Vetk – starodub. collection, individual item 579, p. 2.
29 Sinitsyn 1895, p. 151.
30 Pavel 1885, p. 70.
31 Sapozhnikov 1891, pp. 34–7.
32 Centred on the southern shore of the White Sea. RM-G
33 OR RGB, f. 17, Ye. V. Barsov, no. 343, pp. 36 reverse–38.
34 Pavel 1885, pp. 61, 49.
35 see OR RGB, f. 17, no. 343, pp. 2–42 reverse.
36 *Pustozyorskaya proza* 1989, pp. 252, 254.
37 Barskov 1912, pp. 58–9.
38 MV 1873, no. 169, p. 3.
39 RM 1873, no.192. N. Leskov 'Hellishly-drawn Icons', pp. 1–2.
40 Smirnov 1909, addendum pp. 079–080, second pagination.
41 ORKiR NB MGU, Vetk.-Starodub. sobr., S. F. Mokhovikov collection, pp. 13–18.
42 Porfiriy 1868; see also P. Hetherington, 1974.
43 Restle 1967, p. 193.
44 For more detail, see Peterson 1971, pp. 30–34.
45 Porfiriy 1868, pp. v–vi.
46 OR RGB, f. 17, item 711, p. 197.
47 *Stoglav* 1985, pp. 314–15.
48 Bolshakov 1903, p. 3.
49 Basil the Great 1898, p. 258.
50 OR BAN, f. 67, item 92, p. 45; Grigoriy Yakovlev informs us that many teachers and priors in Priestless communities were simultaneously icon painters: Yakovlev 1888, no. 7, p. 476.
51 OR BAN, f. 67, item 92, pp. 20 and 20 reverse.
52 OR BAN, f. 67, item 92, pp. 20–22 reverse.
53 DDZ, ChOIDR, 1886, book 1, part 5, p. 122.
54 Paul of Aleppo, book 2, p. 160.
55 Expanded holy days: Fedotov 1991, p. 86; for decrees of the 'Priestless' councils: OR BAN, f. 678, item 92, p. 48 reverse.
56 Smirnov 1991, p.167.
57 OR BAN f. 67, item 32, pp. 482[reverse]–483.
58 Bolshakov 1903, pp. 22–23.
59 OR BAN, f. 67, item 92, pp. 21–21 reverse.
60 Bolshakov 1903, p. 3.
61 Ibid.
62 See, for example, Le Goff 1992, p. 261.
63 OR RGB, p. 17, item 711. Icon painting copy-book, p. 1 reverse.
64 Paterik 1702, pp. 159–65.
65 OR RGB, f. 17, item 711, p. 2 reverse, p. 179 reverse.
66 Damascene 1913, p. 401.
67 Bolshakov 1903, p. 17.
68 Zernov 1991, p. 60.
69 Morev 1904, pp. 189–285.
70 PSPR vol. II, 1872, no. 516, pp. 163–4; no. 625, pp. 293–5.
71 PSPR, vol. II, 1872, n. 625, pp. 294–5.
72 OR RGB, f. 17, item 117.11, p. 163 reverse.
73 ORKiR NB MGU. Vetk.-Starodub. Collection, compendium of S. F. Mokhovikov, pp. 3–3 reverse.
74 OR RGB f. 17, no. 117.11, p. 1163 reverse.
75 OR RGB f. 342, item 132, p.74 reverse.
76 OR RGB f. 342, item 132, p. 74 reverse.
77 Cf. Fedotov 1991, p. 53.
78 Bolshakov 1903, pp. 2–3.
79 OR RGB, f. 17, item 117.11, p. 163 reverse.
80 Cited from Uspensky 1989, p. 299.
81 OR RGB f. 17, item 117.11, pp. 164–5 reverse.
82 OR RGB, f. 342, item 132, p. 74 reverse.
83 OR IRLI, f. F. A. Kalikin no. 93, p. 6.
84 ORKiR NB MGU, Vetk.-Starodub. Collection, item no. 580. Ya. S. Kazakov, 'The congress in the village of Gorodets at which a decision was made about the icon of the Lord Sabaoth and Tokarev's error exposed' (pp. 1–2 reverse).
85 See Pustozyorskaya proza 1989, p. 252.
86 OR RGB, f. 17, item 117.11, pp. 170[reverse]–71.
87 Malyshev 1965, p. 334.
88 OR RGB, f. 17, item 397, p. 1 reverse.
89 OR BAN, f. 67, item 49, p. 88 reverse.
90 OR BAN, f. 67, item 49, pp. 91, 92, 93 reverse, 94.
91 Itkina, RRL 1992, cat. no. 88.
92 Mâle 1952, pp. 109–49; ills. 62–3, 65–72.

Part Two: The Icon and Popular Culture

1 P. Florensky *The Iconostasis* (Moscow, 1994), p. 71.
2 Grabar IRI vol. VI, 1914, p. 28.

3 Bogatyryov 1971, pp. 24, 376.
4 Vipper 1939, pp. 8–9.
5 Lotman 1976; Tananayeva 1979; Prokofyev 1983; Sofronova 1983.
6 Bogatyryov 1971, p. 377.
7 For 'vernacular', Białostocki 1976; for 'popular Mannerism', T. Dobrovolsky.
8 Hauser 1976.
9 Shearman 1970, pp. 215–16.
10 Golyshev 1886, p. 1.
11 Forssman 1956, pp. 7–30.
12 Vipper 1978, p. 20.

Chapter Four: East and West

1 Bezobrazov 1861, p. 308.
2 Ostrovsky 1987, p. 73.
3 Dvorzhak 1979, vol. II, p. 95.
4 Shearman 1970, p. 211.
5 Mâle 1958, pp. 167–98.
6 See, for example, Sarabyanov 1993, p. 245.
7 Kondakov 1901, p. 42.
8 Białostocki 1982, ill. 132.
9 Cf. Mâle 1958. pp. 185–6.
10 See Kondakov 1911, pp. 18–19.
11 Zeri 1957 p. 61.
12 On visionary experience in Western art in that period, see Victor I. Stoichita, *Visionary Experience in the Golden Age of Spanish Art* (London, 1995).
13 Cf. Huyghe 1960, pp. 190–93.
14 The Armoury Palace artists comprised a 17th-century royal painting workshop in the Moscow Kremlin. RM-G
15 Chadzidakis 1976 p. 15.
16 Florensky 1971, p. 524.
17 VGV 1843, no. 21.
18 There is a challenge for the translator here. *Litso* is the standard Russian word for 'face'. Its high-style or archaic variant, *lik*, implying the stylized representation of a face, has been translated as 'countenance'. A third related word, *oblichenie*, is rendered 'visage'. RM-G
19 See RZh, 1977, p. 96.
20 Rovinsky 1881–93, Atlas, part 1, no. 3.
21 Rovinsky 1900, p. 23, ill. 32.
22 Le Goff 1991, pp. 28–30, 36–44.
23 I.e., 'Greek manner', the Italian late-medieval painting style, imitative of Byzantine art, that was despised by Giorgio Vasari (1511–74), proponent of the Renaissance. RM-G
24 Garen 1986, p. 34.
25 Buslayev 1908, vol. 1, p. 23.
26 Filimonov 1875, p. 37.
27 Buslayev, vol. 1, 1908, p. 23.
28 Ovchinnikova 1964, p. 31.
29 Sofronova 1994.
30 Lotman 1992 (2), vol. 1, p. 192.
31 IE, vol. 1, p. 457.
32 Barsukov etc. 1987, p. 89.
33 A monastic complex near modern Istra (40 miles west of Moscow), founded by Tsar Aleksey and Patriarch Nikon in 1656. The main church was modelled on the Holy Sepulchre, Jerusalem, and the landscape features were given Palestinian names. RM-G
34 Mâle 1958, p. 184.
35 See Pearsall & Salter 1973.
36 Dvorzhak 1978, vol II, p. 184.
37 Bakhtin 1990, p. 136.
38 See Denisov 1908, p. 148.
39 Denisov 1908, p. 832.
40 Dmitrievsky 1890, pp. 112–13.
41 Zhirmunsky 1914, p. 36.
42 Georgievsky 1895, March, p. 194.
43 In Clark's classification and terminology: Clark 1976, p. 109.
44 Likhachov 1982, p. 158.
45 See H. Maguire *Art and Eloquence in Byzantium* (Princeton, NJ, 1981), pp. 9–21.
46 See Lotman and B. Uspensky 1970, pp. 144–66.
47 Toporov 1979, p. 116.
48 Höpel 1987, pp. 11–29.
49 Sazonova 1991, p. 37.
50 Dimitriy Ivanovich, youngest son of Ivan IV, died in 1591 (aged nine) in mysterious circumstances; regarded subsequently as a martyr. RM-G
51 On this, see Jacques Derrida *The Truth in Painting* (Chicago and London, 1987), pp. 185–254; P. Duro, ed., *The Rhetoric of the Frame: Essays on the Boundary of the Artwork* (Cambridge, 1996).
52 Benua 1912, unnumbered ill.
53 Ernst Gombrich, 'Icones Symbolicae: Philosophies of Symbolism and their Bearing on Art',in Gombrich's *On the Renaissance, II: Symbolic Images* (London, 1985), p. 142.
54 Białostocki 1982, p. 28.
55 see E. A. Maser, *Cesare Ripa, Baroque and Rococo Pictorial Imagery* (New York, 1971).
56 Cf. Sazonova 1991, pp. 87–8.
57 Rovinsky 1900, p. 305.
58 Chernigov 1666; Rovinsky 1900, p. 15,

ill. 23.
59 VI, 1989, ill. p. 65.
60 OR IRLI, f. 4, F.A. Kalikin, item 19, pp.1–12 reverse.
61 Grabar 1968.
62 Damascene 1913, pp. 365–6; see also Acts of the Ecumenical Councils, 1873, p. 297.
63 Anatoliy 1845, pp. 46–7.
64 Vacková 1969, ills. 1, 3, 11, 15, 17.
65 Grabar, vol. VI, 1914, p. 464.
66 Kämpfer 1978, pp. 167–263.
67 Skrine 1978, p. 91.
68 Sarabyanov 1993, pp. 265–6.
69 Filimonov 1876, p. 37; see, too, Antonova and Mnyova, GTG 1963, vol. II, cat 920, ill. 145.
70 Grabar 1936, p. 100.
71 Cf. Golubinsky 1903, pp. 170–78.
72 The Moscow Patriarchate lapsed in 1700; instead of authorizing a new appointment, Peter the Great subsequently devolved its functions on the Synod, in effect a branch of the Civil Service. RM-G
73 *Parsuna* (from the Latin *persona*): an early icon-like portrait, usually of an eminent, recently deceased figure. RM-G
74 Twining 1985, p. 199.
75 See Mario Praz, *Studies in Seventeenth-century Imagery* (Rome, 1975), pp. 152–6.
76 Veniamin 1899, p. 30.
77 Stoyalovich 1988, p. 48.
78 Panchenko 1973, p. 163.
79 Gombrich 1989, p. 290.
80 Dankevich 1893, p. 97.
81 Panchenko 1973, p. 140.
82 Averintsev 1985, p. 300.
83 Cf. Tananayeva 1979, pp. 154–76.
84 See Antonova, Mnyova, GTG 1963, vol. II, cat. 968, ill. 161.
85 See OR RGB, f. 17, no. 324, pp. 35 reverse–36 reverse.
86 Turner 1983, p. 39.
87 Gombrich 1989, p. 282.

Chapter Five: The Middle Ages Delayed

1 Ushakov 1906, p. 47.
2 See Buslayev, vol. II, 1910.
3 Filimonov 1874.
4 Mâle 1951, pp.301–9; 1958, p. 187.
5 Weckwerth 1957, pp 147–85; Białostocki 1982, pp.200–01.
6 Petrov 1902, p. 151.
7 Mâle 1958, p. 176.
8 Antonova, DIPK 1966, cat. 112, p. 134.
9 Hans Belting, *Likeness and Presence: A History of the Image Before the Era of Art* (Chicago and London, 1994), p. 488, ill. 294.
10 See V. A. Chubinskaya 'Zhivopisnaya rama rubezha XVII–XVIII vekov k ikone "Bogomater Donskaya"', in *Kultura i istoriya. Slavyansky mir* (Moscow, 1997), pp. 114–39.
11 SR GRM, f. 122, item 73, pp. 59, 72 reverse.
12 Kondakov 1901, pp. 41–2.
13 SR GRM, f. 122, item 73, pp. 47–8, 53–4.
14 SR GRM, f. 122, item 73, p. 49.
15 Grigorov 1887, pp. 3–5.
16 Foucault 1994, p. 109.
17 Sazonova 1991, pp. 85–6; see 'table'.
18 See Belting 1994, p. 485.
19 'Brotherhood schools', Orthodox lay societies, flourished on the territory of what is now Ukraine and Belarus in response to Counter-Reformation pressures during the 17th century. RM-G
20 Antonova DIPK 1966, ill. 134, cat. 115.
21 Antonova DIPK, 1966, ill. 141, cat. 122.
22 ISM 1991, addendum 1, p. 81; see also ills. 43, 51, 62.
23 Florensky 1985, p. 288.
24 Grabar IRI, vol. VI, 1914, p. 360.
25 Paul of Aleppo vol. II, p. 108.
26 Stebnitsky 1863, pp. 15–16.
27 Smirnov 1979, p. 201.
28 Postnikov 1890, pp. 43, 47.
29 Lann 1930, p. 54 (my italics).
30 Murovyov 1846, pp. 7–8; Poselyanin 1905, p. 105.
31 Vzdornov 1972, p. 64.
32 Rovinsky 1903, p. 25.
33 Rovinsky 1903, p. 26.
34 Kondakov 1911, pp. 118–19.
35 Bessonov 1914, p. 38.
36 Rovinsky 1903, p. 37.
37 On 'highlighted' countenances see Georgievsky 1895, March, p. 208.
38 Trenyov 1903, p. 6.
39 Rovinsky 1903, pp. 20–24.
40 Rovinsky 1903, pp. 39–43.
41 Andrey Rublyov (*c.* 1370–1430), monk, renowned as the 'classic' Russian icon painter of the golden age of the icon. A figure of myth in the 19th century; a few fairly secure attributions have been made since then. RM-G

42 Bessonov 1914, p. 26.
43 Prokhorov 1914, p. 34.
44 OR GMPI, N.L. Safonov, item 10, pp. 2, 31.
45 Lazarev 1971, p. 388; compare Kondakov 1911, p. 89.
46 Rovinsky 1903, pp. 14–16.

Chapter Six: Icons and Popular Art

1 See Kirpichnikov 1895.
2 Propp 1973.
3 Korolyuk 1971, p. 93.
4 VGV, 1843, no. 21.
5 Rovinsky 1900, p. 1.
6 *Lubok*: a popular mass-circulation woodcut, etching or lithograph (similar to those of Épinal, etc.), generally ilustrating a text. RM-G
7 Golyshev 1886, p. 4.
8 See, for more detail, Rovinsky 1976, pp. 221–33.
9 Rovinsky 1900, p. 34.
10 Golyshev 1886, no. 3, p. 684.
11 Quoted from Uspensky 1906, p. 7.
12 Toporov 1987, p. 231.
13 VGV, 1843, no. 21.
14 GMPI, inv. no. 541.
15 See Averintsev 1988, no. 9, p. 232; Toporov 1987, pp. 188, 246.
16 Bogatyryov 1971, p. 372.
17 VGV, 1843, no. 21.
18 Chatzidakis 1976, p. 8.
19 See Garidis 1969.
20 See Freedberg 1991; Milner-Gulland 1999, pp. 171–226.
21 Malevich 1976, pp. 117–8.
22 Shevchenko 1913, pp. 117–8.
23 Larionov 1913, pp. 14–23.
24 Pospelov 1990, ill. 119, p. 230.
25 See Turchin 1993, pp. 6–292.
26 Velimir Khlebnikov (1885–1822), poet and visionary. See R. Cooke, *Velimir Khlebnikov* (Cambridge, 1998); R. Milner-Gulland, 'Khlebnikov's Eye', in C. Kelly and S. Lovell, eds, *Russian Literature, Modernism and the Visual Arts* (Cambridge, 2000). RM-G
27 Bulgakov 1976, p. 3.
28 Alexander Benois (1870–1960), painter and critic, was a founder of the Symbolist World of Art movement and generally hostile to Futurism; Malevich's response has been translated in his *Essays on Art* (1968–), vol. 1, pp. 42–8. See also W. Simmons, *Kasimir Malevich's Black Square* (New York, 1981). RM-G
29 Benua 1916.
30 SR GRM f. 137, item 1186.
31 Voloshin 1914, pp. 26–7.
32 Filonov (1883–1941), a major avant-garde painter, and his followers devised the method of 'Analytic Art', characterized by the quality of 'made-ness' (*sdelannost*, a neologism). RM-G
33 Quoted from Kovtun 1988, p. 32.
34 Larionov 1913, pp. 6–10.
35 Lotman, Uspensky 1977; compare Likhachov, Panchenko and Ponyrko 1984.
36 See Averintsev 1988 [2], p. 120.
37 Tolstoy 1976, p. 300.
38 Danku, RNZh, 1982, pp. 34, 154–6.
39 Lotman 1976, p. 265.
40 Rovinsky 1900, pp. 71–2.
41 Bezobrazov 1861, p. 294.
42 Averintsev 1985, p. 299.
43 Malevich 1922, p. 18.
44 For more detail see Tarasov 1994, pp. 174–95; O. Tarasov, 'Russian Icons and the Avant-garde: Tradition and Change', in *The Art of Holy Russia: Icons from Moscow, 1400–1600*, exh. cat., Royal Academy of Arts, London, 1998, pp. 93–9.
45 Malevich 1921, p. 6.
46 Malevich 1922, p. 37.
47 Malevich 1922, p. 19.
48 See Larionov 1913, p. 23, no. 284.
49 See Billington 1966, p. 36.
50 OR GTG, f. 76, item 9, almanack of UNOVIS, no. 1, p. 3 reverse.
51 OR GTG, f. 76 item 9, almanack of UNOVIS, no. 1, p. 38.

Bibliography

Albums and Catalogues

ADE: *Afonskiye drevnosti. Katalog vystavki iz fondov Ermitazha*, V. N. Zalesskaya, Yu. A. Pyatnitsky and I. N. Ukhanova (St Petersburg, 1992)

DIPK: *Drevnerusskoye iskusstvo v sobranii Pavla Korina*, V. I. Antonova (Moscow, 1966)

GTG: *Gosudarstvennaya Tretyakovskaya Galereya. Katalog drevnerusskoy zhivopisi*, 2 vols, V. I. Antonova (Moscow, 1963)

IB: *Ikonen aus Bulgarien* (Bonn, 1988)

IB: *Irkutskoye barokko: Irkutskiy oblastnoy khudozhestvennyy muzey*, T. A. Dryuchkova (Moscow, 1993)

IHVO: *Ikonen Heilige Bilder der Ostkirche*, Helga Freifrau von Mauchenheim, with a Foreword by W. P. Theunissen (Pattloch, 1987)

IP: *Ikonopis Palekha iz sobraniya Gosudarstvennogo Muzeya palekhskogo iskusstva*, L. Knyazeva (Moscow, 1994)

IP: *Iskusstvo Palekha*, M. Nekrasova (Moscow, 1966)

IPS: *Le immagini devote del popolo siciliano*, G. Cochiara (Palermo, 1982)

IR: *Icona Russa. (Icones de les Colecciones Privades de Moscou Segles XV–XIX)*, Llonja (Palma de Mallorca) 17 May–20 June 1994, G. Vzdornov and B.Dudochkin (Palma de Mallorca, 1994)

IRG: *Ikonen, Russland und Griechenland, 15–18 Jahrhundert*, Galerie Anita Rutz. (Herbst, 1976)

IS: *Ikony staroobrzędowców v zbiorach museum Warmii i Mazur*, G. Kobrzeniecka-Sikorska (Olsztyn, 1993)

ISM: *Iskusstvo stroganovskikh masterov v sobranii Gosudarstvennogo Russkogo muzeya. Issledovaniya i problemy*, Katalog vystavki (Leningrad, 1991)

MBA: *Musée Byzantin, Athènes. Le Monde des grands musées* (1970), no. 25

MI: *Mstjoralaiset Ikonit*, Valamon luostari (Heinävesi, 1992)

PRI: *Pozdnyaya russkaya ikona. Konets XVIII–XIX v*, Katalog vystavki, I. Yarygina (St Petersburg, 1994)

RHI: *Russische Heilige in Ikonen* (Wiss. Berbeitung Dr. E Haustein), Museen der Stadt Recklinghausen, 20 November 1988–15 January 1989

RI: *Russische Ikonen und Kultgerat aus St Petersburg* (Baden-Baden, 1991–2)

RI: *Russkiye ikony XVI-nachala XX veka s nadpisyami, podpisyami i datami*, Katalog vystavki. Gosudarstvennyy Ermitazh. A. S. Kostsova and A. G. Pobedinskaya (Leningrad 1990)

RL: *Russkii lubok XVII–XIX vv*, ed. V. P. Adrianovoy-Peretts (Moscow & Leningrad, 1962)

RNZh: *Rumynskaya narodnaya zhivopis po steklu*, Yu. Danku and D. Danku (Bucharest, 1982)

RRL: *Russkii risovanniy lubok kontsa XVIII-nachala XX veka iz sobraniya Gosudarstvennogo istoricheskogo muzeya*, E. I. Itkina (Moscow, 1992)

RTsI: *Russkoye tserkovnoye iskusstvo XVIII-nachala XX v. v nemuseynykh sobraniyakh Ulyanovskoy oblasti*, catalogue (Ulyanovsk, 1991)

RZh: *Russkaya zhivopis XVI–XVIII vekov. Iz sobraniy GRM, GTG, TsMiAR*, Katalog vystavki, T. A. Ananeva, N. G. Bekeneva & A. S. Loginova (Leningrad, 1977)

VI: *Venäläisiä Ikoneja noin 1780–1915*, Katrija Harri Willamon kokoelma (Espoo, 1989)

ZS: *Zbirka ikona Sekulić. Ubodna reč S. Radojčić* (Belgrade, 1967)

Other Works Cited

Adaryukov, V. Ya., *Arkhiv Dmitriya Aleksandrovicha Rovinskogo*, Sredi kollektsionerov, 1921, nos 6–7

Ariès, P., *Chelovek pered litsom smerti*, trans. from the French by B. K. Ronina (Moscow, 1992)

Arkh, Anatoliy (Martynovskiy), *O ikonopisanii* (Moscow, 1845)

Arkhangelsky, V., *Ocherk istorii grecheskoy tserkvi so vremeni padeniya Konstantinopolya do nashikh dney* (Moscow, 1885)

Averintsev, S. S., *Zametki k budushchey klassifikatsii tipov simvolov*, Problemy izucheniya kulturnogo naslediya, (Moscow, 1985)

Averintsev, S. S. [1], *Vizantiya i Rus: dva tipa dukhovnosti* (Novy Mir, 1988), nos 7 & 9

Averintsev, S. S [2], *Bakhtin, smekh, khristianskaya kultura* (Rossiya-Russia, 1988), no. 6

Bakhtin, M. M., *Tvorchestvo Fransua Rable i narodnaya kultura srednevekovya i Renessansa* (Moscow, 1900)

Barasch, M., *Icon: Studies in the History of an Idea* (New York, 1992)

Barskov, Ya. L., *Pamyatniki perviykh let russkogo staroobryadchestva* (St Petersburg, 1912)

Barsov, Ye. V., *O vozdeystvii apokrifov na obryad i ikonopis*, ZhMNP (December 1885)

Barsukov, S. G., with M. F. Greshchakova, Ye. G. Grigoreva, L. O. Zayonts, Yu. M. Lotman, G. M. Ponomareva and V. Yu. Mitroshkin, *Predvaritelnye zamechaniya po probleme Emblema - simvol - mif v kulture XVIII stoletiya*. Trudy po znakovym sistemam, no. 20 (Tartu, 1987)

Basil the Great [Vasiliy Velikiy], *Tvoreniya* (Sergiyev Posad, 1898), vol. II, chap. 4

Belting, H., *Likeness and Presence: A History of the Image before the Era of Art* (Chicago & London, 1994)

Benua, A., 'Vystavka, posvyashchennaya vremeni imperatritsy Elizavety Petrovny', *Starye gody* (May 1912)

Benua, A., *Poslednyaya futuristicheskaya vystavka* (Rech, 9 January 1916)

Bessonov, I., *Ikonopisaniye v Rossii (Kratkiy ocherk razvitiya russkoy tserkovnoy zhivopisi s drevneyshikh vremen do nastoyashchego vremeni)* (Kaluga, 1914)

Bezobrazov, V. P., *Iz putevykh zapisok*, Russky vestnik, 1861), vol. 34

Białostocki, J., *Pojecie manieryzmu i sztuka polska. Piec vieków mysli o sztuce* (Warsaw, 1976)

Białostocki, J., *Symbole i obrazy w swiecie sztuki* (Warsaw, 1982)

Billington, J. H., *The Icon and the Axe: An Interpretive History of Russian Culture* (New York, 1966)

Bogatyryov, P. G., *Voprosy teorii narodnogo iskusstva* (Moscow, 1971)

Bolshakov, *Podlinnik ikonopisny*, published by S. T. Bolshakova, ed. A. I. Uspenskogo (St Petersburg, 1903)

Borin, V., *Dva pamyatnika ikonografii XVII i XVIII vv.: ikona Azovskoy Bozhey Materi i propis s ney* (Svetilnik, 1914), no. 8

Braudel, F., *Materialnaya tsivilizatsaya, ekonomika i kapitalizm, XV–XVIII vv.*, 3 vols (Moscow, 1986–92), translated from the French

Bryanchaninov, I., *Asketicheskiye opyty* (St Petersburg, 1865)

Bulgakov, S., 'Trup krasoty: Po povodu kartin Pikasso' (1914), in Bulgakov, *Tikhie dumy* (Paris, 1976)

Buslayev, F. I., *Sochineniya*, 2 vols (St Petersburg, 1908–10)

Bylinin, V. K., 'K voprosu o polemike vokrug russkogo ikonopisaniya vo vtoroy polovine XVII v.: "Beseda o pochitanii ikon svyatykh" Simeona Polotskogo' TODRL, vol. 38 (Leningrad, 1985)

Chatzidakis, M., *Considération sur la peinture postbyzantine en Grèce. Communauté et diversité de l'art des pays balkaniques (XVIe siècle – debut du XVIIIe siècle)*, 1-er Congrès international des études balkaniques et sudest européennes (Sofia, 1966)

Chatzidakis, M., *Études sur la peinture postbyzantine* (London, 1976)

Cherniavsky, M., *Tsar and People* (New Haven, CT, 1961)

Chubinskaya, V. A., 'Zhivopisnaya rama rubezha XVII–XVIII vekov k ikone "Bogomater Donskaya"' in *Kultura i istoriya. Slavyansky mir* (Moscow, 1997)

Clark, K., *Landscape into Art* (London, 1976)

Collins, S., *Nyneshnyeye sostoyaniye Rossii, izlozhennoye v pisme k drugu, zhivushchemu v Londone* (Moscow, 1846), translated from the English

Cooke, R., *Velimir Khlebnikov* (Cambridge, 1998)

Cormack, R., *Writing in Gold: Byzantine Society and its Icons* (London, 1985)

Cormack, R., *Painting the Soul: Icons, Death Masks and Shrouds* (London, 1997)

Dagron, G., 'Svyashchennye obrazy i problema portretnogo skhodstva' in A. Lidov, ed., *Chudotvornaya ikona v Vyzantii i Drevney Rusi* (Moscow, 1996)

Dagron, G., *La romanité chrétienne en Orient. Héritages et mutation* (London, 1984)

Dankevich, V., 'Polucheniye pred nastupleniyem zhatvy (Chemu uchit nas zhatva?)', *Khristianskaya beseda*, no. 8 (1893)

de Bruyn, C., *Puteshestviye cherez Moskoviyu* (Moscow, 1873)

Denisov, L. I., *Pravoslavnye monastyri Rossiyskoy imperii* (Moscow, 1908)

Derrida, J. *The Truth in Painting* (Chicago and London, 1987)

Derzhavina, O. A., *'Velikoe zertsalo' i ego sudba na russkoy pochve* (Moscow, 1965)

Dmitrievsky, A., *Puteshestviye po Vostoku i ego nauchnye rezultaty* (Kiev, 1890)

Duchêsne, M., *Le Stoglav ou les cent chapitres* (Paris, 1920)

Duro, P., ed., *The Rhetoric of the Frame: Essays on the Boundary of the Artwork* (Cambridge 1996)

Dvorzhak, M., *Istoriya italyanskogo iskusstva v epokhu Vozrozhdeniya*, 2 vols (Moscow, 1978), translated from the German

Elders' Advice, *Starcheskiye sovety nekotorykh otechestvennykh podvizhnikov blagochestiya XVIII–XIX vv.* (Moscow, 1913)

Fedotov, G. P., *Svyatye Drevney Rusi* (Moscow, 1990)

Fedotov, G. P., *Stikhi Dukhovnye (Russkaya narodnaya vera po dukhovnym stikham)* (Moscow, 1991)

Filaret, *Otvet na voprosy glagolemogo staroobryadtsa po sluchayu besedy o Stoglavom sobore* (KhCh, 1836), vol. 1

Filaret, *Polnoye sobraniye rezolyutsiy Filareta, mitropolita Moskovskogo*, ed. V.S. Markova (Moscow, 1903)

Filimonov, G. D., *Svodnyy ikonopisnyy podlinnik XVIII v. po spisky F. D. Filimonova* (Moscow, 1874)

Filimonov, G. D., *Ikonnye portrety russkikh tsarey*, Vestnik Obshchestva drevnerusskogo iskusstva pri Moskovskom Publichnom muzeye (Moscow, 1875), no. 6

Florensky, P., *Symbolarium (slovar simvolov)*, Trudy po znakovym sistemam, no. 5 (Tartu, 1971)

Florensky, P., 'Ikonostas', in Florensky, *U vodorazdelov mysli*, vol. 1, Stati po iskusstvu (Paris, 1985)

Florensky, P., *The Iconostasis* (Moscow, 1994)

Florovsky, G., *Puti russkogo bogosloviya* (Paris, 1981)

Foucault, M., *Slova i veshchi. Arkheologiya gumanitarnykh nauk* (St Petersburg, 1994), translated from the French

Forssman, E., *Säule und ornament. Studien zum Problem des Manierismus in den nordischen Säulenbüchen und Vorlagssblättern des 16 und 17 Jahrhunderts* (Stockholm, 1956)

Freedberg, D., *The Power of Images: Studies in the History and Theory of Response* (Chicago & London, 1991)

Garen, E., *Problemy italyanskogo Vozrozhdeniya. Izbrannye raboty* (Moscow, 1986)

Garidis, M., *La représentation des 'nations' dans la peinture postbyzantine.* Byzantione (1969), no. 39

Georgievsky, V.T., *Ikonopistsy-suzdaltsy*, Russkoye obozreniye (March–April 1895)

Georgievsky, V. T., *Delo 'O proyavivshikhsya vnov vo Vladimirskoy yeparkhii vo Florishchevoy pustyni moshchakh i chudesakh'*, TVUAKh, kn. 10 (Vladimir, 1908)

Gilferding, A. F., *Poezdka po Gertsegovine, Bosnii i staroy Serbii* (St Petersburg, 1859)

Golubinsky, Ye., *Istoriya kanonizatsii svyatykh v russkoy tserkvi* (Moscow, 1903)

Golyshev, I. A., *Albom risunkov russkikh sinodikov 1651, 1679, 1686 gg* (Mstyora, 1886)

Gombrich, E., 'Icones Symbolicae: Philosophies of Symbolism and their Bearing on Art', in *On the Renaissance, II: Symbolic Images* (London, 1985)

Gombrich, E., 'O zadachakh i granitsakh ikonologii', *Sov. iskusstvoznaniye*, no. 25 (1989), translated from the English

Grabar, A., *L'Empéreur dans l'art byzantin* (Paris, 1936)

Grabar, A., *Christian Iconography: A Study of its Origins* (Princeton, NJ, 1968)

Grabar, I. E., ed., *IRI: Istoriya russkogo iskusstva*, 6 vols (Moscow, 1910–14)

Grammatin, N., 'Poucheniye pri vynose Abalatskoy ikony Bozhiey Materi', *Khristianskaya beseda*, no. 9 (1893)

Grigorov, D. A., *Russkiy ikonopisnyy podlinnik* (St Petersburg, 1887)

Hans the Dane (Gans Datskiy), *Izvestiye o puteshestvii v Rossiyu i Moskvu* (Moscow, 1868)

Hauser, A., *La modernité du seizième siècle* (Paris, 1956)

Herberstein, S., *Zapiski o moskovskikh delakh.* Rossiya XV–XVII v. glazami inostrantsev (Leningrad, 1986), translated from the German

Hetherington, P., *The 'Painter's Manual' of Dionysius of Fourna* (London, 1974)

Höpel, J., *Emblem und Sinnbild: Vom Kunstbuch zum Erbauungsbuch* (Frankfurt, 1987)

Huizinga, J., *Osen srednevekovya [The Waning of the Middle Ages]* (Moscow, 1988)

Juel, J.[=Yul], *Zapiski datskogo poslannika pri Petre Velikom (1709–1711)* (Moscow, 1900)

Kämpfer, F., *Das russische Herrscherbild. Von den Anfängen bis zu Peter dem Grossen. Studien zur entwiklung politischer Ikonographie in byzantinschen Kulturkreis. Beiträge zur Kunst des Christlichen Ostens* (Recklinghausen, 1978), vol. 8

Kämpfer, F., *Predstavleniye o russkom khristianstve i kontseptsiya 'Svyatoy Rusi'*, Tysyacheletiye vvedeniya khristianstva na Rusi, 988–1988, UNESCO – institut slavyanovedeniya i balkanistiki RAN (Moscow, 1993)

Kartashev, A. V., *Ocherki po istorii Russkoy tserkvi*, 2 vols (Paris, 1959)

Kelly, C & Lovell, S., eds, *Russian Literature, Modernism and the Visual Arts* (Cambridge, 2000)

Kirichenko, Ye. I., *Khram Khrista Spasitelya v Moskve. Istoriya proyektirovaniya i sozdaniya sobora. Stranitsy zhizni i gibeli 1813–1913* (Moscow, 1992)

Kirpichnikov, A. I., *Vzaimodeystviye ikonopisi i slovesnosti narodnoy i knizhnoy*, Trudy vosmogo arkheologicheskogo sezda v Moskve, 2 vols (Moscow, 1895)

Kitzinger, E., 'The Cult of Images in the Age before Iconoclasm', in *The Art of Byzantium and the Medieval West: Selected Studies by Ernst Kitzinger* (Bloomington, 1976), pp. 91–150

Kobeko, D. F., *O suzdalskom ikonopisanii. Soobshcheniye* (St Petersburg, 1896)

Kologrivov, I., *Ocherki po istorii russkoy svyatosti* (Brussels, 1961)

Kondakov, N. P., *Ikonografiya Bogomateri. Svyazi grechskoy i russkoy ikonopisi s italyanskoy zhivopisyu rannego Vozrozhdeniya* (St Petersburg, 1911)

Kondakov, N. P., *Puteshestviya po Makedonii* (St Petersburg, 1900)

Kondakov, N. P., *Sovremennoye polozheniye russkoy narodnoy ikonopisi.* PDPI, vol. CXXXIX (St Petersburg, 1901)

Korolyuk, V. D., 'Russkaya krestyanskaya ikonopis. (Traditsiya i razvitiye)', *Études balkaniques*, no. 3 (1971)

Koschmal, W., *Der russische Volksbilderbogen (Von der Religion zum Theater)*, Slavistsche Beiträge, vol. 251 (Munich, 1989)

Kovtun, Ye. F., *Vstupitelnaya statya k katalogu vystavki 'Pavel Nikolayevich Filonov 1883-1941'* (Leningrad, 1988)

Lann, Ye., *Literaturnye mistifikatsii* (Moscow & Leningrad, 1930)

Larionov, *Vystavka ikonopisnykh podlinnikov i lubkov, organizovannaya M. F. Larionovym.* (Moscow, 1913)

Lazarev, V. N., '"Manera Greka" i problema kritskoy shkoly' in Lazarev, *Vizantiyskaya zhivopis*, izbr. raboty (Moscow, 1971)

Lazarev, V. N., *Istoriya vizantiyskoy zhivopisi* (Moscow, 1986)

Le Goff, G., *S nebes na zemlyu (Peremeny v sisteme tsennostnykh orientatsiy na khristianskom Zapade XII–XIII vv.)*, Odissey. Chelovek v istorii. Kulturno-antropologicheskaya istoriya segodnya (Moscow, 1991)

Le Goff, G., *Tsivilizatsiya srednevekovogo Zapada.* (Moscow, 1992)

Leontyev, P., *Ikonopis. Materialy dlya otsenki zemel Vladimirskoy gubernii.* vol. IV, Vyaznikovskiy uyezd. Vyp. III, Promysly krestyanskogo naseleniya (Vladimir, 1903)

Likhachov, D. S., *Gradozashchitnaya semantika Uspenskikh khramov na Rusi,* Uspensky sobor Moskovskogo Kremlya, Materialy i issledovaniya (Moscow, 1985)

Likhachov, D. S., *Poeziya sadov. K semantike sadovo-parkovykh stiley* (Leningrad, 1982)

Likhachov, D. S., Panchenko A. M., Ponyrko, N. V., *Smekh v Drevney Rusi* (Moscow, 1984)

Lotman, Yu, *Khudozhestvennaya priroda russkikh narodnykh kartinok & Narodnaya gravyura i folklor v Rossii* XVIIXIXV *I-XIX vv.* (K 150 letiyu so dnya rozhdeniya D.A. Rovinskogo). Materialy nauchnoy konferentsii, 1975 (Moscow, 1976)

Lotman, Yu. M., Uspensky B.A. *Novye aspekty izucheniya kultury Drevney Rusi.* Voprosy literatury, no. 3 (1977)

Lotman, Yu. M., Uspensky, B. A. *Otzvuki kontseptsii 'Moskva – Tretiy Rim' v ideologii Petra Pervogo (K probleme srednevekovoy traditsii v kulture barokko),* Khudozhestvenny yazyk srednevekovya (Moscow, 1982), trans. in A. Shukman, ed., *The Semiotics of Russian Culture* (Ann Arbor, 1984)

Lotman, Yu. M. (1), *Kultura i vzryv* (Moscow, 1992)

Lotman, Yu. M. (2), 'Simvol v sisteme kultury', in. Lotman, *Izbrannye stati,* vol. I (Tallin, 1992)

Lyadov, I. M., *Razvitiye i upadok kholuyskikh yamarok v Vyaznikovskom uyezde.* EVGSK, vol. I, vyp. II (1876)

Maguire, H., *Art and Eloquence in Byzantium* (Princeton, NJ, 1981)

Majeska, G., *Russian Travelers to Constantinople in the Fourteenth and Fifteenth Centuries* (Washington, DC, 1984)

Maksimov, S. V., 'V doroge (Iz putevykh zapisok)', *Otechestvennye zapiski,* vol. 131 (July 1860)

Maksimov, S. V., *Brodyachaya Rus Khrista-radi,* 2 vols (St Petersburg, 1907)

Mâle, É., *L'art religieux de la fin du XVIe siècle, du XVIIe siècle et du XVIIIe siècle. Études sur l'iconographie aprés le Concile de Trente. Italie-France-Espagne-Flandres* (Paris, 1951)

Mâle, É., *Religious Art from the Twelfth to the Eighteenth Century* (New York, 1958)

Malevich, K., *K voprosu izobrazitelnogo iskusstva* (Vitebsk, 1921)

Malevich, K., *Bog ne skinut: Iskusstvo, tserkov, fabrika* (Vitebsk, 1922)

Malevich, K., *Glavy iz avtobiografii khudozhnika. Podgotovka teksta, predisloviye i primechaniya N. Khardzhiyeva,* K istorii russkogo avangarda (Stockholm, 1976)

Malyshev, V. I., *Novye materialy o protopope Avvakume,* TODRL, XXI (Moscow & Leningrad, 1965)

Maser, E. A., *Cesare Ripa, Baroque and Rococo Pictorial Imagery* (New York, 1971)

Melnikov, P. I., *Na gorakh.* Book I (Moscow, 1986)

Merezhovsky, D. S., *Antikhrist (Petr i Aleksey).* in Merezhovsky, pol. sob. soch. vol. 4 (Moscow, 1914)

Michalski, S., *Protestaci a sztuka: Spór o obrazy w Europie noworzytnej.* (Warsaw, 1989)

Milner-Gulland, R., *The Russians* (Oxford, 1999)

Morev, I., *'Kamen very' mitropolita Stefana Yavorskogo, ego mesto sredi otechestvennykh protivoprotestantskikh sochineniy* (St Petersburg, 1904)

Nicols, R., 'The Icon and the Machine in Russia's Religious Renaissance 1900–1909', paper from the Conference on the Millennium of Christianity in Rus: The Impact of Christianity on the History of the Eastern Slavs. Library of Congress and the Kennan Institure, Washington DC, 27 May 1988. Also in W.Brumfield & M. Velimoirović, *Christianity and the Arts in Russia* (Cambridge, 1991)

Olearius, A., *Opisaniye puteshestviya v Moskoviyu i cherez Moskoviyu v Persiyu i obratno* (St Petersburg, 1906)

Ostrovsky, G., *Zakhary Zograf* (Moscow, 1987)

Ouspensky, L., *Theology of the Icon* (New York, 1992)

Ousterhout, R & Brubaker, L., eds, *Sacred Image: East and West* (Urbana & Chicago, 1995)

Ovchinnikova, Ye. S., *Iosif Vladimirov. Traktat ob iskusstve. (Publikatsiya teksta).* Drevnerusskoye iskusstvo (1964)

Panchenko, A. M., *Russkaya stikhotvornaya kultura XVII v.* (Leningrad, 1973)

Paterik, *Paterik Kievo-Pecherskiy* (Kiev, 1702)

Patterson-Ševčenko, N., 'Icons in the Liturgy', *DOP*, 45 (1991) pp. 45–7

Patterson-Ševčenko, N., 'Servants of the Holy Icon' in *Byzantine East, Latin West. Art Historical Studies in Honor of Kurt Weitzmann* (Princeton, NJ, 1995)

Paul of Aleppo, *Puteshestviye antiokhiyskogo patriarkha Makariya v Rossiyu v polovine XVII vek.* Vyp. 1–3 (Moscow, 1897), translated from the Arabic (also in W. Palmer, *The Patriarch and the Tsar*, London 1875, vol.II)

Pavel, *Kratkiye izvestiya o sushchestvuyushchikh v raskole sektakh, ob ikh proiskhozhdenii, uchenii i obryadakh, o kazhdoy s zamechaniyami* (Moscow, 1885)

Pearsall, D. & Salter, E., *Landscapes and Seasons of the Medieval World* (Toronto and Buffalo, 1973)

Pernstein [=Pernshteyn], J., *Donesenie o Moskovii* (Moscow, 1876)

Peterson, Th. G., 'The Survival of Byzantinism in 18th Century Greek Painting', *Allen Memorial Art Museum Bulletin*, vol. XXIX/I (1971)

Petrov, N. I., *Kollektsiya staroobryadcheskikh ikon i drugikh svyashchennykh predmetov iz Starodubya, sobrannaya V. N. Falkovskim.* Trudy Kievskoy dukhovnoy akademii

(January 1902)

Pospelov, G. G., *'Bubnovyy valet': Primitiv i gorodskoy folklor v moskovkoy zhivopisi 1910-x godov* (Moscow, 1990)

Porfiriy, *Yerminiya, ili Nastavleniye v zhivopisnom iskusstve, sostavlennoye ieromonakhom i zivopistsem Dionisiyem Furnoagrafiontom. 1701-1733 goda*, Publ. Porfiriya, episkopa Chigirinskogo (Kiev, 1868)

Poselyanin, Ye., *Russkaya tserkov i russkiye podvizhniki 18-go veka* (Moscow, 1905)

Poselyanin, Ye., *Bogomater. Polnoye illyustrirovannoye opisanniye Yeyo zemnoy zhizni i posvyashchennykh Yeyo imeni chudotvornykh ikon*, addendum to journal *Russkiy Palomnik*, books 1–4 (1909)

Postnikov, N. M., *Zaly 5-ya i 6-ya arkheologicheskoy vystavki, ustroennoy Imperatorskim Moskovskim arkheologicheskim obshchestvom v pamyat svoego pervogo dvadtsatipyatiletiya*, Sobraniye tserkovnykh drevnostey N. M Postnikova (Moscow, 1890)

Poulsen, F., 'Talking, Weeping, and Bleeding Sculptures: A Chapter of the History of Religious Fraud', in *Acta Archaeologica*, 16 (1945), pp. 178–95

Praz, M., *Studies in Seventeenth-century Imagery* (Rome, 1975)

Prokhorov, S. M., *Ob ikonopisanii i ego tekhnike* (Svetilnik, 1914), no. 1

Prokofyev, V. N., *O tryokh urovnyakh khudozhestvennoy kultury Novogo i Noveyshego vremeni (K probleme primitiva v izobrazitelnykh iskusstvakh)*, Primitiv i yego mesto v khudozhestvennoy kulture Novogo i Noveyshego vremeni, Sb. statey (Moscow, 1983)

Restle, M., *Die byzantinische Wandmalerei in Kleinasien*, vol. 1 (Recklinghausen, 1967)

Rostovsky, D., *Rozysk o raskolnicheskoy brynskoy vere* (Moscow, 1855)

Rovinsky, D. A., *Russkiye narodnye kartinki*. Kn. 1–5, i Atlas, vyp. 1–7 (St Petersburg, 1881–93)

Rovinsky, D. A., *Russkiye narodnye kartinki*, ed. N. P Sobko (St Petersburg, 1900)

Rushchinsky, L. P., *Religiozny i byt russkikh po svedeniyam inostrannykh pisateley XVI–XVII vv* (Moscow, 1871)

Sapozhnikov, D. I., *Samosozhzheniye v russkom raskole* (Moscow, 1891)

Sarabyanov, V., 'Ikonograficheskoye soderzhaniye zakaznykh ikon mitropolita Makariya', *Voprosy iskusstvoznaniya*, no. 4 (1993)

Sazonova, L. I., *Poeziya russkogo barokko (vtoraya polovina XVII – nachalo XVIII v)*

Shearman, J., *Manieryzm* (Warsaw, 1970), 1st pubd as *Mannerism* (Harmondsworth, 1967)

Shevchenko, A., *Neoprimitivizm. Yego teoriya. Yego vozmozhnosti. Yego dostizheniya* (Moscow, 1913)

Shtukenberg, I. F., *Statisticheskiye trudy* (St Petersburg, 1858)

Simmons, W., *Kasimir Malevich's Black Square* (New York, 1981)

Sinitsyn, P. V., *Preobrazhenskoye i okruzhayushchiye ego mesta, ikh proshloye i nastoy-*

ashchyeye (Moscow, 1895)

Sinitsyn, P. V., *Nikolskiy yedinovercheskiy muzhskoy monastyr v Moskve, chto v Preobrazhenskom* (Moscow, 1896)

Sirot, I. M., *Russian Proverbs Deriving from the Bible* (Brussels, 1985)

Skrine, P. H., *The Baroque: Literature and Culture in Seventeenth Century Europe* (London, 1978)

Smirnov, I. P., *O poddelkakh A.I. Sulakadzevym drevnerusskikh pamyatnikov (Mesto mistifikatsii v istorii)*. TODRL, vol. XXXIV (1979)

Smirnov, I. P., *O drevnerusskoy kulture, russkoy natsionalnoy spetsifike i logike istorii* (Venice, 1991)

Smirnov, P. S., *Spory i razdeleniya v russkom raskole v pervoy chetverti XVIII v* (St Petersburg, 1909)

Snessoreva, S., *Zemnaya zhizn Presvyatoy Bogoroditsy i opisaniye svyatykh chydotvornykh Yeyo ikon, chtimykh Pravoslavnoy Tserkovyu, na osnovanii Svyashchennogo Pisaniya i tserkovnykh predaniy, s izobrazheniyami v tekste prazdnikov i ikon Bozhiey Materi* (St Petersburg, 1891)

Sofronova, L. A., 'Problemy khudozhestvennogo primitiva na polskoy stsene XVII–XVIII vv', *Sovetskoye slavyanovedeniye*, no. 3 (1983)

Sofronova, L. A., *Neskolko zamechaniy o simvole barokko (*1994)

Solovyov, V. S., *O raskole v russkom narode i obshchestve.* V.S. Solovyov, pol. sob. soch., 3 vols (Brussels, 1966)

Sosnin, D. *O svyatykh chudotvornykh ikonakh v tserkvi khristianskoy* (St Petersburg, 1833)

St John Damascene, *Tvoreniya*, vol. I (St Petersburg, 1913)

Stebnitsky, M., *S lyudmi drevlego blagochestiya* (St Petersburg, 1863)

Stewart, Ch., *Demons and the Devil* (Princeton, NJ, 1991)

Stoglav, *Rossiyskoye zakonodatelstvo X–XX vekov, t. II. Zakonodatelstvo perioda obrazovaniya i ukrepleniya Russkogo tsentralizovannogo gosudarstva* (Moscow, 1985)

Stoichita, V., *Visionary Experience in the Golden Age of Spanish Art* (London, 1995)

Stoyalovich, L.N., *Zerkalo kak semioticheskaya, gnoseologicheskaya i aksiologicheskaya model*, Trudy po znakovym sistemam, no. 22 (Tartu, 1988)

Tananayeva, L. I., *Sarmatskii portret* (Moscow, 1979)

Tarasov, O., 'The Russian Icon and the Culture of the Modern: The Renaissance of Popular Icon Painting in the Reign of Nicholas II' in *Experiment: A Journal of Russian Culture*, no. 7 (2001), pp. 73-102

Tarasov, O. Yu., *Ikona v tvorchestve K. Malevicha*, Istoriya kultury i poetika (Moscow, 1994)

Tikhonravov, K., *Vladimirskiy sbornik. Materialy dlya statistiki, etnografii, istorii i arkheologii Vladimirskoy gubernii* (Moscow, 1857)

Tolstoy, M. V., *Istoriya russkoy tserkvi.* (*Rasskazy iz istorii Russkoy tserkvi*), Izd.

Spaso-Preobrazhenskogo Valaamskogo monastyrya (1991)

Tolstoy, N. I., *Iz zametok po slavyanskoy demonologii, 2. Kakov oblik dyavolskii?* Narodnaya gravyura i folklor v Rossii XVII–XIX vv. (K 150-letiyu so dnya rozhdeniya D.A. Rovinskogo). Materialy nauchnoy konferentsii, 1975 (Moscow, 1976)

Toporov, V. N., *Ob odnom klasse simvolicheskikh tekstov.* Balkano-Balto-Slavica (Moscow, 1979)

Toporov, V. N., *Ob odnom arkhaichnom indoyevropeyskom elemente v drevnerusskoy dukhovnoy kulture,* Yazyki kultury i problemy perevodimosti (Moscow, 1987)

Toporov, V. N., *O rituale. Vvedeniye v problematiku. Arkhaicheskiy ritual v folklornykh i ranneliteraturnykh pamyatnikakh* (Moscow, 1988)

Trenyov, D. K., *Ikonopis mstyortsev* (Moscow, 1903)

Trubetskoy, Ye., *Umozreniye v kraskakh* (Paris, 1965)

Turchin, V. S., *Po labirintam avangarda* (Moscow, 1993)

Turner, V.[=Terner], *Simvol i ritual* (Moscow, 1983)

Twining, L., *Symbols and Emblems of Early and Medieval Christian Art* (Leningrad, 1885)

Ushakov, N. N., *Istoricheskiye svedeniya ob ikonopisanii i ikonopistsakh Vladimirskoy gubernii* (Vladimir, 1906)

Uspensky, B., *The Semiotics of the Russian Icon* (Lisse, 1976)

Uspensky, B. A., *Antipovedeniye v kulture Drevney Rus,* Problemy izucheniya kulturnogo naslediya (Moscow, 1985)

Uspensky, D., *Narodnye verovaniya v tserkovnoy zhivopisi* (St Petersburg, 1906)

Uspensky, L. A., *Bogosloviye ikony pravoslavnoy tserkvi* (Paris & Moscow, 1989)

Vacková, J., *Epitafní obrazy v Předbělohorských čechách.* Umění, roč, XVIII (1969)

Varkoch, N., *Opisaniye puteshestviya v Moskvu posla rimskogo imperatora, c 22 iyulya 1593* (Moscow, 1875)

Veniamin, *Novaya Skrizhal, ili Obyasneniye o tserkvi, o liturgii i o vsekh sluzhbakh i utvaryakh tserkovnykh.* Izd. 16-e (St Petersburg, 1899)

Vipper, B., *Baroque in Latvia* (Riga, 1939)

Vipper, B., *Arkhitektura russkogo barokko* (Moscow, 1978)

Voloshin, M., *Chemu uchat ikony?* (Appolon, 1914), no. 5

Vzdornov, G. I., *O ponyatiyakh 'shkola' i 'pisma' v zhivopisi Drevney Rusi* (Iskusstvo, 1972), no. 6

Walter, Ch., 'A New Look at the Byzantine Sanctuary Barrier' in *Revue des études byzantines,* vol. 51 (1993), pp. 203–24

Weckwerth, A., 'Der Ursprung des Bildepitaphs', *Zeitschrift für Kunstgeschichte,* no. 20 (1957)

Yakovlev, G., *Izveshcheniye pravednoye o raskole bespopovshchiny* (Bratskoye Slovo, 1888), vol. 1, nos 3–9

Yatsmirsky, A. I., *Iz oblasti starinnoy simvoliki v russkoy ikonografii* (Starye Gody, October 1907)

Zabelin, I., 'Materialy dlya istorii russkoy ikonopisi', *Vremennik Imp. Moskovskogo obshchestva istorii i drevnostey rossiyskikh*, Kn. 7 (1850)

Zabelin, I., *Domashniy byt russkikh tsarey v XVI i XVII stoletiyakh*. Chast 1. (Moscow, 1862)

Zeri, F., *Pittura e Contrariforma. L'arte senza tempo di Scipione da Gaeta* (Turin, 1957)

Zenkovsky, S., *Russkoye staroobryadchestvo. Dukhovnye dvizheniya semnadtsatogo veka* (Munich, 1970)

Zernov, N., *Russkoye religioznoye vozrozhdeniye XX veka* (Parizh, 1991)

Zhirmunsky, V. M., *Nemetskiy romantizm i sovremennaya mistika* (1914)

Zhivov, V. M., Uspensky, B. A., *Metamorfozy antichnogo yazychestva v istorii russkoy kultury XVII–XVIII vv*, Antichnost v kulture i iskusstve posleduyushchikh vekov. Materialy nauchnoy konferentsii, 1982 (Moscow, 1984)

Index

Page numbers in *italics* refer to illustrations;
page numbers followed by 'q' refer to quotations.